to success

Do you like

Choices
+
Control?

Cyclist **+** Entrepreneur Connoisseur **+** Consultant

You're making your way in the world, passionately pursuing your own definition of success. So choose the only business school admissions test that gives you more freedom to do things your way — skip questions, change answers and control which scores schools will see. Show the world's top business schools your best.

Accepted at the world's top-ranked business schools.

Learn more at TakeTheGRE.com

Measuring the Power of Learning.®

2020 EDITION

Best Business Schools

HOW TO ORDER: Additional copies of U.S. News & World Report's **Best Business Schools 2020** guidebook are available for purchase at usnews.com/businessbook or by calling (800) 836-6397. To order custom reprints, please call (877) 652-5295 or email usnews@wrightsmedia.com. For permission to republish articles, data or other content from this book, email permissions@usnews.com.

Northwestern's Kellogg School of Management
ALYSSA SCHUKAR FOR USN&WR

MBA | MFIN | MSBA | MPAc | Ph.D. | ExecEd

WE ARE INNOVATORS. ENTREPRENEURS. #RADYMADE

Attend the top graduate business school in the center of San Diego's innovation economy. Experience the entrepreneurial mindset infused in all curriculum and activities at the Rady School of Management.

ARE YOU RADY?

Rady | School of Management
UNIVERSITY OF CALIFORNIA SAN DIEGO

rady.ucsd.edu

CONTENTS

14

THE BIG PICTURE

CHAPTER 1

EXPLORE YOUR OPTIONS

CHAPTER 2

GO GLOBAL

MELISSA GOLDEN – REDUX FOR USN&WR

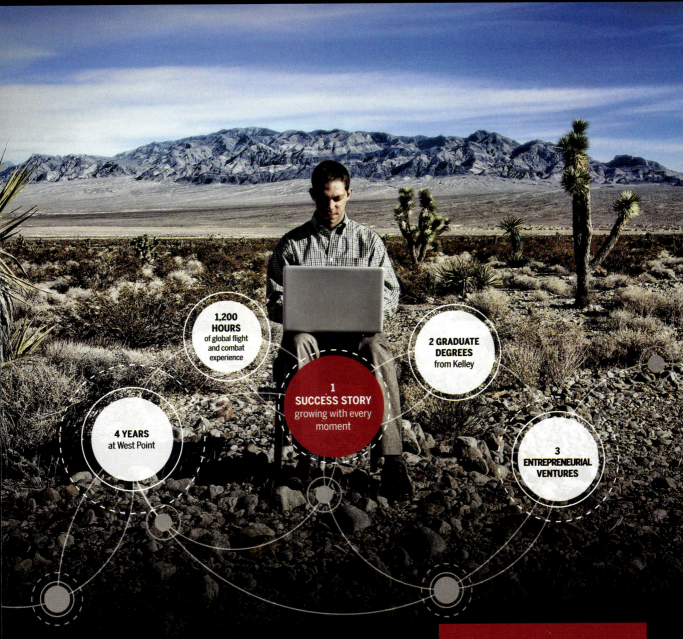

1,200 **HOURS** of global flight and combat experience

4 YEARS at West Point

1 SUCCESS STORY growing with every moment

2 GRADUATE DEGREES from Kelley

3 ENTREPRENEURIAL VENTURES

The pivotal moments in Tony's life mean a lot more than most. Each one starts a chain reaction of new paths, connections and opportunities. Tony earned his MBA and MS from Kelley online, so his moments go much farther.

Start building your momentum
gokelley.iu.edu/EarnYourMBAOnline

KELLEY
SCHOOL OF BUSINESS
GO FROM MOMENT TO MOMENTUM

CHAPTER 4

The U.S. News Rankings

D-1

@ USNEWS.COM/EDUCATION

Prospective business students researching their options will find the U.S. News website (home of the Best Graduate Schools and Best Colleges rankings) full of tips on everything from choosing a school to landing the most generous scholarships. Additional information is added throughout the year, so you'll want to check back often to see what's new on the site. Here's just a sampling of what you'll find to enrich and inform your school search:

Applying to Business School
usnews.com/businessapp

Planning for graduate school involves deciding what to study, finding the right school, and applying to competitive programs. Find out how to plan for the application process, what the ROI of business school can be, and what insider tips you should know.

Paying for Business School
usnews.com/payformba

Higher education is expensive, but students who choose to pursue a business program face especially steep costs. Paying for school involves exploring scholarships, employer reimbursement and student loans, as well as smart financial planning. Learn more about how to navigate your way through paying for an MBA.

Online Education
usnews.com/online

Want to get that MBA without spending time in the classroom? See our rankings of the best online degree programs in business (as well as in education, engineering, computer information technology, criminal justice and nursing). And read time-management and funding tips from students who have completed online degree programs.

Morse Code Blog
usnews.com/morsecode

Get an insider's view of the rankings from Chief Data Strategist Bob Morse, the mastermind behind them. Morse explains the methods we use to rank undergraduate and graduate programs and keeps you up to date on all the commentary and controversy.

Best Graduate Schools
usnews.com/grad

Check out our latest graduate school rankings in business, education, engineering, law, medicine and nursing, as well as the humanities and sciences.

U.S. News Graduate School Compass
usnews.com/gradcompass

Gain access to the U.S. News Graduate School Compass (subscribe at usnews.com/compassdiscount to get a 25 percent discount) and view our profiles of more than 2,000 graduate programs in an array of disciplines. Tap into a wealth of searchable data with tools and an expanded directory of programs. Are you curious about how much you could make coming out of business school? Find out – and get admissions, student body and career data that will help you find your perfect B-school match.

WE GIVE YOU DIRECTION.
YOU LEAD THE WAY.

The University of Tampa's AACSB-accredited graduate business programs prepare students with the invaluable skills and career connections needed for success in today's rapidly evolving global economy. Students benefit from hands-on learning, one-on-one faculty mentoring and a degree from a private, top-ranked university. Within six months of graduation, 98 percent of alumni report achieving their goals, including a new job or a promotion.

AACSB
ACCREDITED

THE UNIVERSITY OF TAMPA IS PROUD TO BE:

- Named by The Princeton Review as one of the best business schools in the world
- Listed in *U.S. News & World Report* among the best MBA programs
- Rated a top graduate business school nationwide by *Bloomberg Businessweek*
- Included on *Forbes'* annual ranking of America's Top Colleges
- Named the #7 best value business school in the U.S. by *Business Insider*

THE UNIVERSITY
OF TAMPA

LEARN MORE AT UT.EDU/GRADINFO OR CALL (813) 258-7409

MBA | Professional MBA | Executive MBA

M.S. in Accounting | M.S. in Cybersecurity | M.S. in Entrepreneurship | M.S. in Finance

M.S. in Marketing | Certificate in Cybersecurity | Certificate in Nonprofit Management

Find the Best B−

Expanding educational choices to boost your career at any stage

STARTUP HUBS, more diverse classes, hands-on learning, STEM-themed and internationally flavored curricula. These are the signs of fast-evolving graduate business programs that are meeting student demand for offerings better tailored to their professional and personal needs. The U.S. News Best Business Schools guidebook takes you inside top MBA programs that have become entrepreneurial engines for their communities. We look at the expanding array of alternatives to the traditional two-year MBA, from one-year professional degrees to certificates and micro-MBAs. We survey a range of experiential learning opportunities, from student-managed investment funds to internship programs – all potential steppingstones to robust career opportunities.

You'll find expert tips on getting in, getting hired, and paying for your education. And, as always, we feature the latest U.S. News rankings of full-time, part-time and executive MBA programs. Enjoy the search! ●

Outside Northwestern's Kellogg School of Management

School for You

EXPLORE YOUR OPTIONS

SPOTLIGHT ON THE B-SCHOOLS AT:

**University of Michigan's
Stephen M. Ross School of Business**
ERIN KIRKLAND FOR USN&WR

Breaking Down the Barriers

Schools hope bias training, more outreach and revamped curricula will increase campus diversity

by **Beth Howard**

DURING ORIENTATION at the Georgia Institute of Technology's Scheller College of Business, first-year MBA student Jasmine Howard received a lesson on the neurochemistry of unconscious bias, which explored "how the brain takes shortcuts and makes stereotyping decisions," she explains. In another exercise, students were asked to stand up if they identified with certain groups or preferences. "There was a mix of visually obvious traits like race and ethnicity, but also some less obvious ones like 'I am or love someone who is LGBTQ or struggling with addiction,'" she says. The point: "To learn on a deeper level all the different aspects that make up a person and what they bring to the table."

Bias training and similar exercises are becoming routine at business schools around the country seeking to boost the ranks of female and traditionally underrepresented groups in graduate programs – and make them feel welcome on campus. The push can't come soon enough. Only 16 percent of GMAT test-takers in the U.S. are from underrepresented populations, according to the Graduate Management Admission Council, which administers the test, and many schools have dismal numbers of minority students.

That's in spite of a growing consensus that diversity in every form – from race and gender to country of origin – improves both the educational experience and the field of business itself, experts say. "You will learn a lot more when you are interacting with people who think differently than you do than if you're dealing with people who already think and believe the same things

Jasmine Howard (in tan blazer) and classmates received bias training at Georgia Tech.

SPOTLIGHT ON

Terry College of Business

UNIVERSITY OF GEORGIA, ATHENS

U.S. NEWS RANK #37

Located in a vibrant college town about 70 miles from Atlanta, the Terry College of Business gives its 100 full-time MBA students plenty of ways to tap into community organizations, small startups and larger corporations in and around the capital city for project-based learning. For example, last year students in a financial technology class worked with tech company Global Payments to help build out its casino and gaming product offerings. As part of an innovative business solutions class, second-year student Kaley Tabor, 26, helped an Athens boutique owner craft a plan to expand her clothing line by developing a marketing toolkit and offering fundraising suggestions.

Students choose from nine concentrations, including risk management, real estate, and human resources. Many add an emphasis in consulting or FinTech. "Being such a small class, we get opportunities to really follow our passions," says Tabor, who is pursuing a focus in brand management. She interned at manufacturer Georgia-Pacific, where she'll start a full-time position after graduation. –*Lindsay Cates*

▶ More @ usnews.com/uga

you do," says Bruce DelMonico, assistant dean for admissions at the Yale School of Management. And research consistently shows that diverse business teams perform better and achieve superior outcomes, such as greater creativity and innovation. Of the more than 700 business leaders surveyed by the University of North Carolina–Chapel Hill in 2016, 95 percent said an inclusive culture is critical to their organization's future success.

No wonder schools are stepping up their efforts to recruit minority candidates for MBAs and other graduate degrees. According to Juliane Iannarelli, senior vice president and chief knowledge officer for AACSB International, a nonprofit that accredits business schools globally, the institutions making the biggest strides are those "tackling multiple dimensions." This can mean engaging minority high school students to think about careers in business, assessing the climate for inclusion and diversity on campus, and staging recruiting events or diversity weekends for prospective business students.

One such event was Women@ ASU, a two-day program for promising female undergraduates and business professionals held at Arizona State University's W. P. Carey School of Business in November 2018. Between panels and tours of the campus, the group heard from students, faculty and alumni about "the ROI of graduate school and finding their life's purpose here," says Pam Delany, director of graduate recruitment and admissions.

Schools are also tapping into pipelines created by organizations like the Forté Foundation, which partners with companies, donors, universities and top MBA programs and offers conferences, networking and training to advance women in business; and

Management Leadership for Tomorrow and The Consortium for Graduate Study in Management, which offer related services and events for African-Americans, Latinos and Native Americans. Similarly, Reaching Out MBA provides mentoring and scholarship support at 46 business schools for LGBTQ students and allies, and the National Black MBA Association identifies and mentors potential black MBA candidates, for example. Schools are also building their own avenues to increase diversity. For instance, Georgia Tech's MBA Pathway offers deferred admission to its own undergraduates, as well as to those from all-women's Agnes Scott College and several historically black colleges in Atlanta. Undergraduate seniors who apply to the program and are accepted are guaranteed MBA admission after completing a minimum of three years of work before starting the program.

Such efforts are beginning to pay off. Over a third of Forté's 54 member B-schools enrolled classes comprised of more than 40 percent women this year, compared with just three schools in 2014. And for the first time, one Forté school, the University of Southern California, achieved gender parity, with women making up 52 percent of the incoming MBA class. "It's just not enough to bring in diverse groups and then leave them to fend for themselves," says Maryam Alavi, Scheller's dean. "It's important that they feel appreciated, respected and supported so everyone can fulfill their potential."

Efforts to do that start during orientation at the University of Michigan–Ann Arbor's Ross School of Business, where first-year students are asked to take a cultural intelligence self-assessment, which

MORE @ USNEWS.COM

INDEX OF BEST BUSINESS SCHOOLS

Check here for our index of the top business schools, which will give you instant online access to the rank of and a wealth of data on every school in our rankings, including the best MBA and other master's business programs. ▶ *usnews.com/bschools*

JOHNS HOPKINS
CAREY BUSINESS SCHOOL

A Business Education that opens minds.
A name that opens doors.

Innovative, curious, and transformative. These are qualities necessary of every successful business leader and the founding principles of the **Johns Hopkins Carey Business School**. It's the business school you would expect from Johns Hopkins.

Learn More: **carey.jhu.edu**

basically measures their intercultural capabilities, or their ability to relate and work effectively in culturally diverse settings. "That's how we begin to normalize conversations around race, gender, sexual orientation, religion and ability," says Taryn Petryk, the school's director of diversity and inclusion. At the beginning of other programs, students take workshops designed to help them identify and address implicit bias and understand identity.

Business schools are also training faculty to be more sensitive to and inclusive of minority perspectives. In fact, they're even ditching biased teaching materials. A 2014 analysis of bestselling case studies used by business schools found that only 13 percent featured a female protagonist. To buck the trend, Yale School of Management has established its own case-writing team. "Increasingly we try to have protagonists who are not white men," DelMonico says. Faculty at the University of Virginia's Darden School of Business participate in periodic forums on engaging minority students, and they get coaching to improve their ability to lead inclusive classroom discussions, according to Martin Davidson, the school's global chief diversity officer and senior associate dean.

Classes that generate awareness of diversity issues are also popping up in the curriculum, such as

Dialogues on Race at University of California-Berkeley's Haas School of Business and Women and Leadership at Duke University's Fuqua School of Business, which explores gender stereotypes, bias and discrimination in organizations. "Negotiating gender identity is as important as knowing the technical aspects of finance

Michigan students share their stories during Diversity Week.

and accounting," says associate professor Ashleigh Shelby Rosette, who created the popular elective. Retired Army Brig. Gen. Rebecca Halstead, one of the first women to lead a unit in combat, paid a visit to the class via Skype in 2018. "When you have someone like that talking to you about leadership style and how she asserted herself in a male-dominated environment and had all this success, it's very inspiring," says second-year MBA student Jeanette Carneglia.

Schools also hold a wide variety of diversity-related events. Last year, Diversity Week at the Georgetown University McDonough School of Business featured a panel on LGBT rights in the non-Western world and a talk with actress Logan Browning of the Netflix series "Dear White People," which delves into racial stereotyping.

The makeup of business school faculty, an area where many schools consistently fall short, is starting to get a sharper focus. "The question is," Iannarelli says, "Do students see

themselves among the individuals that are teaching in business schools and that they are being presented with as having had successful business careers?" Many colleges and universities partner with The PhD Project, an organization dedicated to increasing the number of African-Americans, Hispanic Americans and Native Americans on business school faculties. Since 1994, the organization has shepherded nearly 1,300 minorities into careers in academia. According to Marie Zara, its director of advancement, schools with the most diverse faculties include Rutgers Business School, Howard University School of Business, and Morgan State University's Earl G. Graves School of Business and Management.

In addition to trying to recruit a more diverse faculty, schools often invite successful minority alumni to speak and serve as role models. Last year, Michigan Ross hosted Courtney Schroeder, a 2013 graduate of the program, who is now manager of diversity and inclusion at General Mills. "You have to work with people different from you in the workplace," he told students. "It's the one place we all have to figure it out."

In fact, students like Schroeder are often the

ones leading the charge towards greater diversity. While pursuing his MBA, he spearheaded a proposal to have the school hire its first diversity officer, which was adopted. And like other schools, Ross has scores of student-led clubs that help drive the diversity, equity and inclusion agenda, such as the Hispanic Business Students Association, Black Business Students Association, MBA Council and Michigan Business Women.

Several schools have programs with names like "Manbassadors," which generally encourage men to step up on gender issues or serve as allies for women. These include the Kellogg School of Management at Northwestern University; the Anderson School of Management at the University of California–Los Ange-

les; and the University of Chicago's Booth School of Business. As part of a Manbassadors gathering at Haas in 2018, former Michigan Gov. Jennifer Granholm and her husband Dan Mulhern were invited to discuss the shifting gender roles that arose when she took office in 2003. "He had a really good trajectory for his career but took a back seat in order to be a supportive husband," says Hao Shen, a second-year MBA student who co-organized the event. "He stressed the communication skills that he and Gov. Granholm had to develop to make sure that both their needs were being met."

Students are also making diversity and inclusion part of their scholarship. At Georgia Tech's Scheller School, marketing doctoral candidate Dionne Nickerson has organized workshops for Ph.D. students preparing for careers in business school academia. One session focused on implicit bias in the classroom; another involved having faculty members share examples of how they've worked to make classrooms more inclusive and have dealt with specific challenges – a marketing student making a gross generalization about a particular target market, for example. "That's a chance to create a learning opportunity and really go there as opposed to shying away from the issue or just moving on to the next subject," Nickerson says.

And when MBA student Christina Chavez helped to analyze the earnings of school alumni as part of the Gender Equity Initiative at Haas, she discovered a significant gender pay gap. "A lot of people think that women earn less because they take time off from their careers. But the data showed the gap exists with the very first job," she says. "The fact that the school allows us to do this research is great because talking about it more is how we're going to start making change."

While the move toward greater diversity in business schools isn't always as rapid as some would like to see, Scheller's Alavi puts it this way: "The important thing is that we are making progress and not going backwards." ●

SPOTLIGHT ON

Leeds School of Business

UNIVERSITY OF COLORADO–BOULDER

U.S. NEWS RANK #79

For the 195 or so full-time MBA students at the Leeds School of Business, Boulder offers Rocky Mountain views and a mix of both established firms and startups. Business students can link up with industry executives to network and sharpen their real-world skills through the school's professional mentorship program. They can also work with other graduate students to help seed new business ventures through the university's Deming Center for Entrepreneurship.

Indeed, a certain entrepreneurial spirit is "so much a part of the DNA of this ecosystem," says Dean Sharon Matusik. The curriculum offers specializations in that area, as well as in real estate, finance, marketing and beyond. Sustainability is another draw for some students. MBA candidates can take courses such as "Social Entrepreneurship for Emerging Markets" and "Sustainable Real Estate," and they might go on to work in brand management for organic food and consumer goods companies, say, or in strategic roles at environmental organizations. *–Ann Claire Carnahan*

▶ **More @ usnews.com/cu-boulder**

A Hefty Dose of Tech

Many B-schools are expanding their offerings in cutting-edge areas

by **Arlene Weintraub**

RALPH CAPRIO, 30, was going into the second year of his MBA program at Duke University's Fuqua School of Business when administrators there offered him the chance to get a technical twist on his traditional business degree: By taking eight data-focused courses, he could earn a specialized certificate that would give his MBA a designation in science, technology, engineering and math. Caprio jumped at the opportunity, signing up for classes that trained him in a variety of in-demand technical skills, such as using systems-modeling software and data visualization tools. All told, the coursework put "a quantitative spin on marketing and other core subject areas in business," he says.

After graduating in May of 2018, Caprio landed a job as a senior program manager at Amazon in Seattle, where he was soon deploying his abilities in data analytics. For example, he helped the company figure out how it could cut back on its use of corrugated shipping boxes without damaging the customer experience. "I was able to focus on the analytical side of business," Caprio says. "I learned valuable skills, like how to design marketing campaigns in the tech space, and how to use quantitative analysis to plan the life cycle of a business."

Duke is among a rapidly growing number of schools adding science- and tech-focused courses and programs for MBA and other graduate business students. In 2018, the University of Rochester's Simon Business School began offering a STEM option to all full-time MBA students, regardless of whether they're specializing in marketing, finance or any of the other eight areas the school makes available. Other graduate business schools with STEM programs include those at the University of Wisconsin–Madison and Worcester Polytechnic Institute in Massachusetts.

A formal "STEM designation" for college degree programs was launched during the Obama administration as a way to enhance America's leadership in fields like computer programming, the biological sciences and engineering. The designation was initially designed to attract foreign students by allowing those who qualify to live and work in the U.S. for additional time after graduation. But MBA programs that carry the STEM designation are finding that it has attracted applicants from within the U.S., too.

"There are absolutely benefits to students, whether domestic or international, to have the courses organized in a way that allows them to get the connection between business and technology, and to learn the tools that are relevant for doing more analytic and management-science type of work," says Russ Morgan, senior associate dean for full-time programs at Duke Fuqua. STEM degrees also provide "a good signal to employers that they have pursued this depth of technology competence," he says. In the fall of 2017, Fuqua also launched a stand-alone master's degree program in quantitative management for those who choose not to pursue a full MBA.

These B-schools are responding to two different but complementary demands: Employers are looking for graduates who are comfortable using sophisticated software to parse data and then deploy the results toward improving business practices. And many students are looking for training that will help them balance "soft skills" like marketing, management and communications with technical know-how. The intersection of business and technology might even help attract students who already have backgrounds in science or engineering. At Stanford University's Graduate School of Business, the University of Pennsylvania's Wharton School, and

A business-modeling class at the University of Rochester

the University of Michigan's Stephen M. Ross School of Business, for instance, nearly a third of the MBA classes of 2020 had undergraduate degrees in a STEM field before enrolling. **"Hot skills."** STEM-focused MBA grads are highly valued for a wide variety of jobs, such as helping to automate the trading desks of investment banks, managing the implementation of electronic health records at hospitals, and working at technology consulting firms. "Companies are dealing with an explosion of data that they need to analyze, understand and collate," says Scott Rostan, an adjunct finance professor at the University of

North Carolina Kenan-Flagler Business School, which offers a concentration in data and technology. "Then, they need to figure out how to use that data to improve the services they provide to customers. That creates a lot of job opportunities for well-rounded business school graduates."

Take Mastercard, for example. About 70 percent of the company's 2,400 new hires in 2018 came in with strong training in what the company calls "hot skills," which include blockchain, cybersecurity and artificial intelligence. "Our entire workforce is focused on figuring out how to embed technology in everything we do, and how to make sense of the tsunami of data we have," says Sarah Gretczko, senior vice president for organizational development and people insights at Mastercard. Prospective new hires at the company don't necessarily have to be computer science whizzes, Gretczko adds, "but they do have to embrace technology as a mindset in how they approach their work."

Financial services firms like Mastercard and all of the major banks are actively recruiting STEM-trained graduates, business school administrators report, as are major technology companies like Amazon, Microsoft, Google and Dell. "There's definitely a skill gap right now in the economy," says Wendy Moe, associate dean of master's programs at the University of Maryland's

Firms want tech-savvy grads who can parse data.'

Robert H. Smith School of Business. "You have people with good business and leadership skills, and then you have people with the technology skills. They speak different languages." STEM graduates are attractive to employers because they can "help to fill that gap," she says.

Students who want to pursue STEM-focused degrees can sometimes choose between tacking them onto existing MBA programs or pursuing a specialized master's degree. The latter tend to be more focused on technical coursework than the traditional management-related topics, and they can often be completed in as little as a year. Maryland's business school, for example, offers a number of STEM specialty master's degrees in topics such as quantitative finance and marketing analytics. The University of Iowa's Tippie College of Business recently phased out its full-time MBA program altogether (the spring 2019 class will be the final one) to focus on a range of alternative degree programs, such as two STEM-related master's degrees – one in business analytics and the other in finance.

David Deyak, assistant dean at Tippie, says the school made the change in response to interest from applicants, many of whom want to build their tech expertise without having to take too much time out of the workforce. They want their degrees to

SPOTLIGHT ON

Columbia Business School

COLUMBIA U., NEW YORK CITY

U.S. NEWS RANK #6

To help the 1,300 or so full-time MBA students build a sense of community, Columbia's first-year classes are broken into clusters of 65 to 70 students who take core courses in strategy, economics and other topics together.

Most students cherish the school's deep connections to a wide range of industries in New York, says Michael Malone, associate dean for M.S. and Ph.D. programs. A steady stream of executives from retail, media, health care and finance firms based in the Big Apple visit to speak, co-teach classes and recruit. Electives include immersion seminars on topics like luxury brands and shareholder activism, where teaching happens both in the classroom and during site visits around the city. For example, entrepreneurship seminar students spend time in New York's so-called Silicon Alley to see startups in action.

In addition, Columbia offers weeklong global immersion trips to countries like Cuba, Israel or Brazil. Students can also opt for other offerings like a 10-day backpacking expedition in Chilean Patagonia to learn sustainable environmental practices and leadership approaches. *–Lindsay Cates*

▶ **More @ usnews.com/columbia**

be "more condensed and specialized," Deyak says. The college's two full-time programs run for 15 months over three semesters, with a break before the third term so students can complete summer internships.

At Duke Fuqua, "the goal of the MBA program is to offer students the bread-and-butter management training, and then give them a lot of latitude to choose electives that focus on specialty areas" such as health analytics, financial statement analysis and innovation, Morgan says. By comparison, the Master of Quantitative Management degree requires just 10 months and is more heavily focused on data-analysis training, with options to focus on the technical side of finance, fraud analytics, marketing or strategy, say.

There are often cost advantages to such master's programs, too. At Duke, for example, the quant management degree costs about $95,300 (including living expenses) for students starting in 2018 – half the cost of the full-time MBA.

Real-world tech. As with many more traditional B-school programs, STEM business options tend to have a heavy focus on experiential learning and helping students sharpen their tech skills by solving real-world problems with actual companies. For example, one group of MBA students at Duke analyzed the social media platforms used by the NBA's Milwaukee Bucks basketball team. They used regressions and correlation analyses to determine the best content for the team to post on its feeds so it could better engage fans and leverage that into payments for tickets and merchandise.

Most such programs help students find internships. Caprio, who trained as a mechanical engineer and worked as a consultant before enrolling at Duke, was connected with an internship in one of Amazon's fulfillment centers in Charlotte, North Carolina, where he crunched data to try to figure out how to alleviate shipping

bottlenecks that commonly occur at the busiest times, such as the winter holiday shopping season.

Andrew Ainslie, dean at Simon Business School, believes the combination of technical training and real-world experience provided to students in STEM-focused programs is helping to attract interest in the school's offerings. He expects more than 85 percent of Simon's 2019 graduates will opt into STEM-designated MBA degrees, up from just under 70 percent in 2018.

Ramya Mure, 25, who graduated from Maryland's Smith school with a master's in information systems in December, gained valuable experience in data analysis while completing a class project for Airbnb. She and a group of other students mined data to determine which of the vacation-rental company's properties would be the most popular based on the amenities they offered. Among their discoveries: Apartments that let renters bring pets were among the most highly booked places.

In addition to gaining experience from such hands-on case studies during her classes, Mure nabbed a paid position in the B-school admissions office, where she analyzed data on applicants and made suggestions about how staff could improve their decisions about whom to admit. She was also hired as a research fellow for the Center for Health Information & Decision Systems on campus. She spent a year there using informatics to match patients with telehealth services in a way that would benefit them while also reducing the cost of care for providers.

Mure, who had previously earned a bachelor's degree in computer science in her home country of India, parlayed her work experiences at Maryland into a full-time sales job at Cisco in Raleigh, North Carolina. All in all, the blend of STEM and business in the master's program helped her balance out her expertise, she says. "I love technology, but this degree taught me the organizational strategy and management side of business, too," she says. "That was what I needed to be relevant in an organization." ●

ACADEMIC INSIGHTS
YOUR SCHOOL BY THE NUMBERS

Designed for schools, U.S. News Academic Insights provides instant access to a rich historical archive of undergraduate and graduate school rankings data.

Advanced Visualizations
Take complex data and turn it into six easily understandable and exportable views.

Download Center
Export large data sets from the new Download Center to create custom reports.

Dedicated Account Management
Have access to full analyst support for training, troubleshooting and advanced reporting.

Peer-Group Analysis
Flexibility to create your own peer groups to compare your institution on more than 5 M + data points.

Historical Trending
Find out how institutions have performed over time based on more than 350 metrics.

To request a demo visit **AI.USNEWS.COM**   or call **202.955.2121**

Forging Your Own Path

Students no longer have to settle for the standard two-year MBA

by **Katherine Hobson**

RISTEN KRANZLER knew she wanted to continue her business education. She was less clear on what form that might take. Her nearly $20,000 in undergraduate student loan debt made her wary of a pricey traditional two-year MBA program. But she wanted to move beyond her niche in inventory management and think about the bigger picture. "I didn't have an understanding of the end-to-end supply chain," she says. "I was feeling a little bit stuck."

Then representatives of the University of Minnesota–Twin Cities' Carlson School of Management showed up at work, talking about their master's degree in supply chain management. It's a 12-month program for working professionals with classes mostly in the evening and also on weekends and online. "It seemed like it was designed for me," says Kranzler, now 28, who graduated in 2018. Currently a manager at hearing aid company Starkey Hearing Technologies, she creates standard operating procedures for her supply management team and feels far more prepared to understand strategic decisions across the entire company. Her degree required a bit more explanation to potential employers than an MBA, but it was worth it. "It was absolutely the experience I needed," she says.

While the traditional two-year, residential MBA is still the gold standard for people who want to gain general business skills, there are now many paths to a graduate business education. Some people, like Kranzler, are opting to dig deep with a specialized master's degree. Others want the broader MBA curriculum, but they have enough career focus and relevant experience to earn the degree in a single year. Or they want to pursue an MBA without significantly disrupting their life. Other people don't want the structure or cost of a degree program, but are simply looking to gain new expertise.

"We're seeing alternatives emerge to align to the different needs of different students who are at different points in their careers," says Juliane Iannarelli, senior vice president and chief knowledge officer at AACSB International, which accredits business schools. And, she says, those options work

well in today's environment of lifelong learning, in which people will increasingly need to pick up skills throughout their career. "The model wherein we go to school once, then embark on a career path and perhaps go to school one more time doesn't really align with today's needs," she says.

But the wealth of options can be confusing. Here's what you need to know about key alternatives to the traditional MBA:

For experienced professionals who don't want to leave their job, executive MBA options have become more varied to accommodate students' calendars and interests. Typically, these programs take about 20 months to complete, and classes are concentrated into blocks of time so students can keep working; the average participant already has 14 years of experience.

Columbia Business School has had an EMBA program since

Carlson students start a tour of 3M's Innovation Center with an introductory movie on the dome.

1968, but it has integrated more flexibility and customization particularly as fewer employers are willing to pay the bills. "It's no longer, 'We're a big company; go to an MBA program every Friday for two years, come back, and we'll promote you,'" says Kelley Martin Blanco, assistant dean and dean of students of EMBA programs at Columbia. Students today are more likely to be seeking out a program and paying for it themselves.

Since 2009, Columbia has launched three new EMBA programs: the Saturday option, where all core courses are scheduled for that day; the EMBA-Global Asia program, with most classes in Hong Kong but others in London and New York; and the EMBA-Americas program, for students from the U.S., Canada and Latin America with classes that meet for five-to-six-day blocks every month. (Obviously, employer approval and support is necessary for dayslong absences from the office.) For the right program, plenty of people will commit to regular travel.

Liz Cercado, who had more than 10 years of engineering ex-

S P O T L I G H T   O N

Hankamer School of Business

BAYLOR UNIVERSITY, WACO, TEXAS

In their first year, full-time general MBA students at Baylor's Hankamer School of Business complete the Focus Firm class, where they partner with a company such as AT&T, Nike or Lockheed Martin to address current business problems and provide potential solutions. The course is one of many ways that students can experience hands-on learning. MBA candidate Abby Tisdale, 23, completed an organizational development project at a retirement asset firm, where she shared recommendations on how to improve its internal communications and training. Another option: the Prison Entrepreneurship Program, where MBA candidates help inmates craft business plans.

Through the Robbins Institute for Health Policy and Leadership, healthcare administration MBA students interested in management roles at insurers, hospitals and other care facilities can take specialized courses and complete a seven-month paid executive residency at a hospital or health system. Residents work directly with a mentor to learn about strategic thinking, operations management and other front-line practices. –*Ann Claire Carnahan*

▶ **More @ usnews.com/baylor**

perience at Boeing but wanted an MBA to round out her technical expertise, is one of them. "If we talked about airplane design, fantastic. If we talked about a P&L statement, I didn't have that breadth or familiarity," she says. She chose the 22-month EMBA program at the UCLA Anderson School of Management and makes a monthly commute of more than a thousand miles from her home outside Seattle for Friday and Saturday classes. The travel time and costs (she's paying for the degree and associated expenses) are worth it; Cercado loves the diversity of industries and of life experience in her cohort, and that about a third of her class are female. The program is also filling the gaps in her skills and opening her eyes to fields she hadn't considered, including strategy and entrepreneurship.

Her advice to potential students considering this path: Think of such programs as an additional part-time job, and be flexible. "You need to assess how badly you want it and why you want it. What parameters are you willing to adjust to achieve it?" she says.

Other degree-seekers are willing to leave the workplace, but not for two full years. The one-year MBA, long popular in Europe, has a growing presence in the U.S. as well, including at Emory University's Goizueta Business School, the University of Notre Dame's Mendoza College of Business and Cornell University's Samuel Curtis Johnson Graduate School of Management. Students in one-year programs typically need to absorb much of the core content of an MBA in a single summer, so schools may require more academic or professional credentials than for a two-year program. And there is no time for a summer internship, so an accelerated program may not be a fit for people who want careers in fields such as investment banking that recruit heavily from internship programs, says Mark Nelson, dean of Johnson. They're

also not a natural option for people who lack career focus, he says.

The Johnson Cornell Tech MBA is geared for people with interests and career ambitions in the digital economy, whether that's at a startup or at an established tech company, and begins with a summer of core business courses in Ithaca before moving to the Cornell Tech campus in New York City to come up with new product and service ideas and to build digital and product management skills.

Cornell also has a general one-year MBA program based

in Ithaca, which appealed to Sara Schmitt, 34. She'd worked for a decade at a medical software company and had earned a project management professional credential. Schmitt worried that she was too senior for a traditional program (where students average under five years of work experience) and not yet ready for an EMBA. Cornell's accelerated MBA turned out to be the sweet spot, and Schmitt will graduate this year, looking for future employment in the tech sector. "It's exactly what I expected and wanted," says Schmitt.

Focus is also the hallmark of one-year specialized master's programs. These are often – but not always – for people who are early on in their careers, sometimes right out of college. "If you look at why students choose to get a one-year master's – it's to get a job," says Cherrie Wilkerson, assistant dean for young professional programs at Vanderbilt University's Owen Graduate School of Management. Some students developed an interest in business late enough in college that they missed out on core classes, or went to a school that wasn't on the recruiting trail, says Wilkerson, who oversees the school's Master of Accountancy, Master of Science in finance and Master of Marketing degrees. These narrower degrees allow those people to "get the piece of an MBA" that's most interesting to them, she says. And students take some of their classes with MBA students, which gives them informational and networking opportunities. "The MBAs are leaving the jobs that our students want to move into," she says.

The possibilities include full-time and executive programs. Duke's Fuqua School of Business offers a full-time 10-month Master of Management Studies, giving recent grads the basics of business fundamentals such as accounting and strategy. Georgetown's McDonough School of Business has teamed with the university's Edmund A. Walsh School of Foreign Service to offer a 12-month Master of Arts in international business and policy; students continue to work during the program. The University of Southern California's Marshall School of Business offers a 10-month Friday-Saturday business master's for former or active military personnel looking to transition to the private sector. "The effort we put into career development is immense and intense, and success usually requires folks not simply to shift, but to complete a transformative process," says James Bogle, who spent 23 years as an Army officer before becoming head of the Master of Business for Veterans program.

If you want to brush up your skills or broaden your general knowledge but avoid the time and cost of a formal degree program, you might consider a professional certificate. A report commissioned by AACSB International and other groups found nontraditional options like certificates and digital badges are "gaining credibility and interest." At the University of Texas–Dallas' Jindal School of Management, the noncredit certificate of management is also known

 Credit-bearing or not, a certificate can be valuable on a résumé.'

as a "mini-MBA." "It's the full breadth of topics in a regular MBA program, but it doesn't go nearly as deep," explains David Spivey, executive director of the certificate of management program. It attracts people eager to rise in management, gain responsibility or update their skills.

Students must complete the self-paced program within a year and achieve a 70 or better course grade to earn a certificate. Rutgers Business School has more than 20 different mini-MBA programs for midcareer professionals, from business essentials to digital marketing to intergenerational leadership, some of which offer graduate credits that are accepted toward degrees at Rutgers and other schools. Peter Methot, executive director of the school's executive education program, says they're intended to be "stackable," building on students' existing credentials. In some cases, that means people who already have an MBA return for a mini-MBA in digital marketing – a field that didn't exist when they were getting their degree. Courses are offered both online and in face-to-face weeklong modules.

Credit-bearing or not, a certificate can definitely be valuable on a résumé, advises Hallie Crawford, an Atlanta-based certified career coach. "It shows initiative and that you took the time to do it." That said, these credentials aren't full-fledged degrees and won't be treated as such by employers. It's crucial to do some research to make sure it will help you achieve your long-term goal. AACSB's Iannarelli agrees. Future career success, she says, will come from connecting the dots for your employer – or potential employer – between your coursework and prior work experience and the requirements for the job you want. No degree alone will be the magic bullet. ●

Weatherhead Sch. of Management

CASE WESTERN RESERVE U., CLEVELAND

U.S. NEWS RANK #74

Situated in the heart of Cleveland, the Weatherhead School of Management enrolls about 50 full-time MBA students per year, so classmates can develop close bonds. Each student picks a concentration in finance, operations or marketing, and many intern in those areas with major employers like Goodyear, Cleveland Clinic and Lubrizol Corp., which are headquartered nearby. Almost half of each MBA class has a STEM background, and all students now take business analytics as a core course, says Dean Manoj Malhotra. They can also pursue a thematic focus in sustainability, say, or design and innovation, as well as add electives in hot areas like artificial intelligence and blockchain.

"Companies want creative thinkers that are able to problem-solve," says Kelsey Knutty, 24, a second-year MBA student. Last summer, she interned in KeyBank's human resources department and "heavily used" her newfound design-thinking skills to help create a streamlined onboarding program for new hires and redesign the company's internship program. She'll return to KeyBank full time after she graduates. –*Lindsay Cates*

▶ **More @ usnews.com/cwru**

Where the Action Is

School partnerships with local communities are paying off

by **Margaret Loftus**

AXWELL KUSHNER-LENHOFF landed his first postgrad job at Dow Chemical after earning bachelor's and master's degrees in chemistry from Yale. In just four years, he became communications manager in the office of the chairman and CEO, but Kushner-Lenhoff aspired to move into business management in the clean-technology sector. He looked for an MBA program that would both "fill in the gap in my skill set" and offer hands-on experience. He found it at the University of California-Berkeley's Haas School of Business, a major hub for renewable energy entrepreneurship. In a course called Cleantech to Market, five- or six-person teams, each including MBA students, science and engineering Ph.D.s, and others such as law or policy students, are matched with

A networking event for students and startups tied to Olin's Hatchery

an entrepreneur, a startup or researchers looking to launch a clean-tech product. During the fall semester, students conduct intensive market research into their assigned product, culminating in a 100-page commercialization study and a December symposium where they present their findings and recommend how to bring each offering to market. In the past decade, more than 300 researchers and startup founders have been matched with student teams that worked on 74 technologies, 43 of which ended up being commercialized. Half of those are already profitable or generating revenue.

Kushner-Lenhoff led a team that worked with startup MICROrganic Technologies to conduct an intensive analysis to determine the best early markets for its clean-tech wastewater treatment solution, which eliminates 60 percent of a typical plant's wastewater treatment energy use. His experience with the company (which is now focusing on the food-and-beverage manufacturing market based on his team's work) helped Kushner-Lenhoff hone the skills he needed to redirect his career. After graduating from Haas in 2018, he was hired as a global supply chain manager for battery materials at electric car manufacturer Tesla in Palo Alto, Calif. Mission accomplished, Kushner-Lenhoff says. The course "prepared me for a lot of the work that I currently do, from building a financial model for a new technology to leading an interdisciplinary team."

Haas reflects a trend of business schools carving out

roles as anchors in their communities. Fostering relationships with a range of entities, from startups and Fortune 1000 companies to government agencies and nonprofits, schools are creating opportunities for students to involve themselves in local economies, particularly through consulting and entrepreneurial courses. The collaborations are a win-win for everyone, says Juliane Iannarelli, senior vice president and chief knowledge officer at AACSB International, which accredits business schools. "These programs give students experience, and the business or nonprofit receives perspective and expertise that they wouldn't otherwise have the resources for."

This fall, Indiana University's Kelley School of Business will roll out a redesigned curriculum for its part-time MBA program. All students will have to complete a three-credit consulting gig with an Indianapolis company. The exercise is a domestic version of an offering from Kelley's online MBA curriculum in which students serve as consultants to small businesses in emerging economies like Myanmar and Chile via Skype for 11 weeks and then in

person for one week. "We're now going to bring it home and put it to work here," says Phil Powell, Kelley's associate dean of academic programs.

In Indianapolis, students will be matched with companies in five industries that drive the regional economy – high tech, health care, supply chain and logistics, advanced manufacturing, and commercial real estate – as well as startup enterprises that operate in economically challenged areas. Students might conduct market research to vet a new opportunity, develop an operational plan to move into a new geographic market or redesign workflow in a factory. The days of faculty solely lecturing to classes are numbered, Powell says. "We're going to throw our students in the real world and coach them on how to deliver value. That's what companies are asking for."

Last fall, part-time MBA candidate Dave Nachand, 31, got a taste of that new paradigm when he signed up for the new Kelley pilot consulting course and worked at Indianapolis manufacturer Allison Transmission. With a faculty coach, Nachand and a team of four fellow students conducted research and analysis in Allison's defense division. The students were treated like any external consultant. Says Pat Morello, executive director of defense programs at Allison: "We started off with a set of requirements, and they came back and gave us a project proposal and the resources they needed to accomplish it. They actually had a good mix of short- and midterm recommendations that we could implement right away." An example: using statistical analysis software packages to capture every government solicitation in their space.

Nachand admits that the three-month project, which wrapped up last October, required a major commitment. "There was a lot of information to take in. We were scrolling through government guidelines for the first month," he says. He and his

SPOTLIGHT ON

W. P. Carey School of Business

ARIZONA STATE UNIVERSITY, TEMPE

U.S. NEWS RANK #33

In 2016, the W. P. Carey School of Business rolled out its revamped Forward Focus curriculum, through which all 195 full-time MBA students have access to opportunities such as career coaching; mentoring from industry executives; and courses on leadership, data analytics and entrepreneurship. They can also participate in cross-disciplinary learning labs where B-school students partner with peers across other ASU schools on real community challenges. For instance, in one recent collaboration with ASU's Herberger Institute for Design and the Arts and the local Downtown Tempe Authority, business and architecture students worked together to provide recommendations related to transportation and community development issues in the area.

Along with the retooled curriculum, ASU considers all full-time MBA applicants for scholarships toward tuition and fees for the two-year program, which run about $58,700 for Arizona residents and $96,500 for out-of-staters. *–Mariya Greeley*

▶ More @ usnews.com/asu

teammates, all of whom have full-time jobs, and some, young families, had to carve time out of their already hectic schedules. "It was a rough few months, to be honest. My girlfriend wasn't happy with me."

But in the end, it was worth it. "I took it on because I wanted to grow my consulting skills and grow my career that way," he says. He hopes to move into a consulting role with his current employer or get a job with a consulting firm when he graduates this summer. Plus, working with a local company was important to him. "Indiana is a good manufacturing state – something we take pride in. You want to be a part of that; you want to have a sense of belonging."

Some programs, like the one at Berkeley Haas that launched Kushner-Lenoff into clean-tech, are geared to area industry clusters. Washington University's Olin Business School, for example, has become an innovation hub for St. Louis, which has been on the losing end of globaliza-

Inside the Cortex, the innovation and technology district cofounded by WashU

tion in recent years. Once home to the highest per capita number of Fortune 500 companies of any U.S. city, notes Cliff Holekamp, Olin's academic director for entrepreneurship, St. Louis has seen an expansion of its "eds and meds" – education and health care – sectors. Olin is helping to bolster those sectors, and others, with various programs and initiatives. The school currently touts several courses in which students do pro bono consulting projects to assist local small businesses, startups and nonprofits in these fields. In yet another course, the Hatchery, students learn how to research, model and launch startups themselves.

Abby Cohen, 28, a leader in the city's medical startup community, says the school "is a huge evangelist for entrepreneurs in St. Louis." As a biomedical engineering undergrad, she explored the potential for a smartphone-connected device that measures lung function for people with chronic obstructive pulmonary disease in the Hatchery. She credits the coursework, Olin incubators and feedback from mentors with helping her secure the startup funds and connections to angel investors needed to successfully launch her company, Sparo, with co-founder Andrew Brimer,

another Washington University graduate.

Olin also participates in the Cortex Innovation Community. The 200-acre site, co-founded by WashU and other institutions, is located 4 miles east of campus and has the city's highest concentration of bioscience and tech companies, with lab and shared office space. Some Olin courses are held at Cortex, including a lab on cybersecurity and defense entrepreneurship. While some incubators are situated on campus, Cortex was intentionally not. "We want students to get off campus and into the St. Louis community," Holekamp says. "That's how they build a network here and end up staying."

It's these sorts of programs that prospective students may overlook when comparing MBA programs. "On the surface there can be a fair amount of similarities," says AACSB's Iannarelli. "But often where the differentiation comes in are extracurricular activities and the way a school connects them to the local community." She suggests students find out if faculty are involved in research centers or industries that resonate with their interests.

Connecting with the local community could mean a better job upon graduation. "The best way to rise above the competitive pack is to distinguish yourself with internships and experiential engagements," Holekamp says. "Local entrepreneurial firms provide students opportunity for greater impact on the organization, thus enriching the quality of their work experiences. This helps students develop more compelling personal narratives" with which to compete for opportunities at top international firms. It can also lead to job offers from the local firms where students were engaged, he says – often at higher seniority levels than where they might otherwise have been placed.

Powell sees such partnerships as the wave of the future for B-schools: "We understand we need to step up and deliver more value." Notes Holekamp: "Your local business community is your students' sandbox, so it's really important for the quality of the student experiences to have as high quality a sandbox as possible." ●

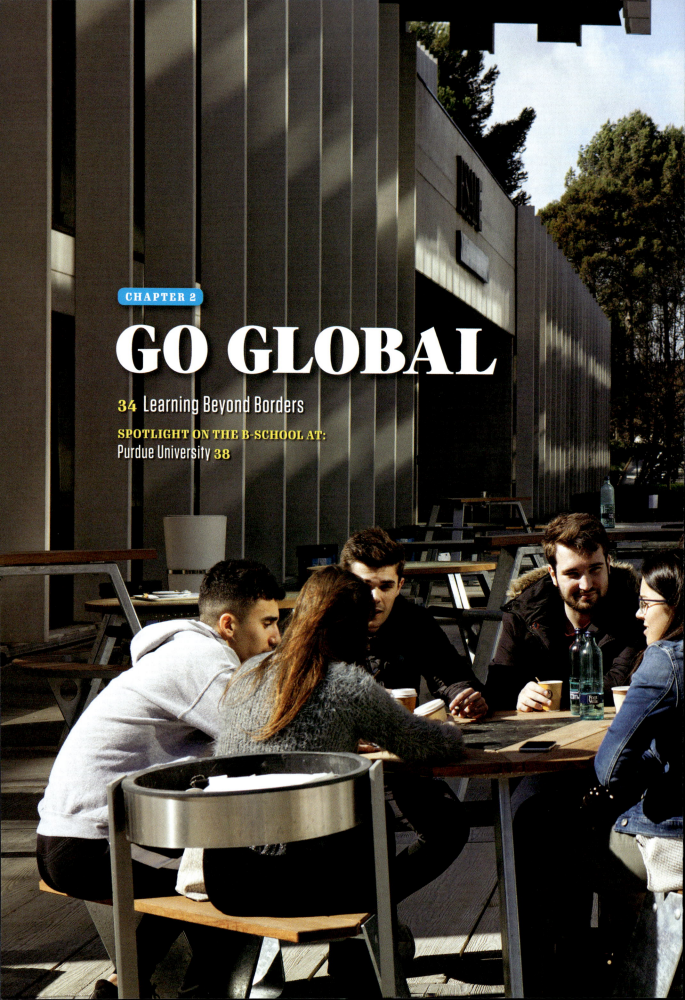

ESADE Business
School, Barcelona
ISABELA ESEVERRI FOR USN&WR

Learning Beyond Borders

Students have new ways to engage with a more connected world

by **Courtney Rubin**

LAST FALL, 23-YEAR-OLD Caroline Wimbleton arrived in Madrid to work in marketing management for Allianz Partners, a global insurance and assistance company. She didn't know anyone in the city, but she knew enough about office culture in Spain to listen carefully in meetings before jumping into the fray. In the U.S., she says, "there is a much stronger sense of self, which is reflected in the dominant leadership style." In contrast, she knew that leaders in Spain tend to prioritize getting collective input rather than that of just one central person.

Wimbleton credits her ease in working with people from different countries and cultures to a new 10-month program she completed in 2018 that simultaneously earned her two business master's degrees and a certificate from schools on three continents. A partnership between the University of Virginia's McIntire School of Commerce, Lingnan (University) College at Sun Yat-sen University in Guangzhou, China; and ESADE Business School in Barcelona, Spain, the program sends students to live and study at all three institutions for stints ranging from nine to 15 weeks. Participants take globally focused courses and study the unique aspects of doing business in the U.S., China and the European Union. Graduates earn a master's in global commerce from UVA, a master's in global strategic management from ESADE, and a certificate in international business from Lingnan. The program debuted in 2016, and the class graduating in 2019 includes 54 students from 13 countries.

Says Wimbleton, who moved to Paris after Madrid for Allianz Partners: "We lived and worked with so many different people you learn that communication is not necessarily just about language."

UVA's program reflects a growing trend among U.S. B-schools to beef up their international offerings for students who want to prepare themselves for a more interconnected global economy. According to a 2016 ranking of the "most international" MBA programs by business education website Poets&Quants, the MIT Sloan School of Management was the top U.S. finisher – in 39th place. But that trend is starting to turn around as U.S. business schools aggressively reimagine their standard curri-

ASIA SCHOOL OF BUSINESS. MBA students being prepped before a factory tour in Malaysia

cula for both traditional MBAs and other professional business master's degrees. Many schools have introduced globally focused courses, such as Chinese Economy and Financial Markets at the University of Chicago Booth School of Business and Israel: Startups and Venture Capital at Harvard Business School.

And since 2016, all full-time MBA students at the Yale School of Management have been required to take a course called Global Virtual Teams, in which they work online with students from a network of international schools to tackle critical business issues. Students might oversee a hypothetical production line, say, making key operations management decisions while getting a feel for working across cultures and time zones. Other institutions are expanding their efforts now with deep immersion programs, academic alliances with global partners, and even a brand-new global business school – all designed to attract more international students and turn domestic ones into effective and culturally sensitive multinational business leaders.

A deep dive. Though study abroad options have been standard fare for years, business schools at Pennsylvania State University, Dartmouth College, Harvard and Rice University have made them core requirements, often in the form of short immersion trips. Rice's Jesse H. Jones Graduate School of Business has required executive MBA students to take so-called global immersion programs for a few years and, starting with the fall 2018 entering class, all MBAs need to complete a mandatory 10-day Global Field Experience before graduating. Much of that time is "dedicated to intensive experiential coursework (including working with in-country experts and business leaders to solve real problems), along with mean-ingful cultural immersion" and "a strategic focus on the big picture," all combined in an experience they can enjoy with their classmates, says Barbara Bennett Ostdiek, senior associate dean of degree programs.

Current students have the option of traveling to either Lima, Peru; Bogota, Colombia; or Mexico City, and Ostdiek expects a continued emphasis on emerging and frontier markets in the years ahead. Other B-schools at the College of William and Mary, the University of Florida and the University of Michigan offer similar opportunities.

A STRONG CULTURAL MIX

U.S. NEWS has compiled a list of the full-time and part-time MBA programs (from among ranked programs) that, for 2018, had the highest percentage of international students enrolled. U.S. News collected this data directly from each MBA program in the fall of 2018 and early 2019. Advantages of choosing a program with a high proportion of international students are that participants can more frequently engage with peers from different cultures, and the curriculum is apt to be more globally oriented. The first data column below indicates the percentage of the full- or part-time 2018 enrollment that was international; the second gives the total full- or part-time enrollment of the program.

MBA PROGRAMS WITH THE MOST INTERNATIONAL STUDENTS

Full Time

School	% international students	'18 enrollment
Stevens Institute of Technology (NJ)	93.4%	595
Babson College (Olin) (MA)	75.0%	344
Syracuse University (Whitman) (NY)	64.4%	45
University of California–Riverside (Anderson)	58.4%	113
Purdue University–West Lafayette (Krannert) (IN)	54.8%	93
University of Arizona (Eller)	50.6%	79
University of Connecticut	50.0%	94
Chapman University (Argyros) (CA)	45.8%	59
College of William and Mary (Mason) (VA)	44.1%	204
University of California–Davis	44.0%	91
University of California–Irvine (Merage)	43.9%	157
University of Rochester (Simon) (NY)	43.1%	209
George Washington University (DC)	41.1%	129
Northeastern University (MA)	39.4%	160
University of Pittsburgh (Katz) (PA)	39.2%	120
University of Illinois–Urbana-Champaign	37.2%	94
Drexel University (LeBow) (PA)	36.8%	38
Case Western Reserve U. (Weatherhead) (OH)	36.8%	95
Iowa State University	36.7%	79
CUNY Bernard M. Baruch College (Zicklin)	36.0%	75

Part Time

School	% international students	'18 enrollment
Indiana University of Pennsylvania (Eberly)	89.8%	98
University of Northern Iowa	70.7%	198
Seton Hall University (Stillman) (NJ)	62.9%	448
Adelphi University (NY)	60.3%	469
California State University–East Bay	51.3%	228
California State University–Fullerton (Mihaylo)	49.4%	316
University of California–Riverside (Anderson)	48.6%	146
University of Texas–Arlington	35.3%	433
University of North Carolina–Charlotte (Belk)	35.2%	375
University of St. Thomas–Houston (TX)	30.7%	179
University of Texas–Dallas	28.2%	720
Indiana University (Kelley)	28.1%	288
California State University–San Bernard	25.0%	204
Bradley University (Foster) (IL)	24.4%	45
Pace University (Lubin) (NY)	24.2%	95
Loyola Marymount University (CA)	23.6%	55
Saginaw Valley State University (MI)	23.3%	60
Chapman University (Argyros) (CA)	22.4%	116
Mercer University–Atlanta (Stetson) (GA)	22.2%	347
Queens University of Charlotte (McColl) (NC)	20.0%	100

Full- and part-time MBA enrollment data are as of March 1, 2019. Only ranked schools are eligible to be included on this list.

The Leonard N. Stern School of Business at New York University still makes international academic experiences optional for most MBA students, but a new one-year fashion-and-luxury MBA requires an intensive week in Milan. This includes a mix of study (class topics include the fine food industry in Italy and the evolution of Italian brands), corporate visits (Lamborghini in Bologna and the Mantero Silk Factory in Como), plus a final project that challenges student teams to create an American marketing plan for an Italian retailer looking to expand its presence in the U.S. market.

MBAs in Stern's traditional two-year program can also opt for one- or two-week "Doing Business in" offerings held in about a dozen countries, including Australia, Israel and South Africa. They talk to academics, make company visits and have cultural experiences. Many students also partner with faculty and go abroad to help solve a real-world business problem through Stern Solutions' experiential learning projects. A former group collaborated with the World Wildlife Fund and the United Arab Emirates' Fujairah municipality to launch the country's first national park. Students spent two weeks in the UAE before the start of the semester, then they worked to come up with a strategy before presenting it by videoconference.

Dual-degree partnerships. Much of the new B-school emphasis on global studies is coming in business master's programs, which are growing fast as an alternative to the MBA. Reflecting this trend, UVA's McIntire program places significant emphasis on tapping the expertise of each school and its locale in the partnership. Business students start at McIntire, where they take advantage of working with a foreign company doing business in the U.S. to study global strategic management, global market research and cross-cultural decision-making. After 15 weeks, students move on to China, where they focus on global finance and operations, and take advantage of visiting high-tech companies in Hong Kong and southern China. Finally, at ESADE in Spain, they focus on entrepreneurship, corporate social responsibility, and innovation and global alliances.

The program is taught in English in all three countries. Students in the coming year will pay approximately $37,400 in tuition, plus roughly $11,000 in housing expenses for the 10 months. Travel expenses are not included. Members of the 2018-2019 class of five dozen students live together during their time on all three continents in cross-cultural residences. There's also a strong emphasis on group work in all classes, so students "are teaching each other all the time" in both formal and less formal ways, says Amanda

SPOTLIGHT ON

Krannert School of Management

PURDUE UNIVERSITY
WEST LAFAYETTE, INDIANA

U.S. NEWS RANK #74

Purdue University's engineering program has long been a top draw, and in fact, more than half of the MBA students at the Krannert School of Management have a STEM background. The campus in West Lafayette is "a sandbox" for people who want to work at the intersection of tech and business, says Dean David Hummels. Students can specialize in manufacturing/technology management, for instance, or technology innovation and entrepreneurship.

Recent MBA grad Steve Sanders, 29, volunteered at the Purdue Foundry, an entrepreneurship hub, where he assisted tech startups in developing their business plans. He was also part of a group that helps the university decide which startups are worth investing in before landing a job as a portfolio business analyst at Elanco, a global animal health company. Also strong in data analytics, Krannert hosts 24-hour "data dives," during which chief data strategists from companies such as Walmart and Cisco allow groups of students to examine their raw data files to help them solve business challenges. *–Lindsay Cates*

▶ **More @ usnews.com/purdue**

Cowen, director of McIntire's M.S. in Global Commerce Program. The cohort has organized an international cooking night, and students often travel to each other's homes over holiday breaks to experience local celebrations and traditions. "They're developing a global network of relationships that continues to be important as they move into their careers," Cowen says. Graduates of the inaugural class have landed jobs at a range of companies including Amazon, Google, Marriott International, Rolls-Royce, Volvo and GSK.

The Yale SOM is also exploring dual-degree partnerships via its new master's initiative, called M2M, with four other schools: the University of British Columbia's Sauder School of Business, HKUST Business School in Hong Kong, HEC Paris, and Brazil's FGV Escola de Administração de Empresas de São Paulo. Students simultaneously earn master's degrees at two of the participating schools in a two-year program and have access to both schools' alumni networks. Giving students the skills to work in a global marketplace is "what recruiters tell us they're looking for," says David Bach, Yale SOM's deputy dean.

Enrollees pay the tuition costs of whichever institutions they attend. Yale's annual tuition and fees for 2018-2019 run about $71,600, while the total cost for a student at HEC Paris, for example, runs about $29,000. Travel and living expenses are not included.

Washington University and the University of Maryland are also offering dual options. The Olin Business School in St. Louis has five different dual-degree programs in which students can pursue a Master of Science in finance from Olin along with a second degree or certificate from a global partner. Maryland debuted a program in 2018 through which students can earn a Master of Quantitative Finance from the school's Robert H. Smith School of Business and a Global Management Program certificate from the S. P. Jain Institute of Management and Research in Mumbai, India.

A global school. The growing interest in international degrees has even led to the creation of a new global MBA school – so new it doesn't even have its own campus yet. The Asia School of Business is a partnership between MIT Sloan and Bank Negara Malaysia, the central bank of Malaysia. The 82 first- and second-year students currently enrolled represent 21 different countries. The program is heavily experiential. "We are teaching [students] how to go into a country they've never been in before and build a business, build networks," says Charles Fine, founding president and dean of ASB and a professor of management at MIT. The program is based in Kuala Lumpur, where classes are currently held in the central bank's training center while a campus is being built.

Over the course of four to five weeks out of each 14-week semester, student teams travel to different countries in Southeast Asia to work with companies on projects. Some recently went to Myanmar, for example, to help Procter & Gamble figure out how to market hair and skin care products there. Students also spend six weeks in the U.S. They first visit New York City, then spend about a month in residence at MIT. The courses in Malaysia cover typical MBA topics like finance and marketing, but students have to be nimble, as scheduling often depends on when MIT professors are able to travel abroad. A course on finance, for instance, might be broken up into several weeklong modules taught in the fall, winter and spring. MIT faculty split teaching duties with a group of 13 local faculty members, who come from 10 different countries.

For now, the classes, all taught in English, are "almost all aligned with MIT Sloan content and are not particularly Asia-specific," Fine says, though they will likely become more specialized as the school recruits and develops more professors locally. The program lasts 20 months and costs roughly $100,000, including

campus housing, travel and lodging costs incurred for the trip to the U.S. Graduates receive an MBA from ASB and a certificate from MIT Sloan.

When she learned about the MIT program, Klara Markus, 29, was already working in Vietnam for Quad Learning, a U.S.-based education tech startup (after working for it in Washington, D.C.), and thinking about business school. "I get the structured learning environment of cases but then I get to balance it with actually doing stuff, and I get to travel to different countries across Southeast Asia," Markus says, speaking by phone from Bangkok, where she was at an end-of-semester school symposium. "There's really no downside." Markus has a political science degree from Yale and has been able to use the ASB experience to win a spot in a leadership development program in the U.S., which should open up more career options for her.

While students may miss some of the traditional opportunities (like large and long-

UNIVERSITY OF VIRGINIA.
UVA students do some team-building at ESADE in Barcelona, a partner school along with another in Guangzhou, China.

established job fairs) that standard MBA programs might offer, 2019 ASB graduate Dante Zannoni, 31, notes that he has gotten more travel and project-based experience than many students in traditional programs. "Right now I'm at a steel mill in Vietnam, and before that I was at a Bangkok bank, one of the largest financial institutions in Southeast Asia," Zannoni says. At a manufacturer in Penang, Malaysia, early in his program, he and his team were able to find upwards of $200,000 in cost savings in the company's operations. "It was way more impactful than spending each day just going over cases that have happened in the past," Zannoni says.

What do potential employers make of students who can bring this kind of international experience with their degree? "They find it very enticing," says Ally Van Deuren, university relations lead for North America with Korn Ferry, an executive search and recruiting firm.

But the particular experience matters. A weeklong study tour will rarely separate you from the pack compared to, say, spending a semester abroad and doing an internship. Bonus points if your experience is in a region of interest to your potential employer. In general, demonstrating substantive experience can really help your résumé rise to the top of the pile. ●

**The Business School
at Harvard**

BRETT ZIEGLER FOR USN&WR

GAIN EXPERIENCE

Bringing the Next **Great Idea** to Life

B-schools now offer entrepreneurs robust support to realize their dreams

by **Elizabeth Gardner**

A**NGELISE HADLEY,** 29, was in the thick of starting EmbraceBox, a hair products subscription service for little girls with curly hair, when she realized how little she knew about the "moving parts" of running a company: developing a marketing strategy, picking an e-commerce platform and handling accounting, budgeting and taxes. Neither her science business degree from the University of Notre Dame (basically a life science major combined with a business minor) nor her day job as a human resources consultant had given her the right skillset. So she headed to the McCombs School of Business at the University of Texas–Austin, where she's concentrating in entrepreneurship and product management and will graduate with an MBA in May 2019. McCombs attracts entrepreneurially minded students with the city's vibrant startup environment and because of the school's resources, says Assistant Dean Tina Mabley. These include summer fellowships and work space for MBA students engaged in launching a startup, competitions for seed money (box, Page 45), and an extensive network of alumni mentors.

"While you're here, it's two years of focusing on your business, which you wouldn't have a chance to do working full time," says Hadley who has a job lined up after she graduates, but plans to continue bootstrapping her business. In a few years, she hopes to be working exclusively on her company. "I foresee getting to a point where I will need outside investment, and I'll be in a much stronger position to speak to investors" with an MBA in hand, she says.

Entrepreneurship is part of America's bedrock. In 2016, the most recent year for which data are available, entrepreneurs launched about 6.5 million businesses, according to the Kauffman Index, which tracks entrepreneurial activity. For ambitious self-starters like these, spending two years of precious development time in graduate school – not to mention losing out on potential income and making a likely six-figure investment in tuition and living costs – may seem too much when success feels so close. But the Kauffman Index also shows fewer than half of those businesses will still be around in five years. So, for many would-be entrepreneurs, investing in a graduate business education can be a worthwhile tradeoff, yielding strong returns in knowledge, contacts with classmates and alumni (who may become investors or collaborators), and easier access to resources and capital.

Brook Stroud, 31, was one student who found the benefits exceeded the costs. Stroud and his brother had spent four years starting and running a company that imported men's accessories from Argentina. "We had a successful product, but we didn't understand financials and

Angelise Hadley participates in an entrepreneurial finance class at ESADE in Barcelona, one of McCombs' study abroad locations.

operations and cash flow," he says. So Stroud enrolled in the full-time two-year MBA program at McCombs. He knew his instincts had been correct when, after taking a business negotiations class, he realized he and his brother could have gotten a better price when they sold their company.

Stroud will graduate this May with a concentration in finance, but he has already launched his second venture – a beverage company called Somerset – using money and resources from winning the school's Entrepreneur Summer Fellowship. "So many people want to help," he says of McCombs' faculty and students. "I'm paying to be here, but I'm getting value back." Another McCombs bonus: Three fellow students were approved to earn independent study credit by working on the Somerset launch.

The University of California-San Diego's Rady School of

Management specializes in turning scientists and engineers into entrepreneurs with full-time, evening and weekend MBA programs. The skills Rady offers in areas like finance, business analytics, sales and marketing are critical for students to succeed in the global innovation-driven economy. "It doesn't matter how great the technology is if there's no customer," says Lada Rasochova, managing director of the Rady Venture Fund and executive director of the California Institute for Innovation and Development at Rady, which manages four university accelerators.

Suman Kanuganti, 38, already had a master's in robotics from the University of Missouri and had held several corporate computer engineering positions when he decided to pursue an MBA at Rady. While attending evening classes part time, he dreamed up Aira, a subscription guidance service for the blind that combines remote support staff with Google Glass technology to help clients navigate daily tasks whenever they call for help. "I used my time at Rady to do my market research on this idea, because I only knew one person," the legally blind friend whose input inspired him originally. "Technologists are always falling in love with the technology and not solving a problem economically. My business education gave me a broader understanding of how things work and how to reach the right people."

Rady's unique three-course Lab to Market sequence, required of all MBA students, has each student take a specific technological innovation through market research and feasibility studies,

SPOTLIGHT ON

Miami Business School

U. OF MIAMI, CORAL GABLES, FLORIDA

Global engagement is a key part of the curriculum at Miami Business School, says Patricia Sanchez Abril, vice dean of graduate business education. Student teams can partner with international executives on consulting projects, like exploring an expansion strategy for a Chinese pharmaceutical firm. Or they can take a global immersion elective that culminates in a two-week trip abroad to learn firsthand about the business and cultural environments in places like Israel, India or Brazil. More than a third of the school's 111 full-time MBA students come from outside the U.S.

"I've been able to branch out," says Geoff Rowan, 29, a second-year MBA student who traveled to Colombia for his own immersion course. In addition to focusing his degree on international business and management, Rowan has also worked on a rebranding project with the school's career services center and explored an interest in entrepreneurship through the startup-oriented Venture Café Miami. Students can also take electives in hot Miami fields like health care and real estate. *–Lindsay Cates*

▶ **More @ usnews.com/miami**

and then develop a business case, a business plan and a go-to-market strategy. After fulfilling the course requirements, Kanuganti used the same process to develop the business plan for Aira, which earned him two more credits and entry into Rady's StartR accelerator, a six-month program that provides students and teams with early-stage companies mentoring, workshops, co-working space, grants up to $5,000, and connections to other funding sources. Aira formally launched in 2014 with Kanuganti as CEO. The company now has 54 employees and has successfully raised some $30 million in venture capital.

Most top schools also offer entrepreneurs more

streamlined or flexible options, alternative master's programs, or even mini- or micro-MBAs, targeting specific knowledge gaps. Harvard Business School, for example, offers a $950, four-week online certificate course in Entrepreneurship Essentials that provides an accelerated look at basics like how to find ideas and build and finance a business.

Along with its standard two-year offerings, Syracuse University's Whitman School of Management offers a one-year master's in entrepreneurship, either on campus or online, which includes some standard MBA program introductions to accounting, finance and marketing but focuses more on courses for entrepreneurs who can choose from four different tracks: New Venture Creation, Corporate Entrepreneurship, Family Business, and Social Entrepreneurship. The one-year program may be better for those with "a strong business background from their undergraduate work," says Alexander McKelvie, professor of entrepreneurship and associate dean for undergraduate and master's education.

Increasingly, schools like Babson College, the University of Southern California, and University of Michigan –Ann Arbor are attracting budding entrepreneurs with their business ac-

celerators, incubators or "hatcheries." At Michigan, students don't need to be enrolled for a business degree to take advantage of the resources of the Ross School of Business.

Anyone involved in the Michigan ecosystem – undergraduates, graduate students, alumni and community members – can benefit from Ross' resources for entrepreneurs, including legal advice, internships, networking groups and events. Startup capital is also available via the Wolverine Venture Fund and the Desai Accelerator, a joint venture between Ross and Michigan's College of Engineering, which is also open to innovative tech-enabled startups unconnected to the school. (Students in undergraduate programs for any field – engineering, computer science, public health, design, even theater – can take courses at Ross for credit toward their degrees, and the university emphasizes cross-disciplinary programs.) "We are working toward everyone being an entrepreneur," says a university spokeswoman, Megha Krishnan.

Elisabeth Michel, 29, who received a master's in public health from Michigan in 2017, knew she not only wanted to address health equity, but also to be an entrepreneur. "I was very intentional about taking courses outside the school of public health," Michel says, and she benefited from Ross classes on strategy, supply chains and organizational leadership.

A startup opportunity occurred sooner than she expected. After some brainstorming, she and two fellow Michigan students focused on the challenge for patients and their families to create timely advance care directives, which spell out an individual's care wishes at the end of life. Often these directives are not available when needed, and their absence can create extra suffering for patients and families and vastly increase costs for health care providers and insurers.

Michel and her two co-founders, Ann Duong, 26 (who has a master's in health informatics, a joint program between the School of Public Health and the School of Information), and Brandon Keelean, 27 (who has a Master of Design from Michigan's Stamps School of Art & Design), developed a web application to help patients and their family members create directives that meet the legal requirements in their state and are accessible by medical providers, family members and others. The three launched their company – Canopy – in 2017, with Michel serving as CEO, Duong as chief technology officer and Keelean as chief design officer.

As well as Ross classes in areas like marketing, supply chain management, negotiating and business strategy, Canopy's founders received free legal services through Michigan Law's Entrepreneurship Clinic and tapped the school's entrepreneurs-in-residence for advice on sales, business plan development, and financial modeling and projections. They also raised enough startup money, through the Desai Accelerator and pitch competitions, to work full time on the company. They will market the application to

health systems, health insurers and employers.

Michel believes the resources and great learning experiences that Ross enabled have boosted the chances that Canopy will succeed. "Entrepreneurship sounds sexy, but people don't talk about the challenges," she says. "If you don't have a foundation to stand on, it's a hard road." ●

GETTING A WINNING START

D **AVID GILBOA,** co-founder and co-CEO at Warby Parker, the now famous eyewear company, had lost his glasses while traveling and was upset at the high cost of replacing them. That led to a discussion with three first-year business school classmates at the University of Pennsylvania's Wharton School about how to make eyewear affordable and the formation of a business school startup team. In 2008, the team entered Wharton's Business Plan Competition (now the Startup Challenge). They were knocked out in the semifinals, which motivated them to prove the judges wrong, says Gilboa, who was then 28. They took the feedback and adapted their plan to build out the company. In 2010, funded with their savings, investments from friends and family, and $2,500 from the Wharton Venture Initiation Program's Snider Seed Award, the founders established Warby Parker initially as an online business. Now valued at about $1.7 billion, it employs more than 1,700 people and has nearly 100 stores across the U.S. and Canada.

Today, many future entrepreneurs like David Gilboa are testing their startup dreams by entering B-school competitions. While the structure varies from school to school, the strongest competitions tend to be nestled in incubators and entrepreneurial or degree programs that offer a range of resources and facilities for students to refine concepts, build management teams, work with mentors, and connect with venture capital funds.

The right stuff. At UCLA's Anderson School of Management, roughly 60 teams of up to six students enter the Knapp Venture Competition. In the spring, 25 semifinal teams participate in Venture Review Night, where they get feedback from volunteer evaluators – faculty, students, staff and alumni who have worked in venture capital or venture capital-backed companies and/or who are subject-matter experts in specific disciplines like biotech and fintech. Finalists get coaching on their presentations and introductions or referrals to potential funders and other resources.

The competition culminates in mid- to late May, when members of the UCLA and Los Angeles entrepreneurial ecosystems gather to watch the finalists give 15-minute presentations and engage in 10-minute question-and-answer sessions with the judges. Last year's finalist teams were awarded a total of $100,000. "It's very Anderson in that members of the community come together to support others and then

share their success," says Elaine Hagan, associate dean of entrepreneurial initiatives. The benefits of these competitions go beyond the access to resources, mentoring and proximity to VC communities. The process forces students to really examine whether their ventures have the right stuff to thrive over the long term.

While pursuing his MBA at Columbia Business School, Oliver Noteware, a former Marine Corps infantry officer, co-founded a virtual reality training company focused on first responders called Street Smarts VR. In 2018, Noteware, 31, entered a competition for startup funding through Columbia's Eugene M. Lang Entrepreneurial Initiative Fund. In the final round, Noteware fielded the judges' questions for his team. The most important: What would his business look like in five years?

Noteware says he realized that sharing his thought process "was more important than my answer." He explained that his team envisioned training law enforcement officers in all of the country's roughly 18,000 departments with virtual reality. To achieve that goal, Street Smarts VR would build on pilot testing and work with departments across the Northeast known to be early adopters of technology and innovative training methods. The judges were impressed enough that Noteware's team received a $50,000 investment.

Because of their appeal, many top B-schools offer such competitions now. As Warby Parker's founders and other budding entrepreneurs have learned, winning may not be as important as participating. –*Barbara Sadick*

Want to Manage Money?

MBA students are at the helm of million-dollar funds

by **Melba Newsome**

IKE MANY BUSINESS school applicants, Brian Purcell, 35, had a specific goal in mind when he quit his day job to get an MBA at the University of North Carolina's Kenan-Flagler Business School. After graduating from Davidson College, Purcell spent six years handling real estate sales and development in Charlotte, North Carolina. He wanted to stay in the industry but move into more of an institutional investing role. "I wanted an MBA program that would help me do that," he explains.

Kenan-Flagler's MBA real estate concentration is well-regarded. But Purcell was particularly intrigued by the chance to get experience helping manage a student-run multimillion-dollar real estate fund with a portfolio of investments ranging from multifamily properties to office space, senior housing and retail. "Our students are responsible for every single thing a private equity fund does, such as running models and dealing with the nitty-gritty of how the assets will perform under different circumstances," says David Hartzell, a real estate professor who serves as faculty advisor. Purcell quickly found that to be true. He joined in the second semester of his first year and worked as a lead fund manager until graduation. He and his fellow students met as a class with Hartzell at least twice a week to discuss every aspect of managing the fund and received credit for two semester courses. When classes were out of session they met via conference call. The year-round commitment required Purcell and his team of managers to meet with real estate developers, visit properties, analyze investments, source deals and report to investors, among other tasks.

Kenan-Flagler is not the only business school offering this kind of direct experience in financial investing. In fact, a growing number of B-schools offer students a chance to manage actual rather than simulated investment portfolios generally combined with for-credit classes that teach investment strategy and offer the guidance of faculty or professional financial advisors. Once an innovation, says Michael D. Wiemer, senior vice president and chief officer Americas for AACSB International, a business school accreditation organization, "it didn't take long for these programs to catch fire because they give the school a big competitive advantage."

The fund experience clearly paid off for Purcell, who

Owen Graduate School of Management

VANDERBILT UNIVERSITY
NASHVILLE, TENNESSEE

U.S. NEWS RANK #29

For the roughly 175 full-time MBA students who enter each year, Owen focuses on creating "personal scale experiences," says Dean Eric Johnson. The average class size is 28, and every student is paired with an executive coach from industry. Matt Sternberg, 29, chose Owen because of its health care offerings. In addition to completing a concentration in the field, the 2018 MBA grad worked on an organizational performance project for Vanderbilt LifeFlight, an emergency medical transport operation, before landing a job as a business strategy manager for a health system solutions and analytics company in Chicago.

The academic year is split into four eight-week "mods," which allows students to take a wide range of classes and pursue electives early. One-week immersion courses are offered in between mods that put MBA candidates on the front lines of fields of interest. Real estate students, for example, might partner with the University of Tennessee's school of architecture in Knoxville to propose a development project to housing professionals. *–Lindsay Cates*
▶ More @ usnews.com/vanderbilt

landed a job as director of portfolio management for a real estate investment company after graduation. Two years later, he became managing director of acquisitions for Asana Partners, a Charlotte-based private equity real estate investment firm focused on retail assets in walkable urban areas around the country. Purcell notes that his work with the fund "uniquely prepared me to perform well in my current position."

Student-led investment funds vary widely from school to school in terms of assets, portfolio composition, investment guidelines and who is eligible to participate. The University of Colorado–Boulder's Deming Center Venture Fund is generally managed by about 15 graduate students from the university's business, law and engineering schools and overseen by an advisory board comprised of faculty members and leaders from the local venture capital and angel investing sector. Investments typically range from $25,000 to $50,000 and can be in any sector but must be tied to the university or the surrounding community. Classroom learning is enhanced by the students' access to angel investors, entrepreneurs and industry partners who help them identify opportunities, negotiate the terms of investment, and execute the deals. The fund recently invested in The Food Corridor, a platform that connects chefs and food entrepreneurs with restaurants that have underused space and equipment. Explains Carlos E. Peña, 30, managing director and MBA candidate, "a big part is not only investing in the now but investing in what you envision the enterprise can be with your support."

The Green and Gold Fund at the University of Alabama–Birmingham's Collat School of Business is open to both graduate and undergraduate students. Each semester, generally over 30 students help manage roughly $550,000 in equity and fixed-income securities by applying professional investment strategies and established risk management principles studied in class.

David Lutomski, 26, completed his Collat MBA in 2018 and now works as an analyst for a wealth management firm in Birmingham. The hours he logged with the Green and Gold Fund as chief investment officer and the research tools he utilized have come in handy. "We used the Bloomberg terminals to look at financial statements and news about the companies to run them through different models," says Lutomski. In addition, "I established guidelines for allocation and made sure we followed the investment policy statement."

The University of Minnesota–Twin Cities' Carlson School of Management considers hands-on experience so important that all full-time MBA students are required to participate in one of four enterprises – investment, brand marketing, consulting or ventures. Rebecca Blumenshine, 36, chose the student-led (MBA and undergraduate) Carlson Funds Enterprise, which oversees approximately $35 million in equity and fixed assets. The Minnesota native had earned a sociology degree and worked in the nonprofit sector for years when she decided to head to graduate school.

While pursuing her master's in public policy at the Humphrey School of Public Affairs, Blumenshine learned about the university's dual-degree programs that allowed her to earn an MBA simultaneously. "I saw it as an opportunity to start building out my quantitative skills, which I wanted to use more in my [public policy] career," she says. The coursework and the fund experience were eye-opening for her, and the latter gave her valuable exposure to managing investments primarily from large financial services firms.

Blumenshine also aided the successful effort to make the Funds

Enterprise a signatory to the Principles for Responsible Investment, which requires it to consider environmental, social and governance factors in its investments. "It is part of our fiscal responsibility to our investors to use all data available and consider all risk factors in our investment decision-making," says Blumenshine.

Curry says the fund helped her focus on the 'story' behind a new initiative.'

The Foster MBA Investment Fund at the University of Washington's Foster School of Business appeals to many participants by teaching not just trading and investing but also by involving students in assessing the value of every component of a business. In their yearlong class, student fund managers learn how to recognize and get ahead of marketplace changes (like is the business following or leading industry trends impacting its bottom line). The fund is divided into various business sectors including grocery, pharmaceuticals, and hotels and leisure.

Working with the faculty advisor and instructor, MBA student Levi Stewart Zurbrugg, 29, manages the grocery retail portfolio. "We start at the industry level and build a hypothesis around what we think will build value. For the grocery sector, that's convenience, product selection and customer experience." When Zurbrugg graduates in June, he will join a mutual fund as a senior investment analyst, thanks in part to his hands-on Foster experience. "Many of our students will never work on Wall Street and don't want to," says Lance Young, faculty advisor and principal lecturer of finance and business economics. "When they get jobs, even if it's at places like Amazon and Microsoft, they have the analytical skills they can take to their jobs and succeed."

Rachel Curry, 32, is a case in point. She wanted to switch from a career in food service management to something in consulting, strategic planning or finance. Unsure of which path to take, Curry believed Foster would provide the broadest course of study. "Lance hammered home the importance of looking at an industry's value proposition and understanding the whole story, how relationships work and what pillars could crumble if there's a big shock to the economy," she says.

As a senior financial analyst now for Amazon's Kindle eBooks team in Seattle, Curry assesses and provides accurate financial data to help prioritize new initiatives. She says the fund helped her focus on the rationale or "story" behind a proposed initiative and then to model financial data to see if it supports the new theory. The process "comes into play with every new model I develop," Curry says. She believes these skills have been key to her success at Amazon. ●

FIND THE BEST ONLINE PROGRAM FOR YOU

Search more than 1,200 online education programs to find one that best fits your needs.

Bachelor's
MBA
Graduate Business
Graduate Criminal Justice
Graduate Education
Graduate Engineering
Graduate Information Technology
Graduate Nursing

U.S.News & WORLD REPORT

Start your search today: usnews.com/education/online-education

A Strategy for the Summer

How to land – and make the most of – an internship

by **Katherine Hobson**

BEFORE MICHAEL LEVIT arrived at Carnegie Mellon University's Tepper School of Business to start his MBA, he was already planning his summer internship. He realized it would be critical in helping him make the transition he wanted from computer programming to investment banking. "I reached out to the school to find out what I needed to be doing to prepare and what the process would look like," says Levit, now 30. He attended a conference in New York to meet with financial industry representatives and gave himself a crash course in finance so he could better shine in interviews once the semester began. Levit's work paid off; he landed a summer internship with JPMorgan Chase & Co., and then a full-time job offer for when he graduates in 2019.

The internship between the first and second years of an MBA program is a key part of the degree. Not every student will end up working full time for his or her internship employer, but the experience is a great way to get a foot in the door. According to a recent survey by the Graduate Management Admission Council, the internship remains a solid avenue to jobs for many business school grads, with most U.S. employers surveyed offering them. U.S. News tapped career experts and successful students for their best advice on landing – and capitalizing on – the internship:

Start early. Career services officials advise getting a jump on things, since informal recruiting and company events can begin in early fall. "We reach out to [students] as soon as we know they're coming," says Naomi Sanchez, assistant dean of MBA Career Management and corporate recruiting at the University of Washington's Michael G. Foster School of Business. Incoming MBA students at Foster take an online course covering all aspects of career search and management, including résumé crafting, self-awareness, networking and case interviewing (discussing how to solve a real business problem). Each September, first-year students undergo six days of training, practicing those skills with each other and with coaches. Like Levit, many pre-MBA students attend conferences or events in the summer to get early insight into different industries. Some conferences target women or specific ethnicities.

Do serious interview prep. Lean on career services for help. You'll need to be able to articulate who you are and connect the dots between your pre-MBA experience, what you're learning in your program, your goals and how these fit the employer's needs, says Jamie Mathews-Mead, senior director of graduate career management at The Ohio State University Fisher College of Business. Readying yourself for that kind of deep conversation can take a lot of practice. "Sometimes MBA students rely and focus on technical skills or GPA or GMAT scores," she says. Those are important, but employers also want to hire people who are likable and with whom they want to work every day.

Know your stuff. Employers don't expect first-year students to have mastered the entire MBA curriculum. But they do want to know that students understand the industry and the company. "Research what the position is all about," Mathews-Mead advises. "Know what employers are looking for and how you can add value." Levit wanted to impress his finance industry interviewers with knowledge that he hadn't yet covered in his coursework. The career services office at Tepper helped him connect with the school's graduate finance association,

introduced him to an online course and recommended an investment banking textbook. That willingness to put in the work showed "my desire to break into the industry," Levit says.

Develop a strategy. The internship is a "pivotal experience" for MBA students who want to switch careers, says Toni Rhorer, associate director of career coaching and programming at Arizona State University's W. P. Carey School of Business. Figure out how to use it to your advantage. Eve Richer worked for an environmental nonprofit and in other industries before opting for an MBA to help her transition to the private sector. For her internship, she wanted to work for a large company where there was potential to make an impact in corporate sustainability. At school, Richer conducted and presented research on the circular economy – designing systems so there's no waste – and ended up at Cisco Systems Inc. in the summer of 2017, working in the circular economy group. She's now a full-time program manager.

Pursue multiple channels. Richer cautions students against putting all their efforts into one recruiting avenue. "Approach the search from different angles," she says. Richer used traditional on-campus recruiting methods, networked with alumni on LinkedIn and cultivated less formal industry con-

nections; her entree to Cisco came when an executive attended her research presentation on the circular economy.

Seize the opportunity. Career services can help prepare you for the internship itself, not just the recruiting process. Sanchez says that second-year peer advisers help first-years by sharing intel on how to succeed in different internships. There's also a lot of work on communications – making presentations and working in teams – so students can thrive during the summer. Once at her internship, Richer says she leapt at the chance to network with people throughout Cisco. "Never be afraid to reach out and ask someone for 30 minutes to learn about their role," she suggests. And maintain your composure, Levit advises. "You're going to be pushed to the limit. If you can do that with a smile and a positive attitude, that goes a very long way."

Keep an open mind. "People think that if Goldman Sachs is their long-term goal, they have to intern with Goldman to get there, but there are 100 different ways to get there," Rhorer says. "It could be solid work experience at a company that doesn't have a big name." Not every intern will get a full-time offer, either, which means it's important to take what you learned during the summer and incorporate it into your résumé and work goals. And if the internship isn't all you'd hoped it would be, do your best and consider it a learning experience, says Stephen Rakas, executive director of the Masters Career Center at Tepper. "I always tell students it's just as important to know what you don't want to do as what you do want to do." ●

Entering a Virtual World

Simulated 3D environments and tech tools are preparing students for the future

by **Linda Childers**

IN A CLASSROOM at the MIT Sloan School of Management, graduate business students are engaged in a complex virtual reality exercise. Using World Climate, a simulated role-playing game, they have been assigned roles as United Nations delegates from different countries and tasked with negotiating a climate agreement to reduce greenhouse gas emissions. The "delegates" debate proposals that might include switching to renewable energy sources or expanding forests to remove carbon dioxide from the atmosphere. On a large computer screen, a simulation model then shows the students – in real time – the impact of their decisions.

The results usually aren't positive in the first round, says John Sterman, professor of management and director of the MIT Sloan Sustainability Initiative and the MIT System Dynamics Group, who co-authored the game. Students may see their proposals lead to rising sea levels wiping out Shanghai or housing being lost in California and Florida. The climate simulation "teaches our business students skills such as improvising, negotiating and public speaking," he notes. In addition, "it reinforces how their decisions can have consequences that last for decades."

Classroom avatars. MIT Sloan is part of a growing number of graduate B-schools worldwide that have integrated different virtual reality tools into their curricula. These can range from virtual "escape rooms" that teach leadership and collaboration to customized programs that can change interiors of retail environments as part of marketing exercises. According to a report published by Gartner, a global research and advisory firm, by the year 2021, 60 percent of higher education institutions in the United States will be using VR to create simulations and put students into immersive environments. A few are already well along in expanding applications.

Stanford University's Graduate School of Business has committed to virtual reality in its two online Learn, Engage, Accelerate, Disrupt – or LEAD – certificate programs, one in corporate innovation and the other in personal leadership. Each one-year, eight-course executive education offering uses the VR platform VirBELA – Virtual Business Education Leadership Assessment – to enable classmates located around the world to create avatars to represent themselves as they gather to chat in a virtual campus space that includes classrooms, meeting rooms and collaborative spaces. Students can talk to each other simply by turning up the volume on their laptops. They can even make presentations in a virtual auditorium.

While the setting may be simulated, the LEAD program provides real case examples and shows students how to "apply the assignments to our jobs," says Leela Parvathaneni, 37, director of consumer and emerging technologies at Align Technology in San Jose, California, who is pursuing the personal leadership certificate and hopes to gain management skills that will help him advance in his career. The immersive 360-degree learning environment features 3D visuals of the Stanford campus including the 285-foot Hoover Tower, the Quad, gardens and more.

"I didn't realize it would feel as if I were in an actual classroom," says Parvathaneni, describing one exercise in ethics and leadership where students, represented by their avatars, gathered in groups to explore how, in the 1970s, Ford Motor Co. had handled a fuel-tank rupture risk in its Pinto models in rear-end collisions. The issue became a PR crisis for the automaker that would impact how it and other companies handled safety and public notification issues in the future. Instead of just listening to a lecture, Parvathaneni says he and his classmates were able to examine Ford's decisions and then have a robust discussion about how the lessons "can be applied to any industry."

Two cohorts, each with about 200 students from over 75 countries, enter the LEAD program every year. VirBELA helps them get to know each other so well, Marineh Lalikian, director of Stanford LEAD says, they often hold in-person meet-ups throughout the world. (Each year, LEAD cohorts can head to Palo Alto for a student-organized three-day reunion event around Silicon Valley and the university.)

Margaret Neale, a Stanford professor, says she is currently working with a company to develop a new virtual negotiation tool to further enhance learning. "Using either their smartphone or computer, students will be able to use a negotiation simulation that reads their facial expressions and offers feedback on how well they did in a simulated job interview," she says. Students will also be able to see an assessment of how they negotiated compared to their peers.

The Rady School of Management at the University of California–San Diego has found similar success using the VirBELA platform as the centerpiece of its global micro-MBA program in partnership with Waseda University in Tokyo. "It provides an interactive forum where students can share ideas and study topics including finance, marketing and leadership," says Jill Farwell, director at Rady's Center for Executive Development. The Japanese students interact with their professors and each other via avatars and are able to get a better idea of American business practices through their coursework.

Cones of silence. Rady hopes next to offer its popular Women's Negotiation and Leadership program on the platform. A locally based instructor will teach women how to build confidence as they acquire essential negotiating and leadership skills. For example, "Students can pair up in virtual classrooms using what we call the 'cones of silence,'" Farwell says. "This allows them to practice their negotiation techniques and give each

other feedback in a private meeting room where they won't be distracted by other students."

The potential of VR to help build leadership and soft skills has caught the attention of other schools. At Fordham University's Gabelli School of Business in New York, for example, Julita Haber, director of the full-time cohort MBA and a communications and media professor, uses VR tools to teach team dynamics as part of the executive MBA program. Working with The Glimpse Group, a consortium of New York-based enterprises creating VR and augmented reality tools (the latter superimpose computer-generated images over the user's view of the real world), the school has been able to "create unique educational experiences," Haber says.

Risky business. In one exercise, students wearing VR headgear are placed at the top of the Tokyo Tower in Japan, where they must encourage each other to overcome a fear of heights and step across a simulated beam 1,092-feet up to change a lightbulb. The immersive experience, which includes a good sound system, is so effective in tricking the brains of participants and can seem so real that they may actually experience increased heart rates and sweating hands. In another exercise individual students must work under time pressure to deactivate a virtual bomb while getting advice from teammates.

Fordham has also begun inviting MBA students to record presentations in front of green screens and 3D VR cameras as part of their data visualization and mixed-reality presentation module. These recordings will be used to create holograms of each team of students, explains Benjamin Cole, interim area chair of strategy and statistics at Fordham. At the same time, he notes, students can improve their public speaking and presentation skills.

Understanding VR technology and how it can "create emotional-physical responses" is vital, Haber says, because it allows students to conceptualize how businesses can apply these tools in new ways, such as increasing brand engagement with customers.

While some administrators have been concerned about the costs of VR tools, these are dropping fast. It's clear that within a few years virtual reality will become a daily reality for many business students. The timing also coincides with the decision of various Fortune 500 businesses like Honeywell, Walmart, Volkswagen and United Parcel Service, to integrate VR into their worker-education programs. As virtual reality tools gain a bigger foothold in more industries, experts say, graduates who have used these technologies as part of their curriculum will be prepared to help take their employers to the next level. ●

Life as an avatar in VirBELA

STANFORD GRADUATE SCHOOL OF BUSINESS

Screenshots of Stanford students' avatars in a virtual classroom and auditorium

THE U.S. NEWS RANKINGS

University of
California–Los Angeles

BRETT ZIEGLER FOR USN&WR

How We Judge Schools

We rely on both objective measures and expert input

by **Robert J. Morse**

EACH YEAR, U.S. NEWS ranks programs in business: MBA programs, both full- and part-time; executive MBA programs; online MBA and other master's degree programs; and undergraduate programs in business. Most of the rankings are based on two types of data: expert opinions about program excellence and statistical indicators that measure the quality of a school's faculty, research and students. In the case of the executive and undergraduate rankings, results are based on opinion alone. Experts were also asked to weigh in on which institutions do the best job of educating students in specialty areas such as accounting, finance and marketing for both MBA and undergraduate business programs.

As you research course offerings and weigh schools' intangible attributes, the data in these pages can help you compare concrete factors such as faculty-student ratio and placement success upon graduation. It's important that you use the rankings to supplement, not substitute for, careful thought and your own research.

Statistical indicators fall into two categories: inputs, or measures of the qualities that students and faculty bring to the educational experience, and outputs, measures of graduates' achievements linked to their degrees. As inputs, for example, we use admission test scores. Output measures for the MBA programs include starting salaries and grads' ability to find jobs. A description of how we ranked full-time

and part-time MBA programs follows here; information on the EMBA, online degree and undergraduate rankings appears with each table.

Full-time MBA programs. The universe that U.S. News considers when ranking MBA programs consists of the 475 programs accredited by AACSB International. We start by surveying all of the schools to collect data on key measures that we consider important indicators of quality, described below. In the most recent fall 2018 and early 2019 data survey, 367 schools responded, with 131 providing the information needed to calculate rankings. In addition, we conduct two peer assessment surveys asking for expert opinion on the quality of education students can expect. While more detailed information can be found at usnews.com/mbameth, the key factors and their weighting in the ranking formula are:

MORE @ USNEWS.COM/BSCHOOL

Visit **usnews.com** regularly while conducting your school search, as U.S. News frequently adds content aimed at helping prospective business students find the best fit and get in. We also occasionally make updates – whether on job placement, test scores, GPA or other factors – when new data become available or new information changes the data.

The University of Washington's Foster Business Library

or more of its 2018 full-time graduates – and at least 50 percent of the graduating class – to be seeking employment. Salary is based on the number of graduates reporting data. Signing bonus is weighted by the proportion of graduates reporting salaries who received a bonus, since not everyone received a signing bonus.

Student selectivity (.25): The strength of full-time students who entered in the fall of 2018 was measured by the average GMAT and GRE scores (65 percent of this measure), average undergraduate grade-point average (30 percent), and the proportion of applicants accepted (5 percent). When fewer than half of full-time students submitted test scores, we adjusted their weighted percentile distributions downward by the percentage of the student body that submitted test scores. A similar adjustment was made when under half of entering MBA students submitted undergraduate grade-point averages.

Overall rank: We examined the data for individual indicators and standardized the value of each one about its mean. The weight applied to each reflects our judgment about its relative importance, as determined in consultation with experts in the field. Final scores were rescaled so the highest-scoring institution was assigned 100; the others' scores were recalculated as a percentage of that top score. Scores were then rounded to the nearest whole number. Schools with a score of 100 accumulated the highest composite score. An institution's rank reflects the number of schools that sit above it; if three are tied at No. 1, for example, the next will be ranked No. 4. Tied schools are listed alphabetically.

Specialty rankings: These rankings are based solely on the opinions of educators at peer schools. B-school deans and MBA program heads were asked to nominate up to 15 programs for excellence. Those receiving the most nominations are listed.

Quality assessment (.40 of the ranking formula): Two peer assessment surveys were conducted in the fall of 2018. Business school deans and directors of accredited MBA programs were asked to rate the overall academic quality of the MBA programs at each school on a scale from marginal (1) to outstanding (5); 45 percent responded. The average score is weighted by .25 in the ranking model. Corporate recruiters and company contacts who hired MBA grads, whose names were supplied by previously ranked MBA programs, also were asked to rate the programs. The last three years' recruiter responses were averaged and are weighted by .15 in the model. Programs that had fewer than 10 recruiter and company responses total were assigned the lowest score for this indicator achieved by any ranked MBA program for the purposes of calculating the rankings. These programs have an N/A instead of a recruiter assessment score published in the tables.

Placement success (.35): Success is based on average starting salary and bonus (40 percent of this measure) and employment rates for full-time 2018 graduates at graduation (20 percent) and at three months later (40 percent). Calculations for MBA placement rates exclude those not seeking jobs and those for whom the school has no information. To be included in the full-time MBA rankings, a program needed 20

Part-time MBA programs. The U.S. News part-time MBA rankings are based on five factors: average peer assessment score (50 percent of the overall score), average GMAT score and GRE scores of part-time MBA students entering in the fall of 2018 (15 percent), average undergraduate GPA (12.5 percent), average number of years of work experience (10 percent), and the percentage of the fall 2018 total MBA program enrollment that is in the part-time program (12.5 percent). As with the full-time programs, adjustments were made when fewer than half of new entrants submitted test scores and GPAs. More detailed information can be found at usnews.com/ptmba-meth.

The average peer assessment score is calculated from a fall 2018 survey that asked business school deans and MBA program directors at each of the nation's 323 part-time MBA programs to rate other programs from marginal (1) to outstanding (5); 55 percent responded. To be eligible, a program had to be accredited by the AACSB and have at least 20 students enrolled part time in both the fall of 2017 and 2018; 287 programs met those criteria. More information about programs can be found at usnews.com and in the directories at the back of this book. ●

Emory University,
tied at No. 21

Best MBA Programs

Rank	School	Overall score	Peer assessment score (5.0=highest)	Recruiter assessment score (5.0=highest)	'18 full-time average undergrad GPA	'18 full-time average GMAT score	'18 full-time acceptance rate	'18 average starting salary and bonus	'18 graduates employed at graduation	Employed 3 months after graduation	'18 out-of-state tuition and fees	'18 total full-time enrollment
1	University of Pennsylvania (Wharton)	100	4.8	4.4	3.60	732	20.7%	$165,528	83.6%	94.6%	$78,948	1,742
2	Stanford University (CA)	99	4.9	4.4	3.73	732	6.1%	$162,704	68.7%	88.1%	$70,590	855
3	Harvard University (MA)	98	4.9	4.4	3.71	731	10.4%	$159,314	79.1%	89.3%	$80,532	1,873
3	Massachusetts Institute of Technology (Sloan)	98	4.7	4.4	3.57	728	13.1%	$159,245	86.0%	93.5%	$76,712	813
3	University of Chicago (Booth) (IL)	98	4.7	4.3	3.58	731	22.9%	$154,722	87.6%	95.5%	$73,209	1,179
6	Columbia University (NY)	95	4.6	4.3	3.60	736	14.5%	$153,351	75.0%	90.1%	$77,404	1,297
6	Northwestern University (Kellogg) (IL)	95	4.6	4.3	3.60	732	21.9%	$151,605	80.4%	92.0%	$73,074	1,304
6	University of California–Berkeley (Haas)	95	4.6	4.3	3.67	726	15.4%	$147,921	75.5%	93.4%	$61,442	590
9	Yale University (CT)	92	4.4	4.2	3.67	724	20.4%	$149,964	77.1%	89.8%	$71,620	723
10	Duke University (Fuqua) (NC)	91	4.4	4.1	3.49	704	22.4%	$155,129	85.4%	94.0%	$70,942	875
10	University of Michigan–Ann Arbor (Ross)	91	4.4	4.1	3.48	720	27.1%	$156,163	89.3%	93.5%	$68,974	832
12	Dartmouth College (Tuck) (NH)	90	4.3	4.0	3.49	722	23.3%	$157,821	80.6%	91.9%	$75,076	576
12	New York University (Stern)	90	4.3	4.0	3.45	716	23.2%	$159,021	83.7%	93.7%	$74,300	772
12	University of Virginia (Darden)	90	4.2	4.1	3.50	718	32.9%	$160,711	87.3%	92.3%	$68,350	660
15	Cornell University (Johnson) (NY)	86	4.3	4.0	3.41	699	33.1%	$154,533	79.7%	91.0%	$69,290	573
16	University of California–Los Angeles (Anderson)	84	4.1	4.0	3.52	716	24.3%	$142,997	69.7%	88.7%	$64,292	723
17	Carnegie Mellon University (Tepper) (PA)	83	4.2	3.8	3.40	690	35.4%	$145,566	81.9%	89.6%	$65,852	465
17	University of Southern California (Marshall)	83	3.9	3.5	3.50	705	28.2%	$151,408	79.2%	95.8%	$70,536	449
19	U. of North Carolina–Chapel Hill (Kenan-Flagler)	81	4.1	3.9	3.34	702	46.6%	$139,627	80.5%	92.1%	$64,479	556
19	University of Texas–Austin (McCombs)	81	4.1	3.9	3.48	702	33.6%	$141,771	75.0%	85.9%	$55,244	551
21	Emory University (Goizueta) (GA)	77	3.8	3.6	3.30	686	40.8%	$145,815	80.0%	92.9%	$63,064	349
21	Indiana University (Kelley)	77	3.9	3.8	3.33	675	38.3%	$125,929	75.6%	95.0%	$52,126	388
21	University of Washington (Foster)	77	3.7	3.1	3.31	696	35.1%	$147,763	83.9%	99.1%	$51,126	223
24	Georgetown University (McDonough) (DC)	76	3.8	3.9	3.34	693	55.2%	$139,215	63.7%	93.8%	$59,052	541
25	University of Florida (Warrington)	75	3.5	3.5	3.55	685	18.8%	$121,558	89.1%	95.7%	$30,630	95
26	Rice University (Jones) (TX)	74	3.6	3.5	3.32	706	39.7%	$129,950	73.6%	94.5%	$61,383	236
26	University of Notre Dame (Mendoza) (IN)	74	3.8	3.6	3.36	671	47.8%	$129,427	73.6%	90.0%	$54,770	281
26	Washington University in St. Louis (Olin) (MO)	74	3.8	3.6	3.50	693	33.4%	$121,215	77.8%	87.9%	$60,760	273
29	Georgia Institute of Technology (Scheller)	73	3.5	3.3	3.40	681	34.5%	$130,206	84.5%	97.2%	$42,196	167
29	Vanderbilt University (Owen) (TN)	73	3.7	3.7	3.30	678	61.8%	$131,381	74.8%	89.9%	$56,750	351
31	Ohio State University (Fisher)	72	3.7	3.2	3.44	676	36.1%	$110,546	80.3%	97.4%	$53,643	181
32	Brigham Young University (Marriott) (UT)	70	3.2	3.4	3.50	672	52.7%	$134,211	78.3%	90.6%	N/A	280
33	Arizona State University (W.P. Carey)	68	3.6	3.4	3.50	694	20.2%	$110,745	57.8%	87.3%	$47,926	195
33	Pennsylvania State U.–University Park (Smeal)	68	3.5	3.3	3.37	657	17.6%	$124,375	72.3%	91.5%	$44,818	117
35	University of Minnesota–Twin Cities (Carlson)	67	3.6	2.8	3.42	682	39.3%	$131,677	64.8%	85.2%	$54,467	188
35	University of Wisconsin–Madison	67	3.6	2.8	3.43	670	33.3%	$112,399	73.6%	90.1%	$40,059	183
37	University of Georgia (Terry)	66	3.5	2.8	3.53	665	32.2%	$105,010	75.6%	90.2%	$34,378	102
38	Michigan State University (Broad)	64	3.5	3.1	3.27	668	44.3%	$121,613	73.3%	86.7%	$50,483	157
38	University of Texas–Dallas	64	3.1	4.2	3.50	671	35.1%	$93,554	54.5%	87.9%	$31,200	101
40	Texas A&M University–College Station (Mays)	63	3.5	3.2	3.33	643	42.1%	$110,963	63.2%	89.5%	$76,606†	123

*Tuition is reported on a per-credit-hour basis. †Total program costs, which may or may not include required fees. Schools receiving fewer than 10 ratings from corporate recruiters have N/A displayed instead of corporate recruiter score. Sources: U.S. News and the schools. Assessment data collected by U.S. News.

Rank	School	Overall score	Peer assessment score (5.0=highest)	Recruiter assessment score (5.0=highest)	'18 full-time average undergrad GPA	'18 full-time average GMAT score	'18 full-time acceptance rate	'18 average starting salary and bonus	'18 graduates employed at graduation	Employed 3 months after graduation	'18 out-of-state tuition and fees	'18 total full-time enrollment
40	University of Maryland–College Park (Smith)	63	3.5	3.1	3.20	638	36.0%	$121,565	74.0%	89.6%	$56,261	155
40	University of Rochester (Simon) (NY)	63	3.3	3.1	3.50	666	32.2%	$121,969	76.9%	93.4%	$46,600	209
43	Boston College (Carroll) (MA)	62	3.5	3.4	3.34	637	44.4%	$105,579	61.9%	82.5%	$51,310	156
43	Southern Methodist University (Cox) (TX)	62	3.3	3.0	3.40	655	46.1%	$113,054	71.8%	87.1%	$53,103	225
43	University of California–Irvine (Merage)	62	3.3	2.8	3.53	667	27.3%	$107,905	57.4%	85.2%	$52,709	157
43	University of Pittsburgh (Katz) (PA)	62	3.3	3.6	3.32	621	34.0%	$93,809	76.8%	91.1%	$71,616†	120
47	Iowa State University	61	2.9	3.6	3.52	607	73.7%	$69,136	92.9%	100.0%	$27,254	79
47	University of California–Davis	61	3.3	3.1	3.22	671	39.0%	$104,855	70.0%	87.5%	$51,813	91
47	University of Illinois–Urbana-Champaign	61	3.6	3.0	3.32	666	39.5%	$100,817	70.5%	90.9%	$79,784†	94
50	Boston University (Questrom) (MA)	60	3.3	3.2	3.30	681	50.6%	$102,041	58.1%	90.6%	$54,144	320
50	University of Alabama (Manderson)	60	3.0	3.2	3.63	650	62.4%	$71,169	77.2%	92.1%	$31,730	314
52	CUNY Bernard M. Baruch College (Zicklin) (NY)	59	3.1	3.5	3.37	637	35.1%	$96,984	63.0%	87.0%	$31,519	75
52	University of Arizona (Eller)	59	3.5	2.8	3.50	665	43.7%	$99,459	42.3%	80.8%	$44,893	79
54	College of William and Mary (Mason) (VA)	58	3.1	3.7	3.40	618	67.6%	$95,961	55.6%	87.3%	$45,980	204
54	University of Tennessee–Knoxville (Haslam)	58	3.3	3.6	3.50	655	48.5%	$81,995	53.1%	83.7%	$43,502	100
54	University of Utah (Eccles)	58	3.3	3.0	3.48	659	50.3%	$83,459	64.7%	80.4%	$31,000	119
57	Baylor University (Hankamer) (TX)	57	3.0	3.1	3.43	607	42.0%	$74,012	74.4%	94.9%	$45,942	84
58	Northeastern University (MA)	56	3.1	3.2	3.33	627	36.4%	$92,665	50.0%	91.4%	$91,640†	160
58	Rutgers, The State U. of N.J.–Newark & New Brunswick	56	3.0	3.2	3.30	683	36.0%	$92,904	57.8%	83.1%	$99,014†	121
58	University of Oklahoma (Price)	56	3.0	3.1	3.45	625	61.3%	$76,950	64.1%	92.3%	$54,000†	69
61	George Washington University (DC)	55	3.2	3.5	3.20	611	60.3%	$103,352	53.3%	83.3%	$55,785	129
61	Texas Christian University (Neeley)	55	3.0	3.0	3.30	631	65.4%	$97,365	72.5%	87.5%	$51,210	92
63	Babson College (Olin) (MA)	54	3.4	3.3	3.25	615	82.3%	$88,685	49.6%	82.6%	$111,952†	344
63	Fordham University (Gabelli) (NY)	54	3.1	3.8	3.18	656	44.2%	$103,588	51.4%	77.1%	$103,598†	100
63	Tulane University (Freeman) (LA)	54	3.2	3.1	3.26	646	70.7%	$93,285	54.3%	82.9%	$57,708	73
66	University at Buffalo–SUNY (NY)	53	2.8	4.1	3.41	592	64.9%	$62,789	63.2%	88.2%	$28,438	209
67	Howard University (DC)	52	2.7	3.4	3.24	485	45.1%	$114,762	75.0%	95.0%	$35,786	50
67	University of Kentucky (Gatton)	52	3.0	3.5	3.50	591	88.3%	$61,288	69.4%	83.9%	$39,964†	65
69	Auburn University (Harbert) (AL)	51	3.0	2.8	3.43	586	40.7%	$68,736	76.7%	90.0%	$54,208	77
69	Louisiana State University–Baton Rouge (Ourso)	51	3.0	2.4	3.40	610	45.2%	$68,261	80.4%	93.5%	$78,215†	84
69	University of California–San Diego (Rady)	51	3.1	3.0	3.50	656	42.1%	$86,247	48.5%	69.7%	$71,176	102
69	University of Missouri (Trulaske)	51	2.9	2.8	3.39	606	55.6%	$69,868	60.5%	94.7%	$66,194†	82
73	Oklahoma State University (Spears)	50	3.0	3.4	3.49	521	48.8%	$62,366	65.7%	88.6%	$876*	53
74	Case Western Reserve U. (Weatherhead) (OH)	49	3.4	3.1	3.20	623	67.9%	$85,860	37.2%	74.4%	$40,760	95
74	Pepperdine University (Graziadio) (CA)	49	3.1	3.2	3.40	633	86.3%	$83,508	54.5%	70.5%	$49,830	116
74	Purdue University–West Lafayette (Krannert) (IN)	49	3.5	3.0	3.26	633	49.4%	$93,927	59.7%	80.6%	$32,966	93
74	University of Massachusetts–Amherst (Isenberg)	49	3.1	3.2	3.49	651	35.4%	$73,357	45.0%	65.0%	$34,132	56
74	University of South Carolina (Moore)	49	3.3	3.0	3.40	651	64.2%	$92,884	40.7%	63.0%	$72,460†	47
79	Clemson University (SC)	48	3.1	3.2	3.37	540	89.7%	$67,171	45.9%	94.6%	$31,592	121
79	Florida State University	48	3.1	3.1	3.68	564	60.8%	$66,402	40.0%	80.0%	$1,110*	54
79	University of Colorado–Boulder (Leeds)	48	3.3	3.1	3.30	609	71.0%	$81,979	41.5%	75.4%	$62,501†	194
79	University of Connecticut	48	3.1	3.1	3.34	601	39.4%	$97,678	37.3%	74.5%	$37,866	94
83	Stevens Institute of Technology (NJ)	47	2.5	4.1	3.10	614	57.4%	$76,537	31.5%	94.2%	$37,250	595
84	Drexel University (LeBow) (PA)	46	2.7	3.3	3.20	607	42.0%	$79,164	47.6%	85.7%	N/A	38
85	Chapman University (Argyros) (CA)	45	2.5	3.6	3.40	625	51.8%	$79,075	50.0%	70.0%	$1,655*	59
85	North Carolina State University (Poole)	45	2.8	1.7	3.35	625	44.6%	$101,074	71.0%	90.3%	$40,874	95
87	University of Arkansas–Fayetteville (Walton)	44	3.1	2.5	N/A	N/A	N/A	$67,165	80.0%	85.7%	N/A	39
87	University of Louisville (KY)	44	2.7	1.7	3.30	619	68.6%	$66,284	85.7%	88.1%	$32,000†	52
89	Binghamton University–SUNY (NY)	43	2.5	3.2	3.51	592	82.2%	$66,903	67.1%	80.0%	$26,746	132
89	Syracuse University (Whitman) (NY)	43	3.1	3.3	3.30	630	75.4%	$80,964	61.9%	71.4%	$1,559*	45
91	University of California–Riverside (Anderson)	42	2.6	2.5	3.29	611	53.3%	$70,211	40.5%	90.5%	$57,209	113
91	University of Denver (Daniels) (CO)	42	2.8	2.9	3.16	603	46.5%	$84,758	41.5%	75.6%	$91,006†	55
93	Rochester Institute of Technology (Saunders) (NY)	41	3.1	3.0	3.24	540	71.2%	$60,284	57.8%	78.3%	$45,808	126

Rank	School	Overall score	Peer assessment score (5.0=highest)	Recruiter assessment score (5.0=highest)	'18 full-time average undergrad GPA	'18 full-time average GMAT score	'18 full-time acceptance rate	'18 average starting salary and bonus	'18 graduates employed at graduation	Employed 3 months after graduation	'18 out-of-state tuition and fees	'18 total full-time enrollment
93	University of Kansas	41	3.1	2.6	3.17	585	72.0%	$69,450	40.0%	80.0%	$1,239*	57
95	University of Houston (Bauer) (TX)	40	2.9	2.9	3.18	611	52.4%	$84,746	43.9%	68.3%	$40,889	70
95	University of South Florida	40	2.6	1.7	3.40	515	37.1%	$43,944	88.9%	100.0%	$913*	52
97	University of Cincinnati (Lindner) (OH)	38	2.8	1.7	3.40	660	62.4%	$76,981	64.7%	74.5%	$43,194†	71
97	University of Oregon (Lundquist)	38	3.2	1.7	3.36	613	67.2%	$81,943	40.8%	61.2%	$41,406	123

School	Peer assessment score (5.0=highest)	Recruiter assessment score (5.0=highest)	'18 full-time average undergrad GPA	'18 full-time average GMAT score	'18 full-time acceptance rate	'18 average starting salary and bonus	'18 graduates employed at graduation	Employed 3 months after graduation	'18 out-of-state tuition and fees	'18 total full-time enrollment
SCHOOLS RANKED 99 THROUGH 131 ARE LISTED HERE ALPHABETICALLY										
Alfred University (NY)	1.7	1.7	N/A	N/A	92.9%	N/A	85.7%	100.0%	$39,010	22
American University (Kogod) (DC)	2.9	3.4	3.29	503	79.5%	$74,866	45.0%	60.0%	$87,896†	63
Appalachian State University (Walker) (NC)	2.2	1.7	3.27	N/A	91.7%	$56,586	48.4%	87.1%	$33,471†	67
Belmont University (Massey) (TN)	2.2	1.7	3.48	546	83.6%	$49,857	40.7%	70.4%	$59,895†	31
Boise State University (ID)	2.6	1.7	3.34	503	93.6%	$63,737	52.2%	82.6%	$26,446	63
Clark University (MA)	2.2	1.7	3.51	505	78.0%	$48,108	22.9%	71.4%	$71,725	84
Clarkson University (NY)	2.2	1.7	3.36	590	90.4%	$64,656	50.0%	93.3%	$53,644†	68
College of Charleston (SC)	2.2	1.7	3.20	527	77.3%	$61,752	69.2%	88.5%	$599†	41
Duquesne University (Palumbo-Donahue) (PA)	2.2	1.7	3.20	565	100.0%	$54,576	20.0%	80.0%	$51,603†	14
John Carroll University (Boler) (OH)	2.4	1.7	3.30	593	98.7%	$55,875	71.4%	71.4%	$900*	93
La Salle University (PA)	2.3	1.7	3.25	496	96.0%	$54,871	46.9%	91.8%	$25,020	48
Louisiana Tech University	2.4	1.7	3.51	527	50.0%	$58,359	56.5%	78.3%	$16,344	33
Mercer University–Atlanta (Stetson) (GA)	2.2	1.7	3.21	518	39.7%	$62,193	47.6%	85.7%	$818*	46
North Carolina A&T State University	2.0	1.7	3.50	510	48.8%	$76,000	100.0%	100.0%	$18,808†	135
Northern Arizona University (Franke)	2.2	1.7	3.36	544	86.0%	$53,778	73.9%	91.3%	$24,056	39
Oregon State University	2.7	1.7	3.37	588	70.7%	$78,787	27.6%	41.4%	$58,926†	146
Pace University (Lubin) (NY)	2.5	2.7	3.40	487	56.2%	$72,000	54.7%	70.3%	$1,267*	187
Quinnipiac University (CT)	2.6	2.4	3.53	600	93.3%	$61,262	47.0%	87.1%	$1,035*	158
San Diego State University (Fowler) (CA)	2.9	2.7	3.31	589	66.4%	$61,250	16.7%	54.2%	$24,240	116
St. John Fisher College (NY)	1.9	1.7	3.50	370	87.3%	$51,062	65.2%	69.6%	$1,130*	53
Texas Tech University (Rawls)	2.8	2.8	3.40	570	57.3%	$62,377	N/A	82.0%	$41,822	105
University at Albany–SUNY (NY)	2.5	1.7	3.40	550	73.3%	$66,633	35.6%	93.3%	$25,374	115
University of Delaware (Lerner)	2.8	1.7	3.10	625	40.2%	$81,815	40.0%	60.0%	$1,000*	101
University of Detroit Mercy (MI)	2.2	1.7	3.40	573	93.5%	$65,166	81.8%	95.5%	$1,579*	31
University of Mississippi	2.8	2.9	3.18	567	28.6%	$61,243	40.5%	75.7%	$1,888*	41
University of New Hampshire (Paul)	2.7	1.7	3.25	515	90.4%	$49,925	12.5%	54.2%	$48,095†	28
University of San Diego (CA)	2.7	2.9	3.20	614	62.1%	$72,628	20.0%	60.0%	$1,475*	80
University of San Francisco (CA)	2.6	1.7	3.31	576	68.7%	$93,917	43.8%	68.8%	$1,475*	65
University of Texas–San Antonio	2.4	1.7	3.40	597	53.2%	$78,125	48.3%	48.3%	$26,197	54
University of Toledo (OH)	2.1	1.7	3.34	459	71.9%	$55,310	8.5%	23.4%	$956*	425
University of Vermont	2.6	1.7	3.30	535	84.2%	$64,130	33.3%	61.9%	$53,785†	41
West Texas A&M University	1.9	1.7	3.41	540	80.0%	$82,057	54.5%	96.4%	$13,908†	150
Willamette University (Atkinson) (OR)	2.2	1.7	3.27	531	67.2%	$62,651	45.8%	79.2%	$42,290	126

Tops in the Specialties

MBA programs ranked best by B-school deans and MBA program directors

ACCOUNTING

1. **University of Texas–Austin** (McCombs)
2. **University of Illinois–Urbana-Champaign**
3. **University of Pennsylvania** (Wharton)
4. **Brigham Young University** (Marriott) (UT)
5. **University of Michigan–Ann Arbor** (Ross)
6. **University of Chicago** (Booth) (IL)
7. **University of Southern California** (Marshall)
8. **Stanford University** (CA)
9. **New York University** (Stern)
10. **Ohio State University** (Fisher)
11. **U. of North Carolina–Chapel Hill** (Kenan-Flagler)
12. **Indiana University** (Kelley)
13. **University of Notre Dame** (Mendoza) (IN)
14. **University of California–Berkeley** (Haas)
15. **Texas A&M University–College Station** (Mays)
16. **Columbia University** (NY)
17. **University of Florida** (Warrington)
18. **Gonzaga University** (WA)
19. **University of Georgia** (Terry)
20. **Fairfield University** (Dolan) (CT)
20. **Loyola Marymount University** (CA)
20. **Loyola University Maryland** (Sellinger)
23. **Northwestern University** (Kellogg) (IL)
24. **Harvard University** (MA)
24. **Seattle University** (Albers) (WA)
24. **Wake Forest University** (NC)

ENTREPRENEURSHIP

1. **Babson College** (Olin) (MA)
2. **Stanford University** (CA)
3. **Massachusetts Institute of Technology** (Sloan)
4. **Harvard University** (MA)
5. **University of California–Berkeley** (Haas)
6. **University of Pennsylvania** (Wharton)
7. **University of Michigan–Ann Arbor** (Ross)
8. **Indiana University** (Kelley)
9. **University of Southern California** (Marshall)
10. **University of Texas–Austin** (McCombs)
11. **Loyola Marymount University** (CA)
12. **University of Arizona** (Eller)
13. **Saint Louis University** (Chaifetz) (MO)
13. **University of Virginia** (Darden)
15. **Cornell University** (Johnson) (NY)
15. **University of San Francisco** (CA)

FINANCE

1. **University of Pennsylvania** (Wharton)
2. **University of Chicago** (Booth) (IL)
3. **New York University** (Stern)
4. **Columbia University** (NY)
5. **Massachusetts Institute of Technology** (Sloan)
6. **Stanford University** (CA)
7. **Harvard University** (MA)
8. **University of California–Berkeley** (Haas)
8. **University of Michigan–Ann Arbor** (Ross)

10. **University of California–Los Angeles** (Anderson)
11. **University of Texas–Austin** (McCombs)
12. **Northwestern University** (Kellogg) (IL)
13. **Carnegie Mellon University** (Tepper) (PA)
13. **Duke University** (Fuqua) (NC)
13. **University of Rochester** (Simon) (NY)
16. **Fordham University** (Gabelli) (NY)
16. **Santa Clara University** (Leavey) (CA)
18. **Creighton University** (Heider) (NE)
19. **Fairfield University** (Dolan) (CT)
19. **St. Joseph's University** (Haub) (PA)
21. **Gonzaga University** (WA)
21. **Xavier University** (Williams) (OH)
23. **Boston College** (Carroll) (MA)
23. **Cornell University** (Johnson) (NY)

INFORMATION SYSTEMS

1. **Massachusetts Institute of Technology** (Sloan)
2. **Carnegie Mellon University** (Tepper) (PA)
3. **University of Arizona** (Eller)
4. **University of Texas–Austin** (McCombs)
5. **Stanford University** (CA)
6. **University of Pennsylvania** (Wharton)
7. **University of Minnesota–Twin Cities** (Carlson)
8. **Georgia Institute of Technology** (Scheller)
9. **University of Maryland–College Park** (Smith)
10. **New York University** (Stern)
11. **Arizona State University** (W.P. Carey)
12. **Indiana University** (Kelley)
13. **Georgia State University** (Robinson)

INTERNATIONAL

1. **University of South Carolina** (Moore)
2. **Harvard University** (MA)
3. **New York University** (Stern)
3. **University of Pennsylvania** (Wharton)
5. **Georgetown University** (McDonough) (DC)
6. **University of California–Berkeley** (Haas)
7. **Columbia University** (NY)
8. **University of Michigan–Ann Arbor** (Ross)
9. **Saint Louis University** (Chaifetz) (MO)
10. **Duke University** (Fuqua) (NC)

MANAGEMENT

1. **Harvard University** (MA)
2. **Stanford University** (CA)
3. **Northwestern University** (Kellogg) (IL)
4. **University of Michigan–Ann Arbor** (Ross)
4. **University of Virginia** (Darden)
6. **Dartmouth College** (Tuck) (NH)
6. **University of Pennsylvania** (Wharton)
8. **University of California–Berkeley** (Haas)
9. **Duke University** (Fuqua) (NC)
10. **Columbia University** (NY)
11. **Yale University** (CT)

12. **Indiana University** (Kelley)
13. **University of California–Los Angeles** (Anderson)
14. **Massachusetts Institute of Technology** (Sloan)
14. **University of Chicago** (Booth) (IL)
16. **Arizona State University** (W.P. Carey)

MARKETING

1. **Northwestern University** (Kellogg) (IL)
2. **Duke University** (Fuqua) (NC)
2. **University of Michigan–Ann Arbor** (Ross)
2. **University of Pennsylvania** (Wharton)
5. **Columbia University** (NY)
6. **Harvard University** (MA)
6. **Stanford University** (CA)
8. **New York University** (Stern)
9. **University of California–Berkeley** (Haas)
9. **University of Chicago** (Booth) (IL)
11. **University of California–Los Angeles** (Anderson)
12. **Indiana University** (Kelley)
13. **University of Texas–Austin** (McCombs)
14. **Fairfield University** (Dolan) (CT)
14. **Loyola Marymount University** (CA)

NONPROFIT

1. **Yale University** (CT)
2. **Harvard University** (MA)
3. **University of California–Berkeley** (Haas)
4. **Stanford University** (CA)
5. **University of Michigan–Ann Arbor** (Ross)
6. **Duke University** (Fuqua) (NC)

PRODUCTION/OPERATIONS

1. **Massachusetts Institute of Technology** (Sloan)
2. **Carnegie Mellon University** (Tepper) (PA)
3. **Purdue University–West Lafayette** (Krannert) (IN)
3. **Stanford University** (CA)
5. **University of Michigan–Ann Arbor** (Ross)
5. **University of Pennsylvania** (Wharton)
7. **Georgia Institute of Technology** (Scheller)
8. **Northwestern University** (Kellogg) (IL)
8. **Columbia University** (NY)
9. **Ohio State University** (Fisher)
11. **Harvard University** (MA)

SUPPLY CHAIN/LOGISTICS

1. **Michigan State University** (Broad)
2. **Massachusetts Institute of Technology** (Sloan)
3. **Arizona State University** (W.P. Carey)
4. **Pennsylvania State U.–University Park** (Smeal)
5. **University of Tennessee–Knoxville** (Haslam)
6. **Ohio State University** (Fisher)
7. **Carnegie Mellon University** (Tepper) (PA)
8. **Purdue University–West Lafayette** (Krannert) (IN)
9. **Stanford University** (CA)
9. **University of Michigan–Ann Arbor** (Ross)
11. **Georgia Institute of Technology** (Scheller)

Best Executive MBA Programs

THE SMART MOVE for successful professionals who would rather not give up their job (and their paycheck) may be to pursue an executive MBA degree. These intensive programs target people who have made strides in their careers already but may need that credential to continue to advance. Classes take place in a concentrated manner, so students come to campus one day a week, say, or for a few days per month.

U.S. News ranked EMBA programs based solely on a fall 2018 survey of B-school deans and MBA program directors, who were asked to nominate up to 15 schools for the excellence of their EMBA programs. Those receiving the most votes in the latest survey are listed here, along with key information (from schools that provided it) about the student body and the cost.

Rank	School	'18 acceptance rate	'18 average age of new entrants	% women enrolled ('18)	% minority students ('18)	% international students ('18)	'18 total EMBA enrollment	'18 total EMBA program cost
1	University of Chicago (Booth) (IL)	N/A	38	21.9%	40.4%	15.8%	183	$189,000
2	Northwestern University (Kellogg) (IL)	N/A	N/A	27.4%	N/A	N/A	514	$104,076*
3	University of Pennsylvania (Wharton)	51.1%	35	28.8%	39.3%	17.2%	458	$205,200
4	Columbia University (NY)	N/A	33	N/A	N/A	N/A	N/A	N/A
5	University of Michigan–Ann Arbor (Ross)	76.3%	38	25.0%	30.7%	7.9%	228	$168,000
6	Duke University (Fuqua) (NC)	94.3%	34	30.5%	30.5%	24.1%	141	$142,400
7	University of California–Berkeley (Haas)	N/A	39	37.3%	N/A	N/A	142	$190,550
8	University of California–Los Angeles (Anderson)	81.0%	38	32.2%	43.8%	7.8%	283	$81,120*
9	New York University (Stern)	64.5%	37	34.5%	39.9%	8.4%	238	$194,876
10	Massachusetts Institute of Technology (Sloan)	N/A	N/A	N/A	N/A	N/A	N/A	N/A
11	Cornell University (Johnson) (NY)	64.2%	35	26.2%	45.4%	8.5%	130	$182,708
12	University of North Carolina–Chapel Hill (Kenan-Flager)	N/A	33	30.4%	34.8%	8.7%	46	N/A
13	Santa Clara University (Leavey) (CA)	92.0%	43	38.9%	72.2%	0%	36	$103,335
14	Marquette University (WI)	94.4%	40	33.3%	16.7%	0%	30	$74,000
14	University of Virginia (Darden)	N/A	34	26.3%	N/A	N/A	266	$133,100
16	St. Joseph's University (Haub) (PA)	88.0%	38	52.5%	29.2%	2.5%	120	N/A
17	Seattle University (Albers) (WA)	48.0%	37	62.2%	11.1%	0%	45	$99,000
18	University of Notre Dame (Mendoza) (IN)	86.4%	35	28.8%	14.4%	1.4%	146	$129,000
18	Emory University (Goizueta) (GA)	78.5%	37	35.8%	38.1%	10.4%	134	$45,000*
20	University of Southern California (Marshall)	80.6%	38	27.0%	53.4%	0.6%	178	$116,728
20	Xavier University (Williams) (OH)	73.3%	41	29.4%	17.6%	0%	17	$61,282
20	Yale University (CT)	N/A	N/A	31.3%	39.6%	8.2%	134	$89,900*
23	Loyola University Chicago (Quinlan) (IL)	73.1%	40	45.7%	31.4%	0%	35	$92,064
23	Southern Methodist University (Cox) (TX)	88.1%	37	19.5%	30.5%	11.7%	128	$116,150
23	University of Washington (Foster)	88.6%	37	37.9%	41.4%	4.3%	140	$108,000

*Annual tuition and fees. Student body and cost data are not used to compute the EMBA ranking. Sources: U.S. News and the schools. Assessment data collected by U.S. News.

▶ **More** @ usnews.com/bschool

Best Part-Time MBA Programs

PART-TIME BUSINESS programs play a vital role for people who can't go to school full time because of family or financial reasons or who simply prefer to keep working. The U.S. News part-time MBA ranking is based on five factors: the opinions of business school deans and MBA directors about program excellence; average GMAT and GRE scores of part-time MBA students entering in the fall of 2018; average undergraduate GPA; average number of years of work experience; and the percentage of the fall 2018 total MBA program enrollment that is in the part-time MBA program. The results were weighted – for more detail on how, see Page 57. Finally, the contenders were ranked by their overall score. To be eligible, a program needed to be accredited by AACSB International and have fall 2017 and fall 2018 part-time MBA program enrollment of 20 or more students. More @ usnews.com/parttime.

Rank	School	Overall score	Peer assessment score (5.0=highest)	'18 part-time average GMAT score	'18 part-time acceptance rate	'18 total part-time enrollment
1	**University of Chicago** (Booth) (IL)	100	4.6	679	N/A	1,322
2	**University of California–Berkeley** (Haas)	99	4.4	693	N/A	823
3	**Northwestern University** (Kellogg) (IL)	98	4.6	673	N/A	776
4	**New York University** (Stern)	96	4.3	665	68.1%	1,207
5	**University of California–Los Angeles** (Anderson)	95	4.2	679	64.4%	938
6	**University of Michigan–Ann Arbor** (Ross)	91	4.3	658	73.8%	429
7	**University of Minnesota–Twin Cities** (Carlson)	88	3.7	606	82.8%	879
8	**University of Texas–Austin** (McCombs)	87	4.0	645	78.7%	445
9	**Carnegie Mellon University** (Tepper) (PA)	86	4.0	649	51.4%	96
9	**Emory University** (Goizueta) (GA)	86	3.8	657	68.5%	264
9	**Indiana University** (Kelley)	86	3.9	633	62.3%	288
12	**Georgetown University** (McDonough) (DC)	85	3.8	655	71.4%	423
12	**University of Washington** (Foster)	85	3.6	631	79.3%	377
14	**Ohio State University** (Fisher)	84	3.7	625	65.1%	356
14	**University of Southern California** (Marshall)	84	3.9	625	75.2%	526
14	**Virginia Tech** (Pamplin)	84	3.3	628	91.1%	206
17	**Georgia Institute of Technology** (Scheller)	83	3.6	613	79.4%	357
17	**Rice University** (Jones) (TX)	83	3.6	637	77.4%	374
17	**University of Massachusetts–Amherst** (Isenberg)	83	3.1	605	89.0%	189
17	**University of Texas–Dallas**	83	3.2	627	72.1%	720
17	**Washington University in St. Louis** (Olin) (MO)	83	3.8	602	82.1%	246
22	**Arizona State University** (W.P. Carey)	82	3.6	607	86.5%	300
22	**Case Western Reserve University** (Weatherhead) (OH)	82	3.4	580	100.0%	162
22	**Santa Clara University** (Leavey) (CA)	82	3.2	627	83.4%	353

Note: The data listed for acceptance rate and enrollment are for informational purposes only and are not used in the computation of the part-time MBA program rankings. N/A=Data were not provided by the school. Sources: U.S. News and the schools. Assessment data collected by U.S. News.

Rank	School	Overall score	Peer assessment score (5.0=highest)	'18 part-time average GMAT score	'18 part-time acceptance rate	'18 total part-time enrollment
22	**University of Iowa** (Tippie)	82	3.3	586	95.3%	923
22	**University of South Carolina** (Moore)	82	3.4	639	94.4%	441
22	**University of Wisconsin–Madison**	82	3.7	611	72.4%	142
28	**Boston College** (Carroll) (MA)	81	3.6	622	96.9%	349
28	**University of California–Davis**	81	3.5	574	82.9%	292
30	**University of Maryland–College Park** (Smith)	80	3.5	581	78.9%	503
30	**Wake Forest University** (NC)	80	3.3	605	93.8%	325
32	**George Mason University** (VA)	79	3.0	568	78.4%	232
32	**University of California–Irvine** (Merage)	79	3.5	566	85.4%	339
32	**University of Florida** (Warrington)	79	3.5	575	64.3%	320
35	**Lehigh University** (PA)	78	2.9	628	74.1%	176
35	**University of California–San Diego** (Rady)	78	3.3	599	78.3%	119
35	**University of North Carolina–Charlotte** (Belk)	78	2.9	606	76.7%	375
35	**University of Richmond** (Robins) (VA)	78	2.9	640	87.1%	90
35	**Villanova University** (PA)	78	3.1	582	78.8%	111
40	**Boston University** (Questrom) (MA)	77	3.3	617	88.7%	649
40	**Loyola University Chicago** (Quinlan) (IL)	77	3.1	559	70.6%	251
40	**Rutgers, The State U. of New Jersey–Newark and New Brunswick**	77	3.1	582	86.7%	1,021
40	**Southern Methodist University** (Cox) (TX)	77	3.4	607	75.0%	219
44	**DePaul University** (Kellstadt) (IL)	76	3.1	604	77.1%	872
44	**Gonzaga University** (WA)	76	2.9	533	58.2%	188
44	**University of Colorado–Boulder** (Leeds)	76	3.3	593	84.1%	159
44	**University of Utah** (Eccles)	76	3.2	543	88.4%	314
48	**Georgia State University** (Robinson)	75	3.2	570	68.0%	320
48	**Marquette University** (WI)	75	2.9	551	83.2%	195
48	**Texas A&M University–College Station** (Mays)	75	3.5	595	81.5%	93
48	**University of Pittsburgh** (Katz) (PA)	75	3.3	562	83.2%	267
52	**Loyola Marymount University** (CA)	74	3.0	580	49.0%	55
52	**Pepperdine University** (Graziadio) (CA)	74	3.1	560	92.8%	505
52	**University of Arizona** (Eller)	74	3.4	610	81.4%	180
52	**University of Georgia** (Terry)	74	3.4	556	91.4%	283
52	**University of Oklahoma** (Price)	74	3.1	607	90.2%	146
57	**Bradley University** (Foster) (IL)	73	2.3	532	96.0%	45
57	**Florida State University**	73	3.1	561	47.6%	113
57	**Fordham University** (Gabelli) (NY)	73	3.1	588	71.0%	140
57	**North Carolina State University** (Poole)	73	2.9	622	70.7%	271
57	**Oregon State University**	73	2.7	577	65.6%	91
57	**Purdue University–West Lafayette** (Krannert) (IN)	73	3.5	536	90.0%	82
57	**Seattle University** (Albers) (WA)	73	2.7	484	70.3%	311
57	**Virginia Commonwealth University**	73	2.7	561	72.1%	151
65	**Oklahoma State University** (Spears)	72	3.0	551	82.6%	75
65	**Old Dominion University** (VA)	72	2.5	552	64.9%	71
65	**University of Alabama–Birmingham**	72	2.8	535	86.8%	350
65	**University of Connecticut**	72	3.1	591	89.1%	980
65	**University of Houston** (Bauer) (TX)	72	2.9	570	83.5%	286
65	**University of Illinois–Chicago** (Liautaud)	72	2.8	554	57.5%	235
65	**University of Illinois–Urbana-Champaign**	72	3.6	N/A	N/A	114
65	**University of Kansas**	72	3.1	580	87.0%	72
65	**University of Washington–Tacoma Milgard**	72	2.4	508	78.6%	65
74	**CUNY Bernard M. Baruch College** (Zicklin) (NY)	71	2.9	570	78.2%	476
74	**Rutgers, The State University of New Jersey–Camden**	71	2.9	530	65.3%	93
74	**Tulane University** (Freeman) (LA)	71	3.2	540	93.5%	135
74	**University of Colorado–Denver**	71	2.7	554	74.8%	440
74	**University of Delaware** (Lerner)	71	2.8	615	75.0%	159
74	**University of Minnesota–Duluth** (Labovitz)	71	2.3	575	94.1%	58

Rank	School	Overall score	Peer assessment score (5.0=highest)	'18 part-time average GMAT score	'18 part-time acceptance rate	'18 total part-time enrollment
74	**University of New Mexico** (Anderson)	71	2.7	526	48.2%	274
81	**Clemson University** (SC)	70	3.1	577	93.4%	417
81	**Creighton University** (Heider) (NE)	70	2.8	563	92.0%	127
81	**Iowa State University**	70	3.0	595	94.1%	41
81	**Kennesaw State University** (Coles) (GA)	70	2.5	556	48.1%	219
81	**Miami University** (Farmer) (OH)	70	2.9	560	77.3%	109
81	**San Diego State University** (Fowler) (CA)	70	2.9	583	65.9%	139
81	**St. Joseph's University** (Haub) (PA)	70	2.8	468	56.3%	205
81	**University of Kentucky** (Gatton)	70	3.0	590	93.7%	175
89	**Butler University** (IN)	69	2.5	553	86.5%	148
89	**Elon University** (Love) (NC)	69	2.6	554	68.3%	127
89	**Fairfield University** (Dolan) (CT)	69	2.6	555	84.8%	51
89	**Illinois State University**	69	2.3	554	97.2%	126
89	**The Citadel** (SC)	69	2.7	438	66.7%	119
89	**University of Central Florida**	69	2.7	N/A	75.9%	536
89	**University of Colorado–Colorado Springs**	69	2.4	564	93.4%	333
89	**University of Wisconsin–Milwaukee** (Lubar)	69	2.7	554	39.2%	245
89	**Wichita State University** (Barton) (KS)	69	2.4	540	80.0%	209
89	**Xavier University** (Williams) (OH)	69	2.8	528	92.6%	573
99	**Babson College** (Olin) (MA)	68	3.4	690	89.9%	229
99	**Bentley University** (MA)	68	3.0	546	86.4%	247
99	**College of William and Mary** (Mason) (VA)	68	3.2	610	100.0%	174
99	**George Washington University** (DC)	68	3.2	535	79.8%	174
99	**Northeastern University** (MA)	68	3.0	579	95.3%	280
99	**Texas State University** (McCoy)	68	2.3	543	40.6%	188
99	**University of Nebraska–Omaha**	68	2.6	561	92.1%	293
99	**University of North Texas**	68	2.4	531	63.4%	304
99	**University of Rochester** (Simon) (NY)	68	3.4	650	91.7%	145
99	**University of South Florida**	68	2.5	571	52.9%	311
109	**California State University–Fullerton** (Mihaylo)	67	2.5	548	70.5%	316
109	**Florida International University**	67	2.7	N/A	61.0%	481
109	**Providence College** (RI)	67	2.4	488	96.7%	161
109	**University of Cincinnati** (Lindner) (OH)	67	2.9	660	77.9%	139
109	**University of Memphis** (Fogelman) (TN)	67	2.8	583	55.2%	115
109	**University of Michigan–Dearborn**	67	2.5	586	59.8%	167
109	**University of North Carolina–Greensboro** (Bryan)	67	2.6	512	85.4%	116
109	**University of Portland** (Pamplin) (OR)	67	2.6	530	59.5%	114
117	**James Madison University** (VA)	66	2.7	490	89.7%	46
117	**St. John's University** (Tobin) (NY)	66	2.6	573	77.0%	361
117	**University of Akron** (OH)	66	2.2	510	61.9%	167
117	**University of Hawaii–Manoa** (Shidler)	66	2.8	552	56.3%	40
117	**University of Louisville** (KY)	66	2.7	536	87.1%	143
117	**University of Massachusetts–Boston**	66	2.7	511	69.8%	256
117	**University of Nevada–Las Vegas**	66	2.6	580	34.6%	158
117	**University of San Francisco** (CA)	66	2.8	504	100.0%	85
117	**University of Scranton** (PA)	66	2.3	531	81.7%	101
117	**University of Tennessee–Chattanooga**	66	2.5	533	82.8%	127
127	**Boise State University** (ID)	65	2.6	547	100.0%	76
127	**Drake University** (IA)	65	2.2	546	90.0%	97
127	**Drexel University** (LeBow) (PA)	65	2.8	469	94.2%	220
127	**Florida Atlantic University**	65	2.4	508	82.1%	163
127	**Loyola University Maryland** (Sellinger)	65	2.8	N/A	N/A	291
127	**Pennsylvania State University–Harrisburg**	65	2.4	538	81.3%	178
127	**Purdue University–Northwest** (IN)	65	2.4	530	72.1%	119

Rank	School	Overall score	Peer assessment score (5.0=highest)	'18 part-time average GMAT score	'18 part-time acceptance rate	'18 total part-time enrollment
127	University of Alabama–Huntsville	65	2.5	489	71.6%	99
127	University of Michigan–Flint	65	2.2	521	57.1%	171
127	University of New Hampshire (Paul)	65	2.6	520	100.0%	146
127	University of Texas–Arlington	65	2.6	506	80.5%	433
127	University of Texas–San Antonio	65	2.3	540	86.2%	196
127	Western Michigan University (Haworth)	65	2.4	512	67.8%	284
140	Rockhurst University (Helzberg) (MO)	64	2.3	499	99.4%	454
140	University at Buffalo–SUNY (NY)	64	2.8	519	99.2%	239
140	University of Denver (Daniels) (CO)	64	2.8	624	73.8%	100
140	University of San Diego (CA)	64	2.7	572	88.2%	108
144	Claremont Graduate University (Drucker) (CA)	63	3.2	N/A	N/A	24
144	Mercer University–Atlanta (Stetson) (GA)	63	2.2	530	70.6%	347
144	New Mexico State University	63	2.3	N/A	86.2%	172
144	Pennsylvania State University–Erie, The Behrend College (Black)	63	2.4	493	100.0%	117
144	Southern Illinois University–Edwardsville	63	2.2	508	87.9%	93
144	Texas Christian University (Neeley)	63	2.9	N/A	N/A	152
144	University of Dayton (OH)	63	2.4	N/A	87.8%	97
144	University of Nevada–Reno	63	2.3	492	97.7%	221
144	University of St. Thomas (MN)	63	2.5	583	100.0%	445
144	Weber State University (Goddard) (UT)	63	2.2	560	86.2%	260
154	Berry College (Campbell) (GA)	62	1.9	480	100.0%	38
154	Louisiana State University–Baton Rouge (Ourso)	62	2.9	497	87.5%	61
154	Loyola University New Orleans (Butt) (LA)	62	2.6	N/A	100.0%	54
154	Portland State University (OR)	62	2.3	540	83.9%	110
154	University of Tulsa (Collins) (OK)	62	2.4	606	93.3%	43
159	Bowling Green State University (OH)	61	2.3	N/A	38.7%	70
159	California State University–Long Beach	61	2.4	545	75.5%	130
159	California State University–San Bernardino	61	2.1	507	66.2%	204
159	Indiana State University	61	2.2	600	100.0%	56
159	Northern Illinois University	61	2.5	N/A	100.0%	294
159	Suffolk University (Sawyer) (MA)	61	2.3	463	82.9%	211
159	University at Albany–SUNY (NY)	61	2.5	540	87.1%	190
159	University of Massachusetts–Lowell (Manning)	61	2.3	550	88.9%	55
159	Wayne State University (MI)	61	2.5	N/A	42.0%	1,319
168	Chapman University (Argyros) (CA)	60	2.5	530	88.5%	116
168	Eastern Michigan University	60	2.1	474	61.2%	207
168	Hofstra University (Zarb) (NY)	60	2.7	512	94.3%	184
168	North Dakota State University	60	2.1	530	80.0%	67
168	Robert Morris University (PA)	60	2.0	618	60.2%	201
168	Seton Hall University (Stillman) (NJ)	60	2.8	493	89.3%	448
168	Stockton University (NJ)	60	1.7	N/A	80.6%	95
168	University of Missouri–Kansas City (Bloch)	60	2.5	N/A	79.1%	247
168	University of Northern Iowa	60	2.2	475	N/A	198
168	University of Tampa (Sykes) (FL)	60	2.4	540	48.3%	83
178	American University (Kogod) (DC)	59	2.9	N/A	N/A	21
178	Belmont University (Massey) (TN)	59	2.3	498	97.6%	138
178	Indiana University–Southeast	59	1.8	547	89.4%	210
178	Oakland University (MI)	59	2.0	501	97.0%	284
178	Quinnipiac University (CT)	59	2.6	690	90.9%	23
178	Shenandoah University (Byrd) (VA)	59	1.8	N/A	70.0%	34
178	Southeast Missouri State University (Harrison)	59	1.8	507	100.0%	61
178	University of Louisiana–Lafayette (Moody)	59	2.2	N/A	82.9%	231
178	University of North Florida (Coggin)	59	2.1	505	52.6%	518
178	Valparaiso University (IN)	59	2.3	610	93.8%	33

Rank	School	Overall score	Peer assessment score (5.0=highest)	'18 part-time average GMAT score	'18 part-time acceptance rate	'18 total part-time enrollment
188	Canisius College (Wehle) (NY)	58	2.3	475	95.3%	211
188	Clark University (MA)	58	2.2	N/A	100.0%	45
188	Duquesne University (Palumbo-Donahue) (PA)	58	2.4	532	91.9%	147
188	Indiana University–South Bend	58	1.8	550	85.7%	80
188	Le Moyne College (NY)	58	2.2	650	100.0%	74
188	Pace University (Lubin) (NY)	58	2.6	580	53.7%	95
188	Queens University of Charlotte (McColl) (NC)	58	2.0	465	92.0%	100
188	Sonoma State University (CA)	58	2.1	475	78.8%	55
188	University of Texas–El Paso	58	2.2	456	90.4%	137
197	Fayetteville State University (NC)	57	1.6	529	88.4%	411
197	Tennessee Technological University	57	1.9	475	82.9%	156
197	Union University (TN)	57	1.6	482	60.8%	112
197	University of California–Riverside (Anderson)	57	2.8	481	88.9%	146
197	University of Central Missouri (Harmon)	57	1.9	520	61.4%	49
197	University of Houston–Clear Lake (TX)	57	2.1	444	80.9%	216
197	University of Illinois–Springfield	57	2.1	498	81.0%	82
197	University of Northern Colorado (Monfort)	57	2.1	485	100.0%	21
197	University of Wisconsin–Whitewater	57	2.1	509	82.0%	126
206	Adelphi University (NY)	56	1.9	416	56.6%	469
206	California State University–Stanislaus	56	1.9	502	100.0%	66
206	Dominican University (Brennan) (IL)	56	1.9	N/A	95.8%	119
206	Monmouth University (NJ)	56	1.9	550	85.1%	148
206	Montclair State University Feliciano (NJ)	56	2.0	N/A	94.5%	286
206	University of Dallas (TX)	56	2.3	430	93.9%	382
206	University of North Carolina–Wilmington (Cameron)	56	2.3	N/A	85.4%	88
213	Bryant University (RI)	55	2.3	445	71.1%	88
213	California State University–East Bay	55	1.9	537	33.9%	228
213	Florida Gulf Coast University (Lutgert)	55	1.9	550	52.6%	108
213	Howard University (DC)	55	2.6	N/A	N/A	21
213	Iona College (NY)	55	2.1	N/A	93.9%	270
213	St. Mary's University (Greehey) (TX)	55	2.2	N/A	51.7%	66
213	Stevens Institute of Technology (NJ)	55	2.5	585	82.0%	329
213	University of Southern Mississippi	55	2.1	550	100.0%	29

School	Peer assessment score (5.0=highest)	'18 part-time average GMAT score	'18 part-time acceptance rate	'18 total part-time enrollment
SCHOOLS RANKED 221 THROUGH 287 ARE LISTED HERE ALPHABETICALLY				
Alfred University (NY)	1.8	N/A	N/A	20
Appalachian State University (Walker) (NC)	2.0	N/A	100.0%	41
Bellarmine University (Rubel) (KY)	1.9	546	93.8%	39
Black Hills State University (SD)	1.7	N/A	N/A	20
Bloomsburg University of Pennsylvania	1.8	490	82.6%	78
California State University–Northridge (Nazarian)	2.4	609	23.2%	108
Central Connecticut State University	1.8	N/A	82.2%	218
Clarion University of Pennsylvania	1.7	N/A	97.7%	71
Cleveland State University (Ahuja) (OH)	2.1	498	79.6%	310
Columbus State University (Turner) (GA)	1.9	450	76.9%	33
Fairleigh Dickinson University (Silberman) (NJ)	2.2	N/A	68.0%	203
Frostburg State University (MD)	1.7	N/A	N/A	135
Georgia Southern University	2.2	471	85.9%	41
Governors State University (IL)	1.5	560	44.4%	87
Grand Valley State University (Seidman) (MI)	2.1	538	71.6%	136

School	Peer assessment score (5.0=highest)	'18 part-time average GMAT score	'18 part-time acceptance rate	'18 total part-time enrollment
Indiana University Northwest	1.7	N/A	N/A	30
Indiana University of Pennsylvania (Eberly)	2.0	460	100.0%	98
Jacksonville University (FL)	2.0	555	100.0%	105
John Carroll University (Boler) (OH)	2.4	N/A	87.5%	57
La Salle University (PA)	2.2	360	100.0%	163
LIU Post (NY)	1.8	410	N/A	21
Manhattan College (NY)	1.9	N/A	66.7%	75
Marshall University (Lewis) (WV)	2.3	N/A	71.1%	67
Meredith College (NC)	1.6	N/A	100.0%	46
Midwestern State University (TX)	1.5	N/A	N/A	49
New Jersey Institute of Technology	2.2	N/A	95.0%	53
Niagara University (NY)	2.0	N/A	57.1%	52
Northeastern Illinois University	2.0	N/A	89.7%	70
Oklahoma City University	1.7	N/A	73.5%	122
Prairie View A&M University (TX)	1.6	N/A	N/A	132
Radford University (VA)	2.0	510	65.5%	32
Ramapo College of New Jersey	1.8	N/A	53.9%	66
Rowan University (Rohrer) (NJ)	2.1	N/A	85.0%	62
SUNY–Oswego (NY)	2.0	400	94.4%	42
Sacred Heart University (Welch) (CT)	2.1	354	92.2%	138
Saginaw Valley State University (MI)	1.8	N/A	60.7%	60
Saint Louis University (Chaifetz) (MO)	3.1	548	81.0%	149
Salisbury University (Perdue) (MD)	1.8	N/A	N/A	30
Savannah State University (GA)	1.8	N/A	51.7%	62
Shippensburg University of Pennsylvania (Grove)	2.0	N/A	49.1%	63
Southern Arkansas University	1.6	453	71.1%	87
Southern Utah University	1.7	520	85.2%	49
St. Bonaventure University (NY)	2.1	505	100.0%	108
St. John Fisher College (NY)	2.0	420	77.3%	70
Stetson University (FL)	2.2	N/A	N/A	25
Texas A&M International University	2.0	N/A	100.0%	46
Texas A&M University–Commerce	2.0	434	74.9%	632
University of Central Arkansas	1.9	N/A	84.6%	22
University of Central Oklahoma	1.9	N/A	N/A	42
University of Detroit Mercy (MI)	2.2	476	100.0%	50
University of Montevallo (AL)	1.6	N/A	100.0%	35
University of New Haven (CT)	2.2	420	100.0%	79
University of North Georgia	1.9	510	72.5%	76
University of South Florida–Sarasota-Manatee	1.8	N/A	34.1%	71
University of Southern Indiana	1.7	550	N/A	176
University of Southern Maine	1.9	N/A	56.0%	52
University of St. Thomas–Houston (TX)	1.8	N/A	97.3%	179
University of Texas–Rio Grande Valley	1.8	N/A	N/A	170
University of West Georgia (Richards)	1.8	414	98.3%	104
University of Wisconsin–Parkside	1.9	N/A	N/A	61
University of Wisconsin–River Falls	1.8	426	100.0%	48
West Texas A&M University	1.7	530	80.0%	25
Western Carolina University (NC)	1.8	375	100.0%	53
Western Illinois University	1.9	N/A	100.0%	73
Western New England University (MA)	1.6	523	82.0%	81
Widener University (PA)	1.9	N/A	92.9%	40
Willamette University (Atkinson) (OR)	2.1	445	100.0%	111

Best Online Programs

OUR RANKINGS OF online business degree programs have been split into two groups: those that deliver the MBA – still the most popular online graduate degree – and non-MBA master's-level business programs. These include degrees in accounting, finance, insurance, marketing and management.

To start, U.S. News surveyed nearly 450 master's-level business programs at regionally accredited institutions that deliver required classes predominantly online. In both the MBA and non-MBA groups, programs were ranked based on their success at promoting student engagement, the training and credentials of their faculty, the selectivity of their admissions processes, the services and technologies available to remote learners, and the opinions of deans and other academics in the disciplines at peer distance-education programs.

Specific indicators include graduation and retention rates, student indebtedness at graduation, the average undergraduate GPAs and standardized test scores of new entrants, proportion of faculty members with terminal degrees, proportion of full-time faculty who are tenured or tenure-track, whether there is program-level accreditation, and whether students can remotely access support services like mentoring and academic advising. In summary, the rankings measure the extent to which online degree programs have achieved academic quality commensurate with that found at strong brick-and-mortar schools. All the ranked programs are listed below; to see more detail on the methodologies, visit **usnews.com/onlinedegrees.**

Best Online MBA Programs

Rank	School	Overall score	Average peer assessment score (5.0=highest)	'18 total enrollment	'18-'19 total program cost[1]	Entrance test required	'18 average undergrad GPA	'18 acceptance rate	'18 full-time faculty with terminal degree	'18 tenured or tenure-track faculty[2]	'18 retention rate	'18 three-year graduation rate
1	Indiana University–Bloomington	100	4.2	934	$67,830	GMAT or GRE	3.4	76%	91%	57%	99%	79%
1	University of North Carolina–Chapel Hill	100	4.2	905	$124,345	N/A	3.2	60%	88%	88%	98%	90%
3	Carnegie Mellon University (PA)	98	4.1	137	$132,000	GMAT or GRE	3.3	54%	97%	90%	98%	97%
4	University of Florida	95	3.8	391	$58,000	GMAT or GRE	3.3	46%	100%	63%	98%	97%
5	University of Southern California	93	3.8	139	$97,512	GMAT or GRE	3.1	53%	87%	47%	100%	N/A
6	Arizona State University	92	3.8	437	$60,074	GMAT or GRE	3.3	61%	88%	45%	98%	89%
6	University of Texas–Dallas	92	3.4	295	$83,428	GMAT or GRE	3.5	43%	78%	35%	82%	47%
8	University of Maryland–College Park	90	3.6	399	$87,318	GMAT or GRE	3.3	65%	97%	50%	91%	82%
9	Auburn University (AL)	88	3.4	372	$34,425	GMAT or GRE	3.4	74%	95%	90%	94%	69%
9	Pennsylvania State U.–World Campus	88	3.3	355	$56,880	N/A	3.3	76%	100%	75%	95%	83%
9	University of Mississippi	88	3.0	116	$31,860	GMAT or GRE	3.5	31%	92%	75%	85%	81%
9	University of Wisconsin MBA Consortium	88	2.9	342	$23,250	GMAT or GRE	3.4	85%	86%	86%	94%	78%
13	Ball State University (IN)	87	2.9	318	$21,000	GMAT or GRE	3.4	63%	100%	97%	92%	76%
13	Lehigh University (PA)	87	2.9	207	$39,075	GMAT or GRE	3.3	61%	75%	69%	97%	71%
13	Villanova University (PA)	87	3.5	249	$64,800	GMAT or GRE	3.2	78%	94%	94%	92%	90%
13	Washington State University	87	3.3	840	$35,000	GMAT or GRE	3.5	60%	86%	64%	94%	68%
17	Creighton University (NE)	84	2.9	117	$37,224	GMAT or GRE	3.3	85%	85%	78%	91%	100%
17	North Carolina State University	84	3.1	312	$78,440	N/A	3.2	69%	80%	68%	97%	84%

N/A=Data were not provided by the school; programs that received insufficient numbers of ratings do not have their peer-assessment scores published.
[1]Tuition is reported for part-time, out-of-state students. [2]Percentage reported of full-time faculty. More detail can be found in the directory of online programs at the back of the book.

Rank	School	Overall score	Average peer assessment score (5.0=highest)	'18 total enrollment	'18-'19 total program cost[1]	Entrance test required	'18 average undergrad GPA	'18 acceptance rate	'18 full-time faculty with terminal degree	'18 tenured or tenure-track faculty[2]	'18 retention rate	'18 three-year graduation rate
17	University of Massachusetts–Amherst	84	3.3	1,403	$35,100	GMAT or GRE	3.3	89%	95%	68%	95%	48%
17	University of Utah	84	3.2	121	$58,800	N/A	3.3	66%	79%	42%	94%	82%
21	Florida State University	83	3.2	211	$29,250	GMAT or GRE	3.3	66%	100%	86%	82%	51%
21	Kennesaw State University (GA)	83	2.8	200	$24,370	GMAT or GRE	3.2	70%	100%	100%	92%	N/A
21	Pepperdine University (CA)	83	3.4	236	$92,040	GMAT or GRE	3.1	67%	82%	36%	93%	72%
21	University of Arizona	83	3.4	313	$18,000	GMAT or GRE	3.3	88%	73%	50%	87%	85%
21	University of Wisconsin–Whitewater	83	2.6	379	$22,968	GMAT or GRE	3.4	73%	100%	100%	95%	75%
26	Mississippi State University	82	2.9	268	$14,235	GMAT or GRE	3.4	71%	100%	100%	91%	49%
26	Rochester Institute of Technology (NY)	82	3.1	47	N/A	None	3.2	52%	82%	82%	92%	94%
26	University of Delaware	82	2.9	357	$39,600	GMAT or GRE	3.3	66%	100%	85%	85%	73%
26	University of Kansas	82	3.2	287	$36,330	GMAT or GRE	3.3	77%	67%	47%	95%	N/A
26	University of Nebraska–Lincoln	82	3.2	503	$30,240	GMAT or GRE	3.3	79%	92%	60%	94%	59%
31	University of North Dakota	81	2.7	127	$20,081	GMAT or GRE	3.3	88%	100%	94%	90%	64%
31	University of North Texas	81	2.6	231	$33,612	GMAT or GRE	3.5	60%	100%	90%	93%	65%
31	University of South Florida–St. Petersburg	81	2.4	317	$32,664	GMAT or GRE	3.4	31%	100%	79%	89%	74%
34	Babson College (MA)	80	3.5	409	$89,564	None	3.1	87%	84%	54%	97%	98%
34	James Madison University (VA)	80	3.0	33	$37,800	GMAT or GRE	3.2	87%	100%	100%	100%	94%
34	Quinnipiac University (CT)	80	2.7	243	$43,010	GMAT or GRE	3.3	62%	100%	84%	91%	72%
34	University of Tennessee–Martin	80	2.4	68	N/A	GMAT or GRE	3.1	68%	100%	100%	84%	82%
38	Oklahoma State University	79	3.0	242	$15,120	GMAT or GRE	3.3	83%	96%	64%	87%	61%
38	Syracuse University (NY)	79	3.4	1,344	$84,186	N/A	3.0	80%	92%	46%	93%	67%
40	Boise State University (ID)	78	2.6	250	$36,750	GMAT or GRE	3.3	91%	78%	100%	94%	69%
40	George Washington University (DC)	78	3.3	431	$101,288	GMAT or GRE	3.3	80%	100%	91%	86%	70%
40	Missouri University of Science & Technology	78	2.3	69	$43,200	GMAT or GRE	3.0	90%	95%	89%	81%	100%
40	SUNY–Oswego	78	2.5	202	$26,748	N/A	3.2	80%	88%	88%	90%	71%
40	University of Nevada–Reno	78	2.6	59	$30,000	GMAT or GRE	3.1	100%	91%	91%	87%	93%
45	Arkansas State University–Jonesboro	77	2.3	164	$20,130	N/A	3.3	57%	100%	100%	59%	33%
45	Drexel University (PA)	77	2.8	214	$64,000	GMAT or GRE	3.2	90%	100%	52%	95%	80%
45	Old Dominion University (VA)	77	2.8	86	$22,720	GMAT or GRE	3.5	74%	93%	93%	85%	55%
45	Stevens Institute of Technology (NJ)	77	2.5	96	$63,180	GMAT or GRE	3.3	84%	97%	38%	85%	61%
45	West Texas A&M University	77	2.1	1,010	$16,035	None	3.4	76%	98%	88%	90%	83%
45	West Virginia University	77	2.7	169	$49,104	GMAT or GRE	3.2	94%	90%	75%	93%	88%
51	Colorado State University	76	3.2	821	N/A	None	3.1	87%	80%	84%	93%	57%
51	Columbus State University (GA)	76	2.1	24	$22,170	GMAT or GRE	3.1	86%	100%	100%	84%	89%
51	Florida Atlantic University	76	2.5	254	$32,000	None	3.2	73%	95%	26%	93%	93%
51	Florida International University	76	2.7	865	$42,000	None	3.3	64%	92%	59%	81%	74%
51	Rutgers University–Camden (NJ)	76	3.0	296	$52,752	GMAT or GRE	3.2	78%	100%	50%	86%	29%
51	University of Massachusetts–Lowell	76	2.7	896	$19,650	N/A	3.4	91%	83%	73%	93%	55%
51	University of New Hampshire	76	2.6	115	$43,680	N/A	3.1	94%	92%	88%	90%	63%
58	Georgia College & State University	75	2.4	54	$22,170	GMAT or GRE	3.1	88%	100%	100%	92%	94%
58	Hofstra University (NY)	75	2.6	45	N/A	GMAT or GRE	3.0	86%	100%	89%	95%	92%
58	Kansas State University	75	3.0	91	$30,000	N/A	3.4	100%	100%	100%	98%	80%
58	Marist College (NY)	75	2.3	217	$28,800	GMAT or GRE	3.3	50%	93%	87%	89%	42%
58	Southern Illinois University–Carbondale	75	2.7	109	$35,868	GMAT or GRE	3.4	74%	100%	92%	84%	74%
58	University of Miami (FL)	75	3.1	56	$85,260	N/A	3.2	34%	100%	100%	N/A	N/A
58	West Chester University of Pennsylvania	75	1.9	550	$15,780	GMAT or GRE	3.4	79%	83%	88%	94%	70%
58	Worcester Polytechnic Institute (MA)	75	2.9	141	$72,624	GMAT or GRE	N/A	80%	89%	56%	95%	90%
66	Georgia Southern University	74	2.4	151	$13,302	GMAT or GRE	2.9	91%	100%	100%	95%	91%
66	Louisiana State University–Baton Rouge	74	2.9	175	$42,462	None	3.2	68%	N/A	N/A	63%	41%
66	University of Cincinnati (OH)	74	3.0	264	$31,198	GMAT or GRE	3.3	64%	88%	56%	96%	59%
66	Western Kentucky University	74	2.4	91	$21,210	N/A	3.4	88%	100%	90%	70%	70%
70	Clarkson University (NY)	73	2.3	184	$56,652	GMAT or GRE	3.3	89%	88%	62%	84%	82%
70	Mercer University–Atlanta (GA)	73	2.5	64	$27,180	GMAT or GRE	3.1	64%	100%	89%	95%	N/A
70	University of Memphis (TN)	73	2.7	130	$36,003	GMAT or GRE	3.4	94%	100%	100%	90%	64%

Rank	School	Overall score	Average peer assessment score (5.0=highest)	'18 total enrollment	'18-'19 total program cost[1]	Entrance test required	'18 average undergrad GPA	'18 acceptance rate	'18 full-time faculty with terminal degree	'18 tenured or tenure-track faculty[2]	'18 retention rate	'18 three-year graduation rate
73	Baylor University (TX)	72	3.1	146	$25,632	None	3.1	74%	86%	86%	76%	65%
73	Central Michigan University	72	2.5	501	N/A	N/A	3.3	68%	83%	83%	73%	72%
73	Robert Morris University (PA)	72	N/A	83	N/A	None	3.3	84%	100%	100%	91%	N/A
73	University of South Dakota	72	2.5	252	$14,883	N/A	3.3	95%	94%	89%	74%	63%
77	American University (DC)	71	N/A	543	$81,984	None	3.1	84%	80%	60%	90%	N/A
77	Louisiana Tech University	71	2.4	58	$12,840	GMAT or GRE	3.3	73%	100%	100%	76%	71%
77	Northeastern University (MA)	71	3.1	692	$80,000	None	3.2	88%	91%	79%	89%	46%
77	Tennessee Technological University	71	2.1	188	$36,420	N/A	3.4	80%	100%	89%	N/A	N/A
77	University of Michigan–Dearborn	71	2.8	177	N/A	GMAT or GRE	3.4	50%	95%	84%	83%	61%
82	College of William and Mary (VA)	70	N/A	401	$59,780	N/A	3.2	96%	86%	57%	93%	N/A
82	Ohio University	70	2.8	842	$36,645	None	3.1	88%	83%	89%	91%	79%
82	SUNY Polytechnic Institute	70	2.4	114	$35,664	GMAT or GRE	3.5	56%	90%	90%	81%	59%
82	St. Mary's College of California	70	2.1	68	$74,400	None	3.0	98%	80%	80%	82%	98%
82	Texas A&M International University	70	2.5	131	$14,760	N/A	3.0	100%	100%	73%	87%	86%
82	University of South Florida	70	2.9	39	$28,800	GMAT or GRE	3.2	48%	100%	60%	66%	N/A
82	University of Tennessee–Chattanooga	70	2.7	197	$24,780	GMAT or GRE	3.4	93%	94%	100%	85%	75%
89	University of Pittsburgh (PA)	69	N/A	350	$103,224	GMAT or GRE	3.3	83%	100%	31%	94%	N/A
90	Cleveland State University (OH)	68	2.3	35	$35,000	GMAT or GRE	2.9	69%	100%	80%	100%	N/A
90	East Carolina University (NC)	68	2.3	857	$33,078	GMAT or GRE	3.3	74%	96%	98%	71%	45%
90	Kent State University (OH)	68	2.8	57	$29,880	GMAT or GRE	3.3	70%	100%	69%	N/A	N/A
90	Longwood University (VA)	68	1.8	34	$44,676	GMAT or GRE	3.2	70%	100%	100%	94%	87%
90	Samford University (AL)	68	2.2	143	$40,000	GMAT or GRE	3.3	88%	100%	100%	99%	72%
90	Southern Utah University	68	1.9	105	$14,570	GMAT or GRE	3.4	85%	78%	78%	81%	N/A
90	The Citadel (SC)	68	2.8	52	$25,020	GMAT or GRE	3.2	52%	100%	94%	15%	N/A
90	University of Alabama–Birmingham	68	2.8	106	$39,168	N/A	3.0	72%	87%	70%	85%	N/A
90	University of Colorado–Colorado Springs	68	2.7	173	N/A	N/A	3.3	72%	100%	93%	72%	38%
90	University of Maine	68	2.5	62	$16,470	GMAT or GRE	3.4	92%	100%	88%	89%	N/A
90	University of West Georgia	68	2.2	94	N/A	GMAT or GRE	3.1	84%	100%	100%	98%	90%
101	Ashland University (OH)	67	1.7	321	$24,450	None	3.2	76%	71%	82%	95%	71%
101	California State University–San Bernardino	67	2.2	170	$36,000	None	3.2	97%	88%	76%	90%	82%
101	Fayetteville State University (NC)	67	1.9	411	$17,789	GMAT or GRE	3.3	95%	100%	93%	75%	45%
101	New Jersey Institute of Technology	67	2.4	115	$61,536	None	3.1	67%	100%	85%	68%	42%
101	St. Joseph's University (PA)	67	2.6	411	N/A	GMAT or GRE	3.3	78%	82%	80%	80%	37%
101	Texas A&M University–Central Texas	67	2.7	194	$23,472	None	3.4	66%	100%	87%	54%	45%
101	Texas A&M University–Commerce	67	2.4	1,033	$18,510	None	3.2	74%	83%	83%	84%	59%
101	University of Massachusetts–Dartmouth	67	2.8	75	N/A	N/A	3.3	95%	79%	79%	81%	54%
109	Southeast Missouri State University	66	2.0	114	$12,672	GMAT or GRE	3.1	88%	96%	78%	67%	55%
109	Texas A&M University–Kingsville	66	2.1	101	$17,831	GMAT or GRE	3.1	98%	100%	100%	89%	70%
109	University of Scranton (PA)	66	2.2	437	$34,740	None	3.2	97%	91%	91%	89%	60%
109	Wichita State University (KS)	66	2.7	231	$8,899	GMAT or GRE	3.4	76%	100%	86%	97%	N/A
113	California Baptist University	65	1.8	144	$23,832	None	3.3	63%	100%	100%	77%	75%
113	Embry-Riddle Aeronautical U.–Worldwide (FL)	65	2.2	931	N/A	None	3.2	91%	100%	50%	87%	37%
113	Fort Hays State University (KS)	65	2.0	134	$12,590	GMAT or GRE	3.4	52%	100%	94%	84%	52%
113	Salisbury University (MD)	65	2.0	21	N/A	GMAT or GRE	3.4	79%	100%	100%	54%	N/A
113	Sam Houston State University (TX)	65	2.2	271	$11,088	N/A	3.4	81%	96%	96%	72%	44%
113	University of Baltimore (MD)	65	2.3	520	$40,320	GMAT or GRE	3.3	99%	95%	76%	90%	59%
119	Baldwin Wallace University (OH)	64	1.5	43	N/A	N/A	3.2	85%	88%	100%	100%	68%
119	California State University–Stanislaus	64	2.0	30	N/A	GMAT or GRE	3.3	94%	100%	100%	N/A	N/A
119	Portland State University (OR)	64	2.6	126	$42,480	N/A	3.3	65%	75%	75%	N/A	N/A
119	Queens University of Charlotte (NC)	64	1.9	119	$40,788	GMAT or GRE	3.0	95%	80%	80%	95%	88%
119	University of Hartford (CT)	64	2.5	513	$25,020	N/A	3.3	42%	77%	77%	N/A	N/A
119	University of Southern Mississippi	64	2.6	69	$15,609	GMAT or GRE	3.3	86%	100%	88%	75%	N/A
119	University of Wyoming	64	N/A	83	$23,640	N/A	3.1	97%	100%	90%	89%	72%
126	Clarion University of Pennsylvania	63	1.8	98	$16,710	GMAT or GRE	3.3	97%	100%	100%	78%	51%

Rank	School	Overall score	Average peer assessment score (5.0=highest)	'18 total enrollment	'18-'19 total program cost[1]	Entrance test required	'18 average undergrad GPA	'18 acceptance rate	'18 full-time faculty with terminal degree	'18 tenured or tenure-track faculty[2]	'18 retention rate	'18 three-year graduation rate
126	DeSales University (PA)	63	1.5	722	N/A	None	3.4	87%	100%	100%	94%	49%
126	Ferris State University (MI)	63	1.9	137	$23,790	GMAT or GRE	3.4	35%	93%	100%	70%	N/A
126	University of Central Missouri	63	2.3	56	$15,309	GMAT or GRE	3.4	47%	100%	100%	80%	N/A
126	University of Washington	63	N/A	47	$1,144	GMAT or GRE	3.4	79%	100%	56%	N/A	N/A
131	Anderson University (SC)	62	N/A	165	$16,560	N/A	N/A	100%	100%	100%	72%	91%
131	Eastern Oregon University	62	N/A	52	$19,980	None	3.3	64%	71%	71%	90%	N/A
131	Frostburg State University (MD)	62	2.0	211	$20,052	GMAT or GRE	3.5	68%	100%	100%	69%	49%
131	Montclair State University (NJ)	62	2.1	218	$25,532	N/A	3.2	58%	89%	95%	83%	N/A
131	Rowan University (NJ)	62	2.0	51	N/A	GMAT or GRE	3.6	59%	90%	90%	95%	82%
131	University of St. Francis (IL)	62	1.7	171	N/A	None	3.3	60%	78%	89%	81%	59%
131	University of Texas–Tyler	62	1.9	1,357	$35,232	GMAT or GRE	3.2	98%	100%	100%	95%	60%
138	Monroe College (NY)	61	1.5	182	$30,312	None	3.0	55%	100%	0%	78%	79%
138	Northwood University (MI)	61	1.8	143	$37,080	None	3.1	68%	100%	0%	84%	N/A
138	Regent University (VA)	61	1.7	529	$27,300	None	3.1	45%	100%	89%	79%	49%
138	University of Louisiana–Monroe	61	2.1	53	$17,490	None	3.3	88%	90%	90%	67%	32%
138	Utica College (NY)	61	2.1	297	N/A	None	3.5	73%	100%	100%	82%	66%
143	Liberty University (VA)	60	1.6	3,942	N/A	None	3.2	32%	100%	0%	73%	41%
143	New Mexico State University	60	2.8	85	$31,720	N/A	3.5	100%	95%	84%	100%	N/A
143	Shippensburg University of Pennsylvania	60	2.1	183	$15,780	None	3.1	97%	100%	100%	83%	N/A
143	Suffolk University (MA)	60	2.5	50	$42,156	GMAT or GRE	3.0	78%	67%	58%	93%	N/A
147	Dakota Wesleyan University (SD)	59	1.6	54	$7,200	None	3.3	71%	80%	80%	83%	80%
147	Jacksonville State University (AL)	59	1.9	89	$11,460	GMAT or GRE	3.4	75%	100%	100%	N/A	57%
147	New England Col. of Business and Finance (MA)	59	1.5	165	$36,420	None	3.2	87%	100%	0%	89%	61%
150	Marymount University (VA)	58	2.2	128	$39,780	GMAT or GRE	3.1	94%	88%	88%	93%	N/A
150	Post University (CT)	58	1.4	495	$26,280	None	3.3	39%	100%	0%	68%	46%
150	University of Denver (CO)	58	N/A	125	$77,940	GMAT or GRE	3.0	96%	67%	44%	N/A	N/A
153	Brenau University (GA)	57	1.6	530	$35,455	None	3.0	61%	93%	100%	61%	61%
153	Campbellsville University (KY)	57	1.4	76	$17,244	GMAT or GRE	3.3	38%	75%	85%	92%	48%
153	Carson-Newman University (TN)	57	N/A	145	$13,500	None	3.2	66%	80%	40%	54%	80%
153	Florida Institute of Technology	57	2.0	948	N/A	None	N/A	45%	100%	0%	77%	50%
153	Herzing University (WI)	57	1.5	243	$26,130	None	3.3	89%	100%	0%	90%	66%
153	La Salle University (PA)	57	2.5	58	$24,981	N/A	3.2	78%	83%	83%	N/A	N/A
153	Lindenwood University (MO)	57	1.5	212	$19,500	None	3.2	52%	100%	0%	95%	27%
153	University of Louisiana–Lafayette	57	N/A	380	$12,800	N/A	3.5	83%	86%	86%	N/A	N/A

Rank	School	Overall score	Average peer assessment score (5.0=highest)	'18 total enrollment	'18-'19 total program cost[1]	Entrance test required	'18 average undergrad GPA	'18 acceptance rate	'18 full-time faculty with terminal degree	'18 tenured or tenure-track faculty[2]	'18 retention rate	'18 three-year graduation rate
161	**Auburn University–Montgomery** (AL)	56	2.3	45	$13,110	N/A	3.2	68%	100%	90%	N/A	N/A
162	**California State University–Dominguez Hills**	55	1.9	59	$15,000	GMAT or GRE	3.1	52%	100%	100%	21%	92%
162	**Colorado State University–Pueblo**	55	N/A	25	$19,800	GMAT or GRE	3.0	72%	100%	89%	42%	N/A
162	**Concordia University–St. Paul** (MN)	55	1.9	382	$27,500	None	N/A	67%	80%	60%	90%	86%
162	**Minnesota State University– Moorhead**	55	2.4	31	$14,948	N/A	N/A	89%	90%	100%	94%	77%
162	**Ohio Dominican University** (OH)	55	1.6	199	$21,600	None	3.2	95%	80%	30%	80%	80%
162	**Upper Iowa University**	55	1.5	344	$20,304	None	3.0	60%	60%	80%	87%	66%
168	**California University of Pennsylvania**	54	1.7	146	$27,864	None	3.1	78%	87%	100%	75%	50%
168	**Cedarville University** (OH)	54	1.5	64	$21,456	None	3.8	79%	N/A	N/A	85%	64%
168	**Franklin Pierce University** (NH)	54	1.7	207	$25,935	None	3.3	100%	100%	0%	77%	55%
168	**Limestone College** (SC)	54	1.5	88	$23,850	GMAT or GRE	2.9	95%	100%	100%	N/A	55%
168	**McKendree University** (IL)	54	1.4	116	$18,360	N/A	N/A	60%	78%	67%	98%	73%
168	**University of La Verne** (CA)	54	1.5	155	N/A	None	3.1	47%	93%	64%	90%	60%
168	**University of Southern Indiana**	54	2.0	643	$12,900	GMAT or GRE	3.1	100%	93%	87%	75%	N/A
175	**Brandman University** (CA)	53	1.6	174	$31,200	None	3.4	100%	100%	0%	85%	63%
175	**Cameron University** (OK)	53	1.5	111	$14,025	N/A	3.6	74%	100%	100%	91%	38%
175	**Charleston Southern University** (SC)	53	1.7	70	$20,625	N/A	3.2	74%	85%	85%	84%	N/A
175	**Concordia U. Wisconsin & Ann Arbor**	53	1.8	203	$27,261	None	N/A	52%	N/A	N/A	77%	36%
175	**Kettering University** (MI)	53	2.0	99	$49,200	None	N/A	62%	100%	100%	N/A	N/A
175	**King University** (TN)	53	1.6	144	$21,780	None	3.2	99%	84%	0%	87%	76%
175	**Lawrence Technological University** (MI)	53	1.7	177	N/A	None	2.8	79%	100%	64%	64%	53%
175	**Olivet Nazarene University** (IL)	53	1.9	144	N/A	None	N/A	92%	N/A	N/A	90%	83%
175	**Stetson University** (FL)	53	2.3	22	N/A	None	3.4	92%	100%	100%	67%	64%
175	**University of North Alabama**	53	1.9	758	$14,450	N/A	3.0	91%	92%	92%	76%	56%
175	**University of the Cumberlands** (KY)	53	1.6	268	$9,450	None	3.1	91%	100%	60%	N/A	N/A
175	**Wright State University** (OH)	53	2.3	751	$52,313	None	3.1	86%	90%	90%	80%	N/A
187	**Colorado Technical University**	52	1.8	2,341	$28,080	None	N/A	100%	100%	0%	93%	65%
187	**Lamar University** (TX)	52	2.0	176	$19,584	N/A	3.3	81%	85%	79%	N/A	N/A
187	**Marshall University** (WV)	52	N/A	24	$15,500	None	3.3	85%	100%	100%	N/A	N/A
187	**University of Houston–Clear Lake** (TX)	52	2.3	139	$38,180	None	N/A	95%	97%	85%	67%	31%
187	**Virginia Commonwealth University**	52	N/A	24	$39,500	N/A	3.2	100%	100%	94%	N/A	N/A
187	**Warner University** (FL)	52	1.4	44	$20,016	None	3.0	71%	100%	0%	92%	64%
193	**Anderson University** (IN)	51	2.2	25	$20,905	None	N/A	54%	87%	100%	N/A	N/A
193	**City University of Seattle** (WA)	51	1.6	790	$33,504	None	N/A	73%	9%	0%	85%	75%
193	**Colorado Christian University**	51	1.8	158	$22,191	None	3.3	64%	67%	0%	76%	53%
193	**Johnson & Wales University** (RI)	51	2.0	548	N/A	None	N/A	71%	73%	0%	79%	62%
193	**Texas Wesleyan University**	51	1.8	105	N/A	N/A	N/A	74%	100%	100%	68%	N/A
198	**Bentley University** (MA)	50	3.0	N/A	$46,200	GMAT or GRE	N/A	N/A	78%	56%	N/A	N/A
198	**Maryville University of St. Louis** (MO)	50	1.7	305	N/A	None	N/A	95%	100%	53%	N/A	N/A
198	**St. Bonaventure University** (NY)	50	2.1	96	$31,710	GMAT or GRE	3.3	95%	77%	69%	N/A	N/A
198	**University of Houston–Victoria** (TX)	50	N/A	834	$29,519	GMAT or GRE	3.1	65%	100%	100%	N/A	N/A
202	**Andrews University** (MI)	49	1.5	31	$18,249	N/A	3.1	80%	100%	100%	81%	N/A
202	**Concordia University Chicago** (IL)	49	1.9	223	$25,560	None	N/A	100%	85%	69%	83%	48%
202	**Dakota State University** (SD)	49	1.8	19	N/A	GMAT or GRE	2.8	100%	88%	100%	87%	64%
202	**Lynn University** (FL)	49	1.5	658	$26,640	None	N/A	89%	88%	0%	96%	79%
202	**National University** (CA)	49	1.4	642	$7,740	None	3.1	100%	81%	0%	75%	62%
202	**Northwest University** (WA)	49	1.8	19	$30,225	None	N/A	100%	100%	100%	12%	62%
202	**University of Alaska–Fairbanks**	49	2.3	N/A	$17,610	N/A	N/A	N/A	71%	71%	N/A	N/A
202	**University of Saint Mary** (KS)	49	1.8	311	N/A	None	N/A	99%	33%	0%	80%	61%
202	**University of the Incarnate Word** (TX)	49	1.5	319	$28,200	None	3.2	87%	100%	0%	76%	62%
202	**Widener University** (PA)	49	1.9	92	N/A	N/A	3.2	79%	100%	100%	83%	N/A
212	**Angelo State University** (TX)	48	1.7	198	$19,021	GMAT or GRE	3.1	94%	83%	75%	100%	N/A
212	**Columbia College** (MO)	48	1.5	275	N/A	None	3.5	98%	100%	100%	85%	69%
212	**Westminster College** (UT)	48	1.7	84	$54,600	GMAT or GRE	N/A	87%	100%	0%	N/A	N/A

School	Average peer assessment score (5.0=highest)	'18 total enrollment	'18-'19 total program cost[1]	Entrance test required	'18 average undergrad GPA	'18 acceptance rate	'18 full-time faculty with terminal degree	'18 tenured or tenure-track faculty[2]	'18 retention rate	'18 three-year graduation rate
MBA PROGRAMS RANKED 215 THROUGH 284 ARE LISTED HERE ALPHABETICALLY										
Abilene Christian University (TX)	2.2	176	$25,956	None	N/A	99%	100%	100%	N/A	N/A
American InterContinental University (IL)	1.3	1,899	$29,328	None	N/A	100%	100%	0%	93%	62%
Baker University (KS)	1.5	162	$26,620	None	N/A	N/A	100%	50%	N/A	N/A
Bay Path University (MA)	1.3	145	N/A	N/A	N/A	N/A	25%	0%	80%	N/A
Belhaven University (MS)	1.6	324	$20,700	None	N/A	67%	100%	56%	90%	58%
Bethel University (TN)	N/A	697	$21,420	None	N/A	81%	100%	0%	86%	66%
Bryan College (TN)	1.6	131	$20,700	None	N/A	100%	100%	0%	N/A	87%
Cardinal Stritch University (WI)	1.7	N/A	$24,840	None	N/A	N/A	N/A	N/A	N/A	N/A
Chatham University (PA)	2.0	14	N/A	None	3.1	100%	100%	0%	N/A	N/A
Cornerstone University (MI)	1.4	84	$21,470	None	N/A	89%	0%	100%	81%	84%
Dallas Baptist University (TX)	1.8	258	$34,524	N/A	N/A	45%	100%	0%	N/A	N/A
Edgewood College (WI)	1.5	N/A	N/A	GMAT or GRE	N/A	N/A	N/A	N/A	N/A	N/A
Florida A&M University	2.2	13	N/A	None	N/A	37%	N/A	N/A	N/A	N/A
Florida Southern College	1.6	16	$34,100	GMAT or GRE	3.4	38%	75%	67%	N/A	N/A
Friends University (KS)	1.5	208	$20,430	None	N/A	94%	44%	100%	80%	88%
Golden Gate University (CA)	N/A	137	$15,750	GMAT or GRE	N/A	75%	N/A	N/A	74%	61%
Governors State University (IL)	1.7	37	$7,308	N/A	3.0	53%	54%	42%	N/A	N/A
Harding University (AR)	N/A	67	$22,068	GMAT or GRE	N/A	100%	N/A	N/A	N/A	N/A
Indiana Institute of Technology	1.7	312	$9,270	None	N/A	97%	N/A	N/A	N/A	N/A
Jackson State University (MS)	2.0	31	N/A	GMAT or GRE	N/A	35%	100%	100%	N/A	N/A
Keiser University (FL)	1.4	493	$6,768	N/A	N/A	100%	100%	0%	59%	68%
Lasell College (MA)	1.5	33	$21,600	None	N/A	95%	75%	0%	69%	80%
Lee University (TN)	N/A	23	N/A	N/A	N/A	100%	100%	100%	80%	N/A
Loyola University New Orleans (LA)	N/A	N/A	$32,720	GMAT or GRE	N/A	N/A	100%	100%	N/A	N/A
Madonna University (MI)	1.3	41	N/A	None	N/A	100%	N/A	N/A	100%	10%
McNeese State University (LA)	2.0	21	N/A	GMAT or GRE	N/A	N/A	100%	100%	N/A	N/A
Mercy College (NY)	1.6	45	N/A	None	N/A	64%	N/A	N/A	N/A	N/A
Mississippi Valley State University	N/A	71	$2,448	None	N/A	73%	83%	83%	N/A	N/A
Montreat College (NC)	N/A	N/A	N/A	N/A	N/A	N/A	100%	75%	N/A	N/A
New England College (NH)	1.6	208	$23,800	None	3.0	98%	N/A	N/A	90%	65%
Nichols College (MA)	N/A	221	$25,200	None	N/A	99%	0%	67%	73%	75%
Northcentral University (AZ)	1.6	N/A	$31,960	None	N/A	100%	100%	0%	N/A	N/A
Northeastern State University (OK)	N/A	76	$8,496	None	N/A	100%	100%	82%	84%	N/A
Northwest Christian University (OR)	1.4	106	$25,020	None	3.2	100%	N/A	N/A	N/A	N/A
Northwest Missouri State University	1.9	216	$13,530	GMAT or GRE	N/A	N/A	100%	85%	66%	N/A
Northwest Nazarene University (ID)	N/A	48	N/A	N/A	N/A	57%	100%	63%	38%	76%
Nova Southeastern University (FL)	1.9	2,387	$37,941	N/A	N/A	82%	93%	0%	84%	N/A
Oklahoma Christian University	N/A	365	$21,780	GMAT or GRE	N/A	N/A	82%	91%	N/A	N/A
Ottawa University–Online (KS)	1.4	23	$7,788	None	N/A	41%	N/A	N/A	83%	60%
Park University (MO)	1.5	1,145	$20,592	None	N/A	86%	100%	100%	95%	N/A
Point Loma Nazarene University (CA)	1.8	29	$35,490	GMAT or GRE	N/A	100%	N/A	N/A	N/A	N/A
Prairie View A&M University (TX)	N/A	110	$4,484	GMAT or GRE	N/A	N/A	100%	100%	N/A	N/A
Regis University (CO)	1.7	645	N/A	None	N/A	69%	50%	0%	84%	46%
Saint Leo University (FL)	N/A	1,913	N/A	None	N/A	N/A	N/A	N/A	N/A	N/A
Southeastern University (FL)	1.6	215	N/A	None	N/A	N/A	100%	0%	N/A	N/A
Southern Arkansas University	1.6	N/A	N/A	GMAT or GRE	N/A	N/A	92%	100%	N/A	N/A
Southwestern College (KS)	1.4	37	N/A	None	N/A	92%	N/A	N/A	83%	60%
St. Francis University (PA)	2.1	65	$31,500	None	N/A	N/A	100%	100%	N/A	N/A
St. Joseph's College New York	1.9	91	$24,522	N/A	N/A	63%	67%	22%	81%	N/A
Tabor College (KS)	1.5	33	$21,682	None	3.0	100%	N/A	N/A	N/A	73%
Tarleton State University (TX)	1.7	146	N/A	GMAT or GRE	N/A	66%	0%	100%	N/A	N/A
Texas A&M University–Texarkana	N/A	176	$4,235	N/A	N/A	N/A	N/A	N/A	N/A	N/A
Thomas Jefferson University (PA)	N/A	N/A	N/A	N/A	N/A	N/A	N/A	N/A	N/A	N/A

School	Average peer assessment score (5.0=highest)	'18 total enrollment	'18-'19 total program cost[1]	Entrance test required	'18 average undergrad GPA	'18 acceptance rate	'18 full-time faculty with terminal degree	'18 tenured or tenure-track faculty[2]	'18 retention rate	'18 three-year graduation rate
MBA PROGRAMS RANKED 215 THROUGH 284 ARE LISTED HERE ALPHABETICALLY CONTINUED										
Tiffin University (OH)	N/A	450	$25,200	None	N/A	72%	N/A	N/A	N/A	N/A
University of Central Arkansas	1.9	136	N/A	GMAT or GRE	N/A	N/A	N/A	N/A	61%	N/A
University of Dayton (OH)	2.8	349	N/A	N/A	N/A	N/A	N/A	N/A	N/A	N/A
University of Findlay (OH)	1.5	326	$22,407	None	3.0	84%	100%	91%	N/A	N/A
University of Lynchburg (VA)	1.6	15	$23,940	GMAT or GRE	3.4	85%	88%	100%	38%	N/A
University of North Carolina–Pembroke	2.1	127	N/A	GMAT or GRE	N/A	99%	94%	94%	N/A	N/A
University of Sioux Falls (SD)	1.7	27	$13,860	None	N/A	100%	67%	83%	N/A	N/A
University of Texas of the Permian Basin	1.8	74	N/A	N/A	N/A	N/A	100%	100%	N/A	N/A
Valdosta State University (GA)	2.3	15	$22,170	GMAT or GRE	N/A	N/A	N/A	N/A	89%	80%
Walsh University (OH)	1.6	178	$12,690	N/A	N/A	90%	91%	91%	33%	N/A
Wayne State College (NE)	N/A	150	N/A	None	N/A	N/A	100%	100%	N/A	N/A
Waynesburg University (PA)	2.0	227	$15,960	N/A	3.1	79%	N/A	N/A	N/A	N/A
Webber International University (FL)	N/A	13	$24,768	None	3.1	42%	100%	0%	100%	N/A
Webster University (MO)	1.6	925	N/A	None	N/A	N/A	100%	100%	N/A	N/A
Western Illinois University	2.2	N/A	N/A	GMAT or GRE	N/A	N/A	100%	100%	N/A	N/A
Western New England University (MA)	1.8	74	$30,564	GMAT or GRE	N/A	82%	74%	74%	N/A	N/A
William Woods University (MO)	1.4	123	N/A	None	3.2	78%	33%	0%	N/A	N/A

Best Online Master's Programs

Rank	School	Overall score	Average peer assessment score (5.0=highest)	'18 total enrollment	'18-'19 total program cost[1]	Entrance test required	'18 average undergrad GPA	'18 acceptance rate	'18 full-time faculty with terminal degree	'18 tenured or tenure-track faculty[2]	'18 retention rate	'18 three-year graduation rate
1	**Indiana University–Bloomington**	100	4.2	273	$39,900	GMAT or GRE	3.4	69%	90%	63%	99%	69%
2	**University of Southern California**	98	3.8	74	$50,301	None	3.2	78%	100%	100%	97%	100%
2	**Villanova University** (PA)	98	3.4	427	$48,024	None	3.3	79%	82%	82%	94%	89%
4	**University of North Carolina–Chapel Hill**	97	4.0	124	N/A	N/A	3.3	56%	67%	53%	81%	100%
5	**Georgetown University** (DC)	95	3.6	115	$75,360	GMAT or GRE	3.3	34%	93%	67%	92%	82%
6	**Arizona State University**	94	3.8	163	$39,660	GMAT or GRE	3.3	65%	95%	37%	94%	93%
7	**University of Texas–Dallas**	93	3.3	637	$56,538	GMAT or GRE	3.4	62%	78%	35%	70%	67%
8	**Pennsylvania State University–World Campus**	91	3.3	641	$31,650	GMAT or GRE	3.2	81%	94%	69%	94%	87%
8	**University of Connecticut**	91	3.3	194	$25,550	GMAT	3.5	89%	56%	44%	91%	86%
10	**University of Alabama**	90	2.9	142	N/A	GMAT or GRE	3.4	83%	97%	97%	95%	91%
11	**Boston University** (MA)	89	3.5	653	$34,370	None	3.2	90%	100%	0%	85%	62%
12	**Florida State University**	87	3.3	122	$19,800	GMAT or GRE	3.2	68%	100%	88%	88%	86%
13	**Auburn University** (AL)	85	3.1	151	$26,565	GMAT or GRE	3.6	64%	100%	96%	96%	74%
14	**Stevens Institute of Technology** (NJ)	82	2.9	145	$58,320	GMAT or GRE	3.4	68%	97%	38%	86%	56%
15	**California State University–Fullerton**	81	2.6	43	$22,920	GMAT or GRE	3.3	77%	100%	100%	81%	81%
15	**Georgia College & State University**	81	2.5	95	$14,010	GMAT or GRE	3.1	88%	100%	100%	89%	83%
17	**Florida International University**	80	2.7	154	$35,000	None	3.2	51%	94%	84%	84%	85%
17	**Rutgers U.–New Brunswick and Newark** (NJ)	80	3.0	261	$36,840	None	3.2	70%	77%	92%	90%	65%
17	**University of Georgia**	80	3.4	33	$24,750	GMAT or GRE	3.2	74%	100%	27%	93%	80%
20	**Creighton University** (NE)	79	2.9	107	$36,900	GMAT or GRE	3.3	69%	91%	87%	89%	65%
20	**Missouri University of Science & Technology**	79	2.0	64	$36,000	GMAT or GRE	3.0	64%	94%	100%	94%	85%
20	**University of Miami** (FL)	79	3.0	119	$64,960	GMAT or GRE	3.1	56%	85%	65%	N/A	66%
23	**Michigan State University**	78	3.6	531	$32,700	None	3.2	95%	100%	60%	95%	85%
24	**University of North Dakota**	77	2.5	59	$14,760	GMAT or GRE	3.3	86%	100%	100%	80%	30%
25	**University of San Diego** (CA)	76	3.0	51	$53,100	None	3.0	93%	100%	100%	93%	83%
26	**Quinnipiac University** (CT)	75	2.8	388	$30,855	None	3.1	85%	100%	100%	76%	62%
26	**West Texas A&M University**	75	2.0	244	$17,885	None	3.5	72%	100%	100%	86%	83%

Rank	School	Overall score	Average peer assessment score (5.0=highest)	'18 total enrollment	'18-'19 total program cost[1]	Entrance test required	'18 average undergrad GPA	'18 acceptance rate	'18 full-time faculty with terminal degree	'18 tenured or tenure-track faculty[2]	'18 retention rate	'18 three-year graduation rate
26	West Virginia University	75	2.5	46	$24,552	GMAT or GRE	3.2	75%	91%	100%	88%	N/A
29	Bentley University (MA)	74	2.9	138	$46,200	GMAT or GRE	3.3	85%	61%	59%	93%	80%
30	St. Joseph's University (PA)	73	2.7	366	N/A	GMAT or GRE	3.1	78%	79%	76%	86%	67%
31	University of Alabama–Birmingham	72	2.6	113	$32,640	GMAT or GRE	3.3	64%	88%	75%	96%	82%
32	Saint Vincent College (PA)	71	N/A	30	$24,552	None	3.0	70%	60%	60%	35%	N/A
33	Mississippi State University	70	2.8	18	$14,235	GMAT or GRE	3.6	100%	100%	100%	100%	N/A
33	University of Illinois–Springfield	70	2.6	146	N/A	GMAT or GRE	3.3	85%	100%	100%	80%	39%
33	University of Massachusetts–Lowell	70	2.7	123	$19,650	N/A	3.3	87%	91%	82%	89%	72%
33	Wright State University (OH)	70	2.4	49	$37,125	None	3.0	91%	100%	100%	96%	98%
37	Oklahoma City University	69	N/A	133	$17,700	None	3.0	88%	100%	100%	96%	89%
37	Thunderbird School of Global Management (AZ)	69	N/A	175	$42,000	None	3.3	84%	100%	71%	98%	N/A
39	American University (DC)	68	2.8	175	$56,384	None	3.1	79%	84%	63%	93%	N/A
39	Colorado State University	68	3.1	148	N/A	GMAT or GRE	3.2	86%	93%	79%	88%	54%
39	George Mason University (VA)	68	2.9	34	N/A	N/A	3.1	92%	63%	63%	83%	N/A
39	Oklahoma State University	68	2.9	81	$11,880	GMAT or GRE	3.2	92%	96%	64%	90%	44%
43	Florida Atlantic University	66	2.3	676	$12,800	None	3.3	71%	95%	36%	95%	73%
43	St. Mary's College of California	66	1.9	89	$45,100	None	3.1	86%	88%	88%	92%	87%
45	George Washington University (DC)	65	3.3	62	$56,430	None	N/A	81%	100%	64%	73%	72%
45	Georgia Southern University	65	2.4	125	$9,486	GMAT or GRE	3.1	96%	100%	100%	86%	61%
45	St. John's University (NY)	65	2.7	39	N/A	GMAT or GRE	3.3	70%	94%	94%	100%	53%
45	University of Cincinnati (OH)	65	2.9	43	$24,630	GMAT or GRE	3.5	93%	100%	0%	100%	57%
49	University of Tulsa (OK)	64	2.4	69	$30,600	N/A	3.2	85%	86%	71%	86%	64%
50	Ferris State University (MI)	63	N/A	31	$20,130	GMAT or GRE	3.5	29%	33%	100%	84%	83%
50	Stetson University (FL)	63	2.1	20	$27,000	GMAT or GRE	3.5	59%	100%	100%	100%	79%
50	Syracuse University (NY)	63	3.3	285	$53,006	N/A	3.1	84%	100%	29%	89%	N/A
53	Eastern Michigan University	62	2.2	56	$30,132	None	3.2	63%	67%	67%	59%	76%
53	Northeastern University (MA)	62	3.0	178	$48,000	None	3.2	84%	96%	65%	71%	60%
55	California University of Pennsylvania	61	N/A	151	$27,864	None	3.1	78%	87%	100%	N/A	N/A
56	University of South Dakota	60	2.3	92	$13,527	GMAT	3.3	80%	100%	100%	76%	33%
57	California State University–Sacramento	59	2.3	88	$22,200	N/A	3.3	83%	100%	70%	N/A	N/A
57	Texas A&M University–Commerce	59	2.2	1,351	$18,510	GMAT or GRE	3.2	74%	83%	83%	81%	54%
59	Embry-Riddle Aeronautical U.–Worldwide (FL)	58	2.2	2,520	N/A	None	3.2	90%	97%	67%	84%	42%
60	Marist College (NY)	57	2.0	319	$33,600	GMAT or GRE	3.3	53%	100%	78%	95%	69%
60	New England Col. of Business and Finance (MA)	57	1.7	157	$30,350	None	3.1	80%	100%	0%	84%	71%
60	Post University (CT)	57	1.3	68	$18,750	None	3.4	36%	100%	0%	100%	84%
60	SUNY Polytechnic Institute	57	2.3	75	$18,315	GMAT or GRE	3.3	96%	86%	86%	86%	48%
60	Southeast Missouri State University	57	2.1	84	N/A	GMAT or GRE	3.4	97%	95%	82%	88%	49%
60	Southern Utah University	57	N/A	141	$14,570	GMAT or GRE	3.4	88%	67%	67%	87%	N/A
60	Stony Brook University–SUNY	57	2.8	184	N/A	None	3.3	98%	N/A	N/A	88%	71%
60	Texas A&M University–Central Texas	57	N/A	50	$23,472	None	3.2	54%	100%	100%	77%	N/A
60	University of Denver (CO)	57	2.8	35	$66,048	None	3.1	56%	100%	86%	92%	69%
69	Marymount University (VA)	56	2.0	115	N/A	None	3.0	100%	100%	100%	84%	54%
70	University of Oklahoma	55	3.3	56	$32,500	None	3.2	79%	92%	85%	N/A	N/A
71	Olivet Nazarene University (IL)	54	N/A	55	N/A	None	N/A	96%	N/A	N/A	90%	94%
71	University of St. Francis (IL)	54	N/A	70	N/A	None	3.1	51%	50%	100%	92%	70%
73	Colorado State University–Global Campus	53	2.3	5,254	$18,000	None	3.0	98%	100%	0%	86%	58%
73	Florida Institute of Technology	53	2.2	677	N/A	None	3.2	57%	100%	0%	75%	52%
73	Warner University (FL)	53	N/A	18	$20,016	None	3.0	69%	100%	0%	92%	40%
76	University of Massachusetts–Dartmouth	52	2.7	13	N/A	N/A	3.3	88%	92%	75%	83%	N/A
76	University of Scranton (PA)	52	2.3	195	$26,850	None	N/A	85%	86%	93%	72%	N/A
78	Clarkson University (NY)	51	1.5	24	$42,564	GMAT or GRE	3.7	75%	78%	44%	100%	62%
78	Northern Arizona University	51	2.2	242	$20,700	None	3.1	99%	94%	44%	90%	65%
78	University of Michigan–Dearborn	51	2.8	33	N/A	GMAT or GRE	3.4	53%	95%	84%	67%	33%
78	Western Carolina University (NC)	51	2.2	220	N/A	None	3.2	91%	100%	0%	78%	52%

Rank	School	Overall score	Average peer assessment score (5.0=highest)	'18 total enrollment	'18-'19 total program cost[1]	Entrance test required	'18 average undergrad GPA	'18 acceptance rate	'18 full-time faculty with terminal degree	'18 tenured or tenure-track faculty[2]	'18 retention rate	'18 three-year graduation rate
82	Duquesne University (PA)	50	2.4	30	$28,590	GMAT or GRE	3.4	95%	83%	83%	71%	N/A
82	Park University (MO)	50	N/A	322	$19,764	None	N/A	79%	100%	100%	85%	N/A
82	Sam Houston State University (TX)	50	2.0	20	$11,088	GMAT	3.5	88%	100%	100%	64%	N/A
85	Union Institute & University (OH)	49	N/A	77	$21,864	None	N/A	96%	100%	0%	95%	79%
86	California Baptist University	48	1.6	48	$19,860	None	3.4	69%	100%	100%	82%	40%
86	Colorado Christian University	48	N/A	140	$20,484	None	3.2	76%	75%	0%	95%	45%
86	New Jersey Institute of Technology	48	2.4	12	$38,460	None	3.3	38%	94%	83%	60%	N/A
89	Clarion University of Pennsylvania	47	1.5	24	$16,710	None	3.4	96%	100%	100%	86%	N/A
89	University of Massachusetts–Boston	47	2.8	97	$20,700	None	N/A	79%	67%	67%	82%	42%
91	Regent University (VA)	46	1.3	378	$21,450	None	3.1	50%	100%	83%	85%	54%
92	Portland State University (OR)	44	2.6	46	$38,064	None	3.2	68%	N/A	N/A	30%	N/A
92	University of Dallas (TX)	44	2.4	174	$37,500	None	3.3	41%	94%	0%	N/A	N/A
94	Granite State College (NH)	42	N/A	143	$17,250	None	3.5	99%	100%	0%	88%	56%
94	Keiser University (FL)	42	N/A	89	N/A	N/A	N/A	99%	100%	0%	50%	47%
94	Lindenwood University (MO)	42	1.4	189	$18,500	None	3.1	56%	100%	0%	85%	69%
94	Troy University (AL)	42	2.1	923	$8,892	GMAT or GRE	N/A	97%	100%	65%	66%	35%
98	Liberty University (VA)	41	1.5	4,935	N/A	None	3.1	61%	99%	0%	68%	27%
98	Minot State University (ND)	41	1.4	79	$9,270	GMAT or GRE	3.3	97%	100%	100%	42%	N/A
100	Campbellsville University (KY)	40	1.1	32	$14,370	GMAT or GRE	3.3	41%	100%	89%	96%	42%
100	University of Houston–Victoria (TX)	40	2.1	33	$26,336	GMAT or GRE	2.9	44%	100%	100%	N/A	N/A
102	Northwood University (MI)	39	1.1	87	$23,610	None	3.0	88%	100%	0%	87%	67%
102	University of Houston–Clear Lake (TX)	39	2.3	72	$38,180	None	N/A	94%	97%	85%	60%	42%
104	Boise State University (ID)	38	2.8	24	$13,500	GMAT or GRE	2.5	100%	100%	100%	N/A	N/A
104	Brandman University (CA)	38	1.2	269	$23,400	None	3.5	100%	100%	0%	79%	74%
104	City University of Seattle (WA)	38	1.7	92	$33,504	None	N/A	71%	63%	0%	76%	41%
104	Johnson & Wales University (RI)	38	1.7	109	N/A	None	N/A	67%	100%	0%	60%	N/A
108	Charleston Southern University (SC)	37	1.6	26	$20,625	N/A	3.3	89%	83%	100%	84%	N/A
108	Concordia University–St. Paul (MN)	37	1.8	216	$15,300	None	N/A	71%	67%	67%	85%	61%
108	Friends University (KS)	37	N/A	52	$20,430	None	N/A	78%	67%	100%	88%	92%
108	Kettering University (MI)	37	1.6	397	$49,200	None	N/A	82%	0%	100%	17%	N/A
108	University of the Incarnate Word (TX)	37	1.6	716	$28,200	None	3.1	98%	100%	0%	84%	72%
113	North Greenville University (SC)	35	N/A	150	$16,680	None	3.4	77%	100%	100%	80%	N/A

School	Average peer assessment score (5.0=highest)	'18 total enrollment	'18-'19 total program cost[1]	Entrance test required	'18 average undergrad GPA	'18 acceptance rate	'18 full-time faculty with terminal degree	'18 tenured or tenure-track faculty[2]	'18 retention rate	'18 three-year graduation rate
MASTER'S PROGRAMS RANKED 114 THROUGH 150 ARE LISTED HERE ALPHABETICALLY										
Abilene Christian University (TX)	N/A	56	$21,630	None	N/A	92%	N/A	N/A	N/A	N/A
Austin Peay State University (TN)	N/A	63	N/A	N/A	3.5	78%	100%	100%	80%	N/A
Baker University (KS)	1.4	65	$22,135	None	N/A	N/A	100%	0%	N/A	N/A
Belhaven University (MS)	1.2	896	$20,700	None	N/A	72%	100%	5%	85%	57%
Bellevue University (NE)	1.5	1,598	$20,700	None	N/A	60%	52%	0%	84%	N/A
California State University–San Bernardino	N/A	170	N/A	None	3.2	97%	N/A	N/A	N/A	N/A
Colorado Technical University	1.6	1,392	$28,080	None	N/A	100%	100%	0%	90%	49%
Concordia University Wisconsin & Ann Arbor	1.4	162	$22,368	None	N/A	66%	N/A	N/A	N/A	N/A
Cornerstone University (MI)	1.3	24	$18,540	None	N/A	100%	N/A	N/A	68%	N/A
Dallas Baptist University (TX)	1.4	30	$34,524	GMAT	N/A	49%	100%	0%	N/A	N/A
East Tennessee State University	N/A	28	$25,416	GMAT or GRE	N/A	N/A	100%	100%	N/A	N/A
Edgewood College (WI)	1.4	N/A	N/A	GMAT or GRE	N/A	N/A	N/A	N/A	N/A	N/A
Golden Gate University (CA)	N/A	839	$15,750	GMAT or GRE	N/A	86%	N/A	N/A	62%	34%
Houston Baptist University (TX)	N/A	26	$18,150	None	N/A	90%	100%	0%	N/A	N/A
Indiana Institute of Technology	1.6	124	$9,270	None	N/A	97%	N/A	N/A	N/A	N/A
LIM College (NY)	N/A	200	$28,500	None	N/A	90%	N/A	N/A	N/A	N/A
Lasell College (MA)	1.4	148	$21,600	None	N/A	93%	38%	0%	76%	67%

School	Average peer assessment score (5.0=highest)	'18 total enrollment	'18-'19 total program cost[1]	Entrance test required	'18 average undergrad GPA	'18 acceptance rate	'18 full-time faculty with terminal degree	'18 tenured or tenure-track faculty[2]	'18 retention rate	'18 three-year graduation rate
MASTER'S PROGRAMS RANKED 114 THROUGH 150 ARE LISTED HERE ALPHABETICALLY										
Maryville University of St. Louis (MO)	1.6	600	N/A	None	N/A	99%	100%	80%	N/A	N/A
Mercer University–Atlanta (GA)	N/A	N/A	N/A	N/A	N/A	N/A	N/A	N/A	N/A	N/A
Mercy College (NY)	1.3	59	N/A	None	N/A	80%	N/A	N/A	N/A	N/A
Montreat College (NC)	N/A	36	N/A	None	N/A	N/A	100%	75%	N/A	N/A
National University (CA)	1.4	675	$7,740	None	2.9	100%	90%	0%	85%	53%
New England College (NH)	1.4	212	$23,020	None	2.9	100%	N/A	N/A	89%	60%
Nichols College (MA)	N/A	105	$21,000	None	N/A	94%	33%	67%	68%	N/A
Nova Southeastern University (FL)	1.8	302	$35,061	N/A	N/A	82%	100%	0%	N/A	N/A
Regis University (CO)	1.8	632	N/A	None	N/A	71%	38%	0%	84%	62%
Rochester Institute of Technology (NY)	3.5	50	N/A	None	3.2	70%	0%	0%	N/A	N/A
Southwestern College (KS)	1.0	81	N/A	None	N/A	85%	N/A	N/A	77%	45%
St. Francis University (PA)	N/A	N/A	$26,250	N/A	N/A	N/A	N/A	N/A	N/A	N/A
St. Joseph's College New York	1.9	48	$24,522	N/A	N/A	63%	67%	22%	74%	N/A
Tarleton State University (TX)	1.4	139	N/A	GMAT or GRE	N/A	81%	0%	95%	N/A	N/A
Trine University (IN)	N/A	81	$10,974	None	N/A	74%	N/A	N/A	N/A	N/A
University of Hartford (CT)	2.4	116	N/A	N/A	N/A	62%	N/A	N/A	N/A	N/A
University of Wisconsin–Platteville	2.1	606	$20,250	None	N/A	75%	0%	0%	96%	37%
Webster University (MO)	1.6	2,199	N/A	None	N/A	N/A	100%	100%	N/A	N/A
Western New England University (MA)	1.7	49	$25,470	GMAT or GRE	N/A	91%	74%	74%	N/A	N/A
William Woods University (MO)	N/A	61	N/A	None	3.1	74%	100%	0%	N/A	N/A

Best Undergraduate Programs

EACH YEAR, U.S. NEWS RANKS undergraduate business programs accredited by AACSB International; the results are based solely on surveys of B-school deans and senior faculty. Participants – two at each AACSB-accredited business program – were asked to rate the quality of business programs with which they're familiar on a scale of 1 (marginal) to 5 (distinguished); 44 percent of those canvassed responded to the most recent survey conducted in the spring of 2018. Two years of data were used to calculate the average peer assessment score. The ranking sorts, in descending order, the under-graduate business programs by their average peer assessment score. In total, 503 schools were ranked; the full list can be found @ **usnews.com/undergrad.**

Deans and faculty members also were asked to nominate the 15 best programs in a number of specialty areas such as accounting, marketing and finance; the schools receiving the most mentions in the 2018 survey appear on page 83. A school or program had to receive seven or more nominations in a specific specialty area to be ranked. The best undergraduate business programs in a specialty are based solely on the results of the peer assessment survey conducted in spring 2018.

Rank	School (State)	Peer assessment score (5.0=highest)
1	University of Pennsylvania (Wharton)	4.8
2	Massachusetts Inst. of Technology (Sloan)	4.6
2	University of California–Berkeley (Haas)	4.6
4	University of Michigan–Ann Arbor (Ross)	4.5
5	New York University (Stern)	4.4
6	Carnegie Mellon University (Tepper) (PA)	4.3
6	University of Texas–Austin (McCombs)	4.3
8	U. of N. Carolina–Chapel Hill (Kenan-Flagler)	4.2
8	University of Virginia (McIntire)	4.2
10	Cornell University (Dyson) (NY)	4.1
10	Indiana University–Bloomington (Kelley)	4.1
10	University of Notre Dame (Mendoza) (IN)	4.1
10	University of Southern California (Marshall)	4.1
14	Washington University in St. Louis (Olin)	4.0
15	Emory University (Goizueta) (GA)	3.9
15	Georgetown University (McDonough) (DC)	3.9
15	Ohio State University–Columbus (Fisher)	3.9
18	University of Illinois–Urbana-Champaign	3.8
18	U. of Minnesota–Twin Cities (Carlson)	3.8
18	Univ. of Wisconsin–Madison	3.8
21	Boston College (Carroll)	3.7
21	Georgia Institute of Technology (Scheller)	3.7

Rank	School (State)	Peer assessment score (5.0=highest)
21	Michigan State University (Broad)	3.7
21	Pennsylvania State U.–Univ. Park (Smeal)	3.7
21	Purdue U.–West Lafayette (Krannert) (IN)	3.7
21	University of Arizona (Eller)	3.7
21	University of Georgia (Terry)	3.7
21	Univ. of Maryland–College Park	3.7
21	University of Washington (Foster)	3.7
30	Arizona State University–Tempe (Carey)	3.6
30	Babson College (MA)	3.6
30	Johns Hopkins University (MD)	3.6
30	Texas A&M U.–College Station (Mays)	3.6
30	University of Florida (Warrington)	3.6
35	Brigham Young Univ.–Provo (Marriott) (UT)	3.5
35	Case Western Reserve U. (Weatherhead) (OH)	3.5
35	University of California–Irvine (Merage)	3.5
35	University of Colorado–Boulder (Leeds)	3.5
35	University of Iowa (Tippie)	3.5
35	University of Pittsburgh	3.5
35	Wake Forest University (NC)	3.5
42	Boston University	3.4
42	George Washington University (DC)	3.4
44	College of William & Mary (Mason) (VA)	3.3

Rank	School (State)	Peer assessment score (5.0=highest)
44	Florida State University	3.3
44	Georgia State University (Robinson)	3.3
44	Pepperdine University (CA)	3.3
44	Southern Methodist University (Cox) (TX)	3.3
44	Syracuse University (Whitman) (NY)	3.3
44	Tulane University (Freeman) (LA)	3.3
44	United States Air Force Academy (CO)	3.3
44	University of Alabama (Culverhouse)	3.3
44	University of Arkansas (Walton)	3.3
44	University of California–San Diego (Rady)	3.3
44	Univ. of Massachusetts–Amherst (Isenberg)	3.3
44	Univ. of Nebraska–Lincoln	3.3
44	University of Oregon (Lundquist)	3.3
44	Univ. of South Carolina (Moore)	3.3
44	University of Utah (Eccles)	3.3
44	Villanova University (PA)	3.3
44	Virginia Tech (Pamplin)	3.3
62	Auburn University (Harbert) (AL)	3.2
62	Baylor University (Hankamer) (TX)	3.2
62	Bentley University (MA)	3.2
62	CUNY–Baruch College (Zicklin)	3.2
62	Fordham University (Gabelli) (NY)	3.2

Note: Peer assessment surveys in 2018 were conducted by U.S. News.
To be ranked in a specialty, an undergraduate business school may have either a program or course offerings in that subject area.

BRETT ZIEGLER FOR USNWR

Rank	School (State)	Peer assessment score (5.0=highest)
62	Miami University–Oxford (Farmer) (OH)	3.2
62	Northeastern U. (D'Amore-McKim) (MA)	3.2
62	Rochester Inst. of Technology (Saunders) (NY)	3.2
62	Santa Clara University (Leavey) (CA)	3.2
62	Temple University (Fox) (PA)	3.2
62	University of Connecticut	3.2
62	University of Kansas	3.2
62	University of Kentucky (Gatton)	3.2
62	University of Miami (FL)	3.2
62	University of Oklahoma (Price)	3.2
62	University of Tennessee (Haslam)	3.2
62	University of Texas–Dallas (Jindal)	3.2
79	Clemson University (SC)	3.1
79	Iowa State University	3.1
79	Loyola Marymount University (CA)	3.1
79	Loyola University Chicago (Quinlan)	3.1
79	Rensselaer Polytechnic Inst. (Lally) (NY)	3.1
79	Rutgers University–New Brunswick (NJ)	3.1
79	Texas Christian University (Neeley)	3.1
79	Univ. of Missouri (Trulaske)	3.1
87	American University (Kogod) (DC)	3.0
87	Brandeis University (MA)	3.0
87	Colorado State University	3.0
87	Creighton University (NE)	3.0
87	DePaul University (Driehaus) (IL)	3.0
87	George Mason University (VA)	3.0
87	Lehigh University (PA)	3.0
87	Marquette University (WI)	3.0
87	North Carolina State U.–Raleigh (Poole)	3.0
87	Oklahoma State University (Spears)	3.0
87	Saint Louis University (Cook)	3.0
87	San Diego State University	3.0
87	University at Buffalo–SUNY	3.0
87	University of California–Riverside	3.0
87	University of Cincinnati (Lindner)	3.0
87	University of Delaware (Lerner)	3.0
87	University of Denver (Daniels)	3.0
87	University of Houston (Bauer)	3.0
87	University of Illinois–Chicago	3.0
87	University of Richmond (Robins) (VA)	3.0
87	Washington State University (Carson)	3.0
108	Binghamton University–SUNY	2.9
108	Cal. Poly. State U.–San Luis Obispo (Orfalea)	2.9
108	Drexel University (LeBow) (PA)	2.9
108	Gonzaga University (WA)	2.9
108	James Madison University (VA)	2.9
108	Kansas State University	2.9
108	Louisiana State U.–Baton Rouge (Ourso)	2.9
108	Loyola University Maryland (Sellinger)	2.9
108	Oregon State University	2.9
108	Rutgers University–Newark (NJ)	2.9
108	Seton Hall University (Stillman) (NJ)	2.9
108	Texas Tech University (Rawls)	2.9
108	United States Coast Guard Academy (CT)	2.9
108	University of Hawaii–Manoa (Shidler)	2.9
108	University of Louisville (KY)	2.9
108	University of Mississippi	2.9
108	University of San Diego	2.9
108	University of San Francisco	2.9
108	Xavier University (Williams) (OH)	2.9
127	Bucknell University (PA)	2.8
127	Butler University (IN)	2.8
127	California State University–Los Angeles	2.8
127	Elon University (Love) (NC)	2.8
127	Florida International University	2.8
127	Hofstra University (Zarb) (NY)	2.8
127	Howard University (DC)	2.8
127	Ohio University	2.8
127	Seattle University (Albers)	2.8
127	St. Joseph's University (Haub) (PA)	2.8
127	University at Albany–SUNY	2.8
127	University of Alabama–Birmingham (Collat)	2.8
127	University of Central Florida	2.8
127	University of Colorado–Denver	2.8
127	University of Montana	2.8
127	University of New Mexico (Anderson)	2.8
127	U. of North Carolina–Charlotte (Belk)	2.8
127	University of Texas–Arlington	2.8
127	Univ. of Wisconsin–Milwaukee (Lubar)	2.8
127	Washington and Lee U. (Williams) (VA)	2.8
147	Ball State University (Miller) (IN)	2.7
147	California State Polytechnic U.–Pomona	2.7
147	The Citadel (SC)	2.7
147	Kennesaw State University (Coles) (GA)	2.7
147	Mississippi State University	2.7
147	Quinnipiac University (CT)	2.7
147	Rutgers University–Camden (NJ)	2.7
147	San Jose State University (Lucas) (CA)	2.7
147	Univ. of Colo.–Colorado Springs	2.7
147	Univ. of Massachusetts–Boston	2.7
147	University of Memphis (Fogelman)	2.7
147	University of Minnesota–Duluth (Labovitz)	2.7
147	Univ. of Missouri–Kansas City (Bloch)	2.7
147	Univ. of Missouri–St. Louis	2.7
147	University of Nevada–Las Vegas (Lee)	2.7
147	University of New Hampshire (Paul)	2.7
147	U. of North Carolina–Greensboro (Bryan)	2.7
147	University of Rhode Island	2.7
147	University of South Florida (Muma)	2.7
147	University of St. Thomas (Opus) (MN)	2.7
147	University of Vermont	2.7
147	Utah State University (Huntsman)	2.7
147	Virginia Commonwealth University	2.7
147	West Virginia University	2.7
147	Worcester Polytechnic Inst. (MA)	2.7
172	Boise State University (ID)	2.6
172	Bradley University (Foster) (IL)	2.6
172	California State U.–Fullerton (Mihaylo)	2.6
172	Chapman University (Argyros) (CA)	2.6
172	Drake University (IA)	2.6
172	Duquesne University (Palumbo) (PA)	2.6
172	Fairfield University (Dolan) (CT)	2.6
172	John Carroll University (Boler) (OH)	2.6
172	Kent State University (OH)	2.6
172	Northern Illinois University	2.6
172	Pace University (Lubin) (NY)	2.6
172	Purdue University–Northwest (IN)	2.6
172	Rollins College (FL)	2.6
172	San Francisco State University	2.6
172	Stevens Institute of Technology (NJ)	2.6
172	St. John's University (Tobin) (NY)	2.6
172	University of Alabama–Huntsville	2.6
172	University of Arkansas–Little Rock	2.6
172	University of Dayton (OH)	2.6
172	University of Evansville (Schroeder) (IN)	2.6
172	University of Idaho	2.6
172	University of Maine	2.6
172	U. of Massachusetts–Dartmouth (Charlton)	2.6
172	University of Nebraska–Omaha	2.6
172	University of Portland (Pamplin) (OR)	2.6
172	University of Wyoming	2.6
172	Valparaiso University (IN)	2.6
199	Bowling Green State University (OH)	2.5
199	Bryant University (RI)	2.5
199	California State University–Long Beach	2.5
199	California State University–Northridge	2.5
199	Clarkson University (NY)	2.5
199	Clark University (MA)	2.5
199	Florida Atlantic University	2.5
199	Illinois Institute of Technology (Stuart)	2.5
199	Illinois State University	2.5
199	Indiana State University	2.5
199	Ithaca College (NY)	2.5
199	Loyola University New Orleans	2.5
199	Morehouse College (GA)	2.5
199	New Jersey Inst. of Technology	2.5
199	New Mexico State University	2.5
199	Northern Arizona University (Franke)	2.5
199	Old Dominion University (Strome) (VA)	2.5
199	Portland State University (OR)	2.5
199	Providence College (RI)	2.5
199	Purdue University–Fort Wayne (Doermer)	2.5
199	Southern Illinois University–Carbondale	2.5
199	Trinity University (TX)	2.5
199	University of Dallas (Gupta)	2.5
199	University of Hartford (Barney) (CT)	2.5
199	Univ. of Massachusetts–Lowell (Manning)	2.5
199	University of Michigan–Dearborn	2.5
199	U. of N. Carolina–Wilmington (Cameron)	2.5
199	University of North Texas	2.5
199	University of Scranton (Kania) (PA)	2.5
199	University of South Dakota (Beacom)	2.5
199	University of Tampa (Sykes) (FL)	2.5
199	Univ. of Tennessee–Chattanooga	2.5
199	University of Texas–San Antonio	2.5
199	University of Tulsa (Collins) (OK)	2.5
199	Wayne State University (MI)	2.5
199	Western Michigan University (Haworth)	2.5

Tops in the Specialties

Undergraduate programs ranked best by B-school deans and senior faculty

ACCOUNTING

1. University of Texas–Austin (McCombs)
2. Brigham Young Univ.–Provo (Marriott) (UT)
2. University of Illinois–Urbana-Champaign
4. University of Michigan–Ann Arbor (Ross)
5. University of Pennsylvania (Wharton)
6. Indiana University–Bloomington (Kelley)
7. University of Notre Dame (Mendoza) (IN)
7. University of Southern California (Marshall)
9. New York University (Stern)
10. Ohio State University–Columbus (Fisher)

ENTREPRENEURSHIP

1. Babson College (MA)
2. Massachusetts Institute of Technology (Sloan)
3. Indiana University–Bloomington (Kelley)
4. University of California–Berkeley (Haas)
4. University of Michigan–Ann Arbor (Ross)
4. U. of North Carolina–Chapel Hill (Kenan-Flagler)
7. University of Pennsylvania (Wharton)
8. University of Texas–Austin (McCombs)
9. University of Southern California (Marshall)
10. University of Arizona (Eller)

FINANCE

1. University of Pennsylvania (Wharton)
2. New York University (Stern)
3. Massachusetts Institute of Technology (Sloan)
4. University of Michigan–Ann Arbor (Ross)
5. University of Texas–Austin (McCombs)
6. University of California–Berkeley (Haas)
7. Indiana University–Bloomington (Kelley)
8. Carnegie Mellon University (Tepper) (PA)
9. Boston College (Carroll)
10. University of Virginia (McIntire)

INSURANCE/RISK MANAGEMENT

1. University of Georgia (Terry)
2. Univ. of Wisconsin–Madison
3. Georgia State University (Robinson)
4. Temple University (Fox) (PA)
5. Florida State University
5. University of Pennsylvania (Wharton)
7. Pennsylvania State U.–Univ. Park (Smeal)
7. University of Texas–Austin (McCombs)
9. Illinois State University
10. New York University (Stern)
10. University of Illinois–Urbana-Champaign

INTERNATIONAL BUSINESS

1. Univ. of South Carolina (Moore)
2. New York University (Stern)
3. Georgetown University (McDonough) (DC)
4. University of California–Berkeley (Haas)
5. University of Pennsylvania (Wharton)
6. Florida International University
6. George Washington University (DC)
8. Fordham University (Gabelli) (NY)
8. Northeastern University (D'Amore-McKim) (MA)
8. University of Michigan–Ann Arbor (Ross)

MANAGEMENT

1. University of Michigan–Ann Arbor (Ross)
2. University of Pennsylvania (Wharton)
3. University of California–Berkeley (Haas)
4. U. of North Carolina–Chapel Hill (Kenan-Flagler)
5. University of Virginia (McIntire)
6. Indiana University–Bloomington (Kelley)
6. Massachusetts Institute of Technology (Sloan)
6. New York University (Stern)
9. University of Texas–Austin (McCombs)
10. Arizona State University–Tempe (Carey)

MANAGEMENT INFORMATION SYSTEMS

1. Massachusetts Institute of Technology (Sloan)
2. Carnegie Mellon University (Tepper) (PA)
3. University of Arizona (Eller)
4. University of Texas–Austin (McCombs)
5. University of Minnesota–Twin Cities (Carlson)
6. Georgia Institute of Technology (Scheller)
6. Indiana University–Bloomington (Kelley)
8. Univ. of Maryland–College Park
9. Georgia State University (Robinson)
10. New York University (Stern)

MARKETING

1. University of Michigan–Ann Arbor (Ross)
2. University of Pennsylvania (Wharton)
3. New York University (Stern)
4. University of Texas–Austin (McCombs)
5. U. of North Carolina–Chapel Hill (Kenan-Flagler)
6. University of California–Berkeley (Haas)
7. Indiana University–Bloomington (Kelley)
8. University of Virginia (McIntire)
9. Univ. of Wisconsin–Madison
10. St. Joseph's University (Haub) (PA)

PRODUCTION/OPERATIONS MANAGEMENT

1. Massachusetts Institute of Technology (Sloan)
2. University of Michigan–Ann Arbor (Ross)
3. University of Pennsylvania (Wharton)
4. Purdue University–West Lafayette (Krannert) (IN)
5. Carnegie Mellon University (Tepper) (PA)
6. University of California–Berkeley (Haas)
7. Georgia Institute of Technology (Scheller)
7. Michigan State University (Broad)
9. Ohio State University–Columbus (Fisher)
10. U. of North Carolina–Chapel Hill (Kenan-Flagler)

QUANTITATIVE ANALYSIS/METHODS

1. Massachusetts Institute of Technology (Sloan)
2. Carnegie Mellon University (Tepper) (PA)
3. University of Pennsylvania (Wharton)
4. New York University (Stern)
5. University of Texas–Austin (McCombs)
6. University of Michigan–Ann Arbor (Ross)
7. Georgia Institute of Technology (Scheller)
8. Purdue University–West Lafayette (Krannert) (IN)
9. Indiana University–Bloomington (Kelley)
10. Arizona State University–Tempe (Carey)

REAL ESTATE

1. University of Pennsylvania (Wharton)
2. Univ. of Wisconsin–Madison
3. University of California–Berkeley (Haas)
4. New York University (Stern)
5. University of Georgia (Terry)
6. University of Southern California (Marshall)
6. University of Texas–Austin (McCombs)
8. University of Florida (Warrington)
9. Cornell University (Dyson) (NY)
10. Georgia State University (Robinson)

SUPPLY CHAIN MANAGEMENT/LOGISTICS

1. Michigan State University (Broad)
2. Arizona State University–Tempe (Carey)
3. Massachusetts Institute of Technology (Sloan)
4. Pennsylvania State U.–Univ. Park (Smeal)
5. Ohio State University–Columbus (Fisher)
6. University of Michigan–Ann Arbor (Ross)
6. University of Tennessee (Haslam)
8. Georgia Institute of Technology (Scheller)
8. Purdue University–West Lafayette (Krannert) (IN)
10. Carnegie Mellon University (Tepper) (PA)

THE INSIDE TRACK

Stanford's Graduate School of Business

PRESTON GANNAWAY FOR USN&WR

Filling in the Picture

Winning essays reveal more than just your achievements

by **Courtney Rubin**

WHEN A NUMBER OF THE TOP 10 U.S. business schools changed their essay prompts for the 2018 application cycle, it wasn't just coincidence. Essays are such a critical (and often tie-breaking) part of the admission process that schools are constantly looking at how they can better invite candidates to show their personality, values, and other please-admit-me qualities schools can't glean from test scores and grades. "Many of the new essays (and recommendation and interview questions) are designed to figure out what the candidate is actually like," says Karen Marks, president and founder of North Star Admissions Consulting in Hanover, New Hampshire. Marks is a former associate director of admissions at Dartmouth's Tuck School of Business, which has a prompt this year that focuses on empathy for others: "Tuck students are nice, and invest generously in one another's success. Share an example of how you helped someone else succeed."

Judi Byers, executive director of admissions and financial aid at Cornell's Samuel Curtis Johnson Graduate School of Management, says Johnson similarly instituted a new Back of Your Résumé prompt at the start of the 2018-2019 admissions season, which asks students to move beyond their professional and academic history and share "the experiences that will give us insight into your character, values, and interests." This way the school can get to "the human side of the candidates and what makes them tick," she explains, including how their values might lead them to contribute once on campus. The new essay idea was inspired by an alumnus' speech. He used the phrase and "it resonated," Byers notes.

Schools – and not just those in the top 10 – want to admit academically qualified students, sure. But they also want to admit those who get along with other people, both because interpersonal skills are highly correlated with future success and because they want to curate a dynamic, interesting class of people who can collaborate, learn from each other, and contribute to the community. They also translate into loyal, happy, involved alums, Marks says.

Your essay is the chance to show the admissions committee things about yourself that can't be gleaned elsewhere in the application. Here's some advice for writing a strong one, no matter what the question.

Do your homework. When someone has done a good job researching a school, "you almost feel like this emotional connection that the applicant has to us as an institution," says Michael Robinson, director of admissions at Columbia Business School, which features an essay this year asking applicants "how will you take advantage of being at the very center of business" after they view a video of Dean Glenn Hubbard discussing the dynamic opportunities offered by the Columbia-New York ecosystem. A good essay is personal and specific about what appeals to you about the school. If you mention meeting an alum, explain what you learned in the talk that drew you to apply. Or, if during a campus visit, you chatted with an interesting professor or sat in on a class, explain how the experience reinforced your perceptions. Then, says Cornell's Byers, connect it back to your candidacy: what you want to accomplish, and what you've done. (She notes: "We can tell when someone has reached out to a faculty member just to be able to say that they have.")

Answer the question. Schools put a lot of thought into their essay prompts because they're trying to elicit important information. Columbia, for example, used to ask applicants to share something future classmates would be "positively sur-

MORE @ USNEWS.COM

ADDITIONAL TIPS FOR GETTING IN
Learn how to get admitted to a top program without a stellar GPA, how to highlight diversity in your application, which schools have the most competitive admissions and more. ▸ *usnews.com/businessapp*

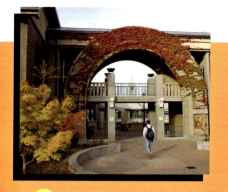

S P O T L I G H T   O N

Haas School of Business

U. OF CALIFORNIA–BERKELEY

U.S. NEWS RANK #6

When she was choosing a business school, Carolyn Chuong Holgate, 30, was struck by the "incredibly talented, yet very down-to-earth" students at Berkeley's Haas School of Business. Its reputation in both the tech sector and in making a difference for society was also appealing to her. Interested in education technology, the 2018 MBA grad led a team to Makererc University in Uganda to help launch a center to improve youth employment rates during her first year. She also interned on the education team at Amazon, and she now works at the company as a senior product manager.

About 80 percent of "Haasies" participate in at least one program through the school's Center for Social Sector Leadership, such as serving on the board of a local nonprofit or tackling an investing project focused on helping others. Most of the school's roughly 590 full-time MBA students choose to concentrate on at least one of the school's 11 "areas of emphasis," which include subjects like corporate social responsibility and energy and clean tech. *–Mariya Greeley*

▶ **More @ usnews.com/berkeley**

prised" to learn about them. Yet students still sent in essays about tragic events like losing a parent, Robinson says. Not answering the question doesn't automatically get your application rejected, but it certainly doesn't help your case for admission.

Donna Swinford, the interim executive director of student recruitment and admissions at the University of Chicago's Booth School of Business, agrees. In the past "no matter what open-ended question we asked, we found applicants wanted to address why they want an MBA and how it fits within their goals." So in 2018, one of the school's two required essays asked simply that. The second essay, however, is open-ended: "How have your interests, leadership experiences, and other passions influenced the choices in your life?" For the latter, a student might write about an impactful book, a critical career choice or opportunities taken or missed. Whatever the topic you choose, Swinford advises, consider when crafting a response that the admissions committee is looking for it to complement the broader application by further filling out your self-portrait. "Too often the essay is used to check boxes," she adds.

Dig deep. Every admissions officer interviewed mentioned the frustration of reading superficial essays. It's not enough just to tell a story. If – as Dartmouth Tuck requests – you're telling how you helped someone else succeed, you need to show the thoughts and the decision-making process behind your actions. If you're writing – as Columbia prompted – about a team failure and what you'd do differently, explain why. That provides key insights into the applicants, says Robinson, "Do they take ownership for their failure? Do they have a growth mindset?"

And in an anecdote about leadership, don't waste space talking about logistics or the scope of the project – facts that reveal nothing about you. You're much better off, Marks advises, talking about interpersonal dynamics, how you build relationships, mistakes that you made, and what you

were thinking throughout the experience. Finally, shorter word counts are not an excuse for a lack of substance. Robinson suggests skeptics read the Gettysburg Address. "See what someone can do with 272 words," he says.

Be yourself. With essays, there's no such thing as bad topics (as long as you're staying within the confines of the prompt), only bad execution. Marks has seen candidates who got into top B-schools talk about reality TV shows, their pets, Ariana Grande, and watching the British royal weddings. How is royal wedding-watching relevant to an MBA essay? The applicant tied it to her interest in marketing. The prompt was about goals, and she was explaining how she sees narrative storytelling – so common in coverage of these kinds of events – as the linchpin of effective marketing. The big point is to "keep it very real," says Marks, who advises clients to choose topics that answer the question but also allow the committee insights into their personality and interests.

Still Kristen Lindeman, associate director of admissions at the Massachusetts Institute of Technology's Sloan School of Management, cautions candidates to avoid creating an idealized version of themselves. Remember, admissions committees will want to see that your essays align with what recommenders say about you.

Show what you can offer. Admissions pros recommend candidates discuss specifically what kind of impact they'll have on the campus community, both during and after their degree. What unique talents or experiences can you share with your classmates and professors? If you believe – as MBA admissions committees do – that past performance is an indicator of future success, can you offer an episode from your past where your skills or ethics affected those around you? "Columbia, for example, does not want students who are more interested in being in New York than engaging with student life," Robinson says. "We're trying to pick people who are going to be active and involved."

Adds Sloan's Lindeman: "When you apply for a job, you never say, 'This is what I'm going to get out of your organization. It's what you're going to bring.'"

Be specific. When Marks begins working with clients, she often asks them to describe their biggest failures, what they're most proud of, how they grew up, and how they spend their free time. She wants them to get in the habit of answering questions with concrete examples. Students can go off the rails if they get too theoretical or avoid personal specifics in responding to prompts about themselves. "Essays are more powerful with tangible examples," she says.

Many MBA programs like to think they offer a transformative experience, and they want to know that it will be for you. Instead of saying where you plan to be in five or 10 years, admissions experts suggest you explain how a school's MBA will help you get there, and what about you and your work experience suggests you will be able to achieve your goals. Sure, adding an MBA to your name may get you a promotion and a raise – or so you hope – but what is it, specifically, that you want to learn? What are your weaknesses, and how will an MBA at that school strengthen them? Writing admissions essays can be a time-consuming process. But

if done well, Tuck's executive director of admissions and financial aid Luke Anthony Pena says you can learn a lot about yourself, your motivations, your goals and how a school can help you grow and achieve those goals. "If you navigate the process and say, 'Thank heavens I'm done,'" he adds, "then you've missed an opportunity." ●

RISING TO THE TOP OF THE PILE

MBA candidates entering in the fall of 2019 at the University of Utah's **David Eccles School of Business** were asked to write three short essays. Here, this successful applicant answers a prompt inviting him to share additional aspects of his life and personality that would help demonstrate why he's a strong candidate for Eccles.

What unique characteristics would you bring to class conversations and group activities? How would you add to the diversity of thought and experience within the classroom? *(Suggested limit: 250 words)*

My background in [professional services] allowed me to experience a wide variety of client industries; **❶ I was involved in everything from physically counting hogs in a [rural] barn owned**

WHY THIS ESSAY WORKED

Says **Brad Vierig**, associate dean of MBA programs and executive education at Eccles: "We look for candidates who will bring a mix of skills, perspectives and experiences. This candidate's essay was so effective because he was able to reflect his impressively varied background and make it clear how his fellow students would be enriched by it."

❶ "Here he shows he's successfully adapted to a mix of environments requiring him to use quantitative, analytical and people skills - all necessary for MBA candidates," Vierig notes. "He also shows he's a hard worker and willing to get his hands dirty. Work ethic and adaptability are also critical qualities we look for."

❷ "We seek to assemble a diverse MBA cohort each year to help shape future leaders who can serve culturally diverse audiences," Vierig says. "We prize candidates who show they're comfortable moving among people of different backgrounds. This applicant's emphasis on his extensive U.S. travel and on his decision to learn Russian while in Eastern Europe is noteworthy."

❸ "The candidate clearly has a lot to share with his classmates, but he also emphasizes how much he loves to learn, and his background shows he means it," Vierig says. "Success in the classroom or in running a startup or corporation also requires a willingness to learn from others. His essay shows he has that openness."

by a Japanese conglomerate, to preparing filings for billions of dollars in public debt and equity capital for a fast-growing datacenter company, to serving regional water and electric utilities and observing the impact of local politics on their planning, to accounting for factories that manufacture military jets and drone-based radar. My role [in investment management] has given me exposure to institutional capital, geographic and tenant-credit considerations in various regions, and to all sectors of traditional real estate development and management. I've also had diverse geographic and cultural experiences, **❷ from living in [Eastern Europe] and learning Russian, to travelling widely (46 states and 38 countries to date);** these varied locations and experiences have provided me with **❸ a wide range of background knowledge and insight that I'll be able to share with fellow students. I love to learn as much as possible** about a wide variety of topics, and I'm excited to continue to expand and share knowledge and experience with my classmates."

Bracketed wording was substituted for proper names to protect student's anonymity.

Smoothing the Rough Spots

Some simple steps can transform weaknesses in your résumé into strengths

by **Stacy Blackman**

WHEN YOU APPLY to an MBA program, particularly at a prestigious business school, the admissions committee will scrutinize every element of your background to determine how well-rounded you are and whether you're up to the program's academic rigors. Of course, not every applicant has a sterling backstory, and you may find yourself concerned that something in your past will hurt your chances to get into your dream school. Understand, though, that you have time before applying to address blemishes in your past. Here are three common challenges for MBA applicants and ways to overcome them.

Nonrigorous undergraduate academics

Your ability to handle the MBA coursework is paramount to your academic success. The admissions team will notice if your undergraduate degree is from a university with a reputation as a party school or if you have a high GPA but the majority of the classes you took were relatively easy. While reviewing your application, the admissions committee will assess any up or down trends in your transcript and look for your exposure to and performance in quantitative classes. If your undergraduate academics are lacking and you're a few years removed from student life, your best course of action is to show that you're aware of these weaknesses by enrolling in a calculus or statistics class at a local community college. You want to show that you can handle the heavy math right now, despite what your transcript may suggest. (If you're a busy professional, then adding to your workload in this way can also demonstrate your ability to multitask – a strength worth highlighting.) Also ask your recommenders to specifically emphasize your quant abilities in their letters of recommendation. The three-pronged approach – adequate GMAT or GRE score, supplemental college coursework, and a sponsor vouching for your skills – should convince the admissions team that your less rigorous classes won't hinder your performance in business school.

Lack of extracurricular activities

This is a significant red flag that you would be wise to address before applying to business school, especially if you are aiming for admission to the most elite MBA programs. Part of what makes business school such an enriching experience is the personal and professional growth that occurs when a diverse group of people come together. Often, an applicant's hobbies and interests outside of work will intrigue the admissions team so much that they want to meet the prospective student.

path. This was something he set up on his own and could do while traveling, as needed. If you're planning to apply to business school for the upcoming admissions season, you may think it's too late to do anything about scant extracurricular or volunteer work. However, in my experience, even if you are less than a year from your application deadlines, you still have enough time to address any shortcomings in your outside activities.

No teamwork

MBA admissions committees seek applicants who are both individually capable and able to work well with others to reach common goals. Teamwork is a hallmark at many elite business schools. Some – such as the University of Pennsylvania's Wharton School and the Stephen M. Ross School of Business at the University of Michigan–Ann Arbor – even require a team-based discussion or exercise as part of the admissions process so they may directly observe applicants' skills in this area. If your professional experience thus far has included little to no work in teams, you'll have to dig deeper to find examples you can share. Luckily, teamwork comes in many forms. Think back to your college days for experiences within a sorority or fraternity, on a sports team or volunteer mission, or participating in a case competition. Next, consider your activities after graduating from college. Can you find examples from a hobby or community service setting or from the active role you played in a political organization or local campaign? Understanding the importance of collaboration and teamwork is vital to growing and learning at B-school. Make sure your application contains examples of your ability to be both an effective leader and team member.

The key is for your application to speak to all of the individual attributes that make you a strong candidate and reveal how you will be a great fit once admitted. If you're still concerned that your efforts to improve in these three areas will not sufficiently sway the admissions committee, emphasize within your application and during your interview that you have a plan for further improvement during your time at business school through classwork and extracurricular activities. This self-awareness and dedication to continual growth will be noted and appreciated. ●

If that doesn't sound like you right now, it's time to make an investment in nurturing another side of your personality. If you're struggling to figure out where to spend your time and energy in a way that feels authentic, think about your past passions and interests. Activities or causes that excited you as a teen or child may still do so – think of ways to incorporate those interests into your life outside of work and build upon them.

Even if you have a grueling work life that involves a lot of travel or leaves you with an unreliable schedule, find an activity to do on your own. I have a client who reached out to the career services department at his undergraduate university and offered to mentor students who want to follow his career

Stacy Blackman *is the author of "The MBA Application Roadmap: The Essential Guide to Getting into a Top Business School" and the founder of Stacy Blackman Consulting, an admissions advisory.*

Paying Your Way

Smart strategies for lightening the financial load

by **Arlene Weintraub**

ATALIE YOUSIF SPENT the last months of her MBA program driving for Uber and Lyft, dog sitting for Rover, delivering groceries for Shipt, and distributing makeup and skin care products for SeneGence. In a good month, the flexible jobs netted her $1,300, and she ended up getting hired to be one family's personal driver for two of those months. The gigs helped Yousif, 27, supplement the nearly $20,000 in scholarships she was able to line up to help pay for the 18-month program at Texas A&M University's Mays Business School, which costs about $112,000 for non-Texas residents. And the jobs are giving her a head start repaying the money she's had to borrow. "I needed more, not just for rent, but also for food, gas and school functions that charge fees," says Yousif, who graduated in December.

No doubt it takes perseverance and ingenuity to pay for an MBA in today's market. The average tuition alone at the top 20 business schools is about $63,000 per year – and then there are living expenses. Seven of the most elite B-schools, including those at Harvard, the University of Pennsylvania and Northwestern University, have all surpassed the $200,000 mark for total costs, according to Poets&Quants, a business school information provider.

Where is a cash-strapped MBA-seeker to turn? Students who used a 529 college savings account to pay for their undergraduate degrees can start by applying any leftover funds to graduate school tuition. Enrolling in an accelerated, online or overseas MBA program might also be a cost-saving move. Here are a few other ways to lower the bill:

Dig deep for scholarships

Most MBA programs will consider all applicants for merit scholarships without requiring an additional essay, with awards ranging from a few thousand dollars per semester to full tuition. Several schools partner with organizations to offer specialized scholarships, such as Reaching Out MBA for LGBTQ students and the Yellow Ribbon Program for military veterans.

It's worth doing some research before applying to see if any schools are handing out money to students in specific demographic groups and/or who plan to work in particular industries. For example, Rice University's Jones Graduate School of Business offers one scholarship for students with a background in agriculture from the central southern Plains region, and another for women interested in commercial real estate. Washington University's Olin Business

Natalie Yousif cobbled together a number of part-time jobs to help cover her expenses at Texas A&M.

School awards scholarships to female students via its participation in the Forté Foundation, a consortium of universities, companies and donors that aims to boost the number of female business school graduates. Olin also offers some full-tuition fellowships for women, though they have to apply separately.

Some private schools are going out of their way to be as affordable for top-tier candidates as public rivals. In the fall of 2018, the University of Denver introduced a scholarship for Colorado residents who have at least a 3.0 undergrad GPA, three years of relevant work experience and a minimum GMAT score of 600 (or 158 per section of the GRE) that slashes the $90,400 price tag of the

MBA to just $45,200. "It's automatic for in-state students who meet the merit threshold," says Brad Rosenwinkel, executive director of graduate admissions and academic services for the university's Daniels College of Business.

The list of external scholarship opportunities continues to grow, too. In 2018, the Graduate Management Admission Council launched a program that awards $1,000 and $2,500 to undergrads planning to pursue an MBA. The winners were selected based on their GMAT scores and an essay on how graduate business schools can improve the world. Websites like GoGrad.org and the Scholly app are good places to search for off-the-radar scholarships. For example, LawnStarter recently offered a $1,000 award to students who had worked in lawn care or were planning to do so. The Paul & Daisy Soros Fellowships for New Americans program awards up to $90,000 to immigrants and children of immigrants.

Get in-state tuition (even when you live elsewhere)

A rapidly growing number of programs are easing the way for out-of-state students. The bulk of Yousif's award came from Texas A&M's in-state tuition waiver scholarship, which brings the bill down to the $87,000 that Texas residents pay. For Yousif, the in-state scholarship provided a welcome alternative to staying at Michigan State University, where she had earned an undergraduate degree in human resources. "I was ready to try something new," says Yousif, who had never even been to Texas before.

Other schools that make similar accommodations for choice out-of-staters include the University of Tennessee and Southern Arkansas University. And some schools lower tuition to in-state levels for students who have participated in service-related programs like the Peace Corps, including Michigan State.

Be transparent about your need – and appeal

Be sure to get all of your applications in promptly, because schools tend to hand out merit scholarships early in the application cycle. You'll also want to fill out the Free Application for Federal Student Aid early if you have any hope of qualifying for a share of the somewhat limited need-based grant money available to graduate business students or if you expect to seek student loans. According to the latest data from GMAC, 45 percent of students applying to full-time MBA programs got merit scholarships and/or need-based aid.

Don't be shy about contacting admissions early and discussing your need for aid, advises Linh Gilles, director of admissions and recruiting at the University of Minnesota–Twin Cities' Carlson School of Management. "In the application there will be different spaces for information to be shared about financial need, so it's important to use that real estate to answer those questions directly," Gilles says. And once you have all of your offers in hand, it's

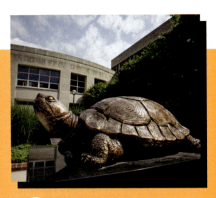

SPOTLIGHT ON

Robert H. Smith School of Business

U. OF MARYLAND—COLLEGE PARK

U.S. NEWS RANK #40

Stephanie Gomez, 27, came to business school after several years of work as a pharmaceutical biochemist. Thanks to coursework that has been heavy on data analytics and an internship at pharma company GlaxoSmithKline, the second-year MBA student has been able to explore firsthand the ways that data and new technology are disrupting how health care companies are doing business. "I knew going into an MBA that would be data-focused would give me an edge," she says.

Teaching future business leaders how to navigate endless amounts of information and ever-changing tech is at the core of Maryland's Smith School of Business, says Wendy Moe, associate dean of master's programs. Students choose to specialize in one of four career tracks – finance, marketing, consulting, or supply chain management – and all of them explore data-driven decision-making within the context of these specific business functions. Marketing students, for example, learn about understanding online targeting methods or models for sales forecasting. –*Ann Claire Carnahan*

▶ **More @ usnews.com/umd**

OK – even wise – to share your options with your top choice, she adds. "Every student who gets admitted and gets awarded a scholarship may not accept the offer, so that provides opportunities for schools to re-award scholarships." It's worthwhile, she notes, to have an open discussion about whether there's anything additional you can do to make yourself attractive.

Join the gig economy

Many schools offer paid teaching assistantships and other on-campus jobs, and they often will tailor the positions to your career goals. Rice has hired students to devise marketing plans for the program and to develop a strategic plan for a new on-campus coffee shop. Campus jobs pay about $20 per hour.

When Adam Rekkbie, 23, decided to start his MBA program at Bentley University in Massachusetts immediately after earning his undergraduate degree there in 2018, he secured merit scholarships to cover 30 percent of the $60,000 tuition for the first year. He also got $16,000 in federal loans and a part-time job at a supermarket. But he wanted to find other paid positions that would offer

THE PAYBACK PICTURE

 U. **S. NEWS HAS** compiled a list of the schools whose 2018 MBA graduates finished up with the heaviest and lightest debt loads. The average amount borrowed reflects what was incurred to pay grad school expenses – for tuition, fees, room, board, books and miscellaneous costs – and omits any undergraduate debt. The figures include all loans taken out by students from private financial institutions and federal, state and local governments. The first column of data indicates what percentage of full- or part-time 2018 graduates completed their programs owing money (and, by extrapolation, what percentage graduated debt free). "Average amount of debt" refers to the amount borrowed by those who incurred debt; it's not an average for all students.

LEAST DEBT

Full Time

School	% of grads with debt	Average amount of debt
Louisiana State U.–Baton Rouge (Ourso)	31%	$15,300
Louisiana Tech University	17%	$15,878
Mercer University–Atlanta, (Stetson) (GA)	60%	$17,343
Northern Arizona University (Franke)	42%	$17,443
West Texas A&M University	54%	$18,000
Binghamton University–SUNY	32%	$18,229
John Carroll University (Boler) (OH)	36%	$19,632
University of Missouri (Trulaske)	12%	$20,261
La Salle University (PA)	45%	$22,495
Baylor University (Hankamer) (TX)	50%	$22,900

Part Time

School	% of grads with debt	Average amount of debt
University of Tulsa (Collins) (OK)	7%	$2,067
West Texas A&M University	22%	$7,400
Loyola University Maryland (Sellinger)	40%	$9,293
Quinnipiac University (CT)	25%	$11,005
University of North Texas	41%	$13,385
SUNY–Oswego	25%	$15,131
Mercer University–Atlanta (Stetson) (GA)	60%	$15,912
University of Central Florida	36%	$16,801
Texas A&M International University	55%	$17,050
University of Akron (OH)	29%	$17,787

MOST DEBT

Full Time

School	% of grads with debt	Average amount of debt
Duke University (Fuqua) (NC)	57%	$115,590
Massachusetts Inst. of Technology (Sloan)	48%	$115,139
University of Virginia (Darden)	54%	$106,489
University of Michigan–Ann Arbor (Ross)	56%	$104,679
U. of North Carolina–Chapel Hill (Kenan-Flagler)	61%	$99,855
University of California–Berkeley (Haas)	45%	$99,328
Stanford University (CA)	46%	$98,690
Yale University (CT)	57%	$98,250
Fordham University (Gabelli) (NY)	25%	$98,199
Pepperdine University (Graziadio) (CA)	30%	$93,267

Part Time

School	% of grads with debt	Average amount of debt
U. of California–Riverside (Anderson)	23%	$120,278
Chapman University (Argyros) (CA)	35%	$92,629
Pepperdine University (Graziadio) (CA)	62%	$89,362
Rice University (Jones) (TX)	27%	$85,458
University of California–Berkeley (Haas)	39%	$83,140
Willamette University (Atkinson) (OR)	66%	$82,451
University of Texas–Austin (McCombs)	55%	$82,191
University of California–Davis	56%	$81,386
University of Michigan–Ann Arbor (Ross)	55%	$78,926
University of California–Irvine (Merage)	66%	$78,081

Student debt data are as of March 1, 2019. Only ranked schools are eligible to be included on this list.

him experience in his chosen field of data analysis, so he signed up with a company called Parker Dewey that matches students with "micro-internships" – short-term gigs that students can complete remotely for companies around the world.

In his first year, Rekkbie completed five micro-internships, each of which paid a fee of between $360 and $450 for about 20 hours of work. He assisted a producer of power tools in analyzing pricing set by the company's main competitors, and he helped write a business plan for a physician hoping to finance a health care start-up. "It's a good learning experience," Rekkbie says. "It pushes me outside of my comfort zone and teaches me to research industries that I'm not familiar with."

Borrow selectively

As a grad student, the government will calculate your need based only on your own assets as reported on the FAFSA, not those of your parents. But borrower beware: Loans for graduate students are not subsidized by Uncle Sam, meaning you will start accruing interest as soon as you sign for your loan. And the interest can build up fast. For the 2018-2019 school year, graduate unsubsidized loans carried interest rates of 6.6 percent and Grad PLUS Loans, which can be used to cover living expenses and other costs not covered by scholarships, racked up rates of 7.6 percent. By contrast, the interest rate on undergraduate loans was 5.05 percent.

Christie St-John, director of MBA admissions at Vanderbilt University's Owen Graduate School of Management, recommends that students consider what they can expect as a starting salary and gauge how long it will take them to pay back their loans. Most Owen graduates are able to get clear in five to 10 years, she says.

What if you determine the cost of an MBA is just too high? Laurie Pickard, 38, came to that conclusion in 2013 while working in international development. Instead, she decided to create her own advanced business education by taking massive open online courses or MOOCs. First she researched typical MBA courses at top-tier business schools, then found MOOC equivalents on sites like Coursera; she also used resources such as iTunes and free courses on university websites. She completed her self-made curriculum in 2016 while working in Rwanda, earning several certificates from Coursera in topics ranging from operations management to financial markets. Pickard estimates she spent less than $1,000 total – 50 times less than the least expensive MBA she could find.

"I didn't want to go into debt. I didn't really want to stop working," says Pickard, who is now employed as an international business consultant and who wrote a book about her experience, "Don't Pay for Your MBA." Employers will take a MOOC education seriously, she says, "if you gain supplemental experience with internships and pursue projects that connect with a career." Besides keeping her job at the U.S. Agency for International Development in Rwanda while studying, Pickard also volunteered to do some book-keeping for the U.S. Embassy's employee association.

Now some business schools are catering to students who want to pursue their degrees via MOOCs. In December 2017, the University of Illinois' Gies College of Business graduated the first cohort of 69 students pursuing its iMBA. The flexible degree program, which can be completed over 24 to 36 months, is offered in partnership with Coursera for under $22,000. ●

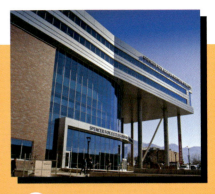

David Eccles School of Business

UNIVERSITY OF UTAH, SALT LAKE CITY

U.S. NEWS RANK #54

All incoming MBA students at the Eccles School of Business choose a concentration in one of 11 areas such as business strategy or marketing. A flexible and cross-disciplinary curriculum encourages them to delve deep into their specialty; indeed, roughly half of the 120 full-time MBA students pick up a joint degree within or outside the business school. Finance and information systems students, for instance, earn a master's in either field and an MBA, while those in the entertainment arts and engineering program blend computer science and the arts to focus on developing and running game-design businesses. (Atari, Pixar and Adobe were founded by Utah grads.)

Students move through core classes in small teams of about five, and one-on-one career coaching helps them identify potential job paths and resources. Kelsey Roderick, 33, a second-year MBA student, credits the coaching with helping her land an internship in customer success at a Salt Lake City software company. She's also enjoyed the school's proximity to national parks and mountains. *–Lindsay Cates*

▶ More @ usnews.com/utah

MORE @ USNEWS.COM

PAYING FOR BUSINESS SCHOOL
Find further tips on how to up your chance for a full ride, get employer assistance in paying off student loans, and slash your debt by volunteering. ▶*usnews.com/mbapay*

7 Experts
on How to Get Hired

YOU WERE A HIGH ACHIEVER IN COLLEGE and now you've made it into a top MBA program. The future looks promising for a great job with a consulting firm, health giant or startup, right? Perhaps. The truth is, employers want more than a polished résumé and glittering recommendations. Getting that dream job is going to require a lot of reflection, research and networking. You might need to put in "10 to 15 hours a week on your career search," says Marla McGraw, director of career management at Michigan State's Eli Broad Graduate School of Management. U.S. News reached out to corporate recruiters as well as career specialists at major MBA programs to get their inside tips for getting an inside track. *–Compiled by Elizabeth Whitehead*

1 RACHEL GROSSBAUM
JPMorgan Chase
MBA Recruiting Lead

START EARLY. If you're interested in a particular sector, like financial services, sign up for related clubs at your school as they can give you information on events employers are putting on for students. We see conferences as great vehicles for us to identify promising potential job candidates early – even before they enter business school. We work with major organizations, many of which target women, like the Forté Foundation, and ethnic diversity, like The Consortium for Graduate Study in Management, that host these gatherings where students can meet employers and learn about different career paths. You can also get valuable experience and showcase your skills by participating in company-sponsored competitions. For example, JPMorgan Chase holds an annual case competition at NYU Stern, where we divide NYU students into teams and give each a case study to work on, like how to handle a media and communications merger. The following day each team then presents its findings to a group of executives from JPMorgan Chase. Take advantage of these opportunities; they can help you get your foot in the door.

2 MARLA MCGRAW
Michigan State U. – Eli Broad Graduate School of Management
Director of Career Management

LOOK FOR THE RIGHT FIT. Students need to choose a career path aligned with their background, skills and values. Initially, it might seem intriguing to pursue a path like high tech in the Bay Area. The benefits could include a flexible, more casual work environment and great perks, but the hours might be longer and the cost of living much higher. Or a student might weigh a job with a big consulting firm that has great resources and major thought leaders versus an opportunity with a small firm where it might be easier to make an impact and gain more responsibility earlier. We really push students to work through their self-assessment before they arrive. We had a student, a musician, who had spent some years handling arrangements for musical groups to perform at religious institutions. He realized he liked business and decided to get his MBA. After going through the self-assessment process, he saw that his experience managing people, schedules, equipment and logistics translated really well to supply chain management, and that's the path he's pursuing.

3 KEITH BEVANS
Bain & Company
Partner, Head of Global Consultant Recruiting

SKIP THE OBVIOUS. If you ask for one-on-one time with a company representative, whether it's a coffee chat on campus or at an industry reception or a casual meetup, know what you want to talk about. Don't ask obvious questions you can answer on Google, like "What is Bain & Company doing in Africa?" Instead, one might ask, "How could I work my passion in machine learning and supply chain analytics into my Bain career?" That's making good use of the interviewer's time and your own. **BONUS TIP** Don't forget interviewing 101 rules: good handshake, nice smile. You want to actually seem like you're having fun and getting energy from the process. If you're not enjoying yourself, then you're probably not going to enjoy the job.

4 PRIYA PRIYADARSHINI
Microsoft
Senior HR Director – Global Early Career Team

TRUST YOUR STORY. I was interviewing a candidate from Nigeria who had done her master's in the U.S. I started

asking her some questions about her professional skills. I saw she was very nervous, so I paused and changed direction. I said, "Tell me something that you're really, really proud of." She told me her family had limited financial resources, so she learned how to design clothes to make money. She began selling them while still an undergrad and started her own company. She said, "That helped me not only understand what it takes to run a company and a business, but also it paid for my education." To further ease her anxiety, I asked her to do a quick sketch for me – she's an amazing artist. In that moment everything changed – her voice, her confidence. She got a sparkle in her eyes. We ended up bringing her on as an intern. I mentored her and then we hired her full time and she's doing amazingly well. What's the lesson? Don't worry about being a little nervous in an interview. As long as you are being authentic, you will be fine.

5 MEGHAN REIBSTEIN
Amazon

Leader – Student Programs

BE CANDID ABOUT SETBACKS.
At Amazon, we look for people who are "vocally self-critical." We'll ask candidates about risks they've taken and where they may have failed. Some candidates will go silent when asked about failure. One project manager candidate talked about all the missteps she'd made during a product launch. I was impressed by her ability to own the failure and the clarity she had around what she learned from it. We want that at Amazon. To be an Amazonian, you must be able to take calculated risks, succeed or fail, and learn.

6 MELANIE SMITH
United Health Group

Senior Director and Talent Partner

GET THE LINKEDIN ADVANTAGE. Because of social media, it doesn't matter anymore where you come from or what your pedigree is. You can network beyond any barriers. If, say, your LinkedIn profile looks great, people will accept your invitation even if they've never heard of you before. I've seen students bring up a topic they're researching or comment on a white paper or video they found online. If they put a hashtag on, like "collaboration," it can catch the eye of people who share a similar thought process and want to connect. It could well help you network into a company you're targeting. **BONUS TIP** Of course, follow up after any meeting or interview. It shows you're organized and appreciative. And mention something meaningful about the conversation, like "of the five company values we discussed, these particularly resonated with me" and then briefly say why.

7 PATRICIA ZETTEK
University of Georgia – Terry College of Business

Director, MBA/MSBA Career Management Center

BE PROACTIVE. It's easy for MBAs to become complacent in their job search. Many sit back and say, "What companies are coming to campus, or who's going to be at the next event to tell us about their opportunities?" But if students restrict their search to just school-sponsored events, they're doing themselves a disservice. The best way to conduct a job search is by researching as many potential careers and employers as possible. That approach means seeking informational interviews with reps from companies who interest them and tapping into the school's alumni network to talk to people doing the work students find interesting. In fact, when choosing an MBA program, you should ask a school about their alumni network. How engaged are they with the Career Center? How invested are they in helping current students? Involved alumni could prove critical to the job search, and longer term success. **BONUS TIP** Resist the temptation to make an informational interview transactional. Don't ask: "What do I need to do for you (or the company) to hire me?" Instead, ask, "What steps did you take at different points in your career? Anything you would have done differently?" "Do you see any areas on my résumé that I should shore up?" Questions like these develop relationships. The ultimate goal? Advisers and mentors who invest in your success. ●

The **Job** Market

Here are some of the fastest-growing, best-paying career options for business grads

by **Mariya Greeley**

BUSINESS OPERATIONS MANAGER

These managers get stuff done. Their specific duties, however, vary widely based on the needs of their company. In manufacturing, say, they might be responsible for increasing production efficiency, managing daily quality assurance operations, or guiding teams through major undertakings like new product development. In any organization, these pros analyze the effectiveness of processes and create policies to optimize productivity. The median salary is just above $100,000, according to the Bureau of Labor Statistics.

MEDICAL AND HEALTH SERVICES MANAGER

Behind the scenes at hospitals, home health care agencies and other facilities, these administrators work to improve how care is delivered and managed. They may balance budgets and oversee patient billing, say, or help implement technology that improves the security of patient records. Careers in health care management are poised to see high growth as the need for services

SPOTLIGHT ON:
MARKETING MANAGEMENT

ANNA SELSER, 29

Emory University
Goizueta Business School, 2017

▶ Growing up, Anna Selser, 29, recalls her family dining on Hamburger Helper. During a stint on the Paleo diet, "LÄRABARs saved my life," she says of the snack bars, which include options that fit the strict regimen. These brands and many others are products of General Mills, where Selser is now an associate marketing manager in Minneapolis. She spent her first year working on Fruit Snacks and now helps manage YQ, a health-conscious Yoplait yogurt brand.

"Anything going on with the brand, I have some part in," Selser says. When YQ launched a new raspberry flavor, Selser worked with research and development to get the flavor right; with operations on the new yogurt's production timeline; and with logistics to meet the shipment date promised to grocery stores, among other tasks. "I am like the business owner," she says.

Selser benefited from taking a mix of team-oriented courses in the MBA program at Emory University's Goizueta Business School. The classes helped Selser, whose background is in engineering, to hone her collaboration and leadership skills. A summer internship at General Mills, during which she worked with the Nature Valley team to develop and test a pipeline of new product ideas, provided the rest of the tools she needed to excel as a full-time associate.

increases with people living and staying active longer. Between 2016 and 2026, jobs for these managers are expected to increase by 20 percent. The median salary in 2017 was about $98,000, according to the BLS.

VENTURE CAPITAL ASSOCIATE

These specialists, usually at VC firms, evaluate pitches from entrepreneurs who hope to get the funding they need to launch or grow their businesses. VC associates analyze market demand, every angle of a startup's business plan, and the entrepreneurs themselves to determine the venture's viability and whether their company should make an investment. The median base salary is about $92,000, according to PayScale, and additional compensation is common, especially for finding companies that succeed and add to the firm's investment fund.

OPERATIONS RESEARCH ANALYST

Applying statistics and strategic thinking, these analysts help systematically improve company performance. They might provide a report with suggestions on how to optimize crew and plane schedules for an airline, for example. As technology advances, companies will look to operations research analysts to cut costs and maximize efficiency, causing their employment opportunities to potentially jump 27 percent between 2016 and 2026. Median salary is about $81,000.

FINANCIAL ANALYST

These specialists' responsibilities can range from helping company leaders make plans using financial data, like deciding whether an expansion is financially feasible, to helping individuals and institutions make stock, bond and other investment decisions. The employment outlook is expected to remain strong in the immediate future, with job growth projected to be around 11 percent over the decade ending in 2026. Median salary is around $84,000, according to government data.

INVESTMENT BANKING ASSOCIATE

These financial pros advise their clients – including corporations, governments and hedge funds – on investing and complicated endeavors such as a merger, financing a big project, or becoming a publicly traded company. The median salary is about $76,000, according to PayScale, but top earners can bring in nearly $125,000. And base salaries are often heavily supplemented by bonuses and commissions, which can make up for the long hours many put in.

FINANCIAL MANAGER

At companies of every type and size, these managers work with their teams to produce financial reports, set long-term earnings goals, direct investments, and propose improvement and growth strategies to top executives. Openings for these pros are expected to grow by 19 percent between 2016 and 2026, much faster than most occupations, because their risk management and money management skills will be in high demand, according to the BLS. Median pay is just over $125,000.

SUPPLY CHAIN MANAGER

If you want to get products from point A (the supplier) to point B (the retailer or customer) in the most efficient way possible, then you need a specialist in supply chain management. Amazon customers can thank these coordination experts for the company's trademark speedy deliveries, for example. They design and supervise logistics policies and practices, including negotiating contracts with suppliers; maintaining the right amount of inventory for fluctuating demand; and traveling to check on production, warehouse or retail locations along the supply chain. Median annual salary is about $81,000, according to PayScale.

MANAGEMENT CONSULTANT

These expert problem solvers often work at a management consulting company like Bain & Co. or Accenture, where they guide other businesses through such challenges as how to reduce costs or better

SPOTLIGHT ON:
DATA SCIENCE

MARK GIANGRECO, 34
Northwestern University
Kellogg School of Management, 2016

▶ **Mark Giangreco, 34, had been working in politics for more than six years when he discovered a passion for analytics while using data to refine a marketing campaign for the Democratic Governors Association. He tackled problems like: How frequently should email solicitations be sent during the campaign cycle to maximize total donations?**

"I liked that you could weave these tiny bits of information into a larger story," says Giangreco, who headed to business school to switch careers and follow this passion full time. He is now a data scientist at HotelTonight, a company that snags deals on unbooked hotel rooms for its customers. On a typical day at the New York City office, Giangreco might analyze the company's supply of hotels and recommend where it should expand offerings or focus its sales efforts. Or he might use data from the customer experience team to anticipate where users need more support.

While at Northwestern University's Kellogg School of Management, Giangreco knew he might have to later fend off skepticism that MBA students have the technical know-how for data science roles. So he took "pretty much every analytics-related course," available and cross-enrolled at Northwestern's engineering school to take classes in machine learning. He also served as a product analytics intern at Groupon, working on the strategy for the company's food delivery and takeout service.

"To get your foot in the door, you have to meet a basic technical bar," Giangreco says, including being familiar with Python, SQL and statistical inference. From there, he advises, let your B-school training shine.

connect with customers. After gathering and analyzing information on the problem, consultants make recommendations for a solution. Openings in management consulting, consistently a favored industry among business school graduates, are expected to increase by 14 percent in the decade ending in 2026. The median salary is around $82,000.

PRODUCT MANAGER

Professionals in this dynamic role develop and manage their assigned products based on data, industry trends and company objectives. Collaborating with a diverse group of stakeholders, including everyone from engineers to executives, they shepherd products from ideation to launch and then back again for improvements. In the technology sector, one might go through this process to develop and implement a new app feature or a device update, for instance. The median salary for these data-savvy leaders is about $82,000, according to PayScale.

ANALYTICS MANAGER

Working with managers across departments and leading a team of math whizzes, analytics managers must have both strong communication and technical skills. They coordinate efforts to collect and analyze raw data – whether from market research, sales or operations – and translate findings into actionable insights for the future of the company. It's a job more and more businesses are specifically looking to fill with B-school grads. Analytics positions are expected to grow faster than average between 2016 and 2026, and according to PayScale, the median salary is approximately $93,000. ●

MORE @ USNEWS.COM

BEST JOBS FOR MBAS
Learn more about the best careers for MBA graduates and, as a bonus, get inside tips from business executives about how to choose the right program and then make the most of it.
▶ *usnews.com/mbajobs*

DIRECTORY OF

Business
Schools

Schools are listed alphabetically by state
within each category; data are accurate
as of March 18, 2019. A key to the terminology
used in the directories can be found at the
beginning of each one.

At UCLA's
Anderson School
of Management

On-Campus MBA Programs

THE BUSINESS directory lists all 475 U.S. schools offering master's programs in business accredited by AACSB International as of summer 2018. Most offer the MBA degree; a few offer the Master of Business. Three hundred and sixty-seven schools responded to the U.S. News survey conducted in the fall of 2018 and early 2019. Schools that did not respond to the survey have abbreviated entries.

KEY TO THE TERMINOLOGY

1. A school whose name is foot-noted with the numeral 1 did not return the U.S. News statistical survey; limited data appear in its entry.
N/A. Not available from the school or not applicable.
Email. The address of the admissions office. If instead of an email address a website is given in this field, the website will automatically present an email screen programmed to reach the admissions office.
Application deadline. For fall 2019 enrollment. "Rolling" means there is no application deadline; the school acts on applications as they are received. "Varies" means deadlines vary according to department or whether applicants are U.S. citizens or foreign nationals.
Tuition. For the 2018-2019 academic year or for the cost of the total graduate business degree program, if specified. Includes required annual student fees.
Credit hour. The cost per credit hour for the 2018-2019 academic year.
Room/board/expenses. For the 2018-2019 academic year.
College-funded aid and international student aid. "Yes" means the school provides its own financial aid to students.
Average indebtedness. Computed for 2018 graduates who

incurred business school debt.
Enrollment. Full-time and part-time program totals are for fall 2018.
Minorities. For fall 2018, percentage of students who are black or African-American, Asian, American Indian or Alaska Native, Native Hawaiian or other Pacific Islander, Hispanic/Latino, or two or more races. The minority numbers were reported by each school.
Acceptance rate. Percentage of applicants to the full-time program who were accepted for fall 2018.
Average Graduate Management Admission Test (GMAT) score. Calculated for full-time students who entered in fall 2018.
Average Graduate Record Examinations (GRE) scores. Verbal, quantitative and writing scores calculated for full-time students who entered in fall 2018.
Average undergraduate grade point average (1.0 to 4.0). For full-time program applicants who entered in fall 2018.
Average age of entrants. Calculated for full-time students who entered in fall 2018.
Average months of work experience. Calculated only for full-time program students who entered in fall 2018. Refers to post-baccalaureate work experience only.
TOEFL requirement. "Yes" means that students from non-English-

speaking countries must submit scores for the Test of English as a Foreign Language.
Minimum TOEFL score. The lowest computer-administered score on the TOEFL accepted for admission.
Most popular departments. Based on highest student demand in the 2018-2019 academic year.
Mean starting base salary for 2018 graduates. Calculated only for graduates who were full-time students, had accepted full-time job offers, and reported salary data. Excludes employer-sponsored students, signing bonuses of any kind and other forms of guaranteed compensation, such as stock options.
Employment locations. For the 2018 graduating class. Calculated only for full-time students who had accepted job offers. Abbreviations: Intl., international; N.E., Northeast (Conn., Maine, Mass., N.H., N.J., N.Y., R.I., Vt.); M.A., Middle Atlantic (Del., D.C., Md., Pa., Va., W.Va.); S., South (Ala., Ark., Fla., Ga., Ky., La., Miss., N.C., S.C., Tenn.); M.W., Midwest (Ill., Ind., Iowa, Kan., Mich., Minn., Mo., Neb., N.D., Ohio, S.D., Wis.); S.W., Southwest (Ariz., Colo., N.M., Okla., Texas); W., West (Alaska, Calif., Hawaii, Idaho, Mont., Nev., Ore., Utah, Wash., Wyo.).

ALABAMA

Auburn University
415 W. Magnolia, Suite 503
Auburn, AL 36849-5240
www.business.auburn.edu/mba
Public
Admissions: (334) 844-4060
Email: mbadmis@auburn.edu
Financial aid: (334) 844-4367
Application deadline: rolling
In-state tuition: full time: $25,318; part time: N/A
Out-of-state tuition: full time: $54,208; part time: N/A
Room/board/expenses: $20,314
College-funded aid: Yes
International student aid: Yes
Average student indebtedness at graduation: $33,071
Full-time enrollment: 77
men: 58%; women: 42%; minorities: 10%; international: 8%
Part-time enrollment: N/A
men: N/A; women: N/A; minorities: N/A; international: N/A
Acceptance rate (full time): 41%
Average GMAT (full time): 586
Average GRE (full time): 148 verbal; 150 quantitative; 3.3 writing
Average GPA (full time): 3.43
Average age of entrants to full-time program: 24
Average months of prior work experience (full time): 11
TOEFL requirement: Yes
Minimum TOEFL score: 79
Most popular departments: finance, management information systems, supply chain management/logistics, quantitative analysis/statistics and operations research
Mean starting base salary for 2018 full-time graduates: $66,999
Employment location for 2018 class: Intl. N/A; N.E. N/A; M.A. N/A; S. 72%; M.W. N/A; S.W. 28%; W. N/A

Auburn University–Montgomery
7400 East Drive
Montgomery, AL 36117
www.aum.edu
Public
Admissions: (334) 244-3623
Email: awarren3@aum.edu
Financial aid: (334) 244-3571
Application deadline: 08/01
In-state tuition: full time: $7,912; part time: N/A
Out-of-state tuition: full time: $16,822; part time: N/A
Room/board/expenses: $9,710
College-funded aid: Yes
International student aid: Yes
Average student indebtedness at graduation: $17,083
Full-time enrollment: 27
men: 41%; women: 59%; minorities: 26%; international: 4%
Part-time enrollment: N/A
men: N/A; women: N/A; minorities: N/A; international: N/A
Acceptance rate (full time): 55%
Average GMAT (full time): 454

Average GRE (full time): N/A verbal; N/A quantitative; N/A writing
Average GPA (full time): 3.32
Average age of entrants to full-time program: 28
TOEFL requirement: Yes
Minimum TOEFL score: 61

Jacksonville State University[1]

700 Pelham Road N
Jacksonville, AL 36265
www.jsu.edu/ccba/
Public
Admissions: (256) 782-5268
Email: graduate@jsu.edu
Financial aid: (256) 782-5006
Tuition: N/A
Room/board/expenses: N/A
Enrollment: N/A

Samford University[1]

800 Lakeshore Drive
Birmingham, AL 35229
www.samford.edu/business
Private
Admissions: (205) 726-2040
Email: gradbusi@samford.edu
Financial aid: (205) 726-2905
Tuition: N/A
Room/board/expenses: N/A
Enrollment: N/A

University of Alabama–Birmingham

710 13th Street South
Birmingham, AL 35233
www.uab.edu/business/
Public
Admissions: (205) 934-8227
Email: gradschool@uab.edu
Financial aid: (205) 934-8223
Application deadline: 08/01
In-state tuition: full time: N/A; part time: $8,150
Out-of-state tuition: full time: N/A; part time: $18,590
Room/board/expenses: N/A
College-funded aid: Yes
International student aid: Yes
Full-time enrollment: N/A
men: N/A; women: N/A; minorities: N/A; international: N/A
Part-time enrollment: 350
men: 42%; women: 58%; minorities: 23%; international: 17%
Average GRE (full time): N/A verbal; N/A quantitative; N/A writing
TOEFL requirement: Yes
Minimum TOEFL score: 80
Most popular departments: accounting, finance, health care administration, marketing, management information systems

University of Alabama–Huntsville

BAB 202
Huntsville, AL 35899
www.uah.edu/business
Public
Admissions: (256) 824-6681
Email: gradbiz@uah.edu
Financial aid: (256) 824-2754

Application deadline: 06/01
In-state tuition: full time: $759/credit hour; part time: $759/credit hour
Out-of-state tuition: full time: $1,655/credit hour; part time: $1,655/credit hour
Room/board/expenses: $18,976
College-funded aid: Yes
International student aid: Yes
Average student indebtedness at graduation: $26,883
Full-time enrollment: 28
men: 61%; women: 39%; minorities: 18%; international: 14%
Part-time enrollment: 99
men: 59%; women: 41%; minorities: 15%; international: 2%
Acceptance rate (full time): 68%
Average GMAT (full time): 560
Average GRE (full time): N/A verbal; N/A quantitative; N/A writing
Average GPA (full time): 3.33
Average age of entrants to full-time program: 27
Average months of prior work experience (full time): 142
TOEFL requirement: Yes
Minimum TOEFL score: 54
Most popular departments: accounting, general management, manufacturing and technology management, supply chain management/logistics, technology

University of Alabama

Box 870223
Tuscaloosa, AL 35487
www.cba.ua.edu/~mba
Public
Admissions: (888) 863-2622
Email: mba@cba.ua.edu
Financial aid: (205) 348-4077
Application deadline: 04/15
In-state tuition: full time: $13,280; part time: N/A
Out-of-state tuition: full time: $31,730; part time: N/A
Room/board/expenses: N/A
College-funded aid: Yes
International student aid: Yes
Full-time enrollment: 314
men: 66%; women: 34%; minorities: 9%; international: 1%
Part-time enrollment: N/A
men: N/A; women: N/A; minorities: N/A; international: N/A
Acceptance rate (full time): 62%
Average GMAT (full time): 650
Average GRE (full time): 154 verbal; 154 quantitative; 3.8 writing
Average GPA (full time): 3.63
Average age of entrants to full-time program: 22
Average months of prior work experience (full time): 33
TOEFL requirement: Yes
Minimum TOEFL score: 79
Most popular departments: consulting, management information systems, production/operations management, supply chain management/logistics, quantitative analysis/statistics and operations research

Mean starting base salary for 2018 full-time graduates: $68,870
Employment location for 2018 class: Intl. 0%; N.E. 2%; M.A. 5%; S. 57%; M.W. 14%; S.W. 16%; W. 6%

University of Montevallo

Morgan Hall 201, Station 6540
Montevallo, AL 35115
www.montevallo.edu/mba/
Public
Admissions: (205) 665-6544
Email: mba@montevallo.edu
Financial aid: (205) 665-6050
Application deadline: rolling
In-state tuition: full time: N/A; total program: $15,750 (part time)
Out-of-state tuition: full time: N/A; total program: $30,240 (part time)
Room/board/expenses: N/A
College-funded aid: Yes
Full-time enrollment: N/A
men: N/A; women: N/A; minorities: N/A; international: N/A
Part-time enrollment: 35
men: 29%; women: 71%; minorities: 29%; international: 6%
Average GRE (full time): N/A verbal; N/A quantitative; N/A writing
TOEFL requirement: Yes
Minimum TOEFL score: 71
Most popular departments: general management

University of North Alabama

UNA Box 5077
Florence, AL 35632
www.una.edu/mba/
Public
Admissions: (256) 765-4103
Email: mbainfo@una.edu
Financial aid: (256) 765-4278
Application deadline: N/A
In-state tuition: full time: N/A; part time: N/A
Out-of-state tuition: full time: N/A; part time: N/A
Room/board/expenses: N/A
Full-time enrollment: 80
men: 55%; women: 45%; minorities: 18%; international: 40%
Part-time enrollment: 460
men: 50%; women: 50%; minorities: 28%; international: 1%
Average GRE (full time): N/A verbal; N/A quantitative; N/A writing
TOEFL requirement: Yes
Minimum TOEFL score: 79

University of South Alabama[1]

307 N. University Boulevard
Mobile, AL 36688
mcob.usouthal.edu
Public
Admissions: (251) 460-6418
Financial aid: N/A
Tuition: N/A
Room/board/expenses: N/A
Enrollment: N/A

University of Alaska–Anchorage[1]

3211 Providence Drive
Anchorage, AK 99508
www.uaa.alaska.edu/cbpp/
Public
Admissions: (907) 786-1480
Email: admissions@uaa.alaska.edu
Financial aid: N/A
Tuition: N/A
Room/board/expenses: N/A
Enrollment: N/A

University of Alaska–Fairbanks[1]

PO Box 756080
Fairbanks, AK 99775-6080
www.uaf.edu/admissions/
Public
Admissions: (800) 478-1823
Email: uaf-admissions@alaska.edu
Financial aid: (888) 474-7256
Tuition: N/A
Room/board/expenses: N/A
Enrollment: N/A

Arizona State University

PO Box 874906
Tempe, AZ 85287-4906
wpcarey.asu.edu/mba-programs
Public
Admissions: (480) 965-3332
Email: wpcareymasters@asu.edu
Financial aid: (480) 965-6890
Application deadline: 04/02
In-state tuition: full time: $29,134; part time: $28,384
Out-of-state tuition: full time: $47,926; part time: $28,114
Room/board/expenses: $19,828
College-funded aid: Yes
International student aid: Yes
Average student indebtedness at graduation: $30,217
Full-time enrollment: 195
men: 60%; women: 40%; minorities: 19%; international: 36%
Part-time enrollment: 300
men: 63%; women: 37%; minorities: 26%; international: 12%
Acceptance rate (full time): 20%
Average GMAT (full time): 694
Average GRE (full time): 157 verbal; 156 quantitative; 4.1 writing
Average GPA (full time): 3.50
Average age of entrants to full-time program: 29
Average months of prior work experience (full time): 65
TOEFL requirement: Yes
Minimum TOEFL score: 80
Most popular departments: entrepreneurship, finance, marketing, supply chain management/logistics, other
Mean starting base salary for 2018 full-time graduates: $100,303

Employment location for 2018 class: Intl. 0%; N.E. 4%; M.A. 3%; S. 8%; M.W. 7%; S.W. 52%; W. 25%

Northern Arizona University

PO Box 15066
Flagstaff, AZ 86011-5066
www.franke.nau.edu/graduateprograms
Public
Admissions: (928) 523-7342
Email: fcb-gradprog@nau.edu
Financial aid: (928) 523-4951
Application deadline: rolling
In-state tuition: full time: $10,970; part time: N/A
Out-of-state tuition: full time: $24,056; part time: N/A
Room/board/expenses: $15,702
College-funded aid: Yes
International student aid: Yes
Average student indebtedness at graduation: $17,443
Full-time enrollment: 39
men: 54%; women: 46%; minorities: 10%; international: 3%
Part-time enrollment: N/A
men: N/A; women: N/A; minorities: N/A; international: N/A
Acceptance rate (full time): 86%
Average GMAT (full time): 544
Average GRE (full time): 152 verbal; 153 quantitative; 3.6 writing
Average GPA (full time): 3.36
Average age of entrants to full-time program: 23
Average months of prior work experience (full time): 29
TOEFL requirement: Yes
Minimum TOEFL score: 83
Mean starting base salary for 2018 full-time graduates: $53,778
Employment location for 2018 class: Intl. N/A; N.E. N/A; M.A. N/A; S. 6%; M.W. N/A; S.W. 83%; W. 11%

University of Arizona

1130 East Helen Street
McClelland Hall, Room 417
Tucson, AZ 85721-0108
ellermba.arizona.edu
Public
Admissions: (520) 621-4008
Email: mba_admissions@eller.arizona.edu
Financial aid: (520) 621-5200
Application deadline: 05/01
In-state tuition: full time: $24,544; part time: $27,000
Out-of-state tuition: full time: $44,893; part time: $27,000
Room/board/expenses: $15,700
College-funded aid: Yes
International student aid: Yes
Average student indebtedness at graduation: $37,436
Full-time enrollment: 79
men: 68%; women: 32%; minorities: 8%; international: 51%
Part-time enrollment: 180
men: 62%; women: 38%; minorities: 36%; international: 4%
Acceptance rate (full time): 44%
Average GMAT (full time): 665

Average GRE (full time): 158 verbal; 158 quantitative; 4.2 writing
Average GPA (full time): 3.50
Average age of entrants to full-time program: 28
Average months of prior work experience (full time): 57
TOEFL requirement: Yes
Minimum TOEFL score: 100
Most popular departments: entrepreneurship, finance, health care administration, marketing, management information systems
Mean starting base salary for 2018 full-time graduates: $93,244
Employment location for 2018 class: Intl. N/A; N.E. 11%; M.A. 0%; S. 0%; M.W. 6%; S.W. 56%; W. 28%

ARKANSAS

Arkansas State University–Jonesboro

PO Box 970
State University, AR 72467
www.astate.edu/business/
Public
Admissions: (870) 972-3035
Email: broe@astate.edu
Financial aid: (870) 972-2310
Application deadline: 06/01
In-state tuition: full time: $267/credit hour; part time: N/A
Out-of-state tuition: full time: $534/credit hour; part time: N/A
Room/board/expenses: $16,458
College-funded aid: Yes
International student aid: Yes
Average student indebtedness at graduation: $40,000
Full-time enrollment: 204
men: 56%; women: 44%; minorities: 13%; international: 24%
Part-time enrollment: N/A
men: N/A; women: N/A; minorities: N/A; international: N/A
Acceptance rate (full time): 80%
Average GMAT (full time): 540
Average GRE (full time): 154 verbal; 151 quantitative; 4.5 writing
Average GPA (full time): 3.50
Average age of entrants to full-time program: 29
Average months of prior work experience (full time): 27
TOEFL requirement: Yes
Minimum TOEFL score: 79
Most popular departments: finance, health care administration, marketing, management information systems, supply chain management/logistics
Mean starting base salary for 2018 full-time graduates: $55,000
Employment location for 2018 class: Intl. N/A; N.E. N/A; M.A. N/A; S. 33%; M.W. N/A; S.W. 33%; W. 33%

Arkansas Tech University

1605 North Coliseum Drive
Russellville, AR 72801
www.atu.edu/business/
Public
Admissions: (479) 968-0398
Email: gradcollege@atu.edu
Financial aid: (479) 968-0399
Application deadline: rolling
In-state tuition: full time: N/A; part time: N/A
Out-of-state tuition: full time: N/A; part time: N/A
Room/board/expenses: N/A
College-funded aid: Yes
International student aid: Yes
Full-time enrollment: N/A
men: N/A; women: N/A; minorities: N/A; international: N/A
Part-time enrollment: N/A
men: N/A; women: N/A; minorities: N/A; international: N/A
Average GRE (full time): N/A verbal; N/A quantitative; N/A writing
TOEFL requirement: Yes
Minimum TOEFL score: N/A

Henderson State University

1100 Henderson Street
Box 7801
Arkadelphia, AR 71999-0001
www.hsu.edu/Academics/GraduateSchool/index.html
Public
Admissions: (870) 230-5126
Email: grad@hsu.edu
Financial aid: (870) 230-5148
Application deadline: rolling
In-state tuition: full time: $6,456; part time: N/A
Out-of-state tuition: full time: $8,064; part time: N/A
Room/board/expenses: N/A
College-funded aid: Yes
Full-time enrollment: 5
men: 80%; women: 20%; minorities: 0%; international: 0%
Part-time enrollment: 55
men: 45%; women: 55%; minorities: 24%; international: 9%
Average GRE (full time): N/A verbal; N/A quantitative; N/A writing
TOEFL requirement: Yes
Minimum TOEFL score: N/A

Southern Arkansas University

100 E. University
Magnolia, AR 71753
web.saumag.edu/graduate/programs/mba/
Public
Admissions: (870) 235-4150
Email: gradstudies@saumag.edu
Financial aid: (870) 235-4023
Application deadline: 07/01
In-state tuition: full time: $279/credit hour; part time: $279/credit hour
Out-of-state tuition: full time: $414/credit hour; part time: $414/credit hour

Room/board/expenses: N/A
College-funded aid: Yes
International student aid: Yes
Full-time enrollment: 20
men: 80%; women: 20%; minorities: 20%; international: 5%
Part-time enrollment: 87
men: 53%; women: 47%; minorities: 14%; international: 8%
Acceptance rate (full time): 88%
Average GMAT (full time): 460
Average GRE (full time): N/A verbal; N/A quantitative; N/A writing
Average GPA (full time): 3.48
Average age of entrants to full-time program: 24
TOEFL requirement: Yes
Minimum TOEFL score: 79
Most popular departments: entrepreneurship, general management, supply chain management/logistics, other

University of Arkansas–Fayetteville

310 Williard J. Walker Hall
Fayetteville, AR 72701
gsb.uark.edu
Public
Admissions: (479) 575-2851
Email: gsb@walton.uark.edu
Financial aid: (479) 575-2711
Application deadline: 04/15
In-state tuition: full time: N/A; part time: N/A
Out-of-state tuition: full time: N/A; part time: N/A
Room/board/expenses: N/A
College-funded aid: Yes
International student aid: Yes
Full-time enrollment: 39
men: 69%; women: 31%; minorities: 0%; international: 18%
Part-time enrollment: N/A
men: N/A; women: N/A; minorities: N/A; international: N/A
Average GRE (full time): N/A verbal; N/A quantitative; N/A writing
TOEFL requirement: Yes
Minimum TOEFL score: 79
Most popular departments: entrepreneurship, finance, marketing, management information systems, supply chain management/logistics
Mean starting base salary for 2018 full-time graduates: $65,748
Employment location for 2018 class: Intl. N/A; N.E. 3%; M.A. 0%; S. 80%; M.W. 3%; S.W. 13%; W. N/A

University of Arkansas–Little Rock[1]

2801 S. University Avenue
Little Rock, AR 72204
ualr.edu/cob
Public
Admissions: (501) 569-3356
Email: mbaadvising@ualr.edu
Financial aid: (501) 569-3035
Tuition: N/A

Room/board/expenses: N/A
Enrollment: N/A

University of Central Arkansas

201 Donaghey
Conway, AR 72035
www.uca.edu/mba
Public
Admissions: (501) 450-5308
Email: markmc@uca.edu
Financial aid: (501) 450-3140
Application deadline: 07/15
In-state tuition: full time: N/A; part time: N/A
Out-of-state tuition: full time: N/A; part time: N/A
Room/board/expenses: $19,368
College-funded aid: Yes
International student aid: No
Average student indebtedness at graduation: $20,091
Full-time enrollment: 21
men: 76%; women: 24%; minorities: 10%; international: 43%
Part-time enrollment: 22
men: 59%; women: 41%; minorities: 23%; international: 0%
Acceptance rate (full time): 81%
Average GRE (full time): N/A verbal; N/A quantitative; N/A writing
TOEFL requirement: Yes
Minimum TOEFL score: 79
Most popular departments: e-commerce, finance, health care administration, international business, quantitative analysis/statistics and operations research

CALIFORNIA

California Polytechnic State University–San Luis Obispo

1 Grand Avenue
San Luis Obispo, CA 93407
www.cob.calpoly.edu/gradbusiness/
Public
Admissions: (805) 756-2311
Email: admissions@calpoly.edu
Financial aid: (805) 756-2927
Application deadline: 04/01
In-state tuition: full time: N/A; part time: N/A
Out-of-state tuition: full time: N/A; part time: N/A
Room/board/expenses: N/A
College-funded aid: Yes
Full-time enrollment: 44
men: 64%; women: 36%; minorities: N/A; international: N/A
Part-time enrollment: N/A
men: N/A; women: N/A; minorities: N/A; international: N/A
Acceptance rate (full time): 77%
Average GMAT (full time): 607
Average GRE (full time): 153 verbal; 154 quantitative; 4.3 writing
Average GPA (full time): 3.30
TOEFL requirement: Yes
Minimum TOEFL score: 80
Most popular departments: accounting, economics, general management, tax, other

California State Polytechnic University–Pomona

3801 W. Temple Avenue
Pomona, CA 91768
mba.cpp.edu
Public
Admissions: (909) 869-5299
Email: admissions@cpp.edu
Financial aid: (909) 869-3700
Application deadline: 06/01
In-state tuition: total program: $26,000 (full time); part time: N/A
Out-of-state tuition: total program: $38,000 (full time); part time: N/A
Room/board/expenses: N/A
College-funded aid: Yes
International student aid: Yes
Full-time enrollment: 72
men: 33%; women: 67%; minorities: 58%; international: 6%
Part-time enrollment: N/A
men: N/A; women: N/A; minorities: N/A; international: N/A
Acceptance rate (full time): 45%
Average GMAT (full time): 521
Average GRE (full time): N/A verbal; N/A quantitative; N/A writing
Average GPA (full time): 3.40
Average months of prior work experience (full time): 96
TOEFL requirement: Yes
Minimum TOEFL score: 80

California State University–Bakersfield[1]

9001 Stockdale Highway
Bakersfield, CA 93311-1099
www.csub.edu/BPA
Public
Admissions: (661) 664-3036
Email: admissions@csub.edu
Financial aid: N/A
Tuition: N/A
Room/board/expenses: N/A
Enrollment: N/A

California State University–Chico

Tehama Hall 301
Chico, CA 95929-0001
www.csuchico.edu/MBA
Public
Admissions: (530) 898-6880
Email: graduatestudies@csuchico.edu
Financial aid: (530) 898-6451
Application deadline: 03/21
In-state tuition: full time: N/A; part time: N/A
Out-of-state tuition: full time: N/A; part time: N/A
Room/board/expenses: N/A
College-funded aid: Yes
International student aid: Yes
Full-time enrollment: 60
men: 60%; women: 40%; minorities: N/A; international: N/A
Part-time enrollment: N/A
men: N/A; women: N/A; minorities: N/A; international: N/A
Acceptance rate (full time): 64%

Average GMAT (full time): 640
Average GRE (full time): N/A verbal, 153 quantitative; N/A writing
Average GPA (full time): 3.20
Average age of entrants to full-time program: 27
Average months of prior work experience (full time): 28
TOEFL requirement: Yes
Minimum TOEFL score: 80

California State University–East Bay

25800 Carlos Bee Boulevard
Hayward, CA 94542
www.csueastbay.edu
Public
Admissions: (510) 885-3973
Email: admissions@csueastbay.edu
Financial aid: (510) 885-2784
Application deadline: 06/01
In-state tuition: total program: $29,800 (full time); total program: $30,000 (part time)
Out-of-state tuition: total program: $29,800 (full time); total program $43,000 (part time)
Room/board/expenses: N/A
College-funded aid: Yes
International student aid: No
Full-time enrollment: 23
men: 43%; women: 57%; minorities: 78%; international: 17%
Part-time enrollment: 228
men: 52%; women: 48%; minorities: 35%; international: 51%
Acceptance rate (full time): 71%
Average GRE (full time): N/A verbal; N/A quantitative; N/A writing
Average GPA (full time): 3.06
Average age of entrants to full-time program: 32
Average months of prior work experience (full time): 60
TOEFL requirement: Yes
Minimum TOEFL score: 79
Most popular departments: finance, general management, human resources management, marketing, supply chain management/logistics

California State University–Fresno[1]

5245 N. Backer Avenue
Fresno, CA 93740-8001
www.craig.csufresno.edu/mba
Public
Admissions: (559) 278-2107
Email: mbainfo@csufresno.edu
Financial aid: N/A
Tuition: N/A
Room/board/expenses: N/A
Enrollment: N/A

California State University–Fullerton

PO Box 6848
Fullerton, CA 92834-6848
business.fullerton.edu/
Public
Admissions: (657) 278-4035
Email: mihaylogradprograms@fullerton.edu

Financial aid: (657) 278-3125
Application deadline: 04/01
In-state tuition: full time: N/A; part time: $347/credit hour
Out-of-state tuition: full time: N/A; part time: N/A/credit hour
Room/board/expenses: N/A
College-funded aid: Yes
International student aid: Yes
Full-time enrollment: N/A
men: N/A; women: N/A; minorities: N/A; international: N/A
Part-time enrollment: 316
men: 55%; women: 45%; minorities: 28%; international: 49%
Average GRE (full time): N/A verbal; N/A quantitative; N/A writing
TOEFL requirement: Yes
Minimum TOEFL score: 80
Most popular departments: accounting, finance, general management, marketing, management information systems

California State University–Long Beach

1250 Bellflower Boulevard
Long Beach, CA 90840-8501
www.csulb.edu/cba-graduate-programs
Public
Admissions: (562) 985-4767
Email: COB-GradPrograms@csulb.edu
Financial aid: (562) 985-4141
Application deadline: 06/01
In-state tuition: total program: $45,600 (full time); part time: $270/credit hour
Out-of-state tuition: total program: $45,600 (full time); part time: $396/credit hour
Room/board/expenses: N/A
College-funded aid: Yes
International student aid: Yes
Full-time enrollment: 58
men: 53%; women: 47%; minorities: 0%; international: 34%
Part-time enrollment: 130
men: 55%; women: 45%; minorities: 0%; international: 9%
Acceptance rate (full time): 68%
Average GMAT (full time): 553
Average GRE (full time): 150 verbal; 149 quantitative; 3.9 writing
Average GPA (full time): 3.25
Average age of entrants to full-time program: 24
Average months of prior work experience (full time): 32
TOEFL requirement: Yes
Minimum TOEFL score: N/A
Most popular departments: entrepreneurship, general management, human resources management

California State University–Los Angeles[1]

5151 State University Drive
Los Angeles, CA 90032-8120
www.calstatela.edu/business/gradprog
Public
Admissions: (323) 343-2810
Email: jratan@calstatela.edu
Financial aid: (323) 343-6260
Tuition: N/A
Room/board/expenses: N/A
Enrollment: N/A

California State University–Northridge

18111 Nordhoff Street
Northridge, CA 91330-8380
www.csun.edu/mba/
Public
Admissions: (818) 677-2467
Email: mba@csun.edu
Financial aid: (818) 677-4085
Application deadline: 05/01
In-state tuition: full time: N/A; part time: $6,940
Out-of-state tuition: full time: N/A; part time: $9,316
Room/board/expenses: N/A
College-funded aid: Yes
International student aid: Yes
Full-time enrollment: N/A
men: N/A; women: N/A; minorities: N/A; international: N/A
Part-time enrollment: 108
men: 56%; women: 44%; minorities: 43%; international: 6%
Average GRE (full time): N/A verbal; N/A quantitative; N/A writing
TOEFL requirement: Yes
Minimum TOEFL score: 79
Most popular departments: accounting, finance, general management, marketing, management information systems

California State University–Sacramento

6000 J Street
Sacramento, CA 95819-6088
www.csus.edu/cba/graduate/index.html
Public
Admissions: (916) 278-7198
Email: mcwilson@csus.edu
Financial aid: (916) 278-6980
Application deadline: 02/15
In-state tuition: total program: $29,520 (full time); part time: $2,866/credit hour
Out-of-state tuition: total program: $29,520 (full time); part time: $2,866/credit hour
Room/board/expenses: N/A
College-funded aid: Yes
International student aid: No
Full-time enrollment: 29
men: 59%; women: 41%; minorities: 34%; international: 0%
Part-time enrollment: 179
men: 55%; women: 45%; minorities: 47%; international: 0%

Acceptance rate (full time): 50%
Average GMAT (full time): 600
Average GRE (full time): N/A verbal; N/A quantitative; N/A writing
Average GPA (full time): 3.24
Average age of entrants to full-time program: 35
Average months of prior work experience (full time): 132
TOEFL requirement: Yes
Minimum TOEFL score: 80
Most popular departments: accounting, entrepreneurship, finance, general management, health care administration

California State University–San Bernardino

5500 University Parkway
San Bernardino, CA 92407
jhbc.csusb.edu/mba
Public
Admissions: (909) 537-5703
Email: mba@csusb.edu
Financial aid: (909) 537-3424
Application deadline: 07/08
In-state tuition: full time: N/A; part time: $413/credit hour
Out-of-state tuition: full time: N/A; part time: $677/credit hour
Room/board/expenses: N/A
College-funded aid: Yes
International student aid: Yes
Full-time enrollment: N/A
men: N/A; women: N/A; minorities: N/A; international: N/A
Part-time enrollment: 204
men: 56%; women: 44%; minorities: 54%; international: 25%
Average GRE (full time): N/A verbal; N/A quantitative; N/A writing
TOEFL requirement: Yes
Minimum TOEFL score: 79
Most popular departments: accounting, entrepreneurship, general management, marketing, other

California State University–Stanislaus

1 University Circle
Turlock, CA 95382
www.csustan.edu/grad
Public
Admissions: (209) 667-3337
Email: ngonzalez4@csustan.edu
Financial aid: (209) 667-3336
Application deadline: 06/30
In-state tuition: full time: N/A; part time: N/A
Out-of-state tuition: full time: N/A; part time: N/A
Room/board/expenses: N/A
College-funded aid: Yes
International student aid: No
Full-time enrollment: N/A
men: N/A; women: N/A; minorities: N/A; international: N/A
Part-time enrollment: 66
men: 36%; women: 64%; minorities: N/A; international: N/A
Average GRE (full time): N/A verbal; N/A quantitative; N/A writing

TOEFL requirement: Yes
Minimum TOEFL score: 80

Chapman University

1 University Drive
Orange, CA 92866
www.chapman.edu/mba
Private
Admissions: (714) 516-7190
Email: mba@chapman.edu
Financial aid: (714) 628-2510
Application deadline: 06/01
Tuition: full time: $1,655/credit hour; part time: $1,655/credit hour
Room/board/expenses: $32,436
College-funded aid: Yes
International student aid: Yes
Average student indebtedness at graduation: $84,128
Full-time enrollment: 59
men: 58%; women: 42%; minorities: 19%; international: 46%
Part-time enrollment: 116
men: 54%; women: 46%; minorities: 37%; international: 22%
Acceptance rate (full time): 52%
Average GMAT (full time): 625
Average GRE (full time): 154 verbal; 157 quantitative; 4.0 writing
Average GPA (full time): 3.40
Average age of entrants to full-time program: 28
Average months of prior work experience (full time): 61
TOEFL requirement: Yes
Minimum TOEFL score: 87
Most popular departments: entrepreneurship, finance, marketing, quantitative analysis/statistics and operations research, other
Mean starting base salary for 2018 full-time graduates: $70,492
Employment location for 2018 class: Intl. 7%; N.E. N/A; M.A. N/A; S. N/A; M.W. N/A; S.W. N/A; W. 93%

Claremont Graduate University

150 E. 10th Street
Claremont, CA 91711
www.cgu.edu/school/drucker-school-of-management/
Private
Admissions: (909) 607-7495
Email: admissions@cgu.edu
Financial aid: (909) 621-8337
Application deadline: 08/15
Tuition: full time: N/A; part time: N/A
Room/board/expenses: N/A
College-funded aid: Yes
International student aid: Yes
Full-time enrollment: 68
men: 63%; women: 37%; minorities: N/A; international: N/A
Part-time enrollment: 24
men: 46%; women: 54%; minorities: N/A; international: N/A
Average GRE (full time): N/A verbal; N/A quantitative; N/A writing
TOEFL requirement: Yes

Minimum TOEFL score: 75
Most popular departments: finance, leadership, marketing, supply chain management/logistics, other

Loyola Marymount University

1 LMU Drive, MS 8387
Los Angeles, CA 90045-2659
mba.lmu.edu
Private
Admissions: (310) 338-2848
Email: Mba.office@lmu.edu
Financial aid: (310) 338-2753
Application deadline: 06/01
Tuition: full time: N/A; total program: $88,500 (part time)
Room/board/expenses: N/A
College-funded aid: Yes
International student aid: Yes
Full-time enrollment: N/A
men: N/A; women: N/A; minorities: N/A; international: N/A
Part-time enrollment: 55
men: 65%; women: 35%; minorities: 35%; international: 24%
Average GRE (full time): N/A verbal; N/A quantitative; N/A writing
TOEFL requirement: Yes
Minimum TOEFL score: 100
Most popular departments: entrepreneurship, finance, general management, human resources management, marketing

Naval Postgraduate School[1]

555 Dyer Road
Monterey, CA 93943
www.nps.edu/academics/schools/GSBPP/
Public
Admissions: N/A
Financial aid: N/A
Tuition: N/A
Room/board/expenses: N/A
Enrollment: N/A

Pepperdine University

24255 Pacific Coast Highway
Malibu, CA 90263-4100
bschool.pepperdine.edu
Private
Admissions: (310) 568-5535
Email: PGBS.Admission@pepperdine.edu
Financial aid: (310) 568-5663
Application deadline: 05/15
Tuition: full time: $49,830; part time: $1,770/credit hour
Room/board/expenses: $19,900
College-funded aid: Yes
International student aid: Yes
Average student indebtedness at graduation: $93,267
Full-time enrollment: 116
men: 59%; women: 41%; minorities: 9%; international: 33%
Part-time enrollment: 505
men: 52%; women: 48%; minorities: 30%; international: 6%
Acceptance rate (full time): 86%

Average GMAT (full time): 633
Average GRE (full time): 151 verbal; 154 quantitative; 3.8 writing
Average GPA (full time): 3.40
Average age of entrants to full-time program: 26
Average months of prior work experience (full time): 61
TOEFL requirement: Yes
Minimum TOEFL score: 90
Most popular departments: finance, general management, leadership, marketing, management information systems
Mean starting base salary for 2018 full-time graduates: $78,380
Employment location for 2018 class: Intl. 6%; N.E. 0%; M.A. 10%; S. 13%; M.W. 3%; S.W. 0%; W. 68%

San Diego State University

5500 Campanile Drive
San Diego, CA 92182-8228
business.sdsu.edu
Public
Admissions: (619) 594-6336
Email: admissions@sdsu.edu
Financial aid: (619) 594-6323
Application deadline: 03/01
In-state tuition: full time: $15,132; total program part time: $10,590
Out-of-state tuition: full time: $24,240; total program part time: $17,718
Room/board/expenses: N/A
College-funded aid: Yes
International student aid: Yes
Average student indebtedness at graduation: $48,500
Full-time enrollment: 116
men: 54%; women: 46%; minorities: 26%; international: 35%
Part-time enrollment: 139
men: 63%; women: 37%; minorities: 35%; international: 6%
Acceptance rate (full time): 66%
Average GMAT (full time): 589
Average GRE (full time): 152 verbal; 153 quantitative; 3.9 writing
Average GPA (full time): 3.31
Average age of entrants to full-time program: 26
Average months of prior work experience (full time): 56
TOEFL requirement: Yes
Minimum TOEFL score: 80
Most popular departments: accounting, entrepreneurship, finance, marketing, management information systems
Mean starting base salary for 2018 full-time graduates: $61,250
Employment location for 2018 class: Intl. N/A; N.E. 0%; M.A. 0%; S. 0%; M.W. 0%; S.W. 0%; W. 100%

San Francisco State University[1]

835 Market Street, Suite 600
San Francisco, CA 94103
mba.sfsu.edu
Public
Admissions: (415) 817-4300
Email: mba@sfsu.edu
Financial aid: (415) 338-1581

Tuition: N/A
Room/board/expenses: N/A
Enrollment: N/A

San Jose State University[1]

1 Washington Square
San Jose, CA 95192-0162
www.sjsu.edu/lucasgsb
Public
Admissions: (408) 924-1000
Email: admissions@sjsu.edu
Financial aid: (408) 283-7500
Tuition: N/A
Room/board/expenses: N/A
Enrollment: N/A

Santa Clara University

Lucas Hall 116
Santa Clara, CA 95053
www.scu.edu/business
Private
Admissions: (408) 554-2752
Email: gradbusiness@scu.edu
Financial aid: (408) 554-4505
Application deadline: 06/01
Tuition: full time: N/A; part time: $1,108/credit hour
Room/board/expenses: N/A
College-funded aid: Yes
International student aid: Yes
Full-time enrollment: N/A
men: N/A; women: N/A; minorities: N/A; international: N/A
Part-time enrollment: 353
men: 58%; women: 42%; minorities: 50%; international: 20%
Average GRE (full time): N/A verbal; N/A quantitative; N/A writing
TOEFL requirement: Yes
Minimum TOEFL score: 100
Most popular departments: entrepreneurship, finance, leadership, marketing, other

Sonoma State University

1801 E. Cotati Avenue
Rohnert Park, CA 94928
www.sonoma.edu/admissions
Public
Admissions: (707) 664-2252
Email: rosanna.kelley@sonoma.edu
Financial aid: (707) 664-2389
Application deadline: 04/30
In-state tuition: full time: N/A; total program: $24,233 (part time)
Out-of-state tuition: full time: N/A; total program: $33,737 (part time)
Room/board/expenses: N/A
College-funded aid: Yes
International student aid: Yes
Full-time enrollment: N/A
men: N/A; women: N/A; minorities: N/A; international: N/A
Part-time enrollment: 55
men: 44%; women: 56%; minorities: 27%; international: 11%
Average GRE (full time): N/A verbal; N/A quantitative; N/A writing
TOEFL requirement: Yes

Minimum TOEFL score: 80
Most popular departments: general management, other

Stanford University

655 Knight Way
Stanford, CA 94305-7298
www.gsb.stanford.edu/mba
Private
Admissions: (650) 723-2766
Email: mba.admissions@gsb.stanford.edu
Financial aid: (650) 723-3282
Application deadline: 04/03
Tuition: full time: $70,590; part time: N/A
Room/board/expenses: $45,207
College-funded aid: Yes
International student aid: Yes
Average student indebtedness at graduation: $98,690
Full-time enrollment: 855
men: 60%; women: 40%; minorities: N/A; international: N/A
Part-time enrollment: N/A
men: N/A; women: N/A; minorities: N/A; international: N/A
Acceptance rate (full time): 6%
Average GMAT (full time): 732
Average GRE (full time): 165 verbal; 165 quantitative; 4.9 writing
Average GPA (full time): 3.73
Average months of prior work experience (full time): 53
TOEFL requirement: Yes
Minimum TOEFL score: 100
Most popular departments: entrepreneurship, finance, general management, leadership, organizational behavior
Mean starting base salary for 2018 full-time graduates: $145,559
Employment location for 2018 class: Intl. N/A; N.E. 16%; M.A. 1%; S. 1%; M.W. 4%; S.W. 3%; W. 77%

St. Mary's College of California[1]

1928 Saint Marys Road
Moraga, CA 94575
www.smcmba.com
Private
Admissions: (925) 631-4503
Email: smcmba@stmarys-ca.edu
Financial aid: (925) 631-4370
Tuition: N/A
Room/board/expenses: N/A
Enrollment: N/A

University of California–Berkeley

545 Student Services Building
Berkeley, CA 94720-1900
mba.haas.berkeley.edu
Public
Admissions: (510) 642-1405
Email: mbaadm@haas.berkeley.edu
Financial aid: (510) 643-0183
Application deadline: 04/04
In-state tuition: full time: $60,987; part time: $3,363/credit hour
Out-of-state tuition: full time: $61,442; part time: $3,363/credit hour
Room/board/expenses: $30,346

College-funded aid: Yes
International student aid: Yes
Average student indebtedness at graduation: $99,328
Full-time enrollment: 590
men: 58%; women: 42%; minorities: 20%; international: 35%
Part-time enrollment: 823
men: 69%; women: 31%; minorities: N/A; international: N/A
Acceptance rate (full time): 15%
Average GMAT (full time): 726
Average GRE (full time): 165 verbal; 164 quantitative; 4.8 writing
Average GPA (full time): 3.67
Average age of entrants to full-time program: 28
Average months of prior work experience (full time): 65
TOEFL requirement: Yes
Minimum TOEFL score: 90
Most popular departments: entrepreneurship, finance, leadership, marketing, technology
Mean starting base salary for 2018 full-time graduates: $127,571
Employment location for 2018 class: Intl. N/A; N.E. 10%; M.A. 1%; S. 1%; M.W. 1%; S.W. 4%; W. 84%

University of California–Davis

1 Shields Avenue
Davis, CA 95616-8609
gsm.ucdavis.edu
Public
Admissions: (530) 752-7658
Email: admissions@gsm.ucdavis.edu
Financial aid: (530) 752-9246
Application deadline: 05/15
In-state tuition: full time: $39,568; part time: $1,520/credit hour
Out-of-state tuition: full time: $51,813; part time: $1,520/credit hour
Room/board/expenses: $25,008
College-funded aid: Yes
International student aid: Yes
Average student indebtedness at graduation: $67,972
Full-time enrollment: 91
men: 59%; women: 41%; minorities: 22%; international: 44%
Part-time enrollment: 292
men: 62%; women: 38%; minorities: 46%; international: 7%
Acceptance rate (full time): 39%
Average GMAT (full time): 671
Average GRE (full time): 162 verbal; 161 quantitative; N/A writing
Average GPA (full time): 3.22
Average age of entrants to full-time program: 30
Average months of prior work experience (full time): 76
TOEFL requirement: Yes
Minimum TOEFL score: 100
Most popular departments: entrepreneurship, finance, marketing, organizational behavior, technology
Mean starting base salary for 2018 full-time graduates: $99,569

Employment location for 2018 class: Intl. 11%; N.E. 3%; M.A. N/A; S. N/A; M.W. N/A; S.W. 3%; W. 83%

University of California–Irvine

5300 SB1, 4293 Pereira Drive
Irvine, CA 92697-3125
merage.uci.edu/
Public
Admissions: (949) 824-4622
Email: mba@merage.uci.edu
Financial aid: (949) 824-7967
Application deadline: 04/01
In-state tuition: full time: $45,288; total program: $95,697 (part time)
Out-of-state tuition: full time: $52,709; total program: $95,697 (part time)
Room/board/expenses: $33,817
College-funded aid: Yes
International student aid: Yes
Average student indebtedness at graduation: $74,973
Full-time enrollment: 157
men: 67%; women: 33%; minorities: 24%; international: 44%
Part-time enrollment: 339
men: 61%; women: 39%; minorities: 62%; international: 4%
Acceptance rate (full time): 27%
Average GMAT (full time): 667
Average GRE (full time): 157 verbal; 159 quantitative; 4.1 writing
Average GPA (full time): 3.53
Average age of entrants to full-time program: 29
Average months of prior work experience (full time): 60
TOEFL requirement: Yes
Minimum TOEFL score: 80
Most popular departments: entrepreneurship, finance, marketing, technology, other
Mean starting base salary for 2018 full-time graduates: $96,297
Employment location for 2018 class: Intl. 4%; N.E. 0%; M.A. 0%; S. 2%; M.W. 2%; S.W. 0%; W. 91%

University of California–Los Angeles

110 Westwood Plaza
Box 951481
Los Angeles, CA 90095-1481
www.anderson.ucla.edu
Public
Admissions: (310) 825-6944
Email: mba.admissions@anderson.ucla.edu
Financial aid: (310) 825-2746
Application deadline: 04/16
In-state tuition: full time: $64,292; part time: $42,420
Out-of-state tuition: full time: $64,292; part time: $42,420
Room/board/expenses: $34,406
College-funded aid: Yes
International student aid: Yes
Full-time enrollment: 723
men: 65%; women: 35%; minorities: 27%; international: 30%

Part-time enrollment: 938
men: 69%; women: 31%; minorities: 46%; international: 10%
Acceptance rate (full time): 24%
Average GMAT (full time): 716
Average GRE (full time): 163 verbal; 163 quantitative; 4.6 writing
Average GPA (full time): 3.52
Average age of entrants to full-time program: 28
Average months of prior work experience (full time): 61
TOEFL requirement: Yes
Minimum TOEFL score: 87
Most popular departments: consulting, entrepreneurship, finance, marketing, technology
Mean starting base salary for 2018 full-time graduates: $121,843
Employment location for 2018 class: Intl. 11%; N.E. 5%; M.A. 2%; S. 1%; M.W. 2%; S.W. 2%; W. 78%

University of California–Riverside

900 University Avenue
Riverside, CA 92521-0203
agsm.ucr.edu
Public
Admissions: (951) 827-6200
Email: ucr_agsm@ucr.edu
Financial aid: (951) 827-7249
Application deadline: 09/01
In-state tuition: full time: $44,963; part time: $1,379/credit hour
Out-of-state tuition: full time: $57,209; part time: N/A/credit hour
Room/board/expenses: $14,950
College-funded aid: Yes
International student aid: Yes
Average student indebtedness at graduation: $67,945
Full-time enrollment: 113
men: 61%; women: 39%; minorities: 34%; international: 58%
Part-time enrollment: 146
men: 58%; women: 42%; minorities: 35%; international: 49%
Acceptance rate (full time): 53%
Average GMAT (full time): 611
Average GRE (full time): 153 verbal; 153 quantitative; 3.6 writing
Average GPA (full time): 3.29
Average age of entrants to full-time program: 26
Average months of prior work experience (full time): 40
TOEFL requirement: Yes
Minimum TOEFL score: 80
Most popular departments: accounting, finance, general management, marketing, supply chain management/logistics
Mean starting base salary for 2018 full-time graduates: $66,976
Employment location for 2018 class: Intl. 16%; N.E. 0%; M.A. 0%; S. 5%; M.W. 0%; S.W. 3%; W. 76%

University of California–San Diego

9500 Gilman Drive, #0553
San Diego, CA 92093-0553
www.rady.ucsd.edu/
Public
Admissions: (858) 534-0864
Email: RadyGradAdmissions@ucsd.edu
Financial aid: (858) 534-4480
Application deadline: 06/01
In-state tuition: full time: $67,873; part time: $35,700
Out-of-state tuition: full time: $71,176; part time: $35,700
Room/board/expenses: $51,468
College-funded aid: Yes
International student aid: Yes
Full-time enrollment: 102
men: 73%; women: 27%; minorities: N/A; international: N/A
Part-time enrollment: 119
men: 62%; women: 38%; minorities: N/A; international: N/A
Acceptance rate (full time): 42%
Average GMAT (full time): 656
Average GRE (full time): 154 verbal; 159 quantitative; 3.9 writing
Average GPA (full time): 3.50
Average age of entrants to full-time program: 29
Average months of prior work experience (full time): 72
TOEFL requirement: Yes
Minimum TOEFL score: 85
Most popular departments: entrepreneurship, finance, general management, marketing, technology
Mean starting base salary for 2018 full-time graduates: $81,398
Employment location for 2018 class: Intl. 4%; N.E. 4%; M.A. 0%; S. 4%; M.W. 4%; S.W. 0%; W. 83%

University of San Diego

5998 Alcala Park
San Diego, CA 92110-2492
www.sandiego.edu/mba
Private
Admissions: (619) 260-4860
Email: gradbus@sandiego.edu
Financial aid: (619) 260-4514
Application deadline: 05/01
Tuition: full time: $1,475/credit hour; part time: $1,475/credit hour
Room/board/expenses: $19,467
College-funded aid: Yes
International student aid: Yes
Average student indebtedness at graduation: $67,340
Full-time enrollment: 80
men: 65%; women: 35%; minorities: 15%; international: 39%
Part-time enrollment: 108
men: 62%; women: 38%; minorities: 31%; international: 4%
Acceptance rate (full time): 62%
Average GMAT (full time): 614
Average GRE (full time): 153 verbal; 155 quantitative; 4.3 writing
Average GPA (full time): 3.20

Average age of entrants to full-time program: 27
Average months of prior work experience (full time): 52
TOEFL requirement: Yes
Minimum TOEFL score: 92
Most popular departments: entrepreneurship, finance, general management, marketing, supply chain management/logistics
Mean starting base salary for 2018 full-time graduates: $71,045

University of San Francisco

101 Howard Street, Suite 500
San Francisco, CA 94105-1080
www.usfca.edu/management/graduate/
Private
Admissions: (415) 422-2221
Email: management@usfca.edu
Financial aid: (415) 422-2020
Application deadline: 06/14
Tuition: full time: $1,475/credit hour; part time: $1,475/credit hour
Room/board/expenses: N/A
College-funded aid: Yes
International student aid: Yes
Full-time enrollment: 65
men: 45%; women: 55%; minorities: 34%; international: 37%
Part-time enrollment: 85
men: 58%; women: 42%; minorities: 46%; international: 2%
Acceptance rate (full time): 69%
Average GMAT (full time): 576
Average GRE (full time): 153 verbal; 155 quantitative; 3.6 writing
Average GPA (full time): 3.31
Average age of entrants to full-time program: 28
Average months of prior work experience (full time): 48
TOEFL requirement: Yes
Minimum TOEFL score: 92
Most popular departments: entrepreneurship, finance, marketing, organizational behavior, quantitative analysis/statistics and operations research
Mean starting base salary for 2018 full-time graduates: $91,389
Employment location for 2018 class: Intl. 6%; N.E. N/A; M.A. N/A; S. N/A; M.W. N/A; S.W. 6%; W. 89%

University of Southern California

University Park
Los Angeles, CA 90089-1421
www.marshall.usc.edu
Private
Admissions: (213) 740-7846
Email: marshallmba@marshall.usc.edu
Financial aid: (213) 740-1111
Application deadline: 04/15
Tuition: full time: $70,536; part time: $1,912/credit hour
Room/board/expenses: $24,980
College-funded aid: Yes
International student aid: Yes

Full-time enrollment: 449
men: 59%; women: 41%; minorities: 30%; international: 30%
Part-time enrollment: 526
men: 66%; women: 34%; minorities: 57%; international: 2%
Acceptance rate (full time): 28%
Average GMAT (full time): 705
Average GRE (full time): 159 verbal; 159 quantitative; 4.4 writing
Average GPA (full time): 3.50
Average age of entrants to full-time program: 28
Average months of prior work experience (full time): 62
TOEFL requirement: Yes
Minimum TOEFL score: 100
Mean starting base salary for 2018 full-time graduates: $122,634
Employment location for 2018 class: Intl. 7%; N.E. 7%; M.A. 1%; S. 3%; M.W. 5%; S.W. 2%; W. 75%

University of the Pacific[1]

3601 Pacific Avenue
Stockton, CA 95211
www.pacific.edu/mba
Private
Admissions: (209) 946-2629
Email: mba@pacific.edu
Financial aid: (209) 946-2421
Tuition: N/A
Room/board/expenses: N/A
Enrollment: N/A

Woodbury University[1]

7500 N. Glenoaks Boulevard
Burbank, CA 91504
woodbury.edu/
Private
Admissions: (818) 252-5221
Email: admissions@woodbury.edu
Financial aid: (818) 252-5273
Tuition: N/A
Room/board/expenses: N/A
Enrollment: N/A

COLORADO

Colorado State University[1]

1270 Campus Delivery
Fort Collins, CO 80523-1270
biz.colostate.edu/Academics/Graduate-Programs/Master-of-Business-Administration
Public
Admissions: (970) 491-1129
Email: gradadmissions@business.colostate.edu
Financial aid: (970) 491-6321
Tuition: N/A
Room/board/expenses: N/A
Enrollment: N/A

Colorado State University–Pueblo[1]

2200 Bonforte Boulevard
Pueblo, CO 81001
hsb.colostate-pueblo.edu
Public
Admissions: (719) 549-2461

Email:
info@colostate-pueblo.edu
Financial aid: N/A
Tuition: N/A
Room/board/expenses: N/A
Enrollment: N/A

University of Colorado–Boulder
995 Regent Drive, 419 UCB
Boulder, CO 80309
www.colorado.edu/business
Public
Admissions: (303) 492-2061
Email: leedsgrad@Colorado.edu
Financial aid: (303) 492-8223
Application deadline: 04/01
In-state tuition: total program:
$53,201 (full time); total
program: $49,800 (part time)
Out-of-state tuition: total
program: $62,501 (full
time); total program:
$49,800 (part time)
Room/board/expenses: $20,500
College-funded aid: Yes
International student aid: Yes
Full-time enrollment: 194
men: 69%; women:
31%; minorities: 14%;
international: 12%
Part-time enrollment: 159
men: 64%; women:
36%; minorities: 11%;
international: 5%
Acceptance rate (full time): 71%
Average GMAT (full time): 609
**Average GRE (full
time):** 156 verbal; 156
quantitative; N/A writing
Average GPA (full time): 3.30
**Average age of entrants to
full-time program:** 28
**Average months of prior work
experience (full time):** 60
TOEFL requirement: Yes
Minimum TOEFL score: 80
Most popular departments:
entrepreneurship, finance,
general management,
real estate, other
**Mean starting base salary for
2018 full-time graduates:** $80,049
**Employment location for
2018 class:** Intl. 2%; N.E.
0%; M.A. 0%; S. 0%; M.W.
4%; S.W. 88%; W. 6%

University of Colorado–Colorado Springs
1420 Austin Bluffs Parkway
Colorado Springs, CO 80918
www.uccs.edu/business/
programs/masters
Public
Admissions: (719) 255-3070
Email: cobgrad@uccs.edu
Financial aid: (719) 255-3460
Application deadline: 06/01
In-state tuition: full time: N/A;
part time: $745/credit hour
Out-of-state tuition: full time: N/A;
part time: $1,298/credit hour
Room/board/expenses: N/A
College-funded aid: Yes
International student aid: Yes
Full-time enrollment: N/A
men: N/A; women:
N/A; minorities: N/A;
international: N/A

Part-time enrollment: 333
men: 54%; women:
46%; minorities: 26%;
international: 3%
**Average GRE (full
time):** N/A verbal; N/A
quantitative; N/A writing
TOEFL requirement: Yes
Minimum TOEFL score: 85
Most popular departments:
accounting, finance, general
management, marketing, other

University of Colorado–Denver
Campus Box 165
PO Box 173364
Denver, CO 80217-3364
business.ucdenver.edu
Public
Admissions: (303) 315-8200
Email: bschool.admissions@
ucdenver.edu
Financial aid: (303) 315-1850
Application deadline: 04/15
In-state tuition: total program:
$42,500 (full time); part
time: $626/credit hour
Out-of-state tuition: total
program: $42,500 (full time);
part time: $1,378/credit hour
Room/board/expenses: N/A
College-funded aid: Yes
International student aid: Yes
Full-time enrollment: 43
men: 51%; women:
49%; minorities: 23%;
international: 9%
Part-time enrollment: 440
men: 60%; women:
40%; minorities: 21%;
international: 4%
Acceptance rate (full time): 72%
Average GMAT (full time): 538
**Average GRE (full
time):** 153 verbal; 149
quantitative; 3.5 writing
Average GPA (full time): 3.30
**Average age of entrants to
full-time program:** 30
TOEFL requirement: Yes
Minimum TOEFL score: 83

University of Denver
2101 S. University Boulevard
Denver, CO 80208
daniels.du.edu/
Private
Admissions: (303) 871-3416
Email: daniels@du.edu
Financial aid: (303) 871-7860
Application deadline: 03/01
Tuition: total program:
$91,006 (full time); part
time: $1,299/credit hour
Room/board/expenses: $19,113
College-funded aid: Yes
International student aid: Yes
Full-time enrollment: 55
men: 64%; women:
36%; minorities: 13%;
international: 13%
Part-time enrollment: 100
men: 65%; women:
35%; minorities: 17%;
international: 4%
Acceptance rate (full time): 46%
Average GMAT (full time): 603
**Average GRE (full
time):** 155 verbal; 155
quantitative; 4.4 writing
Average GPA (full time): 3.16

**Average age of entrants to
full-time program:** 28
**Average months of prior work
experience (full time):** 56
TOEFL requirement: Yes
Minimum TOEFL score: 94
Most popular departments:
accounting, finance,
international business,
marketing, other
**Mean starting base salary for
2018 full-time graduates:** $82,869
**Employment location for
2018 class:** Intl. 6%; N.E.
3%; M.A. 3%; S. 6%; M.W.
10%; S.W. 71%; W. 0%

University of Northern Colorado
800 17th Street
Greeley, CO 80639
mcb.unco.edu/
Public
Admissions: (970) 351-2831
Email: Grad.School@unco.edu
Financial aid: (970) 351-2502
Application deadline: rolling
In-state tuition: full time:
$597/credit hour; part
time: $597/credit hour
Out-of-state tuition: full
time: $597/credit hour; part
time: $597/credit hour
Room/board/expenses: $6,296
College-funded aid: Yes
International student aid: Yes
**Average student indebtedness
at graduation:** $16,622
Full-time enrollment: 15
men: 40%; women:
60%; minorities: 33%;
international: 0%
Part-time enrollment: 21
men: 57%; women:
43%; minorities: 10%;
international: 10%
Acceptance rate (full time): 81%
**Average GRE (full
time):** N/A verbal; N/A
quantitative; N/A writing
Average GPA (full time): 3.25
**Average age of entrants to
full-time program:** 28
TOEFL requirement: Yes
Minimum TOEFL score: 80
Most popular departments:
general management, health
care administration, human
resources management

CONNECTICUT

Central Connecticut State University
1615 Stanley Street
New Britain, CT 06050
www.ccsu.edu/mba
Public
Admissions: (860) 832-2350
Email: graduateadmissions@
ccsu.edu
Financial aid: (860) 832-2200
Application deadline: 06/10
In-state tuition: full time: N/A;
part time: $654/credit hour
Out-of-state tuition: full time: N/A;
part time: $654/credit hour
Room/board/expenses: N/A
College-funded aid: Yes

Full-time enrollment: N/A
men: N/A; women:
N/A; minorities: N/A;
international: N/A
Part-time enrollment: 218
men: 56%; women:
44%; minorities: N/A;
international: N/A
**Average GRE (full
time):** N/A verbal; N/A
quantitative; N/A writing
Minimum TOEFL score: N/A
Most popular departments:
accounting, finance, supply
chain management/logistics,
quantitative analysis/statistics
and operations research, other

Fairfield University
1073 N. Benson Road
Fairfield, CT 06824
www.fairfield.edu/dsb/
graduateprograms/mba/
Private
Admissions: (203) 254-4000
Email: dsbgrad@fairfield.edu
Financial aid: (203) 254-4000
Application deadline: 08/01
Tuition: full time: N/A; part
time: $975/credit hour
Room/board/expenses: N/A
College-funded aid: Yes
International student aid: No
Full-time enrollment: N/A
men: N/A; women:
N/A; minorities: N/A;
international: N/A
Part-time enrollment: 51
men: 63%; women:
37%; minorities: 10%;
international: 6%
**Average GRE (full
time):** N/A verbal; N/A
quantitative; N/A writing
TOEFL requirement: Yes
Minimum TOEFL score: 80
Most popular departments:
accounting, finance, general
management, marketing, other

Quinnipiac University
275 Mount Carmel Avenue
Hamden, CT 06518
www.quinnipiac.edu/
Private
Admissions: (800) 462-1944
Email: graduate@quinnipiac.edu
Financial aid: (203) 582-8384
Application deadline: 07/31
Tuition: full time: $1,035/
credit hour; part time:
$1,035/credit hour
Room/board/expenses: $22,770
College-funded aid: Yes
International student aid: Yes
**Average student indebtedness
at graduation:** $31,081
Full-time enrollment: 158
men: 58%; women:
42%; minorities: 17%;
international: 8%
Part-time enrollment: 23
men: 74%; women:
26%; minorities: 13%;
international: 4%
Acceptance rate (full time): 93%
Average GMAT (full time): 600
**Average GRE (full
time):** 149 verbal; 150
quantitative; N/A writing
Average GPA (full time): 3.53

**Average age of entrants to
full-time program:** 22
**Average months of prior work
experience (full time):** 2
TOEFL requirement: Yes
Minimum TOEFL score: 90
Most popular departments:
finance, general management,
health care administration,
marketing, supply chain
management/logistics
**Mean starting base salary for
2018 full-time graduates:** $60,773
**Employment location for
2018 class:** Intl. 1%; N.E.
90%; M.A. N/A; S. 1%; M.W.
1%; S.W. 2%; W. 6%

Sacred Heart University
5151 Park Avenue
Fairfield, CT 06825
www.sacredheart.edu/
academics/
jackwelchcollegeofbusiness/
Private
Admissions: (203) 365-4716
Email: gradstudies@
sacredheart.edu
Financial aid: (203) 371-7980
Application deadline: rolling
Tuition: full time: N/A; part
time: $935/credit hour
Room/board/expenses: N/A
College-funded aid: No
International student aid: No
Full-time enrollment: N/A
men: N/A; women:
N/A; minorities: N/A;
international: N/A
Part-time enrollment: 138
men: 52%; women:
48%; minorities: 18%;
international: 17%
**Average GRE (full
time):** N/A verbal; N/A
quantitative; N/A writing
TOEFL requirement: Yes
Minimum TOEFL score: 80
Most popular departments:
accounting, finance, human
resources management,
marketing, other

University of Connecticut
100 Constitution Plaza
Hartford, CT 06103
www.business.uconn.edu
Public
Admissions: (860) 728-2419
Email: mba@uconn.edu
Financial aid: (860) 486-2819
Application deadline: 06/01
In-state tuition: full time: $16,256;
part time: $900/credit hour
Out-of-state tuition: full
time: $37,866; part time:
$900/credit hour
Room/board/expenses: $27,000
College-funded aid: Yes
International student aid: Yes
**Average student indebtedness
at graduation:** $44,555
Full-time enrollment: 94
men: 68%; women:
32%; minorities: 14%;
international: 50%
Part-time enrollment: 980
men: 65%; women:
35%; minorities: 35%;
international: 0%

Acceptance rate (full time): 39%
Average GMAT (full time): 601
Average GRE (full time): 152 verbal; 157 quantitative; 3.8 writing
Average GPA (full time): 3.34
Average age of entrants to full-time program: 27
Average months of prior work experience (full time): 54
TOEFL requirement: Yes
Minimum TOEFL score: 90
Most popular departments: finance, general management, marketing, portfolio management, other
Mean starting base salary for 2018 full-time graduates: $89,622
Employment location for 2018 class: Intl. N/A; N.E. 78%; M.A. N/A; S. 17%; M.W. N/A; S.W. N/A; W. 6%

University of Hartford[1]

200 Bloomfield Avenue
West Hartford, CT 06117
www.hartford.edu/barney/
Private
Admissions: (860) 768-5003
Email: knight@hartford.edu
Financial aid: (860) 768-4296
Tuition: N/A
Room/board/expenses: N/A
Enrollment: N/A

University of New Haven

300 Boston Post Road
West Haven, CT 06516
www.newhaven.edu
Private
Admissions: (203) 932-7318
Email: graduate@newhaven.edu
Financial aid: (203) 932-7315
Application deadline: rolling
Tuition: full time: $915/credit hour; part time: $915/credit hour
Room/board/expenses: N/A
College-funded aid: Yes
International student aid: Yes
Full-time enrollment: 124
men: 55%; women: 45%; minorities: 22%; international: 47%
Part-time enrollment: 79
men: 51%; women: 49%; minorities: 33%; international: 6%
Acceptance rate (full time): 86%
Average GMAT (full time): 459
Average GRE (full time): 138 verbal; 140 quantitative; 2.4 writing
Average age of entrants to full-time program: 24
TOEFL requirement: Yes
Minimum TOEFL score: N/A
Most popular departments: accounting, finance, human resources management, sports business, tax

Western Connecticut State University[1]

181 White Street
Danbury, CT 06810
Public
Admissions: N/A
Financial aid: N/A

Tuition: N/A
Room/board/expenses: N/A
Enrollment: N/A

Yale University

165 Whitney Avenue
New Haven, CT 06511-3729
som.yale.edu
Private
Admissions: (203) 432-5635
Email: mba.admissions@yale.edu
Financial aid: (203) 432-5875
Application deadline: 04/16
Tuition: full time: $71,620; part time: N/A
Room/board/expenses: $25,545
College-funded aid: Yes
International student aid: Yes
Average student indebtedness at graduation: $98,250
Full-time enrollment: 723
men: 56%; women: 44%; minorities: 27%; international: 36%
Part-time enrollment: N/A
men: N/A; women: N/A; minorities: N/A; international: N/A
Acceptance rate (full time): 20%
Average GMAT (full time): 724
Average GRE (full time): 165 verbal; 163 quantitative; 4.9 writing
Average GPA (full time): 3.67
Average age of entrants to full-time program: 28
Average months of prior work experience (full time): 58
TOEFL requirement: No
Minimum TOEFL score: N/A
Most popular departments: economics, entrepreneurship, finance, general management, marketing
Mean starting base salary for 2018 full-time graduates: $126,390
Employment location for 2018 class: Intl. N/A; N.E. 48%; M.A. 8%; S. 3%; M.W. 8%; S.W. 7%; W. 27%

DELAWARE

Delaware State University[1]

1200 DuPont Highway
Dover, DE 19901
www.desu.edu/business-administration-mba-program
Public
Admissions: (302) 857-6978
Email: dkim@desu.edu
Financial aid: (302) 857-6250
Tuition: N/A
Room/board/expenses: N/A
Enrollment: N/A

University of Delaware

One South Main Street
Graduate and MBA Programs
Second Floor
Newark, DE 19716
lerner.udel.edu/
Public
Admissions: (302) 831-2221
Email: mbaprogram@udel.edu
Financial aid: (302) 831-8761
Application deadline: 07/01

In-state tuition: full time: $825/credit hour; part time: $825/credit hour
Out-of-state tuition: full time: $1,000/credit hour; part time: $1,000/credit hour
Room/board/expenses: $9,000
College-funded aid: Yes
International student aid: Yes
Average student indebtedness at graduation: $38,425
Full-time enrollment: 101
men: 58%; women: 42%; minorities: 15%; international: 50%
Part-time enrollment: 159
men: 57%; women: 43%; minorities: 30%; international: 5%
Acceptance rate (full time): 40%
Average GMAT (full time): 625
Average GRE (full time): 152 verbal; 159 quantitative; 4.0 writing
Average GPA (full time): 3.10
Average age of entrants to full-time program: 25
Average months of prior work experience (full time): 49
TOEFL requirement: Yes
Minimum TOEFL score: 100
Most popular departments: finance, general management, international business, leadership, quantitative analysis/statistics and operations research
Mean starting base salary for 2018 full-time graduates: $81,815
Employment location for 2018 class: Intl. 4%; N.E. 12%; M.A. 81%; S. N/A; M.W. 4%; S.W. N/A; W. N/A

DISTRICT OF COLUMBIA

American University

4400 Massachusetts Avenue NW
Washington, DC 20016
kogod.american.edu
Private
Admissions: (202) 885-1913
Email: kogodgrad@american.edu
Financial aid: (202) 885-1907
Application deadline: 05/01
Tuition: total program: $87,896 (full time); part time: N/A
Room/board/expenses: $23,200
College-funded aid: Yes
International student aid: Yes
Average student indebtedness at graduation: $92,922
Full-time enrollment: 63
men: 51%; women: 49%; minorities: 33%; international: 38%
Part-time enrollment: 21
men: 48%; women: 52%; minorities: 29%; international: 14%
Acceptance rate (full time): 79%
Average GMAT (full time): 503
Average GRE (full time): 151 verbal; 152 quantitative; 3.8 writing
Average GPA (full time): 3.29
Average age of entrants to full-time program: 28
Average months of prior work experience (full time): 58
TOEFL requirement: Yes
Minimum TOEFL score: 100

Most popular departments: accounting, consulting, finance, international business, quantitative analysis/statistics and operations research
Mean starting base salary for 2018 full-time graduates: $74,699
Employment location for 2018 class: Intl. N/A; N.E. N/A; M.A. 92%; S. N/A; M.W. N/A; S.W. N/A; W. 8%

Georgetown University

Rafik B. Hariri Building
37th and O Streets NW
Washington, DC 20057
msb.georgetown.edu
Private
Admissions: (202) 687-4200
Email: georgetownmba@georgetown.edu
Financial aid: (202) 687-4547
Application deadline: 10/09
Tuition: full time: $59,052; part time: $1,930/credit hour
Room/board/expenses: $27,948
College-funded aid: Yes
International student aid: Yes
Full-time enrollment: 541
men: 70%; women: 30%; minorities: 24%; international: 33%
Part-time enrollment: 423
men: 61%; women: 39%; minorities: 23%; international: 5%
Acceptance rate (full time): 55%
Average GMAT (full time): 693
Average GRE (full time): 159 verbal; 158 quantitative; 4.2 writing
Average GPA (full time): 3.34
Average age of entrants to full-time program: 28
Average months of prior work experience (full time): 67
TOEFL requirement: Yes
Minimum TOEFL score: 100
Most popular departments: consulting, finance, general management, marketing, technology
Mean starting base salary for 2018 full-time graduates: $116,946
Employment location for 2018 class: Intl. N/A; N.E. 31%; M.A. 43%; S. 3%; M.W. 8%; S.W. 1%; W. 15%

George Washington University

2201 G Street NW
Washington, DC 20052
business.gwu.edu/academics/programs/mba/global-mba
Private
Admissions: (202) 994-1212
Email: business@gwu.edu
Financial aid: (202) 994-7850
Application deadline: 06/07
Tuition: full time: $55,785; part time: $1,825/credit hour
Room/board/expenses: $25,300
College-funded aid: Yes
International student aid: Yes
Average student indebtedness at graduation: $87,716
Full-time enrollment: 129
men: 59%; women: 41%; minorities: 22%; international: 41%

Part-time enrollment: 174
men: 56%; women: 44%; minorities: 43%; international: 3%
Acceptance rate (full time): 60%
Average GMAT (full time): 611
Average GRE (full time): 155 verbal; 155 quantitative; 4.0 writing
Average GPA (full time): 3.20
Average age of entrants to full-time program: 28
Average months of prior work experience (full time): 55
TOEFL requirement: Yes
Minimum TOEFL score: 100
Most popular departments: finance, international business, leadership, marketing, quantitative analysis/statistics and operations research
Mean starting base salary for 2018 full-time graduates: $96,363
Employment location for 2018 class: Intl. 6%; N.E. 12%; M.A. 48%; S. 10%; M.W. 10%; S.W. 6%; W. 8%

Howard University

2600 Sixth Street NW, Suite 236
Washington, DC 20059
www.bschool.howard.edu/mba
Private
Admissions: (202) 806-1725
Email: MBA_bschool@howard.edu
Financial aid: (202) 806-2820
Application deadline: 04/01
Tuition: full time: $35,786; part time: $1,840/credit hour
Room/board/expenses: $24,364
College-funded aid: Yes
International student aid: Yes
Average student indebtedness at graduation: $59,810
Full-time enrollment: 50
men: 48%; women: 52%; minorities: 84%; international: 16%
Part-time enrollment: 21
men: 57%; women: 43%; minorities: 95%; international: 5%
Acceptance rate (full time): 45%
Average GMAT (full time): 485
Average GRE (full time): 151 verbal; 150 quantitative; 4.2 writing
Average GPA (full time): 3.24
Average age of entrants to full-time program: 26
Average months of prior work experience (full time): 36
TOEFL requirement: Yes
Minimum TOEFL score: 79
Most popular departments: finance, general management, international business, marketing, supply chain management/logistics
Mean starting base salary for 2018 full-time graduates: $103,164
Employment location for 2018 class: Intl. 0%; N.E. 21%; M.A. 32%; S. 26%; M.W. 5%; S.W. 11%; W. 5%

FLORIDA

Barry University[1]

11300 N.E. Second Avenue
Miami Shores, FL 33161-6695
www.barry.edu/mba
Private
Admissions: (305) 899-3146
Email: dfletcher@mail.barry.edu
Financial aid: (305) 899-3673
Tuition: N/A
Room/board/expenses: N/A
Enrollment: N/A

Florida Atlantic University

777 Glades Road
Boca Raton, FL 33431
www.business.fau.edu
Public
Admissions: (561) 297-3624
Email: graduatecollege@fau.edu
Financial aid: (561) 297-3530
Application deadline: 07/01
In-state tuition: full time: N/A;
part time: $304/credit hour
Out-of-state tuition: full time: N/A;
part time: $928/credit hour
Room/board/expenses: N/A
College-funded aid: Yes
International student aid: Yes
Full-time enrollment: N/A
men: N/A; women:
N/A; minorities: N/A;
international: N/A
Part-time enrollment: 163
men: 51%; women:
49%; minorities: N/A;
international: N/A
Average GRE (full time): N/A verbal; N/A
quantitative; N/A writing
TOEFL requirement: Yes
Minimum TOEFL score: 100
Most popular departments:
accounting, finance,
general management,
health care administration,
international business

Florida Gulf Coast University

10501 FGCU Boulevard S
Fort Myers, FL 33965-6565
www.fgcu.edu/CoB/
Public
Admissions: (239) 590-7908
Email: graduate@fgcu.edu
Financial aid: (239) 590-7920
Application deadline: 05/01
In-state tuition: full time:
N/A/credit hour; part
time: N/A/credit hour
Out-of-state tuition: full
time: N/A/credit hour; part
time: N/A/credit hour
Room/board/expenses: $17,592
College-funded aid: Yes
International student aid: Yes
Full-time enrollment: 35
men: 49%; women:
51%; minorities: 31%;
international: 0%
Part-time enrollment: 108
men: 44%; women:
56%; minorities: 31%;
international: 0%
Acceptance rate (full time): 87%
Average GMAT (full time): 500

Average GRE (full time): 151
verbal; 150 quantitative;
N/A writing
Average GPA (full time): 3.50
**Average age of entrants to
full-time program:** 27
TOEFL requirement: Yes
Minimum TOEFL score: 79
Most popular departments:
accounting, general
management, marketing,
management information
systems

Florida International University

1050 S.W. 112 Avenue, CBC 300
Miami, FL 33199-0001
business.fiu.edu
Public
Admissions: (305) 348-7398
Email: chapman@fiu.edu
Financial aid: (305) 348-7272
Application deadline: 07/01
In-state tuition: total program:
$37,000 (full time); total
program: $48,000 (part time)
Out-of-state tuition: total
program: $47,000 (full
time); total program:
$54,000 (part time)
Room/board/expenses: $18,000
College-funded aid: Yes
International student aid: Yes
Full-time enrollment: 29
men: 34%; women:
66%; minorities: 59%;
international: 38%
Part-time enrollment: 481
men: 42%; women:
58%; minorities: 83%;
international: 6%
Acceptance rate (full time): 35%
Average GMAT (full time): 548
**Average GRE (full
time):** 150 verbal; 150
quantitative; 3.4 writing
Average GPA (full time): 3.40
**Average age of entrants to
full-time program:** 25
**Average months of prior work
experience (full time):** 36
TOEFL requirement: Yes
Minimum TOEFL score: 80
Most popular departments:
finance, general
management, health care
administration, international
business, marketing
**Mean starting base salary for
2018 full-time graduates:** $48,333
**Employment location for
2018 class:** Intl. 0%; N.E.
0%; M.A. 0%; S. 67%; M.W.
0%; S.W. 0%; W. 33%

Florida Southern College

111 Lake Hollingsworth Drive
Lakeland, FL 33801
www.flsouthern.edu/
Private
Admissions: (863) 680-4205
Email: evening@flsouthern.edu
Financial aid: (863) 680-4140
Application deadline: 07/01
Tuition: full time: $775/
credit hour; part time: N/A
Room/board/expenses: N/A
College-funded aid: Yes

International student aid: Yes
**Average student indebtedness
at graduation:** $29,573
Full-time enrollment: 69
men: 57%; women:
43%; minorities: 23%;
international: 7%
Part-time enrollment: N/A
men: N/A; women:
N/A; minorities: N/A;
international: N/A
Acceptance rate (full time): 54%
Average GMAT (full time): 495
**Average GRE (full
time):** N/A verbal; N/A
quantitative; N/A writing
Average GPA (full time): 3.33
**Average age of entrants to
full-time program:** 35
**Average months of prior work
experience (full time):** 93
TOEFL requirement: Yes
Minimum TOEFL score: 79
Most popular departments:
accounting, general
management, health care
administration, supply chain
management/logistics
**Mean starting base salary for
2018 full-time graduates:** $65,950

Florida State University

Graduate Programs
233 Rovetta Building
Tallahassee, FL 32306-1110
business.fsu.edu/academics/
graduate-programs/
masters-degrees
Public
Admissions: (850) 644-6458
Email: gradprograms@
business.fsu.edu
Financial aid: (850) 644-5716
Application deadline: 06/01
In-state tuition: full time:
$480/credit hour; part
time: $480/credit hour
Out-of-state tuition: full time:
$1,110/credit hour; part
time: $1,110/credit hour
Room/board/expenses: $26,027
College-funded aid: Yes
International student aid: Yes
**Average student indebtedness
at graduation:** $24,883
Full-time enrollment: 54
men: 72%; women:
28%; minorities: 17%;
international: 9%
Part-time enrollment: 113
men: 64%; women:
36%; minorities: 27%;
international: 0%
Acceptance rate (full time): 61%
Average GMAT (full time): 564
**Average GRE (full
time):** 153 verbal; 152
quantitative; N/A writing
Average GPA (full time): 3.68
**Average age of entrants to
full-time program:** 24
**Average months of prior work
experience (full time):** 27
TOEFL requirement: Yes
Minimum TOEFL score: 100
Most popular departments:
human resources management,
insurance, management
information systems,
real estate, supply chain
management/logistics

**Mean starting base salary for
2018 full-time graduates:** $64,583
**Employment location for
2018 class:** Intl. 6%; N.E.
13%; M.A. 0%; S. 81%; M.W.
0%; S.W. 0%; W. 0%

Jacksonville University

2800 University Boulevard N
Jacksonville, FL 32211
www.ju.edu
Private
Admissions: (904) 256-7000
Email: admiss@ju.edu
Financial aid: (904) 256-7062
Application deadline: 08/01
Tuition: full time: $793/credit
hour; part time: $793/credit hour
Room/board/expenses: $26,676
College-funded aid: Yes
International student aid: Yes
Full-time enrollment: 55
men: 56%; women:
44%; minorities: 16%;
international: 33%
Part-time enrollment: 105
men: 69%; women:
31%; minorities: 27%;
international: 4%
Acceptance rate (full time): 95%
Average GMAT (full time): 327
**Average GRE (full
time):** 138 verbal; 142
quantitative; 2.5 writing
Average GPA (full time): 3.22
**Average age of entrants to
full-time program:** 24
TOEFL requirement: Yes
Minimum TOEFL score: 79
Most popular departments:
accounting, finance,
general management,
leadership, marketing
**Mean starting base salary for
2018 full-time graduates:** $47,333
**Employment location for 2018
class:** Intl. 0%; N.E. 33%;
M.A. 33%; S. 33%; M.W.
0%; S.W. 0%; W. 0%

Rollins College[1]

1000 Holt Avenue
Winter Park, FL 32789-4499
www.rollins.edu/business/
Private
Admissions: (407) 628-2405
Email: MBAADMISSIONS@
rollins.edu
Financial aid: (407) 646-2395
Tuition: N/A
Room/board/expenses: N/A
Enrollment: N/A

Stetson University

421 N. Woodland Boulevard
DeLand, FL 32723
www.stetson.edu/graduate
Private
Admissions: (386) 822-7100
Email: gradadmissions@
stetson.edu
Financial aid: (800) 688-7120
Application deadline: 08/01
Tuition: full time: $1,020/
credit hour; part time:
$1,020/credit hour
Room/board/expenses: N/A
College-funded aid: Yes
International student aid: Yes

**Average student indebtedness
at graduation:** $24,470
Full-time enrollment: 49
men: 43%; women:
57%; minorities: 24%;
international: 12%
Part-time enrollment: 25
men: 44%; women:
56%; minorities: 56%;
international: 0%
Acceptance rate (full time): 61%
Average GMAT (full time): 497
**Average GRE (full
time):** 149 verbal; 152
quantitative; N/A writing
Average GPA (full time): 3.45
**Average age of entrants to
full-time program:** 24
TOEFL requirement: Yes
Minimum TOEFL score: 90
**Mean starting base salary for
2018 full-time graduates:** $52,429

University of Central Florida

PO Box 161400
Orlando, FL 32816-1400
www.ucf.edu
Public
Admissions: (407) 235-3917
Email: cbagrad@ucf.edu
Financial aid: (407) 823-2827
Application deadline: 07/01
In-state tuition: total program:
$39,000 (full time); part
time: $370/credit hour
Out-of-state tuition: total
program: $39,000 (full time);
part time: $1,194/credit hour
Room/board/expenses: N/A
College-funded aid: Yes
International student aid: Yes
**Average student indebtedness
at graduation:** $17,404
Full-time enrollment: 41
men: 46%; women:
54%; minorities: 56%;
international: 0%
Part-time enrollment: 536
men: 53%; women:
47%; minorities: 47%;
international: 0%
Acceptance rate (full time): 51%
**Average GRE (full
time):** N/A verbal; N/A
quantitative; N/A writing
Average GPA (full time): 3.20
**Average age of entrants to
full-time program:** 26
**Average months of prior work
experience (full time):** 48
TOEFL requirement: Yes
Minimum TOEFL score: 91
Most popular departments:
accounting, entrepreneurship,
general management, human
resources management,
sports business

University of Florida

Hough Hall 310
Gainesville, FL 32611-7152
warrington.ufl.edu/mba/
Public
Admissions: (352) 392-7992
Email: floridamba@
warrington.ufl.edu
Financial aid: (352) 392-1275
Application deadline: 03/15
In-state tuition: full time:
$13,237; part time: $27,475

Out-of-state tuition: full time: $30,630; part time: $27,475
Room/board/expenses: $17,680
College-funded aid: Yes
International student aid: Yes
Average student indebtedness at graduation: $37,035
Full-time enrollment: 95
men: 77%; women: 23%; minorities: 26%; international: 13%
Part-time enrollment: 320
men: 64%; women: 36%; minorities: 34%; international: 11%
Acceptance rate (full time): 19%
Average GMAT (full time): 685
Average GRE (full time): 157 verbal; 153 quantitative; N/A writing
Average GPA (full time): 3.55
Average age of entrants to full-time program: 26
Average months of prior work experience (full time): 41
TOEFL requirement: Yes
Minimum TOEFL score: 80
Most popular departments: consulting, finance, human resources management, international business, marketing
Mean starting base salary for 2018 full-time graduates: $104,538
Employment location for 2018 class: Intl. 5%; N.E. 11%; M.A. 5%; S. 39%; M.W. 16%; S.W. 23%; W. 2%

University of Miami[1]

PO Box 248027
Coral Gables, FL 33124-6520
Private
Admissions: N/A
Financial aid: (305) 284-2270
Tuition: N/A
Room/board/expenses: N/A
Enrollment: N/A

University of North Florida

1 UNF Drive
Jacksonville, FL 32224-2645
www.unf.edu/coggin
Public
Admissions: (904) 620-1360
Email: graduateschool@unf.edu
Financial aid: (904) 620-5555
Application deadline: 08/01
In-state tuition: full time: N/A; part time: $408/credit hour
Out-of-state tuition: full time: N/A; part time: $933/credit hour
Room/board/expenses: N/A
College-funded aid: Yes
International student aid: Yes
Full-time enrollment: N/A
men: N/A; women: N/A; minorities: N/A; international: N/A
Part-time enrollment: 518
men: 50%; women: 50%; minorities: 25%; international: 7%
Average GRE (full time): N/A verbal; N/A quantitative; N/A writing
TOEFL requirement: Yes
Minimum TOEFL score: 80

Most popular departments: accounting, e-commerce, finance, general management, supply chain management/logistics

University of South Florida

4202 Fowler Avenue, BSN 3403
Tampa, FL 33620
www.mba.usf.edu
Public
Admissions: (813) 974-3335
Email: bsn-mba@usf.edu
Financial aid: (813) 974-4700
Application deadline: 07/01
In-state tuition: full time: $467/credit hour; part time: $467/credit hour
Out-of-state tuition: full time: $913/credit hour; part time: $913/credit hour
Room/board/expenses: $28,000
College-funded aid: Yes
International student aid: Yes
Average student indebtedness at graduation: $29,933
Full-time enrollment: 52
men: 52%; women: 48%; minorities: 23%; international: 12%
Part-time enrollment: 311
men: 57%; women: 43%; minorities: 26%; international: 17%
Acceptance rate (full time): 37%
Average GMAT (full time): 515
Average GRE (full time): 150 verbal; 149 quantitative; N/A writing
Average GPA (full time): 3.40
Average age of entrants to full-time program: 24
Average months of prior work experience (full time): 18
TOEFL requirement: Yes
Minimum TOEFL score: 79
Most popular departments: entrepreneurship, finance, leadership, marketing, sports business
Mean starting base salary for 2018 full-time graduates: $43,944

University of South Florida–Sarasota-Manatee

8350 N. Tamiami Trail
Sarasota, FL 34243
usfsm.edu/college-of-business
Public
Admissions: (941) 359-4331
Email: admissions@sar.usf.edu
Financial aid: (941) 359-4200
Application deadline: 07/01
In-state tuition: full time: N/A; part time: $381/credit hour
Out-of-state tuition: full time: N/A; part time: $826/credit hour
Room/board/expenses: N/A
College-funded aid: Yes
International student aid: Yes
Full-time enrollment: N/A
men: N/A; women: N/A; minorities: N/A; international: N/A
Part-time enrollment: 71
men: 59%; women: 41%; minorities: 37%; international: 0%

Average GRE (full time): N/A verbal; N/A quantitative; N/A writing
TOEFL requirement: Yes
Minimum TOEFL score: 79

University of South Florida–St. Petersburg[1]

140 7th Avenue S, BAY III
St. Petersburg, FL 33701
www.usfsp.edu/ktcob
Public
Admissions: (727) 873-4567
Email: applygrad@usfsp.edu
Financial aid: (727) 873-4128
Tuition: N/A
Room/board/expenses: N/A
Enrollment: N/A

University of Tampa

401 W. Kennedy Boulevard
Tampa, FL 33606-1490
grad.ut.edu
Private
Admissions: (813) 257-3642
Email: utgrad@ut.edu
Financial aid: (813) 253-6219
Application deadline: rolling
Tuition: full time: N/A; part time: N/A
Room/board/expenses: N/A
College-funded aid: Yes
International student aid: Yes
Average student indebtedness at graduation: $39,705
Full-time enrollment: 162
men: 54%; women: 46%; minorities: 7%; international: 41%
Part-time enrollment: 83
men: 58%; women: 42%; minorities: 17%; international: 12%
Acceptance rate (full time): 46%
Average GMAT (full time): 560
Average GRE (full time): 149 verbal; 153 quantitative; 4.0 writing
Average GPA (full time): 3.50
Average age of entrants to full-time program: 25
Average months of prior work experience (full time): 45
TOEFL requirement: Yes
Minimum TOEFL score: 90
Most popular departments: accounting, entrepreneurship, finance, marketing, technology
Mean starting base salary for 2018 full-time graduates: $72,375

University of West Florida[1]

11000 University Parkway
Pensacola, FL 32514
uwf.edu
Public
Admissions: (850) 474-2230
Email: mba@uwf.edu
Financial aid: N/A
Tuition: N/A
Room/board/expenses: N/A
Enrollment: N/A

GEORGIA

Augusta University

1120 15th Street
Augusta, GA 30912
www.augusta.edu/hull/
Public
Admissions: (706) 737-1418
Email: hull@augusta.edu
Financial aid: N/A
Application deadline: 06/01
In-state tuition: full time: N/A; part time: $222/credit hour
Out-of-state tuition: full time: N/A; part time: $738/credit hour
Room/board/expenses: N/A
College-funded aid: Yes
Full-time enrollment: N/A
men: N/A; women: N/A; minorities: N/A; international: N/A
Part-time enrollment: 71
men: 51%; women: 49%; minorities: 21%; international: 8%
Average GRE (full time): N/A verbal; N/A quantitative; N/A writing
Minimum TOEFL score: N/A

Berry College

PO Box 495024
Mount Berry, GA 30149-5024
www.berry.edu/academics/campbell/
Private
Admissions: (706) 236-2215
Email: admissions@berry.edu
Financial aid: (706) 236-1714
Application deadline: 07/20
Tuition: full time: $660/credit hour; part time: $660/credit hour
Room/board/expenses: N/A
College-funded aid: Yes
International student aid: Yes
Full-time enrollment: 3
men: 33%; women: 67%; minorities: N/A; international: N/A
Part-time enrollment: 38
men: 63%; women: 37%; minorities: N/A; international: N/A
Acceptance rate (full time): 75%
Average GMAT (full time): 410
Average GRE (full time): 144 verbal; 149 quantitative; N/A writing
Average GPA (full time): 3.13
Average age of entrants to full-time program: 24
Average months of prior work experience (full time): 48
TOEFL requirement: Yes
Minimum TOEFL score: 80
Most popular departments: general management

Clark Atlanta University

223 James P. Brawley Drive SW
Atlanta, GA 30314
www.cau.edu
Private
Admissions: (404) 880-8443
Email: mbaadmissions@cau.edu
Financial aid: (404) 880-6265
Application deadline: 04/01
Tuition: full time: $28,386; part time: N/A
Room/board/expenses: $17,912

College-funded aid: Yes
International student aid: No
Full-time enrollment: 31
men: 39%; women: 61%; minorities: 87%; international: 6%
Part-time enrollment: 2
men: 100%; women: 0%; minorities: 50%; international: 50%
Acceptance rate (full time): 68%
Average GMAT (full time): 351
Average GRE (full time): 145 verbal; 143 quantitative; 3.2 writing
Average GPA (full time): 3.32
Average age of entrants to full-time program: 25
TOEFL requirement: Yes
Minimum TOEFL score: 61
Most popular departments: accounting, marketing
Mean starting base salary for 2018 full-time graduates: $71,000

Clayton State University[1]

2000 Clayton State Boulevard
Morrow, GA 30260-0285
www.clayton.edu/mba
Public
Admissions: (678) 466-4113
Email: graduate@clayton.edu
Financial aid: (678) 466-4185
Tuition: N/A
Room/board/expenses: N/A
Enrollment: N/A

Columbus State University

4225 University Avenue
Columbus, GA 31907
www.columbusstate.edu
Public
Admissions: (706) 507-8800
Email: alexander_viola@columbusstate.edu
Financial aid: (706) 507-8807
Application deadline: 06/30
In-state tuition: total program: $10,455 (full time); part time: $255/credit hour
Out-of-state tuition: total program: $32,805 (full time); part time: $1,000/credit hour
Room/board/expenses: $14,500
College-funded aid: Yes
International student aid: Yes
Full-time enrollment: 21
men: 52%; women: 48%; minorities: 48%; international: 10%
Part-time enrollment: 33
men: 45%; women: 55%; minorities: 27%; international: 6%
Acceptance rate (full time): 60%
Average GRE (full time): 147 verbal; 150 quantitative; 3.0 writing
Average GPA (full time): 3.12
Average age of entrants to full-time program: 24
Average months of prior work experience (full time): 36
TOEFL requirement: Yes
Minimum TOEFL score: 79
Most popular departments: general management, human resources management, leadership

Emory University

1300 Clifton Road NE
Atlanta, GA 30322
www.goizueta.emory.edu
Private
Admissions: (404) 727-6311
Email: mbaadmissions@
emory.edu
Financial aid: (404) 727-6039
Application deadline: 03/09
Tuition: full time: $63,064; total
program: $80,628 (part time)
Room/board/expenses: $25,518
College-funded aid: Yes
International student aid: Yes
**Average student indebtedness
at graduation:** $77,053
Full-time enrollment: 349
men: 70%; women:
30%; minorities: 25%;
international: 26%
Part-time enrollment: 264
men: 64%; women:
36%; minorities: 27%;
international: 11%
Acceptance rate (full time): 41%
Average GMAT (full time): 686
**Average GRE (full
time):** N/A verbal; N/A
quantitative; N/A writing
Average GPA (full time): 3.30
**Average age of entrants to
full-time program:** 28
**Average months of prior work
experience (full time):** 67
TOEFL requirement: Yes
Minimum TOEFL score: 100
Most popular departments:
consulting, finance,
general management,
marketing, production/
operations management
**Mean starting base salary for 2018
full-time graduates:** $120,861
**Employment location for 2018
class:** Intl. 4%; N.E. 13%;
M.A. 5%; S. 58%; M.W.
8%; S.W. 5%; W. 8%

Georgia College & State University[1]

Campus Box 019
Milledgeville, GA 31061
mba.gcsu.edu
Public
Admissions: (478) 445-6283
Email: grad-admit@gcsu.edu
Financial aid: (478) 445-5149
Tuition: N/A
Room/board/expenses: N/A
Enrollment: N/A

Georgia Institute of Technology

800 W. Peachtree Street NW
Atlanta, GA 30332-0520
scheller.gatech.edu
Public
Admissions: (404) 894-8722
Email: mba@scheller.gatech.edu
Financial aid: (404) 894-4160
Application deadline: 06/01
In-state tuition: full time: $31,248;
part time: $1,121/credit hour
Out-of-state tuition: full
time: $42,196; part time:
$1,524/credit hour
Room/board/expenses: $18,736
College-funded aid: Yes
International student aid: Yes

Full-time enrollment: 167
men: 69%; women:
31%; minorities: 22%;
international: 20%
Part-time enrollment: 357
men: 65%; women:
35%; minorities: 29%;
international: 3%
Acceptance rate (full time): 35%
Average GMAT (full time): 681
**Average GRE (full
time):** 159 verbal; 162
quantitative; N/A writing
Average GPA (full time): 3.40
**Average age of entrants to
full-time program:** 28
**Average months of prior work
experience (full time):** 57
TOEFL requirement: Yes
Minimum TOEFL score: 95
Most popular departments:
consulting, entrepreneurship,
production/operations
management, supply
chain management/
logistics, technology
**Mean starting base salary for
2018 full-time graduates:** $112,729

Georgia Southern University

PO Box 8002
Statesboro, GA 30460-8050
coba.georgiasouthern.edu/mba
Public
Admissions: (912) 478-2357
Email: mba@
georgiasouthern.edu
Financial aid: (912) 478-5413
Application deadline: 07/31
In-state tuition: full time: $4,912;
part time: $410/credit hour
Out-of-state tuition: full
time: $14,856; part time:
$1,238/credit hour
Room/board/expenses: N/A
College-funded aid: Yes
International student aid: Yes
Full-time enrollment: 40
men: 80%; women:
20%; minorities: 23%;
international: 13%
Part-time enrollment: 41
men: 68%; women:
32%; minorities: 27%;
international: 2%
**Average GRE (full
time):** N/A verbal; N/A
quantitative; N/A writing
TOEFL requirement: Yes
Minimum TOEFL score: 80

Georgia Southwestern State University[1]

800 Georgia Southwestern
State University Drive
Americus, GA 31709
gsw.edu/
Public
Admissions: N/A
Financial aid: N/A
Tuition: N/A
Room/board/expenses: N/A
Enrollment: N/A

Georgia State University

35 Broad Street
Atlanta, GA 30302-3989
robinson.gsu.edu/
Public
Admissions: (404) 413-7305
Email: rcbgradadmissions@
gsu.edu
Financial aid: (404) 413-2600
Application deadline: 06/01
In-state tuition: full time: N/A;
part time: $491/credit hour
Out-of-state tuition: full time: N/A;
part time: $1,300/credit hour
Room/board/expenses: N/A
College-funded aid: Yes
International student aid: Yes
Full-time enrollment: N/A
men: N/A; women:
N/A; minorities: N/A;
international: N/A
Part-time enrollment: 320
men: 55%; women:
45%; minorities: 46%;
international: 9%
**Average GRE (full
time):** N/A verbal; N/A
quantitative; N/A writing
TOEFL requirement: Yes
Minimum TOEFL score: 90
Most popular departments:
finance, general management,
health care administration,
management information
systems, quantitative
analysis/statistics and
operations research

Kennesaw State University

560 Parliament Garden Way
MD 0401
Kennesaw, GA 30144
graduate.kennesaw.edu/
admissions/
Public
Admissions: (470) 578-4377
Email: ksugrad@kennesaw.edu
Financial aid: (470) 578-2044
Application deadline: 07/01
In-state tuition: full time:
N/A; total program:
$18,456 (part time)
Out-of-state tuition: full
time: N/A; total program:
$50,964 (part time)
Room/board/expenses: N/A
College-funded aid: Yes
International student aid: Yes
Full-time enrollment: N/A
men: N/A; women:
N/A; minorities: N/A;
international: N/A
Part-time enrollment: 219
men: 53%; women:
47%; minorities: 43%;
international: 0%
**Average GRE (full
time):** N/A verbal; N/A
quantitative; N/A writing
TOEFL requirement: Yes
Minimum TOEFL score: 80
Most popular departments:
accounting, economics, general
management, international
business, marketing

Mercer University–Atlanta

3001 Mercer University Drive
Atlanta, GA 30341-4155
business.mercer.edu
Private
Admissions: (678) 547-6300
Email: business.admissions@
mercer.edu
Financial aid: (678) 547-6444
Application deadline: 06/15
Tuition: full time: $818/credit
hour; part time: $755/credit hour
Room/board/expenses: $0
College-funded aid: No
International student aid: No
**Average student indebtedness
at graduation:** $17,343
Full-time enrollment: 46
men: 59%; women:
41%; minorities: 17%;
international: 0%
Part-time enrollment: 347
men: 56%; women:
44%; minorities: 41%;
international: 22%
Acceptance rate (full time): 40%
Average GMAT (full time): 518
**Average GRE (full
time):** 150 verbal; 153
quantitative; N/A writing
Average GPA (full time): 3.21
**Average age of entrants to
full-time program:** 27
**Average months of prior work
experience (full time):** 36
TOEFL requirement: Yes
Minimum TOEFL score: 80
Most popular departments:
accounting, economics,
finance, health care
administration, marketing
**Mean starting base salary for
2018 full-time graduates:** $61,360

Savannah State University

PO Box 20359
Savannah, GA 31404
www.savannahstate.edu/coba/
programs-mba.shtml
Public
Admissions: (912) 358-3393
Email: mba@savannahstate.edu
Financial aid: (912) 358-4162
Application deadline: rolling
In-state tuition: full time:
N/A; part time: N/A
Out-of-state tuition: full
time: N/A; part time: N/A
Room/board/expenses: N/A
College-funded aid: Yes
Full-time enrollment: N/A
men: N/A; women:
N/A; minorities: N/A;
international: N/A
Part-time enrollment: 62
men: 31%; women:
69%; minorities: N/A;
international: N/A
**Average GRE (full
time):** N/A verbal; N/A
quantitative; N/A writing
TOEFL requirement: Yes
Minimum TOEFL score: N/A

University of Georgia

600 South Lumpkin Street
Athens, GA 30602
terry.uga.edu/mba
Public
Admissions: (706) 542-5671
Email: georgiamba@uga.edu
Financial aid: (706) 542-6147
Application deadline: 06/01
In-state tuition: full time:
$15,670; total program:
$56,400 (part time)
Out-of-state tuition: full time:
$34,378; total program:
$72,000 (part time)
Room/board/expenses: $21,874
College-funded aid: Yes
International student aid: Yes
**Average student indebtedness
at graduation:** $36,603
Full-time enrollment: 102
men: 64%; women:
36%; minorities: 13%;
international: 23%
Part-time enrollment: 283
men: 61%; women:
39%; minorities: 36%;
international: 1%
Acceptance rate (full time): 32%
Average GMAT (full time): 665
**Average GRE (full
time):** 157 verbal; 158
quantitative; 4.2 writing
Average GPA (full time): 3.53
**Average age of entrants to
full-time program:** 26
**Average months of prior work
experience (full time):** 39
TOEFL requirement: Yes
Minimum TOEFL score: 100
Most popular departments:
finance, human resources
management, marketing,
management information
systems, production/
operations management
**Mean starting base salary for
2018 full-time graduates:** $95,460
**Employment location for
2018 class:** Intl. 0%; N.E.
5%; M.A. 5%; S. 70%; M.W.
11%; S.W. 0%; W. 8%

University of North Georgia

82 College Circle
Dahlonega, GA 30597
ung.edu/mike-cottrell-
college-of-business/
academic-programs/
the-cottrell-mba.php
Public
Admissions: (706) 864-2077
Email: grads@ung.edu
Financial aid: (706) 864-1412
Application deadline: 04/15
In-state tuition: full time: N/A;
part time: $520/credit hour
Out-of-state tuition: full time: N/A;
part time: $520/credit hour
Room/board/expenses: N/A
College-funded aid: Yes
International student aid: Yes
Full-time enrollment: N/A
men: N/A; women:
N/A; minorities: N/A;
international: N/A
Part-time enrollment: 76
men: 55%; women:
45%; minorities: 26%;
international: 0%

Average GRE (full time): N/A verbal; N/A quantitative; N/A writing
TOEFL requirement: Yes
Minimum TOEFL score: 79
Most popular departments: technology

University of West Georgia

1601 Maple Street
Carrollton, GA 30118-3000
www.westga.edu/academics/business/index.php
Public
Admissions: (678) 839-5355
Email: hudombon@westga.edu
Financial aid: (678) 839-6421
Application deadline: 07/15
In-state tuition: full time: N/A; part time: $6,110
Out-of-state tuition: full time: N/A; part time: $17,900
Room/board/expenses: N/A
College-funded aid: Yes
International student aid: Yes
Full-time enrollment: N/A men: N/A; women: N/A; minorities: N/A; international: N/A
Part-time enrollment: 104 men: 42%; women: 58%; minorities: 34%; international: 8%
Average GRE (full time): N/A verbal; N/A quantitative; N/A writing
TOEFL requirement: Yes
Minimum TOEFL score: N/A
Most popular departments: accounting, economics, finance, general management

Valdosta State University[1]

1500 N. Patterson Street
Valdosta, GA 31698
www.valdosta.edu/lcoba/grad/
Public
Admissions: (229) 245-3822
Email: mschnake@valdosta.edu
Financial aid: (229) 333-5935
Tuition: N/A
Room/board/expenses: N/A
Enrollment: N/A

HAWAII

University of Hawaii–Manoa

2404 Maile Way
Business Administration C-204
Honolulu, HI 96822
www.shidler.hawaii.edu
Public
Admissions: (808) 956-8266
Email: mba@hawaii.edu
Financial aid: (808) 956-7251
Application deadline: N/A
In-state tuition: full time: $887/credit hour; part time: $887/credit hour
Out-of-state tuition: full time: $1,598/credit hour; part time: $1,598/credit hour
Room/board/expenses: $20,500
College-funded aid: Yes
International student aid: Yes

Full-time enrollment: 42 men: 67%; women: 33%; minorities: 64%; international: 7%
Part-time enrollment: 40 men: 45%; women: 55%; minorities: 25%; international: 0%
Acceptance rate (full time): 83%
Average GMAT (full time): 573
Average GRE (full time): 151 verbal; 154 quantitative; 3.3 writing
Average GPA (full time): 3.26
Average age of entrants to full-time program: 30
Average months of prior work experience (full time): 79
TOEFL requirement: Yes
Minimum TOEFL score: N/A
Most popular departments: accounting, entrepreneurship, finance, health care administration, international business

IDAHO

Boise State University

1910 University Drive
MBEB4101
Boise, ID 83725-1600
cobe.boisestate.edu/graduate-programs-overview/
Public
Admissions: (208) 426-3116
Email: graduatebusiness@boisestate.edu
Financial aid: (208) 426-1664
Application deadline: rolling
In-state tuition: full time: $10,364; part time: $7,442
Out-of-state tuition: full time: $26,446; part time: $12,188
Room/board/expenses: N/A
College-funded aid: Yes
International student aid: Yes
Average student indebtedness at graduation: $41,270
Full-time enrollment: 63 men: 54%; women: 46%; minorities: 10%; international: 17%
Part-time enrollment: 76 men: 61%; women: 39%; minorities: 11%; international: 4%
Acceptance rate (full time): 94%
Average GMAT (full time): 503
Average GRE (full time): 156 verbal; 151 quantitative; 3.8 writing
Average GPA (full time): 3.34
Average age of entrants to full-time program: 27
Average months of prior work experience (full time): 29
TOEFL requirement: Yes
Minimum TOEFL score: 95
Mean starting base salary for 2018 full-time graduates: $62,316

Idaho State University[1]

921 S. 8th Ave Stop 8020
Pocatello, ID 83209
www.isu.edu/cob/mba.shtml
Public
Admissions: (208) 282-2966
Email: mba@isu.edu

Financial aid: N/A
Tuition: N/A
Room/board/expenses: N/A
Enrollment: N/A

University of Idaho[1]

PO Box 443161
Moscow, ID 83844-3161
www.uidaho.edu
Public
Admissions: (800) 885-4001
Email: graduateadmissions@uidaho.edu
Financial aid: N/A
Tuition: N/A
Room/board/expenses: N/A
Enrollment: N/A

ILLINOIS

Bradley University

1501 W. Bradley Avenue
Peoria, IL 61625
www.bradley.edu/academic/colleges/fcba/programs/grad/mba/
Private
Admissions: (309) 677-3714
Email: mba@bradley.edu
Financial aid: (309) 677-3085
Application deadline: 08/01
Tuition: full time: N/A; part time: $31,150
Room/board/expenses: N/A
College-funded aid: No
International student aid: Yes
Full-time enrollment: N/A men: N/A; women: N/A; minorities: N/A; international: N/A
Part-time enrollment: 45 men: 69%; women: 31%; minorities: 9%; international: 24%
Average GRE (full time): N/A verbal; N/A quantitative; N/A writing
TOEFL requirement: Yes
Minimum TOEFL score: 79
Most popular departments: accounting, finance, general management

DePaul University

1 E. Jackson Boulevard
Chicago, IL 60604-2287
www.kellstadt.depaul.edu/
Private
Admissions: (312) 362-8810
Email: kgsb@depaul.edu
Financial aid: (312) 362-8091
Application deadline: 08/01
Tuition: full time: N/A; total program: $78,960 (part time)
Room/board/expenses: N/A
College-funded aid: Yes
International student aid: Yes
Full-time enrollment: N/A men: N/A; women: N/A; minorities: N/A; international: N/A
Part-time enrollment: 872 men: 56%; women: 44%; minorities: 31%; international: 2%
Average GRE (full time): N/A verbal; N/A quantitative; N/A writing
TOEFL requirement: Yes
Minimum TOEFL score: 80

Dominican University

7900 West Division Street
River Forest, IL 60305
www.dom.edu/business
Private
Admissions: (708) 524-6562
Email: gbalcazar@dom.edu
Financial aid: (708) 524-6950
Application deadline: rolling
Tuition: full time: N/A; part time: $1,009/credit hour
Room/board/expenses: N/A
College-funded aid: Yes
International student aid: Yes
Full-time enrollment: N/A men: N/A; women: N/A; minorities: N/A; international: N/A
Part-time enrollment: 119 men: 39%; women: 61%; minorities: 39%; international: 18%
Average GRE (full time): N/A verbal; N/A quantitative; N/A writing
TOEFL requirement: Yes
Minimum TOEFL score: 79
Most popular departments: finance, health care administration, international business, marketing, quantitative analysis/statistics and operations research

Eastern Illinois University[1]

600 Lincoln Avenue
Charleston, IL 61920-3099
www.eiu.edu/mba/
Public
Admissions: (217) 581-3028
Email: mba@eiu.edu
Financial aid: (217) 581-6405
Tuition: N/A
Room/board/expenses: N/A
Enrollment: N/A

Governors State University

1 University Parkway
University Park, IL 60484
www.govst.edu
Public
Admissions: (708) 534-4490
Email: admissions@govst.edu
Financial aid: (708) 534-4480
Application deadline: rolling
In-state tuition: full time: N/A; part time: $406/credit hour
Out-of-state tuition: full time: N/A; part time: $812/credit hour
Room/board/expenses: N/A
College-funded aid: Yes
International student aid: No
Full-time enrollment: N/A men: N/A; women: N/A; minorities: N/A; international: N/A
Part-time enrollment: 87 men: 38%; women: 62%; minorities: 59%; international: 1%
Average GRE (full time): N/A verbal; N/A quantitative; N/A writing
TOEFL requirement: Yes
Minimum TOEFL score: 80
Most popular departments: finance, general management, leadership, supply chain management/logistics

---

Illinois Institute of Technology[1]

10 W. 35th Street
Chicago, IL 60616
www.stuart.iit.edu
Private
Admissions: (312) 567-3020
Email: admission@stuart.iit.edu
Financial aid: (312) 567-7219
Tuition: N/A
Room/board/expenses: N/A
Enrollment: N/A

Illinois State University

MBA Program
Campus Box 5570
Normal, IL 61790-5570
business.illinoisstate.edu/mba/
Public
Admissions: (309) 438-2181
Email: admissions@ilstu.edu
Financial aid: (309) 438-2231
Application deadline: 07/01
In-state tuition: full time: N/A; part time: $404/credit hour
Out-of-state tuition: full time: N/A; part time: $838/credit hour
Room/board/expenses: N/A
College-funded aid: Yes
International student aid: Yes
Full-time enrollment: N/A men: N/A; women: N/A; minorities: N/A; international: N/A
Part-time enrollment: 126 men: 58%; women: 42%; minorities: N/A; international: N/A
Average GRE (full time): N/A verbal; N/A quantitative; N/A writing
TOEFL requirement: Yes
Minimum TOEFL score: 80
Most popular departments: finance, human resources management, insurance, leadership, marketing

Loyola University Chicago

820 N. Michigan Avenue
Chicago, IL 60611
www.luc.edu/quinlan/
Private
Admissions: (312) 915-8908
Email: quinlangrad@luc.edu
Financial aid: (773) 508-7704
Application deadline: 07/15
Tuition: full time: N/A; part time: $1,496/credit hour
Room/board/expenses: N/A
College-funded aid: Yes
International student aid: Yes
Full-time enrollment: N/A men: N/A; women: N/A; minorities: N/A; international: N/A
Part-time enrollment: 251 men: 53%; women: 47%; minorities: 28%; international: 7%
Average GRE (full time): N/A verbal; N/A quantitative; N/A writing
TOEFL requirement: Yes
Minimum TOEFL score: 90

Most popular departments:
accounting, finance, health care administration, human resources management, marketing

Northeastern Illinois University

5500 North St. Louis Avenue
Chicago, IL 60625-4699
www.neiu.edu/academics/
college-of-business-and-
management/graduate-
programs-business/master-
business-administration
Public
Admissions: (773) 442-6114
Email: cobm-grad@neiu.edu
Financial aid: N/A
Application deadline: rolling
In-state tuition: full time: $404/credit hour; part time: $404/credit hour
Out-of-state tuition: full time: $808/credit hour; part time: $808/credit hour
Room/board/expenses: $14,175
Full-time enrollment: 17
men: 65%; women: 35%; minorities: 29%; international: 41%
Part-time enrollment: 70
men: 56%; women: 44%; minorities: 36%; international: 6%
Average GRE (full time): N/A verbal; N/A quantitative; N/A writing
TOEFL requirement: Yes
Minimum TOEFL score: 79

Northern Illinois University

Office of MBA Programs
Barsema Hall 203
DeKalb, IL 60115-2897
cob.niu.edu/academics/mba/
index.shtml
Public
Admissions: (866) 648-6221
Email: mba@niu.edu
Financial aid: (815) 753-1300
Application deadline: 07/15
In-state tuition: total program: $26,050 (full time); part time: $896/credit hour
Out-of-state tuition: total program: $36,800 (full time); part time: N/A/credit hour
Room/board/expenses: $15,000
College-funded aid: Yes
International student aid: Yes
Full-time enrollment: 31
men: 61%; women: 39%; minorities: 32%; international: 29%
Part-time enrollment: 294
men: 71%; women: 29%; minorities: N/A; international: N/A
Acceptance rate (full time): 63%
Average GMAT (full time): 450
Average GRE (full time): N/A verbal; N/A quantitative; N/A writing
Average GPA (full time): 3.34
Average age of entrants to full-time program: 24
Average months of prior work experience (full time): 9
TOEFL requirement: Yes
Minimum TOEFL score: 80

Most popular departments:
accounting, leadership, manufacturing and technology management, marketing, management information systems

Northwestern University

2211 Campus Drive
Evanston, IL 60208-2001
www.kellogg.northwestern.edu
Private
Admissions: (847) 491-3308
Email: mbaadmissions@
kellogg.northwestern.edu
Financial aid: (847) 491-3308
Application deadline: 04/10
Tuition: full time: $73,074; part time: $6,950/credit hour
Room/board/expenses: $22,497
College-funded aid: Yes
International student aid: Yes
Full-time enrollment: 1,304
men: 58%; women: 42%; minorities: N/A; international: N/A
Part-time enrollment: 776
men: 72%; women: 28%; minorities: N/A; international: N/A
Acceptance rate (full time): 22%
Average GMAT (full time): 732
Average GRE (full time): N/A verbal; N/A quantitative; N/A writing
Average GPA (full time): 3.60
Average age of entrants to full-time program: 28
Average months of prior work experience (full time): 61
TOEFL requirement: Yes
Minimum TOEFL score: N/A
Most popular departments:
economics, finance, general management, marketing, organizational behavior
Mean starting base salary for 2018 full-time graduates: $128,415
Employment location for 2018 class: Intl. N/A; N.E. 20%; M.A. 3%; S. 4%; M.W. 31%; S.W. 6%; W. 37%

Southern Illinois University–Carbondale

133 Rehn Hall
Carbondale, IL 62901-4625
business.siu.edu/
academics/mba/
Public
Admissions: (618) 453-3030
Email: gradprograms@
business.siu.edu
Financial aid: (618) 453-4334
Application deadline: 07/31
In-state tuition: full time: $13,376; part time: N/A
Out-of-state tuition: full time: $26,053; part time: N/A
Room/board/expenses: $18,313
College-funded aid: Yes
International student aid: Yes
Average student indebtedness at graduation: $38,417
Full-time enrollment: 57
men: 63%; women: 37%; minorities: N/A; international: N/A

Part-time enrollment: N/A
men: N/A; women: N/A; minorities: N/A; international: N/A
Acceptance rate (full time): 69%
Average GMAT (full time): 585
Average GRE (full time): N/A verbal; N/A quantitative; N/A writing
Average GPA (full time): 3.54
Average age of entrants to full-time program: 27
Average months of prior work experience (full time): 60
TOEFL requirement: Yes
Minimum TOEFL score: 80
Most popular departments:
finance, general management, marketing, other

Southern Illinois University–Edwardsville

Box 1051
Edwardsville, IL 62026-1051
www.siue.edu/business
Public
Admissions: (618) 650-3840
Email: mba@siue.edu
Financial aid: (618) 650-3880
Application deadline: rolling
In-state tuition: full time: N/A; part time: $5,163
Out-of-state tuition: full time: N/A; part time: $11,101
Room/board/expenses: N/A
College-funded aid: Yes
International student aid: Yes
Full-time enrollment: N/A
men: N/A; women: N/A; minorities: N/A; international: N/A

Part-time enrollment: 93
men: 58%; women: 42%; minorities: 14%; international: 3%
Average GRE (full time): N/A verbal; N/A quantitative; N/A writing
TOEFL requirement: Yes
Minimum TOEFL score: 79
Most popular departments:
accounting, finance, general management, management information systems

St. Xavier University

3700 West 103rd Street
Chicago, IL 60655
www.sxu.edu/academics/
colleges_schools/gsm/
Private
Admissions: (773) 298-3053
Email: graduateadmission@
sxu.edu
Financial aid: (773) 398-3070
Application deadline: rolling
Tuition: full time: N/A; part time: $999/credit hour
Room/board/expenses: N/A
College-funded aid: Yes
International student aid: Yes
Full-time enrollment: N/A
men: N/A; women: N/A; minorities: N/A; international: N/A
Part-time enrollment: 303
men: 48%; women: 52%; minorities: 47%; international: 0%

Average GRE (full time): N/A verbal; N/A quantitative; N/A writing
TOEFL requirement: Yes
Minimum TOEFL score: 80
Most popular departments:
accounting, finance, general management, human resources management, marketing

University of Chicago

5807 S. Woodlawn Avenue
Chicago, IL 60637
ChicagoBooth.edu
Private
Admissions: (773) 834-3881
Email: admissions@
ChicagoBooth.edu
Financial aid: (773) 702-3964
Application deadline: 04/04
Tuition: full time: $73,209; part time: $7,130/credit hour
Room/board/expenses: $27,099
College-funded aid: Yes
International student aid: Yes
Full-time enrollment: 1,179
men: 59%; women: 41%; minorities: 28%; international: 32%
Part-time enrollment: 1,322
men: 73%; women: 27%; minorities: 25%; international: 19%
Acceptance rate (full time): 23%
Average GMAT (full time): 731
Average GRE (full time): N/A verbal; N/A quantitative; N/A writing
Average GPA (full time): 3.58
Average age of entrants to full-time program: 28
Average months of prior work experience (full time): 60
TOEFL requirement: Yes
Minimum TOEFL score: 104
Most popular departments:
economics, entrepreneurship, finance, organizational behavior, other
Mean starting base salary for 2018 full-time graduates: $131,893
Employment location for 2018 class: Intl. N/A; N.E. 26%; M.A. 3%; S. 37%; M.W. 2%; S.W. 5%; W. 27%

University of Illinois–Chicago

601 South Morgan Street
University Hall, 11th Floor
Chicago, IL 60607
business.uic.edu/liautaud
Public
Admissions: (312) 996-4573
Email: lgsb@uic.edu
Financial aid: (312) 996-3126
Application deadline: 07/15
In-state tuition: full time: N/A; part time: $17,546
Out-of-state tuition: full time: N/A; part time: $25,706
Room/board/expenses: N/A
College-funded aid: Yes
International student aid: Yes
Full-time enrollment: N/A
men: N/A; women: N/A; minorities: N/A; international: N/A
Part-time enrollment: 235
men: 61%; women: 39%; minorities: 38%; international: 10%

Average GRE (full time): N/A verbal; N/A quantitative; N/A writing
TOEFL requirement: Yes
Minimum TOEFL score: 80
Most popular departments:
accounting, finance, general management, human resources management, marketing

University of Chicago

5807 S. Woodlawn Avenue

Average GRE (full time): N/A verbal; N/A quantitative; N/A writing
TOEFL requirement: Yes
Minimum TOEFL score: 80
Most popular departments:
accounting, entrepreneurship, finance, general management, marketing

University of Illinois–Springfield

1 University Plaza
MS UHB 4000
Springfield, IL 62703
www.uis.edu/admissions
Public
Admissions: (888) 977-4847
Email: admissions@uis.edu
Financial aid: (217) 206-6724
Application deadline: N/A
In-state tuition: full time: N/A/credit hour; part time: $329/credit hour
Out-of-state tuition: full time: N/A/credit hour; part time: $675/credit hour
Room/board/expenses: N/A
College-funded aid: Yes
International student aid: Yes
Full-time enrollment: N/A
men: N/A; women: N/A; minorities: N/A; international: N/A
Part-time enrollment: 82
men: 57%; women: 43%; minorities: 15%; international: 18%
Average GRE (full time): N/A verbal; N/A quantitative; N/A writing
TOEFL requirement: Yes
Minimum TOEFL score: 79

University of Illinois–Urbana-Champaign

515 E. Gregory Drive
3019 BIF, MC 520
Champaign, IL 61820
www.mba.illinois.edu
Public
Admissions: (217) 333-8221
Email: mba@illinois.edu
Financial aid: (217) 333-0100
Application deadline: 03/15
In-state tuition: total program: $55,376 (full time); part time: N/A
Out-of-state tuition: total program: $79,784 (full time); part time: N/A
Room/board/expenses: $27,420
College-funded aid: Yes
International student aid: Yes
Full-time enrollment: 94
men: 67%; women: 33%; minorities: 26%; international: 37%
Part-time enrollment: 114
men: 62%; women: 38%; minorities: N/A; international: N/A
Acceptance rate (full time): 39%
Average GMAT (full time): 666
Average GRE (full time): 154 verbal; 154 quantitative; N/A writing
Average GPA (full time): 3.32
Average age of entrants to full-time program: 27
Average months of prior work experience (full time): 46
TOEFL requirement: Yes

Minimum TOEFL score: 102
Most popular departments: consulting, finance, general management, marketing, technology
Mean starting base salary for 2018 full-time graduates: $91,500
Employment location for 2018 class: Intl. 3%; N.E. 8%; M.A. 13%; S. 8%; M.W. 48%; S.W. 15%; W. 8%

Western Illinois University

1 University Circle
Macomb, IL 61455
www.wiu.edu/cbt
Public
Admissions: (309) 298-2442
Email: ca-conrad1@wiu.edu
Financial aid: (309) 298-2446
Application deadline: rolling
In-state tuition: full time: $324/credit hour; part time: $324/credit hour
Out-of-state tuition: full time: $324/credit hour; part time: $324/credit hour
Room/board/expenses: $13,046
College-funded aid: Yes
International student aid: Yes
Average student indebtedness at graduation: $17,548
Full-time enrollment: 32
men: 53%; women: 47%; minorities: 16%; international: 9%
Part-time enrollment: 73
men: 71%; women: 29%; minorities: 12%; international: 4%
Acceptance rate (full time): 100%
Average GRE (full time): N/A verbal; N/A quantitative; N/A writing
Average age of entrants to full-time program: 38
TOEFL requirement: Yes
Minimum TOEFL score: 79
Most popular departments: accounting, economics, finance, general management, supply chain management/logistics

INDIANA

Ball State University[1]

Whitinger Building,147
Muncie, IN 47306
www.bsu.edu/mba/
Public
Admissions: (765) 285-1931
Email: mba@bsu.edu
Financial aid: (765) 285-5600
Tuition: N/A
Room/board/expenses: N/A
Enrollment: N/A

Butler University

4600 Sunset Avenue
Indianapolis, IN 46208-3485
www.butler.edu/mba
Private
Admissions: (317) 940-9842
Email: mba@butler.edu
Financial aid: (317) 940-8200
Application deadline: 07/15
Tuition: full time: N/A; part time: $850/credit hour
Room/board/expenses: N/A
College-funded aid: No

International student aid: No
Full-time enrollment: N/A
men: N/A; women: N/A; minorities: N/A; international: N/A
Part-time enrollment: 148
men: 65%; women: 35%; minorities: 11%; international: 7%
Average GRE (full time): N/A verbal; N/A quantitative; N/A writing
TOEFL requirement: Yes
Minimum TOEFL score: 79
Most popular departments: entrepreneurship, finance, international business, leadership, marketing

Indiana State University

MBA Program
30 N 7th Street
Federal Hall, Room 114
Terre Haute, IN 47809
www.indstate.edu/mba
Public
Admissions: (812) 237-2002
Email: ISU-MBA@ mail.indstate.edu
Financial aid: (800) 841-4744
Application deadline: rolling
In-state tuition: full time: $412/credit hour; part time: $412/credit hour
Out-of-state tuition: full time: $809/credit hour; part time: $809/credit hour
Room/board/expenses: $14,480
College-funded aid: Yes
International student aid: Yes
Average student indebtedness at graduation: $29,050
Full-time enrollment: 35
men: 37%; women: 63%; minorities: 20%; international: 31%
Part-time enrollment: 56
men: 66%; women: 34%; minorities: 13%; international: 13%
Acceptance rate (full time): 61%
Average GMAT (full time): 533
Average GRE (full time): 145 verbal; 150 quantitative; 3.5 writing
Average GPA (full time): 3.23
Average age of entrants to full-time program: 30
Average months of prior work experience (full time): 60
TOEFL requirement: Yes
Minimum TOEFL score: 79
Most popular departments: accounting, finance, marketing, production/operations management, supply chain management/logistics
Mean starting base salary for 2018 full-time graduates: $47,833
Employment location for 2018 class: Intl. 0%; N.E. 0%; M.A. 0%; S. 0%; M.W. 100%; S.W. 0%; W. 0%

Indiana University

1275 E. 10th Street
Suite CG 2010
Bloomington, IN 47405-1703
kelley.iu.edu/programs/ full-time-mba
Public
Admissions: (812) 855-8006

Email: iumba@indiana.edu
Financial aid: (812) 855-1618
Application deadline: 04/15
In-state tuition: full time: $29,224; part time: $17,802
Out-of-state tuition: full time: $52,126; part time: $30,546
Room/board/expenses: $19,000
College-funded aid: Yes
International student aid: Yes
Average student indebtedness at graduation: $57,079
Full-time enrollment: 388
men: 68%; women: 32%; minorities: 23%; international: 32%
Part-time enrollment: 288
men: 83%; women: 17%; minorities: 19%; international: 28%
Acceptance rate (full time): 38%
Average GMAT (full time): 675
Average GRE (full time): 158 verbal; 157 quantitative; 4.5 writing
Average GPA (full time): 3.33
Average age of entrants to full-time program: 28
Average months of prior work experience (full time): 66
TOEFL requirement: Yes
Minimum TOEFL score: 100
Most popular departments: finance, general management, marketing, supply chain management/logistics, other
Mean starting base salary for 2018 full-time graduates: $108,164
Employment location for 2018 class: Intl. 5%; N.E. 9%; M.A. 7%; S. 6%; M.W. 49%; S.W. 6%; W. 19%

Indiana University–Kokomo[1]

2300 S. Washington Street
Kokomo, IN 46904-9003
www.iuk.edu/index.php
Public
Admissions: (765) 455-9275
Financial aid: N/A
Tuition: N/A
Room/board/expenses: N/A
Enrollment: N/A

Indiana University Northwest

3400 Broadway
Gary, IN 46408-1197
www.iun.edu/business/ index.htm
Public
Admissions: (219) 980-6635
Email: iunbiz@iun.edu
Financial aid: (219) 980-6539
Application deadline: 08/01
In-state tuition: full time: N/A; part time: N/A
Out-of-state tuition: full time: N/A; part time: N/A
Room/board/expenses: N/A
College-funded aid: Yes
International student aid: No
Full-time enrollment: N/A
men: N/A; women: N/A; minorities: N/A; international: N/A
Part-time enrollment: 30
men: 57%; women: 43%; minorities: N/A; international: N/A

Average GRE (full time): N/A verbal; N/A quantitative; N/A writing
TOEFL requirement: Yes
Minimum TOEFL score: N/A

Indiana University–South Bend

1700 Mishawaka Avenue
PO Box 7111
South Bend, IN 46634-7111
business.iusb.edu
Public
Admissions: (574) 520-4839
Email: graduate@iusb.edu
Financial aid: (574) 520-4357
Application deadline: 07/15
In-state tuition: full time: N/A; part time: $350/credit hour
Out-of-state tuition: full time: N/A; part time: $785/credit hour
Room/board/expenses: N/A
College-funded aid: Yes
International student aid: Yes
Full-time enrollment: N/A
men: N/A; women: N/A; minorities: N/A; international: N/A
Part-time enrollment: 80
men: 60%; women: 40%; minorities: N/A; international: N/A
Average GRE (full time): N/A verbal; N/A quantitative; N/A writing
TOEFL requirement: Yes
Minimum TOEFL score: N/A
Most popular departments: finance

Indiana University–Southeast

4201 Grant Line Road
New Albany, IN 47150
www.ius.edu/graduatebusiness
Public
Admissions: (812) 941-2364
Email: iusmba@ius.edu
Financial aid: (812) 941-2246
Application deadline: 07/20
In-state tuition: full time: N/A; part time: $427/credit hour
Out-of-state tuition: full time: N/A; part time: $879/credit hour
Room/board/expenses: N/A
College-funded aid: Yes
International student aid: Yes
Full-time enrollment: N/A
men: N/A; women: N/A; minorities: N/A; international: N/A
Part-time enrollment: 210
men: 70%; women: 30%; minorities: 13%; international: 2%
Average GRE (full time): N/A verbal; N/A quantitative; N/A writing
TOEFL requirement: Yes
Minimum TOEFL score: 81

Purdue University–Fort Wayne[1]

2101 E. Coliseum Boulevard
Fort Wayne, IN 46805-1499
www.ipfw.edu/mba
Public
Admissions: (260) 481-6498
Email: mba@ipfw.edu
Financial aid: (260) 481-6820

Tuition: N/A
Room/board/expenses: N/A
Enrollment: N/A

Purdue University–Northwest

2200 169th Street
Hammond, IN 46323
academics.pnw.edu/ business/mba/
Public
Admissions: (219) 989-3150
Email: Kimberly. Nikolovski@pnw.edu
Financial aid: (219) 989-2301
Application deadline: 07/15
In-state tuition: full time: N/A/credit hour; part time: $292/credit hour
Out-of-state tuition: full time: N/A/credit hour; part time: $438/credit hour
Room/board/expenses: N/A
College-funded aid: Yes
Full-time enrollment: N/A
men: N/A; women: N/A; minorities: N/A; international: N/A
Part-time enrollment: 119
men: 55%; women: 45%; minorities: 29%; international: 18%
Average GRE (full time): N/A verbal; N/A quantitative; N/A writing
TOEFL requirement: Yes
Minimum TOEFL score: 80
Most popular departments: accounting, finance, management information systems, quantitative analysis/statistics and operations research, other

Purdue University–West Lafayette

100 S. Grant Street
Rawls Hall, Room 2020
West Lafayette, IN 47907-2076
krannert.purdue.edu/masters/ home.php
Public
Admissions: (765) 494-0773
Email: krannertmasters@ purdue.edu
Financial aid: (765) 494-0998
Application deadline: 05/01
In-state tuition: full time: $22,408; total program: $50,984 (part time)
Out-of-state tuition: full time: $32,966; total program: $59,194 (part time)
Room/board/expenses: $13,030
College-funded aid: Yes
International student aid: Yes
Average student indebtedness at graduation: $63,261
Full-time enrollment: 93
men: 67%; women: 33%; minorities: 12%; international: 55%
Part-time enrollment: 82
men: 66%; women: 34%; minorities: 29%; international: 11%
Acceptance rate (full time): 49%
Average GMAT (full time): 633
Average GRE (full time): 159 verbal; 159 quantitative; 4.5 writing
Average GPA (full time): 3.26

Average age of entrants to full-time program: 28
Average months of prior work experience (full time): 65
TOEFL requirement: Yes
Minimum TOEFL score: 93
Most popular departments: finance, human resources management, marketing, production/operations management, supply chain management/logistics
Mean starting base salary for 2018 full-time graduates: $86,826

University of Notre Dame

204 Mendoza College of Business
Notre Dame, IN 46556
mendoza.nd.edu/programs/mba-programs/
Private
Admissions: (574) 631-8488
Email: mba.business@nd.edu
Financial aid: (574) 631-6436
Application deadline: 04/09
Tuition: full time: $54,770; part time: N/A
Room/board/expenses: $20,650
College-funded aid: Yes
International student aid: Yes
Average student indebtedness at graduation: $64,529
Full-time enrollment: 281
men: 73%; women: 27%; minorities: 15%; international: 27%
Part-time enrollment: N/A
men: N/A; women: N/A; minorities: N/A; international: N/A
Acceptance rate (full time): 48%
Average GMAT (full time): 671
Average GRE (full time): 158 verbal; 156 quantitative; 4.3 writing
Average GPA (full time): 3.36
Average age of entrants to full-time program: 28
Average months of prior work experience (full time): 65
TOEFL requirement: Yes
Minimum TOEFL score: 100
Most popular departments: consulting, finance, leadership, marketing, other
Mean starting base salary for 2018 full-time graduates: $111,178
Employment location for 2018 class: Intl. 3%; N.E. 11%; M.A. 12%; S. 12%; M.W. 38%; S.W. 9%; W. 14%

University of Southern Indiana

8600 University Boulevard
Evansville, IN 47712
www.usi.edu/business/
Public
Admissions: (812) 465-7015
Email: graduate.studies@usi.edu
Financial aid: (812) 464-1767
Application deadline: rolling
In-state tuition: full time: $9,820; part time: $388/credit hour
Out-of-state tuition: full time: $18,704; part time: $757/credit hour
Room/board/expenses: $13,350

College-funded aid: Yes
International student aid: Yes
Full-time enrollment: 165
men: 56%; women: 44%; minorities: 15%; international: 7%
Part-time enrollment: 176
men: 55%; women: 45%; minorities: 16%; international: 1%
Average GRE (full time): 148 verbal; 147 quantitative; 3.3 writing
Average GPA (full time): 3.16
Average age of entrants to full-time program: 27
TOEFL requirement: Yes
Minimum TOEFL score: 79
Most popular departments: general management, health care administration, human resources management, quantitative analysis/statistics and operations research, other

Valparaiso University

Urschel Hall
1909 Chapel Drive
Valparaiso, IN 46383
www.valpo.edu/mba/
Private
Admissions: (219) 465-7952
Email: mba@valpo.edu
Financial aid: (219) 464-5015
Application deadline: 06/30
Tuition: total program: $30,852 (full time); total program: $31,164 (part time)
Room/board/expenses: $21,969
College-funded aid: No
International student aid: No
Average student indebtedness at graduation: $25,792
Full-time enrollment: 3
men: 67%; women 33%; minorities: 0%; international: 0%
Part-time enrollment: 33
men: 52%; women: 48%; minorities: 21%; international: 0%
Acceptance rate (full time): 83%
Average GMAT (full time): 590
Average GRE (full time): N/A verbal; N/A quantitative; N/A writing
Average GPA (full time): 3.02
Average age of entrants to full-time program: 21
Average months of prior work experience (full time): 23
TOEFL requirement: Yes
Minimum TOEFL score: 90
Most popular departments: finance, general management, manufacturing and technology management, technology
Mean starting base salary for 2018 full-time graduates: $60,000
Employment location for 2018 class: Intl. 0%; N.E. 0%; M.A. 0%; S. 0%; M.W. 100%; S.W. 0%; W. 0%

IOWA

Drake University

2847 University Avenue
Des Moines, IA 50311
www.drake.edu/mba
Private
Admissions: (515) 271-2188
Email: cbpa.gradprograms@drake.edu

Financial aid: (515) 271-3048
Application deadline: 08/01
Tuition: full time: N/A; part time: $655/credit hour
Room/board/expenses: N/A
College-funded aid: Yes
International student aid: Yes
Full-time enrollment: N/A
men: N/A; women: N/A; minorities: N/A; international: N/A
Part-time enrollment: 97
men: 55%; women: 45%; minorities: 9%; international: 5%
Average GRE (full time): N/A verbal; N/A quantitative; N/A writing
TOEFL requirement: Yes
Minimum TOEFL score: 80
Most popular departments: finance, general management, health care administration, leadership, other

Iowa State University

1360 Gerdin Business Building
Ames, IA 50011-2027
www.business.iastate.edu
Public
Admissions: (515) 294-8118
Email: busgrad@iastate.edu
Financial aid: N/A
Application deadline: 07/01
In-state tuition: full time: $12,784; part time: $642/credit hour
Out-of-state tuition: full time: $27,254; part time: N/A/credit hour
Room/board/expenses: $13,000
College-funded aid: Yes
International student aid: Yes
Full-time enrollment: 79
men: 61%; women: 39%; minorities: 9%; international: 37%
Part-time enrollment: 41
men: 66%; women: 34%; minorities: 15%; international: 0%
Acceptance rate (full time): 74%
Average GMAT (full time): 607
Average GRE (full time): 150 verbal; 153 quantitative; 4.0 writing
Average GPA (full time): 3.52
Average age of entrants to full-time program: 23
Average months of prior work experience (full time): 14
TOEFL requirement: Yes
Minimum TOEFL score: 100
Most popular departments: finance, marketing, management information systems, supply chain management/logistics, other
Mean starting base salary for 2018 full-time graduates: $66,656
Employment location for 2018 class: Intl. 0%; N.E. 7%; M.A. 0%; S. 7%; M.W. 68%; S.W. 7%; W. 11%

University of Iowa

108 John Pappajohn Business Building, Suite W160
Iowa City, IA 52242-1000
tippie.uiowa.edu/future-graduate-students/mba-programs
Public
Admissions: (800) 622-4692

Email: iowamba@uiowa.edu
Financial aid: N/A
Application deadline: 08/01
In-state tuition: full time: N/A; part time: $30,150
Out-of-state tuition: full time: N/A; part time: $30,150
Room/board/expenses: N/A
College-funded aid: No
International student aid: No
Full-time enrollment: N/A
men: N/A; women: N/A; minorities: N/A; international: N/A
Part-time enrollment: 923
men: 63%; women: 37%; minorities: 12%; international: 5%
Average GRE (full time): N/A verbal; N/A quantitative; N/A writing
TOEFL requirement: Yes
Minimum TOEFL score: 100
Most popular departments: finance, general management, leadership, marketing, quantitative analysis/statistics and operations research

University of Northern Iowa

Curris Business Building 316
Cedar Falls, IA 50614-0123
www.cba.uni.edu/mba/
Public
Admissions: (319) 273-6243
Email: mba@uni.edu
Financial aid: (319) 273-2700
Application deadline: 07/01
In-state tuition: full time: N/A; part time: $606/credit hour
Out-of-state tuition: full time: N/A; part time: $1,187/credit hour
Room/board/expenses: N/A
College-funded aid: Yes
International student aid: No
Full-time enrollment: N/A
men: N/A; women: N/A; minorities: N/A; international: N/A
Part-time enrollment: 198
men: 48%; women: 52%; minorities: 2%; international: 71%
Average GRE (full time): N/A verbal; N/A quantitative; N/A writing
TOEFL requirement: Yes
Minimum TOEFL score: 79
Most popular departments: general management

KANSAS

Emporia State University[1]

1 Kellogg Circle
ESU Box 4039
Emporia, KS 66801-5087
emporia.edu/business/programs/mba
Public
Admissions: (800) 950-4723
Email: gradinfo@emporia.edu
Financial aid: (620) 341-5457
Tuition: N/A
Room/board/expenses: N/A
Enrollment: N/A

Kansas State University

2004 Business Building, 1301 Lovers Lane
Manhattan, KS 66506-0501
www.cba.ksu.edu/cba/
Public
Admissions: (785) 532-7190
Email: gradbusiness@ksu.edu
Financial aid: (785) 532-6420
Application deadline: 02/01
In-state tuition: full time: $419/credit hour; part time: $419/credit hour
Out-of-state tuition: full time: $946/credit hour; part time: $946/credit hour
Room/board/expenses: $22,000
College-funded aid: Yes
International student aid: Yes
Full-time enrollment: 50
men: 66%; women: 34%; minorities: 26%; international: 14%
Part-time enrollment: 15
men: 27%; women: 73%; minorities: 27%; international: 0%
Acceptance rate (full time): 71%
Average GMAT (full time): 555
Average GRE (full time): N/A verbal; N/A quantitative; N/A writing
Average GPA (full time): 3.42
Average age of entrants to full-time program: 27
Average months of prior work experience (full time): 73
TOEFL requirement: Yes
Minimum TOEFL score: 79
Most popular departments: finance, general management, management information systems, supply chain management/logistics

Pittsburg State University[1]

1701 S. Broadway
Pittsburg, KS 66762
www.pittstate.edu/business/departments-programs/mba
Public
Admissions: (620) 235-4180
Email: jsmiller@pittstate.edu
Financial aid: (620) 235-4240
Tuition: N/A
Room/board/expenses: N/A
Enrollment: N/A

University of Kansas

1654 Naismith Drive
Lawrence, KS 66045-7585
www.mba.ku.edu
Public
Admissions: (785) 864-6738
Email: bschoolmba@ku.edu
Financial aid: (785) 864-4700
Application deadline: 06/01
In-state tuition: full time: $681/credit hour; part time: $697/credit hour
Out-of-state tuition: full time: $1,239/credit hour; part time: $1,254/credit hour
Room/board/expenses: $14,000
College-funded aid: Yes
International student aid: Yes
Average student indebtedness at graduation: $32,251

More @ usnews.com/bschool

Full-time enrollment: 57
men: 65%; women:
35%; minorities: 19%;
international: 5%
Part-time enrollment: 72
men: 72%; women:
28%; minorities: 17%;
international: 10%
Acceptance rate (full time): 72%
Average GMAT (full time): 585
Average GRE (full
time): 153 verbal; 155
quantitative; 3.7 writing
Average GPA (full time): 3.17
Average age of entrants to
full-time program: 28
Average months of prior work
experience (full time): 42
TOEFL requirement: Yes
Minimum TOEFL score: N/A
Most popular departments:
finance, general management,
marketing, supply chain
management/logistics
Mean starting base salary for
2018 full-time graduates: $67,000

Washburn University[1]

1700 S.W. College Avenue
Topeka, KS 66621
www.washburn.edu/business
Public
Admissions: N/A
Financial aid: N/A
Tuition: N/A
Room/board/expenses: N/A
Enrollment: N/A

Wichita State University

1845 N. Fairmount, Box 48
Wichita, KS 67260-0048
www.wichita.edu/mba
Public
Admissions: (316) 978-3230
Email: grad.business@
wichita.edu
Financial aid: (316) 978-3430
Application deadline: 07/01
In-state tuition: full time: N/A;
part time: $302/credit hour
Out-of-state tuition: full time: N/A;
part time: $302/credit hour
Room/board/expenses: N/A
College-funded aid: Yes
International student aid: Yes
Full-time enrollment: N/A
men: N/A; women:
N/A; minorities: N/A;
international: N/A
Part-time enrollment: 209
men: 60%; women:
40%; minorities: 24%;
international: 8%
Average GRE (full
time): N/A verbal; N/A
quantitative; N/A writing
TOEFL requirement: Yes
Minimum TOEFL score: 88
Most popular departments:
accounting, finance, health care
administration, management
information systems, supply
chain management/logistics

KENTUCKY

Bellarmine University

2001 Newburg Road
Louisville, KY 40205-0671
www.bellarmine.edu/mba/
Private
Admissions: (502) 272-7200
Email: gradadmissions@
bellarmine.edu
Financial aid: (502) 272-7300
Application deadline: rolling
Tuition: full time: N/A;
part time: N/A
Room/board/expenses: N/A
College-funded aid: Yes
International student aid: Yes
Full-time enrollment: 59
men: 69%; women:
31%; minorities: 10%;
international: 2%
Part-time enrollment: 39
men: 62%; women:
38%; minorities: 15%;
international: 0%
Acceptance rate (full time): 100%
Average GMAT (full time): 450
Average GRE (full
time): 149 verbal; 149
quantitative; 3.3 writing
Average GPA (full time): 3.29
Average age of entrants to
full-time program: 26
TOEFL requirement: Yes
Minimum TOEFL score: 80
Most popular departments:
consulting, finance, leadership,
marketing, quantitative
analysis/statistics and
operations research

Eastern Kentucky University[1]

521 Lancaster Avenue
Richmond, KY 40475
cbt.eku.edu/
Public
Admissions: (859) 622-1742
Email: graduateschool@eku.edu
Financial aid: N/A
Tuition: N/A
Room/board/expenses: N/A
Enrollment: N/A

Morehead State University[1]

Combs Building 214
Morehead, KY 40351
www.moreheadstate.edu/mba
Public
Admissions: (606) 783-2000
Email: admissions@
moreheadstate.edu
Financial aid: N/A
Tuition: N/A
Room/board/expenses: N/A
Enrollment: N/A

Murray State University[1]

109 Business Building
Murray, KY 42071
murraystate.edu/business.aspx
Public
Admissions: (270) 809-3779
Email: Msu.
graduateadmissions@
murraystate.edu

Financial aid: (270) 809-2546
Tuition: N/A
Room/board/expenses: N/A
Enrollment: N/A

Northern Kentucky University[1]

BC 363
Highland Heights, KY 41099
www.nku.edu/academics/cob/
programs/graduate/mba.html
Public
Admissions: (859) 572-6657
Email: wrightk11@nku.edu
Financial aid: (859) 572-6437
Tuition: N/A
Room/board/expenses: N/A
Enrollment: N/A

University of Kentucky

550 South Limestone Street
359 Gatton College of Business
and Economics
Lexington, KY 40506-0034
gatton.uky.edu
Public
Admissions: (859) 257-1306
Email: ukmba@uky.edu
Financial aid: (859) 257-3172
Application deadline: 05/11
In-state tuition: total program:
$34,444 (full time); part
time: $914/credit hour
Out-of-state tuition: total
program: $39,964 (full time);
part time: $1,067/credit hour
Room/board/expenses: $14,000
College-funded aid: Yes
International student aid: Yes
Average student indebtedness
at graduation: $30,923
Full-time enrollment: 65
men: 65%; women:
35%; minorities: 11%;
international: 8%
Part-time enrollment: 175
men: 60%; women: 40%;
minorities: 11%; international: 7%
Acceptance rate (full time): 88%
Average GMAT (full time): 591
Average GRE (full
time): 152 verbal; 154
quantitative; 3.9 writing
Average GPA (full time): 3.50
Average age of entrants to
full-time program: 25
Average months of prior work
experience (full time): 14
TOEFL requirement: Yes
Minimum TOEFL score: 79
Most popular departments:
entrepreneurship, finance,
general management,
marketing, supply chain
management/logistics
Mean starting base salary for
2018 full-time graduates: $60,111
Employment location for
2018 class: Intl. 0%; N.E.
0%; M.A. 0%; S. 60%; M.W.
37%; S.W. 0%; W. 4%

University of Louisville

Belknap Campus
Louisville, KY 40292
business.louisville.edu/uoflmba
Public
Admissions: (502) 852-7257
Email: mba@louisville.edu
Financial aid: (502) 852-5517
Application deadline: 07/01
In-state tuition: total program:
$32,000 (full time); total
program: $32,000 (part time)
Out-of-state tuition: total
program: $32,000 (full
time); total program:
$32,000 (part time)
Room/board/expenses: $13,000
College-funded aid: Yes
International student aid: Yes
Average student indebtedness
at graduation: $30,631
Full-time enrollment: 52
men: 63%; women:
37%; minorities: 25%;
international: 6%
Part-time enrollment: 143
men: 61%; women:
39%; minorities: 31%;
international: 2%
Acceptance rate (full time): 69%
Average GMAT (full time): 619
Average GRE (full
time): 156 verbal; 159
quantitative; 4.0 writing
Average GPA (full time): 3.30
Average age of entrants to
full-time program: 25
Average months of prior work
experience (full time): 48
TOEFL requirement: Yes
Minimum TOEFL score: 83
Most popular departments:
entrepreneurship, finance,
health care administration,
marketing, quantitative
analysis/statistics and
operations research
Mean starting base salary for
2018 full-time graduates: $65,500
Employment location for
2018 class: Intl. 0%; N.E.
0%; M.A. 0%; S. 97%; M.W.
0%; S.W. 0%; W. 3%

Western Kentucky University

434 A. Grise Hall
Bowling Green, KY 42101-1056
www.wku.edu/mba/
Public
Admissions: (270) 745-2446
Email: mba@wku.edu
Financial aid: (270) 745-2755
Application deadline: 04/15
In-state tuition: full time:
$607/credit hour; part
time: N/A/credit hour
Out-of-state tuition: full
time: $899/credit hour; part
time: N/A/credit hour
Room/board/expenses: N/A
College-funded aid: Yes
Full-time enrollment: 26
men: 54%; women:
46%; minorities: 4%;
international: 12%
Part-time enrollment: N/A
men: N/A; women:
N/A; minorities: N/A;
international: N/A

Acceptance rate (full time): 64%
Average GMAT (full time): 499
Average GRE (full
time): N/A verbal; N/A
quantitative; N/A writing
Average GPA (full time): 3.45
Average age of entrants to
full-time program: 23
TOEFL requirement: Yes
Minimum TOEFL score: 79
Most popular departments:
general management

LOUISIANA

Louisiana State University– Baton Rouge

4000 Business Education
Complex
Baton Rouge, LA 70803
www.lsu.edu/business/mba
Public
Admissions: (225) 578-8867
Email: floresmba@lsu.edu
Financial aid: (225) 578-3103
Application deadline: 05/15
In-state tuition: total program:
$44,615 (full time); total
program: $54,566 (part time)
Out-of-state tuition: total
program: $78,215 (full
time); total program:
$84,048 (part time)
Room/board/expenses: $20,000
College-funded aid: Yes
International student aid: Yes
Average student indebtedness
at graduation: $15,300
Full-time enrollment: 84
men: 60%; women:
40%; minorities: 10%;
international: 12%
Part-time enrollment: 61
men: 59%; women:
41%; minorities: 21%;
international: 0%
Acceptance rate (full time): 45%
Average GMAT (full time): 610
Average GRE (full
time): 152 verbal; 152
quantitative; 3.6 writing
Average GPA (full time): 3.40
Average age of entrants to
full-time program: 23
Average months of prior work
experience (full time): 20
TOEFL requirement: Yes
Minimum TOEFL score: 79
Most popular departments:
accounting, consulting, finance,
human resources management,
quantitative analysis/statistics
and operations research
Mean starting base salary for
2018 full-time graduates: $63,911
Employment location for
2018 class: Intl. 2%; N.E.
7%; M.A. 0%; S. 47%; M.W.
2%; S.W. 37%; W. 5%

Louisiana Tech University

PO Box 10318
Ruston, LA 71272
www.latech.edu/gradu-
ate_school
Public
Admissions: (318) 257-2924
Email: gschool@latech.edu
Financial aid: (318) 257-2641

Application deadline: 08/01
In-state tuition: full time: $9,603; part time: $6,307
Out-of-state tuition: full time: $16,344; part time: $9,677
Room/board/expenses: $11,622
College-funded aid: Yes
International student aid: Yes
Average student indebtedness at graduation: $15,878
Full-time enrollment: 33 men: 64%; women: 36%; minorities: 12%; international: 18%
Part-time enrollment: 14 men: 71%; women: 29%; minorities: 21%; international: 0%
Acceptance rate (full time): 50%
Average GMAT (full time): 527
Average GRE (full time): 149 verbal; 156 quantitative; 2.8 writing
Average GPA (full time): 3.51
Average age of entrants to full-time program: 23
Average months of prior work experience (full time): 18
TOEFL requirement: Yes
Minimum TOEFL score: 80
Most popular departments: accounting, finance, general management, marketing, management information systems
Mean starting base salary for 2018 full-time graduates: $57,911
Employment location for 2018 class: Intl. N/A; N.E. N/A; M.A. N/A; S. 81%; M.W. N/A; S.W. 19%; W. N/A

Loyola University New Orleans

6363 St. Charles Avenue
Campus Box 15
New Orleans, LA 70118
www.business.loyno.edu
Private
Admissions: (504) 864-7953
Email: mba@loyno.edu
Financial aid: (504) 865-3333
Application deadline: 06/30
Tuition: full time: $1,005/credit hour; part time: $1,005/credit hour
Room/board/expenses: N/A
College-funded aid: Yes
International student aid: Yes
Average student indebtedness at graduation: $40,306
Full-time enrollment: 19 men: 42%; women: 58%; minorities: 26%; international: 11%
Part-time enrollment: 54 men: 39%; women: 61%; minorities: 31%; international: 7%
Acceptance rate (full time): 100%
Average GMAT (full time): 542
Average GRE (full time): 146 verbal; 147 quantitative; N/A writing
Average age of entrants to full-time program: 26
Average months of prior work experience (full time): 12
TOEFL requirement: Yes
Minimum TOEFL score: 92

Most popular departments: entrepreneurship, finance, marketing, production/operations management, quantitative analysis/statistics and operations research

McNeese State University

PO Box 91660
Lake Charles, LA 70609
www.mcneese.edu/colleges/bus
Public
Admissions: (337) 475-5576
Email: mba@mcneese.edu
Financial aid: (337) 475-5065
Application deadline: N/A
In-state tuition: full time: N/A; part time: N/A
Out-of-state tuition: full time: N/A; part time: N/A
Room/board/expenses: N/A
College-funded aid: Yes
International student aid: No
Full-time enrollment: 38 men: 50%; women: 50%; minorities: 16%; international: 13%
Part-time enrollment: 17 men: 41%; women: 59%; minorities: 24%; international: 0%
Average GRE (full time): N/A verbal; N/A quantitative; N/A writing
TOEFL requirement: Yes
Minimum TOEFL score: N/A

Nicholls State University[1]

PO Box 2015
Thibodaux, LA 70310
www.nicholls.edu/business/
Public
Admissions: (985) 448-4507
Email: becky.leblanc-durocher@nicholls.edu
Financial aid: (985) 448-4048
Tuition: N/A
Room/board/expenses: N/A
Enrollment: N/A

Southeastern Louisiana University

SLU 10735
Hammond, LA 70402
www.selu.edu/acad_research/programs/grad_bus
Public
Admissions: (985) 549-5637
Email: admissions@selu.edu
Financial aid: (985) 549-2244
Application deadline: 07/15
In-state tuition: full time: $8,781; part time: N/A
Out-of-state tuition: full time: $21,259; part time: N/A
Room/board/expenses: $14,436
College-funded aid: Yes
International student aid: Yes
Full-time enrollment: 68 men: 50%; women: 50%; minorities: 9%; international: 15%
Part-time enrollment: N/A men: N/A; women: N/A; minorities: N/A; international: N/A

Acceptance rate (full time): 100%
Average GMAT (full time): 441
Average GRE (full time): 147 verbal; 153 quantitative; N/A writing
Average age of entrants to full-time program: 23
TOEFL requirement: Yes
Minimum TOEFL score: 75
Most popular departments: general management

Southern University and A&M College[1]

PO Box 9723
Baton Rouge, LA 70813
www.subr.edu/index.cfm/page/121
Public
Admissions: (225) 771-5390
Email: gradschool@subr.edu
Financial aid: N/A
Tuition: N/A
Room/board/expenses: N/A
Enrollment: N/A

Tulane University

7 McAlister Drive
New Orleans, LA 70118-5669
freeman.tulane.edu
Private
Admissions: (504) 865-5410
Email: freeman.admissions@tulane.edu
Financial aid: (504) 865-5410
Application deadline: 05/01
Tuition: full time: $57,708; part time: $32,092
Room/board/expenses: $19,970
College-funded aid: Yes
International student aid: Yes
Full-time enrollment: 73 men: 62%; women: 38%; minorities: 27%; international: 15%
Part-time enrollment: 135 men: 59%; women: 41%; minorities: 27%; international: 4%
Acceptance rate (full time): 71%
Average GMAT (full time): 646
Average GRE (full time): 157 verbal; 155 quantitative; N/A writing
Average GPA (full time): 3.26
Average age of entrants to full-time program: 27
Average months of prior work experience (full time): 38
TOEFL requirement: Yes
Minimum TOEFL score: N/A
Most popular departments: entrepreneurship, finance, general management, international business, other
Mean starting base salary for 2018 full-time graduates: $88,150
Employment location for 2018 class: Intl. N/A; N.E. 10%; M.A. 3%; S. 41%; M.W. 3%; S.W. 31%; W. 10%

University of Louisiana–Lafayette

USL Box 43545
Lafayette, LA 70504-3545
gradschool.louisiana.edu/
Public
Admissions: (337) 482-6965
Email: gradschool@louisiana.edu

Financial aid: (337) 482-6506
Application deadline: 06/30
In-state tuition: full time: N/A; part time: $9,790
Out-of-state tuition: full time: N/A; part time: $29,096
Room/board/expenses: N/A
College-funded aid: Yes
International student aid: Yes
Full-time enrollment: N/A men: N/A; women: N/A; minorities: N/A; international: N/A
Part-time enrollment: 231 men: 50%; women: 50%; minorities: 17%; international: 10%
Average GRE (full time): N/A verbal; N/A quantitative; N/A writing
TOEFL requirement: Yes
Minimum TOEFL score: 79
Most popular departments: accounting, finance, health care administration, international business, production/operations management

University of Louisiana–Monroe

700 University Avenue
Monroe, LA 71209
www.ulm.edu/cbss/
Public
Admissions: (318) 342-5430
Email: admissions@ulm.edu
Financial aid: N/A
Application deadline: rolling
In-state tuition: full time: $11,000; part time: N/A
Out-of-state tuition: full time: $23,000; part time: N/A
Room/board/expenses: $6,000
College-funded aid: Yes
International student aid: Yes
Full-time enrollment: 29 men: 52%; women: 48%; minorities: N/A; international: N/A
Part-time enrollment: N/A men: N/A; women: N/A; minorities: N/A; international: N/A
Average GRE (full time): N/A verbal; N/A quantitative; N/A writing
TOEFL requirement: Yes
Minimum TOEFL score: N/A
Most popular departments: general management, health care administration, public administration, other

University of New Orleans[1]

2000 Lakeshore Drive
New Orleans, LA 70148
www.uno.edu/admissions/contact.aspx
Public
Admissions: (504) 280-6595
Email: pec@uno.edu
Financial aid: (504) 280-6603
Tuition: N/A
Room/board/expenses: N/A
Enrollment: N/A

University of Maine

Donald P. Corbett Business Building
Orono, ME 04469-5723
www.umaine.edu/business/mba
Public
Admissions: (207) 581-1973
Email: mba@maine.edu
Financial aid: (207) 581-1324
Application deadline: 05/01
In-state tuition: full time: N/A; part time: $439/credit hour
Out-of-state tuition: full time: N/A; part time: $1,430/credit hour
Room/board/expenses: N/A
College-funded aid: Yes
International student aid: Yes
Full-time enrollment: N/A men: N/A; women: N/A; minorities: N/A; international: N/A
Part-time enrollment: 97 men: 61%; women: 39%; minorities: 5%; international: 1%
Average GRE (full time): N/A verbal; N/A quantitative; N/A writing
TOEFL requirement: Yes
Minimum TOEFL score: 80
Most popular departments: accounting, finance, general management, marketing, quantitative analysis/statistics and operations research

University of Southern Maine

PO Box 9300
Portland, ME 04104
usm.maine.edu/school-of-business
Public
Admissions: N/A
Financial aid: (207) 780-5250
Application deadline: N/A
In-state tuition: full time: N/A; part time: N/A
Out-of-state tuition: full time: N/A; part time: N/A
Room/board/expenses: N/A
College-funded aid: Yes
International student aid: Yes
Full-time enrollment: N/A men: N/A; women: N/A; minorities: N/A; international: N/A
Part-time enrollment: 52 men: 60%; women: 40%; minorities: N/A; international: N/A
Average GRE (full time): N/A verbal; N/A quantitative; N/A writing
TOEFL requirement: Yes
Minimum TOEFL score: 79

Frostburg State University

101 Braddock Road
Frostburg, MD 21532-2303
www.frostburg.edu/colleges/cob/mba/
Public
Admissions: (301) 687-7053
Email: gradservices@frostburg.edu
Financial aid: (301) 687-4301

Application deadline: N/A
In-state tuition: full time:
$433/credit hour; part
time: $433/credit hour
Out-of-state tuition: full
time: $557/credit hour; part
time: $557/credit hour
Room/board/expenses: $7,085
College-funded aid: Yes
International student aid: Yes
Full-time enrollment: 39
men: 51%; women:
49%; minorities: 15%;
international: 0%
Part-time enrollment: 135
men: 44%; women:
56%; minorities: 26%;
international: 1%
**Average GRE (full
time):** N/A verbal; N/A
quantitative; N/A writing
Average GPA (full time): 3.40
**Average age of entrants to
full-time program:** 25
TOEFL requirement: Yes
Minimum TOEFL score: N/A

Johns Hopkins University[1]

3400 N Charles Street
Baltimore, MD 21218
carey.jhu.edu/
Private
Admissions: N/A
Financial aid: N/A
Tuition: N/A
Room/board/expenses: N/A
Enrollment: N/A

Loyola University Maryland

4501 N. Charles Street
Baltimore, MD 21210-2699
www.loyola.edu/sellinger/
Private
Admissions: (410) 617-5020
Email: graduate@loyola.edu
Financial aid: (410) 617-2576
Application deadline: 08/20
Tuition: total program:
$59,450 (full time); part
time: $970/credit hour
Room/board/expenses: $26,400
College-funded aid: Yes
International student aid: Yes
**Average student indebtedness
at graduation:** $16,884
Full-time enrollment: 21
men: 67%; women:
33%; minorities: 29%;
international: 0%
Part-time enrollment: 291
men: 57%; women:
43%; minorities: 23%;
international: 1%
**Average GRE (full
time):** N/A verbal; N/A
quantitative; N/A writing
TOEFL requirement: Yes
Minimum TOEFL score: 80

Morgan State University[1]

1700 E. Cold Spring Lane
Baltimore, MD 21251
www.morgan.edu/sbm
Public
Admissions: (443) 885-3396
Email: gravesschool@
morgan.edu

Financial aid: (443) 885-3170
Tuition: N/A
Room/board/expenses: N/A
Enrollment: N/A

Salisbury University

1101 Camden Avenue
Salisbury, MD 21801-6860
www.salisbury.edu/
Public
Admissions: (410) 543-6161
Email: admissions@
salisbury.edu
Financial aid: (410) 543-6165
Application deadline: 03/01
In-state tuition: full time:
N/A/credit hour; part
time: N/A/credit hour
Out-of-state tuition: full
time: N/A/credit hour; part
time: N/A/credit hour
Room/board/expenses: N/A
College-funded aid: Yes
International student aid: Yes
Full-time enrollment: 39
men: 41%; women:
59%; minorities: 21%;
international: 0%
Part-time enrollment: 30
men: 53%; women:
47%; minorities: 20%;
international: 3%
Acceptance rate (full time): 100%
**Average GRE (full
time):** N/A verbal; N/A
quantitative; N/A writing
**Average age of entrants to
full-time program:** 25
TOEFL requirement: Yes
Minimum TOEFL score: N/A

University of Baltimore[1]

11 W. Mt. Royal Avenue
Baltimore, MD 21201
www.ubalt.edu/mba
Public
Admissions: (410) 837-6565
Email: gradadmission@ubalt.edu
Financial aid: (410) 837-4763
Tuition: N/A
Room/board/expenses: N/A
Enrollment: N/A

University of Maryland– College Park

2308 Van Munching Hall
College Park, MD 20742
www.rhsmith.umd.edu
Public
Admissions: (301) 405-0202
Email: mba_info@
rhsmith.umd.edu
Financial aid: (301) 405-2301
Application deadline: 03/01
In-state tuition: full time: $47,081;
part time: $1,665/credit hour
Out-of-state tuition: full
time: $56,261; part time:
$1,665/credit hour
Room/board/expenses: N/A
College-funded aid: Yes
International student aid: Yes
Full-time enrollment: 155
men: 66%; women:
34%; minorities: 31%;
international: 35%

Part-time enrollment: 503
men: 60%; women:
40%; minorities: 34%;
international: 8%
Acceptance rate (full time): 36%
Average GMAT (full time): 638
**Average GRE (full
time):** 154 verbal; 155
quantitative; 4.0 writing
Average GPA (full time): 3.20
**Average age of entrants to
full-time program:** 29
**Average months of prior work
experience (full time):** 80
TOEFL requirement: Yes
Minimum TOEFL score: 100
Most popular departments:
consulting, entrepreneurship,
finance, general
management, marketing
**Mean starting base salary for 2018
full-time graduates:** $104,966
**Employment location for 2018
class:** Intl. 1%; N.E. 21%;
M.A. 48%; S. 10%; M.W.
4%; S.W. 6%; W. 9%

MASSACHUSETTS

Babson College

231 Forest Street
Babson Park, MA 02457-0310
www.babson.edu/graduate
Private
Admissions: (781) 239-4543
Email: gradadmissions@
babson.edu
Financial aid: (781) 239-4219
Application deadline: rolling
Tuition: total program:
$111,952 (full time); part
time: $1,768/credit hour
Room/board/expenses: $56,204
College-funded aid: Yes
International student aid: Yes
**Average student indebtedness
at graduation:** $67,348
Full-time enrollment: 344
men: 68%; women:
32%; minorities: 8%;
international: 75%
Part-time enrollment: 229
men: 55%; women:
45%; minorities: 18%;
international: 6%
Acceptance rate (full time): 82%
Average GMAT (full time): 615
**Average GRE (full
time):** 152 verbal; 153
quantitative; 4.0 writing
Average GPA (full time): 3.25
**Average age of entrants to
full-time program:** 28
**Average months of prior work
experience (full time):** 65
TOEFL requirement: Yes
Minimum TOEFL score: 100
Most popular departments:
entrepreneurship, finance,
marketing, technology, other
**Mean starting base salary for
2018 full-time graduates:** $85,511
**Employment location for
2018 class:** Intl. N/A; N.E.
82%; M.A. 2%; S. 3%; M.W.
N/A; S.W. 3%; W. 10%

Bentley University

175 Forest Street
Waltham, MA 02452-4705
admissions.bentley.edu/
graduate
Private
Admissions: (781) 891-2108
Email: applygrad@bentley.edu
Financial aid: (781) 891-3441
Application deadline: rolling
Tuition: total program:
$60,600 (full time); part
time: $1,540/credit hour
Room/board/expenses: $21,410
College-funded aid: Yes
International student aid: Yes
**Average student indebtedness
at graduation:** $35,676
Full-time enrollment: 90
men: 54%; women:
46%; minorities: 16%;
international: 47%
Part-time enrollment: 247
men: 50%; women:
50%; minorities: 19%;
international: 4%
Acceptance rate (full time): 68%
Average GMAT (full time): 533
**Average GRE (full
time):** 150 verbal; 152
quantitative; 4.0 writing
Average GPA (full time): 3.30
**Average age of entrants to
full-time program:** 26
**Average months of prior work
experience (full time):** 22
TOEFL requirement: Yes
Minimum TOEFL score: 100
Most popular departments:
finance, leadership, marketing,
management information
systems, quantitative
analysis/statistics and
operations research
**Mean starting base salary for
2018 full-time graduates:** $53,981
**Employment location for
2018 class:** Intl. 18%; N.E.
73%; M.A. N/A; S. N/A; M.W.
N/A; S.W. N/A; W. 9%

Boston College

140 Commonwealth Avenue
Fulton Hall 320
Chestnut Hill, MA 02467
www.bc.edu/mba
Private
Admissions: (617) 552-3920
Email: bcmba@bc.edu
Financial aid: (800) 294-0294
Application deadline: 04/15
Tuition: full time: $51,310; part
time: $1,744/credit hour
Room/board/expenses: $23,335
College-funded aid: Yes
International student aid: Yes
**Average student indebtedness
at graduation:** $63,081
Full-time enrollment: 156
men: 72%; women:
28%; minorities: 14%;
international: 28%
Part-time enrollment: 349
men: 66%; women: 34%;
minorities: 17%; international: 1%
Acceptance rate (full time): 44%
Average GMAT (full time): 637
**Average GRE (full
time):** 158 verbal; 156
quantitative; 4.3 writing
Average GPA (full time): 3.34
**Average age of entrants to
full-time program:** 29

**Average months of prior work
experience (full time):** 57
TOEFL requirement: Yes
Minimum TOEFL score: 100
Most popular departments:
accounting, finance, general
management, marketing,
quantitative analysis/statistics
and operations research
**Mean starting base salary for
2018 full-time graduates:** $97,798
**Employment location for
2018 class:** Intl. 4%; N.E.
83%; M.A. 2%; S. 6%; M.W.
4%; S.W. 0%; W. 2%

Boston University

595 Commonwealth Avenue
Boston, MA 02215-1704
www.bu.edu/questrom
Private
Admissions: (617) 353-2670
Email: mba@bu.edu
Financial aid: N/A
Application deadline: 03/18
Tuition: full time: $54,144; part
time: $1,687/credit hour
Room/board/expenses: $19,519
College-funded aid: Yes
International student aid: Yes
Full-time enrollment: 320
men: 57%; women:
43%; minorities: 18%;
international: 34%
Part-time enrollment: 649
men: 55%; women:
45%; minorities: 22%;
international: 7%
Acceptance rate (full time): 51%
Average GMAT (full time): 681
**Average GRE (full
time):** 154 verbal; 158
quantitative; N/A writing
Average GPA (full time): 3.30
**Average age of entrants to
full-time program:** 27
**Average months of prior work
experience (full time):** 55
TOEFL requirement: Yes
Minimum TOEFL score: 95
Most popular departments:
health care administration,
leadership, marketing, not-
for-profit management, other
**Mean starting base salary for
2018 full-time graduates:** $93,387
**Employment location for
2018 class:** Intl. 9%; N.E.
80%; M.A. 1%; S. 1%; M.W.
3%; S.W. 0%; W. 5%

Brandeis University

415 South Street
Waltham, MA 02454-9110
www.brandeis.edu/global
Private
Admissions: (781) 736-2252
Email: globaladmissions@
brandeis.edu
Financial aid: (781) 736-3700
Application deadline: 04/15
Tuition: full time: $52,913;
part time: N/A
Room/board/expenses: $21,672
College-funded aid: Yes
International student aid: Yes
**Average student indebtedness
at graduation:** $29,657
Full-time enrollment: 30
men: 50%; women:
50%; minorities: 13%;
international: 83%

Part-time enrollment: N/A
men: N/A; women:
N/A; minorities: N/A;
international: N/A
Acceptance rate (full time): 79%
Average GMAT (full time): 577
Average GRE (full time): 151 verbal; 150 quantitative; 4.0 writing
Average GPA (full time): 3.30
Average age of entrants to full-time program: 30
Average months of prior work experience (full time): 81
TOEFL requirement: Yes
Minimum TOEFL score: 100
Most popular departments: finance, marketing, real estate, other
Mean starting base salary for 2018 full-time graduates: $74,786
Employment location for 2018 class: Intl. 10%; N.E. 40%; M.A. 10%; S. N/A; M.W. N/A; S.W. 10%; W. 30%

Clark University
950 Main Street
Worcester, MA 01610
www.clarku.edu/gsom
Private
Admissions: (508) 793-7559
Email: jczub@clarku.edu
Financial aid: (508) 793-7559
Application deadline: 02/01
Tuition: full time $71,725; part time $71,725
Room/board/expenses: $12,000
College-funded aid: Yes
International student aid: Yes
Full-time enrollment: 84
men: 52%; women: 48%; minorities: 13%; international: 36%
Part-time enrollment: 45
men: 47%; women: 53%; minorities: 27%; international: 7%
Acceptance rate (full time): 78%
Average GMAT (full time): 505
Average GRE (full time): 150 verbal; 151 quantitative; 3.5 writing
Average GPA (full time): 3.51
Average age of entrants to full-time program: 27
Average months of prior work experience (full time): 3
TOEFL requirement: Yes
Minimum TOEFL score: N/A
Most popular departments: general management, marketing, quantitative analysis/statistics and operations research, other
Mean starting base salary for 2018 full-time graduates: $48,108

Harvard University
Soldiers Field
Boston, MA 02163
www.hbs.edu
Private
Admissions: (617) 495-6128
Email: admissions@hbs.edu
Financial aid: (617) 495-6640
Application deadline: 01/04
Tuition: full time: $80,532; part time: N/A
Room/board/expenses: $28,592
College-funded aid: Yes
International student aid: Yes
Average student indebtedness at graduation: $90,298

Full-time enrollment: 1,873
men: N/A; women: N/A; minorities: N/A; international: N/A
Part-time enrollment: N/A
men: N/A; women: N/A; minorities: N/A; international: N/A
Acceptance rate (full time): 10%
Average GMAT (full time): 731
Average GRE (full time): 165 verbal; N/A quantitative; N/A writing
Average GPA (full time): 3.71
Average age of entrants to full-time program: 27
Average months of prior work experience (full time): 55
TOEFL requirement: Yes
Minimum TOEFL score: 109
Mean starting base salary for 2018 full-time graduates: $139,339
Employment location for 2018 class: Intl. N/A; N.E. 47%; M.A. 5%; S. 5%; M.W. 8%; S.W. 5%; W. 30%

Hult International Business School–Boston
1 Education Street
Cambridge, MA 02141
www.hult.edu
Private
Admissions: (161) 774-6199
Email: admissions@hult.edu
Financial aid: N/A
Application deadline: rolling
Tuition: full time: N/A; part time: N/A
Room/board/expenses: N/A
College-funded aid: Yes
International student aid: Yes
Full-time enrollment: 258
men: 58%; women: 42%; minorities: N/A; international: N/A
Part-time enrollment: N/A
men: N/A; women: N/A; minorities: N/A; International: N/A
Acceptance rate (full time): 45%
Average GRE (full time): N/A verbal; N/A quantitative; N/A writing
Average GPA (full time): 2.99
Average age of entrants to full-time program: 32
Average months of prior work experience (full time): 92
TOEFL requirement: Yes
Minimum TOEFL score: 90

Massachusetts Institute of Technology
100 Main Street, Building E62
Cambridge, MA 02142
mitsloan.mit.edu/mba
Private
Admissions: (617) 258-5434
Email: mbaadmissions@sloan.mit.edu
Financial aid: (617) 253-4971
Application deadline: 04/08
Tuition: full time: $76,712; part time: N/A
Room/board/expenses: $37,593
College-funded aid: Yes
International student aid: Yes

Average student indebtedness at graduation: $115,139
Full-time enrollment: 813
men: 58%; women: 42%; minorities: 28%; international: 35%
Part-time enrollment: N/A
men: N/A; women: N/A; minorities: N/A; international: N/A
Acceptance rate (full time): 13%
Average GMAT (full time): 728
Average GRE (full time): N/A verbal; N/A quantitative; N/A writing
Average GPA (full time): 3.57
Average age of entrants to full-time program: 28
Average months of prior work experience (full time): 59
TOEFL requirement: No
Minimum TOEFL score: N/A
Most popular departments: entrepreneurship, finance, international business, manufacturing and technology management, production/operations management
Mean starting base salary for 2018 full-time graduates: $135,105
Employment location for 2018 class: Intl. 11%; N.E. 43%; M.A. 3%; S. 2%; M.W. 5%; S.W. 6%; W. 30%

Northeastern University
360 Huntington Avenue
350 Dodge Hall
Boston, MA 02115
www.damore-mckim.northeastern.edu/academic-programs/graduate-programs
Private
Admissions: (617) 373-5992
Email: gradbusiness@northeastern.edu
Financial aid: (617) 373-5899
Application deadline: 04/15
Tuition: total program: $91,640 (full time); total program: $96,414 (part time)
Room/board/expenses: $25,350
College-funded aid: Yes
International student aid: Yes
Full-time enrollment: 160
men: 60%; women: 40%; minorities: 14%; international: 39%
Part-time enrollment: 280
men: 60%; women: 40%; minorities: 21%; international: 4%
Acceptance rate (full time): 36%
Average GMAT (full time): 627
Average GRE (full time): 156 verbal; 153 quantitative; 4.2 writing
Average GPA (full time): 3.33
Average age of entrants to full-time program: 27
Average months of prior work experience (full time): 46
TOEFL requirement: Yes
Minimum TOEFL score: 100
Most popular departments: entrepreneurship, finance, international business, marketing, supply chain management/logistics
Mean starting base salary for 2018 full-time graduates: $89,029

Employment location for 2018 class: Intl. 5%; N.E. 89%; M.A. N/A; S. 2%; M.W. 2%; S.W. 2%; W. N/A

Simmons University[1]
300 The Fenway
Boston, MA 02115
www.simmons.edu/som
Private
Admissions: N/A
Financial aid: N/A
Tuition: N/A
Room/board/expenses: N/A
Enrollment: N/A

Suffolk University
8 Ashburton Place
Boston, MA 02108
www.suffolk.edu/business
Private
Admissions: (617) 573-8302
Email: grad.admission@suffolk.edu
Financial aid: (617) 573-8470
Application deadline: 03/15
Tuition: full time: $1,466/credit hour; part time: $1,466/credit hour
Room/board/expenses: $20,620
College-funded aid: Yes
International student aid: Yes
Average student indebtedness at graduation: $54,276
Full-time enrollment: 95
men: 43%; women: 57%; minorities: 18%; international: 56%
Part-time enrollment: 211
men: 44%; women: 56%; minorities: 24%; international: 7%
Acceptance rate (full time): 69%
Average GMAT (full time): 503
Average GRE (full time): 147 verbal; 145 quantitative; 3.9 writing
Average GPA (full time): 3.38
Average age of entrants to full-time program: 25
Average months of prior work experience (full time): 35
TOEFL requirement: Yes
Minimum TOEFL score: 80
Most popular departments: accounting, finance, marketing, tax

University of Massachusetts–Amherst
121 Presidents Drive
Amherst, MA 01003
www.isenberg.umass.edu/programs/masters/mba
Public
Admissions: (413) 545-5608
Email: grad@isenberg.umass.edu
Financial aid: (413) 545-0801
Application deadline: 04/01
In-state tuition: full time: $16,963; part time: $900/credit hour
Out-of-state tuition: full time: $34,132; part time: $900/credit hour
Room/board/expenses: $15,900
College-funded aid: Yes
International student aid: Yes

Average student indebtedness at graduation: $29,301
Full-time enrollment: 56
men: 54%; women: 46%; minorities: 18%; international: 20%
Part-time enrollment: 189
men: 69%; women: 31%; minorities: 27%; international: 12%
Acceptance rate (full time): 35%
Average GMAT (full time): 651
Average GRE (full time): 158 verbal; 156 quantitative; 4.3 writing
Average GPA (full time): 3.49
Average age of entrants to full-time program: 31
Average months of prior work experience (full time): 74
TOEFL requirement: Yes
Minimum TOEFL score: 100
Most popular departments: entrepreneurship, finance, general management, hotel administration, sports business
Mean starting base salary for 2018 full-time graduates: $73,357
Employment location for 2018 class: Intl. 8%; N.E. 77%; M.A. 8%; S. N/A; M.W. N/A; S.W. 8%; W. N/A

University of Massachusetts–Boston
100 Morrissey Boulevard
Boston, MA 02125-3393
www.umb.edu/cmgrad
Public
Admissions: (617) 287-7720
Email: gradcm@umb.edu
Financial aid: (617) 287-6300
Application deadline: 07/01
In-state tuition: full time: N/A; part time: $760/credit hour
Out-of-state tuition: full time: N/A; part time: $1,470/credit hour
Room/board/expenses: N/A
College-funded aid: Yes
International student aid: Yes
Full-time enrollment: N/A
men: N/A; women: N/A; minorities: N/A; international: N/A
Part-time enrollment: 256
men: 51%; women: 49%; minorities: 31%; international: 4%
Average GRE (full time): N/A verbal; N/A quantitative; N/A writing
TOEFL requirement: Yes
Minimum TOEFL score: 90
Most popular departments: accounting, finance, general management, marketing, management information systems

University of Massachusetts–Dartmouth
285 Old Westport Road
North Dartmouth, MA 02747
www.umassd.edu/charlton/programs/graduate
Public
Admissions: (508) 999-8604
Email: graduate@umassd.edu
Financial aid: (508) 999-8643

Application deadline: 07/01
In-state tuition: full time: $16,337;
part time: N/A/credit hour
Out-of-state tuition: full
time: $29,141; part time:
N/A/credit hour
Room/board/expenses: $16,436
College-funded aid: Yes
International student aid: No
Average student indebtedness
at graduation: $27,449
Full-time enrollment: 130
men: 52%; women:
48%; minorities: 23%;
international: 33%
Part-time enrollment: N/A
men: N/A; women:
N/A; minorities: N/A;
international: N/A
Acceptance rate (full time): 89%
Average GRE (full
time): N/A verbal; N/A
quantitative; N/A writing
Average GPA (full time): 3.38
Average age of entrants to
full-time program: 27
TOEFL requirement: Yes
Minimum TOEFL score: 80
Most popular departments:
general management,
health care administration,
leadership, technology, other
Mean starting base salary for
2018 full-time graduates: $75,200
Employment location for 2018
class: Intl. N/A; N.E. 100%;
M.A. N/A; S. N/A; M.W.
N/A; S.W. N/A; W. N/A

University of Massachusetts– Lowell

1 University Avenue
Lowell, MA 01854
www.uml.edu/grad
Public
Admissions: (978) 934-2390
Email: graduate_
admissions@uml.edu
Financial aid: (978) 934-4220
Application deadline: rolling
In-state tuition: full time:
$810/credit hour; part
time: $810/credit hour
Out-of-state tuition: full time:
$1,465/credit hour; part
time: $1,465/credit hour
Room/board/expenses: $18,782
College-funded aid: Yes
International student aid: Yes
Average student indebtedness
at graduation: $41,674
Full-time enrollment: 38
men: 50%; women:
50%; minorities: 13%;
international: 53%
Part-time enrollment: 55
men: 65%; women:
35%; minorities: 25%;
international: 4%
Acceptance rate (full time): 90%
Average GMAT (full time): 540
Average GRE (full
time): N/A verbal; N/A
quantitative; N/A writing
Average GPA (full time): 3.42
Average age of entrants to
full-time program: 26
Average months of prior work
experience (full time): 50
TOEFL requirement: Yes
Minimum TOEFL score: 100

Most popular departments:
finance, general
management, leadership,
marketing, management
information systems

Western New England University

1215 Wilbraham Road
Springfield, MA 01119-2684
www1.wne.edu/academics/
graduate/index.cfm#?
category=2
Private
Admissions: (800) 325-1122
Email: study@wne.edu
Financial aid: (413) 796-2080
Application deadline: rolling
Tuition: full time: N/A; part
time: $849/credit hour
Room/board/expenses: N/A
College-funded aid: No
International student aid: No
Full-time enrollment: N/A
men: N/A; women:
N/A; minorities: N/A;
international: N/A
Part-time enrollment: 81
men: 48%; women:
52%; minorities: 12%;
international: 1%
Average GRE (full
time): N/A verbal; N/A
quantitative; N/A writing
TOEFL requirement: Yes
Minimum TOEFL score: 79
Most popular departments:
accounting, general
management, leadership, other

Worcester Polytechnic Institute

100 Institute Road
Worcester, MA 01609
business.wpi.edu
Private
Admissions: (508) 831-4665
Email: business@wpi.edu
Financial aid: (508) 831-5469
Application deadline: 07/15
Tuition: total program: $72,624
(full time); total program:
$72,624 (part time)
Room/board/expenses: N/A
College-funded aid: Yes
International student aid: Yes
Full-time enrollment: 14
men: 43%; women:
57%; minorities: 0%;
international: 93%
Part-time enrollment: 5
men: 60%; women:
40%; minorities: 0%;
international: 40%
Acceptance rate (full time): 91%
Average GMAT (full time): 510
Average GRE (full
time): 148 verbal; 143
quantitative; 4.0 writing
Average GPA (full time): 4.00
Average age of entrants to
full-time program: 30
Average months of prior work
experience (full time): 96
TOEFL requirement: Yes
Minimum TOEFL score: 90

Most popular departments:
manufacturing and technology
management, marketing,
management information
systems, production/operations
management, technology

MICHIGAN

Central Michigan University[1]

252 ABSC - Grawn Hall
Mount Pleasant, MI 48859
www.cmich.edu/colleges/cba/
Pages/default.aspx
Public
Admissions: (989) 774-4723
Email: grad@cmich.edu
Financial aid: N/A
Tuition: N/A
Room/board/expenses: N/A
Enrollment: N/A

Eastern Michigan University

Gary M. Owen Building
300 W. Michigan Avenue
Ypsilanti, MI 48197
www.emich.edu/cob/
Public
Admissions: (734) 487-4444
Email: cob.graduate@emich.edu
Financial aid: (734) 487-0455
Application deadline: 05/15
In-state tuition: full time:
N/A; total program:
$27,632 (part time)
Out-of-state tuition: full
time: N/A; total program:
$48,692 (part time)
Room/board/expenses: N/A
College-funded aid: Yes
International student aid: Yes
Full-time enrollment: N/A
men: N/A; women:
N/A; minorities: N/A;
international: N/A
Part-time enrollment: 207
men: 47%; women:
53%; minorities: 21%;
international: 0%
Average GRE (full
time): N/A verbal; N/A
quantitative; N/A writing
TOEFL requirement: Yes
Minimum TOEFL score: 79
Most popular departments:
accounting, finance, general
management, human resources
management, management
information systems

Grand Valley State University

50 Front Avenue SW
Grand Rapids, MI 49504-6424
www.gvsu.edu/Seidman
Public
Admissions: (616) 331-7400
Email: go2gvmba@gvsu.edu
Financial aid: (616) 331-3234
Application deadline: 03/01
In-state tuition: full time: N/A;
part time: $712/credit hour
Out-of-state tuition: full time:
N/A; part time: $712/credit hour
Room/board/expenses: N/A
College-funded aid: Yes
International student aid: Yes

Full-time enrollment: N/A
men: N/A; women:
N/A; minorities: N/A;
international: N/A
Part-time enrollment: 136
men: 62%; women:
38%; minorities: 22%;
international: 0%
Average GRE (full
time): N/A verbal; N/A
quantitative; N/A writing
TOEFL requirement: Yes
Minimum TOEFL score: 80
Most popular departments:
accounting

Lawrence Technological University[1]

21000 West Ten Mile Road
Southfield, MI 48075
Private
Admissions: N/A
Financial aid: N/A
Tuition: N/A
Room/board/expenses: N/A
Enrollment: N/A

Michigan State University

Eppley Center
645 N. Shaw Lane, Room 211
East Lansing, MI 48824-1121
www.mba.msu.edu
Public
Admissions: (517) 355-7604
Email: mba@msu.edu
Financial aid: (517) 432-4109
Application deadline: 04/01
In-state tuition: full time:
$31,867; part time: N/A
Out-of-state tuition: full time:
$50,483; part time: N/A
Room/board/expenses: $21,400
College-funded aid: Yes
International student aid: Yes
Average student indebtedness
at graduation: $51,988
Full-time enrollment: 157
men: 73%; women:
27%; minorities: 19%;
international: 31%
Part-time enrollment: N/A
men: N/A; women:
N/A; minorities: N/A;
international: N/A
Acceptance rate (full time): 44%
Average GMAT (full time): 668
Average GRE (full
time): 155 verbal; 151
quantitative; 4.0 writing
Average GPA (full time): 3.27
Average age of entrants to
full-time program: 27
Average months of prior work
experience (full time): 37
TOEFL requirement: Yes
Minimum TOEFL score: 100
Most popular departments:
consulting, finance, general
management, marketing, supply
chain management/logistics
Mean starting base salary for 2018
full-time graduates: $105,963
Employment location for
2018 class: Intl. 2%; N.E.
26%; M.A. 4%; S. 6%; M.W.
30%; S.W. 13%; W. 19%

Michigan Technological University

1400 Townsend Drive
Houghton, MI 49931-1295
www.mtu.edu/business/
graduate/techmba/
Public
Admissions: (906) 487-3055
Email: techmba@mtu.edu
Financial aid: (906) 487-3055
Application deadline: rolling
In-state tuition: full time: $1,007/
credit hour; part time: N/A
Out-of-state tuition:
full time: $1,007/credit
hour; part time: N/A
Room/board/expenses: $13,621
College-funded aid: Yes
International student aid: Yes
Full-time enrollment: 47
men: 55%; women:
45%; minorities: 6%;
international: 26%
Part-time enrollment: N/A
men: N/A; women:
N/A; minorities: N/A;
international: N/A
Acceptance rate (full time): 22%
Average GRE (full
time): N/A verbal; N/A
quantitative; N/A writing
Average GPA (full time): 3.41
Average age of entrants to
full-time program: 26
Average months of prior work
experience (full time): 53
TOEFL requirement: Yes
Minimum TOEFL score: 95
Most popular departments:
entrepreneurship,
manufacturing and technology
management, technology

Northern Michigan University[1]

1401 Presque Isle Avenue
Marquette, MI 49855
www.nmu.edu/graduatestudies
Public
Admissions: (906) 227-2300
Email: graduate@nmu.edu
Financial aid: (906) 227-2327
Tuition: N/A
Room/board/expenses: N/A
Enrollment: N/A

Oakland University

238 Elliott Hall
275 Varner Drive
Rochester, MI 48309-4485
www.oakland.edu/business/
grad
Public
Admissions: (248) 370-3287
Email: OUGradBusiness@
oakland.edu
Financial aid: (248) 370-2550
Application deadline: 07/15
In-state tuition: full time: N/A;
part time: $738/credit hour
Out-of-state tuition: full time: N/A;
part time: $1,027/credit hour
Room/board/expenses: N/A
College-funded aid: Yes
International student aid: Yes
Full-time enrollment: N/A
men: N/A; women:
N/A; minorities: N/A;
international: N/A

Part-time enrollment: 284
men: 64%; women:
36%; minorities: 14%;
international: 17%
Average GRE (full
time): N/A verbal; N/A
quantitative; N/A writing
TOEFL requirement: Yes
Minimum TOEFL score: 79
Most popular departments:
finance, human
resources management,
international business,
marketing, management
information systems

Saginaw Valley State University

7400 Bay Road
University Center, MI 48710
www.svsu.edu/mba/
Public
Admissions: (989) 964-6096
Email: gradadm@svsu.edu
Financial aid: (989) 964-4103
Application deadline: rolling
In-state tuition: full time:
N/A; part time: $6,945
Out-of-state tuition: full time:
N/A; part time: $13,065
Room/board/expenses: N/A
College-funded aid: Yes
International student aid: Yes
Full-time enrollment: N/A
men: N/A; women:
N/A; minorities: N/A;
international: N/A
Part-time enrollment: 60
men: 62%; women:
38%; minorities: 20%;
international: 23%
Average GRE (full
time): N/A verbal; N/A
quantitative; N/A writing
TOEFL requirement: Yes
Minimum TOEFL score: 79

University of Detroit Mercy

4001 W. McNichols Road
Detroit, MI 48221-3038
business.udmercy.edu
Private
Admissions: (800) 635-5020
Email: admissions@udmercy.edu
Financial aid: (313) 993-3350
Application deadline: rolling
Tuition: full time: $1,579/
credit hour; part time:
$1,579/credit hour
Room/board/expenses: N/A
College-funded aid: Yes
International student aid: Yes
Average student indebtedness
at graduation: $39,096
Full-time enrollment: 31
men: 68%; women:
32%; minorities: 16%;
international: 13%
Part-time enrollment: 50
men: 54%; women:
46%; minorities: 40%;
international: 8%
Acceptance rate (full time): 94%
Average GMAT (full time): 573
Average GRE (full
time): N/A verbal; N/A
quantitative; N/A writing
Average GPA (full time): 3.40
Average age of entrants to
full-time program: 25
TOEFL requirement: No

Minimum TOEFL score: N/A
Mean starting base salary for
2018 full-time graduates: $64,333
Employment location for
2018 class: Intl. N/A; N.E.
N/A; M.A. N/A; S. N/A; M.W.
100%; S.W. N/A; W. N/A

University of Michigan–Ann Arbor

701 Tappan Street
Ann Arbor, MI 48109-1234
michiganross.umich.edu/
Public
Admissions: (734) 763-5796
Email: rossadmissions@
umich.edu
Financial aid: (734) 764-5139
Application deadline: 03/18
In-state tuition: full time:
$63,974; part time: $63,536
Out-of-state tuition: full time:
$68,974; part time: $68,516
Room/board/expenses: $23,860
College-funded aid: Yes
International student aid: Yes
Average student indebtedness
at graduation: $104,679
Full-time enrollment: 832
men: 57%; women:
43%; minorities: 24%;
international: 31%
Part-time enrollment: 429
men: 77%; women:
23%; minorities: 20%;
international: 19%
Acceptance rate (full time): 27%
Average GMAT (full time): 720
Average GRE (full
time): 161 verbal; 159
quantitative; 4.6 writing
Average GPA (full time): 3.48
Average age of entrants to
full-time program: 27
Average months of prior work
experience (full time): 65
TOEFL requirement: Yes
Minimum TOEFL score: N/A
Most popular departments:
consulting, finance, marketing,
production/operations
management, technology
Mean starting base salary for 2018
full-time graduates: $126,500
Employment location for
2018 class: Intl. 9%; N.E.
17%; M.A. 2%; S. 5%; M.W.
34%; S.W. 5%; W. 29%

University of Michigan–Dearborn

19000 Hubbard Drive
Dearborn, MI 48126-2638
umdearborn.edu/cob
Public
Admissions: (313) 593-5460
Email: umd-gradbusiness@
umich.edu
Financial aid: (313) 593-5300
Application deadline: 08/01
In-state tuition: full time: N/A;
part time: $908/credit hour
Out-of-state tuition: full time: N/A;
part time: $1,397/credit hour
Room/board/expenses: N/A
College-funded aid: No
International student aid: Yes
Full-time enrollment: N/A
men: N/A; women:
N/A; minorities: N/A;
international: N/A

Part-time enrollment: 167
men: 65%; women:
35%; minorities: 23%;
international: 7%
Average GRE (full
time): N/A verbal; N/A
quantitative; N/A writing
TOEFL requirement: Yes
Minimum TOEFL score: 84
Most popular departments:
finance, general management,
international business,
marketing, supply chain
management/logistics

University of Michigan–Flint

303 E. Kearsley Street
Flint, MI 48502-1950
www.umflint.edu/som/
graduate-business-programs
Public
Admissions: (810) 762-3171
Email: graduate@umflint.edu
Financial aid: (810) 762-3444
Application deadline: 08/01
In-state tuition: full time: N/A;
part time: $741/credit hour
Out-of-state tuition: full time: N/A;
part time: $924/credit hour
Room/board/expenses: N/A
College-funded aid: Yes
International student aid: Yes
Full-time enrollment: N/A
men: N/A; women:
N/A; minorities: N/A;
international: N/A
Part-time enrollment: 171
men: 58%; women:
42%; minorities: 26%;
international: 11%
Average GRE (full
time): N/A verbal; N/A
quantitative; N/A writing
TOEFL requirement: Yes
Minimum TOEFL score: 84
Most popular departments:
accounting, finance, general
management, health care
administration, leadership

Wayne State University

2771 Woodward Avenue
Detroit, MI 48202
ilitchbusiness.wayne.edu/
Public
Admissions: (313) 577-4511
Email: gradbusiness@wayne.edu
Financial aid: (313) 577-2100
Application deadline: 07/01
In-state tuition: full time: N/A;
part time: $763/credit hour
Out-of-state tuition: full time: N/A;
part time: $1,530/credit hour
Room/board/expenses: N/A
College-funded aid: Yes
International student aid: Yes
Full-time enrollment: N/A
men: N/A; women:
N/A; minorities: N/A;
international: N/A
Part-time enrollment: 1,319
men: 53%; women:
47%; minorities: 27%;
international: 4%
Average GRE (full
time): N/A verbal; N/A
quantitative; N/A writing
TOEFL requirement: Yes
Minimum TOEFL score: 79

Most popular departments:
finance, general management,
marketing, management
information systems, supply
chain management/logistics

Western Michigan University

1903 W Michigan Avenue
Kalamazoo, MI 49008-5480
wmich.edu/mba
Public
Admissions: (269) 387-5133
Email: mba-advising@wmich.edu
Financial aid: (269) 387-6000
Application deadline: 07/15
In-state tuition: full time:
N/A; part time: $8,281
Out-of-state tuition: full time:
N/A; part time: $18,942
Room/board/expenses: N/A
College-funded aid: Yes
International student aid: No
Full-time enrollment: N/A
men: N/A; women:
N/A; minorities: N/A;
international: N/A
Part-time enrollment: 284
men: 62%; women:
38%; minorities: 13%;
international: 17%
Average GRE (full
time): N/A verbal; N/A
quantitative; N/A writing
TOEFL requirement: Yes
Minimum TOEFL score: 80
Most popular departments:
finance, general management,
marketing, management
information systems, other

MINNESOTA

Minnesota State University–Mankato[1]

120 Morris Hall
Mankato, MN 56001
grad.mnsu.edu
Public
Admissions: (507) 389-2321
Financial aid: (507) 389-1419
Tuition: N/A
Room/board/expenses: N/A
Enrollment: N/A

Minnesota State University–Moorhead[1]

1104 7th Avenue South
Moorhead, MN 56563
www.mnstate.edu/graduate/
programs
Public
Admissions: (218) 477-2134
Email: graduate@mnstate.edu
Financial aid: (218) 477-2251
Tuition: N/A
Room/board/expenses: N/A
Enrollment: N/A

St. Cloud State University[1]

720 Fourth Avenue South
St. Cloud, MN 56301-4498
www.stcloudstate.edu/mba
Public
Admissions: (320) 308-3212
Email: mba@stcloudstate.edu
Financial aid: N/A
Tuition: N/A

Room/board/expenses: N/A
Enrollment: N/A

University of Minnesota–Duluth

1318 Kirby Drive
Duluth, MN 55812-2496
lsbe.d.umn.edu/mba
Public
Admissions: (218) 726-8839
Email: LaboMBA@d.umn.edu
Financial aid: (218) 726-8000
Application deadline: 07/15
In-state tuition: full time: $941/
credit hour; part time: N/A
Out-of-state tuition: full time:
N/A/credit hour; part time: N/A
Room/board/expenses: N/A
College-funded aid: Yes
Full-time enrollment: 4
men: 75%; women:
25%; minorities: 25%;
international: 25%
Part-time enrollment: 58
men: 66%; women: 34%;
minorities: 9%; international: 9%
Acceptance rate (full time): 100%
Average GRE (full
time): N/A verbal; N/A
quantitative; N/A writing
Average GPA (full time): 3.38
Average age of entrants to
full-time program: 22
Average months of prior work
experience (full time): 12
TOEFL requirement: Yes
Minimum TOEFL score: 79

University of Minnesota–Twin Cities

321 19th Avenue South,
Suite 4-300
Minneapolis, MN 55455
www.carlsonschool.umn.edu/
degrees/master-business-
administration
Public
Admissions: (612) 625-5555
Email: mba@umn.edu
Financial aid: (612) 626-0302
Application deadline: 04/01
In-state tuition: full time:
$43,523; part time:
$1,400/credit hour
Out-of-state tuition: full
time: $54,467; part time:
$1,400/credit hour
Room/board/expenses: $17,000
College-funded aid: Yes
International student aid: Yes
Average student indebtedness
at graduation: $58,165
Full-time enrollment: 188
men: 68%; women:
32%; minorities: 17%;
international: 22%
Part-time enrollment: 879
men: 68%; women:
32%; minorities: 15%;
international: 6%
Acceptance rate (full time): 39%
Average GMAT (full time): 682
Average GRE (full
time): 160 verbal; 158
quantitative; 4.3 writing
Average GPA (full time): 3.42
Average age of entrants to
full-time program: 28
Average months of prior work
experience (full time): 55
TOEFL requirement: Yes

Minimum TOEFL score: 85
Most popular departments: finance, general management, health care administration, marketing, supply chain management/logistics
Mean starting base salary for 2018 full-time graduates: $113,093
Employment location for 2018 class: Intl. N/A; N.E. 1%; M.A. 3%; S. 1%; M.W. 79%; S.W. 8%; W. 7%

University of St. Thomas

1000 LaSalle Avenue, SCH200
Minneapolis, MN 55403
www.stthomas.edu/business
Private
Admissions: (651) 962-8800
Email: ustmba@stthomas.edu
Financial aid: (651) 962-6550
Application deadline: 08/01
Tuition: total program: $71,370 (full time); total program: $53,056 (part time)
Room/board/expenses: $3,100
College-funded aid: Yes
International student aid: Yes
Average student indebtedness at graduation: $46,899
Full-time enrollment: 67
men: 61%; women: 39%; minorities: 25%; international: 16%
Part-time enrollment: 445
men: 62%; women: 38%; minorities: 14%; international: 3%
Acceptance rate (full time): 85%
Average GMAT (full time): 548
Average GRE (full time): N/A verbal; N/A quantitative; N/A writing
Average GPA (full time): 3.10
Average age of entrants to full-time program: 29
Average months of prior work experience (full time): 64
TOEFL requirement: Yes
Minimum TOEFL score: 80
Most popular departments: accounting, entrepreneurship, finance, general management, marketing

MISSISSIPPI

Jackson State University[1]

1400 J.R. Lynch Street
Jackson, MS 39217
www.jsums.edu/business
Public
Admissions: N/A
Financial aid: N/A
Tuition: N/A
Room/board/expenses: N/A
Enrollment: N/A

Millsaps College[1]

1701 N. State Street
Jackson, MS 39210
millsaps.edu/mba
Private
Admissions: (601) 974-1253
Email: mbamacc@millsaps.edu
Financial aid: (601) 974-1222
Tuition: N/A
Room/board/expenses: N/A
Enrollment: N/A

Mississippi College[1]

200 South Capitol Street
Clinton, MS 39058
www.mc.edu/explore/programs_mba.php
Private
Admissions: N/A
Financial aid: N/A
Tuition: N/A
Room/board/expenses: N/A
Enrollment: N/A

Mississippi State University

PO Box 5288
Mississippi State, MS 39762
www.mba.business.msstate.edu
Public
Admissions: (662) 325-1891
Email: gsb@business.msstate.edu
Financial aid: (662) 325-2450
Application deadline: 03/01
In-state tuition: total program: $13,140 (full time); part time: N/A
Out-of-state tuition: total program: $35,040 (full time); part time: N/A
Room/board/expenses: $19,500
College-funded aid: Yes
International student aid: Yes
Average student indebtedness at graduation: $12,723
Full-time enrollment: 23
men: 61%; women: 39%; minorities: 13%; international: 17%
Part-time enrollment: N/A
men: N/A; women: N/A; minorities: N/A; international: N/A
Acceptance rate (full time): 68%
Average GMAT (full time): 564
Average GRE (full time): 152 verbal; N/A quantitative; N/A writing
Average GPA (full time): 3.48
Average age of entrants to full-time program: 23
Average months of prior work experience (full time): 48
TOEFL requirement: Yes
Minimum TOEFL score: 84
Most popular departments: accounting, marketing, management information systems, other
Mean starting base salary for 2018 full-time graduates: $61,346
Employment location for 2018 class: Intl. N/A; N.E. N/A; M.A. 7%; S. 87%; M.W. 7%; S.W. N/A; W. N/A

University of Mississippi

253 Holman Hall
University, MS 38677
www.olemissbusiness.com/mba
Public
Admissions: (662) 915-5483
Email: amcgee@bus.olemiss.edu
Financial aid: (800) 891-4596
Application deadline: 07/01
In-state tuition: full time: $810/credit hour; part time: N/A
Out-of-state tuition: full time: $1,888/credit hour; part time: N/A
Room/board/expenses: $17,260

College-funded aid: Yes
International student aid: Yes
Average student indebtedness at graduation: $23,478
Full-time enrollment: 41
men: 78%; women: 22%; minorities: 12%; international: 0%
Part-time enrollment: N/A
men: N/A; women: N/A; minorities: N/A; international: N/A
Acceptance rate (full time): 29%
Average GMAT (full time): 567
Average GRE (full time): 153 verbal; 152 quantitative; 3.5 writing
Average GPA (full time): 3.18
Average age of entrants to full-time program: 23
Average months of prior work experience (full time): 21
TOEFL requirement: Yes
Minimum TOEFL score: 99
Mean starting base salary for 2018 full-time graduates: $60,011

University of Southern Mississippi

118 College Drive, #5096
Hattiesburg, MS 39406-5096
usm.edu/business/mba
Public
Admissions: (601) 266-4369
Email: gc-business@usm.edu
Financial aid: (601) 266-4774
Application deadline: 04/01
In-state tuition: total program: $12,936 (full time); part time: $473/credit hour
Out-of-state tuition: total program: $14,936 (full time); part time: $585/credit hour
Room/board/expenses: N/A
College-funded aid: Yes
International student aid: Yes
Full-time enrollment: 26
men: 54%; women: 46%; minorities: 12%; international: 19%
Part-time enrollment: 29
men: 55%; women: 45%; minorities: 31%; international: 0%
Acceptance rate (full time): 89%
Average GMAT (full time): 440
Average GRE (full time): 147 verbal; 146 quantitative; 3.7 writing
Average GPA (full time): 3.43
Average age of entrants to full-time program: 24
Average months of prior work experience (full time): 44
TOEFL requirement: Yes
Minimum TOEFL score: 71
Most popular departments: general management, marketing, sports business, quantitative analysis/statistics and operations research, other

MISSOURI

Drury University[1]

900 North Benton Avenue
Springfield, MO 65802
www.drury.edu/mba/
Private
Admissions: (417) 873-6948
Email: grad@drury.edu
Financial aid: (417) 873-7312

Tuition: N/A
Room/board/expenses: N/A
Enrollment: N/A

Missouri State University[1]

901 S. National Avenue
Glass Hall 400
Springfield, MO 65897
www.mba.missouristate.edu
Public
Admissions: (417) 836-5616
Email: COBGraduatePrograms@MissouriState.edu
Financial aid: (417) 836-5262
Tuition: N/A
Room/board/expenses: N/A
Enrollment: N/A

Missouri University of Science & Technology

1870 Miner Circle
Rolla, MO 65409
bit.mst.edu/
Public
Admissions: (573) 341-4141
Email: grad@mst.edu
Financial aid: (573) 341-4282
Application deadline: 07/15
In-state tuition: full time: $16,016; part time: N/A
Out-of-state tuition: full time: $25,526; part time: N/A
Room/board/expenses: $16,218
College-funded aid: Yes
International student aid: Yes
Full-time enrollment: 13
men: 54%; women: 46%; minorities: 0%; international: 8%
Part-time enrollment: 11
men: 55%; women: 45%; minorities: 27%; international: 9%
Acceptance rate (full time): 53%
Average GRE (full time): N/A verbal; N/A quantitative; N/A writing
Average GPA (full time): 3.65
Average age of entrants to full-time program: 27
TOEFL requirement: Yes
Minimum TOEFL score: 88
Most popular departments: general management, leadership, management information systems, quantitative analysis/statistics and operations research, technology

Rockhurst University

1100 Rockhurst Road
Kansas City, MO 64110
ww2.rockhurst.edu/helzberg
Private
Admissions: (816) 501-4632
Email: mba@rockhurst.edu
Financial aid: (816) 501-4600
Application deadline: rolling
Tuition: full time: N/A; part time: $710/credit hour
Room/board/expenses: N/A
College-funded aid: Yes
International student aid: Yes
Full-time enrollment: N/A
men: N/A; women: N/A; minorities: N/A; international: N/A

Part-time enrollment: 454
men: 62%; women: 38%; minorities: 22%; international: 1%
Average GRE (full time): N/A verbal; N/A quantitative; N/A writing
TOEFL requirement: Yes
Minimum TOEFL score: 80
Most popular departments: accounting, finance, general management, health care administration, quantitative analysis/statistics and operations research

Saint Louis University

3674 Lindell Boulevard
St. Louis, MO 63108
www.slu.edu/business
Private
Admissions: (314) 977-3801
Email: gradbiz@slu.edu
Financial aid: (314) 977-2350
Application deadline: 08/01
Tuition: full time: $47,654; part time: $1,070/credit hour
Room/board/expenses: $21,238
College-funded aid: Yes
International student aid: Yes
Average student indebtedness at graduation: $60,231
Full-time enrollment: 21
men: 62%; women: 38%; minorities: 19%; international: 10%
Part-time enrollment: 149
men: 54%; women: 46%; minorities: 16%; international: 6%
Acceptance rate (full time): 67%
Average GMAT (full time): 608
Average GRE (full time): 151 verbal; 150 quantitative; 3.3 writing
Average GPA (full time): 3.39
Average age of entrants to full-time program: 25
Average months of prior work experience (full time): 14
TOEFL requirement: Yes
Minimum TOEFL score: 88
Most popular departments: finance, general management, international business, marketing, supply chain management/logistics
Mean starting base salary for 2018 full-time graduates: $56,167
Employment location for 2018 class: Intl. N/A; N.E. N/A; M.A. N/A; S. N/A; M.W. 100%; S.W. N/A; W. N/A

Southeast Missouri State University

1 University Plaza, MS 5890
Cape Girardeau, MO 63701
www.semo.edu/mba
Public
Admissions: (573) 651-2590
Email: mba@semo.edu
Financial aid: (573) 651-2253
Application deadline: 08/01
In-state tuition: full time: $277/credit hour; part time: $277/credit hour
Out-of-state tuition: full time: $516/credit hour; part time: $516/credit hour

Room/board/expenses: $679
College-funded aid: Yes
International student aid: Yes
Full-time enrollment: 33
men: 42%; women:
58%; minorities: 6%;
international: 61%
Part-time enrollment: 61
men: 64%; women:
36%; minorities: 15%;
international: 13%
Acceptance rate (full time): 70%
Average GMAT (full time): 506
Average GRE (full
time): 136 verbal; 138
quantitative; 4.0 writing
Average GPA (full time): 3.59
Average age of entrants to
full-time program: 25
TOEFL requirement: Yes
Minimum TOEFL score: 79
Most popular departments:
accounting, finance,
general management,
health care administration,
international business

Truman State University[1]
100 E. Normal
Kirksville, MO 63501
gradstudies.truman.edu
Public
Admissions: (660) 785-4109
Email: gradinfo@truman.edu
Financial aid: (660) 785-4130
Tuition: N/A
Room/board/expenses: N/A
Enrollment: N/A

University of Central Missouri
Ward Edwards 1600
Warrensburg, MO 64093
www.ucmo.edu/mba
Public
Admissions: (660) 543-8192
Email: mba@ucmo.edu
Financial aid: (660) 543-8266
Application deadline: 07/14
In-state tuition: full time:
$464/credit hour; part
time: $464/credit hour
Out-of-state tuition: full
time: $464/credit hour; part
time: $464/credit hour
Room/board/expenses: $8,400
College-funded aid: Yes
International student aid: Yes
Average student indebtedness
at graduation: $18,678
Full-time enrollment: 30
men: 43%; women:
57%; minorities: 20%;
international: 13%
Part-time enrollment: 49
men: 59%; women:
41%; minorities: 14%;
international: 0%
Acceptance rate (full time): 70%
Average GMAT (full time): 460
Average GRE (full
time): 147 verbal; 152
quantitative; 3.3 writing
Average GPA (full time): 3.50
Average age of entrants to
full-time program: 30
Average months of prior work
experience (full time): 36
TOEFL requirement: Yes
Minimum TOEFL score: 79

Most popular departments:
accounting, general
management, health care
administration, management
information systems,
quantitative analysis/statistics
and operations research

University of Missouri– Kansas City
5100 Rockhill Road
Kansas City, MO 64110
www.bloch.umkc.edu/
graduate-program/mba
Public
Admissions: (816) 235-1214
Email: bloch@umkc.edu
Financial aid: (816) 235-1154
Application deadline: 07/10
In-state tuition: full time:
$385/credit hour; part
time: $385/credit hour
Out-of-state tuition: full
time: $993/credit hour; part
time: $993/credit hour
Room/board/expenses: $27,024
College-funded aid: Yes
International student aid: Yes
Full-time enrollment: 36
men: 58%; women:
42%; minorities: 22%;
international: 11%
Part-time enrollment: 247
men: 60%; women:
40%; minorities: 20%;
international: 1%
Average GRE (full
time): N/A verbal; N/A
quantitative; N/A writing
TOEFL requirement: Yes
Minimum TOEFL score: 80

University of Missouri– St. Louis
1 University Boulevard
St. Louis, MO 63121
mba.umsl.edu
Public
Admissions: N/A
Financial aid: (314) 516-5526
Application deadline: 07/01
In-state tuition: full time: N/A;
part time: $477/credit hour
Out-of-state tuition: full time: N/A;
part time: $1,170/credit hour
Room/board/expenses: N/A
College-funded aid: Yes
International student aid: Yes
Full-time enrollment: N/A
men: N/A; women:
N/A; minorities: N/A;
international: N/A
Part-time enrollment: 263
men: 57%; women:
43%; minorities: 17%;
international: 13%
Average GRE (full
time): N/A verbal; N/A
quantitative; N/A writing
TOEFL requirement: Yes
Minimum TOEFL score: N/A

University of Missouri
306 Cornell Hall
Columbia, MO 65211
mba.missouri.edu
Public
Admissions: (573) 882-2750
Email: trulaskemasters@
missouri.edu
Financial aid: (573) 882-2750
Application deadline: 07/15
In-state tuition: total program:
$29,777 (full time); part time: N/A
Out-of-state tuition: total
program: $66,194 (full
time); part time: N/A
Room/board/expenses: $35,200
College-funded aid: Yes
International student aid: Yes
Average student indebtedness
at graduation: $20,261
Full-time enrollment: 82
men: 71%; women:
29%; minorities: 10%;
international: 23%
Part-time enrollment: N/A
men: N/A; women:
N/A; minorities: N/A;
international: N/A
Acceptance rate (full time): 56%
Average GMAT (full time): 606
Average GRE (full
time): 152 verbal; 156
quantitative; 4.0 writing
Average GPA (full time): 3.39
Average age of entrants to
full-time program: 23
Average months of prior work
experience (full time): 18
TOEFL requirement: Yes
Minimum TOEFL score: 80
Most popular departments:
entrepreneurship, finance,
general management, marketing,
quantitative analysis/statistics
and operations research
Mean starting base salary for
2018 full-time graduates: $68,087
Employment location for
2018 class: Intl. 0%; N.E.
0%; M.A. 3%; S. 8%; M.W.
64%; S.W. 0%; W. 17%

Washington University in St. Louis
1 Brookings Drive
Campus Box 1133
St. Louis, MO 63130-4899
olin.wustl.edu/EN-US/
academic-programs/full-
time-MBA/Pages/default.aspx
Private
Admissions: (314) 935-7301
Email: OlinGradAdmissions@
wustl.edu
Financial aid: (314) 935-7301
Application deadline: 03/27
Tuition: full time: $60,760; part
time: $1,740/credit hour
Room/board/expenses: $25,746
College-funded aid: Yes
International student aid: Yes
Average student indebtedness
at graduation: $78,474
Full-time enrollment: 273
men: 59%; women:
41%; minorities: 21%;
international: 34%

Part-time enrollment: 246
men: 66%; women:
34%; minorities: 20%;
international: 5%
Acceptance rate (full time): 33%
Average GMAT (full time): 693
Average GRE (full
time): 156 verbal; 154
quantitative; 4.1 writing
Average GPA (full time): 3.50
Average age of entrants to
full-time program: 28
Average months of prior work
experience (full time): 49
TOEFL requirement: Yes
Minimum TOEFL score: N/A
Most popular departments:
consulting, entrepreneurship,
finance, marketing, supply
chain management/logistics
Mean starting base salary for 2018
full-time graduates: $107,592
Employment location for
2018 class: Intl. 6%; N.E.
8%; M.A. 8%; S. 12%; M.W.
53%; S.W. 7%; W. 6%

MONTANA
University of Montana[1]
32 Campus Drive
Missoula, MT 59812-6808
www.business.umt.edu/
Public
Admissions: N/A
Email: mba@business.umt.edu
Financial aid: N/A
Tuition: N/A
Room/board/expenses: N/A
Enrollment: N/A

NEBRASKA
Creighton University
2500 California Plaza
Omaha, NE 68178-0130
business.creighton.edu
Private
Admissions: (402) 280-2703
Email: GraduateSchool@
creighton.edu
Financial aid: (402) 280-2731
Application deadline: rolling
Tuition: full time: N/A; part
time: $870/credit hour
Room/board/expenses: N/A
College-funded aid: Yes
International student aid: Yes
Full-time enrollment: N/A
men: N/A; women:
N/A; minorities: N/A;
international: N/A
Part-time enrollment: 127
men: 75%; women:
25%; minorities: 16%;
international: 7%
Average GRE (full
time): N/A verbal; N/A
quantitative; N/A writing
TOEFL requirement: Yes
Minimum TOEFL score: 90
Most popular departments:
accounting, finance,
leadership, management
information systems

University of Nebraska–Kearney[1]
905 West 25th Street
Kearney, NE 68849
www.unk.edu
Public
Admissions: (800) 717-7881
Email: gradstudies@unk.edu
Financial aid: N/A
Tuition: N/A
Room/board/expenses: N/A
Enrollment: N/A

University of Nebraska–Lincoln[1]
P.O. Box 880405
730 North 14th Street
Lincoln, NE 68588-0405
business.unl.edu/mba/
Public
Admissions: (402) 472-2338
Email: businessgrad2@unl.edu
Financial aid: (402) 472-2030
Tuition: N/A
Room/board/expenses: N/A
Enrollment: N/A

University of Nebraska–Omaha
6708 Pine Street
Omaha, NE 68182-0048
mba.unomaha.edu
Public
Admissions: (402) 554-4836
Email: mba@unomaha.edu
Financial aid: (402) 554-2327
Application deadline: 07/01
In-state tuition: full time: N/A;
part time: $372/credit hour
Out-of-state tuition: full time:
N/A; part time: $917/credit hour
Room/board/expenses: N/A
College-funded aid: Yes
International student aid: Yes
Full-time enrollment: N/A
men: N/A; women:
N/A; minorities: N/A;
international: N/A
Part-time enrollment: 293
men: 60%; women:
40%; minorities: 13%;
international: 9%
Average GRE (full
time): N/A verbal; N/A
quantitative; N/A writing
TOEFL requirement: Yes
Minimum TOEFL score: 80
Most popular departments: health
care administration, human
resources management, supply
chain management/logistics,
quantitative analysis/statistics
and operations research, other

NEVADA
University of Nevada–Las Vegas
4505 Maryland Parkway
PO Box 456031
Las Vegas, NV 89154-6031
business.unlv.edu
Public
Admissions: (702) 895-3655
Email: lbsmba@unlv.edu
Financial aid: (702) 895-3682
Application deadline: 07/15
In-state tuition: full time:
N/A; total program:
$27,084 (part time)

Out-of-state tuition: full time: N/A; total program: $39,778 (part time)
Room/board/expenses: N/A
College-funded aid: Yes
International student aid: Yes
Full-time enrollment: N/A men: N/A; women: N/A; minorities: N/A; international: N/A
Part-time enrollment: 158 men: 60%; women: 40%; minorities: 37%; international: 10%
Average GRE (full time): N/A verbal; N/A quantitative; N/A writing
TOEFL requirement: Yes
Minimum TOEFL score: 61
Most popular departments: entrepreneurship, finance, hotel administration, marketing, management information systems

University of Nevada–Reno

1664 N. Virginia Street
Reno, NV 89557
www.mba.unr.edu
Public
Admissions: (775) 682-9142
Email: raffiee@unr.edu
Financial aid: (775) 784-4666
Application deadline: 03/15
In-state tuition: full time: N/A; part time: $364/credit hour
Out-of-state tuition: full time: N/A; part time: $666/credit hour
Room/board/expenses: N/A
College-funded aid: Yes
International student aid: Yes
Full-time enrollment: N/A men: N/A; women: N/A; minorities: N/A; international: N/A
Part-time enrollment: 221 men: 51%; women: 49%; minorities: 25%; international: 6%
Average GRE (full time): N/A verbal; N/A quantitative; N/A writing
TOEFL requirement: Yes
Minimum TOEFL score: 79
Most popular departments: entrepreneurship, finance, general management, marketing, management information systems

NEW HAMPSHIRE

Dartmouth College

100 Tuck Hall
Hanover, NH 03755-9000
www.tuck.dartmouth.edu
Private
Admissions: (603) 646-3162
Email: tuck.admissions@tuck.dartmouth.edu
Financial aid: (603) 646-0640
Application deadline: 04/01
Tuition: full time: $75,076; part time: N/A
Room/board/expenses: $35,050
College-funded aid: Yes
International student aid: Yes
Full-time enrollment: 576 men: 55%; women: 45%; minorities: 20%; international: 28%

Part-time enrollment: N/A men: N/A; women: N/A; minorities: N/A; international: N/A
Acceptance rate (full time): 23%
Average GMAT (full time): 722
Average GRE (full time): N/A verbal; N/A quantitative; N/A writing
Average GPA (full time): 3.49
Average age of entrants to full-time program: 28
Average months of prior work experience (full time): 63
TOEFL requirement: Yes
Minimum TOEFL score: N/A
Most popular departments: consulting, finance, general management, marketing, technology
Mean starting base salary for 2018 full-time graduates: $130,022
Employment location for 2018 class: Intl. 9%; N.E. 46%; M.A. 4%; S. 3%; M.W. 11%; S.W. 4%; W. 23%

University of New Hampshire

10 Garrison Avenue
Durham, NH 03824
www.mba.unh.edu
Public
Admissions: (603) 862-1367
Email: paulcollege.grad@unh.edu
Financial aid: (603) 862-3600
Application deadline: 06/01
In-state tuition: total program: $41,095 (full time); part time: $800/credit hour
Out-of-state tuition: total program: $48,095 (full time); part time: $910/credit hour
Room/board/expenses: $20,445
College-funded aid: Yes
International student aid: Yes
Average student indebtedness at graduation: $31,560
Full-time enrollment: 28 men: 75%; women: 25%; minorities: 14%; international: 21%
Part-time enrollment: 146 men: 74%; women: 26%; minorities: 3%; international: 4%
Acceptance rate (full time): 90%
Average GMAT (full time): 515
Average GRE (full time): 154 verbal; 150 quantitative; 3.9 writing
Average GPA (full time): 3.25
Average age of entrants to full-time program: 29
Average months of prior work experience (full time): 68
TOEFL requirement: Yes
Minimum TOEFL score: 80
Most popular departments: entrepreneurship, finance, international business, marketing, quantitative analysis/statistics and operations research
Mean starting base salary for 2018 full-time graduates: $48,508
Employment location for 2018 class: Intl. 33%; N.E. 67%; M.A. 0%; S. 0%; M.W. 0%; S.W. 0%; W. 0%

NEW JERSEY

Fairleigh Dickinson University

1000 River Road
Teaneck, NJ 07666
view2.fdu.edu/academics/silberman-college/
Private
Admissions: (201) 692-2554
Email: grad@fdu.edu
Financial aid: (973) 443-7304
Application deadline: 08/23
Tuition: full time: $1,334/credit hour; part time: $1,334/credit hour
Room/board/expenses: N/A
College-funded aid: Yes
International student aid: Yes
Full-time enrollment: 90 men: 47%; women: 53%; minorities: 23%; international: 11%
Part-time enrollment: 203 men: 56%; women: 44%; minorities: 22%; international: 12%
Acceptance rate (full time): 79%
Average GRE (full time): N/A verbal; N/A quantitative; N/A writing
Average age of entrants to full-time program: 24
TOEFL requirement: Yes
Minimum TOEFL score: 79
Most popular departments: accounting, finance, marketing, supply chain management/logistics

Monmouth University

400 Cedar Avenue
West Long Branch, NJ 07764
www.monmouth.edu
Private
Admissions: (732) 571-3452
Email: gradadm@monmouth.edu
Financial aid: (732) 571-3463
Application deadline: 07/15
Tuition: full time: $1,187/credit hour; part time: $1,187/credit hour
Room/board/expenses: $17,731
College-funded aid: Yes
International student aid: Yes
Average student indebtedness at graduation: $14,780
Full-time enrollment: 30 men: 50%; women: 50%; minorities: 10%; international: 0%
Part-time enrollment: 148 men: 55%; women: 45%; minorities: 9%; international: 8%
Acceptance rate (full time): 97%
Average GRE (full time): N/A verbal; N/A quantitative; N/A writing
Average GPA (full time): 3.60
Average age of entrants to full-time program: 22
TOEFL requirement: Yes
Minimum TOEFL score: 79

Montclair State University

1 Normal Avenue
Montclair, NJ 07043
www.montclair.edu/mba
Public
Admissions: (973) 655-5147

Email: gradschool@montclair.edu
Financial aid: (973) 655-4461
Application deadline: rolling
In-state tuition: full time: $839/credit hour; part time: $839/credit hour
Out-of-state tuition: full time: $839/credit hour; part time: $839/credit hour
Room/board/expenses: $20,084
College-funded aid: Yes
International student aid: Yes
Full-time enrollment: 22 men: 23%; women: 77%; minorities: 41%; international: 5%
Part-time enrollment: 286 men: 42%; women: 58%; minorities: 44%; international: 15%
Acceptance rate (full time): 95%
Average GRE (full time): N/A verbal; N/A quantitative; N/A writing
Average GPA (full time): 3.39
Average age of entrants to full-time program: 26
Average months of prior work experience (full time): 64
TOEFL requirement: Yes
Minimum TOEFL score: 83
Most popular departments: accounting, finance, marketing, management information systems, other

New Jersey Institute of Technology

University Heights
Newark, NJ 07102
management.njit.edu/
Public
Admissions: (973) 596-3300
Email: admissions@njit.edu
Financial aid: (973) 596-3479
Application deadline: 06/01
In-state tuition: full time: $23,374; part time: $1,286
Out-of-state tuition: full time: $33,102; part time: $1,768
Room/board/expenses: $18,000
College-funded aid: Yes
International student aid: Yes
Average student indebtedness at graduation: $33,501
Full-time enrollment: 32 men: 50%; women: 50%; minorities: 63%; international: 19%
Part-time enrollment: 53 men: 62%; women: 38%; minorities: 66%; international: 2%
Acceptance rate (full time): 63%
Average GMAT (full time): 340
Average GRE (full time): N/A verbal; N/A quantitative; N/A writing
Average GPA (full time): 3.03
Average age of entrants to full-time program: 27
Average months of prior work experience (full time): 92
TOEFL requirement: Yes
Minimum TOEFL score: 79
Most popular departments: entrepreneurship, finance, management information systems, technology, other

Ramapo College of New Jersey

505 Ramapo Valley Road
Mahwah, NJ 07430
www.ramapo.edu/admissions/
Public
Admissions: (201) 684-7300
Email: admissions@ramapo.edu
Financial aid: (201) 684-7549
Application deadline: 05/01
In-state tuition: full time: N/A; part time: $983/credit hour
Out-of-state tuition: full time: N/A; part time: $983/credit hour
Room/board/expenses: N/A
College-funded aid: Yes
International student aid: Yes
Full-time enrollment: N/A men: N/A; women: N/A; minorities: N/A; international: N/A
Part-time enrollment: 66 men: 47%; women: 53%; minorities: 27%; international: 0%
Average GRE (full time): N/A verbal; N/A quantitative; N/A writing
TOEFL requirement: Yes
Minimum TOEFL score: 79

Rider University[1]

2083 Lawrenceville Road
Lawrenceville, NJ 08648-3099
www.rider.edu/mba
Private
Admissions: (609) 895-5635
Email: gradadm@rider.edu
Financial aid: (609) 896-5360
Tuition: N/A
Room/board/expenses: N/A
Enrollment: N/A

Rowan University

201 Mullica Hill Road
Glassboro, NJ 08028
www.rowanu.com
Public
Admissions: (856) 256-5435
Email: cgceadmissions@rowan.edu
Financial aid: (856) 256-5141
Application deadline: 07/01
In-state tuition: full time: N/A; part time: N/A
Out-of-state tuition: full time: N/A; part time: N/A
Room/board/expenses: N/A
College-funded aid: Yes
International student aid: No
Average student indebtedness at graduation: $6,928
Full-time enrollment: 33 men: 48%; women: 52%; minorities: 21%; international: 27%
Part-time enrollment: 62 men: 56%; women: 44%; minorities: 26%; international: 0%
Average GRE (full time): N/A verbal; N/A quantitative; N/A writing
TOEFL requirement: Yes
Minimum TOEFL score: 79
Most popular departments: accounting, finance, general management, marketing, management information systems

Rutgers, The State University of New Jersey–Camden

227 Penn Street
Camden, NJ 08102
business.camden.rutgers.edu/
Public
Admissions: (856) 225-6584
Email: Rsbcmba@
camden.rutgers.edu
Financial aid: (856) 225-6039
Application deadline: 08/01
In-state tuition: full time: N/A;
part time: $996/credit hour
Out-of-state tuition: full time: N/A;
part time: $1,688/credit hour
Room/board/expenses: N/A
College-funded aid: Yes
International student aid: Yes
Full-time enrollment: N/A
men: N/A; women:
N/A; minorities: N/A;
international: N/A
Part-time enrollment: 93
men: 57%; women:
43%; minorities: 34%;
international: 9%
**Average GRE (full
time):** N/A verbal; N/A
quantitative; N/A writing
TOEFL requirement: Yes
Minimum TOEFL score: 80
Most popular departments:
finance, general
management, marketing

Rutgers, The State University of New Jersey–Newark and New Brunswick

1 Washington Park
Newark, NJ 07102-3122
www.business.rutgers.edu
Public
Admissions: (973) 353-1234
Email: admit@
business.rutgers.edu
Financial aid: (973) 353-5151
Application deadline: 05/01
In-state tuition: total program:
$59,378 (full time); part
time: $1,122/credit hour
Out-of-state tuition: total
program: $99,014 (full time);
part time: $1,948/credit hour
Room/board/expenses: $26,500
College-funded aid: Yes
International student aid: No
Full-time enrollment: 121
men: 62%; women:
38%; minorities: 35%;
international: 31%
Part-time enrollment: 1,021
men: 61%; women:
39%; minorities: 47%;
international: 2%
Acceptance rate (full time): 36%
Average GMAT (full time): 683
Average GRE (full time): 159
verbal; 157 quantitative;
N/A writing
Average GPA (full time): 3.30
**Average age of entrants to
full-time program:** 29
**Average months of prior work
experience (full time):** 59
TOEFL requirement: Yes
Minimum TOEFL score: 100

Most popular departments:
entrepreneurship, finance,
leadership, marketing, supply
chain management/logistics
**Mean starting base salary for
2018 full-time graduates:** $87,607
**Employment location for
2018 class:** Intl. 5%; N.E.
80%; M.A. 8%; S. 0%; M.W.
3%; S.W. 3%; W. 0%

Seton Hall University

400 S. Orange Avenue
South Orange, NJ 07079
www.shu.edu/academics/
business/
Private
Admissions: (973) 761-9262
Email: busgrad@shu.edu
Financial aid: (973) 761-9350
Application deadline: 05/31
Tuition: full time: N/A; part
time: $1,279/credit hour
Room/board/expenses: N/A
College-funded aid: Yes
International student aid: Yes
Full-time enrollment: N/A
men: N/A; women:
N/A; minorities: N/A;
international: N/A
Part-time enrollment: 448
men: 58%; women:
42%; minorities: 11%;
international: 63%
**Average GRE (full
time):** N/A verbal; N/A
quantitative; N/A writing
TOEFL requirement: Yes
Minimum TOEFL score: 80
Most popular departments:
accounting, finance, general
management, international
business, marketing

Stevens Institute of Technology

1 Castle Point Terrace
Hoboken, NJ 07030
www.stevens.edu/admissions/
graduate-admissions
Private
Admissions: (888) 783-8367
Email: graduate@stevens.edu
Financial aid: (201) 216-5555
Application deadline: 04/01
Tuition: full time: $37,250; part
time: $1,620/credit hour
Room/board/expenses: $17,090
College-funded aid: Yes.
International student aid: Yes
Full-time enrollment: 595
men: 61%; women:
39%; minorities: 2%;
international: 93%
Part-time enrollment: 329
men: 58%; women:
42%; minorities: 27%;
international: 11%
Acceptance rate (full time): 57%
Average GMAT (full time): 614
**Average GRE (full
time):** 149 verbal; 161
quantitative; 3.3 writing
Average GPA (full time): 3.10
**Average age of entrants to
full-time program:** 24
**Average months of prior work
experience (full time):** 28
TOEFL requirement: Yes
Minimum TOEFL score: 74

Most popular departments:
finance, general management,
management information
systems, quantitative
analysis/statistics and
operations research, other
**Mean starting base salary for
2018 full-time graduates:** $72,928

Stockton University

101 Vera King Farris Drive
Galloway, NJ 08205
stockton.edu/graduate/
business-administration.html
Public
Admissions: (609) 626-3640
Email: gradschool@stockton.edu
Financial aid: (609) 652-4203
Application deadline: 07/01
In-state tuition: full time: N/A;
part time: $624/credit hour
Out-of-state tuition: full time: N/A;
part time: $960/credit hour
Room/board/expenses: N/A
College-funded aid: Yes
Full-time enrollment: N/A
men: N/A; women:
N/A; minorities: N/A;
international: N/A
Part-time enrollment: 95
men: 45%; women:
55%; minorities: 24%;
international: 0%
**Average GRE (full
time):** N/A verbal; N/A
quantitative; N/A writing
TOEFL requirement: Yes
Minimum TOEFL score: 80
Most popular departments:
general management

William Paterson University

1600 Valley Road
Wayne, NJ 07470
www.wpunj.edu/MBA
Public
Admissions: (973) 720-3122
Email: graduate@wpunj.edu
Financial aid: (973) 720 3945
Application deadline: rolling
In-state tuition: full time: N/A;
part time: $710/credit hour
Out-of-state tuition: full time: N/A;
part time: $1,107/credit hour
Room/board/expenses: N/A
College-funded aid: Yes
International student aid: Yes
Full-time enrollment: N/A
men: N/A; women:
N/A; minorities: N/A;
international: N/A
Part-time enrollment: 245
men: 52%; women:
48%; minorities: 44%;
international: 5%
**Average GRE (full
time):** N/A verbal; N/A
quantitative; N/A writing
TOEFL requirement: Yes
Minimum TOEFL score: 79
Most popular departments:
accounting, entrepreneurship,
finance, general management,
human resources management

New Mexico State University

P.O. Box 30001, MSC 3AD
Las Cruces, NM 88003-0030
business.nmsu.edu/academics/
graduate-programs/mba
Public
Admissions: (575) 646-8003
Email: mbaprog@nmsu.edu
Financial aid: (575) 646-4105
Application deadline: 07/15
In-state tuition: full time: N/A;
part time: $253/credit hour
Out-of-state tuition: full time:
N/A; part time: $881/credit hour
Room/board/expenses: N/A
College-funded aid: Yes
International student aid: Yes
Full-time enrollment: N/A
men: N/A; women:
N/A; minorities: N/A;
international: N/A
Part-time enrollment: 172
men: 41%; women:
59%; minorities: N/A;
international: N/A
**Average GRE (full
time):** N/A verbal; N/A
quantitative; N/A writing
TOEFL requirement: Yes
Minimum TOEFL score: 79
Most popular departments:
finance, general management,
management information
systems, other

University of New Mexico

MSC05 3090
1 University of New Mexico
Albuquerque, NM 87131-0001
www.mgt.unm.edu
Public
Admissions: (505) 277-3290
Email: andersonadvising@
unm.edu
Financial aid: (505) 277-8900
Application deadline: 04/01
In-state tuition: full time: N/A;
part time: $462/credit hour
Out-of-state tuition: full time: N/A;
part time: $1,128/credit hour
Room/board/expenses: N/A
College-funded aid: Yes
International student aid: Yes
Full-time enrollment: N/A
men: N/A; women:
N/A; minorities: N/A;
international: N/A
Part-time enrollment: 274
men: 53%; women:
47%; minorities: 46%;
international: 8%
**Average GRE (full
time):** N/A verbal; N/A
quantitative; N/A writing
TOEFL requirement: Yes
Minimum TOEFL score: 80
Most popular departments:
finance, production/
operations management,
organizational behavior,
public policy, technology

Adelphi University

1 South Avenue
Garden City, NY 11530
www.adelphi.edu
Private
Admissions: (516) 877-3050
Email: admissions@adelphi.edu
Financial aid: (516) 877-3080
Application deadline: rolling
Tuition: full time: N/A; part
time: $1,260/credit hour
Room/board/expenses: N/A
College-funded aid: Yes
International student aid: Yes
Full-time enrollment: N/A
men: N/A; women:
N/A; minorities: N/A;
international: N/A
Part-time enrollment: 469
men: 58%; women:
42%; minorities: 17%;
international: 60%
**Average GRE (full
time):** N/A verbal; N/A
quantitative; N/A writing
TOEFL requirement: Yes
Minimum TOEFL score: 80
Most popular departments:
accounting, finance,
health care administration,
human resources
management, marketing

Alfred University

One Saxon Drive
Alfred, NY 14802
business.alfred.edu/mba.html
Private
Admissions: (800) 541-9229
Email: gradinquiry@alfred.edu
Financial aid: (607) 871-2159
Application deadline: 08/01
Tuition: full time: $39,010;
part time: $810/credit hour
Room/board/expenses: $15,670
College-funded aid: Yes
International student aid: Yes
**Average student indebtedness
at graduation:** $29,583
Full-time enrollment: 22
men: 64%; women:
36%; minorities: 18%;
international: 14%
Part-time enrollment: 20
men: 55%; women:
45%; minorities: 10%;
international: 5%
Acceptance rate (full time): 93%
**Average GRE (full
time):** N/A verbal; N/A
quantitative; N/A writing
**Average age of entrants to
full-time program:** 23
**Average months of prior work
experience (full time):** 15
TOEFL requirement: Yes
Minimum TOEFL score: 90
Most popular departments:
accounting, general
management, health
care administration
**Employment location for
2018 class:** Intl. N/A; N.E.
77%; M.A. 4%; S. 15%; M.W.
N/A; S.W. 4%; W. N/A

Binghamton University–SUNY

PO Box 6000
Binghamton, NY 13902-6000
www.binghamton.edu/som/
graduate-programs/index.html
Public
Admissions: (607) 777-2317
Email: awheeler@
binghamton.edu
Financial aid: (607) 777-6358
Application deadline: 03/01
In-state tuition: full time:
$17,206; part time: N/A
Out-of-state tuition: full time:
$26,746; part time: N/A
Room/board/expenses: $19,996
College-funded aid: Yes
International student aid: Yes
**Average student indebtedness
at graduation:** $18,229
Full-time enrollment: 132
men: 60%; women:
40%; minorities: 21%;
international: 12%
Part-time enrollment: N/A
men: N/A; women:
N/A; minorities: N/A;
international: N/A
Acceptance rate (full time): 82%
Average GMAT (full time): 592
**Average GRE (full
time):** 151 verbal; 152
quantitative; 4.0 writing
Average GPA (full time): 3.51
**Average age of entrants to
full-time program:** 24
**Average months of prior work
experience (full time):** 37
TOEFL requirement: Yes
Minimum TOEFL score: 96
Most popular departments:
finance, leadership, marketing,
management information
systems, supply chain
management/logistics
**Mean starting base salary for
2018 full-time graduates:** $64,684
**Employment location for
2018 class:** Intl. N/A; N.E.
94%; M.A. N/A; S. 4%; M.W.
N/A; S.W. N/A; W. 2%

Canisius College

2001 Main Street
Buffalo, NY 14208
www.canisius.edu/
Public
Admissions: (800) 950-2505
Email: GradAdm@Canisius.edu
Financial aid: (716) 888-2600
Application deadline: rolling
In-state tuition: full time: $41,420;
part time: $820/credit hour
Out-of-state tuition: full
time: $41,420; part time:
$820/credit hour
Room/board/expenses: $15,368
College-funded aid: Yes
International student aid: Yes
**Average student indebtedness
at graduation:** $29,583
Full-time enrollment: 43
men: 67%; women: 33%;
minorities: 5%; international: 2%
Part-time enrollment: 211
men: 63%; women: 37%;
minorities: 9%; international: 9%
Acceptance rate (full time): 97%
Average GMAT (full time): 501
**Average GRE (full
time):** 150 verbal; 146
quantitative; 3.7 writing

Average GPA (full time): 3.19
**Average age of entrants to
full-time program:** 22
TOEFL requirement: Yes
Minimum TOEFL score: 79
Most popular departments:
accounting, finance,
international business,
marketing, supply chain
management/logistics
**Mean starting base salary for
2018 full-time graduates:** $52,700
**Employment location for 2018
class:** Intl. N/A; N.E. 100%;
M.A. N/A; S. N/A; M.W.
N/A; S.W. N/A; W. N/A

Clarkson University

Snell Hall 322E, Box 5770
Potsdam, NY 13699-5770
www.clarkson.edu/mba
Private
Admissions: (315) 268-6613
Email: busgrad@clarkson.edu
Financial aid: (315) 268-7699
Application deadline: rolling
Tuition: total program: $53,644
(full time); part time: N/A
Room/board/expenses: $21,686
College-funded aid: Yes
International student aid: Yes
**Average student indebtedness
at graduation:** $37,556
Full-time enrollment: 68
men: 59%; women:
41%; minorities: 6%;
international: 18%
Part-time enrollment: N/A
men: N/A; women:
N/A; minorities: N/A;
international: N/A
Acceptance rate (full time): 90%
Average GMAT (full time): 590
**Average GRE (full
time):** 153 verbal; 159
quantitative; 3.9 writing
Average GPA (full time): 3.36
**Average age of entrants to
full-time program:** 23
**Average months of prior work
experience (full time):** 41
TOEFL requirement: Yes
Minimum TOEFL score: 80
Most popular departments:
accounting, entrepreneurship,
health care administration,
supply chain management/
logistics, other
**Mean starting base salary for
2018 full-time graduates:** $62,492
**Employment location for
2018 class:** Intl. N/A; N.E.
76%; M.A. 4%; S. N/A; M.W.
12%; S.W. 4%; W. 4%

College at Brockport–SUNY[1]

119 Hartwell Hall
Brockport, NY 14420
www.brockport.edu/business
Public
Admissions: (585) 395-2525
Email: gradadmit@brockport.edu
Financial aid: (585) 395-2501
Tuition: N/A
Room/board/expenses: N/A
Enrollment: N/A

Columbia University

3022 Broadway
216 Uris Hall
New York, NY 10027
www.gsb.columbia.edu
Private
Admissions: (212) 854-1961
Email: apply@gsb.columbia.edu
Financial aid: (212) 854-4057
Application deadline: 04/10
Tuition: full time: $77,404;
part time: N/A
Room/board/expenses: $28,341
College-funded aid: Yes
International student aid: Yes
Full-time enrollment: 1,297
men: 59%; women:
41%; minorities: N/A;
international: N/A
Part-time enrollment: N/A
men: N/A; women:
N/A; minorities: N/A;
international: N/A
Acceptance rate (full time): 14%
Average GMAT (full time): 736
**Average GRE (full
time):** N/A verbal; N/A
quantitative; N/A writing
Average GPA (full time): 3.60
**Average age of entrants to
full-time program:** 28
**Average months of prior work
experience (full time):** 60
TOEFL requirement: No
Minimum TOEFL score: N/A
Most popular departments:
consulting, entrepreneurship,
finance, health care
administration, real estate
**Mean starting base salary for 2018
full-time graduates:** $130,924

Cornell University

Sage Hall, Cornell University
Ithaca, NY 14853-6201
www.johnson.cornell.edu
Private
Admissions: (607) 255-4526
Email: mba@johnson.cornell.edu
Financial aid: (607) 255-6116
Application deadline: 04/10
Tuition: full time: $69,290;
part time: N/A
Room/board/expenses: $22,900
College-funded aid: Yes
International student aid: Yes
Full-time enrollment: 573
men: 70%; women:
30%; minorities: 21%;
international: 29%
Part-time enrollment: N/A
men: N/A; women:
N/A; minorities: N/A;
international: N/A
Acceptance rate (full time): 33%
Average GMAT (full time): 699
**Average GRE (full
time):** 160 verbal; 160
quantitative; 4.4 writing
Average GPA (full time): 3.41
**Average age of entrants to
full-time program:** 28
**Average months of prior work
experience (full time):** 59
TOEFL requirement: Yes
Minimum TOEFL score: 100
Most popular departments:
consulting, finance, leadership,
marketing, technology
**Mean starting base salary for 2018
full-time graduates:** $126,353

**Employment location for
2018 class:** Intl. N/A; N.E.
61%; M.A. 3%; S. 3%; M.W.
13%; S.W. 6%; W. 13%

CUNY Bernard M. Baruch College

1 Bernard Baruch Way
New York, NY 10010
zicklin.baruch.cuny.edu
Public
Admissions: (646) 312-1300
Email: zicklingradadmissions@
baruch.cuny.edu
Financial aid: (646) 312-1370
Application deadline: N/A
In-state tuition: full time: $18,199;
part time: $705/credit hour
Out-of-state tuition: full
time: $31,519; part time:
$1,080/credit hour
Room/board/expenses: N/A
College-funded aid: Yes
International student aid: Yes
Full-time enrollment: 75
men: 43%; women:
57%; minorities: 17%;
international: 36%
Part-time enrollment: 476
men: 56%; women:
44%; minorities: 31%;
international: 5%
Acceptance rate (full time): 35%
Average GMAT (full time): 637
Average GRE (full time): 157
verbal; 157 quantitative;
N/A writing
Average GPA (full time): 3.37
**Average age of entrants to
full-time program:** 28
**Average months of prior work
experience (full time):** 53
TOEFL requirement: Yes
Minimum TOEFL score: 100
Most popular departments:
accounting, entrepreneurship,
finance, general
management, management
information systems
**Mean starting base salary for
2018 full-time graduates:** $95,343
**Employment location for
2018 class:** Intl. 5%; N.E.
85%; M.A. 3%; S. N/A; M.W.
5%; S.W. N/A; W. 3%

Fordham University

140 W. 62nd Street
New York, NY 10023
www.fordham.edu/gabelli
Private
Admissions: (212) 636-6200
Email: admissionsgb@
fordham.edu
Financial aid: (212) 636-6700
Application deadline: 05/31
Tuition: total program:
$103,598 (full time); part
time: $1,555/credit hour
Room/board/expenses: $35,772
College-funded aid: Yes
International student aid: Yes
**Average student indebtedness
at graduation:** $98,199
Full-time enrollment: 100
men: 60%; women:
40%; minorities: 23%;
international: 34%
Part-time enrollment: 140
men: 53%; women:
47%; minorities: 32%;
international: 3%

Acceptance rate (full time): 44%
Average GMAT (full time): 656
**Average GRE (full
time):** 153 verbal; 152
quantitative; 4.1 writing
Average GPA (full time): 3.18
**Average age of entrants to
full-time program:** 29
**Average months of prior work
experience (full time):** 71
TOEFL requirement: Yes
Minimum TOEFL score: 100
Most popular departments:
finance, general management,
marketing, management
information systems, other
**Mean starting base salary for
2018 full-time graduates:** $99,938
**Employment location for
2018 class:** Intl. N/A; N.E.
88%; M.A. 8%; S. N/A; M.W.
4%; S.W. N/A; W. N/A

Hofstra University

300 Weller Hall
Hempstead, NY 11549
www.hofstra.edu/graduate
Private
Admissions: (516) 463-4723
Email: graduateadmission@
hofstra.edu
Financial aid: (516) 463-8000
Application deadline: rolling
Tuition: full time: $31,518;
part time: $16,830
Room/board/expenses: $22,478
College-funded aid: Yes
International student aid: Yes
Full-time enrollment: 258
men: 59%; women:
41%; minorities: 22%;
international: 48%
Part-time enrollment: 184
men: 58%; women:
42%; minorities: 35%;
international: 7%
Acceptance rate (full time): 91%
Average GMAT (full time): 535
**Average GRE (full
time):** 149 verbal; 156
quantitative; N/A writing
Average GPA (full time): 3.35
**Average age of entrants to
full-time program:** 24
**Average months of prior work
experience (full time):** 44
TOEFL requirement: Yes
Minimum TOEFL score: 80
Most popular departments:
accounting, finance, health
care administration, marketing,
quantitative analysis/statistics
and operations research
**Mean starting base salary for
2018 full-time graduates:** $60,183
**Employment location for
2018 class:** Intl. 10%; N.E.
76%; M.A. 4%; S. 6%; M.W.
0%; S.W. 0%; W. 4%

Iona College

715 North Avenue
New Rochelle, NY 10801
www.iona.edu/academics/
school-of-business.aspx
Private
Admissions: (914) 633-2789
Email: gradadmissions@iona.edu
Financial aid: (914) 633-2497
Application deadline: rolling
Tuition: full time: N/A; part
time: $1,149/credit hour
Room/board/expenses: N/A

College-funded aid: Yes
International student aid: Yes
Full-time enrollment: N/A
men: N/A; women:
N/A; minorities: N/A;
international: N/A
Part-time enrollment: 270
men: 50%; women:
50%; minorities: 38%;
international: 4%
Average GRE (full time): N/A verbal; N/A
quantitative; N/A writing
TOEFL requirement: Yes
Minimum TOEFL score: 80
Most popular departments:
accounting, finance,
general management,
marketing, management
information systems

Ithaca College

953 Danby Road
Ithaca, NY 14850-7002
www.ithaca.edu/gradadmission
Private
Admissions: (607) 274-3124
Email: admission@ithaca.edu
Financial aid: (607) 274-3131
Application deadline: 05/15
Tuition: full time: $976/credit
hour; part time: $976/credit hour
Room/board/expenses: N/A
College-funded aid: Yes
International student aid: Yes
Full-time enrollment: 24
men: 50%; women:
50%; minorities: 33%;
international: 13%
Part-time enrollment: 5
men: 40%; women:
60%; minorities: 20%;
international: 0%
Acceptance rate (full time): 89%
Average GRE (full time): N/A verbal; N/A
quantitative; N/A writing
Average age of entrants to full-time program: 22
TOEFL requirement: Yes
Minimum TOEFL score: 80

Le Moyne College

1419 Salt Springs Road
Syracuse, NY 13214-1301
www.lemoyne.edu/madden
Private
Admissions: (315) 445-5444
Email: business@lemoyne.edu
Financial aid: (315) 445-4400
Application deadline: 07/01
Tuition: full time: $835/credit
hour; part time: $835/credit hour
Room/board/expenses: N/A
College-funded aid: Yes
International student aid: Yes
Average student indebtedness at graduation: $7,243
Full-time enrollment: 21
men: 43%; women:
57%; minorities: 10%;
international: 0%
Part-time enrollment: 74
men: 54%; women:
46%; minorities: 11%;
international: 4%
Acceptance rate (full time): 93%
Average GMAT (full time): 530
Average GRE (full time): 150 verbal; 150
quantitative; 3.3 writing
Average GPA (full time): 3.43

Average age of entrants to full-time program: 22
Average months of prior work experience (full time): 18
TOEFL requirement: Yes
Minimum TOEFL score: 79
Mean starting base salary for 2018 full-time graduates: $53,469
Employment location for 2018 class: Intl. 0%; N.E.
94%; M.A. 0%; S. 0%; M.W.
0%; S.W. 6%; W. 0%

LIU Post

720 Northern Boulevard
Brookville, NY 11548-1300
www.liu.edu/postmba
Private
Admissions: (516) 299-2900
Email: post-enroll@liu.edu
Financial aid: (516) 299-2338
Application deadline: 08/19
Tuition: full time: $1,225/
credit hour; part time:
$1,225/credit hour
Room/board/expenses: $20,750
College-funded aid: Yes
International student aid: Yes
Full-time enrollment: 63
men: 68%; women:
32%; minorities: 17%;
international: 29%
Part-time enrollment: 21
men: 52%; women:
48%; minorities: 33%;
international: 0%
Acceptance rate (full time): 33%
Average GMAT (full time): 453
Average GRE (full time): 145 verbal; 154
quantitative; N/A writing
Average GPA (full time): 3.09
Average age of entrants to full-time program: 26
Average months of prior work experience (full time): 76
TOEFL requirement: Yes
Minimum TOEFL score: 75

Manhattan College

4513 Manhattan College
Parkway
Riverdale, NY 10471
manhattan.edu/
Private
Admissions: (718) 862-8200
Email: gradadmit@
manhattan.edu
Financial aid: (718) 862-7178
Application deadline: rolling
Tuition: full time: $1,120/
credit hour; part time:
$1,120/credit hour
Room/board/expenses: N/A
College-funded aid: Yes
International student aid: No
Full-time enrollment: 31
men: 52%; women:
48%; minorities: 23%;
international: 0%
Part-time enrollment: 75
men: 48%; women:
52%; minorities: 33%;
international: 5%
Acceptance rate (full time): 97%
Average GRE (full time): N/A verbal; N/A
quantitative; N/A writing
Average GPA (full time): 3.23
Average age of entrants to full-time program: 22
TOEFL requirement: Yes
Minimum TOEFL score: 80

Most popular departments:
accounting, economics, finance,
general management, marketing

New York Institute of Technology[1]

1855 Broadway
New York, NY 10023
www.nyit.edu/degrees/
management_mba
Private
Admissions: (516) 686-7520
Email: nyitgrad@nyit.edu
Financial aid: N/A
Tuition: N/A
Room/board/expenses: N/A
Enrollment: N/A

New York University

44 West Fourth Street
New York, NY 10012-1126
www.stern.nyu.edu
Private
Admissions: (212) 998-0600
Email: sternmba@stern.nyu.edu
Financial aid: (212) 998-0790
Application deadline: 03/15
Tuition: full time: $74,300; part
time: $2,228/credit hour
Room/board/expenses: $37,316
College-funded aid: Yes
International student aid: Yes
Full-time enrollment: 772
men: 64%; women:
36%; minorities: 28%;
international: 26%
Part-time enrollment: 1,207
men: 62%; women:
38%; minorities: 25%;
international: 10%
Acceptance rate (full time): 23%
Average GMAT (full time): 716
Average GRE (full time): 163 verbal; 161
quantitative; 4.5 writing
Average GPA (full time): 3.45
Average age of entrants to full-time program: 28
Average months of prior work experience (full time): 63
TOEFL requirement: Yes
Minimum TOEFL score: N/A
Most popular departments:
consulting, finance,
general management,
leadership, marketing
Mean starting base salary for 2018 full-time graduates: $129,059
Employment location for 2018 class: Intl. N/A; N.E.
78%; M.A. 2%; S. 3%; M.W.
2%; S.W. 3%; W. 13%

Niagara University

PO Box 1909
Niagara University, NY 14109
mba.niagara.edu
Private
Admissions: (716) 286-8051
Email: bsemski@niagara.edu
Financial aid: (716) 286-8686
Application deadline: 08/22
Tuition: full time: $895/credit
hour; part time: $895/credit hour
Room/board/expenses: $16,650
College-funded aid: Yes
International student aid: Yes
Full-time enrollment: 211
men: 48%; women:
52%; minorities: 13%;
international: 31%

Part-time enrollment: 52
men: 60%; women:
40%; minorities: 13%;
international: 10%
Acceptance rate (full time): 59%
Average GRE (full time): N/A verbal; N/A
quantitative; N/A writing
Average GPA (full time): 3.31
Average age of entrants to full-time program: 25
TOEFL requirement: Yes
Minimum TOEFL score: 79
Most popular departments:
accounting, finance, general
management, human resources
management, marketing

Pace University

1 Pace Plaza
New York, NY 10038
www.pace.edu/lubin/sections/
explore-programs/
graduate-programs
Private
Admissions: (212) 346-1531
Email: graduateadmission@
pace.edu
Financial aid: (914) 773-3751
Application deadline: 08/01
Tuition: full time: $1,267/
credit hour; part time:
$1,267/credit hour
Room/board/expenses: $23,560
College-funded aid: Yes
International student aid: Yes
Average student indebtedness at graduation: $37,869
Full-time enrollment: 187
men: 45%; women:
55%; minorities: 24%;
international: 47%
Part-time enrollment: 95
men: 44%; women:
56%; minorities: 35%;
international: 24%
Acceptance rate (full time): 56%
Average GMAT (full time): 487
Average GRE (full time): N/A verbal; N/A
quantitative; N/A writing
Average GPA (full time): 3.40
Average age of entrants to full-time program: 25
TOEFL requirement: Yes
Minimum TOEFL score: 90
Most popular departments:
accounting, finance, general
management, human resources
management, marketing
Mean starting base salary for 2018 full-time graduates: $68,824

Rensselaer Polytechnic Institute[1]

110 Eighth Street
Pittsburgh Building 5202
Troy, NY 12180-3590
lallyschool.rpi.edu
Private
Admissions: (518) 276-6565
Email: lallymba@rpi.edu
Financial aid: (518) 276-6565
Tuition: N/A
Room/board/expenses: N/A
Enrollment: N/A

Rochester Institute of Technology

105 Lomb Memorial Drive
Rochester, NY 14623-5608
saunders.rit.edu
Private
Admissions: (585) 475-2229
Email: gradinfo@rit.edu
Financial aid: (585) 475-2186
Application deadline: rolling
Tuition: full time: $45,808;
part time: N/A
Room/board/expenses: $15,100
College-funded aid: Yes
International student aid: Yes
Full-time enrollment: 126
men: 60%; women:
40%; minorities: 12%;
international: 36%
Part-time enrollment: N/A
men: N/A; women:
N/A; minorities: N/A;
international: N/A
Acceptance rate (full time): 71%
Average GMAT (full time): 540
Average GRE (full time): 147 verbal; 148
quantitative; 3.6 writing
Average GPA (full time): 3.24
Average age of entrants to full-time program: 26
TOEFL requirement: Yes
Minimum TOEFL score: 92
Most popular departments:
finance, leadership, marketing,
management information
systems, technology
Mean starting base salary for 2018 full-time graduates: $59,784

St. Bonaventure University

3261 West State Road
St. Bonaventure, NY 14778
www.sbu.edu/admission-aid/
graduate-admissions
Private
Admissions: (716) 375-2021
Email: mretchle@sbu.edu
Financial aid: (716) 375-7888
Application deadline: 10/08
Tuition: full time: $755/credit
hour; part time: $755/credit hour
Room/board/expenses: $15,144
College-funded aid: Yes
International student aid: Yes
Average student indebtedness at graduation: $20,495
Full-time enrollment: 86
men: 49%; women:
51%; minorities: 10%;
international: 8%
Part-time enrollment: 108
men: 52%; women: 48%;
minorities: 9%; international: 1%
Acceptance rate (full time): 96%
Average GMAT (full time): 463
Average GRE (full time): N/A verbal; N/A
quantitative; N/A writing
Average GPA (full time): 3.49
Average age of entrants to full-time program: 23
TOEFL requirement: Yes
Minimum TOEFL score: 79
Most popular departments:
accounting, finance, general
management, marketing

St. John Fisher College

3690 East Avenue
Rochester, NY 14618
www.sjfc.edu/graduate-programs/master-of-business-administration-mba/
Private
Admissions: (585) 385-8064
Email: grad@sjfc.edu
Financial aid: (585) 385-8042
Application deadline: rolling
Tuition: full time: $1,130/credit hour; part time: $1,130/credit hour
Room/board/expenses: N/A
College-funded aid: Yes
International student aid: Yes
Full-time enrollment: 53
men: 45%; women: 55%; minorities: 13%; international: 4%
Part-time enrollment: 70
men: 60%; women: 40%; minorities: 16%; international: 0%
Acceptance rate (full time): 87%
Average GMAT (full time): 370
Average GRE (full time): N/A verbal; N/A quantitative; N/A writing
Average GPA (full time): 3.50
Average age of entrants to full-time program: 22
TOEFL requirement: Yes
Minimum TOEFL score: 80
Mean starting base salary for 2018 full-time graduates: $50,607
Employment location for 2018 class: Intl. N/A; N.E. 100%; M.A. N/A; S. N/A; M.W. N/A; S.W. N/A; W. N/A

St. John's University

8000 Utopia Parkway
Queens, NY 11439
www.stjohns.edu/tobin
Private
Admissions: (718) 990-3060
Email: tobingradnyc@stjohns.edu
Financial aid: (718) 990-2000
Application deadline: 11/01
Tuition: full time: N/A; part time: $1,245/credit hour
Room/board/expenses: N/A
College-funded aid: Yes
International student aid: Yes
Full-time enrollment: N/A
men: N/A; women: N/A; minorities: N/A; international: N/A
Part-time enrollment: 361
men: 54%; women: 46%; minorities: 43%; international: 18%
Average GRE (full time): N/A verbal; N/A quantitative; N/A writing
TOEFL requirement: Yes
Minimum TOEFL score: 80
Most popular departments: accounting, finance, general management, international business, marketing

SUNY–Fredonia[1]

280 Central Ave
Fredonia, NY 14063
home.fredonia.edu/businessadministration
Public

Admissions: N/A
Financial aid: N/A
Tuition: N/A
Room/board/expenses: N/A
Enrollment: N/A

SUNY–New Paltz

1 Hawk Drive
New Paltz, NY 12561
www.newpaltz.edu/graduate
Public
Admissions: (845) 257-3947
Email: gradstudies@newpaltz.edu
Financial aid: (845) 257-3250
Application deadline: rolling
In-state tuition: full time: $16,234; part time: N/A
Out-of-state tuition: full time: $25,774; part time: N/A
Room/board/expenses: N/A
College-funded aid: Yes
International student aid: No
Full-time enrollment: 110
men: 47%; women: 53%; minorities: 22%; international: 7%
Part-time enrollment: N/A
men: N/A; women: N/A; minorities: N/A; international: N/A
Acceptance rate (full time): 93%
Average GMAT (full time): 510
Average GRE (full time): 151 verbal; 152 quantitative; 3.8 writing
Average GPA (full time): 3.48
Average age of entrants to full-time program: 26
TOEFL requirement: Yes
Minimum TOEFL score: 80
Most popular departments: accounting, general management

SUNY–Oswego

138 Rich Hall
Oswego, NY 13126
www.oswego.edu/graduate/
Public
Admissions: (315) 312-3152
Email: gradstudies@oswego.edu
Financial aid: (315) 312-2248
Application deadline: rolling
In-state tuition: full time: $15,538; part time: $619/credit hour
Out-of-state tuition: full time: $25,078; part time: $1,016/credit hour
Room/board/expenses: $18,940
College-funded aid: Yes
International student aid: Yes
Average student indebtedness at graduation: $21,855
Full-time enrollment: 70
men: 66%; women: 34%; minorities: 13%; international: 4%
Part-time enrollment: 42
men: 55%; women: 45%; minorities: 12%; international: 0%
Acceptance rate (full time): 90%
Average GMAT (full time): 483
Average GRE (full time): N/A verbal; N/A quantitative; N/A writing
Average GPA (full time): 3.18
Average age of entrants to full-time program: 22
Average months of prior work experience (full time): 10
TOEFL requirement: Yes

Minimum TOEFL score: 83
Most popular departments: accounting, general management, health care administration, marketing, tax
Mean starting base salary for 2018 full-time graduates: $45,000
Employment location for 2018 class: Intl. N/A; N.E. 100%; M.A. N/A; S. N/A; M.W. N/A; S.W. N/A; W. N/A

SUNY Polytechnic Institute[1]

100 Seymour Road
Utica, NY 13502
www.sunypoly.edu/graduate/mbatm/
Public
Admissions: (315) 792-7347
Email: gradcenter@sunyit.edu
Financial aid: (315) 792-7210
Tuition: N/A
Room/board/expenses: N/A
Enrollment: N/A

Syracuse University

721 University Avenue, Suite 315
Syracuse, NY 13244-2450
whitman.syr.edu/mba/fulltime
Private
Admissions: (315) 443-9214
Email: busgrad@syr.edu
Financial aid: (315) 443-9214
Application deadline: 04/19
Tuition: full time: $1,559/credit hour; part time: N/A
Room/board/expenses: $20,992
College-funded aid: Yes
International student aid: Yes
Average student indebtedness at graduation: $38,000
Full-time enrollment: 45
men: 53%; women: 47%; minorities: 4%; international: 64%
Part-time enrollment: N/A
men: N/A; women: N/A; minorities: N/A; international: N/A
Acceptance rate (full time): 75%
Average GMAT (full time): 630
Average GRE (full time): 159 verbal; 164 quantitative; 5.3 writing
Average GPA (full time): 3.30
Average age of entrants to full-time program: 25
Average months of prior work experience (full time): 33
TOEFL requirement: Yes
Minimum TOEFL score: 100
Most popular departments: entrepreneurship, finance, general management, marketing, supply chain management/logistics
Mean starting base salary for 2018 full-time graduates: $80,964
Employment location for 2018 class: Intl. 7%; N.E. 67%; M.A. 0%; S. 0%; M.W. 13%; S.W. 0%; W. 13%

University at Albany–SUNY

1400 Washington Avenue
Massry Center for Business
Albany, NY 12222
graduatebusiness.albany.edu
Public

Admissions: (518) 442-3980
Email: graduate@albany.edu
Financial aid: (518) 442-5757
Application deadline: 05/01
In-state tuition: full time: $15,834; part time: $619/credit hour
Out-of-state tuition: full time: $25,374; part time: $1,016/credit hour
Room/board/expenses: $2,523
College-funded aid: Yes
International student aid: Yes
Full-time enrollment: 115
men: 70%; women: 30%; minorities: 41%; international: 10%
Part-time enrollment: 190
men: 64%; women: 36%; minorities: 19%; international: 5%
Acceptance rate (full time): 73%
Average GMAT (full time): 550
Average GRE (full time): N/A verbal; N/A quantitative; N/A writing
Average GPA (full time): 3.40
Average months of prior work experience (full time): 60
TOEFL requirement: Yes
Minimum TOEFL score: 90
Most popular departments: finance, human resources management, marketing, management information systems, other
Mean starting base salary for 2018 full-time graduates: $64,000
Employment location for 2018 class: Intl. N/A; N.E. 100%; M.A. N/A; S. N/A; M.W. N/A; S.W. N/A; W. N/A

University at Buffalo–SUNY

203 Alfiero Center
Buffalo, NY 14260-4010
mgt.buffalo.edu/mba
Public
Admissions: (716) 645-3204
Email: som-apps@buffalo.edu
Financial aid: (716) 645-8232
Application deadline: 06/01
In-state tuition: full time: $18,898; part time: N/A/credit hour
Out-of-state tuition: full time: $28,438; part time: $760/credit hour
Room/board/expenses: N/A
College-funded aid: Yes
International student aid: Yes
Full-time enrollment: 209
men: 70%; women: 30%; minorities: 17%; international: 22%
Part-time enrollment: 239
men: 71%; women: 29%; minorities: 15%; international: 5%
Acceptance rate (full time): 65%
Average GMAT (full time): 592
Average GRE (full time): 153 verbal; 151 quantitative; 4.0 writing
Average GPA (full time): 3.41
Average age of entrants to full-time program: 24
Average months of prior work experience (full time): 18
TOEFL requirement: Yes
Minimum TOEFL score: 95
Most popular departments: consulting, finance, health care administration, marketing, other

Mean starting base salary for 2018 full-time graduates: $61,301
Employment location for 2018 class: Intl. N/A; N.E. 88%; M.A. 2%; S. 2%; M.W. 7%; S.W. 2%; W. N/A

University of Rochester

245 Gleason Hall
Rochester, NY 14627
www.simon.rochester.edu
Private
Admissions: (585) 275-3533
Email: admissions@simon.rochester.edu
Financial aid: (585) 275-3533
Application deadline: 05/01
Tuition: full time: $46,600; part time: $1,925/credit hour
Room/board/expenses: $17,765
College-funded aid: Yes
International student aid: Yes
Average student indebtedness at graduation: $40,864
Full-time enrollment: 209
men: 66%; women: 34%; minorities: 29%; international: 43%
Part-time enrollment: 145
men: 59%; women: 41%; minorities: 15%; international: 1%
Acceptance rate (full time): 32%
Average GMAT (full time): 666
Average GRE (full time): 159 verbal; 157 quantitative; 4.2 writing
Average GPA (full time): 3.50
Average age of entrants to full-time program: 28
Average months of prior work experience (full time): 62
TOEFL requirement: Yes
Minimum TOEFL score: N/A
Most popular departments: accounting, consulting, finance, marketing, other
Mean starting base salary for 2018 full-time graduates: $103,709
Employment location for 2018 class: Intl. 11%; N.E. 29%; M.A. 4%; S. 28%; M.W. 9%; S.W. N/A; W. 19%

Yeshiva University[1]

500 West 185th Street
New York, NY 10033
www.yu.edu/syms/
Private
Admissions: N/A
Financial aid: (646) 592-4166
Tuition: N/A
Room/board/expenses: N/A
Enrollment: N/A

Appalachian State University

Box 32037
Boone, NC 28608-2037
mba.appstate.edu
Public
Admissions: (828) 262-2130
Email: mba@appstate.edu
Financial aid: (828) 262-2190
Application deadline: 07/01
In-state tuition: total program: $16,031 (full time); total program: $15,930 (part time)

Out-of-state tuition: total program: $33,471 (full time); total program: $39,636 (part time)
Room/board/expenses: N/A
College-funded aid: Yes
International student aid: Yes
Full-time enrollment: 67 men: 55%; women: 45%; minorities: 9%; international: 3%
Part-time enrollment: 41 men: 56%; women: 44%; minorities: 2%; international: 10%
Acceptance rate (full time): 92%
Average GRE (full time): N/A verbal; N/A quantitative; N/A writing
Average GPA (full time): 3.27
Average age of entrants to full-time program: 24
Average months of prior work experience (full time): 48
TOEFL requirement: Yes
Minimum TOEFL score: 75
Most popular departments: economics, general management, human resources management, management information systems, supply chain management/logistics
Mean starting base salary for 2018 full-time graduates: $56,064

Duke University

100 Fuqua Drive, Box 90120
Durham, NC 27708-0120
www.fuqua.duke.edu/
Private
Admissions: (919) 257-9913
Email: admissions-info@fuqua.duke.edu
Financial aid: (919) 660-7687
Application deadline: 03/20
Tuition: full time: $70,942; part time: N/A
Room/board/expenses: $21,815
College-funded aid: Yes
International student aid: Yes
Average student indebtedness at graduation: $115,590
Full-time enrollment: 875 men: 62%; women: 38%; minorities: 21%; international: 32%
Part-time enrollment: N/A men: N/A; women: N/A; minorities: N/A; international: N/A
Acceptance rate (full time): 22%
Average GMAT (full time): 704
Average GRE (full time): 160 verbal; 159 quantitative; 4.4 writing
Average GPA (full time): 3.49
Average age of entrants to full-time program: 29
Average months of prior work experience (full time): 67
TOEFL requirement: No
Minimum TOEFL score: N/A
Most popular departments: consulting, finance, health care administration, marketing, quantitative analysis/statistics and operations research
Mean starting base salary for 2018 full-time graduates: $127,874
Employment location for 2018 class: Intl. 9%; N.E. 23%; M.A. 8%; S. 19%; M.W. 8%; S.W. 6%; W. 27%

East Carolina University

3203 Bate Building
Greenville, NC 27858-4353
business.ecu.edu/grad/mba
Public
Admissions: (252) 328-6970
Email: gradbus@ecu.edu
Financial aid: (252) 328-6610
Application deadline: 06/01
In-state tuition: full time: $9,736; part time: $7,798
Out-of-state tuition: full time: $22,884; part time: $17,660
Room/board/expenses: $20,268
College-funded aid: Yes
International student aid: Yes
Average student indebtedness at graduation: $37,291
Full-time enrollment: 85 men: 49%; women: 51%; minorities: 24%; international: 1%
Part-time enrollment: 17 men: 59%; women: 41%; minorities: 24%; international: 0%
Acceptance rate (full time): 69%
Average GMAT (full time): 496
Average GRE (full time): 151 verbal; 149 quantitative; 3.7 writing
Average GPA (full time): 3.27
Average age of entrants to full-time program: 24
TOEFL requirement: Yes
Minimum TOEFL score: 78
Most popular departments: health care administration, marketing, supply chain management/logistics, quantitative analysis/statistics and operations research, other

Elon University

100 Campus Drive
Elon, NC 27244-2010
www.elon.edu/u/academics/business/mba/
Private
Admissions: (336) 278-7600
Email: gradadm@elon.edu
Financial aid: (336) 278-7600
Application deadline: rolling
Tuition: full time: N/A; part time: $950/credit hour
Room/board/expenses: N/A
College-funded aid: No
International student aid: No
Full-time enrollment: N/A men: N/A; women: N/A; minorities: N/A; international: N/A
Part-time enrollment: 127 men: 50%; women: 50%; minorities: 22%; international: 3%
Average GRE (full time): N/A verbal; N/A quantitative; N/A writing
TOEFL requirement: Yes
Minimum TOEFL score: 79
Most popular departments: entrepreneurship, general management, human resources management, leadership, marketing

Fayetteville State University

1200 Murchison Road
Newbold Station
Fayetteville, NC 28301-1033
www.uncfsu.edu/academics/colleges-schools-and-departments/broadwell-college-of-business-and-economics/graduate-and-professional-studies-in-business
Public
Admissions: (910) 672-1197
Email: mbaprogram@uncfsu.edu
Financial aid: (910) 672-1325
Application deadline: 06/30
In-state tuition: full time: N/A; part time: $5,969
Out-of-state tuition: full time: N/A; part time: $17,914
Room/board/expenses: N/A
College-funded aid: Yes
International student aid: Yes
Full-time enrollment: N/A men: N/A; women: N/A; minorities: N/A; international: N/A
Part-time enrollment: 411 men: 47%; women: 53%; minorities: 54%; international: 4%
Average GRE (full time): N/A verbal; N/A quantitative; N/A writing
TOEFL requirement: Yes
Minimum TOEFL score: 79
Most popular departments: entrepreneurship, finance, general management, health care administration, production/operations management

Meredith College

3800 Hillsborough Street
Raleigh, NC 27607
www.meredith.edu/master-of-business-administration
Private
Admissions: (919) 760-8058
Email: vcjohnson@meredith.edu
Financial aid: (919) 760-8565
Application deadline: 06/01
Tuition: full time: $940/credit hour; part time: $940/credit hour
Room/board/expenses: $10,718
College-funded aid: Yes
International student aid: Yes
Average student indebtedness at graduation: $38,034
Full-time enrollment: 41 men: 24%; women: 76%; minorities: 46%; international: 10%
Part-time enrollment: 46 men: 20%; women: 80%; minorities: 39%; international: 2%
Acceptance rate (full time): 80%
Average GRE (full time): N/A verbal; N/A quantitative; N/A writing
Average GPA (full time): 3.70
Average age of entrants to full-time program: 33
Average months of prior work experience (full time): 60
TOEFL requirement: Yes
Minimum TOEFL score: 80
Most popular departments: general management, human resources management, other

North Carolina Central University[1]

1801 Fayetteville Street
Durham, NC 27707
www.nccu.edu/academics/business/index.cfm
Public
Admissions: (919) 530-6405
Email: mba@nccu.edu
Financial aid: N/A
Tuition: N/A
Room/board/expenses: N/A
Enrollment: N/A

North Carolina State University

2130 Nelson Hall
Campus Box 8114
Raleigh, NC 27695-8114
www.mba.ncsu.edu
Public

Mean starting base salary for 2018 full-time graduates: $80,000
Employment location for 2018 class: Intl. N/A; N.E. N/A; M.A. N/A; S. 100%; M.W. N/A; S.W. N/A; W. N/A

North Carolina A&T State University

1601 E. Market Street
Greensboro, NC 27411
ncatmba.com
Public
Admissions: (336) 285-2373
Email: cdcampbe@ncat.edu
Financial aid: (336) 334-7973
Application deadline: 07/15
In-state tuition: $6,158 (full time); part time: N/A
Out-of-state tuition: $18,808 (full time); part time: N/A
Room/board/expenses: $7,500
College-funded aid: Yes
International student aid: Yes
Average student indebtedness at graduation: $35,000
Full-time enrollment: 135 men: 41%; women: 59%; minorities: 84%; international: 9%
Part-time enrollment: N/A men: N/A; women: N/A; minorities: N/A; international: N/A
Acceptance rate (full time): 49%
Average GMAT (full time): 510
Average GRE (full time): N/A verbal; N/A quantitative; N/A writing
Average GPA (full time): 3.50
Average age of entrants to full-time program: 26
Average months of prior work experience (full time): 36
TOEFL requirement: Yes
Minimum TOEFL score: 80
Most popular departments: accounting, general management, human resources management, production/operations management, supply chain management/logistics
Mean starting base salary for 2018 full-time graduates: $76,000
Employment location for 2018 class: Intl. N/A; N.E. 20%; M.A. 15%; S. 55%; M.W. N/A; S.W. 10%; W. N/A

Queens University of Charlotte

1900 Selwyn Avenue
Charlotte, NC 28274
mccoll.queens.edu/
Private
Admissions: (704) 337-2224
Email: mccollschool@queens.edu
Financial aid: (704) 337-2225
Application deadline: rolling
Tuition: full time: N/A; part time: $1,133/credit hour
Room/board/expenses: N/A
College-funded aid: Yes
International student aid: Yes
Full-time enrollment: N/A men: N/A; women: N/A; minorities: N/A; international: N/A
Part-time enrollment: 100 men: 54%; women: 46%; minorities: 20%; international: 20%
Average GRE (full time): N/A verbal; N/A quantitative; N/A writing
TOEFL requirement: Yes
Minimum TOEFL score: 79
Most popular departments: finance, health care administration, leadership, other

Admissions: (919) 515-5584
Email: mba@ncsu.edu
Financial aid: (919) 515-2866
Application deadline: 03/01
In-state tuition: full time: $23,901; part time: $1,129/credit hour
Out-of-state tuition: full time: $40,874; part time: $1,961/credit hour
Room/board/expenses: $17,916
College-funded aid: Yes
International student aid: Yes
Average student indebtedness at graduation: $36,288
Full-time enrollment: 95 men: 63%; women: 37%; minorities: 21%; international: 22%
Part-time enrollment: 271 men: 68%; women: 32%; minorities: 27%; international: 20%
Acceptance rate (full time): 45%
Average GMAT (full time): 625
Average GRE (full time): 159 verbal; 159 quantitative; 4.8 writing
Average GPA (full time): 3.35
Average age of entrants to full-time program: 29
Average months of prior work experience (full time): 61
TOEFL requirement: Yes
Minimum TOEFL score: 100
Most popular departments: entrepreneurship, marketing, supply chain management/logistics, technology, other
Mean starting base salary for 2018 full-time graduates: $93,016
Employment location for 2018 class: Intl. N/A; N.E. 5%; M.A. 10%; S. 67%; M.W. 14%; S.W. 0%; W. 5%

University of North Carolina–Chapel Hill

CB 3490, McColl Building
Chapel Hill, NC 27599-3490
www.kenan-flagler.unc.edu
Public
Admissions: (919) 962-3236
Email: mba_info@unc.edu
Financial aid: (919) 962-9096
Application deadline: N/A
In-state tuition: full time:
$49,356; part time: N/A
Out-of-state tuition: full time:
$64,479; part time: N/A
Room/board/expenses: $24,792
College-funded aid: Yes
International student aid: Yes
**Average student indebtedness
at graduation:** $99,855
Full-time enrollment: 556
men: 72%; women:
28%; minorities: 18%;
international: 24%
Part-time enrollment: N/A
men: N/A; women:
N/A; minorities: N/A;
international: N/A
Acceptance rate (full time): 47%
Average GMAT (full time): 702
**Average GRE (full
time):** 159 verbal; 158
quantitative; 4.4 writing
Average GPA (full time): 3.34
**Average age of entrants to
full-time program:** 28
**Average months of prior work
experience (full time):** 65
TOEFL requirement: Yes
Minimum TOEFL score: N/A
Most popular departments:
consulting, entrepreneurship,
finance, marketing, real estate
**Mean starting base salary for 2018
full-time graduates:** $116,543
**Employment location for 2018
class:** Intl. 2%; N.E. 20%;
M.A. 13%; S. 34%; M.W.
7%; S.W. 10%; W. 14%

University of North Carolina–Charlotte

9201 University City Boulevard
Charlotte, NC 28223
www.mba.uncc.edu
Public
Admissions: (704) 687-0815
Email: belkgradprograms@
uncc.edu
Financial aid: (704) 687-7010
Application deadline: rolling
In-state tuition: full time:
N/A; part time: $10,055
Out-of-state tuition: full time:
N/A; part time: $20,131
Room/board/expenses: N/A
College-funded aid: Yes
International student aid: Yes
Full-time enrollment: N/A
men: N/A; women:
N/A; minorities: N/A;
international: N/A
Part-time enrollment: 375
men: 69%; women:
31%; minorities: 23%;
international: 35%
**Average GRE (full
time):** N/A verbal; N/A writing
TOEFL requirement: Yes

Minimum TOEFL score: 83
Most popular departments:
finance, general management,
international business,
marketing, supply chain
management/logistics

University of North Carolina–Greensboro

PO Box 26170
Greensboro, NC 27402-6170
mba.uncg.edu
Public
Admissions: (336) 334-5390
Email: mba@uncg.edu
Financial aid: (336) 334-5702
Application deadline: 06/15
In-state tuition: total program:
$26,184 (full time); total
program: $25,062 (part time)
Out-of-state tuition: total
program: $57,576 (full
time); total program:
$58,694 (part time)
Room/board/expenses: $12,788
College-funded aid: Yes
International student aid: Yes
Full-time enrollment: 57
men: 53%; women:
47%; minorities: 33%;
international: 32%
Part-time enrollment: 116
men: 53%; women:
47%; minorities: 19%;
international: 8%
Acceptance rate (full time): 78%
Average GMAT (full time): 498
**Average GRE (full
time):** 150 verbal; 151
quantitative; 3.3 writing
Average GPA (full time): 3.46
**Average age of entrants to
full-time program:** 24
**Average months of prior work
experience (full time):** 27
TOEFL requirement: Yes
Minimum TOEFL score: 79
Most popular departments:
finance, general management,
marketing, supply chain
management/logistics,
quantitative analysis/statistics
and operations research
**Mean starting base salary for
2018 full-time graduates:** $68,200
**Employment location for 2018
class:** Intl. N/A; N.E. N/A;
M.A. 38%; S. 63%; M.W.
N/A; S.W. N/A; W. N/A

University of North Carolina–Pembroke

PO Box 1510
One University Drive
Pembroke, NC 28372
www.uncp.edu/grad
Public
Admissions: (910) 521-6271
Email: grad@uncp.edu
Financial aid: (910) 521-6255
Application deadline: 08/15
In-state tuition: full time: $7,438;
part time: $2,020/credit hour
Out-of-state tuition: full
time: $18,712; part time:
$4,838/credit hour
Room/board/expenses: $16,635
College-funded aid: Yes
International student aid: Yes

Full-time enrollment: 7
men: 71%; women:
29%; minorities: 14%;
international: 71%
Part-time enrollment: 5
men: 80%; women:
20%; minorities: 80%;
international: 20%
Acceptance rate (full time): 100%
**Average GRE (full
time):** N/A verbal; N/A
quantitative; N/A writing
Average GPA (full time): 3.15
**Average age of entrants to
full-time program:** 25
TOEFL requirement: Yes
Minimum TOEFL score: 80

University of North Carolina–Wilmington

601 S. College Road
Wilmington, NC 28403-5680
www.csb.uncw.edu/
gradprograms
Public
Admissions: (910) 962-3903
Email: wilhelmc@uncw.edu
Financial aid: (910) 962-3177
Application deadline: 06/01
In-state tuition: total
program: $18,850 (full
time); part time: $6,558
Out-of-state tuition: total
program: $18,850 (full
time); part time: $16,929
Room/board/expenses: $16,189
College-funded aid: Yes
International student aid: Yes
Full-time enrollment: 72
men: 57%; women:
43%; minorities: 18%;
international: 10%
Part-time enrollment: 88
men: 75%; women:
25%; minorities: 10%;
international: 0%
Acceptance rate (full time): 90%
**Average GRE (full
time):** N/A verbal; N/A
quantitative; N/A writing
Average GPA (full time): 3.30
**Average age of entrants to
full-time program:** 24
**Average months of prior work
experience (full time):** 24
TOEFL requirement: Yes
Minimum TOEFL score: 79
Most popular departments:
consulting, finance, general
management, marketing

Wake Forest University

PO Box 7659
Winston-Salem, NC 27109-7659
www.business.wfu.edu
Private
Admissions: (336) 758-5422
Email: busadmissions@wfu.edu
Financial aid: (336) 758-4424
Application deadline: rolling
Tuition: full time: N/A;
part time: $38,799
Room/board/expenses: N/A
College-funded aid: Yes
International student aid: Yes
Full-time enrollment: N/A
men: N/A; women:
N/A; minorities: N/A;
international: N/A

Part-time enrollment: 325
men: 65%; women:
35%; minorities: 27%;
international: 2%
**Average GRE (full
time):** N/A verbal; N/A
quantitative; N/A writing
TOEFL requirement: Yes
Minimum TOEFL score: N/A
Most popular departments:
accounting, finance, general
management, leadership

Western Carolina University

Forsyth Building
Cullowhee, NC 28723
business.wcu.edu
Public
Admissions: (828) 227-3174
Email: gradadmissions@
email.wcu.edu
Financial aid: (828) 227-7290
Application deadline: 07/15
In-state tuition: full time:
N/A; part time: N/A
Out-of-state tuition: full
time: N/A; part time: N/A
Room/board/expenses: N/A
College-funded aid: Yes
International student aid: Yes
Full-time enrollment: 22
men: 64%; women:
36%; minorities: 14%;
international: 0%
Part-time enrollment: 53
men: 53%; women:
47%; minorities: 13%;
international: 2%
Acceptance rate (full time): 94%
Average GMAT (full time): 442
**Average GRE (full
time):** 147 verbal; 146
quantitative; 3.0 writing
Average GPA (full time): 3.29
**Average age of entrants to
full-time program:** 32
TOEFL requirement: Yes
Minimum TOEFL score: 79

NORTH DAKOTA

North Dakota State University

NDSU Department 2400
PO Box 6050
Fargo, ND 58108-6050
www.ndsu.edu/business/
programs/graduate/mba/
Public
Admissions: (701) 231-7681
Email: paul.brown@ndsu.edu
Financial aid: N/A
Application deadline: rolling
In-state tuition: total program:
$17,550 (full time); total
program: $17,550 (part time)
Out-of-state tuition: total
program: $25,710 (full
time); total program:
$25,710 (part time)
Room/board/expenses: N/A
College-funded aid: Yes
International student aid: Yes
Full-time enrollment: 14
men: 43%; women:
57%; minorities: 0%;
international: 43%
Part-time enrollment: 67
men: 70%; women: 30%;
minorities: 4%; international: 0%
Acceptance rate (full time): 71%
Average GMAT (full time): 520

**Average GRE (full
time):** N/A verbal; N/A
quantitative; N/A writing
Average GPA (full time): 3.50
**Average age of entrants to
full-time program:** 24
**Average months of prior work
experience (full time):** 36
TOEFL requirement: Yes
Minimum TOEFL score: N/A
Most popular departments:
general management

University of North Dakota[1]

293 Centennial Drive, Stop 8098
Grand Forks, ND 58202-8098
business.und.edu/mba
Public
Admissions: (701) 777-3299
Email: laura.look@und.edu
Financial aid: (701) 777-4409
Tuition: N/A
Room/board/expenses: N/A
Enrollment: N/A

OHIO

Bowling Green State University

371 Business Administration
Building
Bowling Green, OH 43403-0001
www.bgsumba.com
Public
Admissions: (800) 247-8622
Email: mba@bgsu.edu
Financial aid: (419) 372-2651
Application deadline: 03/01
In-state tuition: total program:
$29,868 (full time); total
program: $29,631 (part time)
Out-of-state tuition: total
program: $33,969 (full
time); $29,631 (part time)
Room/board/expenses: $14,154
College-funded aid: Yes
International student aid: Yes
Full-time enrollment: 40
men: 73%; women:
28%; minorities: 40%;
international: 0%
Part-time enrollment: 70
men: 54%; women:
46%; minorities: 17%;
international: 0%
Acceptance rate (full time): 57%
Average GMAT (full time): 432
**Average GRE (full
time):** 148 verbal; 149
quantitative; 3.0 writing
Average GPA (full time): 3.30
**Average age of entrants to
full-time program:** 26
**Average months of prior work
experience (full time):** 24
TOEFL requirement: Yes
Minimum TOEFL score: 80
Most popular departments:
accounting, finance, supply
chain management/logistics

Case Western Reserve University

Peter B. Lewis Building
10900 Euclid Avenue
Cleveland, OH 44106-7235
www.weatherhead.case.edu
Private
Admissions: (216) 368-6702

Email: wsomadmissions@
case.edu
Financial aid: (216) 368-8907
Application deadline: 05/15
Tuition: full time: $40,760;
part time: $22,064
Room/board/expenses: $21,558
College-funded aid: Yes
International student aid: Yes
**Average student indebtedness
at graduation:** $75,516
Full-time enrollment: 95
men: 71%; women:
29%; minorities: 23%;
international: 37%
Part-time enrollment: 162
men: 59%; women:
41%; minorities: 15%;
international: 5%
Acceptance rate (full time): 68%
Average GMAT (full time): 623
**Average GRE (full
time):** 152 verbal; 159
quantitative; 3.7 writing
Average GPA (full time): 3.20
**Average age of entrants to
full-time program:** 27
**Average months of prior work
experience (full time):** 60
TOEFL requirement: No
Minimum TOEFL score: N/A
Most popular departments:
accounting, finance, leadership,
marketing, quantitative
analysis/statistics and
operations research
**Mean starting base salary for
2018 full-time graduates:** $81,881
**Employment location for
2018 class:** Intl. N/A; N.E.
3%; M.A. 13%; S. 0%; M.W.
73%; S.W. 3%; W. 7%

Cleveland State University

1860 E. 18th Street, BU420
Cleveland, OH 44115
www.csuohio.edu/mba
Public
Admissions: (216) 687-5599
Email: cbacsu@csuohio.edu
Financial aid: (216) 687-5411
Application deadline: 08/17
In-state tuition: full time:
$584/credit hour; part
time: $584/credit hour
Out-of-state tuition: full time:
$1,002/credit hour; part
time: $1,002/credit hour
Room/board/expenses: $16,848
College-funded aid: Yes
International student aid: Yes
Full-time enrollment: 163
men: 49%; women:
51%; minorities: 20%;
international: 21%
Part-time enrollment: 310
men: 56%; women:
44%; minorities: 18%;
international: 4%
Acceptance rate (full time): 80%
Average GMAT (full time): 455
**Average GRE (full
time):** N/A verbal; N/A
quantitative; N/A writing
**Average age of entrants to
full-time program:** 31
TOEFL requirement: Yes
Minimum TOEFL score: 78

Most popular departments:
accounting, finance, health care
administration, production/
operations management, supply
chain management/logistics

John Carroll University

1 John Carroll Boulevard
University Heights, OH 44118
boler.jcu.edu/graduate
Private
Admissions: (216) 397-1970
Email: gradbusiness@jcu.edu
Financial aid: (216) 397-4248
Application deadline: 07/15
Tuition: full time: $900/
credit hour; part time:
$900/credit hour
Room/board/expenses: $1,250
College-funded aid: Yes
International student aid: Yes
**Average student indebtedness
at graduation:** $19,632
Full-time enrollment: 93
men: 58%; women: 42%;
minorities: 9%; international: 6%
Part-time enrollment: 57
men: 67%; women:
33%; minorities: 25%;
international: 4%
Acceptance rate (full time): 99%
Average GMAT (full time): 593
**Average GRE (full
time):** N/A verbal; N/A
quantitative; N/A writing
Average GPA (full time): 3.30
**Average age of entrants to
full-time program:** 23
**Average months of prior work
experience (full time):** 26
TOEFL requirement: Yes
Minimum TOEFL score: 79
Most popular departments:
accounting, finance,
human resources
management, international
business, marketing
**Mean starting base salary for
2018 full-time graduates:** $55,875
**Employment location for
2018 class:** Intl. N/A; N.E.
N/A; M.A. N/A; S. N/A; M.W.
92%; S.W. 8%; W. N/A

Kent State University

PO Box 5190
Kent, OH 44242-0001
www.kent.edu/business
Public
Admissions: (330) 672-2282
Email: gradbus@kent.edu
Financial aid: (330) 672-2972
Application deadline: 03/15
In-state tuition: total program:
$18,504 (full time); part time: N/A
Out-of-state tuition: total
program: $34,486 (full
time); part time: N/A
Room/board/expenses: $16,780
College-funded aid: Yes
International student aid: Yes
Full-time enrollment: 32
men: 56%; women:
44%; minorities: 19%;
international: 25%
Part-time enrollment: N/A
men: N/A; women:
N/A; minorities: N/A;
international: N/A
Acceptance rate (full time): 59%

Average GMAT (full time): 504
**Average GRE (full
time):** 151 verbal; 149
quantitative; 3.8 writing
Average GPA (full time): 3.42
**Average age of entrants to
full-time program:** 24
**Average months of prior work
experience (full time):** 12
TOEFL requirement: Yes
Minimum TOEFL score: 80
Most popular departments:
finance, general management,
international business,
management information
systems, supply chain
management/logistics
**Mean starting base salary for
2018 full-time graduates:** $49,687
**Employment location for
2018 class:** Intl. 20%; N.E.
0%; M.A. 10%; S. 0%; M.W.
70%; S.W. 0%; W. 0%

Miami University

800 E. High Street
Oxford, OH 45056
miamioh.edu/fsb/mba/
Public
Admissions: (513) 895-8876
Email: mba@miamioh.edu
Financial aid: (513) 529-8710
Application deadline: rolling
In-state tuition: full time: N/A;
part time: $1,050/credit hour
Out-of-state tuition: full time: N/A;
part time: $1,050/credit hour
Room/board/expenses: N/A
College-funded aid: No
International student aid: No
Full-time enrollment: N/A
men: N/A; women:
N/A; minorities: N/A;
international: N/A
Part-time enrollment: 109
men: 74%; women:
26%; minorities: 17%;
international: 3%
**Average GRE (full
time):** N/A verbal; N/A
quantitative; N/A writing
TOEFL requirement: Yes
Minimum TOEFL score: 95
Most popular departments:
finance, general
management, marketing

Ohio State University

100 Gerlach Hall
2108 Neil Avenue
Columbus, OH 43210-1144
fisher.osu.edu/graduate
Public
Admissions: (614) 292-8511
Email: mba@fisher.osu.edu
Financial aid: (614) 292-8511
Application deadline: 05/15
In-state tuition: full time: $31,139;
part time: $1,698/credit hour
Out-of-state tuition: full
time: $53,643; part time:
$2,948/credit hour
Room/board/expenses: $17,384
College-funded aid: Yes
International student aid: Yes
**Average student indebtedness
at graduation:** $49,781
Full-time enrollment: 181
men: 69%; women:
31%; minorities: 9%;
international: 28%

Part-time enrollment: 356
men: 61%; women:
39%; minorities: 17%;
international: 8%
Acceptance rate (full time): 36%
Average GMAT (full time): 676
**Average GRE (full
time):** 158 verbal; 155
quantitative; N/A writing
Average GPA (full time): 3.44
**Average age of entrants to
full-time program:** 29
**Average months of prior work
experience (full time):** 65
TOEFL requirement: Yes
Minimum TOEFL score: 100
Most popular departments:
finance, leadership, marketing,
production/operations
management, supply chain
management/logistics
**Mean starting base salary for
2018 full-time graduates:** $97,186

Ohio University[1]

1 Ohio University
College of Business Annex, 351
Athens, OH 45701
www.business.ohio.edu
Public
Admissions: (740) 593-2053
Email: mba@ohio.edu
Financial aid: (740) 593-4141
Tuition: N/A
Room/board/expenses: N/A
Enrollment: N/A

University of Akron

CBA 412
Akron, OH 44325-4805
mba.uakron.edu
Public
Admissions: (330) 972-7043
Email: gradcba@uakron.edu
Financial aid: (330) 972-7032
Application deadline: 07/15
In-state tuition: full time: N/A;
part time: $461/credit hour
Out-of-state tuition: full time:
N/A; part time: $767/credit hour
Room/board/expenses: N/A
College-funded aid: Yes
International student aid: Yes
Full-time enrollment: N/A
men: N/A; women:
N/A; minorities: N/A;
international: N/A
Part-time enrollment: 167
men: 66%; women:
34%; minorities: 13%;
international: 6%
**Average GRE (full
time):** N/A verbal; N/A
quantitative; N/A writing
TOEFL requirement: Yes
Minimum TOEFL score: 79
Most popular departments:
accounting, general
management, management
information systems, tax, other

University of Cincinnati

606 Lindner Hall
2925 Campus Green Drive
Cincinnati, OH 45221-0020
www.business.uc.edu/mba
Public
Admissions: (513) 556-7024
Email: graduate@uc.edu
Financial aid: (513) 556-6982

Application deadline: 06/30
In-state tuition: total program:
$31,437 (full time); part
time: $806/credit hour
Out-of-state tuition: total
program: $43,194 (full time);
part time: $806/credit hour
Room/board/expenses: $20,000
College-funded aid: Yes
International student aid: Yes
**Average student indebtedness
at graduation:** $28,782
Full-time enrollment: 71
men: 52%; women:
48%; minorities: 17%;
international: 27%
Part-time enrollment: 139
men: 60%; women:
40%; minorities: 17%;
international: 7%
Acceptance rate (full time): 62%
Average GMAT (full time): 660
**Average GRE (full
time):** 157 verbal; 157
quantitative; 3.6 writing
Average GPA (full time): 3.40
**Average age of entrants to
full-time program:** 27
**Average months of prior work
experience (full time):** 45
TOEFL requirement: Yes
Minimum TOEFL score: 90
Most popular departments:
entrepreneurship, health care
administration, marketing,
real estate, quantitative
analysis/statistics and
operations research
**Mean starting base salary for
2018 full-time graduates:** $75,654
**Employment location for
2018 class:** Intl. 11%; N.E.
3%; M.A. N/A; S. 5%; M.W.
76%; S.W. 3%; W. 3%

University of Dayton

300 College Park Avenue
Dayton, OH 45469-2234
business.udayton.edu/mba
Private
Admissions: (937) 229-3733
Email: mba@udayton.edu
Financial aid: (937) 229-4311
Application deadline: rolling
Tuition: full time: $1,010/
credit hour; part time:
$1,010/credit hour
Room/board/expenses: N/A
College-funded aid: Yes
International student aid: Yes
Full-time enrollment: 20
men: 60%; women:
40%; minorities: N/A;
international: N/A
Part-time enrollment: 97
men: 67%; women:
33%; minorities: N/A;
international: N/A
Acceptance rate (full time): 40%
**Average GRE (full
time):** N/A verbal; N/A
quantitative; N/A writing
Average GPA (full time): 3.39
**Average age of entrants to
full-time program:** 23
TOEFL requirement: Yes
Minimum TOEFL score: 80

University of Toledo

Stranahan Hall North
Room 3130
Toledo, OH 43606-3390
utoledo.edu/business/graduate
Public
Admissions: (419) 530-5689
Email: COBIGradPrograms@
utoledo.edu
Financial aid: (419) 530-5843
Application deadline: 08/01
In-state tuition: full time: $539/
credit hour; part time: N/A
Out-of-state tuition: full time:
$956/credit hour; part time: N/A
Room/board/expenses: $18,061
College-funded aid: Yes
International student aid: Yes
Full-time enrollment: 425
men: 56%; women:
44%; minorities: 9%;
international: 38%
Part-time enrollment: N/A
men: N/A; women:
N/A; minorities: N/A;
international: N/A
Acceptance rate (full time): 72%
Average GMAT (full time): 459
**Average GRE (full
time):** N/A verbal; N/A
quantitative; N/A writing
Average GPA (full time): 3.34
TOEFL requirement: Yes
Minimum TOEFL score: 80
**Mean starting base salary for
2018 full-time graduates:** $55,310
**Employment location for
2018 class:** Intl. N/A; N.E.
5%; M.A. 5%; S. N/A; M.W.
86%; S.W. N/A; W. 5%

Wright State University

3640 Colonel Glenn Highway
Dayton, OH 45435-0001
www.wright.edu/business
Public
Admissions: (937) 775-2953
Email: mba@wright.edu
Financial aid: (937) 775-5721
Application deadline: 08/01
In-state tuition: full time:
$30,690; part time:
N/A/credit hour
Out-of-state tuition: full
time: $52,313; part time:
N/A/credit hour
Room/board/expenses: N/A
College-funded aid: Yes
**Average student indebtedness
at graduation:** $41,296
Full-time enrollment: 580
men: 52%; women:
48%; minorities: 21%;
international: 10%
Part-time enrollment: N/A
men: N/A; women:
N/A; minorities: N/A;
international: N/A
Acceptance rate (full time): 85%
Average GMAT (full time): 505
**Average GRE (full
time):** 149 verbal; 147
quantitative; 3.4 writing
Average GPA (full time): 3.04
**Average age of entrants to
full-time program:** 29
TOEFL requirement: Yes
Minimum TOEFL score: 79

Most popular departments:
economics, finance, general
management, marketing,
quantitative analysis/statistics
and operations research

Xavier University

3800 Victory Parkway
Cincinnati, OH 45207-1221
www.xavier.edu/MBA
Private
Admissions: (513) 745-3348
Email: xumba@xavier.edu
Financial aid: (513) 745-3142
Application deadline: 08/01
Tuition: full time: $815/credit
hour; part time: $815/credit hour
Room/board/expenses: $15,700
College-funded aid: Yes
International student aid: Yes
**Average student indebtedness
at graduation:** $16,926
Full-time enrollment: 48
men: 60%; women:
40%; minorities: 17%;
international: 19%
Part-time enrollment: 573
men: 66%; women:
34%; minorities: 20%;
international: 2%
Acceptance rate (full time): 86%
Average GMAT (full time): 500
**Average GRE (full
time):** 149 verbal; 149
quantitative; 3.6 writing
Average GPA (full time): 3.22
**Average age of entrants to
full-time program:** 25
**Average months of prior work
experience (full time):** 36
TOEFL requirement: Yes
Minimum TOEFL score: 79
Most popular departments:
finance, general management,
marketing, quantitative
analysis/statistics and
operations research, other

Youngstown State University[1]

1 University Plaza
Youngstown, OH 44555
web.ysu.edu/mba
Public
Admissions: N/A
Email: graduateschool@ysu.edu
Financial aid: N/A
Tuition: N/A
Room/board/expenses: N/A
Enrollment: N/A

OKLAHOMA

Oklahoma City University

2501 N Blackwelder
Oklahoma City, OK 73106
www.okcu.edu/mba/
Private
Admissions: (405) 208-5351
Email: gadmissions@okcu.edu
Financial aid: (405) 208-5240
Application deadline: rolling
Tuition: full time: $590/
credit hour; part time:
$590/credit hour
Room/board/expenses: $11,124
College-funded aid: Yes
International student aid: No
**Average student indebtedness
at graduation:** $38,689

Full-time enrollment: 16
men: 56%; women:
44%; minorities: 31%;
international: 31%
Part-time enrollment: 122
men: 60%; women:
40%; minorities: 33%;
international: 1%
Acceptance rate (full time): 79%
**Average GRE (full
time):** N/A verbal; N/A
quantitative; N/A writing
Average GPA (full time): 3.32
**Average age of entrants to
full-time program:** 25
TOEFL requirement: Yes
Minimum TOEFL score: 83
**Mean starting base salary for
2018 full-time graduates:** $41,000

Oklahoma State University

284 Business Building
Stillwater, OK 74078-4022
business.okstate.edu/watson/
mba/index.html
Public
Admissions: (405) 744-2951
Email: spearsmasters@
okstate.edu
Financial aid: (405) 744-6604
Application deadline: 04/15
In-state tuition: full time:
$230/credit hour; part
time: $230/credit hour
Out-of-state tuition: full
time: $876/credit hour; part
time: $876/credit hour
Room/board/expenses: $14,910
College-funded aid: Yes
International student aid: Yes
**Average student indebtedness
at graduation:** $24,544
Full-time enrollment: 53
men: 51%; women:
49%; minorities: 9%;
international: 11%
Part-time enrollment: 75
men: 71%; women:
29%; minorities: 13%;
international: 3%
Acceptance rate (full time): 49%
Average GMAT (full time): 521
**Average GRE (full
time):** 150 verbal; 151
quantitative; 4.0 writing
Average GPA (full time): 3.49
**Average age of entrants to
full-time program:** 23
**Average months of prior work
experience (full time):** 6
TOEFL requirement: Yes
Minimum TOEFL score: 89
Most popular departments:
entrepreneurship, finance,
human resources management,
not-for-profit management,
quantitative analysis/statistics
and operations research
**Mean starting base salary for
2018 full-time graduates:** $61,566
**Employment location for
2018 class:** Intl. N/A; N.E.
N/A; M.A. N/A; S. 16%; M.W.
4%; S.W. 80%; W. N/A

Southeastern Oklahoma State University[1]

1405 N. Fourth Avenue
PMB 4205
Durant, OK 74701-0609
www.se.edu/bus/
Public
Admissions: (580) 745-2176
Email: kluke@se.edu
Financial aid: (580) 745-2186
Tuition: N/A
Room/board/expenses: N/A
Enrollment: N/A

University of Central Oklahoma

100 N University Drive
Box 115
Edmond, OK 73034
business.uco.edu/degrees/mba
Public
Admissions: (405) 974-5445
Email: mba@uco.edu
Financial aid: (405) 974-2727
Application deadline: rolling
In-state tuition: full time:
$393/credit hour; part
time: $393/credit hour
Out-of-state tuition: full
time: $810/credit hour; part
time: $810/credit hour
Room/board/expenses: $18,202
College-funded aid: Yes
International student aid: Yes
**Average student indebtedness
at graduation:** $17,093
Full-time enrollment: 68
men: 60%; women:
40%; minorities: 26%;
international: 13%
Part-time enrollment: 42
men: 57%; women:
43%; minorities: 43%;
international: 2%
Average GMAT (full time): 623
**Average GRE (full
time):** N/A verbal; 149
quantitative; N/A writing
**Average age of entrants to
full-time program:** 31
TOEFL requirement: Yes
Minimum TOEFL score: 83
Most popular departments:
general management, health
care administration

University of Oklahoma

865 Research Parkway
Suite 300
Oklahoma City, OK 73104
ou.edu/mba
Public
Admissions: (405) 325-5623
Email: meganallen@ou.edu
Financial aid: (405) 325-4521
Application deadline: 05/15
In-state tuition: total program:
$34,000 (full time); total
program: $27,000 (part time)
Out-of-state tuition: total
program: $54,000 (full
time); total program:
$42,000 (part time)
Room/board/expenses: $15,000
College-funded aid: Yes
International student aid: Yes

Full-time enrollment: 69
men: 80%; women:
20%; minorities: 13%;
international: 7%
Part-time enrollment: 146
men: 77%; women:
23%; minorities: 16%;
international: 2%
Acceptance rate (full time): 61%
Average GMAT (full time): 625
**Average GRE (full
time):** 159 verbal; 159
quantitative; N/A writing
Average GPA (full time): 3.45
**Average age of entrants to
full-time program:** 24
**Average months of prior work
experience (full time):** 15
TOEFL requirement: Yes
Minimum TOEFL score: 100
Most popular departments:
entrepreneurship, finance,
management information
systems, technology, other
**Mean starting base salary for
2018 full-time graduates:** $75,025
**Employment location for
2018 class:** Intl. 0%; N.E.
3%; M.A. 0%; S. 6%; M.W.
3%; S.W. 83%; W. 6%

University of Tulsa

800 S. Tucker Drive
Tulsa, OK 74104-9700
www.utulsa.edu/graduate/
business
Private
Admissions: (918) 631-2242
Email: graduate-business@
utulsa.edu
Financial aid: (918) 631-2526
Application deadline: 07/01
Tuition: full time: $34,428;
part time: $33,552
Room/board/expenses: $19,630
College-funded aid: Yes
International student aid: Yes
Full-time enrollment: 42
men: 62%; women:
38%; minorities: 21%;
international: 19%
Part-time enrollment: 43
men: 65%; women:
35%; minorities: 14%;
international: 0%
Acceptance rate (full time): 83%
Average GMAT (full time): 526
**Average GRE (full
time):** N/A verbal; N/A
quantitative; N/A writing
Average GPA (full time): 3.50
**Average age of entrants to
full-time program:** 25
**Average months of prior work
experience (full time):** 71
TOEFL requirement: Yes
Minimum TOEFL score: 90
Most popular departments:
accounting, finance, general
management, marketing, other
**Mean starting base salary for
2018 full-time graduates:** $66,068
**Employment location for
2018 class:** Intl. N/A; N.E.
N/A; M.A. N/A; S. N/A; M.W.
8%; S.W. 92%; W. N/A

OREGON

Oregon State University

2751 SW Jefferson Way
Corvallis, OR 97331
mba.oregonstate.edu/
Public
Admissions: (541) 737-5510
Email: mba.info@
oregonstate.edu
Financial aid: (541) 737-3515
Application deadline: 08/20
In-state tuition: total program:
$34,491 (full time); total
program: $36,000 (part time)
Out-of-state tuition: total
program: $58,926 (full
time); total program:
$36,000 (part time)
Room/board/expenses: $16,173
College-funded aid: Yes
International student aid: Yes
**Average student indebtedness
at graduation:** $35,314
Full-time enrollment: 146
men: 53%; women:
47%; minorities: 29%;
international: 30%
Part-time enrollment: 91
men: 48%; women:
52%; minorities: 25%;
international: 0%
Acceptance rate (full time): 71%
Average GMAT (full time): 588
**Average GRE (full
time):** 157 verbal; 152
quantitative; 4.1 writing
Average GPA (full time): 3.37
**Average age of entrants to
full-time program:** 27
**Average months of prior work
experience (full time):** 63
TOEFL requirement: Yes
Minimum TOEFL score: 91
Most popular departments:
entrepreneurship, finance,
leadership, supply chain
management/logistics,
quantitative analysis/statistics
and operations research
**Mean starting base salary for
2018 full-time graduates:** $78,787
**Employment location for
2018 class:** Intl. 29%; N.E.
N/A; M.A. N/A; S. N/A; M.W.
7%; S.W. 7%; W. 57%

Portland State University

PO Box 751
Portland, OR 97207-0751
www.pdx.edu/sba/
the-portland-mba
Public
Admissions: (503) 725-8190
Email: SBGradAdmissions@
pdx.edu
Financial aid: (503) 725-5446
Application deadline: 08/31
In-state tuition: total program:
$49,247 (full time); total
program: $46,351 (part time)
Out-of-state tuition: total
program: $58,130 (full
time); total program:
$55,093 (part time)
Room/board/expenses: $20,000
College-funded aid: Yes
International student aid: Yes
Full-time enrollment: 55
men: 55%; women:
45%; minorities: 24%;
international: 20%

Part-time enrollment: 110
men: 62%; women:
38%; minorities: 21%;
international: 7%
Acceptance rate (full time): 61%
Average GMAT (full time): 527
**Average GRE (full
time):** 153 verbal; 152
quantitative; 3.9 writing
Average GPA (full time): 3.28
**Average age of entrants to
full-time program:** 30
**Average months of prior work
experience (full time):** 131
TOEFL requirement: Yes
Minimum TOEFL score: 80
Most popular departments:
entrepreneurship, finance,
real estate, supply chain
management/logistics, other

University of Oregon

1208 University of Oregon
Eugene, OR 97403-1208
business.uoregon.edu/mba/
Public
Admissions: (541) 346-3306
Email: mbainfo@uoregon.edu
Financial aid: (541) 346-3221
Application deadline: N/A
In-state tuition: full time: $30,510;
part time: $856/credit hour
Out-of-state tuition: full
time: $41,406; part time:
$1,251/credit hour
Room/board/expenses: $15,369
College-funded aid: Yes
International student aid: Yes
**Average student indebtedness
at graduation:** $68,531
Full-time enrollment: 123
men: 61%; women:
39%; minorities: 8%;
international: 18%
Part-time enrollment: 13
men: 77%; women: 23%;
minorities: 0%; international: 0%
Acceptance rate (full time): 67%
Average GMAT (full time): 613
**Average GRE (full
time):** 154 verbal; 154
quantitative; 3.9 writing
Average GPA (full time): 3.36
**Average age of entrants to
full-time program:** 28
**Average months of prior work
experience (full time):** 55
TOEFL requirement: Yes
Minimum TOEFL score: 96
Most popular departments:
accounting, entrepreneurship,
finance, sports business, other
**Mean starting base salary for
2018 full-time graduates:** $79,104
**Employment location for
2018 class:** Intl. 3%; N.E.
3%; M.A. N/A; S. N/A; M.W.
10%; S.W. 7%; W. 77%

University of Portland

5000 N. Willamette Boulevard
Portland, OR 97203-5798
business.up.edu
Private
Admissions: (503) 943-7224
Email: bus-grad@up.edu
Financial aid: (503) 943-7311
Application deadline: 07/15
Tuition: full time: $1,323/
credit hour; part time:
$1,323/credit hour
Room/board/expenses: $12,000
College-funded aid: Yes

International student aid: Yes
**Average student indebtedness
at graduation:** $41,472
Full-time enrollment: 35
men: 54%; women:
46%; minorities: 11%;
international: 40%
Part-time enrollment: 114
men: 59%; women:
41%; minorities: 11%;
international: 9%
Acceptance rate (full time): 60%
Average GMAT (full time): 542
**Average GRE (full
time):** 150 verbal; 158
quantitative; 4.0 writing
Average GPA (full time): 3.29
**Average age of entrants to
full-time program:** 26
**Average months of prior work
experience (full time):** 25
TOEFL requirement: Yes
Minimum TOEFL score: 88
Most popular departments:
finance, manufacturing and
technology management,
marketing, production/
operations management, other

Willamette University

900 State Street
Salem, OR 97301-3922
www.willamette.edu/mba
Private
Admissions: (503) 370-6620
Email: mba-admission@
willamette.edu
Financial aid: (503) 370-6273
Application deadline: 05/01
Tuition: full time: $42,290;
part time: $37,075
Room/board/expenses: $13,600
College-funded aid: Yes
International student aid: Yes
**Average student indebtedness
at graduation:** $58,112
Full-time enrollment: 126
men: 59%; women:
41%; minorities: 33%;
international: 13%
Part-time enrollment: 111
men: 50%; women:
50%; minorities: 23%;
international: 0%
Acceptance rate (full time): 67%
Average GMAT (full time): 531
**Average GRE (full
time):** 151 verbal; 150
quantitative; 3.7 writing
Average GPA (full time): 3.27
**Average age of entrants to
full-time program:** 24
**Average months of prior work
experience (full time):** 15
TOEFL requirement: Yes
Minimum TOEFL score: 88
Most popular departments:
accounting, entrepreneurship,
finance, marketing, production/
operations management
**Mean starting base salary for
2018 full-time graduates:** $61,214
**Employment location for
2018 class:** Intl. N/A; N.E.
14%; M.A. 0%; S. 0%; M.W.
0%; S.W. 3%; W. 83%

PENNSYLVANIA

Bloomsburg University of Pennsylvania

Sutliff Hall, Room 363
400 Second Street
Bloomsburg, PA 17815-1301
cob.bloomu.edu/
Public
Admissions: (570) 389-4394
Email: gradadmissions@
bloomu.edu
Financial aid: (570) 389-4297
Application deadline: 06/01
In-state tuition: full time: N/A;
part time: $516/credit hour
Out-of-state tuition: full time:
N/A; part time: $774/credit hour
Room/board/expenses: N/A
College-funded aid: Yes
International student aid: Yes
Full-time enrollment: N/A
men: N/A; women:
N/A; minorities: N/A;
international: N/A
Part-time enrollment: 78
men: 53%; women:
47%; minorities: N/A;
international: N/A
**Average GRE (full
time):** N/A verbal; N/A
quantitative; N/A writing
TOEFL requirement: Yes
Minimum TOEFL score: 100

Carnegie Mellon University

5000 Forbes Avenue
Pittsburgh, PA 15213
www.cmu.edu/tepper/
programs/mba/index.html
Private
Admissions: (412) 268-2272
Email: mba-admissions@
andrew.cmu.edu
Financial aid: (412) 268-7581
Application deadline: 03/07
Tuition: full time: $65,852;
part time: $50,352
Room/board/expenses: $22,526
College-funded aid: Yes
International student aid: Yes
Full-time enrollment: 465
men: 72%; women:
28%; minorities: 28%;
international: 34%
Part-time enrollment: 96
men: 73%; women:
27%; minorities: 15%;
international: 9%
Acceptance rate (full time): 35%
Average GMAT (full time): 690
**Average GRE (full
time):** 158 verbal; 162
quantitative; 4.0 writing
Average GPA (full time): 3.40
**Average age of entrants to
full-time program:** 28
**Average months of prior work
experience (full time):** 68
TOEFL requirement: Yes
Minimum TOEFL score: 100
Most popular departments:
entrepreneurship, finance,
marketing, management
information systems,
organizational behavior
**Mean starting base salary for 2018
full-time graduates:** $120,382

Clarion University of Pennsylvania

840 Wood Street
Clarion, PA 16214
www.clarion.edu/admissions/
graduate
Public
Admissions: (814) 393-2337
Email: gradstudies@clarion.edu
Financial aid: (800) 672-7171
Application deadline: rolling
In-state tuition: full time:
$516/credit hour; part
time: $516/credit hour
Out-of-state tuition: full
time: $557/credit hour; part
time: $557/credit hour
Room/board/expenses: $10,000
College-funded aid: Yes
International student aid: Yes
**Average student indebtedness
at graduation:** $30,623
Full-time enrollment: 21
men: 62%; women:
38%; minorities: 14%;
international: 0%
Part-time enrollment: 71
men: 54%; women:
46%; minorities: 14%;
international: 0%
Acceptance rate (full time): 100%
**Average GRE (full
time):** N/A verbal; N/A
quantitative; N/A writing
Average GPA (full time): 3.30
**Average age of entrants to
full-time program:** 22
**Average months of prior work
experience (full time):** 20
TOEFL requirement: Yes
Minimum TOEFL score: 80
Most popular departments:
accounting, entrepreneurship,
finance, general management,
health care administration

Drexel University

3141 Chestnut Street
Philadelphia, PA 19104
www.lebow.drexel.edu/
Private
Admissions: (215) 895-6804
Email: mba@drexel.edu
Financial aid: (215) 571-4545
Application deadline: 09/01
Tuition: full time: N/A;
part time: N/A
Room/board/expenses: N/A
College-funded aid: Yes
International student aid: Yes
**Average student indebtedness
at graduation:** $48,102
Full-time enrollment: 38
men: 61%; women:
39%; minorities: 13%;
international: 37%
Part-time enrollment: 220
men: 54%; women:
46%; minorities: 19%;
international: 6%
Acceptance rate (full time): 42%
Average GMAT (full time): 607
**Average GRE (full
time):** N/A verbal; N/A
quantitative; N/A writing
Average GPA (full time): 3.20
**Average age of entrants to
full-time program:** 28
TOEFL requirement: Yes
Minimum TOEFL score: 90

Most popular departments: entrepreneurship, finance, general management, marketing, other
Mean starting base salary for 2018 full-time graduates: $75,182
Employment location for 2018 class: Intl. 6%; N.E. 22%; M.A. 56%; S. N/A; M.W. N/A; S.W. N/A; W. 17%

Duquesne University

600 Forbes Avenue
704 Rockwell Hall
Pittsburgh, PA 15282
www.duq.edu/academics/schools/business/graduate
Private
Admissions: (412) 396-6276
Email: grad-bus@duq.edu
Financial aid: (412) 396-6607
Application deadline: 07/01
Tuition: total program: $51,603 (full time); part time: $1,284/credit hour
Room/board/expenses: $16,186
College-funded aid: Yes
International student aid: Yes
Average student indebtedness at graduation: $35,700
Full-time enrollment: 14 men: 71%; women: 29%; minorities: 36%; international: 21%
Part-time enrollment: 147 men: 68%; women: 32%; minorities: 12%; international: 7%
Acceptance rate (full time): 100%
Average GMAT (full time): 565
Average GRE (full time): 161 verbal; 150 quantitative; 4.0 writing
Average GPA (full time): 3.20
Average age of entrants to full-time program: 25
Average months of prior work experience (full time): 34
TOEFL requirement: Yes
Minimum TOEFL score: 90
Most popular departments: general management, supply chain management/logistics, other
Mean starting base salary for 2018 full-time graduates: $54,384

Indiana University of Pennsylvania

664 Pratt Drive, Room 402
Indiana, PA 15705
www.eberly.iup.edu/mba
Public
Admissions: (724) 357-2222
Email: graduate-admissions@iup.edu
Financial aid: (724) 357-2218
Application deadline: rolling
In-state tuition: full time: $516/credit hour; part time: $516/credit hour
Out-of-state tuition: full time: $774/credit hour; part time: $774/credit hour
Room/board/expenses: $15,500
College-funded aid: Yes
International student aid: Yes
Average student indebtedness at graduation: $22,601

Full-time enrollment: 109 men: 60%; women: 40%; minorities: 2%; international: 81%
Part-time enrollment: 98 men: 58%; women: 42%; minorities: 1%; international: 90%
Acceptance rate (full time): 100%
Average GMAT (full time): 430
Average GRE (full time): N/A verbal; N/A quantitative; N/A writing
Average age of entrants to full-time program: 25
TOEFL requirement: Yes
Minimum TOEFL score: 76
Most popular departments: finance, human resources management, marketing, management information systems, supply chain management/logistics

King's College[1]

133 N. River Street
Wilkes-Barre, PA 18711
www.kings.edu/academics/colleges_and_programs/business
Private
Admissions: (570) 208-5991
Email: gradprograms@kings.edu
Financial aid: N/A
Tuition: N/A
Room/board/expenses: N/A
Enrollment: N/A

Kutztown University of Pennsylvania

PO Box 730
Kutztown, PA 19530
www.kutztown.edu/admissions/graduate-admissions.htm
Public
Admissions: (610) 683-4200
Email: graduate@kutztown.edu
Financial aid: (610) 683-4077
Application deadline: 08/01
In-state tuition: full time: $516/credit hour; part time: $516/credit hour
Out-of-state tuition: full time: $774/credit hour; part time: $774/credit hour
Room/board/expenses: $10,270
College-funded aid: Yes
International student aid: Yes
Full-time enrollment: 12 men: 67%; women: 33%; minorities: 8%; international: 17%
Part-time enrollment: 19 men: 63%; women: 37%; minorities: 0%; international: 5%
Acceptance rate (full time): 85%
Average GMAT (full time): 460
Average GRE (full time): N/A verbal; N/A quantitative; N/A writing
Average GPA (full time): 3.28
Average age of entrants to full-time program: 27
TOEFL requirement: Yes
Minimum TOEFL score: 79

La Salle University

1900 W. Olney Avenue
Philadelphia, PA 19141
www.lasalle.edu/business/programs/mba/
Private
Admissions: (215) 951-1057
Email: mba@lasalle.edu
Financial aid: (215) 951-1070
Application deadline: rolling
Tuition: full time: $25,020; part time: $1,030/credit hour
Room/board/expenses: N/A
College-funded aid: Yes
International student aid: Yes
Average student indebtedness at graduation: $22,495
Full-time enrollment: 48 men: 54%; women: 46%; minorities: 29%; international: 25%
Part-time enrollment: 163 men: 49%; women: 51%; minorities: 26%; international: 1%
Acceptance rate (full time): 96%
Average GMAT (full time): 496
Average GRE (full time): 146 verbal; 137 quantitative; 4.0 writing
Average GPA (full time): 3.25
Average age of entrants to full-time program: 23
Average months of prior work experience (full time): 8
TOEFL requirement: Yes
Minimum TOEFL score: 88
Most popular departments: accounting, finance, general management, marketing, other
Mean starting base salary for 2018 full-time graduates: $54,871
Employment location for 2018 class: Intl. 7%; N.E. 2%; M.A. 87%; S. 2%; M.W. 0%; S.W. 0%; W. 2%

Lehigh University

621 Taylor Street
Bethlehem, PA 18015
www.lehigh.edu/mba
Private
Admissions: (610) 758-4386
Email: mba.admissions@lehigh.edu
Financial aid: (610) 758-5285
Application deadline: 08/01
Tuition: total program: $64,750 (full time); part time: $1,075/credit hour
Room/board/expenses: $18,170
College-funded aid: Yes
International student aid: Yes
Average student indebtedness at graduation: $49,540
Full-time enrollment: 20 men: 60%; women: 40%; minorities: 10%; international: 45%
Part-time enrollment: 176 men: 74%; women: 26%; minorities: 17%; international: 6%
Acceptance rate (full time): 73%
Average GMAT (full time): 590
Average GRE (full time): 154 verbal; 149 quantitative; 4.2 writing
Average GPA (full time): 3.21
Average age of entrants to full-time program: 34
Average months of prior work experience (full time): 105

TOEFL requirement: Yes
Minimum TOEFL score: 94
Most popular departments: entrepreneurship, finance, marketing, supply chain management/logistics, other

Pennsylvania State University–Erie, The Behrend College

5101 Jordan Road
Erie, PA 16563
behrend.psu.edu/
Public
Admissions: (814) 898-7255
Email: behrend.admissions@psu.edu
Financial aid: (814) 898-6162
Application deadline: 06/16
In-state tuition: full time: N/A; part time: N/A
Out-of-state tuition: full time: N/A; part time: N/A
Room/board/expenses: N/A
College-funded aid: Yes
International student aid: No
Average student indebtedness at graduation: $0
Full-time enrollment: N/A men: N/A; women: N/A; minorities: N/A; international: N/A
Part-time enrollment: 117 men: 63%; women: 37%; minorities: 3%; international: 0%
Average GRE (full time): N/A verbal; N/A quantitative; N/A writing
Minimum TOEFL score: N/A
Employment location for 2018 class: Intl. N/A; N.E. N/A; M.A. 92%; S. N/A; M.W. 5%; S.W. 3%; W. N/A

Pennsylvania State University–Great Valley[1]

30 E. Swedesford Road
Malvern, PA 19355
www.sgps.psu.edu
Public
Admissions: (610) 648-3242
Email: gvadmiss@psu.edu
Financial aid: N/A
Tuition: N/A
Room/board/expenses: N/A
Enrollment: N/A

Pennsylvania State University–Harrisburg

777 W. Harrisburg Pike, E355
Middletown, PA 17057-4898
harrisburg.psu.edu/mba
Public
Admissions: (717) 948-6250
Email: mbahbg@psu.edu
Financial aid: (717) 948-6307
Application deadline: 07/18
In-state tuition: full time: $908/credit hour; part time: $908/credit hour
Out-of-state tuition: full time: $1,419/credit hour; part time: $1,419/credit hour
Room/board/expenses: $5,817
College-funded aid: Yes
International student aid: Yes

Full-time enrollment: 20 men: 30%; women: 70%; minorities: 20%; international: 0%
Part-time enrollment: 178 men: 70%; women: 30%; minorities: 20%; international: 0%
Acceptance rate (full time): 70%
Average GMAT (full time): 550
Average GRE (full time): N/A verbal; N/A quantitative; N/A writing
Average GPA (full time): 3.36
Average age of entrants to full-time program: 26
Average months of prior work experience (full time): 29
TOEFL requirement: Yes
Minimum TOEFL score: 80
Most popular departments: accounting, finance, general management, management information systems, supply chain management/logistics

Pennsylvania State University–University Park

220 Business Building
University Park, PA 16802-3000
mba.smeal.psu.edu/
Public
Admissions: (814) 863-0474
Email: smealmba@psu.edu
Financial aid: (814) 865-6301
Application deadline: 04/01
In-state tuition: full time: $28,772; part time: N/A
Out-of-state tuition: full time: $44,818; part time: N/A
Room/board/expenses: $21,950
College-funded aid: Yes
International student aid: Yes
Average student indebtedness at graduation: $40,122
Full-time enrollment: 117 men: 69%; women: 31%; minorities: 21%; international: 33%
Part-time enrollment: N/A men: N/A; women: N/A; minorities: N/A; international: N/A
Acceptance rate (full time): 18%
Average GMAT (full time): 657
Average GRE (full time): 156 verbal; 152 quantitative; 4.0 writing
Average GPA (full time): 3.37
Average age of entrants to full-time program: 29
Average months of prior work experience (full time): 62
TOEFL requirement: Yes
Minimum TOEFL score: 100
Most popular departments: consulting, finance, leadership, marketing, supply chain management/logistics
Mean starting base salary for 2018 full-time graduates: $106,100
Employment location for 2018 class: Intl. 2%; N.E. 7%; M.A. 23%; S. 9%; M.W. 21%; S.W. 23%; W. 14%

Robert Morris University

6001 University Boulevard
Moon Township, PA 15108-1189
rmu.edu/academics/graduate
Private
Admissions: (800) 762-0097
Email: enrollmentoffice@
rmu.edu
Financial aid: (412) 397-6250
Application deadline: N/A
Tuition: full time: N/A; part
time: $955/credit hour
Room/board/expenses: N/A
College-funded aid: Yes
International student aid: Yes
Full-time enrollment: N/A
men: N/A; women:
N/A; minorities: N/A;
international: N/A
Part-time enrollment: 201
men: 64%; women: 36%;
minorities: 3%; international: 4%
**Average GRE (full
time):** N/A verbal; N/A
quantitative; N/A writing
TOEFL requirement: Yes
Minimum TOEFL score: 79
Most popular departments:
general management, human
resources management, tax

Shippensburg University of Pennsylvania

1871 Old Main Drive
Shippensburg, PA 17257
www.ship.edu/mba
Public
Admissions: (717) 477-1231
Email: gradadmiss@ship.edu
Financial aid: (717) 477-1131
Application deadline: rolling
In-state tuition: full time:
$19,950; total program:
$19,950 (part time)
Out-of-state tuition: full time:
$27,690; total program:
$27.690 (part time)
Room/board/expenses: $27,150
College-funded aid: Yes
International student aid: Yes
Full-time enrollment: 18
men: 61%; women:
39%; minorities: 11%;
international: 17%
Part-time enrollment: 63
men: 60%; women:
40%; minorities: 22%;
international: 16%
Acceptance rate (full time): 47%
**Average GRE (full
time):** N/A verbal; N/A
quantitative; N/A writing
**Average age of entrants to
full-time program:** 27
**Average months of prior work
experience (full time):** 42
TOEFL requirement: Yes
Minimum TOEFL score: 68
Most popular departments:
finance, health care
administration, management
information systems,
supply chain management/
logistics, other

St. Joseph's University

5600 City Avenue
Philadelphia, PA 19131
www.sju.edu/majors-programs/
graduate-business/master-
degrees/master-business-
administration-mba
Private
Admissions: (610) 660-1690
Email: sjumba@sju.edu
Financial aid: (610) 660-1346
Application deadline: 07/15
Tuition: full time: N/A; part
time: $1,043/credit hour
Room/board/expenses: N/A
College-funded aid: Yes
International student aid: Yes
Full-time enrollment: N/A
men: N/A; women:
N/A; minorities: N/A;
international: N/A
Part-time enrollment: 205
men: 55%; women:
45%; minorities: 21%;
international: 14%
**Average GRE (full
time):** N/A verbal; N/A
quantitative; N/A writing
TOEFL requirement: Yes
Minimum TOEFL score: 80
Most popular departments:
finance, general management,
human resources management,
marketing, management
information systems

Temple University[1]

Alter Hall, 1801 Liacouras Walk
Philadelphia, PA 19122-6083
sbm.temple.edu/
Public
Admissions: (215) 204-7678
Email: foxinfo@temple.edu
Financial aid: (215) 204-7678
Tuition: N/A
Room/board/expenses: N/A
Enrollment: N/A

University of Pennsylvania

420 Jon M. Huntsman Hall
3730 Walnut Street
Philadelphia, PA 19104
www.wharton.upenn.edu/
Private
Admissions: (215) 898-6183
Email: mbaadmiss@
wharton.upenn.edu
Financial aid: (215) 898-8728
Application deadline: 09/18
Tuition: full time: $78,948;
part time: N/A
Room/board/expenses: $32,952
College-funded aid: Yes
International student aid: Yes
Full-time enrollment: 1,742
men: 56%; women:
44%; minorities: 33%;
international: 33%
Part-time enrollment: N/A
men: N/A; women:
N/A; minorities: N/A;
international: N/A
Acceptance rate (full time): 21%
Average GMAT (full time): 732
**Average GRE (full
time):** N/A verbal; N/A
quantitative; N/A writing
Average GPA (full time): 3.60

**Average age of entrants to
full-time program:** 28
**Average months of prior work
experience (full time):** 60
TOEFL requirement: No
Minimum TOEFL score: N/A
Most popular departments:
entrepreneurship, finance,
general management, health
care administration, other
**Mean starting base salary for 2018
full-time graduates:** $139,670
**Employment location for
2018 class:** Intl. 12%; N.E.
43%; M.A. 8%; S. 5%; M.W.
6%; S.W. 5%; W. 23%

University of Pittsburgh

372 Mervis Hall
Pittsburgh, PA 15260
www.business.pitt.edu/
Public
Admissions: (412) 648-1700
Email: mba@katz.pitt.edu
Financial aid: (412) 648-1700
Application deadline: 04/01
In-state tuition: total program:
$53,264 (full time); part
time: $1,308/credit hour
Out-of-state tuition: total
program: $71,616 (full time);
part time: $2,024/credit hour
Room/board/expenses: $36,034
College-funded aid: Yes
International student aid: Yes
Full-time enrollment: 120
men: 61%; women:
39%; minorities: 24%;
international: 39%
Part-time enrollment: 267
men: 64%; women:
36%; minorities: 10%;
international: 2%
Acceptance rate (full time): 34%
Average GMAT (full time): 621
**Average GRE (full
time):** 153 verbal; 154
quantitative; 4.3 writing
Average GPA (full time): 3.32
**Average age of entrants to
full-time program:** 28
**Average months of prior work
experience (full time):** 55
TOEFL requirement: Yes
Minimum TOEFL score: 100
Most popular departments:
finance, marketing, management
information systems,
production/operations
management, supply chain
management/logistics
**Mean starting base salary for
2018 full-time graduates:** $88,000
**Employment location for
2018 class:** Intl. 2%; N.E.
14%; M.A. 57%; S. 2%; M.W.
6%; S.W. 10%; W. 10%

University of Scranton

800 Linden Street
Scranton, PA 18510-4632
www.scranton.edu
Private
Admissions: (570) 941-4416
Email: gradadmissions@
scranton.edu
Financial aid: (570) 941-7701
Application deadline: rolling
Tuition: full time: N/A; part
time: $965/credit hour
Room/board/expenses: N/A

College-funded aid: Yes
International student aid: Yes
Full-time enrollment: N/A
men: N/A; women:
N/A; minorities: N/A;
international: N/A
Part-time enrollment: 101
men: 47%; women:
53%; minorities: 7%;
international: 12%
**Average GRE (full
time):** N/A verbal; N/A
quantitative; N/A writing
TOEFL requirement: Yes
Minimum TOEFL score: 80
Most popular departments:
accounting, finance, general
management, health care
administration, production/
operations management

Villanova University

Bartley Hall
800 Lancaster Avenue
Villanova, PA 19085
mba.villanova.edu
Private
Admissions: (610) 519-4336
Email: claire.bruno@
villanova.edu
Financial aid: (610) 519-4010
Application deadline: 07/31
Tuition: full time: N/A; part
time: $1,167/credit hour
Room/board/expenses: N/A
College-funded aid: Yes
International student aid: Yes
Full-time enrollment: N/A
men: N/A; women:
N/A; minorities: N/A;
international: N/A
Part-time enrollment: 111
men: 58%; women:
42%; minorities: 12%;
international: 4%
**Average GRE (full
time):** N/A verbal; N/A
quantitative; N/A writing
TOEFL requirement: Yes
Minimum TOEFL score: 90
Most popular departments:
finance, general
management, international
business, marketing

West Chester University of Pennsylvania[1]

1160 McDermott Drive
West Chester, PA 19383
www.wcupa.edu/mba
Public
Admissions: (610) 436-2943
Email: gradstudy@wcupa.edu
Financial aid: (610) 436-2627
Tuition: N/A
Room/board/expenses: N/A
Enrollment: N/A

Widener University

1 University Place
Chester, PA 19013
www.widener.edu/sba
Private
Admissions: (610) 499-4330
Email: sbagradv@
mail.widener.edu
Financial aid: (610) 499-4161
Application deadline: rolling

Tuition: full time: $1,020/
credit hour; part time:
$1,020/credit hour
Room/board/expenses: N/A
College-funded aid: Yes
International student aid: Yes
Full-time enrollment: 27
men: 41%; women:
59%; minorities: 15%;
international: 67%
Part-time enrollment: 40
men: 55%; women:
45%; minorities: 25%;
international: 15%
Acceptance rate (full time): 83%
**Average GRE (full
time):** N/A verbal; N/A
quantitative; N/A writing
Average GPA (full time): 3.32
**Average age of entrants to
full-time program:** 26
TOEFL requirement: Yes
Minimum TOEFL score: N/A

PUERTO RICO

University of Puerto Rico– Rio Piedras[1]

Plaza Universitaria Building,
Torre Norte, 5th Floor
San Juan, PR
business.uprrp.edu
Public
Admissions: (787) 764-0000
Email: mayra.crespo2@upr.edu
Financial aid: (787) 764-0000
Tuition: N/A
Room/board/expenses: N/A
Enrollment: N/A

RHODE ISLAND

Bryant University

1150 Douglas Pike
Smithfield, RI 02917
www.bryant.edu/
Private
Admissions: (401) 232-6707
Email: gradprog@bryant.edu
Financial aid: (401) 232-6020
Application deadline: 04/15
Tuition: full time: $1,118/
credit hour; part time:
$1,118/credit hour
Room/board/expenses: N/A
College-funded aid: Yes
International student aid: Yes
Full-time enrollment: 41
men: 56%; women:
44%; minorities: 29%;
international: 15%
Part-time enrollment: 88
men: 57%; women:
43%; minorities: 19%;
international: 1%
Acceptance rate (full time): 58%
Average GMAT (full time): 464
**Average GRE (full
time):** N/A verbal; N/A
quantitative; N/A writing
Average GPA (full time): 3.45
**Average age of entrants to
full-time program:** 23
TOEFL requirement: Yes
Minimum TOEFL score: 85
Most popular departments:
finance, general management,
international business, supply
chain management/logistics,
quantitative analysis/statistics
and operations research

Providence College

One Cunningham Square
Providence, RI 02918
business.providence.edu/mba/
Private
Admissions: (401) 865-2294
Email: mba@providence.edu
Financial aid: (401) 865-2286
Application deadline: 07/01
Tuition: full time: N/A; total program: $24,700 (part time)
Room/board/expenses: N/A
College-funded aid: Yes
International student aid: Yes
Full-time enrollment: N/A
men: N/A; women:
N/A; minorities: N/A;
international: N/A
Part-time enrollment: 161
men: 59%; women: 41%;
minorities: 9%; international: 6%
**Average GRE (full
time):** N/A verbal; N/A
quantitative; N/A writing
TOEFL requirement: Yes
Minimum TOEFL score: 100
Most popular departments:
accounting, finance, general
management, international
business, marketing

University of Rhode Island[1]

7 Lippitt Road
Kingston, RI 02881
web.uri.edu/business/
Public
Admissions: (401) 874-2842
Email: gradadm@etal.uri.edu
Financial aid: N/A
Tuition: N/A
Room/board/expenses: N/A
Enrollment: N/A

SOUTH CAROLINA

The Citadel

171 Moultrie Street
Charleston, SC 29409
www.citadel.edu/root/bsb
Public
Admissions: (843) 953-5336
Email: cgc@citadel.edu
Financial aid: (843) 953-5187
Application deadline: rolling
In-state tuition: full time: $10,890; part time: $595/credit hour
Out-of-state tuition: full time: $18,540; part time: $1,020/credit hour
Room/board/expenses: $9,699
College-funded aid: Yes
International student aid: Yes
Full-time enrollment: 30
men: 73%; women:
27%; minorities: 23%;
international: 0%
Part-time enrollment: 119
men: 64%; women:
36%; minorities: 13%;
international: 0%
Acceptance rate (full time): 70%
Average GMAT (full time): 570
**Average GRE (full
time):** 142 verbal; 146
quantitative; N/A writing
Average GPA (full time): 3.26
**Average age of entrants to
full-time program:** 27

**Average months of prior work
experience (full time):** 87
TOEFL requirement: Yes
Minimum TOEFL score: 79

Clemson University

1 North Main Street
Greenville, SC 29601
www.clemson.edu/cbbs/
departments/mba
Public
Admissions: (864) 656-8173
Email: mba@clemson.edu
Financial aid: (864) 656-2280
Application deadline: 06/18
In-state tuition: full time: $19,226; part time: $721/credit hour
Out-of-state tuition: full time: $31,592; part time: $1,471/credit hour
Room/board/expenses: $1,400
Full-time enrollment: 121
men: 52%; women:
48%; minorities: 16%;
international: 7%
Part-time enrollment: 417
men: 67%; women:
33%; minorities: 18%;
international: 1%
Acceptance rate (full time): 90%
Average GMAT (full time): 540
**Average GRE (full
time):** N/A verbal; N/A
quantitative; N/A writing
Average GPA (full time): 3.37
**Average age of entrants to
full-time program:** 24
**Average months of prior work
experience (full time):** 44
TOEFL requirement: Yes
Minimum TOEFL score: N/A
Most popular departments:
entrepreneurship, general
management, health care
administration, marketing,
quantitative analysis/statistics
and operations research
**Mean starting base salary for
2018 full-time graduates:** $66,800
**Employment location for
2018 class:** Intl. 0%; N.E.
3%; M.A. N/A; S. 91%; M.W.
6%; S.W. 0%; W. 0%

Coastal Carolina University[1]

PO Box 261954
Conway, SC 29528-6054
www.coastal.edu/
graduatestudies/
Public
Admissions: (843) 349-2394
Email: graduate@coastal.edu
Financial aid: (843) 349-2313
Tuition: N/A
Room/board/expenses: N/A
Enrollment: N/A

College of Charleston

66 George Street
Charleston, SC 29424
www.mbacharleston.com/
Public
Admissions: (843) 953-8112
Email: mba@cofc.edu
Financial aid: (843) 953-5540
Application deadline: 05/01
In-state tuition: total program: $27,873 (full time); part time: N/A

Out-of-state tuition: total program: $599 (full time); part time: N/A
Room/board/expenses: $17,689
College-funded aid: Yes
International student aid: Yes
**Average student indebtedness
at graduation:** $34,099
Full-time enrollment: 41
men: 66%; women:
34%; minorities: 12%;
international: 5%
Part-time enrollment: N/A
men: N/A; women:
N/A; minorities: N/A;
international: N/A
Acceptance rate (full time): 77%
Average GMAT (full time): 527
Average GRE (full time): 154
verbal; 151 quantitative;
N/A writing
Average GPA (full time): 3.20
**Average age of entrants to
full-time program:** 26
TOEFL requirement: Yes
Minimum TOEFL score: 83
Most popular departments:
finance, hotel administration,
marketing
**Mean starting base salary for
2018 full-time graduates:** $57,839
**Employment location for 2018
class:** Intl. N/A; N.E. 18%;
M.A. N/A; S. 68%; M.W.
14%; S.W. N/A; W. N/A

Francis Marion University

Box 100547
Florence, SC 29501
www.fmarion.edu/
business/mba/
Public
Admissions: (843) 661-1424
Email: klawrimore@fmarion.edu
Financial aid: (843) 661-1190
Application deadline: rolling
In-state tuition: full time: $530/
credit hour; part time: N/A
Out-of-state tuition:
full time: $1,061/credit
hour; part time: N/A
Room/board/expenses: N/A
College-funded aid: Yes
Full-time enrollment: 55
men: N/A; women:
N/A; minorities: N/A;
international: N/A
Part-time enrollment: N/A
men: N/A; women:
N/A; minorities: N/A;
international: N/A
**Average GRE (full
time):** N/A verbal; N/A
quantitative; N/A writing
TOEFL requirement: Yes
Minimum TOEFL score: N/A

South Carolina State University

300 College Street NE
Orangeburg, SC 29117
www.scsu.edu/
schoolofgraduatestudies.aspx
Public
Admissions: (803) 536-7133
Email: graduateschool@
scsu.edu
Financial aid: (803) 536-7067
Application deadline: 06/15

In-state tuition: full time:
N/A; part time: N/A
Out-of-state tuition: full
time: N/A; part time: N/A
Room/board/expenses: N/A
College-funded aid: Yes
International student aid: Yes
Full-time enrollment: 20
men: 55%; women:
45%; minorities: 100%;
international: 0%
Part-time enrollment: 6
men: 67%; women:
33%; minorities: 100%;
international: 0%
Acceptance rate (full time): 92%
**Average GRE (full
time):** N/A verbal; N/A
quantitative; N/A writing
TOEFL requirement: Yes
Minimum TOEFL score: 79

University of South Carolina

1014 Greene Street
Columbia, SC 29208
moore.sc.edu/
Public
Admissions: (803) 777-2730
Email: gradinfo@moore.sc.edu
Financial aid: (803) 777-8134
Application deadline: 04/15
In-state tuition: total program:
$44,022 (full time); total
program: $36,464 (part time)
Out-of-state tuition: total
program: $72,460 (full
time); total program:
$36,464 (part time)
Room/board/expenses: $49,589
College-funded aid: Yes
International student aid: Yes
**Average student indebtedness
at graduation:** $54,932
Full-time enrollment: 47
men: 68%; women:
32%; minorities: 11%;
international: 28%
Part-time enrollment: 441
men: 71%; women:
29%; minorities: 22%;
international: 2%
Acceptance rate (full time): 64%
Average GMAT (full time): 651
**Average GRE (full
time):** 155 verbal; 155
quantitative; 4.0 writing
Average GPA (full time): 3.40
**Average age of entrants to
full-time program:** 27
**Average months of prior work
experience (full time):** 48
TOEFL requirement: Yes
Minimum TOEFL score: 95
**Mean starting base salary for
2018 full-time graduates:** $85,923

Winthrop University[1]

Thurmond Building
Rock Hill, SC 29733
www.winthrop.edu/cba
Public
Admissions: (803) 323-2204
Email: gradschool@winthrop.edu
Financial aid: N/A
Tuition: N/A
Room/board/expenses: N/A
Enrollment: N/A

Black Hills State University

1200 University Street
Spearfish, SD 57799
www.bhsu.edu/
Public
Admissions: (605) 642-6919
Email: MBA@bhsu.edu
Financial aid: (605) 718-4113
Application deadline: rolling
In-state tuition: full time:
N/A; N/A (part time)
Out-of-state tuition: full
time: N/A; N/A (part time)
Room/board/expenses: N/A
College-funded aid: Yes
International student aid: Yes
Full-time enrollment: N/A
men: N/A; women:
N/A; minorities: N/A;
international: N/A
Part-time enrollment: 20
men: 50%; women:
50%; minorities: N/A;
international: N/A
**Average GRE (full
time):** N/A verbal; N/A
quantitative; N/A writing
TOEFL requirement: Yes
Minimum TOEFL score: 61

University of South Dakota

414 E. Clark Street
Vermillion, SD 57069
www.usd.edu/mba
Public
Admissions: (605) 658-6533
Email: mba@usd.edu
Financial aid: (605) 677-5446
Application deadline: 06/01
In-state tuition: full time: $326/
credit hour; part time: N/A
Out-of-state tuition: full time:
$627/credit hour; part time: N/A
Room/board/expenses: $8,800
College-funded aid: Yes
International student aid: Yes
**Average student indebtedness
at graduation:** $17,889
Full-time enrollment: 57
men: 54%; women:
46%; minorities: 9%;
international: 11%
Part-time enrollment: N/A
men: N/A; women:
N/A; minorities: N/A;
international: N/A
Acceptance rate (full time): 95%
Average GMAT (full time): 536
**Average GRE (full
time):** N/A verbal; N/A
quantitative; N/A writing
Average GPA (full time): 3.42
**Average age of entrants to
full-time program:** 24
**Average months of prior work
experience (full time):** 30
TOEFL requirement: Yes
Minimum TOEFL score: 79
Most popular departments:
general management,
health care administration,
marketing, production/
operations management,
quantitative analysis/statistics
and operations research
**Mean starting base salary for
2018 full-time graduates:** $47,000

TENNESSEE

Belmont University

1900 Belmont Boulevard
Nashville, TN 37212
www.belmont.edu/business/
graduate/index.html
Private
Admissions: (615) 460-6480
Email: masseyadmissions@
belmont.edu
Financial aid: (615) 460-6403
Application deadline: 06/01
Tuition: total program: $59,895
(full time); total program:
$59,895 (part time)
Room/board/expenses: N/A
College-funded aid: Yes
International student aid: Yes
Full-time enrollment: 31
men: 45%; women: 55%;
minorities: 6%; international: 3%
Part-time enrollment: 138
men: 57%; women:
43%; minorities: 14%;
international: 1%
Acceptance rate (full time): 84%
Average GMAT (full time): 546
**Average GRE (full
time):** N/A verbal; N/A
quantitative; N/A writing
Average GPA (full time): 3.48
**Average age of entrants to
full-time program:** 23
TOEFL requirement: Yes
Minimum TOEFL score: 80
Most popular departments:
entrepreneurship, finance,
general management, health
care administration, marketing
**Mean starting base salary for
2018 full-time graduates:** $48,500
**Employment location for
2018 class:** Intl. 0%; N.E.
5%; M.A. 0%; S. 79%; M.W.
11%; S.W. 5%; W. 0%

East Tennessee State University

PO Box 70699
Johnson City, TN 37614
www.etsu.edu/cbat
Public
Admissions: (423) 439-5314
Email: business@etsu.edu
Financial aid: (423) 439-4300
Application deadline: rolling
In-state tuition: full time:
$9,700; part time: N/A
Out-of-state tuition: full time:
$16,380; part time: N/A
Room/board/expenses: N/A
College-funded aid: Yes
International student aid: Yes
Full-time enrollment: 78
men: 55%; women:
45%; minorities: N/A;
international: N/A
Part-time enrollment: N/A
men: N/A; women:
N/A; minorities: N/A;
international: N/A
Acceptance rate (full time): 92%
Average GMAT (full time): 502
**Average GRE (full
time):** N/A verbal; N/A
quantitative; N/A writing
Average GPA (full time): 3.69
TOEFL requirement: Yes
Minimum TOEFL score: 79
Most popular departments:
general management

Middle Tennessee State University[1]

PO Box 290
Murfreesboro, TN 37132
www.mtsu.edu
Public
Admissions: (615) 898-2840
Email: graduate@mtsu.edu
Financial aid: N/A
Tuition: N/A
Room/board/expenses: N/A
Enrollment: N/A

Tennessee State University[1]

330 N. 10th Avenue
Nashville, TN 37203
www.tnstate.edu/business
Public
Admissions: (615) 963-5145
Email: cobinfo@tnstate.edu
Financial aid: N/A
Tuition: N/A
Room/board/expenses: N/A
Enrollment: N/A

Tennessee Technological University

Box 5023
Cookeville, TN 38505
www.tntech.edu/mba
Public
Admissions: (931) 372-3600
Email: knicewicz@tntech.edu
Financial aid: (931) 372-3073
Application deadline: 07/01
In-state tuition: full time:
$502/credit hour; part
time: $502/credit hour
Out-of-state tuition: full
time: $726/credit hour; part
time: $726/credit hour
Room/board/expenses: $25,600
College-funded aid: Yes
International student aid: Yes
**Average student indebtedness
at graduation:** $10,805
Full-time enrollment: 32
men: 69%; women: 31%;
minorities: 9%; international: 3%
Part-time enrollment: 156
men: 58%; women: 42%;
minorities: 8%; international: 3%
Acceptance rate (full time): 100%
Average GMAT (full time): 475
**Average GRE (full
time):** 150 verbal; 150
quantitative; N/A writing
Average GPA (full time): 3.42
**Average age of entrants to
full-time program:** 28
TOEFL requirement: Yes
Minimum TOEFL score: 79
Most popular departments:
finance, general management,
human resources
management, international
business, management
information systems

Union University

McAfee School of Business
1050 Union University Drive
Jackson, TN 38305
www.uu.edu/academics/
graduate/mba/
Private
Admissions: (731) 661-5341

Email: lperkovic@uu.edu
Financial aid: (731) 661-5213
Application deadline: 08/15
Tuition: full time: N/A; total
program: $22,140 (part time)
Room/board/expenses: N/A
College-funded aid: Yes
International student aid: Yes
Full-time enrollment: N/A
men: N/A; women:
N/A; minorities: N/A;
international: N/A
Part-time enrollment: 112
men: 61%; women:
39%; minorities: N/A;
international: N/A
**Average GRE (full
time):** N/A verbal; N/A
quantitative; N/A writing
TOEFL requirement: Yes
Minimum TOEFL score: 83
Most popular departments:
accounting, general
management, human
resources management,
leadership, marketing

University of Memphis

3675 Central Avenue
Memphis, TN 38152
fcbe.memphis.edu/
Public
Admissions: (901) 678-3721
Email: krishnan@memphis.edu
Financial aid: (901) 678-4825
Application deadline: 07/01
In-state tuition: full time:
$609/credit hour; part
time: $609/credit hour
Out-of-state tuition: full time:
$1,097/credit hour; part
time: $801/credit hour
Room/board/expenses: N/A
College-funded aid: Yes
International student aid: Yes
Full-time enrollment: 34
men: 50%; women:
50%; minorities: 35%;
international: 29%
Part-time enrollment: 115
men: 49%; women:
51%; minorities: 26%;
international: 12%
Acceptance rate (full time): 68%
Average GMAT (full time): 548
**Average GRE (full
time):** 148 verbal; 146
quantitative; 4.0 writing
Average GPA (full time): 3.38
**Average age of entrants to
full-time program:** 27
**Average months of prior work
experience (full time):** 55
TOEFL requirement: Yes
Minimum TOEFL score: 80
Most popular departments:
accounting, finance, general
management, international
business, management
information systems

University of Tennessee–Chattanooga

615 McCallie Avenue
Chattanooga, TN 37403
www.utc.edu/mba
Public
Admissions: (423) 425-4666
Email: christine-estoye@utc.edu

Financial aid: (423) 425-4677
Application deadline: 06/29
In-state tuition: full time: N/A;
part time: $458/credit hour
Out-of-state tuition: full time: N/A;
part time: $906/credit hour
Room/board/expenses: N/A
College-funded aid: Yes
International student aid: No
Full-time enrollment: N/A
men: N/A; women:
N/A; minorities: N/A;
international: N/A
Part-time enrollment: 127
men: 59%; women:
41%; minorities: 17%;
international: 3%
**Average GRE (full
time):** N/A verbal; N/A
quantitative; N/A writing
TOEFL requirement: Yes
Minimum TOEFL score: 79
Most popular departments:
accounting, finance, general
management, marketing, other

University of Tennessee–Knoxville

453 Haslam Business Building
Knoxville, TN 37996-4150
mba.utk.edu
Public
Admissions: (865) 974-5033
Email: mba@utk.edu
Financial aid: (865) 974-3131
Application deadline: rolling
In-state tuition: full time:
$25,314; part time: N/A
Out-of-state tuition: full time:
$43,502; part time: N/A
Room/board/expenses: $16,000
College-funded aid: Yes
International student aid: Yes
**Average student indebtedness
at graduation:** $32,750
Full-time enrollment: 100
men: 71%; women: 29%;
minorities: 2%; international: 7%
Part-time enrollment: N/A
men: N/A; women:
N/A; minorities: N/A;
international: N/A
Acceptance rate (full time): 49%
Average GMAT (full time): 655
**Average GRE (full
time):** 155 verbal; 156
quantitative; N/A writing
Average GPA (full time): 3.50
**Average age of entrants to
full-time program:** 28
**Average months of prior work
experience (full time):** 56
TOEFL requirement: Yes
Minimum TOEFL score: 100
Most popular departments:
entrepreneurship, finance,
marketing, supply chain
management/logistics, other
**Mean starting base salary for
2018 full-time graduates:** $77,995

University of Tennessee–Martin

103 Business Administration
Building
Martin, TN 38238
www.utm.edu/departments/
cbga/mba
Public
Admissions: (731) 881-7012
Email: jcunningham@utm.edu
Financial aid: (731) 881-7040

Application deadline: 07/30
In-state tuition: full time:
$495/credit hour; part
time: $495/credit hour
Out-of-state tuition: full
time: $831/credit hour; part
time: $831/credit hour
Room/board/expenses: N/A
College-funded aid: Yes
International student aid: Yes
**Average student indebtedness
at graduation:** $28,158
Full-time enrollment: 8
men: 75%; women:
25%; minorities: 13%;
international: 0%
Part-time enrollment: 16
men: 31%; women: 69%;
minorities: 6%; international: 0%
Acceptance rate (full time): 86%
Average GMAT (full time): 480
**Average GRE (full
time):** N/A verbal; N/A
quantitative; N/A writing
Average GPA (full time): 3.55
**Average age of entrants to
full-time program:** 30
**Average months of prior work
experience (full time):** 65
TOEFL requirement: Yes
Minimum TOEFL score: 71
Most popular departments: other

Vanderbilt University

401 21st Avenue S
Nashville, TN 37203
business.vanderbilt.edu
Private
Admissions: (615) 322-6469
Email: mba@
owen.vanderbilt.edu
Financial aid: (615) 322-3591
Application deadline: 04/29
Tuition: full time: $56,750;
part time: N/A
Room/board/expenses: $24,500
College-funded aid: Yes
International student aid: Yes
**Average student indebtedness
at graduation:** $81,916
Full-time enrollment: 351
mon: 72%; women:
28%; minorities: 13%;
international: 15%
Part-time enrollment: N/A
men: N/A; women:
N/A; minorities: N/A;
international: N/A
Acceptance rate (full time): 62%
Average GMAT (full time): 678
**Average GRE (full
time):** 157 verbal; 154
quantitative; 4.0 writing
Average GPA (full time): 3.30
**Average age of entrants to
full-time program:** 28
**Average months of prior work
experience (full time):** 66
TOEFL requirement: Yes
Minimum TOEFL score: 100
Most popular departments:
consulting, finance, health care
administration, marketing,
organizational behavior
**Mean starting base salary for
2018 full-time graduates:** $111,168
**Employment location for
2018 class:** Intl. 2%; N.E.
13%; M.A. 2%; S. 51%; M.W.
7%; S.W. 7%; W. 18%

TEXAS

Abilene Christian University[1]

ACU Box 29300
Abilene, TX 79699-9300
www.acu.edu/academics/coba/index.html
Private
Admissions: (800) 460-6228
Email: info@admissions.acu.edu
Financial aid: N/A
Tuition: N/A
Room/board/expenses: N/A
Enrollment: N/A

Baylor University

1 Bear Place, #98013
Waco, TX 76798-8013
www.baylor.edu/mba
Private
Admissions: (254) 710-3718
Email: mba_info@baylor.edu
Financial aid: (254) 710-2611
Application deadline: 05/15
Tuition: full time: $45,942; part time: N/A
Room/board/expenses: $20,500
College-funded aid: Yes
International student aid: Yes
Average student indebtedness at graduation: $22,900
Full-time enrollment: 84
men: 67%; women: 33%; minorities: 21%; international: 11%
Part-time enrollment: N/A
men: N/A; women: N/A; minorities: N/A; international: N/A
Acceptance rate (full time): 42%
Average GMAT (full time): 607
Average GRE (full time): 156 verbal; 154 quantitative; 3.9 writing
Average GPA (full time): 3.43
Average age of entrants to full-time program: 26
Average months of prior work experience (full time): 37
TOEFL requirement: Yes
Minimum TOEFL score: 100
Most popular departments: general management, health care administration, marketing, management information systems, quantitative analysis/statistics and operations research
Mean starting base salary for 2018 full-time graduates: $71,706
Employment location for 2018 class: Intl. 0%; N.E. 3%; M.A. 0%; S. 3%; M.W. 8%; S.W. 84%; W. 3%

Lamar University

4400 Martin Luther King Parkway
Beaumont, TX 77710
lamar.edu/mba
Public
Admissions: (409) 880-8888
Email: gradmissions@lamar.edu
Financial aid: (409) 880-7011
Application deadline: 07/31
In-state tuition: full time: $12,376; part time: N/A
Out-of-state tuition: full time: $22,336; part time: N/A
Room/board/expenses: $13,052

College-funded aid: Yes
International student aid: Yes
Average student indebtedness at graduation: $19,904
Full-time enrollment: 110
men: 45%; women: 55%; minorities: 19%; international: 23%
Part-time enrollment: N/A
men: N/A; women: N/A; minorities: N/A; international: N/A
Acceptance rate (full time): 86%
Average GMAT (full time): 481
Average GRE (full time): N/A verbal; N/A quantitative; N/A writing
Average GPA (full time): 3.22
Average age of entrants to full-time program: 32
TOEFL requirement: Yes
Minimum TOEFL score: 79
Most popular departments: finance, general management, health care administration, leadership, management information systems

Midwestern State University

3410 Taft Boulevard
Wichita Falls, TX 76308
www.msutexas.edu/mba
Public
Admissions: (940) 397-4920
Email: graduateschool@msutexas.edu
Financial aid: (940) 397-4214
Application deadline: 08/01
In-state tuition: full time: N/A; part time: N/A
Out-of-state tuition: full time: N/A; part time: N/A
Room/board/expenses: N/A
College-funded aid: Yes
International student aid: Yes
Full-time enrollment: 20
men: 60%; women: 40%; minorities: N/A; international: N/A
Part-time enrollment: 49
men: 45%; women: 55%; minorities: N/A; international: N/A
Average GRE (full time): N/A verbal; N/A quantitative; N/A writing
TOEFL requirement: Yes
Minimum TOEFL score: 79

Prairie View A&M University

PO Box 519, MS 2300
Prairie View, TX 77446
pvamu.edu/business
Public
Admissions: (936) 261-9217
Email: mba@pvamu.edu
Financial aid: (936) 261-1000
Application deadline: 05/01
In-state tuition: full time: $8,019; part time: $8,019
Out-of-state tuition: full time: $10,170; part time: $10,170
Room/board/expenses: $12,782
College-funded aid: Yes
International student aid: Yes
Full-time enrollment: 57
men: 42%; women: 58%; minorities: 86%; international: 12%

Part-time enrollment: 132
men: 36%; women: 64%; minorities: 95%; international: 2%
Acceptance rate (full time): 84%
Average GRE (full time): N/A verbal; N/A quantitative; N/A writing
Average age of entrants to full-time program: 29
TOEFL requirement: Yes
Minimum TOEFL score: 79
Most popular departments: accounting, finance, general management, international business, management information systems

Rice University

PO Box 2932
Houston, TX 77252-2932
business.rice.edu
Private
Admissions: (713) 348-4918
Email: ricemba@rice.edu
Financial aid: (713) 348-3748
Application deadline: rolling
Tuition: full time: $61,383; total program: $107,883 (part time)
Room/board/expenses: $25,265
College-funded aid: Yes
International student aid: Yes
Average student indebtedness at graduation: $71,793
Full-time enrollment: 236
men: 68%; women: 32%; minorities: 30%; international: 27%
Part-time enrollment: 374
men: 78%; women: 22%; minorities: 30%; international: 9%
Acceptance rate (full time): 40%
Average GMAT (full time): 706
Average GRE (full time): 160 verbal; 157 quantitative; 4.4 writing
Average GPA (full time): 3.32
Average age of entrants to full-time program: 29
Average months of prior work experience (full time): 66
TOEFL requirement: Yes
Minimum TOEFL score: N/A
Most popular departments: entrepreneurship, finance, general management, marketing, other
Mean starting base salary for 2018 full-time graduates: $113,287
Employment location for 2018 class: Intl. 2%; N.E. 5%; M.A. 1%; S. 1%; M.W. 4%; S.W. 86%; W. 1%

Sam Houston State University[1]

PO Box 2056
Huntsville, TX 77341
www.shsu.edu/dept/graduate-admissions
Public
Admissions: (936) 294-1971
Email: graduate@shsu.edu
Financial aid: (936) 294-1724
Tuition: N/A
Room/board/expenses: N/A
Enrollment: N/A

Southern Methodist University

6212 Bishop Boulevard
Dallas, TX 75205
www.coxgrad.com
Private
Admissions: (214) 768-1214
Email: mbainfo@cox.smu.edu
Financial aid: (214) 768-2371
Application deadline: 04/29
Tuition: full time: $53,103; part time: $47,088
Room/board/expenses: $21,485
College-funded aid: Yes
International student aid: Yes
Full-time enrollment: 225
men: 69%; women: 31%; minorities: 17%; international: 15%
Part-time enrollment: 219
men: 64%; women: 36%; minorities: 27%; international: 6%
Acceptance rate (full time): 46%
Average GMAT (full time): 655
Average GRE (full time): 155 verbal; 154 quantitative; 4.0 writing
Average GPA (full time): 3.40
Average age of entrants to full-time program: 28
Average months of prior work experience (full time): 58
TOEFL requirement: Yes
Minimum TOEFL score: 100
Most popular departments: entrepreneurship, finance, marketing, real estate, quantitative analysis/statistics and operations research
Mean starting base salary for 2018 full-time graduates: $102,612
Employment location for 2018 class: Intl. 0%; N.E. 3%; M.A. 3%; S. 0%; M.W. 3%; S.W. 86%; W. 5%

Stephen F. Austin State University[1]

PO Box 13004, SFA Station
Nacogdoches, TX 75962-3004
www.sfasu.edu/cob/
Public
Admissions: (936) 468-2807
Email: gschool@titan.sfasu.edu
Financial aid: N/A
Tuition: N/A
Room/board/expenses: N/A
Enrollment: N/A

St. Mary's University

1 Camino Santa Maria
San Antonio, TX 78228-8607
www.stmarytx.edu/academics/programs/mba-values/
Private
Admissions: (210) 436-3101
Email: kthornton@stmarytx.edu
Financial aid: (210) 436-3141
Application deadline: 07/01
Tuition: full time: $17,890; part time: $17,890
Room/board/expenses: $37,454
College-funded aid: Yes
International student aid: Yes
Full-time enrollment: 46
men: 39%; women: 61%; minorities: 41%; international: 11%

Part-time enrollment: 66
men: 53%; women: 47%; minorities: 55%; international: 12%
Acceptance rate (full time): 74%
Average GMAT (full time): 550
Average GRE (full time): 150 verbal; 148 quantitative; 3.8 writing
Average GPA (full time): 3.14
Average age of entrants to full-time program: 25
TOEFL requirement: Yes
Minimum TOEFL score: 80
Most popular departments: general management

Texas A&M International University

5201 University Boulevard
Western Hemispheric Trade Center, Suite 203
Laredo, TX 78041-1900
www.tamiu.edu
Public
Admissions: (956) 326-3020
Email: graduatedmissions@tamiu.edu
Financial aid: (956) 326-2225
Application deadline: 04/30
In-state tuition: total program: $10,248 (full time); total program: $10,762 (part time)
Out-of-state tuition: total program: $22,698 (full time); total program: $23,212 (part time)
Room/board/expenses: $12,993
College-funded aid: Yes
International student aid: Yes
Average student indebtedness at graduation: $19,718
Full-time enrollment: 17
men: 41%; women: 59%; minorities: 71%; international: 29%
Part-time enrollment: 46
men: 52%; women: 48%; minorities: 96%; international: 2%
Acceptance rate (full time): 100%
Average GRE (full time): N/A verbal; N/A quantitative; N/A writing
Average GPA (full time): 3.30
Average age of entrants to full-time program: 29
Average months of prior work experience (full time): 94
TOEFL requirement: Yes
Minimum TOEFL score: 79
Most popular departments: accounting, finance, general management, international business, management information systems

Texas A&M University–College Station

4117 TAMU
390 Wehner Building
College Station, TX 77843-4117
mays.tamu.edu/mbaprograms
Public
Admissions: (979) 845-4714
Email: mbaprograms@mays.tamu.edu
Financial aid: (979) 845-3236
Application deadline: 04/17

In-state tuition: total program: $53,430 (full time); total program: $89,500 (part time)
Out-of-state tuition: total program: $76,606 (full time); N/A (part time)
Room/board/expenses: $23,038
College-funded aid: Yes
International student aid: Yes
Full-time enrollment: 123 men: 82%; women: 18%; minorities: 24%; international: 22%
Part-time enrollment: 93 men: 60%; women: 40%; minorities: 33%; international: 0%
Acceptance rate (full time): 42%
Average GMAT (full time): 643
Average GRE (full time): 155 verbal; 154 quantitative; 3.9 writing
Average GPA (full time): 3.33
Average age of entrants to full-time program: 29
Average months of prior work experience (full time): 62
TOEFL requirement: Yes
Minimum TOEFL score: 100
Most popular departments: entrepreneurship, finance, marketing, supply chain management/logistics, quantitative analysis/statistics and operations research
Mean starting base salary for 2018 full-time graduates: $101,878
Employment location for 2018 class: Intl. 0%; N.E. 4%; M.A. 4%; S. 10%; M.W. 4%; S.W. 69%; W. 10%

Texas A&M University– Commerce

PO Box 3011
Commerce, TX 75429-3011
www.tamu-commerce.edu/ graduateprograms
Public
Admissions: (903) 886-5163
Email: graduate. school@tamuc.edu
Financial aid: (903) 886-5091
Application deadline: 07/28
In-state tuition: full time: N/A; part time: $6,424
Out-of-state tuition: full time: N/A; part time: $13,894
Room/board/expenses: N/A
College-funded aid: Yes
International student aid: Yes
Full-time enrollment: N/A men: N/A; women: N/A; minorities: N/A; international: N/A
Part-time enrollment: 632 men: 50%; women: 50%; minorities: 47%; international: 6%
Average GRE (full time): N/A verbal; N/A quantitative; N/A writing
TOEFL requirement: Yes
Minimum TOEFL score: 79
Most popular departments: accounting, finance, international business, marketing, other

Texas A&M University– Corpus Christi[1]

6300 Ocean Drive
Corpus Christi, TX 78412-5807
www.cob.tamucc.edu/ prstudents/graduate.html
Public
Admissions: (361) 825-2177
Email: gradweb@tamucc.edu
Financial aid: (361) 825-2338
Tuition: N/A
Room/board/expenses: N/A
Enrollment: N/A

Texas Christian University

PO Box 298540
Fort Worth, TX 76129
www.mba.tcu.edu
Private
Admissions: (817) 257-7531
Email: mbainfo@tcu.edu
Financial aid: (817) 257-7531
Application deadline: 10/15
Tuition: full time: $51,210; part time $36,885
Room/board/expenses: N/A
College-funded aid: Yes
International student aid: Yes
Average student indebtedness at graduation: $47,530
Full-time enrollment: 92 men: 74%; women: 26%; minorities: 10%; international: 23%
Part-time enrollment: 152 men: 71%; women: 29%; minorities: 14%; international: 1%
Acceptance rate (full time): 65%
Average GMAT (full time): 631
Average GRE (full time): 154 verbal; 152 quantitative; 4.0 writing
Average GPA (full time): 3.30
Average age of entrants to full-time program: 28
Average months of prior work experience (full time): 56
TOEFL requirement: Yes
Minimum TOEFL score: N/A
Most popular departments: consulting, finance, health care administration, marketing, supply chain management/logistics
Mean starting base salary for 2018 full-time graduates: $90,765
Employment location for 2018 class: Intl. N/A; N.E. 3%; M.A. 6%; S. 6%; M.W. N/A; S.W. 76%; W. 9%

Texas Southern University[1]

3100 Cleburne Avenue
Houston, TX 77004
www.tsu.edu/academics/ colleges_schools/Jesse_H_ Jones_School_of_Business/
Public
Admissions: (713) 313-7309
Email: haidern@tsu.edu
Financial aid: (713) 313-7480
Tuition: N/A
Room/board/expenses: N/A
Enrollment: N/A

Texas State University

601 University Drive
San Marcos, TX 78666-4616
www.txstate.edu
Public
Admissions: (512) 245-3591
Email: gradcollege@txstate.edu
Financial aid: (512) 245-2315
Application deadline: 06/01
In-state tuition: total program: $24,296 (full time); total program: $24,938 (part time)
Out-of-state tuition: total program: $41,726 (full time); total program: $42,368 (part time)
Room/board/expenses: N/A
College-funded aid: Yes
International student aid: Yes
Average student indebtedness at graduation: $40,000
Full-time enrollment: 24 men: 63%; women: 38%; minorities: 33%; international: 4%
Part-time enrollment: 188 men: 64%; women: 36%; minorities: 30%; international: 6%
Acceptance rate (full time): 38%
Average GMAT (full time): 537
Average GRE (full time): 152 verbal; 153 quantitative; N/A writing
Average GPA (full time): 3.45
Average age of entrants to full-time program: 24
Average months of prior work experience (full time): 61
TOEFL requirement: Yes
Minimum TOEFL score: 78
Most popular departments: general management, health care administration, human resources management, international business, manufacturing and technology management
Mean starting base salary for 2018 full-time graduates: $45,500

Texas Tech University

PO Box 42101
Lubbock, TX 79409-2101
texastechmba.com
Public
Admissions: (806) 834-1455
Email: rawls.mba@ttu.edu
Financial aid: (806) 834-4907
Application deadline: 07/01
In-state tuition: full time: $22,328; part time: $24,600
Out-of-state tuition: full time: $41,822; part time: $27,867
Room/board/expenses: N/A
College-funded aid: Yes
International student aid: Yes
Full-time enrollment: 105 men: 72%; women: 28%; minorities: 41%; international: 8%
Part-time enrollment: 144 men: 67%; women: 33%; minorities: 35%; international: 0%
Acceptance rate (full time): 57%
Average GMAT (full time): 570
Average GRE (full time): 152 verbal; 155 quantitative; 3.6 writing
Average GPA (full time): 3.40
Average age of entrants to full-time program: 24

Average months of prior work experience (full time): 2
TOEFL requirement: Yes
Minimum TOEFL score: 79
Most popular departments: health care administration, other
Mean starting base salary for 2018 full-time graduates: $61,723

Texas Wesleyan University[1]

1201 Wesleyan Street
Fort Worth, TX 76105
txwes.edu/
Private
Admissions: (817) 531-4422
Email: graduate@txwes.edu
Financial aid: (817) 531-4420
Tuition: N/A
Room/board/expenses: N/A
Enrollment: N/A

University of Dallas

1845 East Northgate Drive
Irving, TX 75062
www.udallas.edu/cob/
Private
Admissions: (972) 721-5004
Email: admiss@udallas.edu
Financial aid: (972) 721-5074
Application deadline: rolling
Tuition: full time: N/A/credit hour; part time: $1,250/credit hour
Room/board/expenses: N/A
College-funded aid: Yes
International student aid: Yes
Full-time enrollment: N/A men: N/A; women: N/A; minorities: N/A; international: N/A
Part-time enrollment: 382 men: 56%; women: 44%; minorities: 57%; international: 13%
Average GRE (full time): N/A verbal; N/A quantitative; N/A writing
TOEFL requirement: Yes
Minimum TOEFL score: 80
Most popular departments: accounting, finance, general management, management information systems, technology

University of Houston

334 Melcher Hall, Suite 330
Houston, TX 77204-6021
www.bauer.uh.edu/graduate
Public
Admissions: (713) 743-0700
Email: mba@uh.edu
Financial aid: (713) 743-2062
Application deadline: 06/01
In-state tuition: full time: $25,439; part time: $15,664
Out-of-state tuition: full time: $40,889; part time: $24,934
Room/board/expenses: $15,080
College-funded aid: Yes
International student aid: Yes
Full-time enrollment: 70 men: 74%; women: 26%; minorities: 23%; international: 33%
Part-time enrollment: 286 men: 71%; women: 29%; minorities: 40%; international: 18%
Acceptance rate (full time): 52%
Average GMAT (full time): 611

Average GRE (full time): 152 verbal; 151 quantitative; 3.7 writing
Average GPA (full time): 3.18
Average age of entrants to full-time program: 29
Average months of prior work experience (full time): 56
TOEFL requirement: Yes
Minimum TOEFL score: 100
Mean starting base salary for 2018 full-time graduates: $82,350
Employment location for 2018 class: Intl. N/A; N.E. 4%; M.A. 7%; S. 4%; M.W. 0%; S.W. 86%; W. 0%

University of Houston–Clear Lake

2700 Bay Area Boulevard
Houston, TX 77058
www.uhcl.edu/admissions
Public
Admissions: (281) 283-2500
Email: admissions@uhcl.edu
Financial aid: (281) 283-2480
Application deadline: 08/01
In-state tuition: full time: N/A; part time: $467/credit hour
Out-of-state tuition: full time: N/A; part time: $982/credit hour
Room/board/expenses: N/A
College-funded aid: Yes
International student aid: Yes
Full-time enrollment: N/A men: N/A; women: N/A; minorities: N/A; international: N/A
Part-time enrollment: 216 men: 40%; women: 60%; minorities: 57%; international: 7%
Average GRE (full time): N/A verbal; N/A quantitative; N/A writing
TOEFL requirement: Yes
Minimum TOEFL score: 79
Most popular departments: finance, human resources management, international business, manufacturing and technology management, other

University of Houston–Downtown[1]

320 North Main Street
Houston, TX 77002
www.uhd.edu/admissions/ Pages/admissions-index.aspx
Public
Admissions: (713) 221-8093
Email: gradadmissions@uhd.edu
Financial aid: (713) 221-8041
Tuition: N/A
Room/board/expenses: N/A
Enrollment: N/A

University of Houston–Victoria

University North, Ste 212
3007 N. Ben Wilson
Victoria, TX 77901
www.uhv.edu/business
Public
Admissions: (361) 570-4110
Email: admissions@uhv.edu
Financial aid: (361) 570-4131
Application deadline: rolling

More @ usnews.com/bschool

In-state tuition: full time: $342/credit hour; part time: $342/credit hour
Out-of-state tuition: full time: $757/credit hour; part time: $757/credit hour
Room/board/expenses: N/A
College-funded aid: Yes
International student aid: No
Full-time enrollment: 137 men: 36%; women: 64%; minorities: 42%; international: 1%
Part-time enrollment: 403 men: 45%; women: 55%; minorities: 49%; international: 2%
Average GRE (full time): N/A verbal; N/A quantitative; N/A writing
TOEFL requirement: Yes
Minimum TOEFL score: 61
Most popular departments: accounting, entrepreneurship, finance, general management, international business

University of North Texas

1155 Union Circle, #311160
Denton, TX 76203-5017
www.cob.unt.edu
Public
Admissions: (940) 369-8977
Email: mbacob@unt.edu
Financial aid: (940) 565-2302
Application deadline: 06/15
In-state tuition: full time: $352/credit hour; part time: $252/credit hour
Out-of-state tuition: full time: $767/credit hour; part time: $767/credit hour
Room/board/expenses: $37,784
College-funded aid: Yes
International student aid: Yes
Average student indebtedness at graduation: $17,245
Full-time enrollment: 23 men: 26%; women: 74%; minorities: 43%; international: 4%
Part-time enrollment: 304 men: 61%; women: 39%; minorities: 25%; international: 13%
Acceptance rate (full time): 63%
Average GRE (full time): 154 verbal; 152 quantitative; 3.7 writing
Average GPA (full time): 3.70
Average age of entrants to full-time program: 23
Average months of prior work experience (full time): 12
TOEFL requirement: Yes
Minimum TOEFL score: 79
Most popular departments: accounting, finance, general management, organizational behavior, quantitative analysis/statistics and operations research
Mean starting base salary for 2018 full-time graduates: $53,750
Employment location for 2018 class: Intl. N/A; N.E. N/A; M.A. N/A; S. N/A; M.W. 17%; S.W. 83%; W. N/A

University of St. Thomas–Houston

3800 Montrose Boulevard
Houston, TX 77006
www.stthom.edu/bschool
Private
Admissions: (713) 525-2100
Email: cameron@stthom.edu
Financial aid: (713) 525-2170
Application deadline: 07/15
Tuition: full time: N/A; part time: $1,163/credit hour
Room/board/expenses: N/A
Full-time enrollment: N/A men: N/A; women: N/A; minorities: N/A; international: N/A
Part-time enrollment: 179 men: 43%; women: 57%; minorities: 51%; international: 31%
Average GRE (full time): N/A verbal; N/A quantitative; N/A writing
TOEFL requirement: Yes
Minimum TOEFL score: 79
Most popular departments: accounting, finance, general management, international business, other

University of Texas–Arlington

UTA Box 19377
Arlington, TX 76019-0376
wweb.uta.edu/business/gradbiz
Public
Admissions: (817) 272-3004
Email: gradbiz@uta.edu
Financial aid: (817) 272-3561
Application deadline: 05/15
In-state tuition: full time: N/A; part time: $22,020
Out-of-state tuition: full time: N/A; part time: $44,221
Room/board/expenses: N/A
College-funded aid: Yes
International student aid: Yes
Full-time enrollment: N/A men: N/A; women: N/A; minorities: N/A; international: N/A
Part-time enrollment: 433 men: 43%; women: 57%; minorities: 33%; international: 35%
Average GRE (full time): N/A verbal; N/A quantitative; N/A writing
TOEFL requirement: Yes
Minimum TOEFL score: 79
Most popular departments: accounting, finance, general management, human resources management, management information systems

University of Texas–Austin

Texas MBA Program
Robert B. Rowling Hall
300 W. Martin Luther King Jr. Boulevard
Austin, TX 78712-1750
www.mccombs.utexas.edu/MBA/Full-Time
Public
Admissions: (512) 471-7698
Email: TexasMBA@mccombs.utexas.edu

Financial aid: (512) 471-7698
Application deadline: 04/02
In-state tuition: full time: $41,472; total program: $110,460 (part time)
Out-of-state tuition: full time: $55,244; N/A (part time)
Room/board/expenses: $19,060
College-funded aid: Yes
International student aid: Yes
Average student indebtedness at graduation: $84,043
Full-time enrollment: 551 men: 61%; women: 39%; minorities: 26%; international: 26%
Part-time enrollment: 445 men: 74%; women: 26%; minorities: 35%; international: 8%
Acceptance rate (full time): 34%
Average GMAT (full time): 702
Average GRE (full time): 159 verbal; 158 quantitative; 4.4 writing
Average GPA (full time): 3.48
Average age of entrants to full-time program: 28
Average months of prior work experience (full time): 66
TOEFL requirement: Yes
Minimum TOEFL score: 105
Most popular departments: consulting, entrepreneurship, finance, marketing, management information systems
Mean starting base salary for 2018 full-time graduates: $119,036
Employment location for 2018 class: Intl. 4%; N.E. 9%; M.A. 4%; S. 5%; M.W. 4%; S.W. 57%; W. 17%

University of Texas–Dallas

800 W. Campbell Road, SM 40
Richardson, TX 75080-3021
jindal.utdallas.edu/mba
Public
Admissions: (972) 883-6191
Email: mba@utdallas.edu
Financial aid: (972) 883-2941
Application deadline: 05/01
In-state tuition: full time: $16,768; part time: $16,883
Out-of-state tuition: full time: $31,200; part time: $29,873
Room/board/expenses: $16,000
College-funded aid: Yes
International student aid: Yes
Average student indebtedness at graduation: $28,106
Full-time enrollment: 101 men: 75%; women: 25%; minorities: 21%; international: 32%
Part-time enrollment: 720 men: 65%; women: 35%; minorities: 33%; international: 28%
Acceptance rate (full time): 35%
Average GMAT (full time): 671
Average GRE (full time): 156 verbal; 156 quantitative; 4.0 writing
Average GPA (full time): 3.50
Average age of entrants to full-time program: 28
Average months of prior work experience (full time): 60
TOEFL requirement: Yes
Minimum TOEFL score: 80

Most popular departments: accounting, finance, management information systems, production/operations management, supply chain management/logistics
Mean starting base salary for 2018 full-time graduates: $90,596
Employment location for 2018 class: Intl. N/A; N.E. 7%; M.A. N/A; S. N/A; M.W. 7%; S.W. 79%; W. 7%

University of Texas–El Paso

500 W. University Avenue
El Paso, TX 79968
mba.utep.edu
Public
Admissions: (915) 747-7757
Email: mba@utep.edu
Financial aid: (915) 747-5204
Application deadline: 11/15
In-state tuition: total program: $26,457 (full time); total program: $26,457 (part time)
Out-of-state tuition: total program: $42,158 (full time); total program: $42,158 (part time)
Room/board/expenses: $25,075
College-funded aid: Yes
International student aid: Yes
Average student indebtedness at graduation: $27,725
Full-time enrollment: 38 men: 68%; women: 32%; minorities: 68%; international: 21%
Part-time enrollment: 137 men: 55%; women: 45%; minorities: 81%; international: 9%
Acceptance rate (full time): 88%
Average GMAT (full time): 487
Average GRE (full time): N/A verbal; N/A quantitative; N/A writing
Average GPA (full time): 3.52
Average age of entrants to full-time program: 23
Average months of prior work experience (full time): 49
TOEFL requirement: Yes
Minimum TOEFL score: 100
Most popular departments: finance, general management, health care administration, international business, marketing
Mean starting base salary for 2018 full-time graduates: $89,000
Employment location for 2018 class: Intl. 0%; N.E. 0%; M.A. 0%; S. 0%; M.W. 0%; S.W. 100%; W. 0%

University of Texas of the Permian Basin[1]

4901 E. University
Odessa, TX 79762
www.utpb.edu/
Public
Admissions: (432) 552-2605
Email: Admissions@utpb.edu
Financial aid: (432) 552-2620
Tuition: N/A
Room/board/expenses: N/A
Enrollment: N/A

University of Texas–Rio Grande Valley

1201 W University Dr
Edinburg, TX 78539
www.utrgv.edu/graduate/for-future-students/how-to-apply/index.htm
Public
Admissions: (956) 665-3661
Financial aid: (888) 882-4026
Application deadline: N/A
In-state tuition: full time: $6,889; part time: $426/credit hour
Out-of-state tuition: full time: $14,359; part time: $841/credit hour
Room/board/expenses: $11,440
College-funded aid: Yes
International student aid: Yes
Full-time enrollment: 76 men: 63%; women: 37%; minorities: 37%; international: 54%
Part-time enrollment: 170 men: 55%; women: 45%; minorities: 81%; international: 4%
Acceptance rate (full time): 84%
Average GRE (full time): N/A verbal; N/A quantitative; N/A writing
Average age of entrants to full-time program: 29
TOEFL requirement: Yes
Minimum TOEFL score: 79
Most popular departments: accounting, finance, general management, marketing, management information systems

University of Texas–San Antonio

1 UTSA Circle
San Antonio, TX 78249
www.graduateschool.utsa.edu
Public
Admissions: (210) 458-4331
Email: GraduateAdmissions@utsa.edu
Financial aid: (210) 458-8000
Application deadline: 08/15
In-state tuition: full time: $9,364; part time: $6,374
Out-of-state tuition: full time: $26,197; part time: $17,596
Room/board/expenses: $16,071
College-funded aid: Yes
International student aid: Yes
Full-time enrollment: 54 men: 48%; women: 52%; minorities: 52%; international: 9%
Part-time enrollment: 196 men: 55%; women: 45%; minorities: 46%; international: 4%
Acceptance rate (full time): 53%
Average GMAT (full time): 597
Average GRE (full time): 151 verbal; 152 quantitative; 3.7 writing
Average GPA (full time): 3.40
Average age of entrants to full-time program: 28
Average months of prior work experience (full time): 42
TOEFL requirement: Yes
Minimum TOEFL score: 79

Most popular departments: accounting, finance, general management, management information systems, quantitative analysis/statistics and operations research
Mean starting base salary for 2018 full-time graduates: $77,292
Employment location for 2018 class: Intl. N/A; N.E. N/A; M.A. N/A; S. N/A; M.W. N/A; S.W. 100%; W. N/A

University of Texas–Tyler[1]

3900 University Boulevard
Tyler, TX 75799
www.uttyler.edu/cbt/
Public
Admissions: (903) 566-7360
Email: cbtinfo@uttyler.edu
Financial aid: N/A
Tuition: N/A
Room/board/expenses: N/A
Enrollment: N/A

West Texas A&M University

WTAMU, Box 60768
Canyon, TX 79016
www.wtamu.edu/academics/college-of-business-graduate-programs.aspx
Public
Admissions: (806) 651-2490
Email: ddearmond@wtamu.edu
Financial aid: (806) 651-2059
Application deadline: rolling
In-state tuition: total program: $12,987 (full time); total program: $13,787 (part time)
Out-of-state tuition: total program: $13,908 (full time); total program: $14,708 (part time)
Room/board/expenses: $12,000
College-funded aid: Yes
International student aid: Yes
Average student indebtedness at graduation: $18,000
Full-time enrollment: 150
men: 63%; women: 37%; minorities: 33%; international: 27%
Part-time enrollment: 25
men: 56%; women: 44%; minorities: 44%; international: 0%
Acceptance rate (full time): 80%
Average GMAT (full time): 540
Average GRE (full time): N/A verbal; N/A quantitative; N/A writing
Average GPA (full time): 3.41
Average age of entrants to full-time program: 30
Average months of prior work experience (full time): 74
TOEFL requirement: Yes
Minimum TOEFL score: 79
Most popular departments: accounting, finance, health care administration, marketing, management information systems
Mean starting base salary for 2018 full-time graduates: $81,000

UTAH

Brigham Young University

W-437 TNRB
Provo, UT 84602
mba.byu.edu
Private
Admissions: (801) 422-3500
Email: mba@byu.edu
Financial aid: N/A
Application deadline: 05/01
Tuition: full time: $13,450; part time: N/A
Room/board/expenses: $21,336
College-funded aid: Yes
International student aid: Yes
Full-time enrollment: 280
men: 82%; women: 18%; minorities: 9%; international: 17%
Part-time enrollment: N/A
men: N/A; women: N/A; minorities: N/A; international: N/A
Acceptance rate (full time): 53%
Average GMAT (full time): 672
Average GRE (full time): N/A verbal; N/A quantitative; N/A writing
Average GPA (full time): 3.50
Average age of entrants to full-time program: 29
Average months of prior work experience (full time): 48
TOEFL requirement: Yes
Minimum TOEFL score: 100
Most popular departments: entrepreneurship, finance, human resources management, marketing, supply chain management/logistics
Mean starting base salary for 2018 full-time graduates: $110,971
Employment location for 2018 class: Intl. 6%; N.E. 2%; M.A. 3%; S. 5%; M.W. 19%; S.W. 15%; W. 50%

Southern Utah University

351 W. University Boulevard
Cedar City, UT 84720
www.suu.edu/business
Public
Admissions: (435) 586-7740
Email: businessgrad@suu.edu
Financial aid: (435) 586-7734
Application deadline: 07/01
In-state tuition: full time: $448/credit hour; part time: $486/credit hour
Out-of-state tuition: full time: $1,284/credit hour; part time: $1,403/credit hour
Room/board/expenses: N/A
College-funded aid: Yes
International student aid: Yes
Full-time enrollment: 35
men: 66%; women: 34%; minorities: 14%; international: 20%
Part-time enrollment: 49
men: 67%; women: 33%; minorities: 10%; international: 2%
Acceptance rate (full time): 100%
Average GMAT (full time): 440
Average GRE (full time): 149 verbal; 145 quantitative; N/A writing
Average GPA (full time): 3.37

Average age of entrants to full-time program: 28
TOEFL requirement: Yes
Minimum TOEFL score: 79

University of Utah

1655 E. Campus Center Drive
Room 1113
Salt Lake City, UT 84112-9301
eccles.utah.edu/programs/mba/
Public
Admissions: (801) 585-6291
Email: stephanie.geisler@eccles.utah.edu
Financial aid: (801) 585-6291
Application deadline: 05/01
In-state tuition: full time: $30,000; part time: $29,400
Out-of-state tuition: full time: $31,000; part time: $29,400
Room/board/expenses: N/A
College-funded aid: Yes
International student aid: Yes
Average student indebtedness at graduation: $38,675
Full-time enrollment: 119
men: 76%; women: 24%; minorities: 10%; international: 12%
Part-time enrollment: 314
men: 79%; women: 21%; minorities: 13%; international: 1%
Acceptance rate (full time): 50%
Average GMAT (full time): 659
Average GRE (full time): 159 verbal; 158 quantitative; 3.0 writing
Average GPA (full time): 3.48
Average age of entrants to full-time program: 29
Average months of prior work experience (full time): 52
TOEFL requirement: Yes
Minimum TOEFL score: 100
Most popular departments: entrepreneurship, general management, marketing, quantitative analysis/statistics and operations research, technology
Mean starting base salary for 2018 full-time graduates: $80,991
Employment location for 2018 class: Intl. 3%; N.E. 0%; M.A. 11%; S. 0%; M.W. 0%; S.W. 8%; W. 78%

Utah State University[1]

3500 Old Main Hill
Logan, UT 84322-3500
www.huntsman.usu.edu/mba/
Public
Admissions: (435) 797-3624
Email: HuntsmanMBA@usu.edu
Financial aid: N/A
Tuition: N/A
Room/board/expenses: N/A
Enrollment: N/A

Utah Valley University[1]

800 W. University Parkway
Orem, UT 84058
www.uvu.edu/woodbury
Public
Admissions: (801) 863-8367
Financial aid: N/A
Tuition: N/A
Room/board/expenses: N/A
Enrollment: N/A

Weber State University

2750 N. University Park Boulevard, MC102
Layton, UT 84041-9099
weber.edu/mba
Public
Admissions: (801) 395-3528
Email: mba@weber.edu
Financial aid: (801) 626-7569
Application deadline: 05/01
In-state tuition: full time: N/A; part time: $1,833/credit hour
Out-of-state tuition: full time: N/A; part time: $3,685/credit hour
Room/board/expenses: N/A
College-funded aid: Yes
International student aid: Yes
Full-time enrollment: N/A
men: N/A; women: N/A; minorities: N/A; international: N/A
Part-time enrollment: 260
men: 71%; women: 29%; minorities: N/A; international: N/A
Average GRE (full time): N/A verbal; N/A quantitative; N/A writing
TOEFL requirement: Yes
Minimum TOEFL score: N/A

VERMONT

University of Vermont

55 Colchester Avenue
Burlington, VT 05405
www.uvm.edu/si-mba
Public
Admissions: (802) 656-2699
Email: si-mba@uvm.edu
Financial aid: (802) 656-5700
Application deadline: 07/15
In-state tuition: total program: $33,015 (full time); part time: N/A
Out-of-state tuition: total program: $53,785 (full time); part time: N/A
Room/board/expenses: $12,000
College-funded aid: Yes
International student aid: Yes
Average student indebtedness at graduation: $41,366
Full-time enrollment: 41
men: 59%; women: 41%; minorities: 5%; international: 10%
Part-time enrollment: N/A
men: N/A; women: N/A; minorities: N/A; international: N/A
Acceptance rate (full time): 84%
Average GMAT (full time): 535
Average GRE (full time): 156 verbal; 150 quantitative; 4.0 writing
Average GPA (full time): 3.30
Average age of entrants to full-time program: 28
Average months of prior work experience (full time): 71
TOEFL requirement: Yes
Minimum TOEFL score: 90
Most popular departments: entrepreneurship, other
Mean starting base salary for 2018 full-time graduates: $63,880
Employment location for 2018 class: Intl. N/A; N.E. 100%; M.A. N/A; S. N/A; M.W. N/A; S.W. N/A; W. N/A

VIRGINIA

College of William and Mary

PO Box 8795
Williamsburg, VA 23187-8795
mason.wm.edu
Public
Admissions: (757) 221-2944
Email: admissions@mason.wm.edu
Financial aid: (757) 221-2944
Application deadline: 07/15
In-state tuition: full time: $34,608; part time: $875/credit hour
Out-of-state tuition: full time: $45,980; part time: $1,275/credit hour
Room/board/expenses: N/A
College-funded aid: Yes
International student aid: Yes
Average student indebtedness at graduation: $64,568
Full-time enrollment: 204
men: 71%; women: 29%; minorities: 14%; international: 44%
Part-time enrollment: 174
men: 61%; women: 39%; minorities: 26%; international: 2%
Acceptance rate (full time): 68%
Average GMAT (full time): 618
Average GRE (full time): 152 verbal; 150 quantitative; 4.0 writing
Average GPA (full time): 3.40
Average age of entrants to full-time program: 28
Average months of prior work experience (full time): 60
TOEFL requirement: Yes
Minimum TOEFL score: 90
Most popular departments: consulting, entrepreneurship, finance, marketing, supply chain management/logistics
Mean starting base salary for 2018 full-time graduates: $90,052
Employment location for 2018 class: Intl. 6%; N.E. 6%; M.A. 62%; S. 6%; M.W. 2%; S.W. 4%; W. 15%

George Mason University

4400 University Drive
Fairfax, VA 22030
business.gmu.edu
Public
Admissions: (703) 993-2136
Email: mba@gmu.edu
Financial aid: (703) 993-2353
Application deadline: 04/01
In-state tuition: full time: N/A; part time: $808/credit hour
Out-of-state tuition: full time: N/A; part time: $1,647/credit hour
Room/board/expenses: N/A
College-funded aid: Yes
International student aid: Yes
Full-time enrollment: N/A
men: N/A; women: N/A; minorities: N/A; international: N/A
Part-time enrollment: 232
men: 60%; women: 40%; minorities: 35%; international: 8%
Average GRE (full time): N/A verbal; N/A quantitative; N/A writing

TOEFL requirement: Yes
Minimum TOEFL score: 93

James Madison University

Showker Hall
Harrisonburg, VA 22807
www.jmu.edu/cob/mba
Public
Admissions: (540) 568-6395
Email: michaeld@jmu.edu
Financial aid: (540) 568-7820
Application deadline: 07/01
In-state tuition: full time: N/A; total program: $24,000 (part time)
Out-of-state tuition: full time: N/A; total program: $24,000 (part time)
Room/board/expenses: N/A
College-funded aid: Yes
International student aid: Yes
Full-time enrollment: N/A
men: N/A; women: N/A; minorities: N/A; international: N/A
Part-time enrollment: 46
men: 67%; women: 33%; minorities: 22%; international: 9%
Average GRE (full time): N/A verbal; N/A quantitative; N/A writing
TOEFL requirement: Yes
Minimum TOEFL score: 80
Most popular departments: entrepreneurship, general management, leadership, marketing, organizational behavior

Longwood University[1]

201 High Street
Farmville, VA 23909
www.longwood.edu/business/
Public
Admissions: (877) 267-7883
Email: graduate@longwood.edu
Financial aid: N/A
Tuition: N/A
Room/board/expenses: N/A
Enrollment: N/A

Old Dominion University

1026 Constant Hall
Norfolk, VA 23529
odu.edu/mba
Public
Admissions: (757) 683-3585
Email: mbainfo@odu.edu
Financial aid: (757) 683-3683
Application deadline: 06/01
In-state tuition: total program: $23,353 (full time); total program: $23,353 (part time)
Out-of-state tuition: total program: $55,233 (full time); total program: $55,233 (part time)
Room/board/expenses: $20,363
College-funded aid: Yes
International student aid: Yes
Full-time enrollment: 17
men: 59%; women: 41%; minorities: 6%; international: 53%
Part-time enrollment: 71
men: 49%; women: 51%; minorities: 15%; international: 10%
Average GRE (full time): N/A verbal; N/A quantitative; N/A writing

TOEFL requirement: Yes
Minimum TOEFL score: 79
Most popular departments: entrepreneurship, health care administration, public administration, supply chain management/logistics, other

Radford University

PO Box 6956
Radford, VA 24142
www.radford.edu
Public
Admissions: (540) 831-5724
Email: gradcollege@radford.edu
Financial aid: (540) 831-5408
Application deadline: 08/01
In-state tuition: full time: $3,054; part time: $509/credit hour
Out-of-state tuition: full time: $5,298; part time: $883/credit hour
Room/board/expenses: N/A
College-funded aid: Yes
International student aid: Yes
Full-time enrollment: 8
men: 50%; women: 50%; minorities: 25%; international: 38%
Part-time enrollment: 32
men: 63%; women: 38%; minorities: 6%; international: 6%
Acceptance rate (full time): 75%
Average GMAT (full time): 500
Average GRE (full time): N/A verbal; N/A quantitative; N/A writing
Average GPA (full time): 3.59
Average age of entrants to full-time program: 24
TOEFL requirement: Yes
Minimum TOEFL score: 79
Most popular departments: general management, quantitative analysis/statistics and operations research

Shenandoah University

Halpin Harrison, Room 103
Winchester, VA 22601
www.su.edu/
Private
Admissions: (540) 665-4581
Email: admit@su.edu
Financial aid: (540) 665-4538
Application deadline: 06/15
Tuition: full time: $24,885; part time: $16,305
Room/board/expenses: $18,626
College-funded aid: Yes
International student aid: Yes
Average student indebtedness at graduation: $44,913
Full-time enrollment: 45
men: 73%; women: 27%; minorities: 13%; international: 42%
Part-time enrollment: 34
men: 47%; women: 53%; minorities: 15%; international: 9%
Acceptance rate (full time): 65%
Average GRE (full time): N/A verbal; N/A quantitative; N/A writing
Average GPA (full time): 3.40
Average age of entrants to full-time program: 26
TOEFL requirement: Yes
Minimum TOEFL score: 79

Most popular departments: general management

University of Richmond

102 UR Drive
Richmond, VA 23173
robins.richmond.edu/mba/
Private
Admissions: (804) 289-8553
Email: mba@richmond.edu
Financial aid: (804) 289-8438
Application deadline: 06/15
Tuition: full time: N/A; part time: $1,440/credit hour
Room/board/expenses: N/A
College-funded aid: Yes
International student aid: Yes
Full-time enrollment: N/A
men: N/A; women: N/A; minorities: N/A; international: N/A
Part-time enrollment: 90
men: 64%; women: 36%; minorities: 17%; international: 2%
Average GRE (full time): N/A verbal; N/A quantitative; N/A writing
TOEFL requirement: Yes
Minimum TOEFL score: 100

University of Virginia

PO Box 6550
Charlottesville, VA 22906-6550
www.darden.virginia.edu
Public
Admissions: (434) 924-1817
Email: darden@virginia.edu
Financial aid: (434) 924-7739
Application deadline: 05/01
In-state tuition: full time: $66,032; part time: N/A
Out-of-state tuition: full time: $68,350; part time: N/A
Room/board/expenses: $27,766
College-funded aid: Yes
International student aid: Yes
Average student indebtedness at graduation: $106,489
Full-time enrollment: 660
men: 62%; women: 38%; minorities: N/A; international: N/A
Part-time enrollment: N/A
men: N/A; women: N/A; minorities: N/A; international: N/A
Acceptance rate (full time): 33%
Average GMAT (full time): 718
Average GRE (full time): 164 verbal; 164 quantitative; 4.0 writing
Average GPA (full time): 3.50
Average age of entrants to full-time program: 27
Average months of prior work experience (full time): 61
TOEFL requirement: No
Minimum TOEFL score: N/A
Most popular departments: consulting, entrepreneurship, finance, general management, marketing
Mean starting base salary for 2018 full-time graduates: $127,767
Employment location for 2018 class: Intl. 7%; N.E. 31%; M.A. 18%; S. 12%; M.W. 8%; S.W. 6%; W. 18%

Virginia Commonwealth University

301 W. Main Street
Richmond, VA 23284-4000
business.vcu.edu
Public
Admissions: (804) 828-4622
Email: gsib@vcu.edu
Financial aid: (804) 828-6669
Application deadline: 07/01
In-state tuition: full time: N/A; part time: $674/credit hour
Out-of-state tuition: full time: N/A; part time: $1,386/credit hour
Room/board/expenses: N/A
College-funded aid: Yes
International student aid: Yes
Full-time enrollment: N/A
men: N/A; women: N/A; minorities: N/A; international: N/A
Part-time enrollment: 151
men: 62%; women: 38%; minorities: 32%; international: 3%
Average GRE (full time): N/A verbal; N/A quantitative; N/A writing
TOEFL requirement: Yes
Minimum TOEFL score: 100
Most popular departments: entrepreneurship, finance, general management, international business, quantitative analysis/statistics and operations research

Virginia Tech

1044 Pamplin Hall (0209)
Blacksburg, VA 24061
mba.vt.edu
Public
Admissions: (703) 538-8410
Email: mba@vt.edu
Financial aid: (540) 231-5179
Application deadline: 07/01
In-state tuition: full time: N/A; part time: $1,025/credit hour
Out-of-state tuition: full time: N/A; part time: $1,025/credit hour
Room/board/expenses: N/A
College-funded aid: Yes
International student aid: Yes
Full-time enrollment: N/A
men: N/A; women: N/A; minorities: N/A; international: N/A
Part-time enrollment: 206
men: 61%; women: 39%; minorities: 42%; international: 1%
Average GRE (full time): N/A verbal; N/A quantitative; N/A writing
TOEFL requirement: Yes
Minimum TOEFL score: 90
Most popular departments: finance, general management, international business, management information systems, technology

Eastern Washington University[1]

668 N. Riverpoint Boulevard
Suite A
Spokane, WA 99202-1677
www.ewu.edu/mba
Public
Admissions: (509) 828-1248
Email: mbaprogram@ewu.edu
Financial aid: N/A
Tuition: N/A
Room/board/expenses: N/A
Enrollment: N/A

Gonzaga University

502 E. Boone Avenue
Spokane, WA 99258-0009
www.gonzaga.edu/mba
Private
Admissions: (509) 313-4622
Email: chatman@gonzaga.edu
Financial aid: (509) 313-6568
Application deadline: rolling
Tuition: full time: $975/credit hour; part time: $995/credit hour
Room/board/expenses: $12,425
College-funded aid: Yes
International student aid: Yes
Full-time enrollment: 83
men: 52%; women: 48%; minorities: 17%; international: 10%
Part-time enrollment: 188
men: 56%; women: 44%; minorities: 25%; international: 3%
Acceptance rate (full time): 76%
Average GMAT (full time): 542
Average GRE (full time): N/A verbal; N/A quantitative; N/A writing
Average GPA (full time): 3.54
Average age of entrants to full-time program: 25
TOEFL requirement: Yes
Minimum TOEFL score: 88
Most popular departments: accounting, finance, marketing, production/operations management, tax

Pacific Lutheran University

Morken Center for Learning and Technology, Room 176
Tacoma, WA 98447
www.plu.edu/mba
Private
Admissions: (253) 535-7252
Email: plumba@plu.edu
Financial aid: (253) 535-7164
Application deadline: rolling
Tuition: total program: $45,360 (full time); total program: $45,360 (part time)
Room/board/expenses: $14,256
College-funded aid: Yes
International student aid: Yes
Full-time enrollment: 54
men: 56%; women: 44%; minorities: 30%; international: 4%
Part-time enrollment: 10
men: 40%; women: 60%; minorities: 50%; international: 0%
Acceptance rate (full time): 85%
Average GMAT (full time): 570

Average GRE (full time): 147 verbal; 147 quantitative; 3.5 writing
Average GPA (full time): 3.47
Average age of entrants to full-time program: 27
Average months of prior work experience (full time): 75
TOEFL requirement: Yes
Minimum TOEFL score: 88
Most popular departments: entrepreneurship, general management, health care administration, supply chain management/logistics, technology

Seattle Pacific University[1]

3307 Third Avenue W, Suite 201
Seattle, WA 98119-1950
www.spu.edu/sbe
Public
Admissions: (206) 281-2753
Email: drj@spu.edu
Financial aid: (206) 281-2469
Tuition: N/A
Room/board/expenses: N/A
Enrollment: N/A

Seattle University

901 12th Avenue
PO Box 222000
Seattle, WA 98122-1090
www.seattleu.edu/business/graduate/
Private
Admissions: (206) 296-5904
Email: janshan@seattleu.edu
Financial aid: (206) 220-8020
Application deadline: 08/01
Tuition: full time: N/A; part time: $865/credit hour
Room/board/expenses: N/A
College-funded aid: Yes
International student aid: Yes
Full-time enrollment: N/A
men: N/A; women: N/A; minorities: N/A; international: N/A
Part-time enrollment: 311
men: 45%; women: 55%; minorities: 27%; international: 12%
Average GRE (full time): N/A verbal; N/A quantitative; N/A writing
TOEFL requirement: Yes
Minimum TOEFL score: 92
Most popular departments: accounting, finance, marketing, management information systems, quantitative analysis/statistics and operations research

University of Washington–Bothell[1]

18115 Campus Way NW
Box 358533
Bothell, WA 98011
www.uwb.edu/mba
Public
Admissions: (425) 352-5394
Email: uwbmba@uw.edu
Financial aid: N/A
Tuition: N/A
Room/board/expenses: N/A
Enrollment: N/A

University of Washington

PO Box 353223
Seattle, WA 98195-3223
mba.washington.edu
Public
Admissions: (206) 543-4661
Email: mba@uw.edu
Financial aid: (206) 543-4661
Application deadline: 03/14
In-state tuition: full time: $35,403; part time: $27,096
Out-of-state tuition: full time: $51,126; part time: $27,096
Room/board/expenses: $30,496
College-funded aid: Yes
International student aid: Yes
Average student indebtedness at graduation: $28,968
Full-time enrollment: 223
men: 62%; women: 38%; minorities: 22%; international: 26%
Part-time enrollment: 377
men: 60%; women: 40%; minorities: 28%; international: 7%
Acceptance rate (full time): 35%
Average GMAT (full time): 696
Average GRE (full time): 158 verbal; 157 quantitative; 4.5 writing
Average GPA (full time): 3.31
Average age of entrants to full-time program: 29
Average months of prior work experience (full time): 73
TOEFL requirement: Yes
Minimum TOEFL score: 100
Most popular departments: consulting, entrepreneurship, finance, manufacturing and technology management, marketing
Mean starting base salary for 2018 full-time graduates: $118,355
Employment location for 2018 class: Intl. 5%; N.E. 1%; M.A. 0%; S. 0%; M.W. 2%; S.W. 3%; W. 90%

University of Washington–Tacoma

1900 Commerce Street
Box 358420
Tacoma, WA 98402
www.tacoma.uw.edu/milgard/mba/overview
Public
Admissions: (253) 692-5630
Email: uwtmba@uw.edu
Financial aid: (253) 692-4374
Application deadline: 06/01
In-state tuition: full time: N/A; total program: $46,277 (part time)
Out-of-state tuition: full time: N/A; √$75,264 (part time)
Room/board/expenses: N/A
College-funded aid: Yes
International student aid: Yes
Full-time enrollment: N/A
men: N/A; women: N/A; minorities: N/A; international: N/A
Part-time enrollment: 65
men: 51%; women: 49%; minorities: 29%; international: 0%
Average GRE (full time): N/A verbal; N/A quantitative; N/A writing
TOEFL requirement: Yes
Minimum TOEFL score: 92

Washington State University[1]

PO Box 644744
Pullman, WA 99164-4744
business.wsu.edu/graduate-programs/
Public
Admissions: (509) 335-7617
Email: mba@wsu.edu
Financial aid: (509) 335-9711
Tuition: N/A
Room/board/expenses: N/A
Enrollment: N/A

Western Washington University[1]

516 High Street, MS 9072
Bellingham, WA 98225-9072
www.cbe.wwu.edu/mba/
Public
Admissions: (360) 650-3898
Email: mba@wwu.edu
Financial aid: N/A
Tuition: N/A
Room/board/expenses: N/A
Enrollment: N/A

WEST VIRGINIA

Marshall University

1 John Marshall Drive
Huntington, WV 25755-2020
www.marshall.edu/lcob/
Public
Admissions: (800) 642-9842
Email: johnson73@marshall.edu
Financial aid: (800) 438-5390
Application deadline: 08/01
In-state tuition: full time: N/A; part time: N/A
Out-of-state tuition: full time: N/A; part time: N/A
Room/board/expenses: N/A
College-funded aid: Yes
International student aid: Yes
Full-time enrollment: 117
men: 56%; women: 44%; minorities: N/A; international: N/A
Part-time enrollment: 67
men: 46%; women: 54%; minorities: N/A; international: N/A
Acceptance rate (full time): 79%
Average GRE (full time): N/A verbal; N/A quantitative; N/A writing
Average GPA (full time): 3.26
TOEFL requirement: Yes
Minimum TOEFL score: N/A
Most popular departments: finance, general management, health care administration, human resources management, marketing
Mean starting base salary for 2018 full-time graduates: $54,500

West Virginia University[1]

PO Box 6027
Morgantown, WV 26506
www.be.wvu.edu
Public
Admissions: (304) 293-7811
Email: mba@wvu.edu
Financial aid: (304) 293-5242
Tuition: N/A
Room/board/expenses: N/A
Enrollment: N/A

WISCONSIN

Marquette University

PO Box 1881
Milwaukee, WI 53201-1881
www.marquette.edu/gsm
Private
Admissions: (414) 288-7145
Email: mba@Marquette.edu
Financial aid: (414) 288-7137
Application deadline: rolling
Tuition: full time: N/A; part time: $1,130/credit hour
Room/board/expenses: N/A
College-funded aid: Yes
International student aid: Yes
Full-time enrollment: N/A
men: N/A; women: N/A; minorities: N/A; international: N/A
Part-time enrollment: 195
men: 71%; women: 29%; minorities: 12%; international: 5%
Average GRE (full time): N/A verbal; N/A quantitative; N/A writing
TOEFL requirement: Yes
Minimum TOEFL score: 90
Most popular departments: accounting, finance, human resources management, international business

University of Wisconsin–Eau Claire[1]

Schneider Hall 215
Eau Claire, WI 54702-4004
www.uwec.edu/academics/college-business/
Public
Admissions: (715) 836-5415
Email: uwecmba@uwec.edu
Financial aid: (715) 836-5606
Tuition: N/A
Room/board/expenses: N/A
Enrollment: N/A

University of Wisconsin–La Crosse[1]

1725 State Street
La Crosse, WI 54601
www.uwlax.edu
Public
Admissions: (608) 785-8939
Email: admissions@uwlax.edu
Financial aid: (608) 785-8604
Tuition: N/A
Room/board/expenses: N/A
Enrollment: N/A

University of Wisconsin–Madison

975 University Avenue
Madison, WI 53706-1323
wsb.wisc.edu
Public
Admissions: (608) 262-4000
Email: mba@wsb.wisc.edu
Financial aid: (608) 262-8948
Application deadline: 06/01
In-state tuition: full time: $20,444; part time: $24,695
Out-of-state tuition: full time: $40,059; part time: $24,695
Room/board/expenses: $18,618
College-funded aid: Yes
International student aid: Yes
Average student indebtedness at graduation: $25,737

Full-time enrollment: 183
men: 68%; women: 32%; minorities: 17%; international: 22%
Part-time enrollment: 142
men: 70%; women: 30%; minorities: 11%; international: 4%
Acceptance rate (full time): 33%
Average GMAT (full time): 670
Average GRE (full time): 161 verbal; 157 quantitative; 4.0 writing
Average GPA (full time): 3.43
Average age of entrants to full-time program: 28
Average months of prior work experience (full time): 60
TOEFL requirement: Yes
Minimum TOEFL score: 100
Most popular departments: finance, general management, manufacturing and technology management, marketing, real estate
Mean starting base salary for 2018 full-time graduates: $98,463
Employment location for 2018 class: Intl. 0%; N.E. 4%; M.A. 5%; S. 7%; M.W. 62%; S.W. 9%; W. 13%

University of Wisconsin–Milwaukee

PO Box 742
Milwaukee, WI 53201-9863
lubar.uwm.edu
Public
Admissions: (414) 229-5403
Email: mba-ms@uwm.edu
Financial aid: (414) 229-4541
Application deadline: rolling
In-state tuition: full time: N/A; total program: $36,000 (part time)
Out-of-state tuition: full time: N/A; total program: $53,500 (part time)
Room/board/expenses: N/A
College-funded aid: Yes
International student aid: Yes
Full-time enrollment: N/A
men: N/A; women: N/A; minorities: N/A; international: N/A
Part-time enrollment: 245
men: 61%; women: 39%; minorities: 15%; international: 5%
Average GRE (full time): N/A verbal; N/A quantitative; N/A writing
TOEFL requirement: Yes
Minimum TOEFL score: 79
Most popular departments: accounting, general management, marketing, management information systems, other

University of Wisconsin–Oshkosh[1]

800 Algoma Boulevard
Oshkosh, WI 54901
www.uwosh.edu/cob
Public
Admissions: (800) 633-1430
Email: mba@uwosh.edu
Financial aid: (920) 424-3377
Tuition: N/A
Room/board/expenses: N/A
Enrollment: N/A

More @ usnews.com/bschool

University of Wisconsin–Parkside

900 Wood Road
PO Box 2000
Kenosha, WI 53141-2000
uwp.edu/learn/programs/
mbamasters.cfm
Public
Admissions: (262) 595-2243
Email: admissions@uwp.edu
Financial aid: (262) 595-2574
Application deadline: 08/15
In-state tuition: full time:
N/A; part time: N/A
Out-of-state tuition: full
time: N/A; part time: N/A
Room/board/expenses: N/A
College-funded aid: Yes
International student aid: Yes
Full-time enrollment: 28
men: 50%; women:
50%; minorities: N/A;
international: N/A
Part-time enrollment: 61
men: 54%; women:
46%; minorities: N/A;
international: N/A
**Average GRE (full
time):** N/A verbal; N/A
quantitative; N/A writing
TOEFL requirement: Yes
Minimum TOEFL score: 79

Most popular departments:
finance, general manage-
ment, international
business, marketing,
organizational behavior

University of Wisconsin–River Falls

410 S. Third Street
River Falls, WI 54022-5001
www.uwrf.edu/mba
Public
Admissions: (715) 425-3335
Email: mbacbe@uwrf.edu
Financial aid: (715) 425-4111
Application deadline: rolling
In-state tuition: full time:
$692/credit hour; part
time: $692/credit hour
Out-of-state tuition: full
time: $692/credit hour; part
time: $692/credit hour
Room/board/expenses: N/A
College-funded aid: Yes
International student aid: Yes
Full-time enrollment: 24
men: 63%; women:
38%; minorities: 8%;
international: 63%
Part-time enrollment: 48
men: 65%; women: 35%;
minorities: 8%; international: 6%
Acceptance rate (full time): 100%

Average GMAT (full time): 325
**Average GRE (full
time):** N/A verbal; N/A
quantitative; N/A writing
**Average age of entrants to
full-time program:** 24
TOEFL requirement: Yes
Minimum TOEFL score: 80

University of Wisconsin–Whitewater

800 W. Main Street
Whitewater, WI 53190
www.uww.edu/cobe
Public
Admissions: (262) 472-1945
Email: gradbus@uww.edu
Financial aid: (262) 472-1130
Application deadline: 07/15
In-state tuition: full time: $9,492;
part time: $528/credit hour
Out-of-state tuition: full
time: $19,018; part time:
$1,057/credit hour
Room/board/expenses: $7,000
College-funded aid: Yes
International student aid: Yes
Full-time enrollment: 26
men: 58%; women:
42%; minorities: 12%;
international: 8%

Part-time enrollment: 126
men: 56%; women:
44%; minorities: 13%;
international: 0%
Acceptance rate (full time): 80%
Average GMAT (full time): 511
**Average GRE (full
time):** N/A verbal; N/A
quantitative; N/A writing
Average GPA (full time): 3.30
**Average age of entrants to
full-time program:** 27
**Average months of prior work
experience (full time):** 40
TOEFL requirement: Yes
Minimum TOEFL score: 79
Most popular departments:
accounting, finance, general
management, supply chain
management/logistics, other

WYOMING

University of Wyoming

1000 E. University Avenue
Dept. 3275
Laramie, WY 82071-3275
www.uwyo.edu/mba/
Public
Admissions: (307) 766-5160
Email: admissions@uwyo.edu
Financial aid: (307) 766-3506
Application deadline: 06/30

In-state tuition: full time:
$717/credit hour; part
time: $788/credit hour
Out-of-state tuition: full time:
$1,201/credit hour; part
time: $788/credit hour
Room/board/expenses: N/A
College-funded aid: Yes
International student aid: Yes
Full-time enrollment: 34
men: 74%; women: 26%;
minorities: 3%; international: 0%
Part-time enrollment: 96
men: 67%; women: 33%;
minorities: 7%; international: 0%
Acceptance rate (full time): 63%
Average GMAT (full time): 560
**Average GRE (full
time):** 149 verbal; 153
quantitative; 3.8 writing
Average GPA (full time): 3.18
**Average age of entrants to
full-time program:** 26
**Average months of prior work
experience (full time):** 35
TOEFL requirement: Yes
Minimum TOEFL score: 100
Most popular departments:
finance, international
business, other
**Employment location for
2018 class:** Intl. 0%; N.E.
8%; M.A. 0%; S. 0%; M.W.
23%; S.W. 8%; W. 62%

Online Business Programs

INCLUDED IN THIS directory are 318 regionally accredited U.S. institutions that offer business degree programs that can be completed primarily through distance education. Among them, 301 schools award online MBAs and 156 award Master of Business degrees that are not MBAs; for institutions reporting both, you will find information for each degree type. Data were submitted to U.S. News in a statistical survey conducted in the summer and autumn of 2018. Only schools that provided their data have profiles in this directory.

KEY TO THE TERMINOLOGY

N/A. Not available from the school or not applicable.

Email. The address of the admissions office. If instead of an email address a website is given in this field, the website will automatically present an email screen programmed to reach the admissions office.

Application deadline. For fall 2019 enrollment. "Rolling" means there is no application deadline; the school acts on applications as they are received.

Program can be completed entirely online. "Yes" means there are no requirements to come to campus. "No" indicates some limited face-to-face attendance mandates for events like orientations, group sessions and exams. "Depends" means there may be variation among programs.

Total program cost. For the 2018-2019 academic year, the tuition required to earn the full degree from start to finish. Tuition is for the program with largest enrollment.

Tuition per credit. The cost per credit hour for the 2018-2019 academic year. Tuition is for the program with largest enrollment.

Acceptance rate. Percentage of applicants who were offered admittance during the 2017-2018 academic year.

Test scores required. For the 2017-2018 academic year.

Average Graduate Management Admission Test (GMAT) score. Calculated for students who entered in the 2017-2018 academic year.

Average Graduate Record Examinations (GRE) score. Verbal, quantitative and writing scores calculated for students who entered in the 2017-2018 academic year.

Average age of entrants. Calculated for new entrants in the 2017-2018 academic year.

Students with prior work experience. Calculated for students who entered in the 2017-2018 academic year. Refers to post-baccalaureate work experience only.

Enrollment. The count of students enrolled at least once during the 2017-2018 academic year.

Average class size. Calculation of students per course in October 2017. Includes students attending class on campus in the case of blended courses delivered both online and in person.

Most popular concentrations. Based on highest student demand.

Completion. Includes three distinct elements: the three-year graduation rate among new entrants from the 2014-2015 academic year; the number of credits students need to earn a degree; the estimated time needed for completing the program with the largest enrollment starting in the 2018-2019 academic year.

College-funded aid available. "Yes" means the school provided its own financial aid to students during the 2017-2018 academic year.

Graduates with debt. Calculated for 2017-2018 graduates who incurred business program debt.

ALABAMA

Amridge University
Private

ONLINE MBA PROGRAM(S)

www.amridgeuniversity.edu
Admissions: (888) 790-8080
Email: admissions@amridgeuniversity.edu
Financial aid: (334) 387-7523
Application deadline: rolling
Program can be completed entirely online: Yes
Total program cost: N/A
Tuition per credit: $600 full-time in-state, $725 part-time in-state, $600 full-time out-of-state, $725 part-time out-of-state
Test scores required: No
Most popular MBA concentrations: general management, human resources management, leadership, management information systems, organizational behavior
Completion: Credits needed to graduate: 25

Auburn University (Harbert)
Public

ONLINE MBA PROGRAM(S)

harbert.auburn.edu/
Admissions: (334) 844-4060
Email: mbadmis@auburn.edu
Financial aid: (334) 844-4634
Application deadline: rolling
Program can be completed entirely online: No
Total program cost: $34,425 full-time in-state, $34,425 part-time in-state, $34,425 full-time out-of-state, $34,425 part-time out-of-state
Tuition per credit: $875 full-time in-state, $875 part-time in-state, $875 full-time out-of-state, $875 part-time out-of-state
Acceptance rate: 74.0%
Test scores required: GMAT or GRE
Average GMAT: 576
Average GRE: 154 verbal, 155 quantitative, 3.8 writing
Average age of entrants: 30
Students with prior work experience: 90.0%
Enrollment: 372, 72% men, 28% women, 13% minority, 0% international
Average class size: 54
Most popular MBA concentrations: finance, management information systems, supply chain management/logistics, quantitative analysis/statistics and operations research
Completion: Three year graduation rate: 69%; credits needed to graduate: 39; target time to graduate: 2.5 years
College funded aid available: Domestic: No; International: No
Graduates with debt: 26%; average amount of debt $12,049

ONLINE BUSINESS PROGRAM(S)

harbert.auburn.edu/
Admissions: (334) 844-4060
Email: mbadmis@auburn.edu
Financial aid: (334) 844-4634
Application deadline: rolling

Program can be completed entirely online: No
Total program cost: $26,565
full-time in-state, $26,565
part-time in-state, $26,565
full-time out-of-state, $26,565
part-time out-of-state
Tuition per credit: $875 full-time in-state, $875 part-time in-state, $875 full-time out-of-state, $875 part-time out-of-state
Acceptance rate: 64.0%
Test scores required: GMAT or GRE
Average GMAT: 544
Average GRE: 152 verbal, 152 quantitative, 4.0 writing
Average age of entrants: 33
Students with prior work experience: 80.0%
Enrollment: 151, 61% men, 39% women, 12% minority, 1% international
Average class size: 34
Most popular business concentrations: accounting, finance, management information systems, quantitative analysis/statistics and operations research
Completion: Three year graduation rate: 74%; credits needed to graduate: 30; target time to graduate: 2 years
College funded aid available: Domestic: No; International: No
Graduates with debt: 34%; average amount of debt $15,871

Auburn University–Montgomery

Public

ONLINE MBA PROGRAM(S)

Admissions: (334) 244-3615
Email: admissions@aum.edu
Financial aid: (334) 244-3571
Application deadline: rolling
Program can be completed entirely online: Depends
Total program cost: $11,910
full-time in-state, $11,910
part-time in-state, $13,110
full-time out-of-state, $13,110
part-time out-of-state
Tuition per credit: $397 full-time in-state, $397 part-time in-state, $437 full-time out-of-state, $437 part-time out-of-state
Acceptance rate: 68.0%
Test scores required: GMAT
Average GMAT: 444
Average age of entrants: 28
Enrollment: 45, 51% men, 49% women, 36% minority, 27% international
Average class size: 20
Completion: Credits needed to graduate: 30; target time to graduate: 2 years
College funded aid available: Domestic: Yes; International: No

Jacksonville State University

Public

ONLINE MBA PROGRAM(S)

www.jsu.edu/graduate/index.html
Admissions: (256) 782-5329
Email: graduate@jsu.edu
Financial aid: (256) 782-5006
Application deadline: rolling
Program can be completed entirely online: Yes

Total program cost: $11,460
full-time in-state, $11,460
part-time in-state, $11,460
full-time out-of-state, $11,460
part-time out-of-state
Tuition per credit: $382
full-time in-state, $382
part-time in-state, $382
full-time out-of-state, $382
part-time out-of-state
Acceptance rate: 75.0%
Test scores required: GMAT or GRE
Average GMAT: 456
Average age of entrants: 28
Students with prior work experience: 56.0%
Enrollment: 89, 45% men, 55% women, N/A minority, N/A international
Completion: Three year graduation rate: 57%; credits needed to graduate: 30
College funded aid available: International: Yes

Samford University (Brock)

Private

ONLINE MBA PROGRAM(S)

Admissions: (205) 726-2040
Email: eagambre@samford.edu
Financial aid: (205) 726-2905
Application deadline: rolling
Program can be completed entirely online: Yes
Total program cost: $40,000
full-time in-state, $40,000
part-time in-state, $40,000
full-time out-of-state, $40,000
part-time out-of-state
Tuition per credit: $837 full-time in-state, $837 part-time in-state, $837 full-time out-of-state, $837 part-time out-of-state
Acceptance rate: 88.0%
Test scores required: GMAT or GRE
Average GMAT: 542
Average GRE: 152 verbal, 150 quantitative, 4.0 writing
Average age of entrants: 26
Enrollment: 143, 55% men, 45% women, 15% minority, 6% international
Average class size: 15
Most popular MBA concentrations: entrepreneurship, finance, marketing
Completion: Three year graduation rate: 72%; credits needed to graduate: 36; target time to graduate: 2 years
College funded aid available: Domestic: Yes
Graduates with debt: 8%; average amount of debt $36,048

Troy University

Public

ONLINE BUSINESS PROGRAM(S)

admission.troy.edu
Admissions: (800) 414-5756
Email: admit@troy.edu
Financial aid: (334) 670-3182
Application deadline: rolling
Program can be completed entirely online: Yes
Total program cost: $17,784
full-time in-state, $8,892
part-time in-state, $17,784
full-time out-of-state, $8,892
part-time out-of-state

Tuition per credit: $494
full-time in-state, $494
part-time in-state, $494
full-time out-of-state, $494
part-time out-of-state
Acceptance rate: 97.0%
Test scores required: GMAT or GRE
Average GMAT: 346
Average GRE: 159 verbal, 161 quantitative
Average age of entrants: 35
Enrollment: 923, 43% men, 57% women, 30% minority, 0% international
Average class size: 26
Most popular business concentrations: e-commerce, general management, human resources management, leadership
Completion: Three year graduation rate: 35%; target time to graduate: 2 years
College funded aid available: Domestic: Yes; International: Yes

University of Alabama (Manderson)

Public

ONLINE BUSINESS PROGRAM(S)

www.graduate.ua.edu
Admissions: (205) 348-7221
Email: graduate.school@ua.edu
Financial aid: (205) 348-6756
Application deadline: rolling
Program can be completed entirely online: Yes
Total program cost: N/A
Tuition per credit: $394
full-time in-state, $394
part-time in-state, $394
full-time out-of-state, $394
part-time out-of-state
Acceptance rate: 83.0%
Test scores required: GMAT or GRE
Average GMAT: 587
Average GRE: 150 verbal, 155 quantitative, 4.0 writing
Average age of entrants: 34
Students with prior work experience: 79.0%
Enrollment: 142, 66% men, 34% women, N/A minority, N/A international
Average class size: 22
Most popular business concentrations: general management, marketing, production/operations management
Completion: Three year graduation rate: 91%; credits needed to graduate: 30; target time to graduate: 2 years
College funded aid available: Domestic: Yes; International: Yes
Graduates with debt: 10%; average amount of debt $13,000

University of Alabama–Birmingham

Public

ONLINE MBA PROGRAM(S)

www.uab.edu/graduate/
Admissions: (205) 934-8227
Email: gradschool@uab.edu
Financial aid: (205) 934-8223
Application deadline: rolling
Program can be completed entirely online: Yes

Total program cost: $39,168
full-time in-state, $39,168
part-time in-state, $39,168
full-time out-of-state, $39,168
part-time out-of-state
Tuition per credit: $1,088
full-time in-state, $1,088
part-time in-state, $1,088
full-time out-of-state, $1,088
part-time out-of-state
Acceptance rate: 72.0%
Average GMAT: 527
Average GRE: 141 verbal, 152 quantitative, 4.0 writing
Average age of entrants: 36
Students with prior work experience: 96.0%
Enrollment: 106, 58% men, 42% women, 32% minority, 3% international
Average class size: 27
Most popular MBA concentrations: finance, health care administration, marketing, management information systems
Completion: Credits needed to graduate: 36; target time to graduate: 2 years
College funded aid available: Domestic: Yes; International: Yes

ONLINE BUSINESS PROGRAM(S)

www.uab.edu/graduate/
Admissions: (205) 934-8227
Email: gradschool@uab.edu
Financial aid: (205) 934-8223
Application deadline: rolling
Program can be completed entirely online: Yes
Total program cost: $32,640
full-time in-state, $32,640
part-time in-state, $32,640
full-time out-of-state, $32,640
part-time out-of-state
Tuition per credit: $1,088
full-time in-state, $1,088
part-time in-state, $1,088
full-time out-of-state, $1,088
part-time out-of-state
Acceptance rate: 64.0%
Test scores required: GMAT or GRE
Average GMAT: 536
Average age of entrants: 32
Students with prior work experience: 76.0%
Enrollment: 113, 42% men, 58% women, 22% minority, 0% international
Average class size: 19
Most popular business concentrations: accounting
Completion: Three year graduation rate: 82%; credits needed to graduate: 30; target time to graduate: 2 years
College funded aid available: Domestic: Yes; International: Yes
Graduates with debt: 76%; average amount of debt $44,713

University of North Alabama

Public

ONLINE MBA PROGRAM(S)

www.una.edu/mba/index.html
Admissions: (256) 765-6347
Email: awaddell@una.edu
Financial aid: (256) 765-4279
Application deadline: rolling
Program can be completed entirely online: Yes
Total program cost: $14,450
full-time in-state, $14,450

part-time in-state, $14,450
full-time out-of-state, $14,450
part-time out-of-state
Tuition per credit: $425
full-time in-state, $425
part-time in-state, $425
full-time out-of-state, $425
part-time out-of-state
Acceptance rate: 91.0%
Average GMAT: 451
Average GRE: 149 verbal, 147 quantitative
Average age of entrants: 34
Students with prior work experience: 25.0%
Enrollment: 758, 54% men, 46% women, 26% minority, 3% international
Average class size: 28
Most popular MBA concentrations: finance, general management, health care administration, human resources management, management information systems
Completion: Three year graduation rate: 56%; credits needed to graduate: 34; target time to graduate: 2 years
College funded aid available: Domestic: Yes; International: Yes
Graduates with debt: 31%; average amount of debt $34,277

ALASKA

University of Alaska–Fairbanks

Public

ONLINE MBA PROGRAM(S)

www.uaf.edu/admissions
Admissions: (800) 478-1823
Email: admissions@uaf.edu
Financial aid: (888) 474-7256
Application deadline: rolling
Program can be completed entirely online: Yes
Total program cost: $17,610
full-time in-state, $17,610
part-time in-state, $17,610
full-time out-of-state, $17,610
part-time out-of-state
Tuition per credit: $587 full-time in-state, $587 part-time in-state, $587 full-time out-of-state, $587 part-time out-of-state
Average class size: 19
Most popular MBA concentrations: general management
Completion: Credits needed to graduate: 30; target time to graduate: 2 years
College funded aid available: Domestic: Yes; International: Yes
Graduates with debt: 38%; average amount of debt $16,433

ARIZONA

Arizona State University (Carey)

Public

ONLINE MBA PROGRAM(S)

wpcarey.asu.edu/mba
Admissions: (480) 965-3332
Email: wpcareymasters@asu.edu
Financial aid: (480) 965-6890
Application deadline: Domestic: 07/19; International: 02/05

Program can be completed entirely online: Yes
Total program cost: $57,308 full-time in-state, $60,074 part-time in-state, $60,074 full-time out-of-state, $60,074 part-time out-of-state
Tuition per credit: $1,170 full-time in-state, $1,226 part-time in-state, $1,226 full-time out-of-state, $1,226 part-time out-of-state
Acceptance rate: 61.0%
Test scores required: GMAT or GRE
Average GMAT: 590
Average GRE: 153 verbal, 151 quantitative, 3.9 writing
Average age of entrants: 32
Students with prior work experience: 92.0%
Enrollment: 437, 70% men, 30% women, 28% minority, 2% international
Average class size: 61
Most popular MBA concentrations: finance, international business, marketing, supply chain management/logistics
Completion: Three year graduation rate: 89%; credits needed to graduate: 49; target time to graduate: 2 years
College funded aid available: Domestic: Yes; International: Yes
Graduates with debt: 49%; average amount of debt $59,637

ONLINE BUSINESS PROGRAM(S)

wpcarey.asu.edu/masters-programs
Admissions: (480) 965-3332
Email: wpcareymasters@asu.edu
Financial aid: (480) 965-6890
Application deadline: Domestic: 07/19; International: 02/05
Program can be completed entirely online: Yes
Total program cost: $39,660 full-time in-state, $39,660 part-time in-state, $39,660 full-time out-of-state, $39,660 part-time out-of-state
Tuition per credit: $1,322 full-time in-state, $1,322 part-time in-state, $1,322 full-time out-of-state, $1,322 part-time out-of-state
Acceptance rate: 65.0%
Test scores required: GMAT or GRE
Average GMAT: 625
Average GRE: 154 verbal, 154 quantitative, 3.9 writing
Average age of entrants: 33
Students with prior work experience: 90.0%
Enrollment: 163, 75% men, 25% women, 34% minority, 6% international
Average class size: 34
Most popular business concentrations: management information systems
Completion: Three year graduation rate: 93%; credits needed to graduate: 30; target time to graduate: 1.5 years
College funded aid available: Domestic: Yes; International: Yes
Graduates with debt: 59%; average amount of debt $42,490

Northcentral University
Private

ONLINE MBA PROGRAM(S)

www.ncu.edu
Admissions: (866) 776-0331
Email: information@ncu.edu
Financial aid: (888) 327-2877
Application deadline: rolling
Program can be completed entirely online: Yes
Total program cost: $31,960 full-time in-state, $31,960 part-time in-state, $31,960 full-time out-of-state, $31,960 part-time out-of-state
Tuition per credit: $1,022 full-time in-state, $1,022 part-time in-state, $1,022 full-time out-of-state, $1,022 part-time out-of-state
Acceptance rate: 100.0%
Test scores required: No
Average class size: 1
Most popular MBA concentrations: entrepreneurship, finance, general management, health care administration, human resources management
Completion: Target time to graduate: 1.5 years

Northern Arizona University
Public

ONLINE BUSINESS PROGRAM(S)

nau.edu/gradcol/admissions/
Admissions: (928) 523-4348
Email: graduate@nau.edu
Financial aid: (928) 523-4951
Application deadline: rolling
Program can be completed entirely online: Yes
Total program cost: $20,700 full-time in-state, $20,700 part-time in-state, $20,700 full-time out-of-state, $20,700 part-time out-of-state
Tuition per credit: $575 full-time in-state, $575 part-time in-state, $575 full-time out-of-state, $575 part-time out-of-state
Acceptance rate: 99.0%
Test scores required: No
Average age of entrants: 37
Enrollment: 242, 38% men, 62% women, 36% minority, 0% international
Average class size: 12
Most popular business concentrations: leadership, public administration
Completion: Three year graduation rate: 65%; credits needed to graduate: 36; target time to graduate: 2 years
College funded aid available: Domestic: Yes; International: Yes
Graduates with debt: 66%; average amount of debt $40,642

Thunderbird School of Global Management
Public

ONLINE BUSINESS PROGRAM(S)

thunderbird.asu.edu/
Admissions: (602) 496-7000
Email: admissions.tbird@asu.edu
Financial aid: (480) 965-1127
Application deadline: rolling

Program can be completed entirely online: Yes
Total program cost: $42,000 full-time in-state, $42,000 part-time in-state, $42,000 full-time out-of-state, $42,000 part-time out-of-state
Tuition per credit: $1,050 full-time in-state, $1,050 part-time in-state, $1,050 full-time out-of-state, $1,050 part-time out-of-state
Acceptance rate: 84.0%
Test scores required: No
Average age of entrants: 32
Students with prior work experience: 100.0%
Enrollment: 175, 65% men, 35% women, 33% minority, 7% international
Average class size: 33
Most popular business concentrations: finance, international business, marketing
Completion: Credits needed to graduate: 40; target time to graduate: 2 years
College funded aid available: Domestic: Yes; International: Yes

University of Arizona (Eller)
Public

ONLINE MBA PROGRAM(S)

ellermba.arizona.edu/
Admissions: (520) 621-2281
Email: pjorden@eller.arizona.edu
Financial aid: (520) 621-5065
Application deadline: rolling
Program can be completed entirely online: Yes
Total program cost: $27,000 full-time in-state, $18,000 part-time in-state, $27,000 full-time out-of-state, $18,000 part-time out-of-state
Tuition per credit: $1,000 full-time in-state, $1,000 part-time in-state, $1,000 full-time out-of-state, $1,000 part-time out-of-state
Acceptance rate: 88.0%
Test scores required: GMAT or GRE
Average GMAT: 553
Average age of entrants: 34
Students with prior work experience: 97.0%
Enrollment: 313, 72% men, 28% women, 29% minority, 3% international
Average class size: 43
Most popular MBA concentrations: entrepreneurship, finance, general management, marketing, management information systems
Completion: Three year graduation rate: 85%; credits needed to graduate: 45; target time to graduate: 2 years
College funded aid available: Domestic: Yes; International: Yes
Graduates with debt: 43%; average amount of debt $47,286

Arkansas State University–Jonesboro
Public

ONLINE MBA PROGRAM(S)

www.astate.edu/college/graduate-school
Admissions: (870) 972-3035
Email: broe@astate.edu
Financial aid: (870) 972-2310
Application deadline: rolling
Program can be completed entirely online: Yes
Total program cost: $20,130 full-time in-state, $20,130 part-time in-state, $20,130 full-time out-of-state, $20,130 part-time out-of-state
Tuition per credit: $610 full-time in-state, $610 part-time in-state, $610 full-time out-of-state, $610 part-time out-of-state
Acceptance rate: 57.0%
Average GMAT: 544
Average GRE: 150 verbal, 149 quantitative, 4.0 writing
Average age of entrants: 32
Students with prior work experience: 91.0%
Enrollment: 164, 56% men, 44% women, 23% minority, 0% international
Average class size: 20
Most popular MBA concentrations: finance, marketing, supply chain management/logistics
Completion: Three year graduation rate: 33%; credits needed to graduate: 33; target time to graduate: 2 years
Graduates with debt: 41%; average amount of debt $38,816

Harding University
Private

ONLINE MBA PROGRAM(S)

www.harding.edu/mba
Admissions: (501) 279-5789
Email: mba@harding.edu
Financial aid: (501) 279-5278
Application deadline: rolling
Program can be completed entirely online: Yes
Total program cost: $22,068 full-time in-state, $22,068 part-time in-state, $22,068 full-time out-of-state, $22,068 part-time out-of-state
Tuition per credit: $613 full-time in-state, $613 part-time in-state, $613 full-time out-of-state, $613 part-time out-of-state
Acceptance rate: 100.0%
Test scores required: GMAT or GRE
Average age of entrants: 28
Enrollment: 67, 64% men, 36% women, 9% minority, 4% international
Completion: Credits needed to graduate: 36; target time to graduate: 2 years
College funded aid available: Domestic: Yes; International: Yes

Southern Arkansas University
Public

ONLINE MBA PROGRAM(S)

www.saumag.edu/graduate
Admissions: (870) 235-4150
Email: kkbloss@saumag.edu
Financial aid: (870) 235-4025
Application deadline: rolling
Program can be completed entirely online: Yes
Total program cost: N/A
Tuition per credit: $285 full-time in-state, $285 part-time in-state, $437 full-time out-of-state, $437 part-time out-of-state
Test scores required: GMAT or GRE
Average class size: 18
Most popular MBA concentrations: entrepreneurship, general management, supply chain management/logistics
Completion: Credits needed to graduate: 30; target time to graduate: 2 years
College funded aid available: Domestic: Yes; International: Yes

University of Central Arkansas
Public

ONLINE MBA PROGRAM(S)

Admissions: (501) 450-3124
Financial aid: (501) 450-3140
Application deadline: rolling
Program can be completed entirely online: Yes
Total program cost: N/A
Tuition per credit: $325 full-time in-state, $325 part-time in-state, $325 full-time out-of-state, $325 part-time out-of-state
Test scores required: GMAT or GRE
Enrollment: 136, 54% men, 46% women, 19% minority, 16% international
Most popular MBA concentrations: finance, health care administration, management information systems
Completion: Credits needed to graduate: 30
College funded aid available: Domestic: Yes
Graduates with debt: 31%; average amount of debt $20,091

Brandman University
Private

ONLINE MBA PROGRAM(S)

www.brandman.edu/admissions
Admissions: (800) 746-0082
Email: adminfo@brandman.edu
Financial aid: (800) 746-0082
Application deadline: rolling
Program can be completed entirely online: Yes
Total program cost: $31,200 full-time in-state, $31,200 part-time in-state, $31,200 full-time out-of-state, $31,200 part-time out-of-state
Tuition per credit: $650 full-time in-state, $650 part-time in-state, $650

full-time out-of-state, $650 part-time out-of-state
Acceptance rate: 100.0%
Test scores required: No
Average age of entrants: 34
Enrollment: 174, 42% men, 58% women, 44% minority, 0% international
Average class size: 21
Most popular MBA concentrations: general management, health care administration, human resources management, leadership, marketing
Completion: Three year graduation rate: 63%; credits needed to graduate: 48; target time to graduate: 2 years
College funded aid available: Domestic: Yes; International: Yes
Graduates with debt: 74%; average amount of debt $53,544

ONLINE BUSINESS PROGRAM(S)
www.brandman.edu/admissions
Admissions: (800) 746-0082
Email: adminfo@brandman.edu
Financial aid: (800) 746-0082
Application deadline: rolling
Program can be completed entirely online: Yes
Total program cost: $23,400
full-time in-state, $23,400
part-time in-state, $23,400
full-time out-of-state, $23,400
part-time out-of-state
Tuition per credit: $650
full-time in-state, $650
part-time in-state, $650
full-time out-of-state, $650
part-time out-of-state
Acceptance rate: 100.0%
Test scores required: No
Average age of entrants: 36
Enrollment: 269, 44% men, 56% women, 40% minority, 0% international
Average class size: 21
Most popular business concentrations: human resources management, leadership, public administration
Completion: Three year graduation rate: 74%; credits needed to graduate: 36; target time to graduate: 1.5 years
College funded aid available: Domestic: Yes; International: Yes
Graduates with debt: 50%; average amount of debt $54,854

California Baptist University

Private

ONLINE MBA PROGRAM(S)
www.cbuonline.edu
Admissions: (951) 343-3927
Email: cbuonline@calbaptist.edu
Financial aid: (951) 343-4236
Application deadline: rolling
Program can be completed entirely online: Yes
Total program cost: $23,832
full-time in-state, $23,832
part-time in-state, $23,832
full-time out-of-state, $23,832
part-time out-of-state
Tuition per credit: $662
full-time in-state, $662
part-time in-state, $662
full-time out-of-state, $662
part-time out-of-state
Acceptance rate: 63.0%
Test scores required: No

Average age of entrants: 31
Students with prior work experience: 100.0%
Enrollment: 144, 44% men, 56% women, 58% minority, 0% international
Average class size: 17
Most popular MBA concentrations: accounting, general management
Completion: Three year graduation rate: 75%; credits needed to graduate: 36; target time to graduate: 1.5 years
College funded aid available: Domestic: Yes; International: Yes
Graduates with debt: 81%; average amount of debt $41,252

ONLINE BUSINESS PROGRAM(S)
www.cbuonline.edu
Admissions: (951) 343-3927
Email: cbuonline@calbaptist.edu
Financial aid: (951) 343-4236
Application deadline: rolling
Program can be completed entirely online: Yes
Total program cost: $19,860
full-time in-state, $19,860
part-time in-state, $19,860
full-time out-of-state, $19,860
part-time out-of-state
Tuition per credit: $662
full-time in-state, $662
part-time in-state, $662
full-time out-of-state, $662
part-time out-of-state
Acceptance rate: 69.0%
Test scores required: No
Average age of entrants: 33
Students with prior work experience: 100.0%
Enrollment: 48, 31% men, 69% women, 44% minority, 0% international
Average class size: 15
Most popular business concentrations: accounting
Completion: Three year graduation rate: 40%; credits needed to graduate: 30; target time to graduate: 1 year
College funded aid available: Domestic: Yes; International: Yes
Graduates with debt: 85%; average amount of debt $34,167

California State University–Dominguez Hills

Public

ONLINE MBA PROGRAM(S)
mbaonline.csudh.edu
Admissions: (310) 243-3646
Email: mbaonline@csudh.edu
Financial aid: (310) 243-3691
Application deadline: rolling
Program can be completed entirely online: Yes
Total program cost: $15,000
full-time in-state, $15,000
part-time in-state, $15,000
full-time out-of-state, $15,000
part-time out-of-state
Tuition per credit: $497 full-time in-state, $497 part-time in-state, $497 full-time out-of-state, $497 part-time out-of-state
Acceptance rate: 52.0%
Test scores required: GMAT or GRE
Average GMAT: 488
Average GRE: 145 verbal, 145 quantitative, 4.0 writing

Students with prior work experience: 95.0%
Enrollment: 59, 47% men, 53% women, 66% minority, 0% international
Average class size: 20
Most popular MBA concentrations: finance, general management, human resources management, international business, marketing
Completion: Three year graduation rate: 92%; credits needed to graduate: 30; target time to graduate: 1.5 years
College funded aid available: Domestic: No; International: No

California State University–Fullerton (Mihaylo)

Public

ONLINE BUSINESS PROGRAM(S)
business.fullerton.edu/msit
Admissions: (657) 278-2574
Email: msit@fullerton.edu
Financial aid: (657) 278-3128
Application deadline: Domestic: 06/30
Program can be completed entirely online: No
Total program cost: $8,970
full-time in-state, $10,410
part-time in-state, $20,850
full-time out-of-state, $22,920
part-time out-of-state
Tuition per credit: $299 full-time in-state, $347 part-time in-state, $695 full-time out-of-state, $743 part-time out-of-state
Acceptance rate: 77.0%
Test scores required: GMAT or GRE
Average GMAT: 510
Average GRE: 152 verbal, 151 quantitative, 4.0 writing
Average age of entrants: 33
Students with prior work experience: 100.0%
Enrollment: 43, 81% men, 19% women, 51% minority, 7% international
Average class size: 30
Most popular business concentrations: e-commerce, manufacturing and technology management, management information systems, technology
Completion: Three year graduation rate: 81%; credits needed to graduate: 30; target time to graduate: 1.5 years
College funded aid available: Domestic: Yes; International: No
Graduates with debt: 56%; average amount of debt $18,354

California State University–Sacramento

Public

ONLINE BUSINESS PROGRAM(S)
www.csus.edu/cba/graduate/
Admissions: (916) 278-2895
Email: cbagrad@csus.edu
Financial aid: (916) 278-2676
Application deadline: Domestic: 03/01
Program can be completed entirely online: Yes
Total program cost: $22,200
full-time in-state, $22,200

part-time in-state, $22,200
full-time out-of-state, $22,200
part-time out-of-state
Tuition per credit: $740 full-time in-state, $740 part-time in-state, $740 full-time out-of-state, $740 part-time out-of-state
Acceptance rate: 83.0%
Average GMAT: 534
Average age of entrants: 34
Students with prior work experience: 93.0%
Enrollment: 88, 34% men, 66% women, N/A minority, N/A international
Average class size: 20
Most popular business concentrations: accounting
Completion: Credits needed to graduate: 30; target time to graduate: 1.5 years
College funded aid available: Domestic: Yes; International: No

California State University– San Bernardino

Public

ONLINE MBA PROGRAM(S)
jhbc.csusb.edu/mba
Admissions: (909) 537-5703
Email: mbaonline@csusb.edu
Financial aid: (909) 537-7651
Application deadline: rolling
Program can be completed entirely online: Yes
Total program cost: $36,000
full-time in-state, $36,000
part-time in-state, $36,000
full-time out-of-state, $36,000
part-time out-of-state
Tuition per credit: $750 full-time in-state, $750 part-time in-state, $750 full-time out-of-state, $750 part-time out-of-state
Acceptance rate: 97.0%
Test scores required: No
Average age of entrants: 40
Students with prior work experience: 100.0%
Enrollment: 170, 51% men, 49% women, 55% minority, 4% international
Average class size: 23
Most popular MBA concentrations: general management
Completion: Three year graduation rate: 82%; credits needed to graduate: 48; target time to graduate: 1.5 years
College funded aid available: Domestic: No; International: No
Graduates with debt: 69%; average amount of debt $21,966

ONLINE BUSINESS PROGRAM(S)
jhbc.csusb.edu/mba
Admissions: (909) 537-5703
Email: mbaonline@csusb.edu
Financial aid: (909) 537-7651
Application deadline: N/A
Program can be completed entirely online: Yes
Total program cost: N/A
Tuition per credit:
Acceptance rate: 97.0%
Test scores required: No
Average age of entrants: 40
Students with prior work experience: 100.0%
Enrollment: 170, 51% men, 49% women, 55% minority, 4% international

Most popular business concentrations: general management

California State University–Stanislaus

Public

ONLINE MBA PROGRAM(S)
www.csustan.edu/omba
Admissions: (209) 667-3683
Email: kkidd@csustan.edu
Financial aid: (209) 667-3337
Application deadline: Domestic: 06/30; International: 06/30
Program can be completed entirely online: Yes
Total program cost: N/A
Tuition per credit: $800
full-time in-state, $800
part-time in-state, $800
full-time out-of-state, $800
part-time out-of-state
Acceptance rate: 94.0%
Test scores required: GMAT or GRE
Average GMAT: 508
Average GRE: 147 verbal, 143 quantitative, 4.0 writing
Average age of entrants: 29
Students with prior work experience: 97.0%
Enrollment: 30, 57% men, 43% women, N/A minority, N/A international
Completion: Credits needed to graduate: 30; target time to graduate: 2 years
College funded aid available: Domestic: No; International: No

Golden Gate University

Private

ONLINE MBA PROGRAM(S)
www.ggu.edu
Admissions: (415) 442-7224
Email: info@ggu.edu
Financial aid: (415) 442-6632
Application deadline: rolling
Program can be completed entirely online: Yes
Total program cost: $25,200
full-time in-state, $15,750
part-time in-state, $25,200
full-time out-of-state, $15,750
part-time out-of-state
Tuition per credit: $1,050
full-time in-state, $1,050
part-time in-state, $1,050
full-time out-of-state, $1,050
part-time out-of-state
Acceptance rate: 75.0%
Test scores required: GMAT or GRE
Average age of entrants: 38
Enrollment: 137, 45% men, 55% women, 49% minority, 6% international
Average class size: 11
Most popular MBA concentrations: finance, general management, human resources management, public administration
Completion: Three year graduation rate: 61%; credits needed to graduate: 54; target time to graduate: 2.5 years
College funded aid available: Domestic: Yes

ONLINE BUSINESS PROGRAM(S)
www@ggu.edu
Admissions: (415) 442-7224

Email: info@ggu.edu
Financial aid: (415) 442-6632
Application deadline: rolling
Program can be completed entirely online: Yes
Total program cost: $25,200
full-time in-state, $15,750
part-time in-state, $25,200
full-time out-of-state, $15,750
part-time out-of-state
Tuition per credit: $1,050
full-time in-state, $1,050
part-time in-state, $1,050
full-time out-of-state, $1,050
part-time out-of-state
Acceptance rate: 86.0%
Test scores required: GMAT or GRE
Average age of entrants: 35
Enrollment: 839, 45% men, 55% women, 31% minority, 8% international
Average class size: 13
Most popular business concentrations: accounting, finance, human resources management, tax, technology
Completion: Three year graduation rate: 34%; credits needed to graduate: 45; target time to graduate: 2.5 years
College funded aid available: Domestic: Yes; International: No

National University

Private

ONLINE MBA PROGRAM(S)

www.nu.edu/onlineeducation.html
Admissions: (855) 355-6288
Email: onlineadmissions@nu.edu
Financial aid: (858) 642-8513
Application deadline: rolling
Program can be completed entirely online: Yes
Total program cost: $15,480
full-time in-state, $7,740
part-time in-state, $15,480
full-time out-of-state, $7,740
part-time out-of-state
Tuition per credit: $430
full-time in-state, $430
part-time in-state, $430
full-time out-of-state, $430
part-time out-of-state
Acceptance rate: 100.0%
Test scores required: No
Average age of entrants: 34
Enrollment: 642, 51% men, 49% women, 49% minority, 16% international
Average class size: 25
Most popular MBA concentrations: general management
Completion: Three year graduation rate: 62%; credits needed to graduate: 63; target time to graduate: 3 years
College funded aid available: Domestic: Yes; International: Yes
Graduates with debt: 36%; average amount of debt $13,725

ONLINE BUSINESS PROGRAM(S)

www.nu.edu/onlineeducation.html
Admissions: (855) 355-6288
Email: onlineadmissions@nu.edu
Financial aid: (858) 642-8513
Application deadline: rolling
Program can be completed entirely online: Yes
Total program cost: $15,480
full-time in-state, $7,740
part-time in-state, $15,480

---

full-time out-of-state, $7,740
part-time out-of-state
Tuition per credit: $430
full-time in-state, $430
part-time in-state, $430
full-time out-of-state, $430
part-time out-of-state
Acceptance rate: 100.0%
Test scores required: No
Average age of entrants: 37
Enrollment: 675, 44% men, 56% women, 56% minority, 2% international
Average class size: 20
Most popular business concentrations: accounting, general management, human resources management, leadership
Completion: Three year graduation rate: 53%; credits needed to graduate: 54; target time to graduate: 3 years
College funded aid available: Domestic: Yes; International: Yes
Graduates with debt: 50%; average amount of debt $30,694

Pepperdine University (Graziadio)

Private

ONLINE MBA PROGRAM(S)

bschool.pepperdine.edu/
Admissions: (310) 568-5535
Email: PGBS.Admission@pepperdine.edu
Financial aid: (310) 568-5530
Application deadline: rolling
Program can be completed entirely online: No
Total program cost: $92,040
full-time in-state, $92,040
part-time in-state, $92,040
full-time out-of-state, $92,040
part-time out-of-state
Tuition per credit: $1,770
full-time in-state, $1,770
part-time in-state, $1,770
full-time out-of-state, $1,770
part-time out-of-state
Acceptance rate: 67.0%
Test scores required: GMAT or GRE
Average GMAT: 591
Average GRE: 153 verbal, 151 quantitative, 4.0 writing
Average age of entrants: 32
Students with prior work experience: 98.0%
Enrollment: 236, 50% men, 50% women, 32% minority, 2% international
Average class size: 23
Most popular MBA concentrations: finance, general management, leadership, marketing, management information systems
Completion: Three year graduation rate: 72%; credits needed to graduate: 52; target time to graduate: 2 years
College funded aid available: Domestic: Yes; International: Yes
Graduates with debt: 81%; average amount of debt $96,094

Point Loma Nazarene University

Private

ONLINE MBA PROGRAM(S)

Admissions: (866) 692-4723
Email: gradinfo@pointloma.edu
Financial aid: (619) 563-2849
Application deadline: rolling
Program can be completed entirely online: Yes
Total program cost: $35,490
full-time in-state, $35,490
part-time in-state, $35,490
full-time out-of-state, $35,490
part-time out-of-state
Tuition per credit: $845
full-time in-state, $845
part-time in-state, $845
full-time out-of-state, $845
part-time out-of-state
Acceptance rate: 100.0%
Test scores required: GMAT or GRE
Average age of entrants: 31
Enrollment: 29, 59% men, 41% women, 48% minority, 0% international
Completion: Credits needed to graduate: 42
College funded aid available: Domestic: Yes; International: Yes

St. Mary's College of California

Private

ONLINE MBA PROGRAM(S)

www.stmarys-ca.edu/graduate-business
Admissions: (925) 631-4888
Email: smcmba@stmarys-ca.edu
Financial aid: (925) 631-4836
Application deadline: Domestic: 04/15; International: 04/01
Program can be completed entirely online: No
Total program cost: $74,400
full-time in-state, $74,400
part-time in-state, $74,400
full-time out-of-state, $74,400
part-time out-of-state
Tuition per credit: $1,550
full-time in-state, $1,550
part-time in-state, $1,550
full-time out-of-state, $1,550
part-time out-of-state
Acceptance rate: 98.0%
Test scores required: No
Average age of entrants: 40
Students with prior work experience: 100.0%
Enrollment: 68, 57% men, 43% women, 49% minority, 0% international
Average class size: 26
Most popular MBA concentrations: entrepreneurship
Completion: Three year graduation rate: 98%; credits needed to graduate: 48; target time to graduate: 1.5 years
College funded aid available: Domestic: Yes; International: Yes
Graduates with debt: 80%; average amount of debt $63,000

ONLINE BUSINESS PROGRAM(S)

www.stmarys-ca.edu/graduate-business
Admissions: (925) 631-4888
Email: smcmba@stmarys-ca.edu
Financial aid: (925) 631-4686

Application deadline: Domestic: 01/02; International: 01/02
Program can be completed entirely online: No
Total program cost: $45,100
full-time in-state, $45,100
part-time in-state, $45,100
full-time out-of-state, $45,100
part-time out-of-state
Tuition per credit: $1,025
full-time in-state, $1,025
part-time in-state, $1,025
full-time out-of-state, $1,025
part-time out-of-state
Acceptance rate: 86.0%
Test scores required: No
Average GMAT: 571
Average GRE: 133 verbal, 140 quantitative
Average age of entrants: 31
Students with prior work experience: 99.0%
Enrollment: 89, 49% men, 51% women, 48% minority, 17% international
Average class size: 18
Completion: Three year graduation rate: 87%; credits needed to graduate: 44; target time to graduate: 1.5 years
College funded aid available: Domestic: Yes; International: Yes
Graduates with debt: 80%; average amount of debt $41,000

University of La Verne

Private

ONLINE MBA PROGRAM(S)

laverne.edu/admission/graduate/
Admissions: (909) 448-4086
Email: laverneonline@laverne.edu
Financial aid: (800) 649-0160
Application deadline: rolling
Program can be completed entirely online: Yes
Total program cost: N/A
Tuition per credit: $855
full-time in-state, $855
part-time in-state, $855
full-time out-of-state, $855
part-time out-of-state
Acceptance rate: 47.0%
Test scores required: No
Average age of entrants: 33
Enrollment: 155, 43% men, 57% women, 55% minority, 0% international
Average class size: 16
Most popular MBA concentrations: finance, general management, leadership, marketing, supply chain management/logistics
Completion: Three year graduation rate: 60%; credits needed to graduate: 33; target time to graduate: 2.5 years
College funded aid available: Domestic: Yes; International: Yes
Graduates with debt: 48%; average amount of debt $55,760

University of San Diego

Private

ONLINE BUSINESS PROGRAM(S)

www.sandiego.edu/msscm
Admissions: (619) 260-4860
Email: msscminfo@sandiego.edu
Financial aid: (619) 260-4720
Application deadline: rolling

Program can be completed entirely online: No
Total program cost: $53,100
part-time in-state, $53,100
part-time out-of-state
Tuition per credit: $1,475
full-time in-state, $1,475
part-time in-state, $1,475
full-time out-of-state, $1,475
part-time out-of-state
Acceptance rate: 93.0%
Test scores required: No
Average age of entrants: 36
Students with prior work experience: 100.0%
Enrollment: 51, 57% men, 43% women, 49% minority, 2% international
Average class size: 14
Most popular business concentrations: supply chain management/logistics
Completion: Three year graduation rate: 83%; credits needed to graduate: 36; target time to graduate: 2 years
College funded aid available: Domestic: Yes
Graduates with debt: 37%; average amount of debt $46,773

University of Southern California (Marshall)

Private

ONLINE MBA PROGRAM(S)

onlinemba.marshall.usc.edu/admissions/
Admissions: (877) 779-6643
Email: onlinemba@marshall.usc.edu
Financial aid: (213) 740-4444
Application deadline: rolling
Program can be completed entirely online: No
Total program cost: $97,512
full-time in-state, $97,512
part-time in-state, $97,512
full-time out-of-state, $97,512
part-time out-of-state
Tuition per credit: $1,912
full-time in-state, $1,912
part-time in-state, $1,912
full-time out-of-state, $1,912
part-time out-of-state
Acceptance rate: 53.0%
Test scores required: GMAT or GRE
Average GMAT: 648
Average GRE: 151 verbal, 155 quantitative, 4.0 writing
Average age of entrants: 34
Students with prior work experience: 100.0%
Enrollment: 139, 69% men, 31% women, 54% minority, 1% international
Average class size: 37
Completion: Credits needed to graduate: 51; target time to graduate: 1.5 years
College funded aid available: Domestic: Yes; International: Yes
Graduates with debt: 51%; average amount of debt $36,477

ONLINE BUSINESS PROGRAM(S)

www.marshall.usc.edu/
Admissions: (213) 740-9507
Email: learning@marshall.usc.edu
Financial aid: (213) 740-4444
Application deadline: rolling
Program can be completed entirely online: Depends

Total program cost: $50,301
full-time in-state, $50,301
part-time in-state, $50,301
full-time out-of-state, $50,301
part-time out-of-state
Tuition per credit: $1,863
full-time in-state, $1,863
part-time in-state, $1,863
full-time out-of-state, $1,863
part-time out-of-state
Acceptance rate: 78.0%
Test scores required: No
Average GMAT: 650
Average GRE: 152 verbal, 159
quantitative, 3.5 writing
Average age of entrants: 34
Students with prior work
experience: 47.0%
Enrollment: 74, 61% men,
39% women, N/A minority,
N/A international
Average class size: 40
Most popular business
concentrations: accounting,
production/operations
management, supply chain
management/logistics,
quantitative analysis/statistics
and operations research, tax
Completion: Three year
graduation rate: 100%; credits
needed to graduate: 27; target
time to graduate: 1.5 years
College funded aid
available: Domestic: Yes;
International: Yes
Graduates with debt:
52%; average amount
of debt $32,000

COLORADO

Colorado Christian University
Private

ONLINE MBA PROGRAM(S)

www.ccu.edu/ccu/mba/
admission/
Admissions: (303) 963-3311
Email: asievers@ccu.edu
Financial aid: (303) 963-3040
Application deadline: rolling
Program can be completed
entirely online: Yes
Total program cost: $22,191
full-time in-state, $22,191
part-time in-state, $22,191
full-time out-of-state, $22,191
part-time out-of-state
Tuition per credit: $569
full-time in-state, $569
part-time in-state, $569
full-time out-of-state, $569
part-time out-of-state
Acceptance rate: 64.0%
Test scores required: No
Average age of entrants: 36
Enrollment: 158, 45%
men, 55% women, 40%
minority, 0% international
Average class size: 8
Most popular MBA
concentrations: accounting,
health care administration,
leadership
Completion: Three year
graduation rate: 53%; credits
needed to graduate: 39; target
time to graduate: 1.5 years
College funded aid
available: Domestic: Yes;
International: Yes
Graduates with debt: 53%;
average amount of debt $32,698

ONLINE BUSINESS PROGRAM(S)

www.ccu.edu/ccu/grad/
Admissions: (303) 963-3311
Email: AdmissionsSupport@
ccu.edu
Financial aid: (303) 963-3040
Application deadline: rolling
Program can be completed
entirely online: Yes
Total program cost: $20,484
full-time in-state, $20,484
part-time in-state, $20,484
full-time out-of-state, $20,484
part-time out-of-state
Tuition per credit: $569
full-time in-state, $569
part-time in-state, $569
full-time out-of-state, $569
part-time out-of-state
Acceptance rate: 76.0%
Test scores required: No
Average age of entrants: 36
Enrollment: 140, 44%
men, 56% women, 38%
minority, 0% international
Average class size: 8
Most popular business
concentrations: leadership
Completion: Three year
graduation rate: 45%; credits
needed to graduate: 36; target
time to graduate: 1.5 years
College funded aid available:
Domestic: No; International: No
Graduates with debt: 47%;
average amount of debt $32,038

Colorado State University
Public

ONLINE MBA PROGRAM(S)

biz.colostate.edu/academics/
graduate-programs/mba/
online-mba/how-to-apply
Admissions: (970) 491-1129
Email: gradadmissions@
business.colostate.edu
Financial aid: (970) 491-6321
Application deadline: rolling
Program can be completed
entirely online: Yes
Total program cost: N/A
Tuition per credit: $974 full-time
in-state, $974 part-time in-state,
$974 full-time out-of-state,
$974 part-time out-of-state
Acceptance rate: 87.0%
Test scores required: No
Average GMAT: 453
Average GRE: 150 verbal, 150
quantitative, 4.0 writing
Average age of entrants: 34
Students with prior work
experience: 98.0%
Enrollment: 821, 61%
men, 39% women, 20%
minority, 1% international
Average class size: 35
Most popular MBA
concentrations: finance, general
management, leadership,
marketing, supply chain
management/logistics
Completion: Three year
graduation rate: 57%; credits
needed to graduate: 42; target
time to graduate: 2.5 years
College funded aid available:
Domestic: Yes; International: No
Graduates with debt: 32%;
average amount of debt $42,684

ONLINE BUSINESS PROGRAM(S)

biz.colostate.edu/cismaster/
pages.apply.aspx
Admissions: (970) 491-1129

Email: gradadmissions@
business.colostate.edu
Financial aid: (970) 491-6321
Application deadline: rolling
Program can be completed
entirely online: Yes
Total program cost: N/A
Tuition per credit: $842
full-time in-state, $842
part-time in-state, $842
full-time out-of-state, $842
part-time out-of-state
Acceptance rate: 86.0%
Test scores required:
GMAT or GRE
Average GRE: 157 verbal, 154
quantitative, 4.0 writing
Average age of entrants: 35
Students with prior work
experience: 79.0%
Enrollment: 148, 72% men,
28% women, 27% minority,
2% international
Average class size: 27
Most popular business
concentrations: e-commerce,
management information
systems, quantitative analysis/
statistics and operations
research, technology
Completion: Three year
graduation rate: 54%; credits
needed to graduate: 33; target
time to graduate: 2.5 years
College funded aid available:
Domestic: Yes; International: No
Graduates with debt:
31%; average amount
of debt $28,900

Colorado State University– Global Campus
Public

ONLINE BUSINESS PROGRAM(S)

csuglobal.edu/graduate/
admissions/admissions-process
Admissions: (800) 920-6723
Email: Admissions@
CSUGlobal.edu
Financial aid: (800) 462-7845
Application deadline: rolling
Program can be completed
entirely online: Yes
Total program cost: $18,000
full-time in-state, $18,000
part-time in-state, $18,000
full-time out-of-state, $18,000
part-time out-of-state
Tuition per credit: $500
full-time in-state, $500
part-time in-state, $500
full-time out-of-state, $500
part-time out-of-state
Acceptance rate: 98.0%
Test scores required: No
Average age of entrants: 35
Enrollment: 5,254, 38%
men, 62% women, 30%
minority, 0% international
Average class size: 9
Most popular business
concentrations: accounting,
finance, general management,
human resources
management, leadership
Completion: Three year
graduation rate: 58%; credits
needed to graduate: 36; target
time to graduate: 2 years
College funded aid
available: Domestic: Yes;
International: Yes
Graduates with debt: 61%;
average amount of debt $39,927

Colorado State University–Pueblo
Public

ONLINE MBA PROGRAM(S)

www.csupueblo.edu/
admissions/index.html
Admissions: (719) 549-2462
Email: info@csupueblo.edu
Financial aid: (719) 549-2753
Application deadline: rolling
Program can be completed
entirely online: Yes
Total program cost: $19,800
full-time in-state, $19,800
part-time in-state, $19,800
full-time out-of-state, $19,800
part-time out-of-state
Tuition per credit: $550
full-time in-state, $550
part-time in-state, $550
full-time out-of-state, $550
part-time out-of-state
Acceptance rate: 72.0%
Test scores required:
GMAT or GRE
Average GMAT: 480
Average GRE: 160 verbal, 150
quantitative, 4.0 writing
Average age of entrants: 37
Enrollment: 25, 48% men,
52% women, 56% minority,
0% international
Average class size: 18
Completion: Credits needed
to graduate: 36; target time
to graduate: 2 years
College funded aid
available: Domestic: Yes;
International: Yes
Graduates with debt: 17%;
average amount of debt $35,411

Colorado Technical University
Proprietary

ONLINE MBA PROGRAM(S)

www.coloradotech.edu/
admissions
Admissions: (855) 230-0555
Email: enroll@coloradotech.edu
Financial aid: (847) 851-7167
Application deadline: rolling
Program can be completed
entirely online: Yes
Total program cost: $28,080
full-time in-state, $28,080
part-time in-state, $28,080
full-time out-of-state, $28,080
part-time out-of-state
Tuition per credit: $585
full-time in-state, $585
part-time in-state, $585
full-time out-of-state, $585
part-time out-of-state
Acceptance rate: 100.0%
Test scores required: No
Average age of entrants: 37
Enrollment: 2,341, 37%
men, 63% women, 49%
minority, 0% international
Average class size: 20
Most popular MBA concentrations:
entrepreneurship, general
management, health care
administration, human
resources management
Completion: Three year
graduation rate: 65%; credits
needed to graduate: 48; target
time to graduate: 1.5 years
College funded aid
available: Domestic: Yes;
International: Yes

Graduates with debt: 83%;
average amount of debt $27,017

ONLINE BUSINESS PROGRAM(S)

www.coloradotech.edu/
admissions
Admissions: (855) 230-0555
Email: enroll@coloradotech.edu
Financial aid: (847) 851-7167
Application deadline: rolling
Program can be completed
entirely online: Yes
Total program cost: $28,080
full-time in-state, $28,080
part-time in-state, $28,080
full-time out-of-state, $28,080
part-time out-of-state
Tuition per credit: $585
full-time in-state, $585
part-time in-state, $585
full-time out-of-state, $585
part-time out-of-state
Acceptance rate: 100.0%
Test scores required: No
Average age of entrants: 38
Enrollment: 1,392, 40%
men, 60% women, 52%
minority, 0% international
Average class size: 21
Most popular business
concentrations: accounting,
health care administration,
organizational behavior,
technology
Completion: Three year
graduation rate: 49%; credits
needed to graduate: 48; target
time to graduate: 1.5 years
College funded aid
available: Domestic: Yes;
International: Yes
Graduates with debt: 82%;
average amount of debt $26,450

Regis University
Private

ONLINE MBA PROGRAM(S)

www.regis.edu/cps/admissions/
applying-to-college-for-
professional%20studies/
graduate-admissions.aspx
Admissions: (800) 388-2366
Email: regisadm@regis.edu
Financial aid: (303) 964-5449
Application deadline: rolling
Program can be completed
entirely online: Yes
Total program cost: N/A
Tuition per credit: $950
full-time in-state, $950
part-time in-state, $950
full-time out-of-state, $950
part-time out-of-state
Acceptance rate: 69.0%
Test scores required: No
Average age of entrants: 32
Enrollment: 645, 48%
men, 52% women, 31%
minority, 6% international
Average class size: 18
Most popular MBA
concentrations: accounting,
general management,
leadership, marketing
Completion: Three year
graduation rate: 46%; credits
needed to graduate: 39; target
time to graduate: 2 years
College funded aid available:
Domestic: Yes
Graduates with debt: 58%;
average amount of debt $45,304

ONLINE BUSINESS PROGRAM(S)

www.regis.edu/cbe/
admissions.aspx
Admissions: (800) 388-2366

Email: regisadm@regis.edu
Financial aid: (303) 458-4126
Application deadline: rolling
Program can be completed entirely online: Yes
Total program cost: N/A
Tuition per credit: $850 full-time in-state, $850 part-time in-state, $850 full-time out-of-state, $850 part-time out-of-state
Acceptance rate: 71.0%
Test scores required: No
Average age of entrants: 34
Enrollment: 632, 33% men, 67% women, 33% minority, 1% international
Average class size: 19
Most popular business concentrations: accounting, human resources management, leadership, not-for-profit management
Completion: Three year graduation rate: 62%; credits needed to graduate: 30; target time to graduate: 2 years
College funded aid available: Domestic: Yes; International: Yes
Graduates with debt: 70%; average amount of debt $49,776

University of Colorado–Boulder (Leeds)
Public

ONLINE BUSINESS PROGRAM(S)
www.colorado.edu/business/admissions
Admissions: (303) 492-8397
Email: leedsgrad@colorado.edu
Financial aid: N/A
Application deadline: N/A
Program can be completed entirely online: Yes
Total program cost: N/A
Tuition per credit: $1,023 full-time in-state, $1,023 part-time in-state, $1,432 full-time out-of-state, $1,432 part-time out of state
Most popular business concentrations: supply chain management/logistics

University of Colorado–Colorado Springs
Public

ONLINE MBA PROGRAM(S)
www.uccs.edu/business/programs/masters/online-mba
Admissions: (719) 255-3122
Email: cobgrad@uccs.edu
Financial aid: (719) 255-3460
Application deadline: rolling
Program can be completed entirely online: Yes
Total program cost: N/A
Tuition per credit: $714 full-time in-state, $809 part-time in-state, $858 full-time out-of-state, $858 part-time out-of-state
Acceptance rate: 72.0%
Average GMAT: 544
Average GRE: 153 verbal, 151 quantitative, 4.0 writing
Average age of entrants: 32
Enrollment: 173, 47% men, 53% women, 22% minority, 3% international

---

Average class size: 23
Most popular MBA concentrations: finance, general management, health care administration, international business
Completion: Three year graduation rate: 38%; credits needed to graduate: 36; target time to graduate: 3 years
College funded aid available: Domestic: No; International: Yes
Graduates with debt: 57%; average amount of debt $31,555

University of Denver (Daniels)
Private

ONLINE MBA PROGRAM(S)
onlinemba.du.edu/admissions/
Admissions: (303) 871-3934
Email: admissions@onlinemba.du.edu
Financial aid: (303) 871-4020
Application deadline: rolling
Program can be completed entirely online: Yes
Total program cost: $77,940 full-time in-state, $77,940 part-time in-state, $77,940 full-time out-of-state, $77,940 part-time out-of-state
Tuition per credit: $1,299 full-time in-state, $1,299 part-time in-state, $1,299 full-time out-of-state, $1,299 part-time out-of-state
Acceptance rate: 96.0%
Test scores required: GMAT or GRE
Average GMAT: 492
Average GRE: 148 verbal, 142 quantitative, 4.5 writing
Average age of entrants: 36
Students with prior work experience: 100.0%
Enrollment: 125, 59% men, 41% women, 20% minority, 0% international
Most popular MBA concentrations: finance, marketing
Completion: Credits needed to graduate: 60; target time to graduate: 2 years
College funded aid available: Domestic: No; International: No

ONLINE BUSINESS PROGRAM(S)
daniels.du.edu/graduate-students/admissions
Admissions: (303) 732-6186
Email: daniels@du.edu
Financial aid: (303) 871-4098
Application deadline: Domestic: 05/01; International: 03/15
Program can be completed entirely online: No
Total program cost: $66,048 full-time in-state, $66,048 part-time in-state, $66,048 full-time out-of-state, $66,048 part-time out-of-state
Tuition per credit: $1,372 full-time in-state, $1,372 part-time in-state, $1,372 full-time out-of-state, $1,372 part-time out-of-state
Acceptance rate: 56.0%
Test scores required: No
Average age of entrants: 37
Students with prior work experience: 100.0%
Enrollment: 35, 80% men, 20% women, 14% minority, 0% international
Average class size: 8

Most popular business concentrations: real estate
Completion: Three year graduation rate: 69%; credits needed to graduate: 48; target time to graduate: 1.5 years
College funded aid available: Domestic: Yes; International: Yes
Graduates with debt: 45%

CONNECTICUT

Post University
Proprietary

ONLINE MBA PROGRAM(S)
post.edu/admissions/online-students/graduate
Admissions: (203) 596-6164
Email: adpadmissions@post.edu
Financial aid: (203) 591-5641
Application deadline: rolling
Program can be completed entirely online: Yes
Total program cost: $26,280 full-time in-state, $26,280 part-time in-state, $26,280 full-time out-of-state, $26,280 part-time out-of-state
Tuition per credit: $730 full-time in-state, $730 part-time in-state, $730 full-time out-of-state, $730 part-time out-of-state
Acceptance rate: 39.0%
Test scores required: No
Average age of entrants: 34
Students with prior work experience: 100.0%
Enrollment: 495, 56% men, 44% women, 24% minority, 16% international
Average class size: 11
Most popular MBA concentrations: entrepreneurship, finance, leadership
Completion: Three year graduation rate: 46%; credits needed to graduate: 36; target time to graduate: 3 years
College funded aid available: Domestic: Yes; International: Yes
Graduates with debt: 58%

ONLINE BUSINESS PROGRAM(S)
post.edu/admissions
Admissions: (203) 596-6164
Email: adpadmissions@post.edu
Financial aid: (800) 345-2562
Application deadline: rolling
Program can be completed entirely online: Yes
Total program cost: $18,750 full-time in-state, $18,750 part-time in-state, $18,750 full-time out-of-state, $18,750 part-time out-of-state
Tuition per credit: $625 full-time in-state, $625 part-time in-state, $625 full-time out-of-state, $625 part-time out-of-state
Acceptance rate: 36.0%
Test scores required: No
Average age of entrants: 35
Students with prior work experience: 75.0%
Enrollment: 68, 35% men, 65% women, 25% minority, 0% international
Average class size: 6
Most popular business concentrations: accounting
Completion: Three year graduation rate: 84%; credits needed to graduate: 30; target time to graduate: 2 years

---

College funded aid available: Domestic: Yes; International: Yes
Graduates with debt: 56%

Quinnipiac University
Private

ONLINE MBA PROGRAM(S)
www.qu.edu/schools/business/programs/mba.html
Admissions: (877) 403-4277
Email: quonlineadmissions@quinnipiac.edu
Financial aid: (203) 582-3638
Application deadline: rolling
Program can be completed entirely online: Yes
Total program cost: $43,010 full-time in-state, $43,010 part-time in-state, $43,010 full-time out-of-state, $43,010 part-time out-of-state
Tuition per credit: $935 full-time in-state, $935 part-time in-state, $935 full-time out-of-state, $935 part-time out-of-state
Acceptance rate: 62.0%
Test scores required: GMAT or GRE
Average GMAT: 540
Average GRE: 152 verbal, 152 quantitative, 4.3 writing
Average age of entrants: 34
Students with prior work experience: 98.0%
Enrollment: 243, 56% men, 44% women, 15% minority, 0% international
Average class size: 29
Most popular MBA concentrations: finance, general management, health care administration, marketing, supply chain management/logistics
Completion: Three year graduation rate: 72%; credits needed to graduate: 46; target time to graduate: 4 years
College funded aid available: Domestic: No; International: No
Graduates with debt: 73%; average amount of debt $39,090

ONLINE BUSINESS PROGRAM(S)
quonline.quinnipiac.edu/
Admissions: (203) 582-7265
Email: Vincent.VanOss@quinnipiac.edu
Financial aid: (203) 582-8384
Application deadline: rolling
Program can be completed entirely online: Yes
Total program cost: $30,855 full-time in-state, $30,855 part-time in-state, $30,855 full-time out-of-state, $30,855 part-time out-of-state
Tuition per credit: $935 full-time in-state, $935 part-time in-state, $935 full-time out-of-state, $935 part-time out-of-state
Acceptance rate: 85.0%
Test scores required: No
Average GMAT: 540
Average age of entrants: 37
Students with prior work experience: 98.0%
Enrollment: 388, 43% men, 57% women, 28% minority, 0% international
Average class size: 26

Most popular business concentrations: general management, health care administration, human resources management, leadership, quantitative analysis/statistics and operations research
Completion: Three year graduation rate: 62%; credits needed to graduate: 33; target time to graduate: 2 years
College funded aid available: Domestic: No; International: No
Graduates with debt: 28%; average amount of debt $17,303

University of Connecticut
Public

ONLINE BUSINESS PROGRAM(S)
www.msaccounting.business.uconn.edu
Admissions: (860) 486-8180
Email: ricki.livingston@business.uconn.edu
Financial aid: (860) 486-2819
Application deadline: rolling
Program can be completed entirely online: No
Total program cost: $25,550 full-time in-state, $25,550 part-time in-state, $25,550 full-time out-of-state, $25,550 part-time out-of-state
Tuition per credit: $850 full-time in-state, $850 part-time in-state, $850 full-time out-of-state, $850 part-time out-of-state
Acceptance rate: 89.0%
Test scores required: GMAT
Average GMAT: 597
Average age of entrants: 26
Students with prior work experience: 61.0%
Enrollment: 194, 56% men, 44% women, 24% minority, 0% international
Average class size: 29
Most popular business concentrations: accounting
Completion: Three year graduation rate: 86%; credits needed to graduate: 30; target time to graduate: 1 year
College funded aid available: Domestic: No; International: No
Graduates with debt: 40%; average amount of debt $18,000

University of Hartford (Barney)
Private

ONLINE MBA PROGRAM(S)
www.hartford.edu/barney/graduate/graduate-programs/mba/admission/default.aspx
Admissions: (860) 768-5003
Email: mbainfo@hartford.edu
Financial aid: (860) 768-4296
Application deadline: rolling
Program can be completed entirely online: Yes
Total program cost: $25,020 full-time in-state, $25,020 part-time in-state, $25,020 full-time out-of-state, $25,020 part-time out-of-state
Tuition per credit: $695 full-time in-state, $695 part-time in-state, $695 full-time out-of-state, $695 part-time out-of-state

Acceptance rate: 42.0%
Average GMAT: 565
Average age of entrants: 31
Enrollment: 513, 51% men,
49% women, N/A minority,
N/A international
Average class size: 25
Most popular MBA
concentrations: finance, general
management, insurance,
marketing, quantitative
analysis/statistics and
operations research
Completion: Credits needed
to graduate: 36; target time
to graduate: 2 years

ONLINE BUSINESS PROGRAM(S)

www.hartford.edu/
barney/graduate
Admissions: (860) 768-4198
Email: msat@hartford.edu
Financial aid: (860) 768-4296
Application deadline: rolling
Program can be completed
entirely online: Yes
Total program cost: N/A
Tuition per credit: $695
full-time in-state, $695
part-time in-state, $695
full-time out-of-state, $695
part-time out-of-state
Acceptance rate: 62.0%
Average age of entrants: 31
Enrollment: 116, 53% men,
47% women, N/A minority,
N/A international
Average class size: 12
Completion: Credits needed
to graduate: 30; target time
to graduate: 1.5 years

DELAWARE

University of Delaware (Lerner)

Public

ONLINE MBA PROGRAM(S)

business.online.udel.edu/mba
Admissions: (302) 831-4626
Email: onlinemba@udel.edu
Financial aid: (302) 831-8189
Application deadline: rolling
Program can be completed
entirely online: Yes
Total program cost: $39,600
full-time in-state, $39,600
part-time in-state, $39,600
full-time out-of-state, $39,600
part-time out-of-state
Tuition per credit: $900
full-time in-state, $900
part-time in-state, $900
full-time out-of-state, $900
part-time out-of-state
Acceptance rate: 66.0%
Test scores required:
GMAT or GRE
Average GMAT: 593
Average GRE: 153 verbal, 156
quantitative, 4.3 writing
Average age of entrants: 35
Students with prior work
experience: 79.0%
Enrollment: 357, 58%
men, 42% women, 20%
minority, 4% international
Average class size: 22
Most popular MBA
concentrations: finance,
health care administration,
international business,
leadership
Completion: Three year
graduation rate: 73%; credits
needed to graduate: 44; target
time to graduate: 1.5 years

College funded aid
available: Domestic: Yes;
International: Yes
Graduates with debt: 71%;
average amount of debt $31,014

DISTRICT OF COLUMBIA

American University (Kogod)

Private

ONLINE MBA PROGRAM(S)

www.onlinebusiness.
american.edu
Admissions: (202) 885-2831
Email: admissions@
onlinebusiness.american.edu
Financial aid: (202) 885-6500
Application deadline: rolling
Program can be completed
entirely online: Depends
Total program cost: $81,984
full-time in-state, $81,984
part-time in-state, $81,984
full-time out-of-state, $81,984
part-time out-of-state
Tuition per credit: $1,708
full-time in-state, $1,708
part-time in-state, $1,708
full-time out-of-state, $1,708
part-time out-of-state
Acceptance rate: 84.0%
Test scores required: No
Average GMAT: 580
Average GRE: 155 verbal, 151
quantitative, 4.0 writing
Average age of entrants: 31
Students with prior work
experience: 98.0%
Enrollment: 543, 52%
men, 48% women, 56%
minority, 0% international
Average class size: 11
Most popular MBA
concentrations: consulting,
finance, general
management, marketing
Completion: Credits needed
to graduate: 48; target time
to graduate: 2 years
College funded aid
available: Domestic: Yes;
International: Yes
Graduates with debt: 64%;
average amount of debt $82,668

ONLINE BUSINESS PROGRAM(S)

www.onlinebusiness.
american.edu
Admissions: (202) 885-2831
Email: admissions@
onlinebusiness.american.edu
Financial aid: (202) 885-6500
Application deadline: rolling
Program can be completed
entirely online: Depends
Total program cost: $56,384
full-time in-state, $56,384
part-time in-state, $56,384
full-time out-of-state, $56,384
part-time out-of-state
Tuition per credit: $1,708
full-time in-state, $1,708
part-time in-state, $1,708
full-time out-of-state, $1,708
part-time out-of-state
Acceptance rate: 79.0%
Test scores required: No
Average GRE: 160 verbal, 157
quantitative, 4.0 writing
Average age of entrants: 33
Students with prior work
experience: 98.0%
Enrollment: 175, 50% men,
50% women, 50% minority,
0% international
Average class size: 13

Most popular business
concentrations: consulting,
finance, marketing, management
information systems,
quantitative analysis/statistics
and operations research
Completion: Credits needed
to graduate: 33; target time
to graduate: 1.5 years
College funded aid
available: Domestic: Yes;
International: Yes
Graduates with debt: 61%;
average amount of debt $42,653

George Washington University

Private

ONLINE MBA PROGRAM(S)

business.gwu.edu/programs/
online-programs/
Admissions: (202) 994-1212
Email: business@gwu.edu
Financial aid: (202) 994-6620
Application deadline: Domestic:
07/12; International: 07/12
Program can be completed
entirely online: Yes
Total program cost: $101,288
full-time in-state, $101,288
part-time in-state, $101,288
full-time out-of-state, $101,288
part-time out-of-state
Tuition per credit: $1,825
full-time in-state, $1,825
part-time in-state, $1,825
full-time out-of-state, $1,825
part-time out-of-state
Acceptance rate: 80.0%
Test scores required:
GMAT or GRE
Average GMAT: 590
Average GRE: 151 verbal, 147
quantitative, 4.0 writing
Average age of entrants: 37
Students with prior work
experience: 31.0%
Enrollment: 431, 52% men,
48% women, 47% minority,
3% international
Average class size: 38
Most popular MBA
concentrations: consulting,
entrepreneurship, finance,
health care administration,
international business
Completion: Three year
graduation rate: 70%; credits
needed to graduate: 55; target
time to graduate: 3 years
College funded aid available:
Domestic: Yes; International: No
Graduates with debt: 49%;
average amount of debt $73,159

ONLINE BUSINESS PROGRAM(S)

business.gwu.edu/programs/
online-programs/
Admissions: (202) 994-1212
Email: business@gwu.edu
Financial aid: (202) 994-5729
Application deadline: rolling
Program can be completed
entirely online: No
Total program cost: $56,430
full-time in-state, $56,430
part-time in-state, $56,430
full-time out-of-state, $56,430
part-time out-of-state
Tuition per credit: $1,710
full-time in-state, $1,710
part-time in-state, $1,710
full-time out-of-state, $1,710
part-time out-of-state
Acceptance rate: 81.0%
Test scores required: No

Average GRE: 153 verbal, 150
quantitative, 4.0 writing
Average age of entrants: 38
Students with prior work
experience: 96.0%
Enrollment: 62, 47% men,
53% women, 47% minority,
3% international
Average class size: 28
Completion: Three year
graduation rate: 72%; credits
needed to graduate: 33; target
time to graduate: 2.5 years
College funded aid available:
Domestic: Yes; International: No
Graduates with debt: 17%;
average amount of debt $43,687

Georgetown University (McDonough)

Private

ONLINE BUSINESS PROGRAM(S)

msbonline.georgetown.edu/
admissions
Admissions: (866) 531-4825
Email: msfadmissions@
georgetown.edu
Financial aid: (202) 687-4547
Application deadline: Domestic:
06/01; International: 06/01
Program can be completed
entirely online: No
Total program cost: $75,360
full-time in-state, $75,360
part-time in-state, $75,360
full-time out-of-state, $75,360
part-time out-of-state
Tuition per credit: $2,355
full-time in-state, $2,355
part-time in-state, $2,355
full-time out-of-state, $2,355
part-time out-of-state
Acceptance rate: 34.0%
Test scores required:
GMAT or GRE
Average GMAT: 670
Average GRE: 153 verbal, 151
quantitative, 4.0 writing
Average age of entrants: 30
Students with prior work
experience: 83.0%
Enrollment: 115, 71% men,
29% women, 35% minority,
0% international
Average class size: 45
Most popular business
concentrations: finance
Completion: Three year
graduation rate: 82%; credits
needed to graduate: 32; target
time to graduate: 2 years
College funded aid
available: Domestic: Yes;
International: Yes
Graduates with debt: 48%;
average amount of debt $60,705

FLORIDA

Embry-Riddle Aeronautical University–Worldwide

Private

ONLINE MBA PROGRAM(S)

worldwide.erau.edu/admissions/
Admissions: (800) 522-6787
Email: wwadmissions@erau.edu
Financial aid: (866) 567-7202
Application deadline: rolling
Program can be completed
entirely online: Yes
Total program cost: N/A

Tuition per credit: $665
full-time in-state, $665
part-time in-state, $665
full-time out-of-state, $665
part-time out-of-state
Acceptance rate: 91.0%
Test scores required: No
Average GMAT: 640
Average GRE: 145 verbal, 141
quantitative, 3.0 writing
Average age of entrants: 33
Enrollment: 931, 79% men,
21% women, 28% minority,
8% international
Average class size: 14
Most popular MBA
concentrations: finance,
international business,
leadership, marketing,
technology
Completion: Three year
graduation rate: 37%; credits
needed to graduate: 33; target
time to graduate: 2 years
College funded aid
available: Domestic: Yes;
International: Yes
Graduates with debt: 16%;
average amount of debt $11,120

ONLINE BUSINESS PROGRAM(S)

worldwide.erau.edu/admissions
Admissions: (800) 522-6787
Email: wwadmissions@erau.edu
Financial aid: (866) 567-7202
Application deadline: rolling
Program can be completed
entirely online: Yes
Total program cost: N/A
Tuition per credit: $665
full-time in-state, $665
part-time in-state, $665
full-time out-of-state, $665
part-time out-of-state
Acceptance rate: 90.0%
Test scores required: No
Average GMAT: 497
Average GRE: 150 verbal, 150
quantitative, 3.0 writing
Average age of entrants: 36
Enrollment: 2,520, 71%
men, 29% women, 34%
minority, 2% international
Average class size: 11
Most popular business
concentrations: general
management, leadership,
manufacturing and technology
management, supply chain
management/logistics
Completion: Three year
graduation rate: 42%; credits
needed to graduate: 30; target
time to graduate: 2 years
College funded aid
available: Domestic: Yes;
International: Yes
Graduates with debt: 16%;
average amount of debt $12,362

Florida A&M University

Public

ONLINE MBA PROGRAM(S)

elearning.famu.edu/
pos-sbi.php#pos
Admissions: (850) 599-3796
Email: famuonline@famu.edu
Financial aid: (850) 599-3730
Application deadline: rolling
Program can be completed
entirely online: Yes
Total program cost: N/A
Tuition per credit: $792 full-time
in-state, $792 part-time in-state,
$792 full-time out-of-state,
$792 part-time out-of-state

Acceptance rate: 37.0%
Test scores required: No
Average age of entrants: 37
Students with prior work experience: 100.0%
Enrollment: 13, 69% men, 31% women, 100% minority, 0% international
Most popular MBA concentrations: general management
Completion: Credits needed to graduate: 43

Florida Atlantic University

Public

ONLINE MBA PROGRAM(S)

business.fau.edu
Admissions: (561) 297-2470
Email: omba@fau.edu
Financial aid: (561) 297-3530
Application deadline: rolling
Program can be completed entirely online: Yes
Total program cost: $32,000
full-time in-state, $32,000 part-time in-state, $32,000 full-time out-of-state, $32,000 part-time out-of-state
Tuition per credit: $800
full-time in-state, $800 part-time in-state, $800 full-time out-of-state, $800 part-time out-of-state
Acceptance rate: 73.0%
Test scores required: No
Average GRE: 146 verbal, 148 quantitative, 3.2 writing
Average age of entrants: 31
Students with prior work experience: 90.0%
Enrollment: 254, 40% men, 60% women, N/A minority, N/A international
Average class size: 36
Most popular MBA concentrations: general management, international business, marketing, management information systems, sports business
Completion: Three year graduation rate: 93%; credits needed to graduate: 40; target time to graduate: 2 years
College funded aid available: Domestic: Yes; International: Yes
Graduates with debt: 75%; average amount of debt $38,500

ONLINE BUSINESS PROGRAM(S)

business.fau.edu
Admissions: (561) 297-0525
Email: jknox6@fau.edu
Financial aid: (561) 297-3530
Application deadline: rolling
Program can be completed entirely online: Yes
Total program cost: $19,200
full-time in-state, $12,800 part-time in-state, $19,200 full-time out-of-state, $12,800 part-time out-of-state
Tuition per credit: $1,067
full-time in-state, $1,067 part-time in-state, $1,067 full-time out-of-state, $1,067 part-time out-of-state
Acceptance rate: 71.0%
Test scores required: No
Average GMAT: 560
Average age of entrants: 33

Enrollment: 676, 37% men, 63% women, N/A minority, N/A international
Average class size: 31
Most popular business concentrations: accounting, health care administration, tax
Completion: Three year graduation rate: 73%; credits needed to graduate: 30; target time to graduate: 2 years
College funded aid available: Domestic: Yes; International: No

Florida Institute of Technology

Private

ONLINE MBA PROGRAM(S)

www.fit.edu
Admissions: (321) 674-7118
Email: gradadm-olocp@fit.edu
Financial aid: (321) 674-8070
Application deadline: rolling
Program can be completed entirely online: Yes
Total program cost: N/A
Tuition per credit: $896
full-time in-state, $896 part-time in-state, $896 full-time out-of-state, $896 part-time out-of-state
Acceptance rate: 45.0%
Test scores required: No
Average GRE: 146 verbal, 145 quantitative
Average age of entrants: 34
Enrollment: 948, 49% men, 51% women, 41% minority, 1% international
Average class size: 18
Most popular MBA concentrations: general management, health care administration, production/operations management, supply chain management/logistics
Completion: Three year graduation rate: 50%; credits needed to graduate: 36; target time to graduate: 2 years
College funded aid available: Domestic: No; International: No
Graduates with debt: 59%; average amount of debt $40,962

ONLINE BUSINESS PROGRAM(S)

www.fit.edu
Admissions: (321) 674-7118
Email: gradadm-olocp@fit.edu
Financial aid: (321) 674-8070
Application deadline: rolling
Program can be completed entirely online: Yes
Total program cost: N/A
Tuition per credit: $777 full-time in-state, $777 part-time in-state, $777 full-time out-of-state, $777 part-time out-of-state
Acceptance rate: 57.0%
Test scores required: No
Average age of entrants: 34
Enrollment: 677, 67% men, 33% women, 39% minority, 2% international
Average class size: 18
Most popular business concentrations: health care administration, production/operations management, supply chain management/logistics, technology
Completion: Three year graduation rate: 52%; credits needed to graduate: 33; target time to graduate: 2 years

College funded aid available:
Domestic: No; International: No
Graduates with debt: 28%; average amount of debt $41,464

Florida International University

Public

ONLINE MBA PROGRAM(S)

Admissions: (305) 348-3125
Email: chapman@fiu.edu
Financial aid: (305) 348-4234
Application deadline: rolling
Program can be completed entirely online: Depends
Total program cost: $42,000
full-time in-state, $42,000 part-time in-state, $42,000 full-time out-of-state, $42,000 part-time out-of-state
Tuition per credit: $1,000
full-time in-state, $1,000 part-time in-state, $1,000 full-time out-of-state, $1,000 part-time out-of-state
Acceptance rate: 64.0%
Test scores required: No
Average GMAT: 500
Average age of entrants: 32
Students with prior work experience: 100.0%
Enrollment: 865, 48% men, 52% women, 75% minority, 1% international
Average class size: 11
Most popular MBA concentrations: finance, general management, health care administration, international business, marketing
Completion: Three year graduation rate: 74%; credits needed to graduate: 42; target time to graduate: 1.5 years
College funded aid available: Domestic: Yes
Graduates with debt: 76%; average amount of debt $48,902

ONLINE BUSINESS PROGRAM(S)

Admissions: (305) 348-3125
Email: chapman@fiu.edu
Financial aid: (305) 348-4234
Application deadline: rolling
Program can be completed entirely online: Yes
Total program cost: $35,000
full-time in-state, $35,000 part-time in-state, $35,000 full-time out-of-state, $35,000 part-time out-of-state
Tuition per credit: $921 full-time in-state, $921 part-time in-state, $921 full-time out-of-state, $921 part-time out-of-state
Acceptance rate: 51.0%
Test scores required: No
Average GMAT: 582
Average GRE: 150 verbal, 153 quantitative, 3.9 writing
Average age of entrants: 33
Students with prior work experience: 100.0%
Enrollment: 154, 25% men, 75% women, 80% minority, 1% international
Average class size: 11
Most popular business concentrations: health care administration, human resources management, international business, real estate
Completion: Three year graduation rate: 85%; credits needed to graduate: 36; target time to graduate: 1 year

College funded aid available:
Domestic: No; International: No
Graduates with debt: 80%; average amount of debt $42,881

Florida Southern College

Private

ONLINE MBA PROGRAM(S)

www.flsouthern.edu/sage/graduate/master-of-business-administration.aspx
Admissions: (863) 680-4205
Email: evening@flsouthern.edu
Financial aid: (863) 680-4140
Application deadline: rolling
Program can be completed entirely online: No
Total program cost: $34,100
full-time in-state, $34,100 part-time in-state, $34,100 full-time out-of-state, $34,100 part-time out-of-state
Tuition per credit: $775 full-time in-state, $775 part-time in-state, $775 full-time out-of-state, $775 part-time out-of-state
Acceptance rate: 38.0%
Test scores required: GMAT or GRE
Average GRE: 149 verbal, 146 quantitative, 3.0 writing
Average age of entrants: 23
Students with prior work experience: 100.0%
Enrollment: 16, 56% men, 44% women, 19% minority, 0% international
Average class size: 7
Most popular MBA concentrations: general management
Completion: Credits needed to graduate: 44; target time to graduate: 2 years
College funded aid available: Domestic: Yes; International: Yes
Graduates with debt: 50%

Florida State University

Public

ONLINE MBA PROGRAM(S)

admissions.fsu.edu/gradapp
Admissions: (850) 644-6458
Email: graduateadmissions@business.fsu.edu
Financial aid: (850) 644-0539
Application deadline: rolling
Program can be completed entirely online: Yes
Total program cost: $29,250
full-time in-state, $29,250 part-time in-state, $29,250 full-time out-of-state, $29,250 part-time out-of-state
Tuition per credit: $750 full-time in-state, $750 part-time in-state, $750 full-time out-of-state, $750 part-time out-of-state
Acceptance rate: 66.0%
Test scores required: GMAT or GRE
Average GMAT: 575
Average GRE: 157 verbal, 154 quantitative
Average age of entrants: 34
Students with prior work experience: 99.0%
Enrollment: 211, 72% men, 28% women, 23% minority, 1% international
Average class size: 41

Most popular MBA concentrations: general management, real estate
Completion: Three year graduation rate: 51%; credits needed to graduate: 39; target time to graduate: 2.5 years
College funded aid available: Domestic: Yes; International: Yes
Graduates with debt: 42%; average amount of debt $45,819

ONLINE BUSINESS PROGRAM(S)

admissions.fsu.edu/gradapp
Admissions: (850) 644-6458
Email: graduateadmissions@business.fsu.edu
Financial aid: (850) 644-0539
Application deadline: Domestic: 06/01; International: 06/01
Program can be completed entirely online: Yes
Total program cost: $19,800
full-time in-state, $19,800 part-time in-state, $19,800 full-time out-of-state, $19,800 part-time out-of-state
Tuition per credit: $600
full-time in-state, $600 part-time in-state, $600 full-time out-of-state, $600 part-time out-of-state
Acceptance rate: 68.0%
Test scores required: GMAT or GRE
Average GMAT: 535
Average GRE: 151 verbal, 148 quantitative
Average age of entrants: 36
Students with prior work experience: 98.0%
Enrollment: 122, 57% men, 43% women, 30% minority, 1% international
Average class size: 19
Most popular business concentrations: insurance, management information systems
Completion: Three year graduation rate: 86%; credits needed to graduate: 33; target time to graduate: 2 years
College funded aid available: Domestic: Yes; International: Yes
Graduates with debt: 31%; average amount of debt $37,915

Keiser University

Private

ONLINE MBA PROGRAM(S)

www.keiseruniversity.edu/
Admissions: (954) 776-4476
Financial aid: (954) 318-1620
Application deadline: rolling
Program can be completed entirely online: Yes
Total program cost: $27,072
full-time in-state, $6,768 part-time in-state, $27,072 full-time out-of-state, $6,768 part-time out-of-state
Tuition per credit: $1,128
full-time in-state, $1,128 part-time in-state, $1,128 full-time out-of-state, $1,128 part-time out-of-state
Acceptance rate: 100.0%
Average age of entrants: 37
Enrollment: 493, 40% men, 60% women, 62% minority, 8% international
Average class size: 12
Most popular MBA concentrations: accounting,

general management, health care administration, international business, marketing
Completion: Three year graduation rate: 68%; target time to graduate: 2 years

ONLINE BUSINESS PROGRAM(S)

www.keiseruniversity.edu/
Admissions: (954) 318-1620
Email: tdelvecchio@
keiseruniversity.edu
Financial aid: (954) 318-1620
Application deadline: N/A
Program can be completed entirely online: Yes
Total program cost: N/A
Tuition per credit: $1,128
full-time in-state, $1,128
part-time in-state, $1,128
full-time out-of-state, $1,128
part-time out-of-state
Acceptance rate: 99.0%
Average age of entrants: 40
Enrollment: 89, 34% men, 66% women, 82% minority, 0% international
Average class size: 15
Most popular business concentrations: accounting, general management, leadership
Completion: Three year graduation rate: 47%; target time to graduate: 1.5 years

Lynn University

Private

ONLINE MBA PROGRAM(S)

onlinemba.lynn.edu/admissions/
Admissions: (561) 237-7834
Email: spruitt@lynn.edu
Financial aid: (561) 237-7973
Application deadline: rolling
Program can be completed entirely online: Yes
Total program cost: $26,640
full-time in-state, $26,640
part-time in-state, $26,640
full-time out-of-state, $26,640
part-time out-of-state
Tuition per credit: $740 full-time in-state, $740 part-time in-state, $740 full-time out-of-state, $740 part-time out-of-state
Acceptance rate: 89.0%
Test scores required: No
Average age of entrants: 29
Enrollment: 658, 50% men, 50% women, 27% minority, 25% international
Average class size: 18
Most popular MBA concentrations: entrepreneurship, finance, human resources management, international business, marketing
Completion: Three year graduation rate: 79%; credits needed to graduate: 36; target time to graduate: 1 year
College funded aid available: Domestic: Yes; International: Yes
Graduates with debt: 49%; average amount of debt $35,307

Nova Southeastern University

Private

ONLINE MBA PROGRAM(S)

www.business.nova.edu
Admissions: (954) 262-5119
Email: sumulong@nova.edu

Financial aid: (954) 262-7456
Application deadline: rolling
Program can be completed entirely online: Yes
Total program cost: $37,941
full-time in-state, $37,941
part-time in-state, $37,941
full-time out-of-state, $37,941
part-time out-of-state
Tuition per credit: $899
full-time in-state, $899
part-time in-state, $899
full-time out-of-state, $899
part-time out-of-state
Acceptance rate: 82.0%
Enrollment: 2,387, 36% men, 64% women, 66% minority, 11% international
Average class size: 20
Most popular MBA concentrations: entrepreneurship, finance, general management, human resources management, marketing
Completion: Credits needed to graduate: 39; target time to graduate: 2.5 years
College funded aid available: Domestic: Yes; International: Yes

ONLINE BUSINESS PROGRAM(S)

business.nova.edu
Admissions: (800) 672-7223
Email: sumulong@nova.edu
Financial aid: (954) 262-7456
Application deadline: rolling
Program can be completed entirely online: Depends
Total program cost: $35,061
full-time in-state, $35,061
part-time in-state, $35,061
full-time out-of-state, $35,061
part-time out-of-state
Tuition per credit: $899
full-time in-state, $899
part-time in-state, $899
full-time out-of-state, $899
part-time out-of-state
Acceptance rate: 82.0%
Enrollment: 302, 36% men, 64% women, 72% minority, 2% international
Average class size: 20
Most popular business concentrations: accounting, public administration, real estate, tax
Completion: Credits needed to graduate: 40; target time to graduate: 2.5 years
College funded aid available: Domestic: Yes

Saint Leo University

Private

ONLINE MBA PROGRAM(S)

www.saintleo.edu/
graduate-admissions
Admissions: (352) 588-7573
Email: mark.russum@
saintleo.edu
Financial aid: (813) 226-4858
Application deadline: rolling
Program can be completed entirely online: Yes
Total program cost: N/A
Tuition per credit:
Test scores required: No
Enrollment: 1,913, N/A minority, N/A international
Most popular MBA concentrations: accounting, health care administration, human resources management, marketing, management information systems

Completion: Credits needed to graduate: 36

Southeastern University

Private

ONLINE MBA PROGRAM(S)

seu.edu
Admissions: (863) 667-5999
Email: admission@seu.edu
Financial aid: (863) 667-8760
Application deadline: rolling
Program can be completed entirely online: Yes
Total program cost: N/A
Tuition per credit: $525
full-time in-state, $525
part-time in-state, $525
full-time out-of-state, $525
part-time out-of-state
Test scores required: No
Enrollment: 215, 51% men, 49% women, N/A minority, N/A international
Average class size: 17
Most popular MBA concentrations: leadership
Completion: Credits needed to graduate: 39; target time to graduate: 2 years

Stetson University

Private

ONLINE MBA PROGRAM(S)

www.stetson.edu/graduate
Admissions: (386) 822-7100
Email: gradadmissions@
stetson.edu
Financial aid: (386) 822-7120
Application deadline: rolling
Program can be completed entirely online: Yes
Total program cost: N/A
Tuition per credit: $1,020
full-time in-state, $1,020
part-time in-state, $1,020
full-time out-of-state, $1,020
part-time out-of-state
Acceptance rate: 92.0%
Test scores required: No
Average age of entrants: 33
Enrollment: 22, 36% men, 64% women, 36% minority, 0% international
Average class size: 10
Most popular MBA concentrations: general management
Completion: Three year graduation rate: 64%; credits needed to graduate: 30; target time to graduate: 2.5 years
College funded aid available: Domestic: No; International: Yes
Graduates with debt: 50%; average amount of debt $41,346

ONLINE BUSINESS PROGRAM(S)

www.stetson.edu/graduate
Admissions: (386) 822-7100
Email: gradadmissions@
stetson.edu
Financial aid: (386) 822-7120
Application deadline: rolling
Program can be completed entirely online: Yes
Total program cost: $27,000
full-time in-state, $27,000
part-time in-state, $27,000
full-time out-of-state, $27,000
part-time out-of-state
Tuition per credit: $900
full-time in-state,
$900 part-time in-state,

$900 full-time out-of-state,
$900 part-time out-of-state
Acceptance rate: 59.0%
Test scores required: GMAT or GRE
Average GMAT: 553
Average GRE: 159 verbal, 152 quantitative
Average age of entrants: 33
Enrollment: 20, 35% men, 65% women, 20% minority, 5% international
Average class size: 10
Most popular business concentrations: accounting, tax
Completion: Three year graduation rate: 79%; credits needed to graduate: 30; target time to graduate: 1 year
College funded aid available: Domestic: Yes
Graduates with debt: 70%; average amount of debt $22,432

University of Florida (Hough)

Public

ONLINE MBA PROGRAM(S)

www.floridamba.ufl.edu
Admissions: (352) 392-7992
Email: FloridaMBA@
warrington.ufl.edu
Financial aid: (352) 273-4960
Application deadline: rolling
Program can be completed entirely online: Depends
Total program cost: $58,000
part-time in-state, $58,000
part-time out-of-state
Tuition per credit: $531
full-time in-state, $1,208
part-time in-state, $1,255
full-time out-of-state, $1,208
part-time out-of-state
Acceptance rate: 46.0%
Test scores required: GMAT or GRE
Average GMAT: 588
Average GRE: 152 verbal, 151 quantitative
Average age of entrants: 29
Students with prior work experience: 100.0%
Enrollment: 391, 64% men, 36% women, 32% minority, 3% international
Average class size: 42
Most popular MBA concentrations: entrepreneurship, finance, general management, international business, marketing
Completion: Three year graduation rate: 97%; credits needed to graduate: 48; target time to graduate: 2 years
College funded aid available: Domestic: No; International: No
Graduates with debt: 50%; average amount of debt $54,664

University of Miami

Private

ONLINE MBA PROGRAM(S)

miami.edu/online
Admissions: (800) 411-2290
Email: onlineinfo@miami.edu
Financial aid: (305) 284-3115
Application deadline: rolling
Program can be completed entirely online: Yes
Total program cost: $85,260
full-time in-state,
$85,260 part-time in-state,

$85,260 full-time out-of-state,
$85,260 part-time out-of-state
Tuition per credit: $2,030
full-time in-state, $2,030
part-time in-state, $2,030
full-time out-of-state, $2,030
part-time out-of-state
Acceptance rate: 34.0%
Average GMAT: 620
Average age of entrants: 33
Students with prior work experience: 100.0%
Enrollment: 56, 68% men, 32% women, 25% minority, 0% international
Average class size: 24
Completion: Credits needed to graduate: 42; target time to graduate: 2 years
College funded aid available: Domestic: Yes; International: Yes
Graduates with debt: 50%; average amount of debt $50,000

ONLINE BUSINESS PROGRAM(S)

miami.edu/online
Admissions: (800) 411-2290
Email: onlineinfo@miami.edu
Financial aid: (305) 284-3115
Application deadline: rolling
Program can be completed entirely online: Yes
Total program cost: $64,960
full-time in-state, $64,960
part-time in-state, $64,960
full-time out-of-state, $64,960
part-time out-of-state
Tuition per credit: $2,030
full-time in-state, $2,030
part-time in-state, $2,030
full-time out-of-state, $2,030
part-time out-of-state
Acceptance rate: 56.0%
Test scores required: GMAT or GRE
Average GMAT: 655
Average age of entrants: 32
Students with prior work experience: 97.0%
Enrollment: 119, 61% men, 39% women, 22% minority, 0% international
Average class size: 13
Completion: Three year graduation rate: 66%; credits needed to graduate: 32; target time to graduate: 1.5 years
College funded aid available: Domestic: Yes; International: Yes
Graduates with debt: 25%; average amount of debt $30,000

University of South Florida

Public

ONLINE MBA PROGRAM(S)

www.usf.edu/business/
graduate/mba-online/
Admissions: (813) 974-3335
Email: aartis@usf.edu
Financial aid: (813) 974-4700
Application deadline: rolling
Program can be completed entirely online: Depends
Total program cost: $28,800
full-time in-state, $28,800
part-time in-state, $28,800
full-time out-of-state, $28,800
part-time out-of-state
Tuition per credit: $900
full-time in-state, $900
part-time in-state, $900

full-time out-of-state, $900
part-time out-of-state
Acceptance rate: 48.0%
Test scores required:
GMAT or GRE
Average GMAT: 563
Average GRE: 144 verbal,
155 quantitative
Average age of entrants: 32
**Students with prior work
experience:** 100.0%
Enrollment: 39, 67% men,
33% women, 31% minority,
0% international
Average class size: 6
Completion: Credits needed
to graduate: 32; target time
to graduate: 2 years
College funded aid available:
Domestic: No; International: No

University of South Florida–St. Petersburg (Tiedemann)
Public

ONLINE MBA PROGRAM(S)
www.usfsp.edu/mba
Admissions: (727) 873-4622
Email: mba@usfsp.edu
Financial aid: (727) 873-4128
Application deadline: rolling
**Program can be completed
entirely online:** Yes
Total program cost: $16,617
full-time in-state, $16,617
part-time in-state, $32,664
full-time out-of-state, $32,664
part-time out-of-state
Tuition per credit: $462
full-time in-state, $462
full-time out-of-state, $907
part-time out-of-state
Acceptance rate: 31.0%
Test scores required:
GMAT or GRE
Average GMAT: 523
Average GRE: 152 verbal, 150
quantitative, 3.6 writing
Average age of entrants: 32
**Students with prior work
experience:** 86.0%
Enrollment: 317, 54% men,
46% women, 27% minority,
2% international
Average class size: 27
**Most popular MBA
concentrations:** finance, general
management, international
business, management
information systems
Completion: Three year
graduation rate: 74%; credits
needed to graduate: 36; target
time to graduate: 2 years
**College funded aid
available:** Domestic: Yes;
International: Yes
Graduates with debt: 36%;
average amount of debt $36,576

Warner University
Private

ONLINE MBA PROGRAM(S)
Admissions: (863) 638-7212
Email: admissions@warner.edu
Financial aid: (863) 638-7202
Application deadline: rolling
**Program can be completed
entirely online:** Depends
Total program cost: $20,016
full-time in-state, $20,016
part-time in-state, $20,016

full-time out-of-state, $20,016
part-time out-of-state
Tuition per credit: $556
full-time in-state, $556
part-time in-state, $556
full-time out-of-state, $556
part-time out-of-state
Acceptance rate: 71.0%
Test scores required: No
Average age of entrants: 31
Enrollment: 44, 55% men,
45% women, 52% minority,
2% international
Average class size: 9
**Most popular MBA
concentrations:** accounting,
human resources management,
international business
Completion: Three year
graduation rate: 64%; credits
needed to graduate: 36; target
time to graduate: 2 years
**College funded aid
available:** Domestic: Yes;
International: Yes
Graduates with debt: 38%;
average amount of debt $42,796

ONLINE BUSINESS PROGRAM(S)
Admissions: (863) 638-7212
Email: admissions@warner.edu
Financial aid: (863) 638-7202
Application deadline: rolling
**Program can be completed
entirely online:** Depends
Total program cost: $20,016
full-time in-state, $20,016
part-time in-state, $20,016
full-time out-of-state, $20,016
part-time out-of-state
Tuition per credit: $556
full-time in-state, $556
part-time in-state, $556
full-time out-of-state, $556
part-time out-of-state
Acceptance rate: 69.0%
Test scores required: No
Average age of entrants: 33
Enrollment: 18, 61% men,
39% women, 56% minority,
6% international
Average class size: 13
**Most popular business
concentrations:** general
management
Completion: Three year
graduation rate: 40%; credits
needed to graduate: 36; target
time to graduate: 2 years
**College funded aid
available:** Domestic: Yes;
International: Yes
Graduates with debt: 76%;
average amount of debt $33,778

Webber International University
Private

ONLINE MBA PROGRAM(S)
webber.edu/admissions/apply/
Admissions: (863) 638-2910
Email: admissions@webber.edu
Financial aid: (863) 638-2929
Application deadline: rolling
**Program can be completed
entirely online:** Yes
Total program cost: $24,768
full-time in-state, $24,768
part-time in-state, $24,768
full-time out-of-state, $24,768
part-time out-of-state
Tuition per credit: $688
full-time in-state, $688
part-time in-state, $688
full-time out-of-state, $688
part-time out-of-state
Acceptance rate: 42.0%

Test scores required: No
**Students with prior work
experience:** 20.0%
Enrollment: 13, 62% men,
38% women, 23% minority,
0% international
Average class size: 6
**Most popular MBA
concentrations:** international
business
Completion: Credits needed
to graduate: 36; target time
to graduate: 1.5 years
**College funded aid
available:** Domestic: Yes;
International: Yes
Graduates with debt: 75%;
average amount of debt $27,124

GEORGIA

Brenau University
Private

ONLINE MBA PROGRAM(S)
www.brenau.edu/
admissions/grad/
Admissions: (770) 534-6162
Email: ngoss@brenau.edu
Financial aid: (770) 534-6152
Application deadline: rolling
**Program can be completed
entirely online:** Yes
Total program cost: $35,445
full-time in-state, $35,445
part-time in-state, $35,455
full-time out-of-state, $35,455
part-time out-of-state
Tuition per credit: $695
full-time in-state, $695
part-time in-state, $695
full-time out-of-state, $695
part-time out-of-state
Acceptance rate: 61.0%
Test scores required: No
Average age of entrants: 34
**Students with prior work
experience:** 100.0%
Enrollment: 530, 25% men,
75% women, N/A minority,
N/A international
Average class size: 13
**Most popular MBA
concentrations:** accounting,
general management,
health care administration,
human resources
management, production/
operations management
Completion: Three year
graduation rate: 61%; credits
needed to graduate: 45; target
time to graduate: 2 years
College funded aid available:
Domestic: No; International: No
Graduates with debt: 76%;
average amount of debt $52,305

Columbus State University (Turner)
Public

ONLINE MBA PROGRAM(S)
admissions.columbusstate.edu/
grad/index.php
Admissions: (706) 507-8800
Email: admissions@
columbusstate.edu
Financial aid: (706) 507-8898
Application deadline: Domestic:
06/30; International: 06/01
**Program can be completed
entirely online:** No
Total program cost: $22,170
part-time in-state, $22,170
part-time out-of-state

Tuition per credit: $739 full-time
in-state, $739 part-time in-state,
$739 full-time out-of-state,
$739 part-time out-of-state
Acceptance rate: 86.0%
Test scores required:
GMAT or GRE
Average GMAT: 540
Average GRE: 150 verbal, 148
quantitative, 3.2 writing
Average age of entrants: 29
**Students with prior work
experience:** 100.0%
Enrollment: 24, 50% men,
50% women, 75% minority,
0% international
Average class size: 5
**Most popular MBA
concentrations:** general
management
Completion: Three year
graduation rate: 89%; credits
needed to graduate: 30; target
time to graduate: 1.5 years
**College funded aid
available:** Domestic: Yes;
International: Yes
Graduates with debt: 50%;
average amount of debt $28,225

Georgia College & State University (Bunting)
Public

ONLINE MBA PROGRAM(S)
webmba.gcsu.edu
Admissions: (478) 445-5115
Email: mba@gcsu.edu
Financial aid: (478) 445-5149
Application deadline: rolling
**Program can be completed
entirely online:** No
Total program cost: $22,170
full-time in-state, $22,170
part-time in-state, $22,170
full-time out-of-state, $22,170
part-time out-of-state
Tuition per credit: $739 full-time
in-state, $739 part-time in-state,
$739 full-time out-of-state,
$739 part-time out-of-state
Acceptance rate: 88.0%
Test scores required:
GMAT or GRE
Average GMAT: 557
Average age of entrants: 36
**Students with prior work
experience:** 100.0%
Enrollment: 54, 59% men,
41% women, 35% minority,
0% international
Average class size: 14
Completion: Three year
graduation rate: 94%; credits
needed to graduate: 30; target
time to graduate: 1.5 years
College funded aid available:
Domestic: Yes; International: No
Graduates with debt: 28%;
average amount of debt $22,697

ONLINE BUSINESS PROGRAM(S)
mlscm.gcsu.edu
Admissions: (478) 445-5115
Email: mlscm@gcsu.edu
Financial aid: (478) 445-5149
Application deadline: rolling
**Program can be completed
entirely online:** No
Total program cost: $14,010
full-time in-state, $14,010
part-time in-state, $14,010
full-time out-of-state, $14,010
part-time out-of-state
Tuition per credit: $467 full-time
in-state, $467 part-time in-state,

$467 full-time out-of-state,
$467 part-time out-of-state
Acceptance rate: 88.0%
Test scores required:
GMAT or GRE
Average GMAT: 541
Average GRE: 161 verbal, 144
quantitative, 3.8 writing
Average age of entrants: 35
**Students with prior work
experience:** 100.0%
Enrollment: 95, 59% men,
41% women, 29% minority,
1% international
Average class size: 27
Completion: Three year
graduation rate: 83%; credits
needed to graduate: 30; target
time to graduate: 1.5 years
College funded aid available:
Domestic: No; International: No
Graduates with debt: 45%;
average amount of debt $24,042

Georgia Southern University
Public

ONLINE MBA PROGRAM(S)
cogs.georgiasouthern.edu/
admission/
Admissions: (912) 478-5384
Email: gradadmissions@
georgiasouthern.edu
Financial aid: (912) 478-5413
Application deadline: rolling
**Program can be completed
entirely online:** No
Total program cost: $13,302
full-time in-state, $13,302
part-time in-state, $13,302
full-time out-of-state, $13,302
part-time out-of-state
Tuition per credit: $739 full-time
in-state, $739 part-time in-state,
$739 full-time out-of-state,
$739 part-time out-of-state
Acceptance rate: 91.0%
Test scores required:
GMAT or GRE
Average GMAT: 503
Average GRE: 155 verbal, 152
quantitative, 3.0 writing
Average age of entrants: 34
Enrollment: 151, 59% men,
41% women, 33% minority,
2% international
Average class size: 24
**Most popular MBA
concentrations:** general
management
Completion: Three year
graduation rate: 91%; credits
needed to graduate: 30; target
time to graduate: 2 years
College funded aid available:
Domestic: No; International: No
Graduates with debt: average
amount of debt $26,935

ONLINE BUSINESS PROGRAM(S)
cogs.georgiasouthern.edu/
admission/
Admissions: (912) 478-5384
Email: gradadmissions@
georgiasouthern.edu
Financial aid: (912) 478-5413
Application deadline: rolling
**Program can be completed
entirely online:** Yes
Total program cost: $9,486
full-time in-state, $9,486
part-time in-state, $9,486
full-time out-of-state, $9,486
part-time out-of-state
Tuition per credit: $527 full-time
in-state, $527 part-time in-state,

$527 full-time out-of-state, $527 part-time out-of-state
Acceptance rate: 96.0%
Test scores required: GMAT or GRE
Average GMAT: 491
Average GRE: 157 verbal, 156 quantitative, 4.0 writing
Average age of entrants: 29
Enrollment: 125, 40% men, 60% women, N/A minority, N/A international
Average class size: 32
Most popular business concentrations: accounting, economics
Completion: Three year graduation rate: 61%; credits needed to graduate: 30; target time to graduate: 2 years
College funded aid available: Domestic: Yes; International: No
Graduates with debt: average amount of debt $31,684

Kennesaw State University (Coles)

Public

ONLINE MBA PROGRAM(S)

graduate.kennesaw.edu/ admissions/
Admissions: (470) 578-4377
Email: ksugrad@kennesaw.edu
Financial aid: (470) 578-2044
Application deadline: rolling
Program can be completed entirely online: Depends
Total program cost: $24,370 full-time in-state, $24,370 part-time in-state, $24,370 full-time out-of-state, $24,370 part-time out-of-state
Tuition per credit: $383 full-time in-state, $383 part-time in-state, $383 full-time out-of-state, $383 part-time out-of-state
Acceptance rate: 70.0%
Test scores required: GMAT or GRE
Average GMAT: 560
Average GRE: 151 verbal, 155 quantitative, 4.0 writing
Average age of entrants: 36
Students with prior work experience: 100.0%
Enrollment: 200, 52% men, 49% women, 47% minority, 0% international
Average class size: 32
Completion: Credits needed to graduate: 30; target time to graduate: 1.5 years
College funded aid available: Domestic: Yes; International: Yes
Graduates with debt: 47%; average amount of debt $14,724

Mercer University–Atlanta (Stetson)

Private

ONLINE MBA PROGRAM(S)

Admissions: (678) 547-6159
Email: whiteside_l@mercer.edu
Financial aid: (678) 547-6467
Application deadline: rolling
Program can be completed entirely online: Yes
Total program cost: $27,180 full-time in-state, $27,180 part-time in-state, $27,180 full-time out-of-state, $27,180 part-time out-of-state

Tuition per credit: $755 full-time in-state, $755 part-time in-state, $755 full-time out-of-state, $755 part-time out-of-state
Acceptance rate: 64.0%
Test scores required: GMAT or GRE
Average GMAT: 523
Average GRE: 152 verbal, 153 quantitative
Average age of entrants: 33
Students with prior work experience: 93.0%
Enrollment: 64, 44% men, 56% women, N/A minority, N/A international
Average class size: 19
Most popular MBA concentrations: economics, entrepreneurship, finance, health care administration, marketing
Completion: Credits needed to graduate: 36; target time to graduate: 2 years
College funded aid available: Domestic: Yes; International: No
Graduates with debt: 70%; average amount of debt $20,000

ONLINE BUSINESS PROGRAM(S)

business.mercer.edu/ programs/online-mba/
Admissions: (678) 547-6300
Email: business. admissions@mercer.edu
Financial aid: (678) 547-6444
Application deadline: N/A
Total program cost: N/A
Tuition per credit:

University of Georgia (Terry)

Public

ONLINE BUSINESS PROGRAM(S)

www.terry.uga.edu/mbt
Admissions: (706) 542-3589
Email: cpiercy@uga.edu
Financial aid: (706) 542-6147
Application deadline: rolling
Program can be completed entirely online: Yes
Total program cost: $24,750 full-time in-state, $24,750 part-time in-state, $24,750 full-time out-of-state, $24,750 part-time out-of-state
Tuition per credit: $825 full-time in-state, $825 part-time in-state, $825 full-time out-of-state, $825 part-time out-of-state
Acceptance rate: 74.0%
Test scores required: GMAT or GRE
Average GMAT: 500
Average GRE: 148 verbal, 149 quantitative, 3.5 writing
Average age of entrants: 32
Students with prior work experience: 65.0%
Enrollment: 33, 76% men, 24% women, 39% minority, 6% international
Average class size: 18
Most popular business concentrations: e-commerce, entrepreneurship, management information systems, technology
Completion: Three year graduation rate: 80%; credits needed to graduate: 30; target time to graduate: 2 years
College funded aid available: Domestic: No; International: No

Graduates with debt: 61%; average amount of debt $17,555

University of West Georgia

Public

ONLINE MBA PROGRAM(S)

www.westga.edu/academics/ program_page.php?program_ id=189
Admissions: (678) 839-5355
Email: hudombon@westga.edu
Financial aid: (678) 839-6421
Application deadline: Domestic: 07/30; International: 06/01
Program can be completed entirely online: Depends
Total program cost: N/A
Tuition per credit: $739 full-time in-state, $739 part-time in-state, $739 full-time out-of-state, $739 part-time out-of-state
Acceptance rate: 84.0%
Test scores required: GMAT or GRE
Average GMAT: 404
Average GRE: 146 verbal, 146 quantitative, 3.5 writing
Enrollment: 94, 52% men, 48% women, 39% minority, 2% international
Average class size: 19
Most popular MBA concentrations: accounting
Completion: Three year graduation rate: 90%; credits needed to graduate: 30; target time to graduate: 1.5 years
Graduates with debt: 43%; average amount of debt $35,145

Valdosta State University (Langdale)

Public

ONLINE MBA PROGRAM(S)

www.valdosta.edu/academics/ graduate-school/
Admissions: (229) 333-5694
Email: rlwaters@valdosta.edu
Financial aid: (229) 333-5935
Application deadline: N/A
Program can be completed entirely online: Yes
Total program cost: $22,170 full-time in-state, $22,170 part-time in-state, $22,170 full-time out-of-state, $22,170 part-time out-of-state
Tuition per credit: $739 full-time in-state, $739 part-time in-state, $739 full-time out-of-state, $739 part-time out-of-state
Test scores required: GMAT or GRE
Enrollment: 15, 33% men, 67% women, 47% minority, 0% international
Average class size: 8
Most popular MBA concentrations: general management, health care administration
Completion: Three year graduation rate: 80%; credits needed to graduate: 30; target time to graduate: 1.5 years
College funded aid available: Domestic: Yes; International: Yes
Graduates with debt: 63%; average amount of debt $38,444

IDAHO

Boise State University

Public

ONLINE MBA PROGRAM(S)

degree.boisestate.edu/ admissions.aspx
Admissions: (855) 290-3840
Email: OnlineMBA@ boisestate.edu
Financial aid: (208) 426-1664
Application deadline: rolling
Program can be completed entirely online: Yes
Total program cost: $36,750 full-time in-state, $36,750 part-time in-state, $36,750 full-time out-of-state, $36,750 part-time out-of-state
Tuition per credit: $750 full-time in-state, $750 part-time in-state, $750 full-time out-of-state, $750 part-time out-of-state
Acceptance rate: 91.0%
Test scores required: GMAT or GRE
Average GMAT: 550
Average GRE: 169 verbal, 165 quantitative, 3.9 writing
Average age of entrants: 34
Students with prior work experience: 95.0%
Enrollment: 250, 73% men, 27% women, 16% minority, 1% international
Average class size: 34
Completion: Three year graduation rate: 69%; credits needed to graduate: 49; target time to graduate: 2 years
College funded aid available: Domestic: Yes; International: Yes
Graduates with debt: 28%; average amount of debt $43,239

ONLINE BUSINESS PROGRAM(S)

online.boisestate.edu/ masters-degrees/ accountancy/admissions/
Admissions: (208) 426-5921
Email: online@boisestate.edu
Financial aid: (208) 426-1664
Application deadline: rolling
Program can be completed entirely online: Yes
Total program cost: $13,500 full-time in-state, $13,500 part-time in-state, $13,500 full-time out-of-state, $13,500 part-time out-of-state
Tuition per credit: $450 full-time in-state, $450 part-time in-state, $450 full-time out-of-state, $450 part-time out-of-state
Acceptance rate: 100.0%
Test scores required: GMAT or GRE
Average GRE: 156 verbal, 154 quantitative, 3.7 writing
Average age of entrants: 32
Enrollment: 24, 50% men, 50% women, 21% minority, 0% international
Average class size: 11
Completion: Credits needed to graduate: 30; target time to graduate: 2 years
College funded aid available: Domestic: Yes; International: Yes

Northwest Nazarene University

Private

ONLINE MBA PROGRAM(S)

www.nnu.edu
Admissions: (208) 467-8000
Email: admissions@nnu.edu
Financial aid: (208) 467-8593
Application deadline: rolling
Program can be completed entirely online: Yes
Total program cost: N/A
Tuition per credit: $595 full-time in-state, $595 part-time in-state, $595 full-time out-of-state, $595 part-time out-of-state
Acceptance rate: 57.0%
Average age of entrants: 35
Enrollment: 48, 58% men, 42% women, 21% minority, 0% international
Average class size: 15
Most popular MBA concentrations: accounting, health care administration, leadership
Completion: Three year graduation rate: 76%; credits needed to graduate: 42; target time to graduate: 1.5 years
College funded aid available: Domestic: No; International: No
Graduates with debt: 63%; average amount of debt $23,302

ILLINOIS

American InterContinental University

Proprietary

ONLINE MBA PROGRAM(S)

www.aiuniv.edu/admissions
Admissions: (877) 701-3800
Email: enroll@aiuonline.edu
Financial aid: (877) 221-5800
Application deadline: rolling
Program can be completed entirely online: Yes
Total program cost: $29,328 full-time in-state, $29,328 part-time in-state, $29,328 full-time out-of-state, $29,328 part-time out-of-state
Tuition per credit: $611 full-time in-state, $611 part-time in-state, $611 full-time out-of-state, $611 part-time out-of-state
Acceptance rate: 100.0%
Test scores required: No
Average age of entrants: 39
Enrollment: 1,899, 30% men, 70% women, 61% minority, 0% international
Average class size: 14
Most popular MBA concentrations: general management, health care administration, human resources management, production/operations management
Completion: Three year graduation rate: 62%; credits needed to graduate: 48; target time to graduate: 1 year
College funded aid available: Domestic: Yes; International: Yes
Graduates with debt: 83%; average amount of debt $32,260

Concordia University Chicago

Private

ONLINE MBA PROGRAM(S)

gradschool.cuchicago.edu/
academics/mba/admissions/
Admissions: (708) 209-4093
Email: grad.admission@
cuchicago.edu
Financial aid: (708) 209-3347
Application deadline: rolling
**Program can be completed
entirely online:** Yes
Total program cost: $25,560
full-time in-state, $25,560
part-time in-state, $25,560
full-time out-of-state, $25,560
part-time out-of-state
Tuition per credit: $710 full-time
in-state, $710 part-time in-state,
$710 full-time out-of-state,
$710 part-time out-of-state
Acceptance rate: 100.0%
Test scores required: No
Average age of entrants: 33
Enrollment: 223, 36%
men, 64% women, 51%
minority, 1% international
Average class size: 11
**Most popular MBA
concentrations:** finance,
general management,
health care administration,
leadership, sports business
Completion: Three year
graduation rate: 48%; credits
needed to graduate: 36; target
time to graduate: 2 years
**College funded aid
available:** Domestic: Yes;
International: Yes

Governors State University

Public

ONLINE MBA PROGRAM(S)

www.govst.edu/admissions/
Admissions: (708) 534-4490
Email: admissions@govst.edu
Financial aid: (708) 534-4480
Application deadline: rolling
**Program can be completed
entirely online:** Yes
Total program cost: $14,616
full-time in-state, $7,308
part-time in-state, $14,616
full-time out-of-state, $7,308
part-time out-of-state
Tuition per credit: $406
full-time in-state, $406
part-time in-state, $406
full-time out-of-state, $406
part-time out-of-state
Acceptance rate: 53.0%
Average GMAT: 560
Average age of entrants: 32
Enrollment: 37, 43% men,
57% women, 59% minority,
0% international
Average class size: 17
Completion: Credits
needed to graduate: 36
**College funded aid
available:** Domestic: Yes;
International: Yes
Graduates with debt: 100%;
average amount of debt $46,844

Judson University

Private

ONLINE MBA PROGRAM(S)

www.judsonu.edu/admissions/
Admissions: (847) 628-2510
Email: admissions@judsonu.edu
Financial aid: (847) 628-2531
Application deadline: rolling
**Program can be completed
entirely online:** Yes
Total program cost: N/A
Tuition per credit: $665
full-time in-state, $665
part-time in-state, $665
full-time out-of-state, $665
part-time out-of-state
Acceptance rate: 75.0%
Test scores required: No
Average age of entrants: 44
Enrollment: 9, 22% men,
78% women, 33% minority,
0% international
Average class size: 10
**Most popular MBA
concentrations:** leadership,
not-for-profit management,
organizational behavior
Completion: Credits needed
to graduate: 37; target time
to graduate: 1.5 years
College funded aid available:
Domestic: Yes

McKendree University

Private

ONLINE MBA PROGRAM(S)

www.mckendree.edu/
admission/info/graduate/
index.php
Admissions: (618) 537-6576
Email: graduate@mckendree.edu
Financial aid: (618) 537-6530
Application deadline: rolling
**Program can be completed
entirely online:** Yes
Total program cost: $18,360
full-time in-state, $18,360
part-time in-state, $18,360
full-time out-of-state, $18,360
part-time out-of-state
Tuition per credit: $510 full-time
in-state, $510 part-time in-state,
$510 full-time out-of-state,
$510 part-time out-of-state
Acceptance rate: 60.0%
Average age of entrants: 30
Enrollment: 116, 37% men,
63% women, 12% minority,
1% international
Average class size: 14
**Most popular MBA
concentrations:** general
management, human
resources management
Completion: Three year
graduation rate: 73%; credits
needed to graduate: 36; target
time to graduate: 2 years
Graduates with debt: 51%;
average amount of debt $29,669

Olivet Nazarene University

Private

ONLINE MBA PROGRAM(S)

graduate.olivet.edu
Admissions: (877) 965-4838
Email: gradadmissions@
olivet.edu
Financial aid: N/A
Application deadline: rolling
**Program can be completed
entirely online:** Yes
Total program cost: N/A
Tuition per credit: $675 full-time
in-state, $675 part-time in-state,
$675 full-time out-of-state,
$675 part-time out-of-state
Acceptance rate: 92.0%
Test scores required: No
Enrollment: 144, N/A minority,
N/A international
Average class size: 11
**Most popular MBA
concentrations:** health care
administration, leadership,
not-for-profit management
Completion: Three year
graduation rate: 83%; credits
needed to graduate: 36
**College funded aid
available:** Domestic: Yes;
International: Yes
Graduates with debt: 80%;
average amount of debt $31,025

ONLINE BUSINESS PROGRAM(S)

Admissions: (877) 965-4838
Email: gradadmissions@
olivet.edu
Financial aid: (877) 965-4838
Application deadline: rolling
**Program can be completed
entirely online:** Yes
Total program cost: N/A
Tuition per credit: $675 full-time
in-state, $675 part-time in-state,
$675 full-time out-of-state,
$675 part-time out-of-state
Acceptance rate: 96.0%
Test scores required: No
Enrollment: 55, N/A minority,
N/A international
Average class size: 10
Completion: Three year
graduation rate: 94%; credits
needed to graduate: 36; target
time to graduate: 2 years
**College funded aid
available:** Domestic: Yes;
International: Yes
Graduates with debt:
48%; average amount
of debt $20,694

Southern Illinois University–Carbondale

Public

ONLINE MBA PROGRAM(S)

onlinegrad.business.siu.edu
Admissions: (618) 453-3030
Email: GradPrograms@
business.siu.edu
Financial aid: (618) 453-4334
Application deadline: Domestic:
06/01; International: 04/15
**Program can be completed
entirely online:** Yes
Total program cost: $35,868
full-time in-state, $35,868
part-time in-state, $35,868
full-time out-of-state, $35,868
part-time out-of-state
Tuition per credit: $854
full-time in-state, $854
part-time in-state, $854
full-time out-of-state, $854
part-time out-of-state
Acceptance rate: 74.0%
Test scores required:
GMAT or GRE
Average GMAT: 525
Average age of entrants: 35
**Students with prior work
experience:** 95.0%
Enrollment: 109, 62% men,
38% women, 21% minority,
0% international

University of Illinois–Springfield

Public

ONLINE BUSINESS PROGRAM(S)

www.uis.edu/admissions
Admissions: (888) 977-4847
Email: admissions@uis.edu
Financial aid: (217) 206-6724
Application deadline: rolling
**Program can be completed
entirely online:** Yes
Total program cost: N/A
Tuition per credit: $403
full-time in-state, $403
part-time in-state, $403
full-time out-of-state, $403
part-time out-of-state
Acceptance rate: 85.0%
Test scores required:
GMAT or GRE
Average age of entrants: 32
**Students with prior work
experience:** 90.0%
Enrollment: 146, 65% men,
35% women, 37% minority,
11% international
Average class size: 18
**Most popular business
concentrations:** management
information systems
Completion: Three year
graduation rate: 39%; credits
needed to graduate: 36; target
time to graduate: 2.5 years
**College funded aid
available:** Domestic: Yes;
International: Yes
Graduates with debt: 27%;
average amount of debt $34,134

University of St. Francis

Private

ONLINE MBA PROGRAM(S)

www.stfrancis.edu/admissions/
graduate
Admissions: (800) 735-7500
Email: admissions@stfrancis.edu
Financial aid: (866) 890-8331
Application deadline: rolling
**Program can be completed
entirely online:** Yes
Total program cost: N/A
Tuition per credit: $798 full-time
in-state, $798 part-time in-state,
$798 full-time out-of-state,
$798 part-time out-of-state
Acceptance rate: 60.0%
Test scores required: No
Average age of entrants: 34
Enrollment: 171, 33% men,
67% women, 28% minority,
1% international
Average class size: 13
**Most popular MBA
concentrations:** finance,
general management, health
care administration, human
resources management, supply
chain management/logistics

Average class size: 22
**Most popular MBA
concentrations:** general
management
Completion: Three year
graduation rate: 74%; credits
needed to graduate: 42; target
time to graduate: 2 years
College funded aid available:
Domestic: No; International: No
Graduates with debt: 35%;
average amount of debt $38,417

Completion: Three year
graduation rate: 59%; credits
needed to graduate: 36; target
time to graduate: 2 years
**College funded aid
available:** Domestic: Yes;
International: Yes
Graduates with debt: 52%;
average amount of debt $34,681

ONLINE BUSINESS PROGRAM(S)

www.stfrancis.edu/
admissions/graduate
Admissions: (800) 735-7500
Email: admissions@stfrancis.edu
Financial aid: (866) 890-8331
Application deadline: rolling
**Program can be completed
entirely online:** Yes
Total program cost: N/A
Tuition per credit: $748 full-time
in-state, $748 part-time in-state,
$748 full-time out-of-state,
$748 part-time out-of-state
Acceptance rate: 51.0%
Test scores required: No
Average age of entrants: 38
Enrollment: 70, 33% men,
67% women, 33% minority,
4% international
Average class size: 13
**Most popular business
concentrations:** general
management, health care
administration, human
resources management
Completion: Three year
graduation rate: 70%; credits
needed to graduate: 36; target
time to graduate: 2 years
**College funded aid
available:** Domestic: Yes;
International: Yes
Graduates with debt: 61%;
average amount of debt $34,103

Western Illinois University

Public

ONLINE MBA PROGRAM(S)

www.wiu.edu/cbt/mba
Admissions: (309) 298-2442
Email: grad-office@wiu.edu
Financial aid: (309) 298-2446
Application deadline: rolling
**Program can be completed
entirely online:** Yes
Total program cost: N/A
Tuition per credit: $324
full-time in-state, $324
part-time in-state, $324
full-time out-of-state, $324
part-time out-of-state
Test scores required:
GMAT or GRE
Average class size: 16
**Most popular MBA
concentrations:** accounting,
finance, general management,
international business, supply
chain management/logistics
Completion: Credits needed
to graduate: 33; target time
to graduate: 2 years
**College funded aid
available:** Domestic: Yes;
International: Yes

INDIANA

Anderson University

Private

ONLINE MBA PROGRAM(S)

anderson.edu/entry
Admissions: (765) 641-3043
Email: agsenrollment@
anderson.edu
Financial aid: (765) 641-4180
Application deadline: rolling
**Program can be completed
entirely online:** Yes
Total program cost: $20,905
full-time in-state, $20,905
part-time in-state, $20,905
full-time out-of-state, $20,905
part-time out-of-state
Tuition per credit: $565
full-time in-state, $565
part-time in-state, $565
full-time out-of-state, $565
part-time out-of-state
Acceptance rate: 54.0%
Test scores required: No
Average age of entrants: 30
Enrollment: 25, 52% men,
48% women, 16% minority,
4% international
Average class size: 16
Most popular MBA concentrations:
entrepreneurship,
finance, international
business, leadership
Completion: Credits needed
to graduate: 37; target time
to graduate: 2 years
College funded aid available:
Domestic: No; International: No

Ball State University (Miller)

Public

ONLINE MBA PROGRAM(S)

www.bsu.edu/academics/
collegesanddepartments/mba/
admissions
Admissions: (765) 285-1931
Email: mba@bsu.edu
Financial aid: (765) 285-5600
Application deadline: rolling
**Program can be completed
entirely online:** Yes
Total program cost: $14,820
full-time in-state, $14,820
part-time in-state, $21,000
full-time out-of-state, $21,000
part-time out-of-state
Tuition per credit: $410 full-time
in-state, $410 part-time in-state,
$616 full-time out-of-state,
$616 part-time out-of-state
Acceptance rate: 63.0%
Test scores required:
GMAT or GRE
Average GMAT: 539
Average GRE: 154 verbal, 156
quantitative, 4.0 writing
Average age of entrants: 28
**Students with prior work
experience:** 87.0%
Enrollment: 318, 63% men,
37% women, 10% minority,
3% international
Average class size: 32
Most popular MBA concentrations:
entrepreneurship,
finance, health care
administration, supply chain
management/logistics
Completion: Three year
graduation rate: 76%; credits
needed to graduate: 30; target
time to graduate: 2 years

**College funded aid
available:** Domestic: Yes;
International: Yes
Graduates with debt: 48%;
average amount of debt $32,331

Indiana Institute of Technology

Private

ONLINE MBA PROGRAM(S)

cps.indianatech.edu/
Admissions: (800) 288-1766
Email: cps@indianatech.edu
Financial aid: (260) 422-5561
Application deadline: rolling
**Program can be completed
entirely online:** Yes
Total program cost: $9,270
full-time in-state, $9,270
part-time in-state, $9,270
full-time out-of-state, $9,270
part-time out-of-state
Tuition per credit: $515 full-time
in-state, $515 part-time in-state,
$515 full-time out-of-state,
$515 part-time out-of-state
Acceptance rate: 97.0%
Test scores required: No
Average age of entrants: 33
Enrollment: 312, 43%
men, 57% women, 33%
minority, 7% international
Average class size: 13
**Most popular MBA
concentrations:** accounting,
general management,
health care administration,
human resources
management, marketing
Completion: Target time
to graduate: 2 years

ONLINE BUSINESS PROGRAM(S)

cps.indianatech.edu/
Admissions: (800) 288-1766
Email: cps@indianatech.edu
Financial aid: (260) 422-5561
Application deadline: rolling
**Program can be completed
entirely online:** Yes
Total program cost: $9,270
full-time in-state, $9,270
part-time in-state, $9,270
full-time out-of-state, $9,270
part-time out-of-state
Tuition per credit: $515 full-time
in-state, $515 part-time in-state,
$515 full-time out-of-state,
$515 part-time out-of-state
Acceptance rate: 97.0%
Test scores required: No
Average age of entrants: 36
Enrollment: 124, 39% men,
61% women, 48% minority,
2% international
Average class size: 13
**Most popular business
concentrations:** general
management, leadership
Completion: Target time
to graduate: 2 years

Indiana University–Bloomington (Kelley)

Public

ONLINE MBA PROGRAM(S)

kelley.iu.edu/onlinemba/
admissions/page36806.html
Admissions: (877) 785-4713
Email: kdirect@indiana.edu
Financial aid: (812) 856-7026
Application deadline: rolling
**Program can be completed
entirely online:** No

Total program cost: $67,830
full-time in-state, $67,830
part-time in-state, $67,830
full-time out-of-state, $67,830
part-time out-of-state
Tuition per credit: $1,330
full-time in-state, $1,330
part-time in-state, $1,330
full-time out-of-state, $1,330
part-time out-of-state
Acceptance rate: 76.0%
Test scores required:
GMAT or GRE
Average GMAT: 638
Average GRE: 157 verbal, 159
quantitative, 4.0 writing
Average age of entrants: 31
**Students with prior work
experience:** 100.0%
Enrollment: 934, 74% men,
26% women, 17% minority,
12% international
Average class size: 31
**Most popular MBA
concentrations:** finance, general
management, marketing, supply
chain management/logistics,
quantitative analysis/statistics
and operations research
Completion: Three year
graduation rate: 79%; credits
needed to graduate: 51; target
time to graduate: 3 years
**College funded aid
available:** Domestic: Yes;
International: Yes
Graduates with debt: 45%;
average amount of debt $55,829

ONLINE BUSINESS PROGRAM(S)

kelley.iu.edu/onlinemba/
Admissions: (877) 785-4713
Email: ajherman@indiana.edu
Financial aid: (812) 856-7026
Application deadline: rolling
**Program can be completed
entirely online:** Depends
Total program cost: $39,900
full-time in-state, $39,900
part-time in-state, $39,900
full-time out-of-state, $39,900
part-time out-of-state
Tuition per credit: $1,330
full-time in-state, $1,330
part-time in-state, $1,330
full-time out-of-state, $1,330
part-time out-of-state
Acceptance rate: 69.0%
Test scores required:
GMAT or GRE
Average GMAT: 629
Average GRE: 157 verbal, 158
quantitative, 4.0 writing
Average age of entrants: 35
**Students with prior work
experience:** 98.0%
Enrollment: 273, 74% men,
26% women, 19% minority,
13% international
Average class size: 32
**Most popular business
concentrations:** finance, general
management, marketing, supply
chain management/logistics,
quantitative analysis/statistics
and operations research
Completion: Three year
graduation rate: 69%; target
time to graduate: 2 years
**College funded aid
available:** Domestic: Yes;
International: Yes
Graduates with debt: 52%;
average amount of debt $41,820

Trine University

Private

ONLINE BUSINESS PROGRAM(S)

www.trine.edu/adult-studies/
admission/index.aspx
Admissions: (260) 665-4149
Email: cgps@trine.edu
Financial aid: (260) 665-4130
Application deadline: rolling
**Program can be completed
entirely online:** Yes
Total program cost: $10,974
full-time in-state, $10,974
part-time in-state, $10,974
full-time out-of-state, $10,974
part-time out-of-state
Tuition per credit: $354
full-time in-state, $354
part-time in-state, $354
full-time out-of-state, $354
part-time out-of-state
Acceptance rate: 74.0%
Test scores required: No
Enrollment: 81, N/A minority,
N/A international
**Most popular business
concentrations:** leadership
Completion: Credits needed
to graduate: 31; target
time to graduate: 1 year
College funded aid available:
Domestic: No; International: No

University of Southern Indiana

Public

ONLINE MBA PROGRAM(S)

www.usi.edu/graduatestudies/
Admissions: (812) 465-7015
Email: Graduate.
Studies@usi.edu
Financial aid: (812) 464-1767
Application deadline: rolling
**Program can be completed
entirely online:** Yes
Total program cost: $12,900
full-time in-state, $12,900
part-time in-state, $12,900
full-time out-of-state, $12,900
part-time out-of-state
Tuition per credit: $430
full-time in-state, $430
part-time in-state, $430
full-time out-of-state, $430
part-time out-of-state
Acceptance rate: 100.0%
Test scores required:
GMAT or GRE
Average GMAT: 495
Average GRE: 150 verbal, 151
quantitative, 3.5 writing
Average age of entrants: 33
**Students with prior work
experience:** 5.0%
Enrollment: 643, 51% men,
49% women, 17% minority,
2% international
Average class size: 50
**Most popular MBA
concentrations:** accounting,
health care administration,
human resources management,
industrial management
Completion: Credits needed
to graduate: 30; target time
to graduate: 1.5 years
**College funded aid
available:** Domestic: Yes;
International: Yes
Graduates with debt: 44%;
average amount of debt $19,595

IOWA

Drake University

Private

ONLINE MBA PROGRAM(S)

Admissions: (844) 254-4221
Email: Enrollments@drake.edu
Financial aid: (515) 271-2011
Application deadline: rolling
**Program can be completed
entirely online:** Yes
Total program cost: $27,300
full-time in-state, $27,300
part-time in-state, $27,300
full-time out-of-state, $27,300
part-time out-of-state
Tuition per credit: $700
full-time in-state, $700
part-time in-state, $700
full-time out-of-state, $700
part-time out-of-state
Test scores required:
GMAT or GRE
Average age of entrants: 0
Enrollment: N/A, N/A minority,
N/A international
**Most popular MBA
concentrations:** health
care administration, public
administration, quantitative
analysis/statistics and
operations research
Completion: Target time
to graduate: 2 years
College funded aid available:
Domestic: No; International: No

Upper Iowa University

Private

ONLINE MBA PROGRAM(S)

uiu.edu/future/index.html
Admissions: (563) 425-5253
Email: wissmiller@uiu.edu
Financial aid: (563) 425-5170
Application deadline: rolling
**Program can be completed
entirely online:** Yes
Total program cost: $20,304
full-time in-state, $20,304
part-time in-state, $20,304
full-time out-of-state, $20,304
part-time out-of-state
Tuition per credit: $564
full-time in-state, $564
part-time in-state, $564
full-time out-of-state, $564
part-time out-of-state
Acceptance rate: 60.0%
Test scores required: No
Average age of entrants: 34
Enrollment: 344, 39% men,
61% women, 21% minority,
4% international
Average class size: 13
**Most popular MBA
concentrations:** accounting,
finance, general management,
human resources management
Completion: Three year
graduation rate: 66%; credits
needed to graduate: 36; target
time to graduate: 2 years
**College funded aid
available:** Domestic: Yes;
International: Yes
Graduates with debt:
58%; average amount
of debt $60,003

KANSAS

Baker University
Private

ONLINE MBA PROGRAM(S)
www.bakeru.edu/spgs/mba/
Admissions: (913) 491-4432
Email: ruth.miller@bakeru.edu
Financial aid: (785) 594-4595
Application deadline: rolling
Program can be completed entirely online: Yes
Total program cost: $26,620 part-time in-state, $26,620 full-time out-of-state, $26,620 part-time out-of-state
Tuition per credit: $670 full-time in-state, $670 part-time in-state, $670 full-time out-of-state, $670 part-time out-of-state
Test scores required: No
Enrollment: 162, 44% men, 56% women, 28% minority, 0% international
Average class size: 15
Most popular MBA concentrations: finance, health care administration, human resources management
Completion: Credits needed to graduate: 33; target time to graduate: 2 years
College funded aid available: Domestic: Yes; International: No

ONLINE BUSINESS PROGRAM(S)
www.bakeru.edu
Admissions: (913) 491-4432
Email: ruth.miller@bakeru.edu
Financial aid: (785) 594-4595
Application deadline: rolling
Program can be completed entirely online: Yes
Total program cost: $22,135 full-time in-state, $22,135 part-time in-state, $22,135 full-time out-of-state, $22,135 part-time out-of-state
Tuition per credit: $555 full-time in-state, $555 part-time in-state, $555 full-time out-of-state, $555 part-time out-of-state
Test scores required: No
Enrollment: 65, 57% men, 43% women, 32% minority, 0% international
Average class size: 13
Most popular business concentrations: finance, health care administration, human resources management, leadership
Completion: Credits needed to graduate: 39; target time to graduate: 2 years
College funded aid available: Domestic: Yes; International: No

Fort Hays State University
Public

ONLINE MBA PROGRAM(S)
www.fhsu.edu/mba
Admissions: (785) 628-5696
Email: gradcoordinator@fhsu.edu
Financial aid: (785) 628-4494
Application deadline: rolling
Program can be completed entirely online: Yes
Total program cost: $12,590 full-time in-state, $12,590 part-time in-state, $12,590

full-time out-of-state, $12,590 part-time out-of-state
Tuition per credit: $400 full-time in-state, $400 part-time in-state, $400 full-time out-of-state, $400 part-time out-of-state
Acceptance rate: 52.0%
Test scores required: GMAT or GRE
Average GMAT: 440
Average GRE: 150 verbal, 151 quantitative, 3.5 writing
Average age of entrants: 32
Students with prior work experience: 69.0%
Enrollment: 134, 47% men, 53% women, 18% minority, 1% international
Average class size: 23
Most popular MBA concentrations: finance, general management, health care administration, human resources management, marketing
Completion: Three year graduation rate: 52%; credits needed to graduate: 34; target time to graduate: 2 years
College funded aid available: Domestic: Yes; International: Yes
Graduates with debt: 44%; average amount of debt $31,871

Friends University
Private

ONLINE MBA PROGRAM(S)
www.friends.edu/admissions/
Admissions: (316) 295-5872
Email: learn@friends.edu
Financial aid: (316) 295-5120
Application deadline: rolling
Program can be completed entirely online: Yes
Total program cost: $20,430 full-time in-state, $20,430 part-time in-state, $20,430 full-time out-of-state, $20,430 part-time out-of-state
Tuition per credit: $681 full-time in-state, $681 part-time in-state, $681 full-time out-of-state, $681 part-time out-of-state
Acceptance rate: 94.0%
Test scores required: No
Average age of entrants: 34
Enrollment: 208, 43% men, 57% women, 29% minority, 0% international
Average class size: 10
Most popular MBA concentrations: accounting, health care administration, human resources management, supply chain management/logistics
Completion: Three year graduation rate: 88%; credits needed to graduate: 30; target time to graduate: 2 years
College funded aid available: Domestic: No; International: No
Graduates with debt: 61%; average amount of debt $30,432

ONLINE BUSINESS PROGRAM(S)
www.friends.edu/admissions/
Admissions: (316) 295-5872
Email: learn@friends.edu
Financial aid: (316) 295-5120
Application deadline: rolling
Program can be completed entirely online: Yes
Total program cost: $20,430 full-time in-state, $20,430

part-time in-state, $20,430 full-time out-of-state, $20,430 part-time out-of-state
Tuition per credit: $681 full-time in-state, $681 part-time in-state, $681 full-time out-of-state, $681 part-time out-of-state
Acceptance rate: 78.0%
Test scores required: No
Average age of entrants: 33
Enrollment: 52, 50% men, 50% women, 46% minority, 0% international
Average class size: 8
Most popular business concentrations: health care administration, management information systems
Completion: Three year graduation rate: 92%; credits needed to graduate: 33; target time to graduate: 2 years
College funded aid available: Domestic: Yes; International: Yes
Graduates with debt: 89%; average amount of debt $36,865

Kansas State University
Public

ONLINE MBA PROGRAM(S)
www.k-state.edu/onlinemba
Admissions: (785) 532-6191
Email: grad@ksu.edu
Financial aid: (785) 532-6420
Application deadline: rolling
Program can be completed entirely online: No
Total program cost: $30,000 full-time in-state, $30,000 part-time in-state, $30,000 full-time out-of-state, $30,000 part-time out-of-state
Tuition per credit: $833 full-time in-state, $833 part-time in-state, $833 full-time out-of-state, $833 part-time out-of-state
Acceptance rate: 100.0%
Test scores required: GMAT
Average GRE: 155 verbal, 159 quantitative, 4.7 writing
Average age of entrants: 31
Students with prior work experience: 100.0%
Enrollment: 91, 62% men, 38% women, 18% minority, 0% international
Average class size: 14
Most popular MBA concentrations: general management
Completion: Three year graduation rate: 80%; credits needed to graduate: 33; target time to graduate: 2.5 years
College funded aid available: Domestic: Yes; International: Yes
Graduates with debt: 61%; average amount of debt $59,101

Ottawa University–Online
Private

ONLINE MBA PROGRAM(S)
www.ottawa.edu/adult-and-graduate/admissions/
Admissions: (913) 266-8625
Email: admiss.kc@ottawa.edu
Financial aid: (602) 749-5120
Application deadline: rolling

Program can be completed entirely online: Yes
Total program cost: $11,682 full-time in-state, $7,788 part-time in-state, $11,682 full-time out-of-state, $7,788 part-time out-of-state
Tuition per credit: $649 full-time in-state, $649 part-time in-state, $649 full-time out-of-state, $649 part-time out-of-state
Acceptance rate: 41.0%
Test scores required: No
Average age of entrants: 42
Students with prior work experience: 0.0%
Enrollment: 23, 35% men, 65% women, 35% minority, 0% international
Average class size: 12
Most popular MBA concentrations: health care administration, leadership, production/operations management
Completion: Three year graduation rate: 60%; credits needed to graduate: 36; target time to graduate: 2 years
College funded aid available: Domestic: Yes; International: No
Graduates with debt: 70%; average amount of debt $31,965

Southwestern College
Private

ONLINE MBA PROGRAM(S)
ps.sckans.edu/admissions-center
Admissions: (888) 684-5335
Email: enrollment@sckans.edu
Financial aid: (620) 229-6387
Application deadline: rolling
Program can be completed entirely online: Yes
Total program cost: N/A
Tuition per credit: $695 full-time in-state, $695 part-time in-state, $695 full-time out-of-state, $695 part-time out-of-state
Acceptance rate: 92.0%
Test scores required: No
Average age of entrants: 31
Enrollment: 37, 62% men, 38% women, 24% minority, 0% international
Average class size: 3
Most popular MBA concentrations: finance, general management
Completion: Three year graduation rate: 60%; credits needed to graduate: 33; target time to graduate: 2 years
College funded aid available: Domestic: Yes; International: No
Graduates with debt: 58%; average amount of debt $47,045

ONLINE BUSINESS PROGRAM(S)
ps.sckans.edu/admissions-center
Admissions: (888) 684-5335
Email: enrollment@sckans.edu
Financial aid: (620) 229-6387
Application deadline: rolling
Program can be completed entirely online: Yes
Total program cost: N/A
Tuition per credit: $629 full-time in-state, $629 part-time in-state, $629 full-time out-of-state, $629 part-time out-of-state
Acceptance rate: 85.0%

Test scores required: No
Average age of entrants: 36
Enrollment: 81, 68% men, 32% women, 25% minority, 0% international
Average class size: 4
Most popular business concentrations: general management, leadership
Completion: Three year graduation rate: 45%; credits needed to graduate: 33; target time to graduate: 2 years
College funded aid available: Domestic: Yes; International: No
Graduates with debt: 36%; average amount of debt $28,320

Tabor College
Private

ONLINE MBA PROGRAM(S)
tabor.edu/online/admissions-enrollment/
Admissions: (316) 729-6333
Email: learn@tabor.edu
Financial aid: (316) 729-6333
Application deadline: rolling
Program can be completed entirely online: Yes
Total program cost: $21,682 full-time in-state, $21,682 part-time in-state, $21,682 full-time out-of-state, $21,682 part-time out-of-state
Tuition per credit: $547 full-time in-state, $547 part-time in-state, $547 full-time out-of-state, $547 part-time out-of-state
Acceptance rate: 100.0%
Test scores required: No
Average age of entrants: 25
Enrollment: 33, 64% men, 36% women, 24% minority, 0% international
Average class size: 12
Most popular MBA concentrations: leadership
Completion: Three year graduation rate: 73%; credits needed to graduate: 36; target time to graduate: 2 years
College funded aid available: Domestic: Yes; International: Yes

University of Kansas
Public

ONLINE MBA PROGRAM(S)
onlinemba.ku.edu/admissions
Admissions: (785) 864-6738
Email: onlineinfo@ku.edu
Financial aid: (785) 864-4700
Application deadline: rolling
Program can be completed entirely online: Yes
Total program cost: $36,330 full-time in-state, $36,330 part-time in-state, $36,330 full-time out-of-state, $36,330 part-time out-of-state
Tuition per credit: $865 full-time in-state, $865 part-time in-state, $865 full-time out-of-state, $865 part-time out-of-state
Acceptance rate: 77.0%
Test scores required: GMAT or GRE
Average GMAT: 569
Average age of entrants: 33
Students with prior work experience: 92.0%
Enrollment: 287, 65% men, 35% women, 17% minority, 1% international

More @ usnews.com/bschool

Average class size: 63
Most popular MBA concentrations: finance, general management, leadership, marketing
Completion: Credits needed to graduate: 42; target time to graduate: 2.5 years
College funded aid available: Domestic: No; International: No
Graduates with debt: 41%; average amount of debt $34,000

University of St. Mary

Private

ONLINE MBA PROGRAM(S)

www.stmary.edu/admissions.aspx
Admissions: (913) 758-6308
Email: John.Shultz@stmary.edu
Financial aid: (913) 758-6172
Application deadline: rolling
Program can be completed entirely online: Yes
Total program cost: N/A
Tuition per credit: $630 full-time in-state, $630 part-time in-state, $630 full-time out-of-state, $630 part-time out-of-state
Acceptance rate: 99.0%
Test scores required: No
Enrollment: 311, 42% men, 58% women, 34% minority, 0% international
Average class size: 14
Most popular MBA concentrations: general management, health care administration, human resources management, leadership, marketing
Completion: Three year graduation rate: 61%; credits needed to graduate: 36; target time to graduate: 2 years
Graduates with debt: 43%; average amount of debt $38,094

Wichita State University (Barton)

Public

ONLINE MBA PROGRAM(S)

Admissions: (316) 978-3095
Email: wsugradschool@wichita.edu
Financial aid: (316) 978-3430
Application deadline: rolling
Program can be completed entirely online: Yes
Total program cost: $7,247 full-time in-state, $3,623 part-time in-state, $17,797 full-time out-of-state, $8,899 part-time out-of-state
Tuition per credit: $302 full-time in-state, $302 part-time in-state, $742 full-time out-of-state, $742 part-time out-of-state
Acceptance rate: 76.0%
Test scores required: GMAT or GRE
Average GRE: 148 verbal, 150 quantitative, 3.8 writing
Average age of entrants: 29
Enrollment: 231, 61% men, 39% women, 23% minority, 9% international
Average class size: 16
Most popular MBA concentrations: general management, marketing

Completion: Credits needed to graduate: 36
College funded aid available: Domestic: Yes; International: Yes
Graduates with debt: 33%; average amount of debt $25,875

Campbellsville University

Private

ONLINE MBA PROGRAM(S)

www.campbellsville.edu/
Admissions: (270) 789-5221
Email: mkbamwine@campbellsville.edu
Financial aid: (270) 789-5013
Application deadline: rolling
Program can be completed entirely online: Yes
Total program cost: $17,244 full-time in-state, $17,244 part-time in-state, $17,244 full-time out-of-state, $17,244 part-time out-of-state
Tuition per credit: $479 full-time in-state, $479 part-time in-state, $479 full-time out-of-state, $479 part-time out-of-state
Acceptance rate: 38.0%
Test scores required: GMAT or GRE
Average GMAT: 325
Average GRE: 148 verbal, 142 quantitative, 3.0 writing
Average age of entrants: 32
Students with prior work experience: 0.0%
Enrollment: 76, 50% men, 50% women, 11% minority, 3% international
Average class size: 68
Most popular MBA concentrations: health care administration, human resources management, international business, marketing, technology
Completion: Three year graduation rate: 48%; credits needed to graduate: 36; target time to graduate: 2 years
College funded aid available: Domestic: No; International: No
Graduates with debt: 49%; average amount of debt $32,316

ONLINE BUSINESS PROGRAM(S)

www.campbellsville.edu/
Admissions: (270) 789-5221
Email: mkbamwine@campbellsville.edu
Financial aid: (270) 789-5013
Application deadline: rolling
Program can be completed entirely online: Yes
Total program cost: $14,370 part-time in-state, $14,370 full-time out-of-state, $14,370 part-time out-of-state
Tuition per credit: $479 full-time in-state, $479 part-time in-state, $479 full-time out-of-state, $479 part-time out-of-state
Acceptance rate: 41.0%
Test scores required: GMAT or GRE
Average age of entrants: 42
Enrollment: 32, 53% men, 47% women, 22% minority, 0% international
Average class size: 45
Most popular business concentrations: general management, leadership

Completion: Three year graduation rate: 42%; credits needed to graduate: 30; target time to graduate: 2 years
College funded aid available: Domestic: No; International: No
Graduates with debt: 63%; average amount of debt $22,965

University of Pikeville

Private

ONLINE MBA PROGRAM(S)

www.upike.edu/admissions
Admissions: (606) 218-5251
Email: wewantyou@upike.edu
Financial aid: (606) 218-5247
Application deadline: rolling
Program can be completed entirely online: Yes
Total program cost: $5,400 full-time in-state, $2,700 part-time in-state, $5,400 full-time out-of-state, $2,700 part-time out-of-state
Tuition per credit: $450 full-time in-state, $450 part-time in-state, $450 full-time out-of-state, $450 part-time out-of-state
Test scores required: No
Most popular MBA concentrations: health care administration
Completion: Target time to graduate: 2.5 years

University of the Cumberlands

Private

ONLINE MBA PROGRAM(S)

www.ucumberlands.edu/
Admissions: (606) 539-4390
Email: mba@ucumberlands.edu
Financial aid: (606) 539-4220
Application deadline: rolling
Program can be completed entirely online: Yes
Total program cost: $9,450 full-time in-state, $9,450 part-time in-state, $9,450 full-time out-of-state, $9,450 part-time out-of-state
Tuition per credit: $315 full-time in-state, $315 part-time in-state, $315 full-time out-of-state, $315 part-time out-of-state
Acceptance rate: 91.0%
Test scores required: No
Average age of entrants: 32
Students with prior work experience: 94.0%
Enrollment: 268, N/A minority, N/A international
Average class size: 24
Most popular MBA concentrations: accounting, entrepreneurship, general management, health care administration
Completion: Credits needed to graduate: 30
College funded aid available: Domestic: No; International: No
Graduates with debt: 33%

Western Kentucky University (Ford)

Public

ONLINE MBA PROGRAM(S)

www.wku.edu/mba/
Admissions: (270) 745-5458
Email: gfcb@wku.edu
Financial aid: (270) 745-2755

Application deadline: rolling
Program can be completed entirely online: Depends
Total program cost: $21,210 full-time in-state, $21,210 part-time in-state, $21,210 full-time out-of-state, $21,210 part-time out-of-state
Tuition per credit: $707 full-time in-state, $707 part-time in-state, $707 full-time out-of-state, $707 part-time out-of-state
Acceptance rate: 88.0%
Average GMAT: 528
Average age of entrants: 30
Enrollment: 91, 53% men, 47% women, 7% minority, 0% international
Average class size: 16
Most popular MBA concentrations: accounting, finance, marketing, organizational behavior
Completion: Three year graduation rate: 70%; credits needed to graduate: 33; target time to graduate: 2 years
Graduates with debt: 38%; average amount of debt $21,577

Louisiana State University– Baton Rouge (Ourso)

Public

ONLINE MBA PROGRAM(S)

lsuonline.lsu.edu/programs/master-business-administration.aspx
Admissions: (225) 578-8867
Email: lwhitm3@lsu.edu
Financial aid: (225) 578-3103
Application deadline: rolling
Program can be completed entirely online: Yes
Total program cost: $42,462 full-time in-state, $42,462 part-time in-state, $42,462 full-time out-of-state, $42,462 part-time out-of-state
Tuition per credit: $1,011 full-time in-state, $1,011 part-time in-state, $1,011 full-time out-of-state, $1,011 part-time out-of-state
Acceptance rate: 68.0%
Test scores required: No
Average GMAT: 460
Average GRE: 155 verbal, 156 quantitative, 4.5 writing
Average age of entrants: 34
Students with prior work experience: 100.0%
Enrollment: 175, 72% men, 28% women, 24% minority, 1% international
Average class size: 25
Completion: Three year graduation rate: 41%; credits needed to graduate: 42; target time to graduate: 2.5 years
College funded aid available: Domestic: No; International: No
Graduates with debt: 52%; average amount of debt $49,864

Louisiana Tech University

Public

ONLINE MBA PROGRAM(S)

www.latech.edu/graduate_school
Admissions: (318) 257-2924
Email: gschool@latech.edu
Financial aid: (318) 257-2641
Application deadline: rolling
Program can be completed entirely online: Yes
Total program cost: $13,765 full-time in-state, $12,840 part-time in-state, $13,765 full-time out-of-state, $12,840 part-time out-of-state
Tuition per credit: $412 full-time in-state, $365 part-time in-state, $412 full-time out-of-state, $365 part-time out-of-state
Acceptance rate: 73.0%
Test scores required: GMAT or GRE
Average GMAT: 475
Average GRE: 151 verbal, 151 quantitative, 4.0 writing
Average age of entrants: 26
Students with prior work experience: 82.0%
Enrollment: 58, 53% men, 47% women, 16% minority, 0% international
Average class size: 30
Most popular MBA concentrations: general management
Completion: Three year graduation rate: 71%; credits needed to graduate: 30; target time to graduate: 1.5 years
College funded aid available: Domestic: No; International: No
Graduates with debt: 21%; average amount of debt $12,316

Loyola University New Orleans (Butt)

Private

ONLINE MBA PROGRAM(S)

online.loyno.edu/graduate-admissions-requirements/
Admissions: (844) 490-6766
Email: mba@loyno.edu
Financial aid: (504) 865-3333
Application deadline: rolling
Program can be completed entirely online: Yes
Total program cost: $32,720 full-time in-state, $32,720 part-time in-state, $32,720 full-time out-of-state, $32,720 part-time out-of-state
Tuition per credit: $818 full-time in-state, $818 part-time in-state, $818 full-time out-of-state, $818 part-time out-of-state
Test scores required: GMAT or GRE
Most popular MBA concentrations: entrepreneurship, finance, general management, marketing, production/operations management
Completion: Credits needed to graduate: 40; target time to graduate: 1.5 years
College funded aid available: Domestic: No; International: N

McNeese State University (Burton)

Public

ONLINE MBA PROGRAM(S)

www.becomeacowboy.com
Admissions: (337) 475-5504
Email: admissions@mcneese.edu
Financial aid: (337) 475-5068
Application deadline: Domestic:
05/01; International: 05/01
**Program can be completed
entirely online:** Yes
Total program cost: N/A
Tuition per credit: $900
full-time in-state, $900
part-time in-state, $1,432
full-time out-of-state, $1,432
part-time out-of-state
Test scores required:
GMAT or GRE
Enrollment: 21, 38% men,
62% women, 14% minority,
0% international
Average class size: 10
Completion: Credits
needed to graduate: 30
College funded aid available:
Domestic: No; International: No

University of Louisiana–Lafayette (Moody)

Public

ONLINE MBA PROGRAM(S)

gradschool.louisiana.edu/apply
Admissions: (337) 482-6965
Email: gradschool@louisiana.edu
Financial aid: (337) 482-6506
Application deadline: rolling
**Program can be completed
entirely online:** Yes
Total program cost: $12,800
full-time in-state, $12,800
part-time in-state, $12,800
full-time out-of-state, $12,800
part-time out-of-state
Tuition per credit: $387 full-time
in-state, $387 part-time in-state,
$387 full-time out-of-state,
$387 part-time out-of-state
Acceptance rate: 83.0%
Average age of entrants: 32
Enrollment: 380, 50% men,
50% women, N/A minority,
N/A international
Average class size: 37
**Most popular MBA
concentrations:** finance,
general management,
health care administration,
human resources
management, production/
operations management
Completion: Credits needed
to graduate: 33; target time
to graduate: 2 years
College funded aid available:
Domestic: Yes; International: No

University of Louisiana–Monroe

Public

ONLINE MBA PROGRAM(S)

www.ulm.edu/gradschool
Admissions: (318) 342-1041
Email: gradadmissions@ulm.edu
Financial aid: (318) 342-5329
Application deadline: rolling
**Program can be completed
entirely online:** Yes
Total program cost: $17,490

full-time in-state, $17,490
part-time in-state, $17,490
full-time out-of-state, $17,490
part-time out-of-state
Tuition per credit: $583
full-time in-state, $583
part-time in-state, $583
full-time out-of-state, $583
part-time out-of-state
Acceptance rate: 88.0%
Test scores required: No
Average GMAT: 514
Average GRE: 155 verbal, 147
quantitative, 3.0 writing
Average age of entrants: 31
**Students with prior work
experience:** 100.0%
Enrollment: 53, 55% men,
45% women, 23% minority,
2% international
Average class size: 15
**Most popular MBA
concentrations:** general
management
Completion: Three year
graduation rate: 32%; credits
needed to graduate: 30; target
time to graduate: 2 years
**College funded aid
available:** Domestic: Yes;
International: Yes
Graduates with debt: 67%;
average amount of debt $24,267

MAINE

University of Maine

Public

ONLINE MBA PROGRAM(S)

Admissions: (207) 581-3072
Email: umaineonline@maine.edu
Financial aid: N/A
Application deadline: rolling
**Program can be completed
entirely online:** Yes
Total program cost: $13,170
full-time in-state, $13,170
part-time in-state, $16,470
full-time out-of-state, $16,470
part-time out-of-state
Tuition per credit: $439
full-time in-state, $439
part-time in-state, $549
full-time out-of-state, $549
part-time out-of-state
Acceptance rate: 92.0%
Test scores required:
GMAT or GRE
Average GMAT: 573
Average age of entrants: 32
Enrollment: 62, 53% men,
47% women, 6% minority,
2% international
Average class size: 21
**Most popular MBA
concentrations:** accounting,
general management
Completion: Credits needed
to graduate: 30; target time
to graduate: 2 years
**College funded aid
available:** Domestic: Yes;
International: Yes

MARYLAND

Frostburg State University

Public

ONLINE MBA PROGRAM(S)

www.frostburg.edu/academics/
majorminors/graduate/
ms-business-administration.php
Admissions: (301) 687-4595
Email: vmmazer@frostburg.edu

Financial aid: (301) 687-4301
Application deadline: rolling
**Program can be completed
entirely online:** Yes
Total program cost: $15,588
full-time in-state, $15,588
part-time in-state, $20,052
full-time out-of-state, $20,052
part-time out-of-state
Tuition per credit: $433
full-time in-state, $433
part-time in-state, $557
full-time out-of-state, $557
part-time out-of-state
Acceptance rate: 68.0%
Test scores required:
GMAT or GRE
Average GMAT: 470
Average GRE: 162 verbal, 146
quantitative, 4.0 writing
Average age of entrants: 32
Enrollment: 211, 48%
men, 52% women, 22%
minority, 1% international
Average class size: 17
**Most popular MBA
concentrations:** general
management
Completion: Three year
graduation rate: 49%; credits
needed to graduate: 36; target
time to graduate: 3 years
Graduates with debt:
33%; average amount
of debt $33,950

Morgan State University (Graves)

Public

ONLINE MBA PROGRAM(S)

www.morgan.edu/online
Admissions: (443) 885-4720
Email: online@morgan.edu
Financial aid: (443) 885-3170
Application deadline: Domestic:
05/01; International: 04/01
**Program can be completed
entirely online:** Yes
Total program cost: $30,000
full-time in-state, $30,000
full-time out-of-state
Tuition per credit: $3,300
full-time in-state, $3,300
part-time in-state, $3,300
full-time out-of-state, $3,300
part-time out-of-state
Acceptance rate: 75.0%
Test scores required:
GMAT or GRE
Average age of entrants: 31
Enrollment: 4, 25% men,
75% women, 100% minority,
0% international
Average class size: 11
Completion: Credits needed
to graduate: 36; target time
to graduate: 2 years
College funded aid available:
Domestic: Yes; International: No

ONLINE BUSINESS PROGRAM(S)

www.morgan.edu/
online_education/
online_admissions.html
Admissions: (443) 885-3396
Email: joseph.wells@morgan.edu
Financial aid: (443) 885-3172
Application deadline: Domestic:
03/15; International: 03/15
**Program can be completed
entirely online:** Yes
Total program cost: $30,000
full-time in-state, $30,000
full-time out-of-state
Tuition per credit: $433
full-time in-state, $433
part-time in-state, $851

full-time out-of-state, $851
part-time out-of-state
Acceptance rate: 92.0%
Test scores required: No
Average age of entrants: 32
**Students with prior work
experience:** 100.0%
Enrollment: 9, 56% men,
44% women, 44% minority,
56% international
Average class size: 18
Completion: Credits needed
to graduate: 30; target time
to graduate: 2 years
**College funded aid
available:** Domestic: Yes;
International: Yes

Salisbury University

Public

ONLINE MBA PROGRAM(S)

www.salisbury.edu/
explore-academics/
graduate-studies.aspx
Admissions: (410) 677-0047
Email: mba@salisbury.edu
Financial aid: (410) 543-6165
Application deadline: N/A
**Program can be completed
entirely online:** Yes
Total program cost: $22,950
full-time in-state, $22,950
full-time out-of-state
Tuition per credit: $765 full-time
in-state, $765 part-time in-state,
$765 full-time out-of-state,
$765 part-time out-of-state
Acceptance rate: 79.0%
Test scores required:
GMAT or GRE
Average GMAT: 465
Average age of entrants: 29
**Students with prior work
experience:** 71.0%
Enrollment: 21, 62% men,
38% women, 29% minority,
5% international
Average class size: 11
Completion: Credits needed
to graduate: 30; target
time to graduate: 1 year
**College funded aid
available:** Domestic: Yes;
International: Yes
Graduates with debt: 22%;
average amount of debt $29,816

University of Baltimore

Public

ONLINE MBA PROGRAM(S)

www.ubalt.edu/admission/
graduate/index.cfm
Admissions: (410) 837-6565
Email: admission@ubalt.edu
Financial aid: (410) 837-4772
Application deadline: rolling
**Program can be completed
entirely online:** Yes
Total program cost: $40,320
full-time in-state, $40,320
part-time in-state, $40,320
full-time out-of-state, $40,320
part-time out-of-state
Tuition per credit: $840
full-time in-state, $840
part-time in-state, $840
full-time out-of-state, $840
part-time out-of-state
Acceptance rate: 99.0%
Test scores required:
GMAT or GRE
Average GMAT: 494

Average GRE: 148 verbal, 145
quantitative, 4.0 writing
Average age of entrants: 31
Enrollment: 520, 48%
men, 52% women, 42%
minority, 6% international
Average class size: 27
**Most popular MBA
concentrations:** general
management
Completion: Three year
graduation rate: 59%; credits
needed to graduate: 36; target
time to graduate: 3 years
**College funded aid
available:** Domestic: Yes;
International: Yes
Graduates with debt: 42%;
average amount of debt $46,585

University of Maryland–College Park (Smith)

Public

ONLINE MBA PROGRAM(S)

onlinemba.umd.edu/
Admissions: (877) 807-8741
Email: admissions@
onlineprograms.umd.edu
Financial aid: (301) 314-9565
Application deadline: rolling
**Program can be completed
entirely online:** No
Total program cost: $87,318
full-time in-state, $87,318
part-time in-state, $87,318
full-time out-of-state, $87,318
part-time out-of-state
Tuition per credit: $1,617
full-time in-state, $1,617
part-time in-state, $1,617
full-time out-of-state, $1,617
part-time out-of-state
Acceptance rate: 65.0%
Test scores required:
GMAT or GRE
Average GMAT: 554
Average GRE: 154 verbal, 152
quantitative, 4.0 writing
Average age of entrants: 33
**Students with prior work
experience:** 100.0%
Enrollment: 399, 64%
men, 36% women, 40%
minority, 1% international
Average class size: 18
**Most popular MBA
concentrations:** finance,
general management,
marketing, management
information systems, supply
chain management/logistics
Completion: Three year
graduation rate: 82%; credits
needed to graduate: 54; target
time to graduate: 2 years
**College funded aid
available:** Domestic: Yes;
International: Yes

MASSACHUSETTS

Babson College (Olin)

Private

ONLINE MBA PROGRAM(S)

www.babson.edu/admission/
graduate/
Admissions: (781) 239-4317
Email: gradadmissions@
babson.edu
Financial aid: (781) 239-4219
Application deadline: rolling
**Program can be completed
entirely online:** No

Total program cost: $89,564
full-time in-state, $89,564
part-time in-state, $89,564
full-time out-of-state, $89,564
part-time out-of-state
Tuition per credit: $1,907
full-time in-state, $1,907
part-time in-state, $1,907
full-time out-of-state, $1,907
part-time out-of-state
Acceptance rate: 87.0%
Test scores required: No
Average age of entrants: 33
Students with prior work
experience: 100.0%
Enrollment: 409, 58%
men, 42% women, 27%
minority, 6% international
Average class size: 35
Most popular MBA concentrations:
entrepreneurship, marketing
Completion: Three year
graduation rate: 98%; credits
needed to graduate: 46; target
time to graduate: 2 years
College funded aid available:
Domestic: Yes
Graduates with debt: 61%;
average amount of debt $65,478

Bay Path University

Private

ONLINE MBA PROGRAM(S)

graduate.baypath.edu/
Admissions: (413) 565-1332
Email: graduate@baypath.edu
Financial aid: (413) 565-1256
Application deadline: N/A
Total program cost: N/A
Tuition per credit: $830
full-time in-state, $830
part-time in-state, $830
full-time out-of-state, $830
part-time out-of-state
Enrollment: 145, 10% men,
90% women, N/A minority,
N/A international
Completion: Target time
to graduate: 1.5 years
Graduates with debt: 53%;
average amount of debt $7,535

Bentley University

Private

ONLINE MBA PROGRAM(S)

Admissions: (781) 891-2108
Email: applygrad@bentley.edu
Financial aid: (781) 891-3441
Application deadline: rolling
Program can be completed
entirely online: Yes
Total program cost: $46,200
full-time in-state, $46,200
part-time in-state, $46,200
full-time out-of-state, $46,200
part-time out-of-state
Tuition per credit: $1,540
full-time in-state, $1,540
part-time in-state, $1,540
full-time out-of-state, $1,540
part-time out-of-state
Test scores required:
GMAT or GRE
Average class size: N/A
Most popular MBA
concentrations: leadership
Completion: Credits needed
to graduate: 45; target time
to graduate: 1.5 years
College funded aid
available: Domestic: Yes;
International: Yes

ONLINE BUSINESS PROGRAM(S)

Admissions: (781) 891-2108
Email: applygrad@bentley.edu
Financial aid: (781) 891-3441
Application deadline: rolling
Program can be completed
entirely online: Depends
Total program cost: $46,200
full-time in-state, $46,200
part-time in-state, $46,200
full-time out-of-state, $46,200
part-time out-of-state
Tuition per credit: $1,540
full-time in-state, $1,540
part-time in-state, $1,540
full-time out-of-state, $1,540
part-time out-of-state
Acceptance rate: 85.0%
Test scores required:
GMAT or GRE
Average GMAT: 591
Average GRE: 153 verbal, 158
quantitative, 4.0 writing
Average age of entrants: 29
Students with prior work
experience: 48.0%
Enrollment: 138, 44% men,
56% women, 17% minority,
16% international
Average class size: 26
Most popular business
concentrations: tax
Completion: Three year
graduation rate: 80%; credits
needed to graduate: 30; target
time to graduate: 2 years
College funded aid
available: Domestic: Yes;
International: Yes
Graduates with debt: 37%;
average amount of debt $32,982

Boston University

Private

ONLINE BUSINESS PROGRAM(S)

www.bu.edu/met/
admissions/apply-now/
graduate-degree-program/
Admissions: (617) 358-8162
Email: adsadmissions@bu.edu
Financial aid: (617) 358-3993
Application deadline: rolling
Program can be completed
entirely online: Yes
Total program cost: $34,370
part-time in-state, $34,370
part-time out-of-state
Tuition per credit: $880
full-time in-state, $880
part-time in-state, $880
full-time out-of-state, $880
part-time out-of-state
Acceptance rate: 90.0%
Test scores required: No
Average GMAT: 643
Average GRE: 155 verbal, 155
quantitative, 3.9 writing
Average age of entrants: 33
Students with prior work
experience: 100.0%
Enrollment: 653, 49% men,
51% women, 33% minority,
13% international
Average class size: 37
Most popular business
concentrations: finance,
international business,
marketing, supply chain
management/logistics,
quantitative analysis/statistics
and operations research
Completion: Three year
graduation rate: 62%; credits
needed to graduate: 40; target
time to graduate: 3 years
College funded aid
available: Domestic: Yes;
International: Yes

Graduates with debt: 47%;
average amount of debt $37,787

Lasell College

Private

ONLINE MBA PROGRAM(S)

www.lasell.edu/admissions/
graduate-admission.html
Admissions: (617) 243-2400
Email: gradinfo@lasell.edu
Financial aid: (617) 243-2227
Application deadline: rolling
Program can be completed
entirely online: Yes
Total program cost: $21,600
full-time in-state, $21,600
part-time in-state, $21,600
full-time out-of-state, $21,600
part-time out-of-state
Tuition per credit: $600
full-time in-state, $600
part-time in-state, $600
full-time out-of-state, $600
part-time out-of-state
Acceptance rate: 95.0%
Test scores required: No
Average age of entrants: 37
Enrollment: 33, 27% men,
73% women, 30% minority,
0% international
Average class size: 11
Most popular MBA
concentrations: general
management
Completion: Three year
graduation rate: 80%; credits
needed to graduate: 36; target
time to graduate: 2 years
College funded aid available:
Domestic: No; International: No

ONLINE BUSINESS PROGRAM(S)

www.lasell.edu/admissions/
graduate-admission.html
Admissions: (617) 243-2400
Email: gradinfo@lasell.edu
Financial aid: (617) 243-2227
Application deadline: rolling
Program can be completed
entirely online: Yes
Total program cost: $21,600
full-time in-state, $21,600
part-time in-state, $21,600
full-time out-of-state, $21,600
part-time out-of-state
Tuition per credit: $600
full-time in-state, $600
part-time in-state, $600
full-time out-of-state, $600
part-time out-of-state
Acceptance rate: 93.0%
Test scores required: No
Average age of entrants: 30
Enrollment: 148, 32% men,
68% women, 20% minority,
20% international
Average class size: 12
Most popular business
concentrations: general
management, hotel
administration, human
resources management,
marketing
Completion: Three year
graduation rate: 67%; credits
needed to graduate: 36; target
time to graduate: 1.5 years
College funded aid available:
Domestic: No; International: No
Graduates with debt: 46%;
average amount of debt $39,471

New England College of Business and Finance

Proprietary

ONLINE MBA PROGRAM(S)

www.necb.edu/admissions/
about-admissions/
Admissions: (617) 603-6937
Email: john.alonso@necb.edu
Financial aid: (205) 795-9605
Application deadline: rolling
Program can be completed
entirely online: Yes
Total program cost: $36,420
full-time in-state, $36,420
part-time in-state, $36,420
full-time out-of-state, $36,420
part-time out-of-state
Tuition per credit: $1,012
full-time in-state, $1,012
part-time in-state, $1,012
full-time out-of-state, $1,012
part-time out-of-state
Acceptance rate: 87.0%
Test scores required: No
Average age of entrants: 34
Students with prior work
experience: 93.0%
Enrollment: 165, 30% men,
70% women, 35% minority,
0% international
Average class size: 11
Most popular MBA
concentrations: finance, health
care administration, human
resources management
Completion: Three year
graduation rate: 61%; credits
needed to graduate: 36; target
time to graduate: 1.5 years
College funded aid
available: Domestic: Yes;
International: Yes
Graduates with debt: 70%;
average amount of debt $29,842

ONLINE BUSINESS PROGRAM(S)

www.necb.edu/admissions/
about-admissions/
Admissions: (617) 603-6937
Email: john.alonso@necb.edu
Financial aid: (205) 795-9605
Application deadline: rolling
Program can be completed
entirely online: Yes
Total program cost: $30,350
full-time in-state, $30,350
part-time in-state, $30,350
full-time out-of-state, $30,350
part-time out-of-state
Tuition per credit: $1,012
full-time in-state, $1,012
part-time in-state, $1,012
full-time out-of-state, $1,012
part-time out-of-state
Acceptance rate: 80.0%
Test scores required: No
Average age of entrants: 38
Students with prior work
experience: 98.0%
Enrollment: 157, 22% men,
78% women, 36% minority,
3% international
Average class size: 7
Most popular business
concentrations: accounting,
finance, health care
administration, human
resources management
Completion: Three year
graduation rate: 71%; credits
needed to graduate: 30; target
time to graduate: 1.5 years
College funded aid
available: Domestic: Yes;
International: Yes
Graduates with debt: 64%;
average amount of debt $24,683

Nichols College

Private

ONLINE MBA PROGRAM(S)

gps.nichols.edu/
Admissions: (508) 213-2159
Email: gps@nichols.edu
Financial aid: (508) 213-2340
Application deadline: rolling
Program can be completed
entirely online: Yes
Total program cost: $25,200
full-time in-state, $25,200
part-time in-state, $25,200
full-time out-of-state, $25,200
part-time out-of-state
Tuition per credit: $700
full-time in-state, $700
part-time in-state, $700
full-time out-of-state, $700
part-time out-of-state
Acceptance rate: 99.0%
Test scores required: No
Average age of entrants: 28
Students with prior work
experience: 82.0%
Enrollment: 221, 46%
men, 54% women, 16%
minority, 1% international
Average class size: 15
Most popular MBA
concentrations: accounting,
leadership, organizational
behavior
Completion: Three year
graduation rate: 75%; credits
needed to graduate: 36; target
time to graduate: 2 years
College funded aid available:
Domestic: No; International: No

ONLINE BUSINESS PROGRAM(S)

gps.nichols.edu/
Admissions: (508) 213-2159
Email: gps@nichols.edu
Financial aid: (508) 213-2340
Application deadline: rolling
Program can be completed
entirely online: Yes
Total program cost: $21,000
full-time in-state, $21,000
part-time in-state, $21,000
full-time out-of-state, $21,000
part-time out-of-state
Tuition per credit: $700
full-time in-state, $700
part-time in-state, $700
full-time out-of-state, $700
part-time out-of-state
Acceptance rate: 94.0%
Test scores required: No
Average age of entrants: 31
Enrollment: 105, 44% men,
56% women, 9% minority,
2% international
Average class size: 15
Most popular business
concentrations: accounting,
organizational behavior
Completion: Credits needed
to graduate: 30; target time
to graduate: 2 years
College funded aid available:
Domestic: No; International: No
Graduates with debt: 51%

Northeastern University

Private

ONLINE MBA PROGRAM(S)

onlinebusiness.
northeastern.edu/
Admissions: (866) 890-0347
Email: onlinegradbusiness@
northeastern.edu
Financial aid: (617) 373-5899

Application deadline: rolling
Program can be completed entirely online: Yes
Total program cost: $80,000
full-time in-state, $80,000
part-time in-state, $80,000
full-time out-of-state, $80,000
part-time out-of-state
Tuition per credit: $1,600
full-time in-state, $1,600
part-time in-state, $1,600
full-time out-of-state, $1,600
part-time out-of-state
Acceptance rate: 88.0%
Test scores required: No
Average age of entrants: 35
Students with prior work experience: 100.0%
Enrollment: 692, 59% men, 41% women, 26% minority, 5% international
Average class size: 18
Most popular MBA concentrations: entrepreneurship, finance, international business, marketing, supply chain management/logistics
Completion: Three year graduation rate: 46%; credits needed to graduate: 50; target time to graduate: 2 years
College funded aid available: Domestic: Yes; International: Yes

ONLINE BUSINESS PROGRAM(S)

onlinebusiness.
northeastern.edu/
Admissions: (866) 890-0347
Email: onlinegradbusiness@northeastern.edu
Financial aid: (617) 373-5899
Application deadline: rolling
Program can be completed entirely online: Yes
Total program cost: $48,000
full-time in-state, $48,000
part-time in-state, $48,000
full-time out-of-state, $48,000
part-time out-of-state
Tuition per credit: $1,600
full-time in-state, $1,600
part-time in-state, $1,600
full-time out-of-state, $1,600
part-time out-of-state
Acceptance rate: 84.0%
Test scores required: No
Average age of entrants: 38
Students with prior work experience: 94.0%
Enrollment: 178, 61% men, 39% women, 24% minority, 6% international
Average class size: 12
Most popular business concentrations: finance, tax
Completion: Three year graduation rate: 60%; credits needed to graduate: 30; target time to graduate: 1.5 years
College funded aid available: Domestic: Yes; International: Yes

Suffolk University (Sawyer)

Private

ONLINE MBA PROGRAM(S)

www.suffolk.edu/admission/grad.php
Admissions: (617) 573-8302
Email: gradadmission@suffolk.edu
Financial aid: (617) 573-8470
Application deadline: rolling
Program can be completed entirely online: Yes

Total program cost: $42,156
part-time in-state, $42,156
part-time out-of-state
Tuition per credit: $1,171
full-time in-state, $1,171
part-time in-state, $1,171
full-time out-of-state, $1,171
part-time out-of-state
Acceptance rate: 78.0%
Test scores required: GMAT or GRE
Average GMAT: 530
Average GRE: 148 verbal, 144 quantitative, 4.0 writing
Average age of entrants: 28
Students with prior work experience: 91.0%
Enrollment: 50, 40% men, 60% women, 24% minority, 0% international
Average class size: 12
Completion: Credits needed to graduate: 36; target time to graduate: 2 years
College funded aid available: Domestic: Yes; International: Yes
Graduates with debt: 57%; average amount of debt $53,936

University of Massachusetts–Amherst (Isenberg)

Public

ONLINE MBA PROGRAM(S)

www.isenberg.umass.edu
Admissions: (413) 545-5608
Email: grad@isenberg.umass.edu
Financial aid: (413) 545-0801
Application deadline: rolling
Program can be completed entirely online: Yes
Total program cost: $35,100
full-time in-state, $35,100
part-time in-state, $35,100
full-time out-of-state, $35,100
part-time out-of-state
Tuition per credit: $900
full-time in-state, $900
part-time in-state, $900
full-time out-of-state, $900
part-time out-of-state
Acceptance rate: 89.0%
Test scores required: GMAT or GRE
Average GMAT: 600
Average GRE: 157 verbal, 158 quantitative, 4.1 writing
Average age of entrants: 37
Students with prior work experience: 100.0%
Enrollment: 1,403, 67% men, 33% women, 25% minority, 6% international
Average class size: 49
Most popular MBA concentrations: finance, health care administration, marketing, management information systems, production/operations management
Completion: Three year graduation rate: 48%; credits needed to graduate: 39; target time to graduate: 4 years
College funded aid available: Domestic: No; International: No
Graduates with debt: 17%; average amount of debt $40,795

University of Massachusetts–Boston

Public

ONLINE BUSINESS PROGRAM(S)

www.umb.edu/admissions/grad
Admissions: (617) 287-6400
Email: bos.gadm@umb.edu
Financial aid: (617) 287-6300
Application deadline: Domestic: 06/01; International: 06/01
Program can be completed entirely online: Yes
Total program cost: $20,700
part-time in-state, $20,700
full-time out-of-state, $20,700
part-time out-of-state
Tuition per credit: $575 full-time in-state, $575 part-time in-state, $575 full-time out-of-state, $575 part-time out-of-state
Acceptance rate: 79.0%
Test scores required: No
Average age of entrants: 34
Enrollment: 97, 23% men, 77% women, 26% minority, 8% international
Average class size: 11
Most popular business concentrations: health care administration, leadership, organizational behavior, public administration, public policy
Completion: Three year graduation rate: 42%; credits needed to graduate: 36; target time to graduate: 2 years
College funded aid available: Domestic: Yes; International: No
Graduates with debt: 39%; average amount of debt $37,281

University of Massachusetts–Dartmouth (Charlton)

Public

ONLINE MBA PROGRAM(S)

www.umassd.edu/programs/business-administration-mba-online
Admissions: (508) 999-9202
Email: online@umassd.edu
Financial aid: (508) 999-8643
Application deadline: rolling
Program can be completed entirely online: Yes
Total program cost: N/A
Tuition per credit: $553
full-time in-state, $553
part-time in-state, $553
full-time out-of-state, $553
part-time out-of-state
Acceptance rate: 95.0%
Average GMAT: 483
Average age of entrants: 33
Enrollment: 75, 52% men, 48% women, 20% minority, 1% international
Average class size: 21
Most popular MBA concentrations: general management
Completion: Three year graduation rate: 54%; credits needed to graduate: 30; target time to graduate: 2 years
College funded aid available: International: No
Graduates with debt: 59%; average amount of debt $42,021

ONLINE BUSINESS PROGRAM(S)

www.umassd.edu/programs/healthcare-management-ms-online
Admissions: (508) 999-9202
Email: online@umassd.edu
Financial aid: (508) 999-8643
Application deadline: rolling
Program can be completed entirely online: Yes
Total program cost: N/A
Tuition per credit: $553
full-time in-state, $553
part-time in-state, $553
full-time out-of-state, $553
part-time out-of-state
Acceptance rate: 88.0%
Average age of entrants: 34
Enrollment: 13, 38% men, 62% women, 46% minority, 0% international
Average class size: 22
Most popular business concentrations: health care administration
Completion: Credits needed to graduate: 30; target time to graduate: 2 years
College funded aid available: International: No

University of Massachusetts–Lowell

Public

ONLINE MBA PROGRAM(S)

continuinged.uml.edu/online/mba/
Admissions: (800) 656-4723
Email: mba@uml.edu
Financial aid: (978) 934-4220
Application deadline: rolling
Program can be completed entirely online: Yes
Total program cost: $19,650
full-time in-state, $19,650
part-time in-state, $19,650
full-time out-of-state, $19,650
part-time out-of-state
Tuition per credit: $655
full-time in-state, $655
part-time in-state, $655
full-time out-of-state, $655
part-time out-of-state
Acceptance rate: 91.0%
Average GMAT: 544
Average age of entrants: 34
Students with prior work experience: 86.0%
Enrollment: 896, 65% men, 35% women, 18% minority, 5% international
Average class size: 27
Most popular MBA concentrations: finance, international business, leadership, marketing, management information systems
Completion: Three year graduation rate: 55%; credits needed to graduate: 30; target time to graduate: 3 years
College funded aid available: Domestic: Yes; International: No
Graduates with debt: 16%; average amount of debt $31,717

ONLINE BUSINESS PROGRAM(S)

continuinged.uml.edu/online/mba/
Admissions: (800) 656-4723
Email: mba@uml.edu
Financial aid: (978) 934-4220
Application deadline: rolling
Program can be completed entirely online: Yes

Total program cost: $19,650
full-time in-state, $19,650
part-time in-state, $19,650
full-time out-of-state, $19,650
part-time out-of-state
Tuition per credit: $655
full-time in-state, $655
part-time in-state, $655
full-time out-of-state, $655
part-time out-of-state
Acceptance rate: 87.0%
Average age of entrants: 28
Students with prior work experience: 88.0%
Enrollment: 123, 57% men, 43% women, 33% minority, 5% international
Average class size: 23
Most popular business concentrations: accounting, entrepreneurship, finance
Completion: Three year graduation rate: 72%; credits needed to graduate: 30; target time to graduate: 3 years
College funded aid available: Domestic: Yes; International: No
Graduates with debt: 44%; average amount of debt $18,768

Western New England University

Private

ONLINE MBA PROGRAM(S)

www1.wne.edu/admissions/graduate/index.cfm
Admissions: (800) 325-1122
Email: study@wne.edu
Financial aid: (413) 796-2080
Application deadline: rolling
Program can be completed entirely online: Yes
Total program cost: $30,564
part-time in-state, $30,564
part-time out-of-state
Tuition per credit: $849
full-time in-state, $849
part-time in-state, $849
full-time out-of-state, $849
part-time out-of-state
Acceptance rate: 82.0%
Test scores required: GMAT or GRE
Average GMAT: 523
Average age of entrants: 29
Students with prior work experience: 78.0%
Enrollment: 74, 54% men, 46% women, 9% minority, 1% international
Most popular MBA concentrations: accounting, general management, leadership
Completion: Credits needed to graduate: 36; target time to graduate: 2 years
College funded aid available: Domestic: No; International: No

ONLINE BUSINESS PROGRAM(S)

www1.wne.edu/admissions/graduate/index.cfm
Admissions: (800) 325-1122
Email: study@wne.edu
Financial aid: (413) 796-2080
Application deadline: rolling
Program can be completed entirely online: Depends
Total program cost: $25,470
full-time in-state, $25,470
part-time in-state, $25,470
full-time out-of-state, $25,470
part-time out-of-state
Tuition per credit: $849
full-time in-state, $849
part-time in-state, $849

full-time out-of-state, $849
Acceptance rate: 91.0%
Test scores required:
GMAT or GRE
Average GMAT: 485
Average age of entrants: 29
**Students with prior work
experience:** 65.0%
Enrollment: 49, 51% men,
49% women, 6% minority,
0% international
**Most popular business
concentrations:** accounting,
leadership
Completion: Credits needed
to graduate: 30; target time
to graduate: 2 years
College funded aid available:
Domestic: No; International: No

Worcester Polytechnic Institute
Private

ONLINE MBA PROGRAM(S)

business.wpi.edu
Admissions: (508) 831-4665
Email: business@wpi.edu
Financial aid: (508) 831-5469
Application deadline: rolling
**Program can be completed
entirely online:** No
Total program cost: $72,624
full-time in-state, $72,624
part-time in-state, $72,624
full-time out-of-state, $72,624
part-time out-of-state
Tuition per credit: $1,513
full-time in-state, $1,513
part-time in-state, $1,513
full-time out-of-state, $1,513
part-time out-of-state
Acceptance rate: 80.0%
Test scores required:
GMAT or GRE
Average GRE: 150 verbal, 152
quantitative, 3.6 writing
Average age of entrants: 30
**Students with prior work
experience:** 100.0%
Enrollment: 141, 63% men,
37% women, 16% minority,
8% international
Average class size: 20
**Most popular MBA
concentrations:** manufacturing
and technology
management, production/
operations management,
organizational behavior,
supply chain management/
logistics, technology
Completion: Three year
graduation rate: 90%; credits
needed to graduate: 48; target
time to graduate: 2.5 years
**College funded aid
available:** Domestic: Yes;
International: Yes
Graduates with debt: 50%;
average amount of debt $10,000

Andrews University
Private

ONLINE MBA PROGRAM(S)

www.andrews.edu/grad/
admissions/
Admissions: (269) 471-6321
Email: graduate@andrews.edu
Financial aid: (269) 471-6040
Application deadline: rolling

**Program can be completed
entirely online:** Yes
Total program cost: $18,249
full-time in-state, $18,249
part-time in-state, $18,249
full-time out-of-state, $18,249
part-time out-of-state
Tuition per credit: $553
full-time in-state, $553
part-time in-state, $553
full-time out-of-state, $553
part-time out-of-state
Acceptance rate: 80.0%
Test scores required: GMAT
Average GMAT: 475
Average age of entrants: 28
**Students with prior work
experience:** 36.0%
Enrollment: 31, 45% men,
55% women, N/A minority,
N/A international
Average class size: 9
**Most popular MBA
concentrations:** general
management
Completion: Credits needed
to graduate: 33; target time
to graduate: 2 years
College funded aid available:
Domestic: No; International: No

Central Michigan University
Public

ONLINE MBA PROGRAM(S)

global.cmich.edu/onlinemba/
default.aspx?dc=mba
Admissions: (877) 268-4636
Email: cmuglobal@cmich.edu
Financial aid: (989) 774-3674
Application deadline: rolling
**Program can be completed
entirely online:** Yes
Total program cost: N/A
Tuition per credit: $625
full-time in-state, $625
part-time in-state, $625
full-time out-of-state, $625
part-time out-of-state
Acceptance rate: 68.0%
Test scores required: GMAT
Average GMAT: 499
Average age of entrants: 32
Enrollment: 501, 51% men,
49% women, 19% minority,
1% international
Average class size: 28
**Most popular MBA
concentrations:** general
management, human
resources management,
marketing, management
information systems, supply
chain management/logistics
Completion: Three year
graduation rate: 72%; credits
needed to graduate: 36; target
time to graduate: 2.5 years
**College funded aid
available:** Domestic: Yes;
International: Yes
Graduates with debt: 19%;
average amount of debt $26,455

Cornerstone University
Private

ONLINE MBA PROGRAM(S)

www.cornerstone.edu/
pgs-business-degrees
Admissions: (800) 947-2382
Email: pgs.information@
cornerstone.edu
Financial aid: (616) 222-1424

Application deadline: rolling
**Program can be completed
entirely online:** Yes
Total program cost: $21,470
full-time in-state, $21,470
part-time in-state, $21,470
full-time out-of-state, $21,470
part-time out-of-state
Tuition per credit: $565
full-time in-state, $565
part-time in-state, $565
full-time out-of-state, $565
part-time out-of-state
Acceptance rate: 89.0%
Test scores required: No
Average age of entrants: 34
Enrollment: 84, 46% men,
54% women, 27% minority,
2% international
Average class size: 8
**Most popular MBA
concentrations:** finance,
health care administration,
international business
Completion: Three year
graduation rate: 84%; credits
needed to graduate: 38; target
time to graduate: 2 years
College funded aid available:
Domestic: No; International: No

ONLINE BUSINESS PROGRAM(S)

www.cornerstone.edu/
pgs-business-degrees
Admissions: (800) 947-2382
Email: pgs.information@
cornerstone.edu
Financial aid: (616) 222-1424
Application deadline: rolling
**Program can be completed
entirely online:** Yes
Total program cost: $18,540
full-time in-state, $18,540
part-time in-state, $18,540
full-time out-of-state, $18,540
part-time out-of-state
Tuition per credit: $515 full-time
in-state, $515 part-time in-state,
$515 full-time out-of-state,
$515 part-time out-of-state
Acceptance rate: 100.0%
Test scores required: No
Average age of entrants: 45
**Students with prior work
experience:** 100.0%
Enrollment: 24, 25% men,
75% women, 50% minority,
0% international
Average class size: 8
**Most popular business
concentrations:** leadership
Completion: Credits needed
to graduate: 36; target time
to graduate: 1.5 years
College funded aid available:
Domestic: No; International: No

Eastern Michigan University
Public

ONLINE BUSINESS PROGRAM(S)

cob.emich.edu
Admissions: (734) 487-4444
Email: cob_graduate@emich.edu
Financial aid: (734) 487-1048
Application deadline: rolling
**Program can be completed
entirely online:** Yes
Total program cost: $30,132
full-time in-state, $30,132
part-time in-state, $30,132
full-time out-of-state, $30,132
part-time out-of-state
Tuition per credit: $762 full-time
in-state, $762 part-time in-state,
$762 full-time out-of-state,
$762 part-time out-of-state

Acceptance rate: 63.0%
Test scores required: No
Average age of entrants: 29
Enrollment: 56, 20% men,
80% women, 25% minority,
0% international
Average class size: 16
**Most popular business
concentrations:** marketing
Completion: Three year
graduation rate: 76%; credits
needed to graduate: 36; target
time to graduate: 2 years
College funded aid available:
Domestic: Yes; International: No
Graduates with debt: 75%;
average amount of debt $24,790

Ferris State University
Public

ONLINE MBA PROGRAM(S)

www.ferris.edu/mba-online/
Admissions: (231) 591-3932
Email: tetsworc@ferris.edu
Financial aid: (231) 591-2115
Application deadline: rolling
**Program can be completed
entirely online:** Yes
Total program cost: $23,790
full-time in-state, $23,790
part-time in-state, $23,790
full-time out-of-state, $23,790
part-time out-of-state
Tuition per credit: $610 full-time
in-state, $610 part-time in-state,
$610 full-time out-of-state,
$610 part-time out-of-state
Acceptance rate: 35.0%
Test scores required:
GMAT or GRE
Average GMAT: 420
Average GRE: 149 verbal, 150
quantitative, 4.0 writing
Average age of entrants: 25
**Students with prior work
experience:** 100.0%
Enrollment: 137, 42% men,
58% women, N/A minority,
N/A international
Average class size: 20
**Most popular MBA
concentrations:** accounting,
general management,
leadership, supply chain
management/logistics
Completion: Credits needed
to graduate: 39; target time
to graduate: 2 years
**College funded aid
available:** Domestic: Yes;
International: Yes
Graduates with debt: 46%;
average amount of debt $37,910

ONLINE BUSINESS PROGRAM(S)

ferris.edu/admissions/
homepage.htm
Admissions: (231) 591-3932
Email: CharlotteTetsworth@
ferris.edu
Financial aid: (231) 591-2115
Application deadline: rolling
**Program can be completed
entirely online:** Yes
Total program cost: $20,130
full-time in-state, $20,130
part-time in-state, $20,130
full-time out-of-state, $20,130
part-time out-of-state
Tuition per credit: $610 full-time
in-state, $610 part-time in-state,
$610 full-time out-of-state,
$610 part-time out-of-state
Acceptance rate: 29.0%
Test scores required:
GMAT or GRE

Average GRE: 145 verbal, 155
quantitative, 3.0 writing
Average age of entrants: 27
**Students with prior work
experience:** 100.0%
Enrollment: 31, 48% men,
52% women, 6% minority,
35% international
Average class size: 12
**Most popular business
concentrations:** management
information systems
Completion: Three year
graduation rate: 83%; credits
needed to graduate: 33; target
time to graduate: 1.5 years
**College funded aid
available:** Domestic: Yes;
International: Yes
Graduates with debt: 36%;
average amount of debt $41,440

Kettering University
Private

ONLINE MBA PROGRAM(S)

Admissions: (810) 762-9575
Email: kuonline@kettering.edu
Financial aid: (810) 762-7491
Application deadline: rolling
**Program can be completed
entirely online:** Yes
Total program cost: $49,200
full-time in-state, $49,200
part-time in-state, $49,200
full-time out-of-state, $49,200
part-time out-of-state
Tuition per credit: $912 full-time
in-state, $912 part-time in-state,
$912 full-time out-of-state,
$912 part-time out-of-state
Acceptance rate: 62.0%
Test scores required: No
Average age of entrants: 29
**Students with prior work
experience:** 100.0%
Enrollment: 99, 64% men,
36% women, 19% minority,
1% international
Average class size: 12
**Most popular MBA
concentrations:** general
management, leadership,
production/operations
management, supply
chain management/
logistics, technology
Completion: Credits needed
to graduate: 40; target time
to graduate: 1.5 years
**College funded aid
available:** Domestic: Yes;
International: Yes
Graduates with debt: 12%;
average amount of debt $4,880

ONLINE BUSINESS PROGRAM(S)

Admissions: (810) 762-9575
Email: kuonline@kettering.edu
Financial aid: (810) 762-7491
Application deadline: rolling
**Program can be completed
entirely online:** Yes
Total program cost: $49,200
full-time in-state, $49,200
part-time in-state, $49,200
full-time out-of-state, $49,200
part-time out-of-state
Tuition per credit: $912 full-time
in-state, $912 part-time in-state,
$912 full-time out-of-state,
$912 part-time out-of-state
Acceptance rate: 82.0%
Test scores required: No
Average age of entrants: 27
**Students with prior work
experience:** 100.0%

Enrollment: 397, 76% men, 24% women, 20% minority, 10% international
Average class size: 12
Most popular business concentrations: general management, leadership, production/operations management, supply chain management/logistics
Completion: Credits needed to graduate: 40; target time to graduate: 2.5 years
College funded aid available: Domestic: Yes; International: Yes
Graduates with debt: average amount of debt $4,800

Lawrence Technological University

Private

ONLINE MBA PROGRAM(S)

www.ltu.edu/futurestudents/
Admissions: (800) 225-5588
Email: admissions@ltu.edu
Financial aid: (248) 204-2126
Application deadline: rolling
Program can be completed entirely online: Yes
Total program cost: N/A
Tuition per credit: $1,150 full-time in-state, $1,150 part-time in-state, $1,150 full-time out-of-state, $1,150 part-time out-of-state
Acceptance rate: 79.0%
Test scores required: No
Average age of entrants: 30
Enrollment: 177, 62% men, 38% women, 25% minority, 14% international
Average class size: 20
Most popular MBA concentrations: finance, marketing, management information systems
Completion: Three year graduation rate: 53%; credits needed to graduate: 36; target time to graduate: 3 years
College funded aid available: Domestic: Yes; International: Yes
Graduates with debt: 35%; average amount of debt $64,303

Madonna University

Private

ONLINE MBA PROGRAM(S)

www.madonna.edu/grad
Admissions: (734) 432-5667
Email: grad@madonna.edu
Financial aid: (734) 432-5662
Application deadline: rolling
Program can be completed entirely online: Yes
Total program cost: N/A
Tuition per credit: $835 full-time in-state, $835 part-time in-state, $835 full-time out-of-state, $835 part-time out-of-state
Acceptance rate: 100.0%
Test scores required: No
Average age of entrants: 22
Enrollment: 41, 41% men, 59% women, N/A minority, 100% international
Average class size: 16
Completion: Three year graduation rate: 10%; credits

needed to graduate: 45; target time to graduate: 3 years
College funded aid available: Domestic: No; International: No

Michigan State University (Broad)

Public

ONLINE BUSINESS PROGRAM(S)

www.michiganstateuniversityonline.com/programs/masters-degree/ms-management-strategy-leadership/
Admissions: (517) 355-1878
Email: MS-MGT@broad.msu.edu
Financial aid: (517) 432-1155
Application deadline: rolling
Program can be completed entirely online: Yes
Total program cost: $32,700 full-time in-state, $32,700 part-time in-state, $32,700 full-time out-of-state, $32,700 part-time out-of-state
Tuition per credit: $1,090 full-time in-state, $1,090 part-time in-state, $1,090 full-time out-of-state, $1,090 part-time out-of-state
Acceptance rate: 95.0%
Test scores required: No
Average age of entrants: 38
Students with prior work experience: 89.0%
Enrollment: 531, 66% men, 34% women, 6% minority, 0% international
Average class size: 29
Completion: Three year graduation rate: 85%; credits needed to graduate: 30; target time to graduate: 1.5 years
College funded aid available: Domestic: No; International: No
Graduates with debt: 42%; average amount of debt $45,604

Northwood University

Private

ONLINE MBA PROGRAM(S)

www.northwood.edu/academics/graduate/admissions-requirements.aspx
Admissions: (989) 837-4895
Email: rca@northwood.edu
Financial aid: (800) 622-9000
Application deadline: rolling
Program can be completed entirely online: Yes
Total program cost: $37,080 full-time in-state, $37,080 part-time in-state, $37,080 full-time out-of-state, $37,080 part-time out-of-state
Tuition per credit: $1,030 full-time in-state, $1,030 part-time in-state, $1,030 full-time out-of-state, $1,030 part-time out-of-state
Acceptance rate: 68.0%
Test scores required: No
Average age of entrants: 33
Enrollment: 143, 48% men, 52% women, N/A minority, N/A international
Average class size: 19
Most popular MBA concentrations: general management
Completion: Credits needed to graduate: 36; target time to graduate: 2 years

College funded aid available: Domestic: Yes; International: Yes
Graduates with debt: 72%; average amount of debt $41,858

ONLINE BUSINESS PROGRAM(S)

www.northwood.edu/graduate/admission-requirements.aspx
Admissions: (989) 837-4168
Email: luziusk@northwood.edu
Financial aid: (800) 622-9000
Application deadline: rolling
Program can be completed entirely online: Yes
Total program cost: $23,610 full-time in-state, $23,610 part-time in-state, $23,610 full-time out-of-state, $23,610 part-time out-of-state
Tuition per credit: $787 full-time in-state, $787 part-time in-state, $787 full-time out-of-state, $787 part-time out-of-state
Acceptance rate: 88.0%
Test scores required: No
Average age of entrants: 38
Students with prior work experience: 100.0%
Enrollment: 87, 43% men, 57% women, N/A minority, N/A international
Average class size: 11
Most popular business concentrations: finance, leadership
Completion: Three year graduation rate: 67%; credits needed to graduate: 30; target time to graduate: 2 years
College funded aid available: Domestic: No; International: No
Graduates with debt: 86%; average amount of debt $45,417

University of Michigan–Dearborn

Public

ONLINE MBA PROGRAM(S)

umdearborn.edu/cob/grad-programs/
Admissions: (313) 593-5460
Email: umd-gradbusiness@umich.edu
Financial aid: (313) 593-5300
Application deadline: rolling
Program can be completed entirely online: Yes
Total program cost: N/A
Tuition per credit: $908 full-time in-state, $908 part-time in-state, $1,397 full-time out-of-state, $1,397 part-time out-of-state
Acceptance rate: 50.0%
Test scores required: GMAT or GRE
Average GMAT: 592
Average GRE: 154 verbal, 156 quantitative, 4.0 writing
Average age of entrants: 31
Students with prior work experience: 100.0%
Enrollment: 177, 63% men, 37% women, 21% minority, 3% international
Average class size: 28
Most popular MBA concentrations: finance, international business
Completion: Three year graduation rate: 61%; credits needed to graduate: 48; target time to graduate: 2.5 years
College funded aid available: Domestic: Yes; International: Yes

Graduates with debt: 26%; average amount of debt $49,715

ONLINE BUSINESS PROGRAM(S)

umdearborn.edu/cob/grad-programs/
Admissions: (313) 593-5460
Email: umd-gradbusiness@umich.edu
Financial aid: (313) 593-5300
Application deadline: rolling
Program can be completed entirely online: Yes
Total program cost: N/A
Tuition per credit: $908 full-time in-state, $908 part-time in-state, $1,397 full-time out-of-state, $1,397 part-time out-of-state
Acceptance rate: 53.0%
Test scores required: GMAT or GRE
Average GRE: 163 verbal, 161 quantitative, 5.0 writing
Average age of entrants: 31
Students with prior work experience: 100.0%
Enrollment: 33, 67% men, 33% women, 30% minority, 6% international
Average class size: 28
Most popular business concentrations: finance
Completion: Three year graduation rate: 33%; credits needed to graduate: 30; target time to graduate: 1.5 years
College funded aid available: Domestic: Yes; International: Yes
Graduates with debt: 63%; average amount of debt $42,845

MINNESOTA

Concordia University–St. Paul

Private

ONLINE MBA PROGRAM(S)

www.csp.edu/admission/graduate/
Admissions: (651) 641-8230
Email: graduateadmission@csp.edu
Financial aid: (651) 603-6300
Application deadline: rolling
Program can be completed entirely online: Yes
Total program cost: $27,500 full-time in-state, $27,500 part-time in-state, $27,500 full-time out-of-state, $27,500 part-time out-of-state
Tuition per credit: $625 full-time in-state, $625 part-time in-state, $625 full-time out-of-state, $625 part-time out-of-state
Acceptance rate: 67.0%
Test scores required: No
Average age of entrants: 32
Enrollment: 382, 45% men, 55% women, 25% minority, 13% international
Average class size: 12
Most popular MBA concentrations: general management, health care administration
Completion: Three year graduation rate: 86%; credits needed to graduate: 44; target time to graduate: 3 years
College funded aid available: Domestic: Yes; International: Yes

Graduates with debt: 61%; average amount of debt $35,666

ONLINE BUSINESS PROGRAM(S)

www.csp.edu/admission/graduate/
Admissions: (651) 641-8230
Email: graduateadmission@csp.edu
Financial aid: (651) 603-6300
Application deadline: rolling
Program can be completed entirely online: Yes
Total program cost: $15,300 full-time in-state, $15,300 part-time in-state, $15,300 full-time out-of-state, $15,300 part-time out-of-state
Tuition per credit: $475 full-time in-state, $475 part-time in-state, $475 full-time out-of-state, $475 part-time out-of-state
Acceptance rate: 71.0%
Test scores required: No
Average age of entrants: 32
Enrollment: 216, 24% men, 76% women, 27% minority, 0% international
Average class size: 12
Most popular business concentrations: human resources management, leadership
Completion: Three year graduation rate: 61%; credits needed to graduate: 36; target time to graduate: 2 years
College funded aid available: Domestic: Yes; International: Yes
Graduates with debt: 65%; average amount of debt $26,561

Minnesota State University–Moorhead

Public

ONLINE MBA PROGRAM(S)

www.mnstate.edu/graduate/admission.aspx
Admissions: (218) 477-2134
Email: graduate@mnstate.edu
Financial aid: (218) 477-2251
Application deadline: rolling
Program can be completed entirely online: Yes
Total program cost: $14,948 full-time in-state, $14,948 part-time in-state, $14,948 full-time out-of-state, $14,948 part-time out-of-state
Tuition per credit: $404 full-time in-state, $404 part-time in-state, $404 full-time out-of-state, $404 part-time out-of-state
Acceptance rate: 89.0%
Test scores required: GMAT
Average GMAT: 426
Average age of entrants: 30
Enrollment: 31, 48% men, 52% women, N/A minority, N/A international
Average class size: 15
Most popular MBA concentrations: general management, health care administration
Completion: Three year graduation rate: 77%; credits needed to graduate: 37; target time to graduate: 2 years
College funded aid available: Domestic: Yes

MISSISSIPPI

Belhaven University

Private

ONLINE MBA PROGRAM(S)

online.belhaven.edu
Admissions: (601) 965-7043
Email: onlineadmission@
belhaven.edu
Financial aid: (601) 968-5920
Application deadline: rolling
**Program can be completed
entirely online:** Yes
Total program cost: $20,700
full-time in-state, $20,700
part-time in-state, $20,700
full-time out-of-state, $20,700
part-time out-of-state
Tuition per credit: $550
full-time in-state, $550
part-time in-state, $550
full-time out-of-state, $550
part-time out-of-state
Acceptance rate: 67.0%
Test scores required: No
Average age of entrants: 33
**Students with prior work
experience:** 32.0%
Enrollment: 324, 24%
men, 76% women, 74%
minority, 0% international
Average class size: 13
**Most popular MBA
concentrations:** health care
administration, human
resources management,
leadership, sports business
Completion: Three year
graduation rate: 58%; credits
needed to graduate: 36; target
time to graduate: 2 years
**College funded aid
available:** Domestic: Yes;
International: Yes
Graduates with debt: 82%;
average amount of debt $47,437

ONLINE BUSINESS PROGRAM(S)

online.belhaven.edu
Admissions: (601) 965-7043
Email: onlineadmission@
belhaven.edu
Financial aid: (601) 968-5920
Application deadline: rolling
**Program can be completed
entirely online:** Yes
Total program cost: $20,700
full-time in-state, $20,700
part-time in-state, $20,700
full-time out-of-state, $20,700
part-time out-of-state
Tuition per credit: $550
full-time in-state, $550
part-time in-state, $550
full-time out-of-state, $550
part-time out-of-state
Acceptance rate: 72.0%
Test scores required: No
Average age of entrants: 33
Enrollment: 896, 22%
men, 78% women, 83%
minority, 0% international
Average class size: 13
**Most popular business
concentrations:** health care
administration, human
resources management,
leadership, public
administration, sports business
Completion: Three year
graduation rate: 57%; credits
needed to graduate: 36; target
time to graduate: 2 years
College funded aid available:
Domestic: Yes; International: No
Graduates with debt: 87%;
average amount of debt $51,869

Jackson State University

Public

ONLINE MBA PROGRAM(S)

www.jsums.edu/
graduateschool/
Admissions: (601) 979-4327
Financial aid: (601) 979-2227
Application deadline:
Domestic: 03/15
**Program can be completed
entirely online:** Yes
Total program cost: N/A
Tuition per credit: $462
full-time in-state, $462
part-time in-state, $462
full-time out-of-state, $462
part-time out-of-state
Acceptance rate: 35.0%
Test scores required:
GMAT or GRE
Enrollment: 31, 58% men,
42% women, 90% minority,
3% international
Average class size: 20
**Most popular MBA
concentrations:** economics,
entrepreneurship, finance,
general management, marketing
Completion: Credits needed
to graduate: 30; target
time to graduate: 1 year
College funded aid available:
Domestic: No; International: No
Graduates with debt: 82%;
average amount of debt $36,987

Mississippi State University

Public

ONLINE MBA PROGRAM(S)

distance.msstate.edu/mba
Admissions: (662) 325-7281
Email: csmith@
business.msstate.edu
Financial aid: (662) 325-2450
Application deadline: rolling
**Program can be completed
entirely online:** Yes
Total program cost: $14,235
full-time in-state, $14,235
part-time in-state, $14,235
full-time out-of-state, $14,235
part-time out-of-state
Tuition per credit: $475 full-time
in-state, $475 part-time in-state,
$475 full-time out-of-state,
$475 part-time out-of-state
Acceptance rate: 71.0%
Test scores required:
GMAT or GRE
Average GMAT: 588
Average GRE: 154 verbal, 155
quantitative, 3.9 writing
Average age of entrants: 29
Enrollment: 268, 75% men,
25% women, 9% minority,
2% international
Average class size: 25
**Most popular MBA
concentrations:** general
management, industrial
management, marketing,
management information
systems, quantitative
analysis/statistics and
operations research
Completion: Three year
graduation rate: 49%; credits
needed to graduate: 30; target
time to graduate: 2 years
**College funded aid
available:** Domestic: Yes;
International: Yes

Graduates with debt: 24%;
average amount of debt $28,512

ONLINE BUSINESS PROGRAM(S)

distance.msstate.edu/msis
Admissions: (662) 325-7281
Email: csmith@
business.msstate.edu
Financial aid: (662) 325-2450
Application deadline: rolling
**Program can be completed
entirely online:** Yes
Total program cost: $14,235
full-time in-state, $14,235
part-time in-state, $14,235
full-time out-of-state, $14,235
part-time out-of-state
Tuition per credit: $475 full-time
in-state, $475 full-time out-of-state,
$475 part-time out-of-state
Acceptance rate: 100.0%
Test scores required:
GMAT or GRE
Average GMAT: 607
Average GRE: 155 verbal, 150
quantitative, 4.2 writing
Average age of entrants: 29
Enrollment: 18, 78% men,
22% women, 17% minority,
6% international
Average class size: 11
**Most popular business
concentrations:** accounting,
finance, general management,
marketing, management
information systems
Completion: Credits needed
to graduate: 30; target time
to graduate: 2 years
**College funded aid
available:** Domestic: Yes;
International: Yes
Graduates with debt: 50%;
average amount of debt $33,533

Mississippi Valley State University

Public

ONLINE MBA PROGRAM(S)

Admissions: N/A
Financial aid: N/A
Application deadline: rolling
Total program cost: $4,896
full-time in-state, $2,448
part-time in-state, $4,896
full-time out-of-state, $2,448
part-time out-of-state
Tuition per credit: $408
full-time in-state, $408
part-time in-state, $408
full-time out-of-state, $408
part-time out-of-state
Acceptance rate: 73.0%
Test scores required: No
Average age of entrants: 31
**Students with prior work
experience:** 0.0%
Enrollment: 71, 37% men,
63% women, 97% minority,
0% international
Completion: Credits
needed to graduate: 30
**College funded aid
available:** Domestic: Yes;
International: Yes
Graduates with debt: 100%;
average amount of debt $16,989

University of Mississippi

Public

ONLINE MBA PROGRAM(S)

www.olemissbusiness.com/
mba/pmba/index.html
Admissions: (662) 915-5483
Email: ajones@bus.olemiss.edu
Financial aid: (800) 891-4596
Application deadline: rolling
**Program can be completed
entirely online:** Yes
Total program cost: $31,860
full-time in-state, $31,860
part-time in-state, $31,860
full-time out-of-state, $31,860
part-time out-of-state
Tuition per credit: $810 full-time
in-state, $810 part-time in-state,
$810 full-time out-of-state,
$810 part-time out-of-state
Acceptance rate: 31.0%
Test scores required:
GMAT or GRE
Average GMAT: 566
Average GRE: 154 verbal, 156
quantitative, 3.6 writing
Average age of entrants: 31
**Students with prior work
experience:** 100.0%
Enrollment: 116, 78% men,
22% women, N/A minority,
N/A international
Average class size: 39
Completion: Three year
graduation rate: 81%; credits
needed to graduate: 36; target
time to graduate: 2 years
College funded aid available:
Domestic: No; International: No
Graduates with debt: 26%;
average amount of debt $22,774

University of Southern Mississippi

Public

ONLINE MBA PROGRAM(S)

Admissions: (601) 266-4369
Email: graduateschool@usm.edu
Financial aid: (601) 266-4774
Application deadline: Domestic:
06/01; International: 05/01
**Program can be completed
entirely online:** Depends
Total program cost: $12,771
full-time in-state, $15,609
part-time in-state, $12,771
full-time out-of-state, $15,609
part-time out-of-state
Tuition per credit: $387 full-time
in-state, $473 part-time in-state,
$387 full-time out-of-state,
$473 part-time out-of-state
Acceptance rate: 86.0%
Test scores required:
GMAT or GRE
Average GMAT: 423
Average GRE: 149 verbal, 148
quantitative, 3.6 writing
Average age of entrants: 29
**Students with prior work
experience:** 95.0%
Enrollment: 69, 55% men,
45% women, 17% minority,
1% international
Average class size: 17
**Most popular MBA
concentrations:** sports business,
quantitative analysis/statistics
and operations research
Completion: Credits needed
to graduate: 33; target time
to graduate: 2 years
College funded aid available:
Domestic: No; International: No

MISSOURI

Columbia College

Private

ONLINE MBA PROGRAM(S)

www.ccis.edu/onlinemba/
Admissions: (573) 875-7352
Email: onlinegrad@ccis.edu
Financial aid: (573) 875-7362
Application deadline: rolling
**Program can be completed
entirely online:** Yes
Total program cost: N/A
Tuition per credit: $490
full-time in-state, $490
part-time in-state, $490
full-time out-of-state, $490
part-time out-of-state
Acceptance rate: 98.0%
Test scores required: No
Average age of entrants: 36
**Students with prior work
experience:** 78.0%
Enrollment: 275, 42%
men, 58% women, 26%
minority, 1% international
Average class size: 11
**Most popular MBA
concentrations:** accounting,
general management, human
resources management
Completion: Three year
graduation rate: 69%; credits
needed to graduate: 36; target
time to graduate: 2.5 years
College funded aid available:
Domestic: No; International: No
Graduates with debt: 55%;
average amount of debt $51,450

Lindenwood University

Private

ONLINE MBA PROGRAM(S)

www.lindenwood.edu/
admissions/
Admissions: (636) 949-4933
Email: online@lindenwood.edu
Financial aid: (636) 949-4814
Application deadline: rolling
**Program can be completed
entirely online:** Yes
Total program cost: $19,500
full-time in-state, $19,500
part-time in-state, $19,500
full-time out-of-state, $19,500
part-time out-of-state
Tuition per credit: $500
full-time in-state, $500
part-time in-state, $500
full-time out-of-state, $500
part-time out-of-state
Acceptance rate: 52.0%
Test scores required: No
Average age of entrants: 33
**Students with prior work
experience:** 74.0%
Enrollment: 212, 42% men,
58% women, 25% minority,
2% international
Average class size: 17
**Most popular MBA
concentrations:** accounting,
general management,
leadership, not-for-
profit management
Completion: Three year
graduation rate: 27%; credits
needed to graduate: 39; target
time to graduate: 1.5 years
**College funded aid
available:** Domestic: Yes;
International: Yes
Graduates with debt: 39%;
average amount of debt $30,151

ONLINE BUSINESS PROGRAM(S)

www.lindenwood.edu/
admissions/
Admissions: (636) 949-4933
Email: online@lindenwood.edu
Financial aid: (636) 949-4925
Application deadline: rolling
Program can be completed entirely online: Yes
Total program cost: $18,500 full-time in-state, $18,500 part-time in-state, $18,500 full-time out-of-state, $18,500 part-time out-of-state
Tuition per credit: $500 full-time in-state, $500 part-time in-state, $500 full-time out-of-state, $500 part-time out-of-state
Acceptance rate: 56.0%
Test scores required: No
Average age of entrants: 33
Students with prior work experience: 53.0%
Enrollment: 189, 24% men, 76% women, 38% minority, 3% international
Average class size: 16
Most popular business concentrations: accounting, leadership, not-for-profit management, public administration
Completion: Three year graduation rate: 69%; credits needed to graduate: 36; target time to graduate: 1.5 years
College funded aid available: Domestic: Yes; International: Yes
Graduates with debt: 75%; average amount of debt $37,442

Maryville University of St. Louis

Private

ONLINE MBA PROGRAM(S)

www.maryville.edu/admissions
Admissions: (314) 529-9571
Email: gradprograms@maryville.edu
Financial aid: (314) 529-9360
Application deadline: rolling
Program can be completed entirely online: Yes
Total program cost: N/A
Tuition per credit: $714 full-time in-state, $714 part-time in-state, $714 full-time out-of-state, $714 part-time out-of-state
Acceptance rate: 95.0%
Test scores required: No
Average age of entrants: 31
Enrollment: 305, 41% men, 59% women, 27% minority, 1% international
Average class size: 15
Most popular MBA concentrations: general management, health care administration, human resources management, technology
Completion: Credits needed to graduate: 36; target time to graduate: 2 years
College funded aid available: Domestic: Yes; International: Yes
Graduates with debt: 76%; average amount of debt $38,485

ONLINE BUSINESS PROGRAM(S)

online.maryville.edu/
Admissions: (314) 529-9571
Email: gradprograms@maryville.edu

Financial aid: (314) 529-9360
Application deadline: rolling
Program can be completed entirely online: Yes
Total program cost: N/A
Tuition per credit: $816 full-time in-state, $816 part-time in-state, $816 full-time out-of-state, $816 part-time out-of-state
Acceptance rate: 99.0%
Test scores required: No
Average age of entrants: 35
Enrollment: 600, 61% men, 39% women, 32% minority, 2% international
Average class size: 15
Completion: Credits needed to graduate: 36; target time to graduate: 2 years
College funded aid available: Domestic: Yes; International: Yes
Graduates with debt: 73%; average amount of debt $42,912

Missouri University of Science & Technology

Public

ONLINE MBA PROGRAM(S)

futurestudents.mst.edu/
Admissions: (573) 341-4165
Email: admissions@mst.edu
Financial aid: (573) 341-4282
Application deadline: rolling
Program can be completed entirely online: Yes
Total program cost: $43,200 full-time in-state, $43,200 part-time in-state, $43,200 full-time out-of-state, $43,200 part-time out-of-state
Tuition per credit: $1,200 full-time in-state, $1,200 part-time in-state, $1,200 full-time out-of-state, $1,200 part-time out-of-state
Acceptance rate: 90.0%
Test scores required: GMAT or GRE
Average GMAT: 620
Average GRE: 147 verbal, 160 quantitative, 3.0 writing
Average age of entrants: 33
Students with prior work experience: 89.0%
Enrollment: 69, 54% men, 46% women, 26% minority, 1% international
Average class size: 17
Most popular MBA concentrations: entrepreneurship, general management, leadership, marketing, management information systems
Completion: Three year graduation rate: 100%; credits needed to graduate: 36; target time to graduate: 1.5 years
College funded aid available: Domestic: Yes; International: Yes
Graduates with debt: 35%; average amount of debt $3,550

ONLINE BUSINESS PROGRAM(S)

futurestudents.mst.edu/
Admissions: (573) 341-4075
Email: lynns@mst.edu
Financial aid: (573) 341-4282
Application deadline: rolling
Program can be completed entirely online: Yes
Total program cost: $36,000 full-time in-state, $36,000 part-time in-state, $36,000 full-time out-of-state, $36,000 part-time out-of-state

Tuition per credit: $1,200 full-time in-state, $1,200 part-time in-state, $1,200 full-time out-of-state, $1,200 part-time out-of-state
Acceptance rate: 64.0%
Test scores required: GMAT or GRE
Average GMAT: 545
Average GRE: 149 verbal, 160 quantitative, 3.0 writing
Average age of entrants: 25
Students with prior work experience: 89.0%
Enrollment: 64, 45% men, 55% women, 23% minority, 0% international
Average class size: 16
Most popular business concentrations: leadership, management information systems, supply chain management/logistics, technology
Completion: Three year graduation rate: 85%; credits needed to graduate: 30; target time to graduate: 3 years
College funded aid available: Domestic: Yes; International: Yes
Graduates with debt: 25%; average amount of debt $19,737

Northwest Missouri State University

Public

ONLINE MBA PROGRAM(S)

www.nwmissouri.edu/online/admissions.htm
Admissions: (660) 562-1562
Email: admissions@nwmissouri.edu
Financial aid: (660) 562-1363
Application deadline: rolling
Program can be completed entirely online: Yes
Total program cost: $13,530 full-time in-state, $13,530 part-time in-state, $13,530 full-time out-of-state, $13,530 part-time out-of-state
Tuition per credit: $400 full-time in-state, $400 part-time in-state, $400 full-time out-of-state, $400 part-time out-of-state
Test scores required: GMAT or GRE
Enrollment: 216, 50% men, 50% women, 18% minority, 3% international
Average class size: 23
Most popular MBA concentrations: general management, human resources management, marketing
Completion: Credits needed to graduate: 33; target time to graduate: 2 years
College funded aid available: Domestic: Yes; International: Yes

Park University

Private

ONLINE MBA PROGRAM(S)

www.park.edu/admissions/graduate/index.html
Admissions: (816) 559-5625
Email: gradschool@park.edu
Financial aid: (816) 584-6714
Application deadline: rolling

Program can be completed entirely online: Yes
Total program cost: $20,592 full-time in-state, $20,592 part-time in-state, $20,592 full-time out-of-state, $20,592 part-time out-of-state
Tuition per credit: $624 full-time in-state, $624 part-time in-state, $624 full-time out-of-state, $624 part-time out-of-state
Acceptance rate: 86.0%
Test scores required: No
Average age of entrants: 36
Enrollment: 1,145, 52% men, 48% women, 44% minority, 8% international
Average class size: 19
Most popular MBA concentrations: finance, general management, human resources management, management information systems
Completion: Credits needed to graduate: 33; target time to graduate: 2 years
College funded aid available: Domestic: Yes; International: Yes
Graduates with debt: 51%; average amount of debt $20,955

ONLINE BUSINESS PROGRAM(S)

www.park.edu/admissions/graduate/index.html
Admissions: (816) 559-5625
Email: gradschool@park.edu
Financial aid: (816) 584-6714
Application deadline: rolling
Program can be completed entirely online: Yes
Total program cost: $19,764 full-time in-state, $19,764 part-time in-state, $19,764 full-time out-of-state, $19,764 part-time out-of-state
Tuition per credit: $549 full-time in-state, $549 part-time in-state, $549 full-time out-of-state, $549 part-time out-of-state
Acceptance rate: 79.0%
Test scores required: No
Average age of entrants: 35
Enrollment: 322, 33% men, 67% women, 49% minority, 4% international
Average class size: 14
Most popular business concentrations: accounting, finance, human resources management, international business, management information systems
Completion: Credits needed to graduate: 36; target time to graduate: 2 years
College funded aid available: Domestic: Yes; International: Yes
Graduates with debt: 48%; average amount of debt $34,702

Southeast Missouri State University (Harrison)

Public

ONLINE MBA PROGRAM(S)

www.semo.edu/admissions
Admissions: (573) 651-2590
Email: admissions@semo.edu
Financial aid: (573) 651-2253
Application deadline: rolling

Program can be completed entirely online: Yes
Total program cost: $12,672 full-time in-state, $12,672 part-time in-state, $12,672 full-time out-of-state, $12,672 part-time out-of-state
Tuition per credit: $384 full-time in-state, $384 part-time in-state, $384 full-time out-of-state, $384 part-time out-of-state
Acceptance rate: 88.0%
Test scores required: GMAT or GRE
Average GMAT: 512
Average GRE: 152 verbal, 154 quantitative
Average age of entrants: 33
Enrollment: 114, 72% men, 28% women, 19% minority, 4% international
Average class size: 21
Most popular MBA concentrations: general management, health care administration, sports business
Completion: Three year graduation rate: 55%; credits needed to graduate: 33
College funded aid available: Domestic: Yes; International: Yes
Graduates with debt: 24%

ONLINE BUSINESS PROGRAM(S)

www.semo.edu/admissions
Admissions: (573) 651-2590
Email: admissions@semo.edu
Financial aid: (573) 651-2253
Application deadline: rolling
Program can be completed entirely online: Yes
Total program cost: N/A
Tuition per credit: $347 full-time in-state, $347 part-time in-state, $347 full-time out-of-state, $347 part-time out-of-state
Acceptance rate: 97.0%
Test scores required: GMAT or GRE
Average GMAT: 387
Average GRE: 146 verbal, 150 quantitative
Average age of entrants: 32
Enrollment: 84, 20% men, 80% women, 18% minority, 4% international
Average class size: 23
Most popular business concentrations: general management, health care administration
Completion: Three year graduation rate: 49%; credits needed to graduate: 30; target time to graduate: 2.5 years
College funded aid available: Domestic: Yes; International: Yes
Graduates with debt: 11%

University of Central Missouri (Harmon)

Public

ONLINE MBA PROGRAM(S)

www.ucmo.edu/mba
Admissions: (660) 543-8192
Email: mba@ucmo.edu
Financial aid: (660) 543-8266
Application deadline: rolling
Program can be completed entirely online: Yes
Total program cost: $15,309 full-time in-state, $15,309 part-time in-state, $15,309 full-time out-of-state, $15,309 part-time out-of-state

Tuition per credit: $464
full-time in-state, $464
part-time in-state, $464
full-time out-of-state, $464
part-time out-of-state
Acceptance rate: 47.0%
Test scores required:
GMAT or GRE
Average GMAT: 530
Average GRE: 149 verbal, 150
quantitative, 3.5 writing
Average age of entrants: 31
Students with prior work
experience: 79.0%
Enrollment: 56, 50% men,
50% women, 29% minority,
14% international
Average class size: 16
Most popular MBA
concentrations: general
management, health care
administration, international
business, marketing,
sports business
Completion: Credits needed
to graduate: 33; target time
to graduate: 1.5 years
College funded aid
available: Domestic: Yes;
International: Yes
Graduates with debt: 32%;
average amount of debt $22,580

Webster University

Private

ONLINE MBA PROGRAM(S)

www.webster.edu/admissions/
graduate/
Admissions: (314) 246-7646
Email: mcwill@webster.edu
Financial aid: (314) 246-7080
Application deadline: rolling
Program can be completed
entirely online: Yes
Total program cost: N/A
Tuition per credit: $780 full-time
in-state, $780 part-time in-state,
$780 full-time out-of-state,
$780 part-time out-of-state
Test scores required: No
Enrollment: 925, 51%
men, 49% women, 50%
minority, 0% international
Average class size: 14
Most popular MBA
concentrations: finance, general
management, human resources
management, leadership, supply
chain management/logistics
Completion: Credits needed
to graduate: 36; target time
to graduate: 2.5 years
College funded aid available:
Domestic: No; International: No
Graduates with debt:
49%; average amount
of debt $54,630

ONLINE BUSINESS PROGRAM(S)

www.webster.edu/
admissions/graduate/
Admissions: (314) 246-7646
Email: mcwill@webster.edu
Financial aid: (314) 246-7080
Application deadline: rolling
Program can be completed
entirely online: Yes
Total program cost: N/A
Tuition per credit: $780 full-time
in-state, $780 part-time in-state,
$780 full-time out-of-state,
$780 part-time out-of-state
Test scores required: No
Enrollment: 2,199, 50%
men, 50% women, 59%
minority, 0% international
Average class size: 14

Most popular business
concentrations: general
management, human
resources management,
leadership, management
information systems, supply
chain management/logistics
Completion: Credits needed
to graduate: 36; target time
to graduate: 2.5 years
College funded aid available:
Domestic: No; International: No
Graduates with debt: 45%;
average amount of debt $57,899

William Woods University

Private

ONLINE MBA PROGRAM(S)

www.williamwoods.edu/
admissions/online/index.html
Admissions: (800) 995-3159
Email: admissions@
williamwoods.edu
Financial aid: (573) 592-1793
Application deadline: rolling
Program can be completed
entirely online: Yes
Total program cost: N/A
Tuition per credit: $350
full-time in-state, $350
part-time in-state, $350
full-time out-of-state, $350
part-time out-of-state
Acceptance rate: 78.0%
Test scores required: No
Average age of entrants: 33
Enrollment: 123, 44%
men, 56% women, 22%
minority, 2% international
Average class size: 12
Most popular MBA concentrations:
entrepreneurship
Completion: Credits needed
to graduate: 30; target time
to graduate: 2 years
College funded aid
available: Domestic: Yes;
International: Yes
Graduates with debt: 52%;
average amount of debt $22,076

ONLINE BUSINESS PROGRAM(S)

www.williamwoods.edu/
admissions/index.html
Admissions: (800) 995-3159
Email: admissions@
williamwoods.edu
Financial aid: (573) 592-1793
Application deadline: rolling
Program can be completed
entirely online: Yes
Total program cost: N/A
Tuition per credit: $350
full-time in-state, $350
part-time in-state, $350
full-time out-of-state, $350
part-time out-of-state
Acceptance rate: 74.0%
Test scores required: No
Average age of entrants: 34
Enrollment: 61, 31% men,
69% women, 28% minority,
0% international
Average class size: 5
Most popular business
concentrations: health
care administration
Completion: Credits needed
to graduate: 30; target time
to graduate: 2 years
College funded aid available:
Domestic: Yes; International: No

NEBRASKA

Bellevue University

Private

ONLINE BUSINESS PROGRAM(S)

Admissions: (402) 557-7282
Email: dubay@bellevue.edu
Financial aid: (402) 557-7095
Application deadline: rolling
Program can be completed
entirely online: Yes
Total program cost: $20,700
full-time in-state, $20,700
part-time in-state, $20,700
full-time out-of-state, $20,700
part-time out-of-state
Tuition per credit: $575 full-time
in-state, $575 part-time in-state,
$575 full-time out-of-state,
$575 part-time out-of-state
Acceptance rate: 60.0%
Test scores required: No
Average age of entrants: 37
Enrollment: 1,598, 39%
men, 61% women, 40%
minority, 1% international
Average class size: 13
Most popular business
concentrations: general
management, health care
administration, human
resources management,
leadership, management
information systems
Completion: Credits needed
to graduate: 36; target time
to graduate: 2.5 years
College funded aid
available: Domestic: Yes;
International: Yes
Graduates with debt:
68%; average amount
of debt $34,000

Creighton University

Private

ONLINE MBA PROGRAM(S)

gradschool.creighton.edu/
future-students
Admissions: (402) 280-2703
Email: gradschool@
creighton.edu
Financial aid: (402) 280-2351
Application deadline: rolling
Program can be completed
entirely online: Yes
Total program cost: $37,224
full-time in-state, $37,224
part-time in-state, $37,224
full-time out-of-state, $37,224
part-time out-of-state
Tuition per credit: $1,128
full-time in-state, $1,128
part-time in-state, $1,128
full-time out-of-state, $1,128
part-time out-of-state
Acceptance rate: 85.0%
Test scores required:
GMAT or GRE
Average GMAT: 503
Average GRE: 154 verbal, 152
quantitative, 5.0 writing
Average age of entrants: 31
Students with prior work
experience: 81.0%
Enrollment: 117, 62% men,
38% women, 16% minority,
1% international
Average class size: 15
Most popular MBA
concentrations: accounting,
finance, leadership
Completion: Three year
graduation rate: 100%; credits
needed to graduate: 33; target
time to graduate: 2.5 years

College funded aid
available: Domestic: Yes;
International: Yes
Graduates with debt: 30%;
average amount of debt $21,138

ONLINE BUSINESS PROGRAM(S)

gradschool.creighton.edu/
future-students
Admissions: (402) 280-2703
Email: gradschool@
creighton.edu
Financial aid: (402) 280-2351
Application deadline: rolling
Program can be completed
entirely online: Yes
Total program cost: $36,900
full-time in-state, $36,900
part-time in-state, $36,900
full-time out-of-state, $36,900
part-time out-of-state
Tuition per credit: $1,230
full-time in-state, $1,230
part-time in-state, $1,230
full-time out-of-state, $1,230
part-time out-of-state
Acceptance rate: 69.0%
Test scores required:
GMAT or GRE
Average GMAT: 547
Average GRE: 154 verbal, 152
quantitative, 4.0 writing
Average age of entrants: 34
Students with prior work
experience: 80.0%
Enrollment: 107, 79% men,
21% women, 14% minority,
1% international
Average class size: 14
Most popular business
concentrations: finance
Completion: Three year
graduation rate: 65%; credits
needed to graduate: 30; target
time to graduate: 2.5 years
College funded aid
available: Domestic: Yes;
International: Yes
Graduates with debt:
60%; average amount
of debt $35,308

University of Nebraska–Lincoln

Public

ONLINE MBA PROGRAM(S)

business.unl/mba/
Admissions: (402) 472-2338
Email: businessgrad@unl.edu
Financial aid: (402) 472-3484
Application deadline: Domestic:
07/01; International: 04/01
Program can be completed
entirely online: Yes
Total program cost: $30,240
full-time in-state, $30,240
part-time in-state, $30,240
full-time out-of-state, $30,240
part-time out-of-state
Tuition per credit: $630
full-time in-state, $630
part-time in-state, $630
full-time out-of-state, $630
part-time out-of-state
Acceptance rate: 79.0%
Test scores required:
GMAT or GRE
Average GMAT: 609
Average GRE: 155 verbal, 157
quantitative, 4.0 writing
Average age of entrants: 33
Students with prior work
experience: 91.0%
Enrollment: 503, 78% men,
22% women, 11% minority,
5% international
Average class size: 41

Most popular MBA
concentrations: finance,
international business,
marketing, supply chain
management/logistics,
quantitative analysis/statistics
and operations research
Completion: Three year
graduation rate: 59%; credits
needed to graduate: 48; target
time to graduate: 3 years
College funded aid available:
Domestic: No; International: No
Graduates with debt: 15%;
average amount of debt $27,733

Wayne State College

Public

ONLINE MBA PROGRAM(S)

Admissions: (402) 375-7234
Financial aid: (402) 375-7430
Application deadline: N/A
Program can be completed
entirely online: Yes
Total program cost: N/A
Tuition per credit: $361 full-time
in-state, $361 part-time in-state,
$361 full-time out-of-state,
$361 part-time out-of-state
Test scores required: No
Enrollment: 150, N/A minority,
N/A international

NEVADA

University of Nevada–Reno

Public

ONLINE MBA PROGRAM(S)

www.unr.edu/grad/admissions
Admissions: (775) 784-4652
Email: ealdrich@unr.edu
Financial aid: (775) 784-4666
Application deadline: rolling
Program can be completed
entirely online: Yes
Total program cost: $30,000
full-time in-state, $30,000
part-time in-state, $30,000
full-time out-of-state, $30,000
part-time out-of-state
Tuition per credit: $833
full-time in-state, $833
part-time in-state, $833
full-time out-of-state, $833
part-time out-of-state
Acceptance rate: 100.0%
Test scores required:
GMAT or GRE
Average GMAT: 457
Average GRE: 153 verbal, 150
quantitative, 3.5 writing
Average age of entrants: 38
Students with prior work
experience: 100.0%
Enrollment: 59, 59% men,
41% women, 25% minority,
0% international
Average class size: 30
Completion: Three year
graduation rate: 93%; credits
needed to graduate: 36; target
time to graduate: 2 years
Graduates with debt: 42%;
average amount of debt $19,042

NEW HAMPSHIRE

Franklin Pierce University

Private

ONLINE MBA PROGRAM(S)

www.franklinpierce.edu/
academics/gradstudies/
apply.htm
Admissions: (800) 325-1090
Email: cgps@franklinpierce.edu
Financial aid: (877) 372-7347
Application deadline: rolling
Program can be completed entirely online: Yes
Total program cost: $25,935
full-time in-state, $25,935
part-time in-state, $25,935
full-time out-of-state, $25,935
part-time out-of-state
Tuition per credit: $665
full-time in-state, $665
part-time in-state, $665
full-time out-of-state, $665
part-time out-of-state
Acceptance rate: 100.0%
Test scores required: No
Average age of entrants: 30
Students with prior work experience: 61.0%
Enrollment: 207, 48% men,
52% women, 14% minority,
4% international
Average class size: 15
Most popular MBA concentrations: health care
administration, human
resources management,
leadership, sports business
Completion: Three year
graduation rate: 55%; credits
needed to graduate: 39; target
time to graduate: 2 years
College funded aid available: Domestic: Yes;
International: Yes
Graduates with debt: 58%;
average amount of debt $27,563

Granite State College

Public

ONLINE BUSINESS PROGRAM(S)

Admissions: N/A
Financial aid: N/A
Application deadline: rolling
Program can be completed entirely online: Yes
Total program cost: $16,140
full-time in-state, $16,140
part-time in-state, $17,250
full-time out-of-state, $17,250
part-time out-of-state
Tuition per credit: $538
full-time in-state, $538
part-time in-state, $575
full-time out-of-state, $575
part-time out-of-state
Acceptance rate: 99.0%
Test scores required: No
Average age of entrants: 38
Students with prior work experience: 67.0%
Enrollment: 143, 41% men,
59% women, 8% minority,
0% international
Average class size: 7
Most popular business concentrations: general
management, human
resources management,
leadership, not-for-profit
management, production/
operations management
Completion: Three year
graduation rate: 56%; credits

needed to graduate: 30; target
time to graduate: 1.5 years
College funded aid available:
Domestic: Yes
Graduates with debt: 50%;
average amount of debt $17,275

New England College

Private

ONLINE MBA PROGRAM(S)

www.nec.edu/sgps/prospective
Admissions: (603) 428-2252
Email: graduateadmission@
nec.edu
Financial aid: (603) 428-2226
Application deadline: rolling
Program can be completed entirely online: Yes
Total program cost: $23,800
full-time in-state, $23,800
part-time in-state, $23,800
full-time out-of-state, $23,800
part-time out-of-state
Tuition per credit: $595
full-time in-state, $595
part-time in-state, $595
full-time out-of-state, $595
part-time out-of-state
Acceptance rate: 98.0%
Test scores required: No
Average age of entrants: 36
Enrollment: 208, 53%
men, 47% women, 18%
minority, 2% international
Average class size: 12
Most popular MBA concentrations: health care
administration, leadership,
not-for-profit management,
sports business
Completion: Three year
graduation rate: 65%; credits
needed to graduate: 40; target
time to graduate: 1.5 years
College funded aid available:
Domestic: No; International: No
Graduates with debt: 32%;
average amount of debt $18,647

ONLINE BUSINESS PROGRAM(S)

www.nec.edu/sgps/prospective
Admissions: (603) 428-2252
Email: graduateadmission@
nec.edu
Financial aid: (603) 428-2226
Application deadline: rolling
Program can be completed entirely online: Yes
Total program cost: $23,020
full-time in-state, $23,020
part-time in-state, $23,020
full-time out-of-state, $23,020
part-time out-of-state
Tuition per credit: $565
full-time in-state, $565
part-time in-state, $565
full-time out-of-state, $565
part-time out-of-state
Acceptance rate: 100.0%
Test scores required: No
Average age of entrants: 41
Enrollment: 212, 31% men,
69% women, 15% minority,
1% international
Average class size: 13
Most popular business concentrations: accounting,
health care administration,
not-for-profit management,
production/operations
management, real estate
Completion: Three year
graduation rate: 60%; credits
needed to graduate: 40; target
time to graduate: 1.5 years
College funded aid available:
Domestic: No; International: No

Graduates with debt: 76%;
average amount of debt $25,856

University of New Hampshire (Paul)

Public

ONLINE MBA PROGRAM(S)

Admissions: (603) 862-1367
Email: paulcollege.grad@unh.edu
Financial aid: (603) 862-3671
Application deadline: Domestic:
06/01; International: 06/01
Program can be completed entirely online: Yes
Total program cost: $38,400
full-time in-state, $38,400
part-time in-state, $43,680
full-time out-of-state, $43,680
part-time out-of-state
Tuition per credit: $800
full-time in-state, $800
part-time in-state, $910
full-time out-of-state, $910
part-time out-of-state
Acceptance rate: 94.0%
Average GMAT: 550
Average GRE: 152 verbal, 154
quantitative, 3.8 writing
Average age of entrants: 34
Students with prior work experience: 98.0%
Enrollment: 115, 61% men,
39% women, 12% minority,
2% international
Average class size: 17
Most popular MBA concentrations: finance,
international business,
marketing, quantitative
analysis/statistics and
operations research
Completion: Three year
graduation rate: 63%; credits
needed to graduate: 48; target
time to graduate: 2 years
College funded aid available: Domestic: Yes;
International: Yes
Graduates with debt: 31%;
average amount of debt $33,954

NEW JERSEY

Montclair State University

Public

ONLINE MBA PROGRAM(S)

Admissions: (973) 655-5147
Email: gradschool@
montclair.edu
Financial aid: (973) 655-7600
Application deadline: rolling
Program can be completed entirely online: Yes
Total program cost: $25,532
part-time in-state, $25,532
part-time out-of-state
Tuition per credit: $709 full-time
in-state, $709 part-time in-state,
$709 full-time out-of-state,
$709 part-time out-of-state
Acceptance rate: 58.0%
Average GMAT: 493
Average GRE: 147 verbal, 146
quantitative, 3.3 writing
Average age of entrants: 31
Students with prior work experience: 8.0%
Enrollment: 218, 32%
men, 68% women, 44%
minority, 1% international
Average class size: 19

Most popular MBA concentrations: human
resources management
Completion: Credits needed
to graduate: 36; target time
to graduate: 2 years
College funded aid available:
Domestic: Yes; International: No

New Jersey Institute of Technology

Public

ONLINE MBA PROGRAM(S)

www.njit.edu/admissions
Admissions: (973) 596-3306
Email: stephen.eck@njit.edu
Financial aid: (973) 596-3476
Application deadline: rolling
Program can be completed entirely online: Depends
Total program cost: $52,848
full-time in-state, $52,848
part-time in-state, $61,536
full-time out-of-state, $61,536
part-time out-of-state
Tuition per credit: $1,101
full-time in-state, $1,101
part-time in-state, $1,282
full-time out-of-state, $1,282
part-time out-of-state
Acceptance rate: 67.0%
Test scores required: No
Average GMAT: 558
Average GRE: 147 verbal, 153
quantitative, 3.0 writing
Average age of entrants: 32
Students with prior work experience: 96.0%
Enrollment: 115, 64%
men, 36% women, 46%
minority, 1% international
Average class size: 24
Most popular MBA concentrations: finance, general
management, marketing,
management information
systems, technology
Completion: Three year
graduation rate: 42%; credits
needed to graduate: 48; target
time to graduate: 3.5 years
College funded aid available:
Domestic: No; International: No
Graduates with debt:
75%; average amount
of debt $53,599

ONLINE BUSINESS PROGRAM(S)

www.njit.edu/admissions
Admissions: (973) 596-3306
Email: eck@njit.edu
Financial aid: (973) 596-3476
Application deadline: rolling
Program can be completed entirely online: Depends
Total program cost: $33,030
full-time in-state, $33,030
part-time in-state, $38,460
full-time out-of-state, $38,460
part-time out-of-state
Tuition per credit: $1,101
full-time in-state, $1,101
part-time in-state, $1,282
full-time out-of-state, $1,282
part-time out-of-state
Acceptance rate: 38.0%
Test scores required: No
Average GRE: 154 verbal,
154 quantitative
Average age of entrants: 33
Students with prior work experience: 50.0%
Enrollment: 12, 83% men,
17% women, 50% minority,
0% international
Average class size: 24

Most popular business concentrations: general
management, management
information systems,
organizational behavior,
technology
Completion: Credits needed
to graduate: 30; target time
to graduate: 2 years
College funded aid available:
Domestic: No; International: No
Graduates with debt: 29%;
average amount of debt $27,703

Rowan University (Rohrer)

Public

ONLINE MBA PROGRAM(S)

rowanu.com/graduate/
admissions
Admissions: (856) 256-4747
Email: global@rowan.edu
Financial aid: (856) 256-5141
Application deadline: rolling
Program can be completed entirely online: Yes
Total program cost: N/A
Tuition per credit: $909
full-time in-state, $909
part-time in-state, $909
full-time out-of-state, $909
part-time out-of-state
Acceptance rate: 59.0%
Test scores required:
GMAT or GRE
Average GMAT: 490
Average age of entrants: 27
Enrollment: 51, 45% men,
55% women, 18% minority,
2% international
Average class size: 20
Most popular MBA concentrations: general
management
Completion: Three year
graduation rate: 82%; credits
needed to graduate: 36; target
time to graduate: 2 years
College funded aid available: Domestic: Yes;
International: Yes
Graduates with debt:
38%; average amount
of debt $34,503

Rutgers University–Camden

Public

ONLINE MBA PROGRAM(S)

online.rutgers.edu/
master-business-admin/
Admissions: (856) 225-6452
Email: Rsbcmba@
camden.rutgers.edu
Financial aid: (856) 225-6039
Application deadline: rolling
Program can be completed entirely online: Yes
Total program cost: $52,752
full-time in-state, $52,752
part-time in-state, $52,752
full-time out-of-state, $52,752
part-time out-of-state
Tuition per credit: $1,256
full-time in-state, $1,256
part-time in-state, $1,256
full-time out-of-state, $1,256
part-time out-of-state
Acceptance rate: 78.0%
Test scores required:
GMAT or GRE
Average GMAT: 578
Average GRE: 152 verbal, 152
quantitative, 5.2 writing

Average age of entrants: 33
Students with prior work
experience: 100.0%
Enrollment: 296, 55%
men, 45% women, 46%
minority, 0% international
Average class size: 33
Most popular MBA
concentrations: finance, general
management, international
business, marketing
Completion: Three year
graduation rate: 29%; credits
needed to graduate: 42; target
time to graduate: 3 years
College funded aid available:
Domestic: No; International: No
Graduates with debt: 47%;
average amount of debt $51,995

Rutgers University–New Brunswick and Newark

Public

ONLINE BUSINESS PROGRAM(S)

www.business.rutgers.edu/
admissions
Admissions: (973) 353-1234
Email: rkwan@
business.rutgers.edu
Financial aid: (973) 353-1234
Application deadline: rolling
Program can be completed
entirely online: Yes
Total program cost: $36,840
full-time in-state, $36,840
part-time in-state, $36,840
full-time out-of-state, $36,840
part-time out-of-state
Tuition per credit: $1,228
full-time in-state, $1,228
part-time in-state, $1,228
full-time out-of-state, $1,228
part-time out-of-state
Acceptance rate: 70.0%
Test scores required: No
Average GRE: 145 verbal,
170 quantitative
Average age of entrants: 34
Students with prior work
experience: 97.0%
Enrollment: 261, 57% men,
43% women, 34% minority,
3% international
Average class size: 16
Most popular business
concentrations:
accounting, supply chain
management/logistics
Completion: Three year
graduation rate: 65%; credits
needed to graduate: 30; target
time to graduate: 3 years
College funded aid available:
Domestic: Yes; International: No
Graduates with debt: 45%;
average amount of debt $26,842

Stevens Institute of Technology

Private

ONLINE MBA PROGRAM(S)

www.stevens.edu/admissions/
graduate-admissions
Admissions: (888) 783-8367
Email: graduate@stevens.edu
Financial aid: (201) 216-8142
Application deadline: rolling
Program can be completed
entirely online: Yes
Total program cost: $60,735
full-time in-state, $63,180
part-time in-state, $60,735
full-time out-of-state, $63,180
part-time out-of-state

Tuition per credit: $1,620
full-time in-state, $1,620
part-time in-state, $1,620
full-time out-of-state, $1,620
part-time out-of-state
Acceptance rate: 84.0%
Test scores required:
GMAT or GRE
Average GMAT: 569
Average GRE: 157 verbal, 156
quantitative, 4.0 writing
Average age of entrants: 35
Students with prior work
experience: 100.0%
Enrollment: 96, 59% men,
41% women, 36% minority,
0% international
Average class size: 18
Most popular MBA
concentrations: general
management, management
information systems,
quantitative analysis/statistics
and operations research
Completion: Three year
graduation rate: 61%; credits
needed to graduate: 39; target
time to graduate: 2 years
College funded aid
available: Domestic: Yes;
International: Yes
Graduates with debt: 21%;
average amount of debt $35,203

ONLINE BUSINESS PROGRAM(S)

www.stevens.edu/admissions/
graduate-admissions
Admissions: (888) 783-8367
Email: graduate@stevens.edu
Financial aid: (201) 216-5555
Application deadline: rolling
Program can be completed
entirely online: Yes
Total program cost: $53,940
full-time in-state, $58,320
part-time in-state, $53,940
full-time out-of-state, $58,320
part-time out-of-state
Tuition per credit: $1,620
full-time in-state, $1,620
part-time in-state, $1,620
full-time out-of-state, $1,620
part-time out-of-state
Acceptance rate: 68.0%
Test scores required:
GMAT or GRE
Average GMAT: 603
Average GRE: 152 verbal, 158
quantitative, 4.0 writing
Average age of entrants: 32
Students with prior work
experience: 89.0%
Enrollment: 145, 64%
men, 36% women, 33%
minority, 0% international
Average class size: 18
Most popular business
concentrations: general
management, management
information systems,
quantitative analysis/statistics
and operations research
Completion: Three year
graduation rate: 56%; credits
needed to graduate: 36; target
time to graduate: 2 years
College funded aid
available: Domestic: Yes;
International: Yes
Graduates with debt: 16%;
average amount of debt $39,584

New Mexico State University

Public

ONLINE MBA PROGRAM(S)

gradadmissions.nmsu.edu
Admissions: (575) 646-3836
Email: gradinfo@nmsu.edu
Financial aid: (575) 646-4105
Application deadline: rolling
Program can be completed
entirely online: No
Total program cost: $9,097
full-time in-state, $9,097
part-time in-state, $31,720
full-time out-of-state, $31,720
part-time out-of-state
Tuition per credit: $253
full-time in-state, $253
part-time in-state, $881
full-time out-of-state, $881
part-time out-of-state
Acceptance rate: 100.0%
Average age of entrants: 30
Enrollment: 85, 36% men,
64% women, 51% minority,
0% international
Average class size: 20
Most popular MBA
concentrations: finance
Completion: Credits
needed to graduate: 36
College funded aid
available: Domestic: Yes;
International: Yes

Clarkson University

Private

ONLINE MBA PROGRAM(S)

www.clarkson.edu/
graduate-admissions/
Admissions: (518) 631-9831
Email: graduate@clarkson.edu
Financial aid: N/A
Application deadline: rolling
Program can be completed
entirely online: No
Total program cost: $56,652
full-time in-state, $56,652
part-time in-state, $56,652
full-time out-of-state, $56,652
part-time out-of-state
Tuition per credit: $1,174
full-time in-state, $1,174
part-time in-state, $1,174
full-time out-of-state, $1,174
part-time out-of-state
Acceptance rate: 89.0%
Test scores required:
GMAT or GRE
Average GRE: 152 verbal, 149
quantitative, 4.0 writing
Average age of entrants: 32
Students with prior work
experience: 92.0%
Enrollment: 184, 53% men,
47% women, 16% minority,
6% international
Average class size: 14
Most popular MBA
concentrations: general
management, health care
administration, supply chain
management/logistics
Completion: Three year
graduation rate: 82%; credits
needed to graduate: 48; target
time to graduate: 2 years
College funded aid
available: Domestic: Yes;
International: Yes

Graduates with debt: 36%;
average amount of debt $18,789

ONLINE BUSINESS PROGRAM(S)

www.clarkson.edu/
graduate-admissions/
Admissions: (518) 631-9831
Email: graduate@clarkson.edu
Financial aid: N/A
Application deadline: rolling
Program can be completed
entirely online: No
Total program cost: $42,564
full-time in-state, $42,564
part-time in-state, $42,564
full-time out-of-state, $42,564
part-time out-of-state
Tuition per credit: $1,174
full-time in-state, $1,174
part-time in-state, $1,174
full-time out-of-state, $1,174
part-time out-of-state
Acceptance rate: 75.0%
Test scores required:
GMAT or GRE
Average age of entrants: 41
Students with prior work
experience: 50.0%
Enrollment: 24, 29% men,
71% women, 4% minority,
4% international
Average class size: 9
Completion: Three year
graduation rate: 62%; credits
needed to graduate: 36; target
time to graduate: 1.5 years
College funded aid
available: Domestic: Yes;
International: Yes
Graduates with debt: 40%;
average amount of debt $10,674

D'Youville College

Private

ONLINE MBA PROGRAM(S)

www.dyc.edu/academics/
schools-and-departments/arts-
sciences-education/programs-
and-degrees/mba.aspx
Admissions: (716) 829-7600
Email: graduateadmissions@
dyc.edu
Financial aid: (716) 829-7500
Application deadline: rolling
Program can be completed
entirely online: Yes
Total program cost: $18,000
full-time in-state, $18,000
part-time in-state, $18,000
full-time out-of-state, $18,000
part-time out-of-state
Tuition per credit: $500
full-time in-state, $500
part-time in-state, $500
full-time out-of-state, $500
part-time out-of-state
Acceptance rate: 71.0%
Test scores required: No
Average age of entrants: 36
Enrollment: 5, 60% men,
40% women, 20% minority,
0% international
Most popular MBA
concentrations: general
management
Completion: Credits
needed to graduate: 36
College funded aid
available: Domestic: Yes;
International: Yes

Hofstra University (Zarb)

Private

ONLINE MBA PROGRAM(S)

www.hofstra.edu/graduate
Admissions: (800) 463-7672
Email: graduateadmission@
hofstra.edu
Financial aid: (516) 463-8000
Application deadline: rolling
Program can be completed
entirely online: Depends
Total program cost: $61,875
full-time in-state, $61,875
full-time out-of-state
Tuition per credit: $1,375
full-time in-state, $1,375
part-time in-state, $1,375
full-time out-of-state, $1,375
part-time out-of-state
Acceptance rate: 86.0%
Test scores required:
GMAT or GRE
Average age of entrants: 36
Students with prior work
experience: 96.0%
Enrollment: 45, 64% men,
36% women, 56% minority,
0% international
Average class size: 17
Most popular MBA
concentrations: accounting,
finance, general management,
health care administration
Completion: Three year
graduation rate: 92%; credits
needed to graduate: 45; target
time to graduate: 2 years
College funded aid
available: Domestic: Yes;
International: Yes
Graduates with debt: 50%

LIM College

Proprietary

ONLINE BUSINESS PROGRAM(S)

www.limcollege.edu/
admissions/online-admissions
Admissions: (844) 957-2720
Email: LIMonline@limcollege.edu
Financial aid: (212) 752-1530
Application deadline: rolling
Program can be completed
entirely online: Yes
Total program cost: $28,500
full-time in-state, $28,500
part-time in-state, $28,500
full-time out-of-state, $28,500
part-time out-of-state
Tuition per credit: $950
full-time in-state, $950
part-time in-state, $950
full-time out-of-state, $950
part-time out-of-state
Acceptance rate: 90.0%
Test scores required: No
Average age of entrants: 28
Enrollment: 200, 51%
minority, 0% international
Completion: Credits needed
to graduate: 30; target
time to graduate: 1 year

Marist College

Private

ONLINE MBA PROGRAM(S)

www.marist.edu/admission/
graduate/
Admissions: (845) 575-3800
Email: graduate@marist.edu
Financial aid: (845) 575-3000
Application deadline: rolling

Program can be completed
entirely online: Yes
Total program cost: $28,800
full-time in-state, $28,800
part-time in-state, $28,800
full-time out-of-state, $28,800
part-time out-of-state
Tuition per credit: $800
full-time in-state, $800
part-time in-state, $800
full-time out-of-state, $800
part-time out-of-state
Acceptance rate: 50.0%
Test scores required:
GMAT or GRE
Average GMAT: 548
Average GRE: 157 verbal, 152
quantitative, 3.9 writing
Average age of entrants: 30
Students with prior work
experience: 93.0%
Enrollment: 217, 52% men,
48% women, 16% minority,
0% international
Average class size: 25
Most popular MBA
concentrations: finance, general
management, health care
administration, leadership
Completion: Three year
graduation rate: 42%; credits
needed to graduate: 36; target
time to graduate: 2 years
College funded aid
available: Domestic: Yes;
International: Yes
Graduates with debt: 25%;
average amount of debt $32,750

ONLINE BUSINESS PROGRAM(S)

www.marist.edu/
admission/graduate/
Admissions: (845) 575-3800
Email: graduate@marist.edu
Financial aid: (845) 575-3230
Application deadline: rolling
Program can be completed
entirely online: Yes
Total program cost: $33,600
full-time in-state, $33,600
part-time in-state, $33,600
full-time out-of-state, $33,600
part-time out-of-state
Tuition per credit: $800
full-time in-state, $800
part-time in-state, $800
full-time out-of-state, $800
part-time out-of-state
Acceptance rate: 53.0%
Test scores required:
GMAT or GRE
Average GRE: 149 verbal, 145
quantitative, 3.8 writing
Average age of entrants: 35
Students with prior work
experience: 97.0%
Enrollment: 319, 48% men,
52% women, 39% minority,
0% international
Average class size: 23
Most popular business
concentrations: health care
administration, leadership,
not-for-profit management,
public administration
Completion: Three year
graduation rate: 69%; credits
needed to graduate: 42; target
time to graduate: 2 years
College funded aid
available: Domestic: Yes;
International: Yes
Graduates with debt: 56%;
average amount of debt $40,041

Mercy College

Private

ONLINE MBA PROGRAM(S)

www.mercy.edu/admissions/
Admissions: (877) 637-2946
Email: admissions@mercy.edu
Financial aid: (877) 637-2946
Application deadline: rolling
Program can be completed
entirely online: Yes
Total program cost: N/A
Tuition per credit: $891 full-time
in-state, $891 part-time in-state,
$891 full-time out-of-state,
$891 part-time out-of-state
Acceptance rate: 64.0%
Test scores required: No
Average age of entrants: 28
Enrollment: 45, 38% men,
62% women, 67% minority,
0% international
Average class size: 18
Most popular MBA
concentrations: finance, general
management, international
business, marketing,
quantitative analysis/statistics
and operations research
Completion: Credits needed
to graduate: 57; target
time to graduate: 1 year

ONLINE BUSINESS PROGRAM(S)

www.mercy.edu/admissions/
Admissions: (877) 637-2946
Email: admissions@mercy.edu
Financial aid: (877) 637-2946
Application deadline: rolling
Program can be completed
entirely online: Yes
Total program cost: N/A
Tuition per credit: $891 full-time
in-state, $891 part-time in-state,
$891 full-time out-of-state,
$891 part-time out-of-state
Acceptance rate: 80.0%
Test scores required: No
Enrollment: 59, 14% men,
86% women, 76% minority,
0% international
Average class size: 18
Most popular business
concentrations: accounting,
human resources
management, leadership
Completion: Credits needed
to graduate: 57; target time
to graduate: 2 years
College funded aid available:
Domestic: Yes

Molloy College

Private

ONLINE MBA PROGRAM(S)

www.molloy.edu/admissions/
graduate-admissions
Admissions: (516) 323-4000
Email: admissions@molloy.edu
Financial aid: (516) 323-4200
Application deadline: rolling
Program can be completed
entirely online: Yes
Total program cost: N/A
Tuition per credit: $1,155
full-time in-state, $1,155
part-time in-state, $1,155
full-time out-of-state, $1,155
part-time out-of-state
Acceptance rate: 50.0%
Test scores required: No
Enrollment: 1, 0% men,
100% women, N/A minority,
0% international
Most popular MBA
concentrations: finance, general

management, health care
administration, marketing
Completion: Credits needed
to graduate: 33; target
time to graduate: 1 year
College funded aid available:
Domestic: Yes; International: No

Monroe College

Proprietary

ONLINE MBA PROGRAM(S)

www.monroecollege.edu/
online-learning/
Admissions: (718) 933-6700
Financial aid: (718) 933-6700
Application deadline: rolling
Program can be completed
entirely online: Depends
Total program cost: $30,312
full-time in-state, $30,312
part-time in-state, $30,312
full-time out-of-state, $30,312
part-time out-of-state
Tuition per credit: $842
full-time in-state, $842
part-time in-state, $842
full-time out-of-state, $842
part-time out-of-state
Acceptance rate: 55.0%
Test scores required: No
Average age of entrants: 32
Students with prior work
experience: 96.0%
Enrollment: 182, 21% men,
79% women, 76% minority,
17% international
Average class size: 14
Most popular MBA concentrations:
entrepreneurship, finance,
general management, health
care administration, marketing
Completion: Three year
graduation rate: 79%; credits
needed to graduate: 37; target
time to graduate: 3 years
College funded aid
available: Domestic: Yes;
International: Yes
Graduates with debt: 92%;
average amount of debt $29,516

Rochester Institute of Technology

Private

ONLINE MBA PROGRAM(S)

www.rit.edu/emba/
admissions-requirements
Admissions: (585) 475-2729
Email: awilliams@
saunders.rit.edu
Financial aid: (585) 475-2186
Application deadline: rolling
Program can be completed
entirely online: No
Total program cost: $78,000
full-time in-state, $78,000
full-time out-of-state
Tuition per credit: $1,660
full-time in-state, $1,660
part-time in-state, $1,660
full-time out-of-state, $1,660
part-time out-of-state
Acceptance rate: 52.0%
Test scores required: No
Average age of entrants: 39
Students with prior work
experience: 100.0%
Enrollment: 47, 51% men,
49% women, 6% minority,
2% international
Average class size: 17

Completion: Three year
graduation rate: 94%; credits
needed to graduate: 47; target
time to graduate: 1.5 years
College funded aid
available: Domestic: Yes;
International: Yes
Graduates with debt: 36%;
average amount of debt $45,073

ONLINE BUSINESS PROGRAM(S)

Admissions: (585) 475-2729
Email: sgriffin@saunders.rit.edu
Financial aid: (585) 475-2186
Application deadline: rolling
Program can be completed
entirely online: Yes
Total program cost: N/A
Tuition per credit: $1,081
full-time in-state, $1,081
part-time in-state, $1,081
full-time out-of-state, $1,081
part-time out-of-state
Acceptance rate: 70.0%
Test scores required: No
Average age of entrants: 36
Students with prior work
experience: 100.0%
Enrollment: 50, 36% men,
64% women, 16% minority,
24% international
Most popular business
concentrations: human
resources management,
leadership
Completion: Credits
needed to graduate: 33
College funded aid available:
Domestic: No; International: No

SUNY Polytechnic Institute

Public

ONLINE MBA PROGRAM(S)

sunypoly.edu/admissions/
graduate.html
Admissions: (315) 792-7347
Email: graduate@sunypoly.edu
Financial aid: (315) 792-7210
Application deadline: Domestic:
07/01; International: 07/01
Program can be completed
entirely online: Yes
Total program cost: $29,712
full-time in-state, $29,712
part-time in-state, $35,664
full-time out-of-state, $35,664
part-time out-of-state
Tuition per credit: $619 full-time
in-state, $619 part-time in-state,
$743 full-time out-of-state,
$743 part-time out-of-state
Acceptance rate: 56.0%
Test scores required:
GMAT or GRE
Average GMAT: 492
Average GRE: 147 verbal, 146
quantitative, 3.0 writing
Average age of entrants: 32
Enrollment: 114, 53% men,
47% women, 16% minority,
0% international
Average class size: 24
Most popular MBA
concentrations: e-commerce,
finance, health care
administration, human
resources management,
marketing
Completion: Three year
graduation rate: 59%; credits
needed to graduate: 48; target
time to graduate: 1.5 years
College funded aid
available: Domestic: Yes;
International: Yes

ONLINE BUSINESS PROGRAM(S)

sunypoly.edu/
office-graduate-studies.html
Admissions: (315) 792-7347
Email: graduate@sunypoly.edu
Financial aid: (315) 792-7210
Application deadline: Domestic:
07/01; International: 07/01
Program can be completed
entirely online: Yes
Total program cost: $15,246
full-time in-state, $15,246
part-time in-state, $18,315
full-time out-of-state, $18,315
part-time out-of-state
Tuition per credit: $462
full-time in-state, $462
part-time in-state, $555
full-time out-of-state, $555
part-time out-of-state
Acceptance rate: 96.0%
Test scores required:
GMAT or GRE
Average GMAT: 524
Average GRE: 154 verbal, 151
quantitative, 3.5 writing
Average age of entrants: 31
Enrollment: 75, 44% men,
56% women, 32% minority,
0% international
Average class size: 17
Most popular business
concentrations: accounting
Completion: Three year
graduation rate: 48%; credits
needed to graduate: 33; target
time to graduate: 1.5 years
College funded aid
available: Domestic: Yes;
International: Yes

SUNY–Oswego

Public

ONLINE MBA PROGRAM(S)

www.oswego.edu/mba
Admissions: (315) 312-3152
Email: mba@oswego.edu
Financial aid: (315) 312-2248
Application deadline: rolling
Program can be completed
entirely online: Yes
Total program cost: $22,284
full-time in-state, $22,284
part-time in-state, $26,748
full-time out-of-state, $26,748
part-time out-of-state
Tuition per credit: $619 full-time
in-state, $619 part-time in-state,
$743 full-time out-of-state,
$743 part-time out-of-state
Acceptance rate: 80.0%
Test scores required: GMAT
Average GMAT: 548
Average age of entrants: 31
Students with prior work
experience: 92.0%
Enrollment: 202, 57%
men, 43% women, 20%
minority, 1% international
Average class size: 19
Most popular MBA
concentrations: accounting,
finance, general
management, health care
administration, marketing
Completion: Three year
graduation rate: 71%; credits
needed to graduate: 36; target
time to graduate: 2 years
College funded aid
available: Domestic: Yes;
International: Yes
Graduates with debt: 45%;
average amount of debt $35,224

St. Bonaventure University

Private

ONLINE MBA PROGRAM(S)

www.sbu.edu/admission-aid/graduate-admissions
Admissions: (716) 375-2411
Email: gradsch@sbu.edu
Financial aid: (716) 375-7888
Application deadline: Domestic: 08/10; International: 06/01
Program can be completed entirely online: Yes
Total program cost: $31,710 full-time in-state, $31,710 part-time in-state, $31,710 full-time out-of-state, $31,710 part-time out-of-state
Tuition per credit: $755 full-time in-state, $755 part-time in-state, $755 full-time out-of-state, $755 part-time out-of-state
Acceptance rate: 95.0%
Test scores required: GMAT or GRE
Average GMAT: 455
Average age of entrants: 32
Students with prior work experience: 74.0%
Enrollment: 96, 46% men, 54% women, 17% minority, 0% international
Average class size: 15
Most popular MBA concentrations: accounting, finance, general management, marketing
Completion: Credits needed to graduate: 42; target time to graduate: 2 years
College funded aid available: Domestic: No; International: No
Graduates with debt: 27%; average amount of debt $30,470

St. John's University (Tobin)

Private

ONLINE BUSINESS PROGRAM(S)

www.stjohns.edu/admission-aid/graduate-admission
Admissions: (718) 277-5113
Email: steigera@stjohns.edu
Financial aid: (718) 990-2000
Application deadline: Domestic: 06/01; International: 06/01
Program can be completed entirely online: Yes
Total program cost: N/A
Tuition per credit: $1,245 full-time in-state, $1,245 part-time in-state, $1,245 full-time out-of-state, $1,245 part-time out-of-state
Acceptance rate: 70.0%
Test scores required: GMAT or GRE
Average GMAT: 580
Average age of entrants: 39
Students with prior work experience: 100.0%
Enrollment: 39, 62% men, 38% women, 15% minority, 3% international
Average class size: 15
Most popular business concentrations: accounting, tax
Completion: Three year graduation rate: 53%; credits needed to graduate: 33; target time to graduate: 2 years
College funded aid available: Domestic: Yes; International: Yes

Graduates with debt: 54%; average amount of debt $43,174

St. Joseph's College New York

Private

ONLINE MBA PROGRAM(S)

www.sjcny.edu/online/admissions/graduate
Admissions: (631) 687-4501
Email: online@sjcny.edu
Financial aid: (631) 687-2611
Application deadline: rolling
Program can be completed entirely online: Yes
Total program cost: $23,961 full-time in-state, $24,522 part-time in-state, $23,961 full-time out-of-state, $24,522 part-time out-of-state
Tuition per credit: $650 full-time in-state, $650 part-time in-state, $650 full-time out-of-state, $650 part-time out-of-state
Acceptance rate: 63.0%
Average age of entrants: 33
Enrollment: 91, 27% men, 73% women, 25% minority, 0% international
Average class size: 14
Most popular MBA concentrations: health care administration
Completion: Credits needed to graduate: 36; target time to graduate: 2 years
College funded aid available: Domestic: No; International: No
Graduates with debt: 40%; average amount of debt $45,858

ONLINE BUSINESS PROGRAM(S)

www.sjcny.edu/online/admissions/graduate
Admissions: (631) 687-4501
Email: online@sjcny.edu
Financial aid: (631) 687-2611
Application deadline: rolling
Program can be completed entirely online: Yes
Total program cost: $23,961 full-time in-state, $24,522 part-time in-state, $23,961 full-time out-of-state, $24,522 part-time out-of-state
Tuition per credit: $650 full-time in-state, $650 part-time in-state, $650 full-time out-of-state, $650 part-time out-of-state
Acceptance rate: 63.0%
Average age of entrants: 34
Enrollment: 48, 23% men, 77% women, 42% minority, 0% international
Average class size: 14
Most popular business concentrations: general management, health care administration, human resources management
Completion: Credits needed to graduate: 36; target time to graduate: 2 years
College funded aid available: Domestic: No; International: No
Graduates with debt: 50%; average amount of debt $43,185

Stony Brook University–SUNY

Public

ONLINE BUSINESS PROGRAM(S)

www.stonybrook.edu/spd/
Admissions: (631) 632-7050
Email: SPD@stonybrook.edu
Financial aid: (631) 632-6840
Application deadline: Domestic: 07/01; International: 04/01
Program can be completed entirely online: Yes
Total program cost: N/A
Tuition per credit: $462 full-time in-state, $462 part-time in-state, $944 full-time out-of-state, $944 part-time out-of-state
Acceptance rate: 98.0%
Test scores required: No
Average age of entrants: 30
Students with prior work experience: 100.0%
Enrollment: 184, 17% men, 83% women, 40% minority, 0% international
Average class size: 20
Most popular business concentrations: human resources management
Completion: Three year graduation rate: 71%; credits needed to graduate: 30; target time to graduate: 2.5 years
College funded aid available: International: No
Graduates with debt: 39%; average amount of debt $26,677

Syracuse University (Whitman)

Private

ONLINE MBA PROGRAM(S)

onlinebusiness.syr.edu/admissions
Admissions: (315) 443-9214
Email: admissions@onlinebusiness.syr.edu
Financial aid: (315) 443-1513
Application deadline: rolling
Program can be completed entirely online: No
Total program cost: $84,186 full-time in-state, $84,186 part-time in-state, $84,186 full-time out-of-state, $84,186 part-time out-of-state
Tuition per credit: $1,559 full-time in-state, $1,559 part-time in-state, $1,559 full-time out-of-state, $1,559 part-time out-of-state
Acceptance rate: 80.0%
Average GMAT: 597
Average GRE: 155 verbal, 156 quantitative, 4.0 writing
Average age of entrants: 35
Students with prior work experience: 100.0%
Enrollment: 1,344, 69% men, 31% women, 39% minority, 1% international
Average class size: 18
Most popular MBA concentrations: entrepreneurship, finance, general management, marketing, supply chain management/logistics
Completion: Three year graduation rate: 67%; credits needed to graduate: 54; target time to graduate: 2 years
College funded aid available: Domestic: No; International: No

Graduates with debt: 62%; average amount of debt $78,700

ONLINE BUSINESS PROGRAM(S)

onlinebusiness.syr.edu/admissions
Admissions: (315) 443-9214
Email: admissions@onlinebusiness.syr.edu
Financial aid: (315) 443-1513
Application deadline: rolling
Program can be completed entirely online: No
Total program cost: $53,006 full-time in-state, $53,006 part-time in-state, $53,006 full-time out-of-state, $53,006 part-time out-of-state
Tuition per credit: $1,559 full-time in-state, $1,559 part-time in-state, $1,559 full-time out-of-state, $1,559 part-time out-of-state
Acceptance rate: 84.0%
Average GMAT: 619
Average GRE: 152 verbal, 152 quantitative, 4.0 writing
Average age of entrants: 37
Students with prior work experience: 100.0%
Enrollment: 285, 57% men, 43% women, 38% minority, 1% international
Average class size: 18
Most popular business concentrations: accounting, entrepreneurship
Completion: Credits needed to graduate: 30; target time to graduate: 1 year
College funded aid available: Domestic: No; International: No
Graduates with debt: 88%; average amount of debt $55,398

Utica College

Private

ONLINE MBA PROGRAM(S)

programs.online.utica.edu/programs/mba"(315) 792-3010
Admissions: admiss@utica.edu
Email: (315) 792-3215
Financial aid: rolling
Application deadline: Yes
Program can be completed entirely online:
Total program cost: $650 full-time in-state, $650 part-time in-state, $650 full-time out-of-state, $650 part-time out-of-state
Tuition per credit: 73.0%
Acceptance rate: No
Average GRE: 32
Students with prior work experience: 297, 46% men, 54% women, 24% minority, 2% international
Enrollment: 14
Average class size: Accounting, Entrepreneurship, Health Care Administration, Insurance
Most popular MBA concentrations: three year graduation rate: 66%; credits needed to graduate: 60; target time to graduate: 2 years
Completion: Domestic: no; international: no
College funded aid available: 52%; average amount of debt $6,277
Graduates with debt: N/A

East Carolina University

Public

ONLINE MBA PROGRAM(S)

business.ecu.edu/grad/degrees
Admissions: (252) 328-6970
Email: gradbus@ecu.edu
Financial aid: (252) 328-6610
Application deadline: rolling
Program can be completed entirely online: Yes
Total program cost: $11,807 full-time in-state, $11,807 part-time in-state, $33,078 full-time out-of-state, $33,078 part-time out-of-state
Tuition per credit: $358 full-time in-state, $358 part-time in-state, $1,002 full-time out-of-state, $1,002 part-time out-of-state
Acceptance rate: 74.0%
Test scores required: GMAT or GRE
Average GMAT: 506
Average GRE: 151 verbal, 150 quantitative, 3.4 writing
Average age of entrants: 32
Enrollment: 857, 53% men, 47% women, 23% minority, 2% international
Average class size: 27
Most popular MBA concentrations: finance, health care administration, marketing, management information systems, supply chain management/logistics
Completion: Three year graduation rate: 45%; credits needed to graduate: 54; target time to graduate: 3 years
College funded aid available: Domestic: Yes; International: Yes
Graduates with debt: 43%; average amount of debt $31,439

Fayetteville State University

Public

ONLINE MBA PROGRAM(S)

www.uncfsu.edu/mba
Admissions: (910) 672-2910
Email: mbaprogram@uncfsu.edu
Financial aid: (910) 672-1325
Application deadline: rolling
Program can be completed entirely online: Yes
Total program cost: $7,128 full-time in-state, $7,128 part-time in-state, $17,789 full-time out-of-state, $17,789 part-time out-of-state
Tuition per credit: $198 full-time in-state, $198 part-time in-state, $494 full-time out-of-state, $494 part-time out-of-state
Acceptance rate: 95.0%
Test scores required: GMAT or GRE
Average GMAT: 528
Average GRE: 149 verbal, 146 quantitative, 3.1 writing
Average age of entrants: 36
Students with prior work experience: 94.0%
Enrollment: 411, 47% men, 53% women, 54% minority, 4% international
Average class size: 24
Most popular MBA concentrations: finance, general

management, health care administration, marketing
Completion: Three year graduation rate: 45%; credits needed to graduate: 36; target time to graduate: 2 years
College funded aid available: Domestic: Yes; International: Yes
Graduates with debt: 33%; average amount of debt $8,409

Montreat College
Private

ONLINE MBA PROGRAM(S)
www.montreat.edu/adultstudies
Admissions: N/A
Email: admissions@montreat.edu
Financial aid: (828) 669-8012
Application deadline: rolling
Program can be completed entirely online: Yes
Total program cost: N/A
Tuition per credit: $510 full-time in-state, $510 part-time in-state, $510 full-time out-of-state, $510 part-time out-of-state
Test scores required: GMAT
Completion: Credits needed to graduate: 30; target time to graduate: 2 years

ONLINE BUSINESS PROGRAM(S)
Admissions: N/A
Financial aid: N/A
Application deadline: rolling
Program can be completed entirely online: Yes
Total program cost: N/A
Tuition per credit: $510 full-time in-state, $510 part-time in-state, $510 full-time out-of-state, $510 part-time out-of-state
Test scores required: No
Enrollment: 36, 31% men, 69% women, 36% minority, 0% international
Average class size: 10
Completion: Credits needed to graduate: 36; target time to graduate: 2 years

North Carolina State University (Poole)
Public

ONLINE MBA PROGRAM(S)
mba.ncsu.edu/admissions/
Admissions: (919) 513-5584
Email: jennifer_arthur@ncsu.edu
Financial aid: (919) 515-2866
Application deadline: rolling
Program can be completed entirely online: No
Total program cost: $45,160 full-time in-state, $45,160 part-time in-state, $78,440 full-time out-of-state, $78,440 part-time out-of-state
Tuition per credit: $1,129 full-time in-state, $1,129 part-time in-state, $1,961 full-time out-of-state, $1,961 part-time out-of-state
Acceptance rate: 69.0%
Average GMAT: 603
Average GRE: 154 verbal, 153 quantitative, 4.0 writing
Average age of entrants: 36
Students with prior work experience: 100.0%
Enrollment: 312, 66% men, 34% women, 22% minority, 3% international

Average class size: 15
Most popular MBA concentrations: entrepreneurship, finance, marketing, supply chain management/logistics
Completion: Three year graduation rate: 84%; credits needed to graduate: 40; target time to graduate: 3 years
College funded aid available: Domestic: Yes; International: Yes
Graduates with debt: 30%; average amount of debt $44,344

Queens University of Charlotte (McColl)
Private

ONLINE MBA PROGRAM(S)
online.queens.edu/master-of-business-administration-online-overview
Admissions: (704) 337-2465
Email: info@online.queens.edu
Financial aid: (704) 337-2512
Application deadline: rolling
Program can be completed entirely online: No
Total program cost: $40,788 full-time in-state, $40,788 part-time in-state, $40,788 full-time out-of-state, $40,788 part-time out-of-state
Tuition per credit: $1,133 full-time in-state, $1,133 part-time in-state, $1,133 full-time out-of-state, $1,133 part-time out-of-state
Acceptance rate: 95.0%
Test scores required: GMAT or GRE
Average GRE: 153 verbal, 159 quantitative, 4.0 writing
Average age of entrants: 32
Students with prior work experience: 100.0%
Enrollment: 119, 44% men, 56% women, 39% minority, 1% international
Average class size: 18
Completion: Three year graduation rate: 88%; credits needed to graduate: 36; target time to graduate: 2 years
College funded aid available: Domestic: Yes; International: Yes
Graduates with debt: 53%; average amount of debt $48,618

University of North Carolina–Chapel Hill (Kenan-Flagler)
Public

ONLINE MBA PROGRAM(S)
onlinemba.unc.edu/admissions/admissions-overview/
Admissions: (919) 962-8919
Email: OnlineMBA@unc.edu
Financial aid: (919) 962-0135
Application deadline: rolling
Program can be completed entirely online: Depends
Total program cost: $124,345 full-time in-state, $124,345 part-time in-state, $124,345 full-time out-of-state, $124,345 part-time out-of-state
Tuition per credit: $1,884 full-time in-state, $1,884 part-time in-state, $1,884 full-time out-of-state, $1,884 part-time out-of-state

Acceptance rate: 60.0%
Average GMAT: 649
Average GRE: 158 verbal, 161 quantitative, 4.3 writing
Average age of entrants: 34
Students with prior work experience: 100.0%
Enrollment: 905, 72% men, 28% women, 25% minority, 4% international
Average class size: 14
Most popular MBA concentrations: consulting, finance, general management, leadership, marketing
Completion: Three year graduation rate: 90%; credits needed to graduate: 66; target time to graduate: 2 years
College funded aid available: Domestic: Yes; International: Yes
Graduates with debt: 41%; average amount of debt $71,550

ONLINE BUSINESS PROGRAM(S)
onlinemac.unc.edu
Admissions: (919) 962-3209
Email: mac_info@unc.edu
Financial aid: (919) 962-0135
Application deadline: rolling
Program can be completed entirely online: No
Total program cost: N/A
Tuition per credit: $1,418 full-time in-state, $1,418 part-time in-state, $1,418 full-time out-of-state, $1,418 part-time out-of-state
Acceptance rate: 56.0%
Average GMAT: 626
Average GRE: 156 verbal, 156 quantitative, 4.1 writing
Average age of entrants: 34
Students with prior work experience: 90.0%
Enrollment: 124, 49% men, 51% women, N/A minority, N/A international
Average class size: 12
Most popular business concentrations: accounting
Completion: Three year graduation rate: 100%; credits needed to graduate: 48; target time to graduate: 2 years
College funded aid available: Domestic: Yes; International: Yes
Graduates with debt: 49%; average amount of debt $51,950

University of North Carolina–Pembroke
Public

ONLINE MBA PROGRAM(S)
www.uncp.edu/grad
Admissions: (910) 521-6271
Email: grad@uncp.edu
Financial aid: (910) 521-6255
Application deadline: rolling
Program can be completed entirely online: Yes
Total program cost: N/A
Tuition per credit: $224 full-time in-state, $224 part-time in-state, $776 full-time out-of-state, $776 part-time out-of-state
Acceptance rate: 99.0%
Test scores required: GMAT or GRE
Average age of entrants: 31

Enrollment: 127, 38% men, 62% women, 42% minority, 1% international
Most popular MBA concentrations: accounting, finance, general management, international business, marketing
Completion: Credits needed to graduate: 36
College funded aid available: Domestic: Yes; International: Yes
Graduates with debt: 62%; average amount of debt $28,800

Western Carolina University
Public

ONLINE BUSINESS PROGRAM(S)
www.wcu.edu/apply/distance-online-programs/index.aspx
Admissions: (828) 227-7397
Email: distance@wcu.edu
Financial aid: (828) 227-7290
Application deadline: rolling
Program can be completed entirely online: Yes
Total program cost: N/A
Tuition per credit: $291 full-time in-state, $291 part-time in-state, $845 full-time out-of-state, $845 part-time out-of-state
Acceptance rate: 91.0%
Test scores required: No
Average age of entrants: 35
Enrollment: 220, 54% men, 46% women, 36% minority, 1% international
Average class size: 16
Most popular business concentrations: entrepreneurship, sports business
Completion: Three year graduation rate: 52%; credits needed to graduate: 36; target time to graduate: 2 years
College funded aid available: Domestic: Yes; International: Yes

NORTH DAKOTA

Minot State University
Public

ONLINE BUSINESS PROGRAM(S)
www.minotstateu.edu/graduate/future_students/admission_requirements.shtml
Admissions: (701) 858-3413
Email: penny.brandt@minotstateu.edu
Financial aid: (701) 858-3875
Application deadline: Domestic: 07/30; International: 05/30
Program can be completed entirely online: Yes
Total program cost: $9,270 full-time in-state, $9,270 part-time in-state, $9,270 full-time out-of-state, $9,270 part-time out-of-state
Tuition per credit: $309 full-time in-state, $309 part-time in-state, $309 full-time out-of-state, $309 part-time out-of-state
Acceptance rate: 97.0%
Test scores required: GMAT or GRE

Average GRE: 140 verbal, 139 quantitative, 2.7 writing
Enrollment: 79, 37% men, 63% women, 30% minority, 0% international
Average class size: 15
Most popular business concentrations: general management, management information systems, sports business
Completion: Credits needed to graduate: 30; target time to graduate: 2 years
College funded aid available: Domestic: Yes; International: Yes

University of North Dakota
Public

ONLINE MBA PROGRAM(S)
und.edu/programs/business-administration-mba/index.html
Admissions: (701) 777-5892
Email: kate.menzies@und.edu
Financial aid: (701) 777-4409
Application deadline: rolling
Program can be completed entirely online: Yes
Total program cost: $20,081 full-time in-state, $20,081 part-time in-state, $20,081 full-time out-of-state, $20,081 part-time out-of-state
Tuition per credit: $404 full-time in-state, $404 part-time in-state, $404 full-time out-of-state, $404 part-time out-of-state
Acceptance rate: 88.0%
Test scores required: GMAT or GRE
Average GMAT: 585
Average GRE: 157 verbal, 154 quantitative, 3.5 writing
Average age of entrants: 30
Enrollment: 127, 81% men, 19% women, 6% minority, 8% international
Average class size: 24
Most popular MBA concentrations: economics, entrepreneurship, general management, health care administration, marketing
Completion: Three year graduation rate: 64%; credits needed to graduate: 43; target time to graduate: 2.5 years
College funded aid available: Domestic: No
Graduates with debt: 21%; average amount of debt $26,893

ONLINE BUSINESS PROGRAM(S)
und.edu/programs/applied-economics-ms/how-to-apply.html
Admissions: (701) 777-5892
Email: kate.menzies@und.edu
Financial aid: (701) 777-4409
Application deadline: rolling
Program can be completed entirely online: Yes
Total program cost: $14,760 full-time in-state, $14,760 part-time in-state, $14,760 full-time out-of-state, $14,760 part-time out-of-state
Tuition per credit: $404 full-time in-state, $404 part-time in-state, $404 full-time out-of-state, $404 part-time out-of-state
Acceptance rate: 86.0%

Test scores required: GMAT or GRE
Average GMAT: 680
Average GRE: 156 verbal, 156 quantitative, 4.0 writing
Average age of entrants: 30
Enrollment: 59, 88% men, 12% women, 17% minority, 7% international
Average class size: 18
Most popular business concentrations: economics
Completion: Three year graduation rate: 30%; credits needed to graduate: 30; target time to graduate: 2 years
College funded aid available: Domestic: No; International: No
Graduates with debt: 25%; average amount of debt $8,667

OHIO

Ashland University
Private

ONLINE MBA PROGRAM(S)
Admissions: (419) 289-5214
Email: mba@ashland.edu
Financial aid: (419) 289-5002
Application deadline: rolling
Program can be completed entirely online: Yes
Total program cost: $24,450 full-time in-state, $24,450 part-time in-state, $24,450 full-time out-of-state, $24,450 part-time out-of-state
Tuition per credit: $815 full-time in-state, $815 part-time in-state, $815 full-time out-of-state, $815 part-time out-of-state
Acceptance rate: 76.0%
Test scores required: No
Average GMAT: 510
Average GRE: 158 verbal, 148 quantitative, 4.0 writing
Average age of entrants: 25
Students with prior work experience: 90.0%
Enrollment: 321, 52% men, 48% women, 24% minority, 0% international
Average class size: 29
Most popular MBA concentrations: finance, human resources management, production/operations management, supply chain management/logistics
Completion: Three year graduation rate: 71%; credits needed to graduate: 30; target time to graduate: 2 years
College funded aid available: Domestic: No; International: No
Graduates with debt: 62%; average amount of debt $29,245

Baldwin Wallace University
Private

ONLINE MBA PROGRAM(S)
www.bw.edu/graduate-admission/
Admissions: (440) 826-2064
Email: lspencer@bw.edu
Financial aid: (440) 826-2081
Application deadline: rolling
Program can be completed entirely online: No
Total program cost: N/A
Tuition per credit: $948 full-time in-state, $948 part-time in-state, $948

full-time out-of-state, $948 part-time out-of-state
Acceptance rate: 85.0%
Test scores required: GMAT
Average age of entrants: 38
Students with prior work experience: 100.0%
Enrollment: 43, 58% men, 42% women, 14% minority, 0% international
Average class size: 12
Most popular MBA concentrations: general management
Completion: Three year graduation rate: 68%; credits needed to graduate: 38; target time to graduate: 2 years
College funded aid available: Domestic: Yes; International: Yes
Graduates with debt: 29%; average amount of debt $27,374

Cedarville University
Private

ONLINE MBA PROGRAM(S)
www.cedarville.edu/admissions/graduate.aspx
Admissions: (888) 233-2784
Email: gradadmissions@cedarville.edu
Financial aid: (937) 766-7866
Application deadline: rolling
Program can be completed entirely online: Yes
Total program cost: $21,456 full-time in-state, $21,456 part-time in-state, $21,456 full-time out-of-state, $21,456 part-time out-of-state
Tuition per credit: $596 full-time in-state, $596 part-time in-state, $596 full-time out-of-state, $596 part-time out-of-state
Acceptance rate: 79.0%
Test scores required: No
Average age of entrants: 29
Students with prior work experience: 0.0%
Enrollment: 64, 53% men, 47% women, 22% minority, 2% international
Average class size: 7
Most popular MBA concentrations: health care administration, production/operations management, quantitative analysis/statistics and operations research
Completion: Three year graduation rate: 64%; credits needed to graduate: 36; target time to graduate: 2 years
College funded aid available: Domestic: No; International: No
Graduates with debt: 53%; average amount of debt $19,692

Cleveland State University (Ahuja)
Public

ONLINE MBA PROGRAM(S)
www.csuohio.edu/graduate-admissions
Admissions: (216) 687-9370
Email: d.easler@csuohio.edu
Financial aid: (216) 687-5411
Application deadline: rolling
Program can be completed entirely online: Yes
Total program cost: $35,000 full-time in-state, $35,000

part-time in-state, $35,000 full-time out-of-state, $35,000 part-time out-of-state
Tuition per credit: $584 full-time in-state, $584 part-time in-state, $1,002 full-time out-of-state, $1,002 part-time out-of-state
Acceptance rate: 69.0%
Test scores required: GMAT or GRE
Average GMAT: 495
Average GRE: 153 verbal, 150 quantitative, 3.7 writing
Average age of entrants: 28
Enrollment: 35, 63% men, 37% women, 20% minority, 3% international
Average class size: 30
Most popular MBA concentrations: general management
Completion: Target time to graduate: 1 year
College funded aid available: Domestic: Yes; International: Yes

Kent State University
Public

ONLINE MBA PROGRAM(S)
www.kent.edu/business/onlinemba
Admissions: (330) 672-2282
Email: gradbus@kent.edu
Financial aid: (330) 672-6000
Application deadline: rolling
Program can be completed entirely online: Yes
Total program cost: $29,880 full-time in-state, $29,880 part-time in-state, $29,880 full-time out-of-state, $29,880 part-time out-of-state
Tuition per credit: $830 full-time in-state, $830 part-time in-state, $830 full-time out-of-state, $830 part-time out-of-state
Acceptance rate: 70.0%
Test scores required: GMAT or GRE
Average GMAT: 515
Average GRE: 154 verbal, 148 quantitative, 3.8 writing
Average age of entrants: 33
Students with prior work experience: 100.0%
Enrollment: 57, 46% men, 54% women, 2% minority, 2% international
Average class size: 24
Most popular MBA concentrations: international business, supply chain management/logistics
Completion: Credits needed to graduate: 36; target time to graduate: 2 years
College funded aid available: Domestic: No; International: No
Graduates with debt: 17%; average amount of debt $26,239

Ohio Dominican University
Private

ONLINE MBA PROGRAM(S)
ohiodominican.edu
Admissions: (614) 251-4721
Email: naughtoj@ohiodominican.edu
Financial aid: (614) 251-4954
Application deadline: rolling

Program can be completed entirely online: Yes
Total program cost: $21,600 full-time in-state, $21,600 part-time in-state, $21,600 full-time out-of-state, $21,600 part-time out-of-state
Tuition per credit: $600 full-time in-state, $600 part-time in-state, $600 full-time out-of-state, $600 part-time out-of-state
Acceptance rate: 95.0%
Test scores required: No
Average age of entrants: 32
Enrollment: 199, 55% men, 45% women, 23% minority, 5% international
Average class size: 19
Completion: Three year graduation rate: 80%; credits needed to graduate: 36; target time to graduate: 2 years
College funded aid available: Domestic: No; International: No
Graduates with debt: 52%; average amount of debt $34,863

Ohio University
Public

ONLINE MBA PROGRAM(S)
onlinemba.ohio.edu
Admissions: (800) 622-3124
Email: mba@ohio.edu
Financial aid: (740) 593-9853
Application deadline: rolling
Program can be completed entirely online: Yes
Total program cost: $35,980 part-time in-state, $36,645 part-time out-of-state
Tuition per credit: $1,025 full-time in-state, $1,025 part-time in-state, $1,044 full-time out-of-state, $1,044 part-time out-of-state
Acceptance rate: 88.0%
Test scores required: No
Average age of entrants: 34
Students with prior work experience: 100.0%
Enrollment: 842, 59% men, 41% women, 24% minority, 1% international
Average class size: 55
Most popular MBA concentrations: finance, general management, health care administration
Completion: Three year graduation rate: 79%; credits needed to graduate: 35; target time to graduate: 2 years
College funded aid available: Domestic: No; International: No
Graduates with debt: 47%; average amount of debt $12,161

Tiffin University
Private

ONLINE MBA PROGRAM(S)
www.tiffin.edu/admissions/graduate
Admissions: (800) 968-6446
Email: grad@tiffin.edu
Financial aid: (419) 448-3375
Application deadline: rolling
Program can be completed entirely online: Yes
Total program cost: $25,200 full-time in-state, $25,200 part-time in-state, $25,200 full-time out-of-state, $25,200 part-time out-of-state

Program can be completed entirely online: Yes
Total program cost: $21,600 full-time in-state, $21,600 part-time in-state, $21,600 full-time out-of-state, $21,600 part-time out-of-state
Tuition per credit: $600 full-time in-state, $600 part-time in-state, $600 full-time out-of-state, $600 part-time out-of-state
Acceptance rate: 95.0%
Test scores required: No
Average age of entrants: 32
Enrollment: 199, 55% men, 45% women, 23% minority, 5% international
Average class size: 19

Tuition per credit: $700 full-time in-state, $700 part-time in-state, $700 full-time out-of-state, $700 part-time out-of-state
Acceptance rate: 72.0%
Test scores required: No
Average age of entrants: 31
Enrollment: 450, 43% men, 57% women, N/A minority, N/A international
Most popular MBA concentrations: general management, international business, leadership, marketing, sports business
Completion: Credits needed to graduate: 36
College funded aid available: Domestic: Yes

Union Institute and University
Private

ONLINE BUSINESS PROGRAM(S)
www.myunion.edu/admissions
Admissions: (800) 861-6400
Email: admissions@myunion.edu
Financial aid: (513) 487-1126
Application deadline: Domestic: 08/01; International: 08/01
Program can be completed entirely online: Yes
Total program cost: $21,864 full-time in-state, $21,864 part-time in-state, $21,864 full-time out-of-state, $21,864 part-time out-of-state
Tuition per credit: $600 full-time in-state, $600 part-time in-state, $600 full-time out-of-state, $600 part-time out-of-state
Acceptance rate: 96.0%
Test scores required: No
Average age of entrants: 42
Students with prior work experience: 89.0%
Enrollment: 77, 51% men, 49% women, 61% minority, 0% international
Average class size: 15
Most popular business concentrations: leadership
Completion: Three year graduation rate: 79%; credits needed to graduate: 36; target time to graduate: 1 year
College funded aid available: Domestic: Yes; International: Yes

University of Cincinnati
Public

ONLINE MBA PROGRAM(S)
aponline.uc.edu/programs/master-of-business-administration.aspx#admissions
Admissions: (513) 556-7024
Email: jason.dickman@uc.edu
Financial aid: (513) 556-3076
Application deadline: rolling
Program can be completed entirely online: Yes
Total program cost: $28,920 full-time in-state, $30,628 part-time in-state, $40,677 full-time out-of-state, $31,198 part-time out-of-state

Tuition per credit: $964 full-time in-state, $806 part-time in-state, $1,356 full-time out-of-state, $821 part-time out-of-state
Acceptance rate: 64.0%
Test scores required: GMAT or GRE
Average GMAT: 643
Average GRE: 155 verbal, 154 quantitative, 4.6 writing
Average age of entrants: 33
Students with prior work experience: 56.0%
Enrollment: 264, 59% men, 41% women, 18% minority, 2% international
Average class size: 51
Most popular MBA concentrations: health care administration, marketing
Completion: Three year graduation rate: 59%; credits needed to graduate: 38; target time to graduate: 1.5 years
College funded aid available: Domestic: Yes; International: Yes
Graduates with debt: 34%; average amount of debt $47,381

ONLINE BUSINESS PROGRAM(S)
aponline.uc.edu/programs/ms-in-taxation.aspx
Admissions: (513) 556-7024
Email: jason.dickman@uc.edu
Financial aid: (513) 556-3076
Application deadline: rolling
Program can be completed entirely online: Yes
Total program cost: $28,920 full-time in-state, $24,180 part-time in-state, $36,180 full-time out-of-state, $24,630 part-time out-of-state
Tuition per credit: $964 full-time in-state, $806 part-time in-state, $1,206 full-time out-of-state, $821 part-time out-of-state
Acceptance rate: 93.0%
Test scores required: GMAT or GRE
Average GMAT: 463
Average age of entrants: 36
Students with prior work experience: 44.0%
Enrollment: 43, 56% men, 44% women, 21% minority, 0% international
Average class size: 21
Completion: Three year graduation rate: 57%; credits needed to graduate: 30; target time to graduate: 2 years
College funded aid available: Domestic: Yes; International: Yes
Graduates with debt: 44%; average amount of debt $36,341

University of Dayton
Private

ONLINE MBA PROGRAM(S)
onlinemba.udayton.edu/admission/
Admissions: (937) 229-1850
Email: gradadmission@udayton.edu
Financial aid: (937) 229-4113
Application deadline: rolling
Program can be completed entirely online: No
Total program cost: N/A
Tuition per credit:

Enrollment: 349, 60% men, 40% women, 24% minority, 4% international
Completion: Credits needed to graduate: 30

University of Findlay
Private

ONLINE MBA PROGRAM(S)
www.findlay.edu
Admissions: (800) 472-9502
Email: admissions@findlay.edu
Financial aid: (419) 434-4791
Application deadline: rolling
Program can be completed entirely online: Yes
Total program cost: $22,407 full-time in-state, $22,407 part-time in-state, $22,407 full-time out-of-state, $22,407 part-time out-of-state
Tuition per credit: $679 full-time in-state, $679 part-time in-state, $679 full-time out-of-state, $679 part-time out-of-state
Acceptance rate: 84.0%
Test scores required: No
Average age of entrants: 23
Enrollment: 326, 51% men, 49% women, 2% minority, 16% international
Average class size: 20
Most popular MBA concentrations: accounting, finance, general management, health care administration, human resources management
Completion: Credits needed to graduate: 33; target time to graduate: 2 years
College funded aid available: Domestic: Yes; International: Yes

Walsh University
Private

ONLINE MBA PROGRAM(S)
www.walsh.edu/graduate-programs
Admissions: (330) 490-7181
Email: adice@walsh.edu
Financial aid: (330) 490-7146
Application deadline: rolling
Program can be completed entirely online: Yes
Total program cost: $12,690 full-time in-state, $8,460 part-time in-state, $12,690 full-time out-of-state, $12,690 part-time out-of-state
Tuition per credit: $705 full-time in-state, $705 part-time in-state, $705 full-time out-of-state, $705 part-time out-of-state
Acceptance rate: 90.0%
Enrollment: 178, 46% men, 54% women, 8% minority, 3% international
Average class size: 13
Most popular MBA concentrations: entrepreneurship, general management, health care administration, leadership, marketing
Completion: Credits needed to graduate: 36; target time to graduate: 1 year
College funded aid available: Domestic: Yes; International: No
Graduates with debt: 61%; average amount of debt $43,265

Wright State University (Soin)
Public

ONLINE MBA PROGRAM(S)
business.wright.edu/master-of-business-administration
Admissions: (937) 775-2437
Email: mba@wright.edu
Financial aid: (937) 775-5721
Application deadline: rolling
Program can be completed entirely online: No
Total program cost: $30,690 full-time in-state, $30,690 part-time in-state, $52,313 full-time out-of-state, $52,313 part-time out-of-state
Tuition per credit: $660 full-time in-state, $660 part-time in-state, $1,125 full-time out-of-state, $1,125 part-time out-of-state
Acceptance rate: 86.0%
Test scores required: No
Average GMAT: 455
Average GRE: 163 verbal, 150 quantitative, 4.0 writing
Average age of entrants: 29
Enrollment: 751, 53% men, 47% women, 19% minority, 12% international
Average class size: 30
Most popular MBA concentrations: economics, finance, general management, marketing, quantitative analysis/statistics and operations research
Completion: Credits needed to graduate: 46; target time to graduate: 2 years
College funded aid available: Domestic: Yes; International: Yes
Graduates with debt: 38%; average amount of debt $41,296

ONLINE BUSINESS PROGRAM(S)
www.wright.edu/graduate-school/admissions/apply-now
Admissions: (937) 775-2895
Email: Donald.Hopkins@wright.edu
Financial aid: (937) 775-5721
Application deadline: rolling
Program can be completed entirely online: Depends
Total program cost: $20,958 full-time in-state, $21,780 part-time in-state, $35,536 full-time out-of-state, $37,125 part-time out-of-state
Tuition per credit: $600 full-time in-state, $660 part-time in-state, $1,125 full-time out-of-state, $1,125 part-time out-of-state
Acceptance rate: 91.0%
Test scores required: No
Average GRE: 150 verbal, 156 quantitative, 4.0 writing
Students with prior work experience: 100.0%
Enrollment: 49, 69% men, 31% women, 39% minority, 0% international
Average class size: 24
Most popular business concentrations: management information systems, supply chain management/logistics
Completion: Three year graduation rate: 98%; credits needed to graduate: 33; target time to graduate: 1 year
College funded aid available: Domestic: Yes

Graduates with debt: 47%; average amount of debt $26,335

OKLAHOMA

Cameron University
Public

ONLINE MBA PROGRAM(S)
www.cameron.edu/business/graduate
Admissions: (580) 581-2289
Email: admissions@cameron.edu
Financial aid: (580) 581-2293
Application deadline: rolling
Program can be completed entirely online: Yes
Total program cost: $10,560 full-time in-state, $10,560 part-time in-state, $14,025 full-time out-of-state, $14,025 part-time out-of-state
Tuition per credit: $320 full-time in-state, $320 part-time in-state, $425 full-time out-of-state, $425 part-time out-of-state
Acceptance rate: 74.0%
Average GMAT: 433
Average age of entrants: 34
Enrollment: 111, 53% men, 47% women, 18% minority, 28% international
Average class size: 13
Completion: Three year graduation rate: 38%; credits needed to graduate: 33; target time to graduate: 2 years
College funded aid available: Domestic: Yes; International: Yes
Graduates with debt: 28%; average amount of debt $21,245

Northeastern State University
Public

ONLINE MBA PROGRAM(S)
academics.nsuok.edu/graduatecollege/applyforadmission.aspx
Admissions: (918) 444-2093
Email: mccolluj@nsuok.edu
Financial aid: (918) 444-3410
Application deadline: rolling
Program can be completed entirely online: No
Total program cost: $8,460 full-time in-state, $8,460 part-time in-state, $8,496 full-time out-of-state, $8,496 part-time out-of-state
Tuition per credit: $235 full-time in-state, $235 part-time in-state, $236 full-time out-of-state, $236 part-time out-of-state
Acceptance rate: 100.0%
Test scores required: No
Average age of entrants: 30
Enrollment: 76, 51% men, 49% women, 51% minority, 5% international
Average class size: 17
Completion: Credits needed to graduate: 36; target time to graduate: 2 years
College funded aid available: Domestic: Yes; International: Yes

---

Oklahoma Christian University
Private

ONLINE MBA PROGRAM(S)
Admissions: (405) 425-5562
Email: gsb@oc.edu
Financial aid: (405) 425-5191
Application deadline: rolling
Program can be completed entirely online: Yes
Total program cost: $21,780 full-time in-state, $21,780 part-time in-state, $21,780 full-time out-of-state, $21,780 part-time out-of-state
Tuition per credit: $605 full-time in-state, $605 part-time in-state, $605 full-time out-of-state, $605 part-time out-of-state
Test scores required: GMAT or GRE
Enrollment: 365, 51% men, 49% women, N/A minority, N/A international
Average class size: 13
Most popular MBA concentrations: accounting, finance, international business, leadership, manufacturing and technology management
Completion: Credits needed to graduate: 36; target time to graduate: 1 year
College funded aid available: Domestic: Yes; International: Yes

Oklahoma City University
Private

ONLINE BUSINESS PROGRAM(S)
www.okcu.edu/admissions/graduate/
Admissions: (405) 208-5094
Email: maharrington@okcu.edu
Financial aid: (405) 208-5154
Application deadline: rolling
Program can be completed entirely online: Depends
Total program cost: $17,700 full-time in-state, $17,700 part-time in-state, $17,700 full-time out-of-state, $17,700 part-time out-of-state
Tuition per credit: $590 full-time in-state, $590 part-time in-state, $590 full-time out-of-state, $590 part-time out-of-state
Acceptance rate: 88.0%
Test scores required: No
Average age of entrants: 33
Students with prior work experience: 100.0%
Enrollment: 133, 67% men, 33% women, 23% minority, 0% international
Average class size: 17
Most popular business concentrations: economics, finance, general management, leadership, public policy
Completion: Three year graduation rate: 89%; credits needed to graduate: 30; target time to graduate: 2 years
College funded aid available: Domestic: Yes; International: No
Graduates with debt: 30%; average amount of debt $28,641

Oklahoma State University (Spears)

Public

ONLINE MBA PROGRAM(S)

business.okstate.edu/watson/mba/admission.html
Admissions: (405) 744-2951
Email: spearsmasters@okstate.edu
Financial aid: (405) 744-6604
Application deadline: Domestic: 07/01; International: 03/01
Program can be completed entirely online: Yes
Total program cost: $9,677 full-time in-state, $9,677 part-time in-state, $15,120 full-time out-of-state, $15,120 part-time out-of-state
Tuition per credit: $230 full-time in-state, $230 part-time in-state, $360 full-time out-of-state, $360 part-time out-of-state
Acceptance rate: 83.0%
Test scores required: GMAT or GRE
Average GMAT: 567
Average GRE: 156 verbal, 153 quantitative, 4.0 writing
Average age of entrants: 29
Students with prior work experience: 92.0%
Enrollment: 242, 76% men, 24% women, 18% minority, 1% international
Average class size: 22
Most popular MBA concentrations: entrepreneurship, human resources management, management information systems, not-for-profit management
Completion: Three year graduation rate: 61%; credits needed to graduate: 42; target time to graduate: 3 years
College funded aid available: Domestic: Yes; International: No
Graduates with debt: 11%; average amount of debt $33,732

ONLINE BUSINESS PROGRAM(S)

business.okstate.edu/watson/
Admissions: (405) 744-2951
Email: spearsmasters@okstate.edu
Financial aid: (405) 744-6604
Application deadline: Domestic: 07/01; International: 03/01
Program can be completed entirely online: Yes
Total program cost: $7,605 full-time in-state, $7,605 part-time in-state, $11,880 full-time out-of-state, $11,880 part-time out-of-state
Tuition per credit: $230 full-time in-state, $230 part-time in-state, $360 full-time out-of-state, $360 part-time out-of-state
Acceptance rate: 92.0%
Test scores required: GMAT or GRE
Average GMAT: 543
Average GRE: 153 verbal, 153 quantitative, 4.0 writing
Average age of entrants: 33
Students with prior work experience: 90.0%
Enrollment: 81, 81% men, 19% women, 32% minority, 2% international
Average class size: 22

Most popular business concentrations: entrepreneurship, marketing, management information systems
Completion: Three year graduation rate: 44%; credits needed to graduate: 33; target time to graduate: 2 years
College funded aid available: Domestic: No; International: No
Graduates with debt: 17%; average amount of debt $27,969

University of Oklahoma

Public

ONLINE BUSINESS PROGRAM(S)

www.ou.edu/content/admissions/apply/graduate.html
Admissions: (405) 325-6765
Email: gradadm@ou.edu
Financial aid: (405) 325-4521
Application deadline: rolling
Program can be completed entirely online: Yes
Total program cost: $32,500 full-time in-state, $32,500 part-time in-state, $32,500 full-time out-of-state, $32,500 part-time out-of-state
Tuition per credit: $985 full-time in-state, $985 part-time in-state, $985 full-time out-of-state, $985 part-time out-of-state
Acceptance rate: 79.0%
Test scores required: No
Average GMAT: 550
Average age of entrants: 36
Students with prior work experience: 100.0%
Enrollment: 56, 46% men, 54% women, 23% minority, 0% international
Average class size: 21
Most popular business concentrations: accounting
Completion: Credits needed to graduate: 33; target time to graduate: 2 years
College funded aid available: Domestic: Yes; International: No

University of Tulsa (Collins)

Private

ONLINE BUSINESS PROGRAM(S)

business.utulsa.edu/
Admissions: (918) 631-2242
Email: graduate-business@utulsa.edu
Financial aid: (918) 631-2527
Application deadline: rolling
Program can be completed entirely online: Depends
Total program cost: $30,600 full-time in-state, $30,600 part-time in-state, $30,600 full-time out-of-state, $30,600 part-time out-of-state
Tuition per credit: $900 full-time in-state, $900 part-time in-state, $900 full-time out-of-state, $900 part-time out-of-state
Acceptance rate: 85.0%
Average age of entrants: 38
Students with prior work experience: 100.0%
Enrollment: 69, 86% men, 14% women, 9% minority, 9% international
Average class size: 14

Completion: Three year graduation rate: 64%; credits needed to graduate: 34; target time to graduate: 2 years
College funded aid available: Domestic: No; International: No
Graduates with debt: 21%; average amount of debt $35,665

OREGON

Eastern Oregon University

Public

ONLINE MBA PROGRAM(S)

www.eou.edu/mba/
Admissions: (541) 962-3529
Email: kristin.johnson@eou.edu
Financial aid: (541) 962-3550
Application deadline: rolling
Program can be completed entirely online: Yes
Total program cost: $19,980 full-time in-state, $19,980 part-time in-state, $19,980 full-time out-of-state, $19,980 part-time out-of-state
Tuition per credit: $444 full-time in-state, $444 part-time in-state, $444 full-time out-of-state, $444 part-time out-of-state
Acceptance rate: 64.0%
Test scores required: No
Enrollment: 52, 42% men, 58% women, 17% minority, 12% international
Average class size: 18
Most popular MBA concentrations: general management
Completion: Credits needed to graduate: 45; target time to graduate: 1.5 years
College funded aid available: Domestic: No; International: No
Graduates with debt: 80%; average amount of debt $39,490

Northwest Christian University

Private

ONLINE MBA PROGRAM(S)

www.nwcu.edu/graduate/majors/business-administration-gd/
Admissions: (541) 684-7201
Email: admissions@nwcu.edu
Financial aid: (541) 684-7291
Application deadline: rolling
Program can be completed entirely online: Yes
Total program cost: $25,020 full-time in-state, $25,020 part-time in-state, $25,020 full-time out-of-state, $25,020 part-time out-of-state
Tuition per credit: $695 full-time in-state, $695 part-time in-state, $695 full-time out-of-state, $695 part-time out-of-state
Acceptance rate: 100.0%
Test scores required: No
Average age of entrants: 33
Students with prior work experience: 86.0%
Enrollment: 106, 43% men, 57% women, 30% minority, 0% international
Completion: Credits needed to graduate: 36; target time to graduate: 1 year

Oregon State University

Public

ONLINE MBA PROGRAM(S)

mba.oregonstate.edu/admissions/application-process/
Admissions: (541) 737-5510
Email: Matt.Alex@oregonstate.edu
Financial aid: (541) 737-2241
Application deadline: rolling
Program can be completed entirely online: Yes
Total program cost: $48,000 full-time in-state, $48,000 part-time in-state, $48,000 full-time out-of-state, $48,000 part-time out-of-state
Tuition per credit: $800 full-time in-state, $800 part-time in-state, $800 full-time out-of-state, $800 part-time out-of-state
Test scores required: GMAT or GRE
Most popular MBA concentrations: general management, leadership, marketing, supply chain management/logistics, quantitative analysis/statistics and operations research
Completion: Credits needed to graduate: 45; target time to graduate: 2 years
College funded aid available: Domestic: Yes; International: No

Portland State University

Public

ONLINE MBA PROGRAM(S)

thehealthcaremba.org/
Admissions: (503) 725-8001
Email: SBGradAdmissions@pdx.edu
Financial aid: N/A
Application deadline: Domestic: 06/01; International: 06/01
Program can be completed entirely online: No
Total program cost: $42,480 part-time in-state, $42,480 part-time out-of-state
Tuition per credit: $590 full-time in-state, $590 part-time in-state, $590 full-time out-of-state, $590 part-time out-of-state
Acceptance rate: 65.0%
Average GMAT: 430
Average GRE: 154 verbal, 148 quantitative, 3.8 writing
Average age of entrants: 36
Students with prior work experience: 100.0%
Enrollment: 126, 52% men, 48% women, 32% minority, 0% international
Average class size: 42
Most popular MBA concentrations: health care administration
Completion: Credits needed to graduate: 72; target time to graduate: 3 years

ONLINE BUSINESS PROGRAM(S)

www.pdx.edu/sba/graduate-business-programs-admissions
Admissions: (503) 725-8001
Email: gradadmissions.sba@pdx.edu
Financial aid: (503) 725-5442

Application deadline: rolling

Program can be completed entirely online: No
Total program cost: $31,152 full-time in-state, $31,152 part-time in-state, $38,064 full-time out-of-state, $38,064 part-time out-of-state
Tuition per credit: $649 full-time in-state, $649 part-time in-state, $790 full-time out-of-state, $790 part-time out-of-state
Acceptance rate: 68.0%
Test scores required: No
Average age of entrants: 32
Students with prior work experience: 74.0%
Enrollment: 46, 54% men, 46% women, 28% minority, 2% international
Average class size: 32
Most popular business concentrations: supply chain management/logistics, tax
Completion: Credits needed to graduate: 52; target time to graduate: 2 years
College funded aid available: Domestic: Yes; International: Yes

PENNSYLVANIA

California University of Pennsylvania

Public

ONLINE MBA PROGRAM(S)

www.calu.edu/academics/graduate/
Admissions: (724) 938-5712
Email: popielarcheck@calu.edu
Financial aid: (724) 938-4415
Application deadline: rolling
Program can be completed entirely online: Yes
Total program cost: $18,576 full-time in-state, $18,576 part-time in-state, $27,864 full-time out-of-state, $27,864 part-time out-of-state
Tuition per credit: $516 full-time in-state, $516 part-time in-state, $774 full-time out-of-state, $774 part-time out-of-state
Acceptance rate: 78.0%
Test scores required: No
Average age of entrants: 32
Enrollment: 146, 53% men, 47% women, 14% minority, 0% international
Average class size: 31
Most popular MBA concentrations: entrepreneurship, health care administration
Completion: Three year graduation rate: 50%; credits needed to graduate: 36; target time to graduate: 1.5 years
College funded aid available: Domestic: Yes
Graduates with debt: 36%; average amount of debt $47,958

ONLINE BUSINESS PROGRAM(S)

www.calu.edu/academics/online-programs/index.htm
Admissions: (724) 938-4000
Email: calugo@calu.edu
Financial aid: N/A
Application deadline: rolling
Program can be completed entirely online: Yes
Total program cost: $18,576 full-time in-state, $18,576 part-time in-state, $27,864 full-time out-of-state, $27,864 part-time out-of-state

Tuition per credit: $516 full-time in-state, $516 part-time in-state, $774 full-time out-of-state, $774 part-time out-of-state
Acceptance rate: 78.0%
Test scores required: No
Average age of entrants: 32
Enrollment: 151, 47% men, 53% women, 17% minority, 0% international
Average class size: 31
Most popular business concentrations: entrepreneurship, general management, health care administration, international business, leadership
Completion: Credits needed to graduate: 36; target time to graduate: 1 year
College funded aid available: Domestic: Yes; International: Yes
Graduates with debt: 36%; average amount of debt $47,958

Carnegie Mellon University (Tepper)

Private

ONLINE MBA PROGRAM(S)

www.cmu.edu/tepper/programs/mba/admissions/index.html
Admissions: (412) 268-2273
Email: mba-admissions@andrew.cmu.edu
Financial aid: (412) 268-7581
Application deadline: Domestic: 04/18; International: 04/18
Program can be completed entirely online: No
Total program cost: $132,000 part-time in-state, $132,000 part-time out-of-state
Tuition per credit: $2,063 full-time in-state, $2,063 part-time in-state, $2,063 full-time out-of-state, $2,063 part-time out-of-state
Acceptance rate: 54.0%
Test scores required: GMAT or GRE
Average GMAT: 669
Average GRE: 158 verbal, 161 quantitative, 4.0 writing
Average age of entrants: 29
Students with prior work experience: 100.0%
Enrollment: 137, 70% men, 30% women, 36% minority, 7% international
Average class size: 22
Most popular MBA concentrations: entrepreneurship, finance, marketing, production/operations management, technology
Completion: Three year graduation rate: 97%; credits needed to graduate: 64; target time to graduate: 2.5 years
College funded aid available: Domestic: No; International: No
Graduates with debt: 45%; average amount of debt $88,172

Chatham University

Private

ONLINE MBA PROGRAM(S)

www.chatham.edu/admission/
Admissions: (412) 365-1290
Email: admission@chatham.edu
Financial aid: (412) 365-2781
Application deadline: rolling

Program can be completed entirely online: Yes
Total program cost: N/A
Tuition per credit: $930 full-time in-state, $930 part-time in-state, $930 full-time out-of-state, $930 part-time out-of-state
Acceptance rate: 100.0%
Test scores required: No
Students with prior work experience: 100.0%
Enrollment: 14, 14% men, 86% women, 7% minority, 7% international
Average class size: 15
Most popular MBA concentrations: health care administration
Completion: Credits needed to graduate: 36; target time to graduate: 2 years
College funded aid available: Domestic: Yes

Clarion University of Pennsylvania

Public

ONLINE MBA PROGRAM(S)

www.clarion.edu/admissions
Admissions: (814) 393-2306
Email: gradstudies@clarion.edu
Financial aid: (814) 393-2315
Application deadline: rolling
Program can be completed entirely online: Yes
Total program cost: $15,480 full-time in-state, $15,480 part-time in-state, $16,710 full-time out-of-state, $16,710 part-time out-of-state
Tuition per credit: $516 full-time in-state, $516 part-time in-state, $557 full-time out-of-state, $557 part-time out-of-state
Acceptance rate: 97.0%
Test scores required: GMAT or GRE
Average age of entrants: 28
Students with prior work experience: 95.0%
Enrollment: 98, 54% men, 46% women, 15% minority, 0% international
Average class size: 27
Most popular MBA concentrations: accounting, entrepreneurship, finance, health care administration, not-for-profit management
Completion: Three year graduation rate: 51%; credits needed to graduate: 36; target time to graduate: 2.5 years
College funded aid available: Domestic: Yes; International: Yes
Graduates with debt: 38%; average amount of debt $30,623

ONLINE BUSINESS PROGRAM(S)

www.clarion.edu/admissions
Admissions: (814) 393-2306
Email: gradstudies@clarion.edu
Financial aid: (814) 393-2315
Application deadline: rolling
Program can be completed entirely online: Yes
Total program cost: $15,480 full-time in-state, $15,480 part-time in-state, $16,710 full-time out-of-state, $16,710 part-time out-of-state
Tuition per credit: $516 full-time in-state, $516 part-time in-state, $557 full-time out-of-state, $557 part-time out-of-state

Acceptance rate: 96.0%
Test scores required: No
Average age of entrants: 29
Students with prior work experience: 71.0%
Enrollment: 24, 42% men, 58% women, 13% minority, 0% international
Average class size: 18
Most popular business concentrations: accounting
Completion: Credits needed to graduate: 30; target time to graduate: 1.5 years
College funded aid available: Domestic: Yes; International: Yes
Graduates with debt: 60%; average amount of debt $26,641

DeSales University

Private

ONLINE MBA PROGRAM(S)

www.desales.edu/admissions-financial-aid/graduate-admissions-aid
Admissions: (610) 282-1100
Email: gradadmissions@desales.edu
Financial aid: (610) 282-1100
Application deadline: rolling
Program can be completed entirely online: Yes
Total program cost: N/A
Tuition per credit: $840 full-time in-state, $840 part-time in-state, $840 full-time out-of-state, $840 part-time out-of-state
Acceptance rate: 87.0%
Test scores required: No
Average age of entrants: 34
Students with prior work experience: 100.0%
Enrollment: 722, 46% men, 54% women, N/A minority, N/A international
Average class size: 11
Most popular MBA concentrations: accounting, finance, general management, health care administration, production/operations management
Completion: Three year graduation rate: 49%; credits needed to graduate: 36; target time to graduate: 2.5 years
College funded aid available: Domestic: Yes; International: Yes
Graduates with debt: 33%; average amount of debt $14,171

Drexel University (LeBow)

Private

ONLINE MBA PROGRAM(S)

www.lebow.drexel.edu/academics/graduate/resources/admissions
Admissions: (215) 895-1671
Email: lebowgrad@drexel.edu
Financial aid: (215) 571-4545
Application deadline: rolling
Program can be completed entirely online: Yes
Total program cost: $64,000 part-time in-state, $64,000 part-time out-of-state
Tuition per credit: $1,306 full-time in-state, $1,306 part-time in-state, $1,306 full-time out-of-state, $1,306 part-time out-of-state

Acceptance rate: 90.0%
Test scores required: GMAT or GRE
Average GMAT: 508
Average GRE: 153 verbal, 151 quantitative
Average age of entrants: 33
Students with prior work experience: 100.0%
Enrollment: 214, 57% men, 43% women, 29% minority, 5% international
Average class size: 31
Most popular MBA concentrations: entrepreneurship, finance, general management, health care administration, marketing
Completion: Three year graduation rate: 80%; credits needed to graduate: 49; target time to graduate: 2.5 years
College funded aid available: Domestic: Yes; International: Yes
Graduates with debt: 46%; average amount of debt $57,513

Duquesne University (Palumbo-Donahue)

Private

ONLINE BUSINESS PROGRAM(S)

www.duq.edu/academics/schools/business/graduate
Admissions: (412) 396-6276
Email: grad-bus@duq.edu
Financial aid: (412) 396-6607
Application deadline: rolling
Program can be completed entirely online: Yes
Total program cost: $28,590 full-time in-state, $28,590 part-time in-state, $28,590 full-time out-of-state, $28,590 part-time out-of-state
Tuition per credit: $953 full-time in-state, $953 part-time in-state, $953 full-time out-of-state, $953 part-time out-of-state
Acceptance rate: 95.0%
Test scores required: GMAT or GRE
Average GRE: 138 verbal, 150 quantitative, 2.0 writing
Average age of entrants: 34
Students with prior work experience: 86.0%
Enrollment: 30, 53% men, 47% women, 17% minority, 0% international
Average class size: 8
Completion: Credits needed to graduate: 30; target time to graduate: 2 years
College funded aid available: Domestic: No; International: No
Graduates with debt: 100%; average amount of debt $34,663

La Salle University

Private

ONLINE MBA PROGRAM(S)

online.lasalle.edu/admissions.aspx
Admissions: (215) 951-1100
Email: onlinegrad@lasalle.edu
Financial aid: (215) 951-1974
Application deadline: rolling
Program can be completed entirely online: Yes
Total program cost: $24,981 full-time in-state, $24,981 part-time in-state, $24,981 full-time out-of-state, $24,981 part-time out-of-state

Tuition per credit: $757 full-time in-state, $757 part-time in-state, $757 full-time out-of-state, $757 part-time out-of-state
Acceptance rate: 78.0%
Average GMAT: 475
Average GRE: 147 verbal, 155 quantitative, 4.0 writing
Average age of entrants: 32
Students with prior work experience: 90.0%
Enrollment: 58, 52% men, 48% women, 31% minority, 0% international
Average class size: 12
Most popular MBA concentrations: accounting, finance, general management, marketing, management information systems
Completion: Credits needed to graduate: 36; target time to graduate: 1.5 years
College funded aid available: Domestic: No; International: No

Lehigh University

Private

ONLINE MBA PROGRAM(S)

www.lehigh.edu/mba
Admissions: (610) 758-4450
Email: business@lehigh.edu
Financial aid: (610) 758-5289
Application deadline: rolling
Program can be completed entirely online: No
Total program cost: $39,075 full-time in-state, $39,075 part-time in-state, $39,075 full-time out-of-state, $39,075 part-time out-of-state
Tuition per credit: $1,075 full-time in-state, $1,075 part-time in-state, $1,075 full-time out-of-state, $1,075 part-time out-of-state
Acceptance rate: 61.0%
Test scores required: GMAT or GRE
Average GMAT: 620
Average GRE: 158 verbal, 158 quantitative, 4.5 writing
Average age of entrants: 34
Students with prior work experience: 100.0%
Enrollment: 207, 75% men, 25% women, 16% minority, 6% international
Average class size: 24
Most popular MBA concentrations: finance, international business, marketing, supply chain management/logistics
Completion: Three year graduation rate: 71%; credits needed to graduate: 36; target time to graduate: 3 years
College funded aid available: Domestic: Yes; International: Yes
Graduates with debt: 9%; average amount of debt $23,958

Pennsylvania State University–World Campus

Public

ONLINE MBA PROGRAM(S)

www.worldcampus.psu.edu/degrees-and-certificates/penn-state-online-mba-degree-program/apply
Admissions: (814) 863-0474

Email: psuonlinemba@psu.edu
Financial aid: (800) 252-3592
Application deadline: rolling
Program can be completed entirely online: No
Total program cost: $56,880 full-time in-state, $56,880 part-time in-state, $56,880 full-time out-of-state, $56,880 part-time out-of-state
Tuition per credit: $1,185 full-time in-state, $1,185 part-time in-state, $1,185 full-time out-of-state, $1,185 part-time out-of-state
Acceptance rate: 76.0%
Average GMAT: 573
Average GRE: 153 verbal, 154 quantitative, 3.8 writing
Average age of entrants: 33
Students with prior work experience: 99.0%
Enrollment: 355, 67% men, 33% women, 21% minority, 4% international
Average class size: 31
Most popular MBA concentrations: entrepreneurship, finance, general management
Completion: Three year graduation rate: 83%; credits needed to graduate: 48; target time to graduate: 2.5 years
College funded aid available: Domestic: Yes; International: Yes
Graduates with debt: 56%; average amount of debt $43,373

ONLINE BUSINESS PROGRAM(S)

www.worldcampus.psu.edu/admissions
Admissions: (800) 252-3592
Email: wdadmissions@outreach.psu.edu
Financial aid: (800) 252-3592
Application deadline: rolling
Program can be completed entirely online: Depends
Total program cost: $31,650 full-time in-state, $31,650 part-time in-state, $31,650 full-time out-of-state, $31,650 part-time out-of-state
Tuition per credit: $1,055 full-time in-state, $1,055 part-time in-state, $1,055 full-time out-of-state, $1,055 part-time out-of-state
Acceptance rate: 81.0%
Test scores required: GMAT or GRE
Average GMAT: 540
Average GRE: 155 verbal, 153 quantitative, 4.0 writing
Average age of entrants: 34
Students with prior work experience: 98.0%
Enrollment: 641, 68% men, 32% women, 22% minority, 12% international
Average class size: 23
Most popular business concentrations: accounting, entrepreneurship, finance, supply chain management/logistics
Completion: Three year graduation rate: 87%; credits needed to graduate: 30; target time to graduate: 2 years
College funded aid available: Domestic: Yes; International: Yes
Graduates with debt: 22%; average amount of debt $29,950

Robert Morris University
Private

ONLINE MBA PROGRAM(S)

www.rmu.edu/online
Admissions: (412) 397-6300
Email: onlineadmissions@rmu.edu
Financial aid: (412) 397-6250
Application deadline: rolling
Program can be completed entirely online: Yes
Total program cost: N/A
Tuition per credit: $955 full-time in-state, $955 part-time in-state, $955 full-time out-of-state, $955 part-time out-of-state
Acceptance rate: 84.0%
Test scores required: No
Average GMAT: 530
Average age of entrants: 30
Students with prior work experience: 100.0%
Enrollment: 83, 69% men, 31% women, 10% minority, 0% international
Average class size: 17
Most popular MBA concentrations: general management
Completion: Credits needed to graduate: 30; target time to graduate: 1.5 years
College funded aid available: Domestic: Yes;
Graduates with debt: 20%; average amount of debt $25,690

ONLINE BUSINESS PROGRAM(S)

www.rmu.edu/online
Admissions: (412) 397-6300
Email: onlineadmissions@rmu.edu
Financial aid: (412) 397-6250
Application deadline: rolling
Program can be completed entirely online: Yes
Total program cost: N/A
Tuition per credit: $930 full-time in-state, $930 part-time in-state, $930 full-time out-of-state, $930 part-time out-of-state
Acceptance rate: 55.0%
Average age of entrants: 31
Students with prior work experience: 100.0%
Enrollment: 8, 38% men, 63% women, 13% minority, 0% international
Average class size: 10
Most popular business concentrations: human resources management
Completion: Credits needed to graduate: 30; target time to graduate: 1.5 years
College funded aid available: Domestic: No; International: No
Graduates with debt: 57%; average amount of debt $45,270

Saint Vincent College
Private

ONLINE BUSINESS PROGRAM(S)

www.stvincent.edu/admission-aid/graduate-students
Admissions: N/A
Financial aid: N/A
Application deadline: rolling
Program can be completed entirely online: Depends

Total program cost: $24,552 full-time in-state, $24,552 part-time in-state, $24,552 full-time out-of-state, $24,552 part-time out-of-state
Tuition per credit: $682 full-time in-state, $682 part-time in-state, $682 full-time out-of-state, $682 part-time out-of-state
Acceptance rate: 70.0%
Test scores required: No
Average age of entrants: 31
Students with prior work experience: 92.0%
Enrollment: 30, 70% men, 30% women, 17% minority, 3% international
Average class size: 10
Most popular business concentrations: general management, leadership, production/operations management, organizational behavior, quantitative analysis/statistics and operations research
Completion: Credits needed to graduate: 6; target time to graduate: 2 years
College funded aid available: Domestic: Yes; International: Yes
Graduates with debt: 15%

Seton Hill University
Private

ONLINE MBA PROGRAM(S)

www.setonhill.edu/admissions/graduate-admissions/
Admissions: (724) 838-4208
Email: gadmit@setonhill.edu
Financial aid: (724) 830-1010
Application deadline: rolling
Program can be completed entirely online: Yes
Total program cost: $28,440 full-time in-state, $28,440 part-time in-state, $28,440 full-time out-of-state, $28,440 part-time out-of-state
Tuition per credit: $790 full-time in-state, $790 part-time in-state, $790 full-time out-of-state, $790 part-time out-of-state
Test scores required: No
Enrollment: 2, 100% men, 0% women, N/A minority, N/A international
Completion: Credits needed to graduate: 36; target time to graduate: 1 year
College funded aid available: Domestic: Yes; International: No
Graduates with debt: 36%; average amount of debt $34,309

Shippensburg University of Pennsylvania (Grove)
Public

ONLINE MBA PROGRAM(S)

www.ship.edu/graduate
Admissions: (717) 477-1231
Email: gradadmiss@ship.edu
Financial aid: (717) 477-1131
Application deadline: rolling
Program can be completed entirely online: Depends
Total program cost: $15,480 full-time in-state, $15,480 part-time in-state, $15,780 full-time out-of-state, $15,780 part-time out-of-state

Tuition per credit: $516 full-time in-state, $516 part-time in-state, $526 full-time out-of-state, $526 part-time out-of-state
Acceptance rate: 97.0%
Test scores required: No
Average age of entrants: 32
Enrollment: 183, 61% men, 39% women, 13% minority, 0% international
Average class size: 19
Most popular MBA concentrations: finance, health care administration, management information systems, supply chain management/logistics, quantitative analysis/statistics and operations research
Completion: Credits needed to graduate: 30; target time to graduate: 2 years
College funded aid available: Domestic: Yes; International: Yes
Graduates with debt: 56%

St. Francis University
Private

ONLINE MBA PROGRAM(S)

www.francis.edu/admissions/
Admissions: (814) 472-3026
Email: nbauman@francis.edu
Financial aid: (814) 472-3945
Application deadline: rolling
Program can be completed entirely online: Yes
Total program cost: $31,500 full-time in-state, $31,500 part-time in-state, $31,500 full-time out-of-state, $31,500 part-time out-of-state
Tuition per credit: $875 full-time in-state, $875 part-time in-state, $875 full-time out-of-state, $875 part-time out-of-state
Test scores required: No
Enrollment: 65, 6% minority, 0% international
Average class size: 15
Most popular MBA concentrations: accounting, finance, health care administration, human resources management, marketing
Completion: Credits needed to graduate: 45; target time to graduate: 2 years
College funded aid available: Domestic: Yes
Graduates with debt: 40%; average amount of debt $9,780

ONLINE BUSINESS PROGRAM(S)

www.francis.edu/admissions/
Admissions: N/A
Financial aid: (814) 472-3010
Application deadline: rolling
Program can be completed entirely online: Yes
Total program cost: $26,250 full-time in-state, $26,250 part-time in-state, $26,250 full-time out-of-state, $26,250 part-time out-of-state
Tuition per credit: $875 full-time in-state, $875 part-time in-state, $875 full-time out-of-state, $875 part-time out-of-state
Most popular business concentrations: accounting, finance, health care administration, marketing, management information systems

College funded aid available: Domestic: Yes; International: Yes

St. Joseph's University (Haub)
Private

ONLINE MBA PROGRAM(S)

www.sju.edu/majors-programs/graduate-business
Admissions: (610) 660-1690
Email: sjumba@sju.edu
Financial aid: (610) 660-1346
Application deadline: rolling
Program can be completed entirely online: Yes
Total program cost: N/A
Tuition per credit: $1,043 full-time in-state, $1,043 part-time in-state, $1,043 full-time out-of-state, $1,043 part-time out-of-state
Acceptance rate: 78.0%
Test scores required: GMAT or GRE
Average GMAT: 486
Average GRE: 144 verbal, 145 quantitative, 3.8 writing
Average age of entrants: 31
Students with prior work experience: 72.0%
Enrollment: 411, 58% men, 42% women, 20% minority, 0% international
Average class size: 18
Most popular MBA concentrations: finance, general management, health care administration, marketing, management information systems
Completion: Three year graduation rate: 37%; credits needed to graduate: 33; target time to graduate: 2.5 years
College funded aid available: Domestic: Yes; International: Yes
Graduates with debt: 36%; average amount of debt $45,240

ONLINE BUSINESS PROGRAM(S)

www.sju.edu/majors-programs/graduate-business
Admissions: (610) 660-1690
Email: sjums@sju.edu
Financial aid: (610) 660-1346
Application deadline: rolling
Program can be completed entirely online: Yes
Total program cost: N/A
Tuition per credit: $1,043 full-time in-state, $1,043 part-time in-state, $1,043 full-time out-of-state, $1,043 part-time out-of-state
Acceptance rate: 78.0%
Test scores required: GMAT or GRE
Average GMAT: 506
Average GRE: 153 verbal, 151 quantitative, 3.5 writing
Average age of entrants: 33
Students with prior work experience: 66.0%
Enrollment: 366, 58% men, 42% women, 31% minority, 0% international
Average class size: 17
Most popular business concentrations: finance, human resources management, marketing, management information systems

Completion: Three year graduation rate: 67%; credits needed to graduate: 30; target time to graduate: 2 years
College funded aid available: Domestic: Yes; International: Yes
Graduates with debt: 54%; average amount of debt $34,947

Thomas Jefferson University

Private

ONLINE MBA PROGRAM(S)

online.jefferson.edu/
Admissions: (855) 865-5565
Email: online@email.jefferson.edu
Financial aid: (215) 951-2940
Application deadline: N/A
Total program cost: N/A
Tuition per credit: $750 full-time in-state, $750 part-time in-state, $750 full-time out-of-state, $750 part-time out-of-state
College funded aid available: Domestic: Yes; International: Yes

University of Pittsburgh (Katz)

Public

ONLINE MBA PROGRAM(S)

www.katz.business.pitt.edu/apply
Admissions: (412) 648-1659
Email: MBA@KATZ.PITT.EDU
Financial aid: (412) 648-1700
Application deadline: rolling
Program can be completed entirely online: No
Total program cost: $45,564 full-time in-state, $66,708 part-time in-state, $63,912 full-time out-of-state, $103,224 part-time out-of-state
Tuition per credit: $759 full-time in-state, $1,308 part-time in-state, $1,065 full-time out-of-state, $2,024 part-time out-of-state
Acceptance rate: 83.0%
Test scores required: GMAT or GRE
Average GMAT: 562
Average GRE: 155 verbal, 152 quantitative, 3.9 writing
Average age of entrants: 28
Students with prior work experience: 93.0%
Enrollment: 350, 66% men, 34% women, 12% minority, 1% international
Average class size: 40
Most popular MBA concentrations: finance, marketing, management information systems, production/operations management, supply chain management/logistics
Completion: Credits needed to graduate: 51; target time to graduate: 3 years

University of Scranton

Private

ONLINE MBA PROGRAM(S)

elearning.scranton.edu/
Admissions: (866) 373-9547
Email: onlineprograms@scranton.edu

Financial aid: (570) 941-7700
Application deadline: rolling
Program can be completed entirely online: Yes
Total program cost: $34,740 full-time in-state, $34,740 part-time in-state, $34,740 full-time out-of-state, $34,740 part-time out-of-state
Tuition per credit: $965 full-time in-state, $965 part-time in-state, $965 full-time out-of-state, $965 part-time out-of-state
Acceptance rate: 97.0%
Test scores required: No
Average age of entrants: 32
Students with prior work experience: 100.0%
Enrollment: 437, 54% men, 46% women, 23% minority, 3% international
Average class size: 14
Most popular MBA concentrations: accounting, general management, health care administration, international business, production/operations management
Completion: Three year graduation rate: 60%; credits needed to graduate: 36; target time to graduate: 2 years
College funded aid available: Domestic: No; International: No
Graduates with debt: 23%; average amount of debt $15,847

ONLINE BUSINESS PROGRAM(S)

elearning.scranton.edu/macc
Admissions: (866) 373-9547
Email: onlineprograms@scranton.edu
Financial aid: (570) 941-7700
Application deadline: rolling
Program can be completed entirely online: Yes
Total program cost: $26,850 full-time in-state, $26,850 part-time in-state, $26,850 full-time out-of-state, $26,850 part-time out-of-state
Tuition per credit: $895 full-time in-state, $895 part-time in-state, $895 full-time out-of-state, $895 part-time out-of-state
Acceptance rate: 85.0%
Test scores required: No
Average age of entrants: 34
Students with prior work experience: 27.0%
Enrollment: 195, 41% men, 59% women, 27% minority, 5% international
Average class size: 16
Most popular business concentrations: accounting, finance
Completion: Credits needed to graduate: 30; target time to graduate: 2 years
College funded aid available: Domestic: No; International: No

Villanova University

Private

ONLINE MBA PROGRAM(S)

www.villanova.edu/business/graduate
Admissions: (610) 519-4336
Email: claire.bruno@villanova.edu
Financial aid: (610) 519-4010
Application deadline: rolling

Program can be completed entirely online: No
Total program cost: $64,800 full-time in-state, $64,800 part-time in-state, $64,800 full-time out-of-state, $64,800 part-time out-of-state
Tuition per credit: $1,350 full-time in-state, $1,350 part-time in-state, $1,350 full-time out-of-state, $1,350 part-time out-of-state
Acceptance rate: 78.0%
Test scores required: GMAT or GRE
Average GMAT: 560
Average GRE: 158 verbal, 156 quantitative, 4.0 writing
Average age of entrants: 33
Students with prior work experience: 100.0%
Enrollment: 249, 59% men, 41% women, 14% minority, 1% international
Average class size: 21
Most popular MBA concentrations: accounting, economics, finance, general management, marketing
Completion: Three year graduation rate: 90%; credits needed to graduate: 48; target time to graduate: 2 years
College funded aid available: Domestic: Yes; International: Yes
Graduates with debt: 62%; average amount of debt $43,395

ONLINE BUSINESS PROGRAM(S)

Admissions: (610) 519-4336
Email: claire.bruno@villanova.edu
Financial aid: (610) 519-4010
Application deadline: rolling
Program can be completed entirely online: Yes
Total program cost: $48,024 full-time in-state, $48,024 part-time in-state, $48,024 full-time out-of-state, $48,024 part-time out-of-state
Tuition per credit: $1,334 full-time in-state, $1,334 part-time in-state, $1,334 full-time out-of-state, $1,334 part-time out-of-state
Acceptance rate: 79.0%
Test scores required: No
Average GMAT: 636
Average GRE: 155 verbal, 156 quantitative, 4.0 writing
Average age of entrants: 34
Students with prior work experience: 99.0%
Enrollment: 427, 58% men, 42% women, 21% minority, 3% international
Average class size: 21
Most popular business concentrations: accounting, finance, general management, production/operations management, technology
Completion: Three year graduation rate: 89%; credits needed to graduate: 36; target time to graduate: 2 years
College funded aid available: Domestic: Yes; International: Yes
Graduates with debt: 48%; average amount of debt $25,553

Waynesburg University

Private

ONLINE MBA PROGRAM(S)

www.waynesburg.edu/academics/graduate-and-professional-studies/master-business-administration
Admissions: (724) 743-4420
Email: dmariner@waynesburg.edu
Financial aid: (724) 852-3208
Application deadline: rolling
Program can be completed entirely online: Yes
Total program cost: $15,960 full-time in-state, $15,960 part-time in-state, $15,960 full-time out-of-state, $15,960 part-time out-of-state
Tuition per credit: $665 full-time in-state, $665 part-time in-state, $665 full-time out-of-state, $665 part-time out-of-state
Acceptance rate: 79.0%
Average age of entrants: 34
Enrollment: 227, 60% men, 40% women, 11% minority, 0% international
Average class size: 9
Most popular MBA concentrations: finance, leadership
Completion: Credits needed to graduate: 36
College funded aid available: Domestic: No; International: No
Graduates with debt: 75%; average amount of debt $20,500

West Chester University of Pennsylvania

Public

ONLINE MBA PROGRAM(S)

www.wcupa.edu/grad
Admissions: (610) 436-2943
Email: gradstudy@wcupa.edu
Financial aid: (610) 436-2627
Application deadline: rolling
Program can be completed entirely online: Yes
Total program cost: $15,480 full-time in-state, $15,480 part-time in-state, $15,780 full-time out-of-state, $15,780 part-time out-of-state
Tuition per credit: $516 full-time in-state, $516 part-time in-state, $526 full-time out-of-state, $526 part-time out-of-state
Acceptance rate: 79.0%
Test scores required: GMAT or GRE
Average GMAT: 518
Average GRE: 155 verbal, 151 quantitative, 4.1 writing
Average age of entrants: 31
Students with prior work experience: 98.0%
Enrollment: 550, 61% men, 39% women, 17% minority, 0% international
Average class size: 29
Most popular MBA concentrations: entrepreneurship, finance, general management, leadership, production/operations management

Completion: Three year graduation rate: 70%; credits needed to graduate: 30; target time to graduate: 1.5 years
College funded aid available: Domestic: Yes; International: Yes
Graduates with debt: 31%; average amount of debt $22,463

Widener University

Private

ONLINE MBA PROGRAM(S)

onlineprograms.widener.edu/mba/online-mba-program
Admissions: N/A
Financial aid: N/A
Application deadline: rolling
Program can be completed entirely online: Yes
Total program cost: N/A
Tuition per credit: $1,004 full-time in-state, $1,004 part-time in-state, $1,004 full-time out-of-state, $1,004 part-time out-of-state
Acceptance rate: 79.0%
Test scores required: GMAT
Average GMAT: 480
Enrollment: 92, 47% men, 53% women, 42% minority, 0% international
Average class size: 13
Most popular MBA concentrations: general management, health care administration
Completion: Credits needed to graduate: 33; target time to graduate: 2 years
College funded aid available: International: No

RHODE ISLAND

Bryant University

Private

ONLINE MBA PROGRAM(S)

gradschool.bryant.edu/
Admissions: (401) 232-6230
Email: graduateprograms@bryant.edu
Financial aid: (401) 232-6020
Application deadline: rolling
Program can be completed entirely online: Yes
Total program cost: N/A
Tuition per credit: $717 full-time in-state, $717 part-time in-state, $717 full-time out-of-state, $717 part-time out-of-state
Completion: Credits needed to graduate: 30; target time to graduate: 1.5 years

Johnson & Wales University

Private

ONLINE MBA PROGRAM(S)

online.jwu.edu/
Admissions: (401) 598-4400
Email: onlineadmissions@jwu.edu
Financial aid: (401) 598-2499
Application deadline: rolling
Program can be completed entirely online: Yes
Total program cost: N/A
Tuition per credit: $742 full-time in-state, $742 part-time in-state, $742 full-time out-of-state, $742 part-time out-of-state
Acceptance rate: 71.0%

Test scores required: No
Average age of entrants: 29
Enrollment: 548, 31%
men, 69% women, 39%
minority, 1% international
Average class size: 15
**Most popular MBA
concentrations:** finance,
general management, hotel
administration, human
resources management, supply
chain management/logistics
Completion: Three year
graduation rate: 62%; credits
needed to graduate: 36; target
time to graduate: 2 years
College funded aid available:
Domestic: No; International: No
Graduates with debt: 88%

ONLINE BUSINESS PROGRAM(S)

online.jwu.edu/
Admissions: (401) 598-4400
Email: onlineadmissions@
jwu.edu
Financial aid: (401) 598-2499
Application deadline: rolling
**Program can be completed
entirely online:** Yes
Total program cost: N/A
Tuition per credit: $742 full-time
in-state, $742 part-time in-state,
$742 full-time out-of-state,
$742 part-time out-of-state
Acceptance rate: 67.0%
Test scores required: No
Average age of entrants: 32
Enrollment: 109, 75% men,
25% women, 43% minority,
3% international
Average class size: 15
**Most popular business
concentrations:** finance, human
resources management,
not-for-profit management
Completion: Credits needed
to graduate: 30; target time
to graduate: 1.5 years
College funded aid available:
Domestic: No; International: No
Graduates with debt: 76%

SOUTH CAROLINA

Anderson University
Private

ONLINE MBA PROGRAM(S)

Admissions: N/A
Financial aid: N/A
Application deadline: N/A
Total program cost: $16,560
full-time in-state, $16,560
part-time in-state, $16,560
full-time out-of-state, $16,560
part-time out-of-state
Tuition per credit: $450
full-time in-state, $450
part-time in-state, $450
full-time out-of-state, $450
part-time out-of-state
Acceptance rate: 100.0%
Enrollment: 165, 50% men,
50% women, N/A minority,
N/A international
Average class size: 15
Completion: Three year
graduation rate: 91%; target
time to graduate: 1.5 years
Graduates with debt: 63%;
average amount of debt $33,769

ONLINE BUSINESS PROGRAM(S)

Admissions: N/A
Financial aid: N/A
Application deadline: N/A
Total program cost: $13,500
full-time in-state, $13,500

part-time in-state, $13,500
full-time out-of-state, $13,500
part-time out-of-state
Tuition per credit: $450
full-time in-state, $450
part-time in-state, $450
full-time out-of-state, $450
part-time out-of-state
Completion: Target time
to graduate: 1.5 years

Charleston Southern University
Private

ONLINE MBA PROGRAM(S)

www.csuniv.edu/mba
Admissions: (843) 863-7050
Email: jsbrown@csuniv.edu
Financial aid: (843) 863-7050
Application deadline: rolling
**Program can be completed
entirely online:** Depends
Total program cost: $20,625
full-time in-state, $20,625
part-time in-state, $20,625
full-time out-of-state, $20,625
part-time out-of-state
Tuition per credit: $625
full-time in-state, $625
part-time in-state, $625
full-time out-of-state, $625
part-time out-of-state
Acceptance rate: 74.0%
Average age of entrants: 31
**Students with prior work
experience:** 0.0%
Enrollment: 70, 43% men,
57% women, N/A minority,
N/A international
Average class size: 12
**Most popular MBA
concentrations:** finance,
general management,
leadership, management
information systems
Completion: Credits needed
to graduate: 33; target time
to graduate: 2 years
College funded aid available:
Domestic: No; International: No
Graduates with debt: 60%;
average amount of debt $10,500

ONLINE BUSINESS PROGRAM(S)

www.csuniv.edu/mba
Admissions: (843) 863-7050
Email: jsbrown@csuniv.edu
Financial aid: (843) 863-7050
Application deadline: rolling
**Program can be completed
entirely online:** Depends
Total program cost: $20,625
full-time in-state, $20,625
part-time in-state, $20,625
full-time out-of-state, $20,625
part-time out-of-state
Tuition per credit: $625
full-time in-state, $625
part-time in-state, $625
full-time out-of-state, $625
part-time out-of-state
Acceptance rate: 89.0%
Average age of entrants: 32
**Students with prior work
experience:** 0.0%
Enrollment: 26, 42% men,
58% women, N/A minority,
N/A international
Average class size: 12
**Most popular business
concentrations:** leadership
Completion: Credits needed
to graduate: 33; target time
to graduate: 2 years
College funded aid available:
Domestic: No; International: No

Graduates with debt: 60%;
average amount of debt $10,500

The Citadel
Public

ONLINE MBA PROGRAM(S)

www.citadel.edu/root/mba
Admissions: (843) 953-5089
Email: cgc@citadel.edu
Financial aid: (843) 953-5187
Application deadline: rolling
**Program can be completed
entirely online:** Yes
Total program cost: $25,020
full-time in-state, $25,020
part-time in-state, $25,020
full-time out-of-state, $25,020
part-time out-of-state
Tuition per credit: $695
full-time in-state, $695
part-time in-state, $695
full-time out-of-state, $695
part-time out-of-state
Acceptance rate: 52.0%
Test scores required:
GMAT or GRE
Average GMAT: 430
Average GRE: 149 verbal,
148 quantitative
Average age of entrants: 34
**Students with prior work
experience:** 100.0%
Enrollment: 52, 67% men,
33% women, 13% minority,
0% international
Average class size: 17
Most popular MBA concentrations:
entrepreneurship, finance,
leadership, supply chain
management/logistics
Completion: Credits needed
to graduate: 36; target time
to graduate: 6 years
College funded aid available:
Domestic: Yes; International: No
Graduates with debt: 100%;
average amount of debt $24,039

Coastal Carolina University (Wall)
Public

ONLINE MBA PROGRAM(S)

Admissions: (843) 349-2761
Email: gradbus@coastal.edu
Financial aid: (843) 349-2313
Application deadline: N/A
Total program cost: N/A
Tuition per credit: $588
full-time in-state, $588
part-time in-state, $1,067
full-time out-of-state, $1,067
part-time out-of-state
Enrollment: 1, 100% men,
0% women, 100% minority,
0% international

Limestone College
Private

ONLINE MBA PROGRAM(S)

www.limestone.edu/
online-mba-programs
Admissions: (866) 381-8445
Email: mba@limestone.edu
Financial aid: (864) 488-8231
Application deadline: rolling
**Program can be completed
entirely online:** No
Total program cost: $23,850
full-time in-state, $23,850
part-time in-state, $23,850
full-time out-of-state, $23,850
part-time out-of-state

Tuition per credit: $650
full-time in-state, $650
part-time in-state, $650
full-time out-of-state, $650
part-time out-of-state
Acceptance rate: 95.0%
Test scores required:
GMAT or GRE
Average GRE: 149 verbal, 153
quantitative, 4.1 writing
Average age of entrants: 34
Enrollment: 88, 43% men,
57% women, 45% minority,
1% international
Average class size: 12
Completion: Three year
graduation rate: 55%; credits
needed to graduate: 36; target
time to graduate: 2.5 years
College funded aid available:
Domestic: No; International: No
Graduates with debt: 45%;
average amount of debt $21,333

North Greenville University
Private

ONLINE BUSINESS PROGRAM(S)

www.ngu.edu/graduate-
admissions-page.php
Admissions: (864) 663-7507
Email: justin.pitts@ngu.edu
Financial aid: (864) 977-7058
Application deadline: rolling
**Program can be completed
entirely online:** Yes
Total program cost: $16,680
full-time in-state, $16,680
part-time in-state, $16,680
full-time out-of-state, $16,680
part-time out-of-state
Tuition per credit: $450
full-time in-state, $450
part-time in-state, $450
full-time out-of-state, $450
part-time out-of-state
Acceptance rate: 77.0%
Test scores required: No
Average age of entrants: 34
**Students with prior work
experience:** 100.0%
Enrollment: 150, 47% men,
53% women, N/A minority,
N/A international
Average class size: 12
**Most popular business
concentrations:** accounting,
human resources
management, marketing,
organizational behavior
Completion: Credits needed
to graduate: 36; target time
to graduate: 1.5 years
**College funded aid
available:** Domestic: Yes;
International: Yes
Graduates with debt: 35%;
average amount of debt $10,000

Winthrop University
Public

ONLINE MBA PROGRAM(S)

Admissions: N/A
Financial aid: N/A
Application deadline: rolling
**Program can be completed
entirely online:** Yes
Total program cost: $36,780
part-time in-state, $36,780
part-time out-of-state
Tuition per credit: $980
part-time in-state, $980
part-time out-of-state
Test scores required:
GMAT or GRE

Enrollment: N/A, N/A minority,
N/A international
**Most popular MBA
concentrations:** leadership,
marketing
Completion: Credits
needed to graduate: 36

SOUTH DAKOTA

Dakota State University
Public

ONLINE MBA PROGRAM(S)

dsu.edu/graduate-students/mba
Admissions: (605) 256-5165
Email: gradoffice@dsu.edu
Financial aid: (605) 256-5152
Application deadline: rolling
**Program can be completed
entirely online:** Yes
Total program cost: N/A
Tuition per credit: $451 full-time
in-state, $451 part-time in-state,
$451 full-time out-of-state,
$451 part-time out-of-state
Acceptance rate: 100.0%
Test scores required:
GMAT or GRE
Average age of entrants: 29
Enrollment: 19, 58% men,
42% women, 11% minority,
5% international
Average class size: 12
**Most popular MBA
concentrations:** general
management
Completion: Three year
graduation rate: 64%; credits
needed to graduate: 36; target
time to graduate: 2 years
**College funded aid
available:** Domestic: Yes;
International: Yes

Dakota Wesleyan University
Private

ONLINE MBA PROGRAM(S)

www.dwu.edu/admissions
Admissions: (605) 995-2650
Email: admissions@dwu.edu
Financial aid: (605) 995-2656
Application deadline: rolling
**Program can be completed
entirely online:** Yes
Total program cost: $14,400
full-time in-state, $7,200
part-time in-state, $14,400
full-time out-of-state, $7,200
part-time out-of-state
Tuition per credit: $400
full-time in-state, $400
part-time in-state, $400
full-time out-of-state, $400
part-time out-of-state
Acceptance rate: 71.0%
Test scores required: No
Average age of entrants: 32
**Students with prior work
experience:** 100.0%
Enrollment: 54, 54% men,
46% women, 17% minority,
0% international
Average class size: 9
**Most popular MBA
concentrations:** leadership
Completion: Three year
graduation rate: 80%; credits
needed to graduate: 36; target
time to graduate: 1.5 years
College funded aid available:
Domestic: No; International: No

Graduates with debt: 50%;
average amount of debt $22,229

University of Sioux Falls

Private

ONLINE MBA PROGRAM(S)

usiouxfalls.edu/mba
Admissions: (605) 331-6708
Email: mba@usiouxfalls.edu
Financial aid: (605) 331-6621
Application deadline: rolling
Program can be completed entirely online: Yes
Total program cost: $13,860
full-time in-state, $13,860
part-time in-state, $13,860
full-time out-of-state, $13,860
part-time out-of-state
Tuition per credit: $385
full-time in-state, $385
part-time in-state, $385
full-time out-of-state, $385
part-time out-of-state
Acceptance rate: 100.0%
Test scores required: No
Average age of entrants: 32
Enrollment: 27, 70% men,
30% women, N/A minority,
N/A international
Average class size: 22
Most popular MBA concentrations: general
management, health
care administration
Completion: Credits needed
to graduate: 36; target time
to graduate: 2 years
College funded aid available:
Domestic: Yes; International: No
Graduates with debt: 50%

University of South Dakota

Public

ONLINE MBA PROGRAM(S)

www.usd.edu/graduate-school/
apply-now
Admissions: (605) 658-6136
Email: Brittany.E.Wagner@
usd.edu
Financial aid: (605) 658-6250
Application deadline: rolling
Program can be completed entirely online: No
Total program cost: $14,883
full-time in-state, $14,883
part-time in-state, $14,883
full-time out-of-state, $14,883
part-time out-of-state
Tuition per credit: $451 full-time
in-state, $451 part-time in-state,
$451 full-time out-of-state,
$451 part-time out-of-state
Acceptance rate: 95.0%
Test scores required: GMAT
Average GMAT: 526
Average age of entrants: 31
Students with prior work experience: 86.0%
Enrollment: 252, 67% men,
33% women, 8% minority,
5% international
Average class size: 30
Most popular MBA concentrations: general
management, health
care administration,
marketing, supply chain
management/logistics
Completion: Three year
graduation rate: 63%; credits
needed to graduate: 33; target
time to graduate: 2.5 years

College funded aid available:
Domestic: No; International: No
Graduates with debt: 27%;
average amount of debt $27,698

ONLINE BUSINESS PROGRAM(S)

www.usd.edu/academics/
graduate-studies
Admissions: (605) 658-6138
Email: grad@usd.edu
Financial aid: (605) 677-5446
Application deadline: rolling
Program can be completed entirely online: Yes
Total program cost: $13,527
full-time in-state, $13,527
part-time in-state, $13,527
full-time out-of-state, $13,527
part-time out-of-state
Tuition per credit: $451 full-time
in-state, $451 part-time in-state,
$451 full-time out-of-state,
$451 part-time out-of-state
Acceptance rate: 80.0%
Test scores required: GMAT
Average GMAT: 525
Average age of entrants: 33
Students with prior work experience: 95.0%
Enrollment: 92, 49% men,
51% women, 12% minority,
12% international
Average class size: 33
Most popular business concentrations: accounting
Completion: Three year
graduation rate: 33%; credits
needed to graduate: 30; target
time to graduate: 2 years
College funded aid available:
Domestic: No; International: No
Graduates with debt: 15%;
average amount of debt $20,891

TENNESSEE

Austin Peay State University

Public

ONLINE BUSINESS PROGRAM(S)

www.apsu.edu/
grad-studies/management.php
Admissions: (931) 221-7662
Email: gradadmissions@
apsu.edu
Financial aid: (931) 221-7907
Application deadline: rolling
Program can be completed entirely online: Yes
Total program cost: N/A
Tuition per credit: $440
full-time in-state, $440
part-time in-state, $660
full-time out-of-state, $660
part-time out-of-state
Acceptance rate: 78.0%
Average GMAT: 442
Average age of entrants: 31
Students with prior work experience: 0.0%
Enrollment: 63, 44% men,
56% women, 22% minority,
0% international
Average class size: 15
Most popular business concentrations: general
management
Completion: Credits needed
to graduate: 30; target
time to graduate: 1 year
College funded aid available:
Domestic: Yes

Bethel University

Private

ONLINE MBA PROGRAM(S)

bethelsuccess.net/programs/
graduate/
Admissions: (844) 415-2151
Email: bevilla@bethelu.edu
Financial aid: (731) 352-8412
Application deadline: rolling
Program can be completed entirely online: Yes
Total program cost: $21,420
full-time in-state, $21,420
part-time in-state, $21,420
full-time out-of-state, $21,420
part-time out-of-state
Tuition per credit: $595
full-time in-state, $595
part-time in-state, $595
full-time out-of-state, $595
part-time out-of-state
Acceptance rate: 81.0%
Test scores required: No
Average age of entrants: 38
Enrollment: 697, 33%
men, 67% women, 58%
minority, 0% international
Average class size: 20
Most popular MBA concentrations: general
management, health care
administration, human
resources management
Completion: Three year
graduation rate: 66%; credits
needed to graduate: 36; target
time to graduate: 2 years
College funded aid available: Domestic: No
Graduates with debt: 80%;
average amount of debt $26,148

Bryan College

Private

ONLINE MBA PROGRAM(S)

www.bryan.edu/adult-education
Admissions: (877) 256-7008
Email: ags@bryan.edu
Financial aid: (423) 775-7460
Application deadline: rolling
Program can be completed entirely online: Yes
Total program cost: $20,700
full-time in-state, $20,700
part-time in-state, $20,700
full-time out-of-state, $20,700
part-time out-of-state
Tuition per credit: $575 full-time
in-state, $575 part-time in-state,
$575 full-time out-of-state,
$575 part-time out-of-state
Acceptance rate: 100.0%
Test scores required: No
Students with prior work experience: 96.0%
Enrollment: 131, 47% men,
53% women, N/A minority,
N/A international
Average class size: 12
Most popular MBA concentrations: general
management, human resources
management, marketing
Completion: Three year
graduation rate: 87%; credits
needed to graduate: 36; target
time to graduate: 1.5 years
College funded aid available:
Domestic: Yes; International: No

Carson-Newman University

Private

ONLINE MBA PROGRAM(S)

www.cn.edu/admissions
Admissions: (865) 471-2000
Email: admitme@cn.edu
Financial aid: (800) 678-9061
Application deadline: rolling
Program can be completed entirely online: Yes
Total program cost: $13,500
full-time in-state, $13,500
part-time in-state, $13,500
full-time out-of-state, $13,500
part-time out-of-state
Tuition per credit: $450
full-time in-state, $450
part-time in-state, $450
full-time out-of-state, $450
part-time out-of-state
Acceptance rate: 66.0%
Test scores required: No
Average GRE: 155 verbal, 150
quantitative, 5.0 writing
Average age of entrants: 28
Enrollment: 145, 59% men,
41% women, N/A minority,
N/A international
Average class size: 15
Most popular MBA concentrations: general
management, leadership,
marketing, sports business
Completion: Three year
graduation rate: 80%; credits
needed to graduate: 30; target
time to graduate: 1.5 years
College funded aid available: Domestic: Yes;
International: Yes
Graduates with debt: 25%;
average amount of debt $13,540

East Tennessee State University

Public

ONLINE BUSINESS PROGRAM(S)

www.etsu.edu/admissions/
Admissions: (423) 439-4213
Email: admissions@etsu.edu
Financial aid: (423) 439-6932
Application deadline: N/A
Program can be completed entirely online: Yes
Total program cost: $19,944
full-time in-state, $19,944
part-time in-state, $25,416
full-time out-of-state, $25,416
part-time out-of-state
Tuition per credit: $554
full-time in-state, $554
part-time in-state, $706
full-time out-of-state, $706
part-time out-of-state
Test scores required:
GMAT or GRE
Enrollment: 28, N/A minority,
N/A international
Most popular business concentrations: marketing
Completion: Credits needed
to graduate: 36; target time
to graduate: 2 years
College funded aid available:
Domestic: Yes

King University

Private

ONLINE MBA PROGRAM(S)

www.king.edu/admissions
Admissions: (800) 362-0014
Email: admissions@king.edu
Financial aid: (423) 652-4725
Application deadline: rolling
Program can be completed entirely online: Yes
Total program cost: $21,780
full-time in-state, $21,780
part-time in-state, $21,780
full-time out-of-state, $21,780
part-time out-of-state
Tuition per credit: $605
full-time in-state, $605
part-time in-state, $605
full-time out-of-state, $605
part-time out-of-state
Acceptance rate: 99.0%
Test scores required: No
Average age of entrants: 33
Students with prior work experience: 100.0%
Enrollment: 144, 32%
men, 68% women, 15%
minority, 1% international
Average class size: 14
Most popular MBA concentrations: general
management, human
resources management,
marketing, management
information systems
Completion: Three year
graduation rate: 76%; credits
needed to graduate: 36; target
time to graduate: 1.5 years
College funded aid available:
Domestic: No; International: No
Graduates with debt: 86%;
average amount of debt $38,543

Lee University

Private

ONLINE MBA PROGRAM(S)

www.leeuniversity.edu/
adult-learning
Admissions: (423) 614-8670
Email: dal@leeuniversity.edu
Financial aid: (423) 614-8300
Application deadline: rolling
Program can be completed entirely online: Yes
Total program cost: N/A
Tuition per credit: $710 full-time
in-state, $710 part-time in-state,
$710 full-time out-of-state,
$710 part-time out-of-state
Acceptance rate: 100.0%
Test scores required: GMAT
Average age of entrants: 37
Enrollment: 23, 61% men,
39% women, 22% minority,
4% international
Average class size: 11
Completion: Credits needed
to graduate: 32; target time
to graduate: 2 years
College funded aid available: Domestic: Yes;
International: Yes
Graduates with debt: 83%;
average amount of debt $19,693

Tennessee Technological University

Public

ONLINE MBA PROGRAM(S)

www.tntech.edu/cob/mba/
requirements/
Admissions: (931) 372-3600
Email: knicewicz@tntech.edu
Financial aid: (931) 372-3073
Application deadline: rolling
**Program can be completed
entirely online:** Yes
Total program cost: $14,640
full-time in-state, $14,640
part-time in-state, $36,420
full-time out-of-state, $36,420
part-time out-of-state
Tuition per credit: $488
full-time in-state, $488
part-time in-state, $726
full-time out-of-state, $726
part-time out-of-state
Acceptance rate: 80.0%
Average GMAT: 493
Average GRE: 149 verbal, 148
quantitative, 3.3 writing
Average age of entrants: 28
Enrollment: 188, 53% men,
47% women, N/A minority,
N/A international
Average class size: 25
**Most popular MBA
concentrations:** finance, general
management, human resources
management, international
business, management
information systems
Completion: Credits needed
to graduate: 30; target time
to graduate: 1.5 years
**College funded aid
available:** Domestic: Yes;
International: Yes
Graduates with debt: 22%;
average amount of debt $8,815

Tusculum College

Private

ONLINE MBA PROGRAM(S)

home.tusculum.edu/aos/
admission/
Admissions: (423) 636-7312
Email: abascom@tusculum.edu
Financial aid: (423) 636-7377
Application deadline: rolling
**Program can be completed
entirely online:** Yes
Total program cost: $12,750
full-time in-state, $12,750
part-time in-state, $12,750
full-time out-of-state, $12,750
part-time out-of-state
Tuition per credit: $425
full-time in-state, $425
part-time in-state, $425
full-time out-of-state, $425
part-time out-of-state
Test scores required: No
Completion: Target time
to graduate: 1 year
College funded aid available:
Domestic: Yes; International: No

University of Memphis (Fogelman)

Public

ONLINE MBA PROGRAM(S)

www.memphis.edu/
Admissions: (901) 678-2111
Email: Eric.Stokes@
memphis.edu

Financial aid: (901) 678-3687
Application deadline: rolling
**Program can be completed
entirely online:** Yes
Total program cost: $19,899
full-time in-state, $19,899
part-time in-state, $36,003
full-time out-of-state, $36,003
part-time out-of-state
Tuition per credit: $603
full-time in-state, $603
part-time in-state, $1,091
full-time out-of-state, $1,091
part-time out-of-state
Acceptance rate: 94.0%
Test scores required:
GMAT or GRE
Average GMAT: 555
Average GRE: 155 verbal, 150
quantitative, 4.0 writing
Average age of entrants: 30
**Students with prior work
experience:** 53.0%
Enrollment: 130, 65% men,
35% women, 27% minority,
0% international
Average class size: 44
**Most popular MBA
concentrations:** accounting,
finance, general management,
marketing, management
information systems
Completion: Three year
graduation rate: 64%; credits
needed to graduate: 33; target
time to graduate: 2 years
**College funded aid
available:** Domestic: Yes;
International: Yes
Graduates with debt: 39%;
average amount of debt $23,989

University of Tennessee–Chattanooga

Public

ONLINE MBA PROGRAM(S)

www.utc.edu/college-business/
academic-programs/graduate-
programs/mba/admissions.php
Admissions: (423) 425-5708
Email: cobgraduate@utc.edu
Financial aid: (423) 425-4677
Application deadline: rolling
**Program can be completed
entirely online:** Yes
Total program cost: $23,088
full-time in-state, $23,088
part-time in-state, $24,780
full-time out-of-state, $24,780
part-time out-of-state
Tuition per credit: $642
full-time in-state, $642
part-time in-state, $689
full-time out-of-state, $689
part-time out-of-state
Acceptance rate: 93.0%
Test scores required:
GMAT or GRE
Average GMAT: 508
Average GRE: 152 verbal, 147
quantitative, 4.0 writing
Average age of entrants: 30
Enrollment: 197, 53% men,
47% women, 20% minority,
2% international
Average class size: 25
**Most popular MBA
concentrations:** general
management, health
care administration
Completion: Three year
graduation rate: 75%; credits
needed to graduate: 36; target
time to graduate: 2 years

**College funded aid
available:** Domestic: Yes;
International: Yes
Graduates with debt: 71%;
average amount of debt $34,414

University of Tennessee–Martin

Public

ONLINE MBA PROGRAM(S)

www.utm.edu/gradstudies/
index.php
Admissions: (731) 881-7012
Email: graduatestudies@utm.edu
Financial aid: (731) 881-7031
Application deadline: rolling
**Program can be completed
entirely online:** Yes
Total program cost: N/A
Tuition per credit: $532
full-time in-state, $532
part-time in-state, $585
full-time out-of-state, $585
part-time out-of-state
Acceptance rate: 68.0%
Test scores required:
GMAT or GRE
Average GMAT: 552
Average GRE: 156 verbal, 151
quantitative, 3.5 writing
Average age of entrants: 39
**Students with prior work
experience:** 100.0%
Enrollment: 68, 57% men,
43% women, 16% minority,
0% international
Average class size: 15
**Most popular MBA
concentrations:** general
management
Completion: Three year
graduation rate: 82%; credits
needed to graduate: 38; target
time to graduate: 2 years
**College funded aid
available:** Domestic: Yes; International: No
Graduates with debt: 57%;
average amount of debt $37,286

TEXAS

Abilene Christian University

Private

ONLINE MBA PROGRAM(S)

www.acu.edu/admissions-aid/
online-graduate/admissions.html
Admissions: (855) 219-7300
Email: gradonline@acu.edu
Financial aid: (800) 460-6228
Application deadline: rolling
**Program can be completed
entirely online:** Yes
Total program cost: $25,956
full-time in-state, $25,956
part-time in-state, $25,956
full-time out-of-state, $25,956
part-time out-of-state
Tuition per credit: $721 full-time
in-state, $721 part-time in-state,
$721 full-time out-of-state,
$721 part-time out-of-state
Acceptance rate: 99.0%
Test scores required: No
Enrollment: 176, 56%
men, 44% women, 39%
minority, 1% international
Average class size: 18
**Most popular MBA
concentrations:** general
management, health care
administration, marketing,
supply chain management/

logistics, quantitative
analysis/statistics and
operations research
Completion: Credits needed
to graduate: 36; target time
to graduate: 2 years
College funded aid available:
Domestic: No; International: No

ONLINE BUSINESS PROGRAM(S)

www.acu.edu/admissions-aid/
online-graduate.html
Admissions: (855) 219-7300
Email: gradonline@acu.edu
Financial aid: (800) 460-6228
Application deadline: rolling
**Program can be completed
entirely online:** Yes
Total program cost: $21,630
full-time in-state, $21,630
part-time in-state, $21,630
full-time out-of-state, $21,630
part-time out-of-state
Tuition per credit: $721 full-time
in-state, $721 part-time in-state,
$721 full-time out-of-state,
$721 part-time out-of-state
Acceptance rate: 92.0%
Test scores required: No
Enrollment: 56, 61% men,
39% women, 54% minority,
5% international
**Most popular business
concentrations:** marketing,
supply chain management/
logistics, quantitative
analysis/statistics and
operations research
Completion: Credits needed
to graduate: 30; target time
to graduate: 2 years

Angelo State University

Public

ONLINE MBA PROGRAM(S)

www.angelo.edu/dept/
graduate-studies/
Admissions: (325) 942-2169
Email: graduate.studies@
angelo.edu
Financial aid: (325) 942-2246
Application deadline: rolling
**Program can be completed
entirely online:** Yes
Total program cost: $6,571
full-time in-state, $6,571
part-time in-state, $19,021
full-time out-of-state, $19,021
part-time out-of-state
Tuition per credit: $220
full-time in-state, $220
part-time in-state, $635
full-time out-of-state, $635
part-time out-of-state
Acceptance rate: 94.0%
Test scores required:
GMAT or GRE
Average GMAT: 426
Average GRE: 151 verbal,
149 quantitative
Average age of entrants: 31
Enrollment: 198, 62%
men, 38% women, 38%
minority, 5% international
Average class size: 25
**Most popular MBA
concentrations:** general
management
Completion: Credits needed
to graduate: 30; target
time to graduate: 1 year
College funded aid available:
Domestic: No; International: No
Graduates with debt: 35%;
average amount of debt $18,185

Baylor University (Hankamer)

Private

ONLINE MBA PROGRAM(S)

www.baylor.edu/business/
onlinemba
Admissions: (254) 710-7858
Email: ashley_coffer@baylor.edu
Financial aid: (254) 710-2611
Application deadline: rolling
**Program can be completed
entirely online:** Yes
Total program cost: $51,264
full-time in-state, $25,632
part-time in-state, $51,264
full-time out-of-state, $25,632
part-time out-of-state
Tuition per credit: $1,068
full-time in-state, $1,068
part-time in-state, $1,068
full-time out-of-state, $1,068
part-time out-of-state
Acceptance rate: 74.0%
Test scores required: No
Average GMAT: 620
Average age of entrants: 35
**Students with prior work
experience:** 100.0%
Enrollment: 146, 63% men,
37% women, 34% minority,
0% international
Average class size: 54
**Most popular MBA
concentrations:** general
management
Completion: Three year
graduation rate: 65%; credits
needed to graduate: 48; target
time to graduate: 1 year
**College funded aid
available:** Domestic: Yes;
International: Yes
Graduates with debt: 62%;
average amount of debt $57,658

Dallas Baptist University

Private

ONLINE MBA PROGRAM(S)

Admissions: (214) 333-5242
Email: graduate@dbu.edu
Financial aid: (214) 333-5363
Application deadline: rolling
**Program can be completed
entirely online:** Yes
Total program cost: $34,524
full-time in-state, $34,524
part-time in-state, $34,524
full-time out-of-state, $34,524
part-time out-of-state
Tuition per credit: $959
full-time in-state, $959
part-time in-state, $959
full-time out-of-state, $959
part-time out-of-state
Acceptance rate: 45.0%
Test scores required: GMAT
Enrollment: 258, 48% men,
52% women, 33% minority,
34% international
Average class size: 13
**Most popular MBA
concentrations:** finance, general
management, health care
administration, marketing
Completion: Credits needed
to graduate: 36; target time
to graduate: 2.5 years
**College funded aid
available:** Domestic: Yes;
International: Yes

ONLINE BUSINESS PROGRAM(S)
dbu.edu/graduate
Admissions: (214) 333-5242
Email: graduate@dbu.edu
Financial aid: (214) 333-5363
Application deadline: rolling
Program can be completed entirely online: Yes
Total program cost: $34,524 full-time in-state, $34,524 part-time in-state, $34,524 full-time out-of-state, $34,524 part-time out-of-state
Tuition per credit: $959 full-time in-state, $959 part-time in-state, $959 full-time out-of-state, $959 part-time out-of-state
Acceptance rate: 49.0%
Test scores required: GMAT
Enrollment: 30, 30% men, 70% women, 50% minority, 13% international
Average class size: 13
Most popular business concentrations: general management, health care administration, human resources management
Completion: Credits needed to graduate: 36; target time to graduate: 2.5 years
College funded aid available: Domestic: Yes; International: Yes

Houston Baptist University

Private

ONLINE BUSINESS PROGRAM(S)
www.hbu.edu/online-learning/
Admissions: (855) 428-1960
Email: OnlineAdmissions@HBU.edu
Financial aid: (281) 649-3747
Application deadline: rolling
Program can be completed entirely online: Yes
Total program cost: $18,150 full-time in-state, $18,150 part-time in-state, $18,150 full-time out-of-state, $18,150 part-time out-of-state
Tuition per credit: $550 full-time in-state, $550 part-time in-state, $550 full-time out-of-state, $550 part-time out-of-state
Acceptance rate: 90.0%
Test scores required: No
Average age of entrants: 33
Students with prior work experience: 58.0%
Enrollment: 26, 4% men, 96% women, 73% minority, 0% international
Average class size: 17
Most popular business concentrations: human resources management
Completion: Credits needed to graduate: 33; target time to graduate: 2 years
College funded aid available: Domestic: Yes; International: Yes

Lamar University

Public

ONLINE MBA PROGRAM(S)
Admissions: (409) 880-8888
Email: gradmissions@lamar.edu
Financial aid: (409) 880-7011
Application deadline: rolling

Program can be completed entirely online: Yes
Total program cost: $19,584 full-time in-state, $19,584 part-time in-state, $19,584 full-time out-of-state, $19,584 part-time out-of-state
Tuition per credit: $318 full-time in-state, $318 part-time in-state, $318 full-time out-of-state, $318 part-time out-of-state
Acceptance rate: 81.0%
Test scores required: GMAT
Average GMAT: 510
Average age of entrants: 38
Enrollment: 176, 45% men, 55% women, 35% minority, 1% international
Average class size: 28
Most popular MBA concentrations: health care administration, leadership, management information systems
Completion: Credits needed to graduate: 36
College funded aid available: Domestic: No
Graduates with debt: 37%; average amount of debt $27,002

Prairie View A&M University

Public

ONLINE MBA PROGRAM(S)
www.pvamu.edu/business/
Admissions: (936) 261-9215
Email: mba@pvamu.edu
Financial aid: (936) 261-1000
Application deadline: rolling
Program can be completed entirely online: Yes
Total program cost: $2,384 full-time in-state, $1,608 part-time in-state, $6,696 full-time out-of-state, $4,484 part-time out-of-state
Tuition per credit: $317 full-time in-state, $317 part-time in-state, $796 full-time out-of-state, $796 part-time out-of-state
Test scores required: GMAT or GRE
Enrollment: 110, 39% men, 61% women, 91% minority, 3% international
Average class size: 30
Completion: Credits needed to graduate: 36
College funded aid available: International: No
Graduates with debt: 72%; average amount of debt $40,981

Rice University (Jones)

Private

ONLINE MBA PROGRAM(S)
business.rice.edu/department/mba-recruiting-and-admissions
Admissions: N/A
Financial aid: (713) 348-3886
Application deadline: rolling
Program can be completed entirely online: Yes
Total program cost: N/A
Tuition per credit: $1,935 full-time in-state, $1,935 part-time in-state, $1,935 full-time out-of-state, $1,935 part-time out-of-state
Completion: Target time to graduate: 2 years

Sam Houston State University

Public

ONLINE MBA PROGRAM(S)
www.shsu.edu/~coba/programs/graduate.html
Admissions: (936) 294-1971
Email: graduate@shsu.edu
Financial aid: (936) 294-1774
Application deadline: Domestic: 08/01; International: 06/25
Program can be completed entirely online: Yes
Total program cost: $11,088 full-time in-state, $11,088 part-time in-state, $11,088 full-time out-of-state, $11,088 part-time out-of-state
Tuition per credit: $308 full-time in-state, $308 part-time in-state, $308 full-time out-of-state, $308 part-time out-of-state
Acceptance rate: 81.0%
Test scores required: GMAT
Average age of entrants: 33
Enrollment: 271, 58% men, 42% women, 34% minority, 2% international
Average class size: 16
Most popular MBA concentrations: economics, finance, general management
Completion: Three year graduation rate: 44%; credits needed to graduate: 36; target time to graduate: 2 years
College funded aid available: Domestic: Yes; International: Yes
Graduates with debt: 40%; average amount of debt $36,832

ONLINE BUSINESS PROGRAM(S)
www.shsu.edu/~coba/programs/graduate.html
Admissions: (936) 294-1971
Email: graduate@shsu.edu
Financial aid: (936) 294-1774
Application deadline: Domestic: 08/01; International: 06/25
Program can be completed entirely online: Yes
Total program cost: $11,088 full-time in-state, $11,088 part-time in-state, $11,088 full-time out-of-state, $11,088 part-time out-of-state
Tuition per credit: $308 full-time in-state, $308 part-time in-state, $308 full-time out-of-state, $308 part-time out-of-state
Acceptance rate: 88.0%
Test scores required: GMAT
Average age of entrants: 43
Enrollment: 20, 65% men, 35% women, 55% minority, 0% international
Average class size: 16
Most popular business concentrations: production/operations management
Completion: Credits needed to graduate: 36; target time to graduate: 2 years
College funded aid available: Domestic: Yes; International: Yes

St. Edward's University

Private

ONLINE BUSINESS PROGRAM(S)
Admissions: (512) 448-8500
Email: seu.admit@stedwards.edu
Financial aid: (512) 448-8523
Application deadline: N/A
Total program cost: N/A
Tuition per credit: $1,540 full-time in-state, $1,540 part-time in-state, $1,540 full-time out-of-state, $1,540 part-time out-of-state
Enrollment: N/A, N/A minority, N/A international
Completion: Credits needed to graduate: 30

Tarleton State University

Public

ONLINE MBA PROGRAM(S)
www.tarleton.edu/graduate/future/admissions.html
Admissions: (254) 968-9104
Email: coba@tarleton.edu
Financial aid: (254) 968-9070
Application deadline: Domestic: 08/21; International: 06/15
Program can be completed entirely online: Yes
Total program cost: N/A
Tuition per credit: $222 full-time in-state, $222 part-time in-state, $637 full-time out-of-state, $637 part-time out-of-state
Acceptance rate: 66.0%
Test scores required: GMAT or GRE
Enrollment: 146, 51% men, 49% women, 45% minority, 0% international
Completion: Credits needed to graduate: 30
Graduates with debt: 75%; average amount of debt $23,450

ONLINE BUSINESS PROGRAM(S)
www.tarleton.edu/graduate/future/admissions.html
Admissions: (254) 968-9104
Email: coba@tarleton.edu
Financial aid: (254) 968-9070
Application deadline: Domestic: 08/21; International: 06/15
Program can be completed entirely online: Yes
Total program cost: N/A
Tuition per credit: $222 full-time in-state, $222 part-time in-state, $637 full-time out-of-state, $637 part-time out-of-state
Acceptance rate: 81.0%
Test scores required: GMAT or GRE
Enrollment: 139, 35% men, 65% women, 46% minority, 0% international
Most popular business concentrations: human resources management, management information systems
Completion: Credits needed to graduate: 30
Graduates with debt: 73%; average amount of debt $52,750

Texas A&M University-Central Texas

Public

ONLINE MBA PROGRAM(S)
www.tamuct.edu/graduate-studies/index.html
Admissions: (254) 519-5447
Email: graduatestudies@tamuct.edu
Financial aid: (254) 501-5854
Application deadline: Domestic: 07/01; International: 03/01
Program can be completed entirely online: Yes
Total program cost: $8,532 full-time in-state, $8,532 part-time in-state, $23,472 full-time out-of-state, $23,472 part-time out-of-state
Tuition per credit: $237 full-time in-state, $237 part-time in-state, $652 full-time out-of-state, $652 part-time out-of-state
Acceptance rate: 66.0%
Test scores required: No
Average GRE: 138 verbal, 140 quantitative
Average age of entrants: 36
Enrollment: 194, 44% men, 56% women, 57% minority, 1% international
Average class size: 15
Most popular MBA concentrations: general management, human resources management, marketing, management information systems
Completion: Three year graduation rate: 45%; credits needed to graduate: 36; target time to graduate: 2 years
College funded aid available: Domestic: Yes; International: Yes
Graduates with debt: 65%; average amount of debt $32,655

ONLINE BUSINESS PROGRAM(S)
www.tamuct.edu/graduate-studies/index.html
Admissions: (254) 519-5447
Email: graduatestudies@tamuct.edu
Financial aid: (254) 501-5854
Application deadline: rolling
Program can be completed entirely online: Yes
Total program cost: $8,532 full-time in-state, $8,532 part-time in-state, $23,472 full-time out-of-state, $23,472 part-time out-of-state
Tuition per credit: $237 full-time in-state, $237 part-time in-state, $652 full-time out-of-state, $652 part-time out-of-state
Acceptance rate: 54.0%
Test scores required: No
Average GRE: 144 verbal, 144 quantitative
Average age of entrants: 38
Enrollment: 50, 52% men, 48% women, 64% minority, 2% international
Average class size: 16
Most popular business concentrations: human resources management, leadership, marketing, management information systems, organizational behavior
Completion: Credits needed to graduate: 36; target time to graduate: 2 years

College funded aid
available: Domestic: Yes;
International: Yes
Graduates with debt: 33%;
average amount of debt $36,907

Texas A&M International University

Public

ONLINE MBA PROGRAM(S)

www.tamiu.edu/prospect/
graduate.shtml
Admissions: (956) 326-3020
Email: GraduateSchool@
tamiu.edu
Financial aid: (956) 326-2225
Application deadline: rolling
Program can be completed
entirely online: Yes
Total program cost: $2,310
full-time in-state, $2,310
part-time in-state, $14,760
full-time out-of-state, $14,760
part-time out-of-state
Tuition per credit: $77 full-time
in-state, $77 part-time in-state,
$492 full-time out-of-state,
$492 part-time out-of-state
Acceptance rate: 100.0%
Average GMAT: 500
Average GRE: 143 verbal, 140
quantitative, 3.0 writing
Average age of entrants: 31
Students with prior work
experience: 93.0%
Enrollment: 131, 60% men,
40% women, 66% minority,
30% international
Average class size: 24
Most popular MBA
concentrations: general
management, international
business
Completion: Three year
graduation rate: 86%; credits
needed to graduate: 30; target
time to graduate: 2 years
College funded aid available:
Domestic: Yes; International: No
Graduates with debt: 13%;
average amount of debt $20,255

Texas A&M University–Commerce

Public

ONLINE MBA PROGRAM(S)

www.tamu-commerce.edu/
graduateprograms
Admissions: (903) 886-5163
Email: graduate.
school@tamuc.edu
Financial aid: (903) 886-5096
Application deadline: rolling
Program can be completed
entirely online: Yes
Total program cost: $6,060
full-time in-state, $6,060
part-time in-state, $18,510
full-time out-of-state, $18,510
part-time out-of-state
Tuition per credit: $202
full-time in-state, $202
part-time in-state, $617
full-time out-of-state, $617
part-time out-of-state
Acceptance rate: 74.0%
Test scores required: No
Average GMAT: 435
Average GRE: 144 verbal, 143
quantitative, 2.0 writing
Average age of entrants: 31

Students with prior work
experience: 81.0%
Enrollment: 1,033, 53%
men, 47% women, 47%
minority, 5% international
Average class size: 26
Most popular MBA
concentrations: accounting,
finance, general
management, marketing
Completion: Three year
graduation rate: 59%; credits
needed to graduate: 30; target
time to graduate: 2 years
College funded aid
available: Domestic: Yes;
International: Yes
Graduates with debt: 45%;
average amount of debt $29,519

ONLINE BUSINESS PROGRAM(S)

www.tamu-commerce.edu/
graduateprograms
Admissions: (903) 886-5163
Email: graduate.
school@tamuc.edu
Financial aid: (903) 886-5091
Application deadline: rolling
Program can be completed
entirely online: Yes
Total program cost: $6,060
full-time in-state, $6,060
part-time in-state, $18,510
full-time out-of-state, $18,510
part-time out-of-state
Tuition per credit: $202
full-time in-state, $202
part-time in-state, $617
full-time out-of-state, $617
part-time out-of-state
Acceptance rate: 74.0%
Test scores required:
GMAT or GRE
Average GMAT: 463
Average GRE: 143 verbal, 146
quantitative, 2.0 writing
Average age of entrants: 30
Students with prior work
experience: 74.0%
Enrollment: 1,351, 44%
men, 56% women, 44%
minority, 15% international
Average class size: 26
Most popular business
concentrations: accounting,
finance, general
management, marketing
Completion: Three year
graduation rate: 54%; credits
needed to graduate: 30; target
time to graduate: 2 years
College funded aid
available: Domestic: Yes;
International: Yes
Graduates with debt: 36%;
average amount of debt $33,448

Texas A&M University–Kingsville

Public

ONLINE MBA PROGRAM(S)

www.tamuk.edu/cba
Admissions: (361) 593-2501
Email: Jesus.Carmona@
tamuk.edu
Financial aid: (361) 593-2175
Application deadline: Domestic:
07/15; International: 06/01
Program can be completed
entirely online: Yes
Total program cost: $5,791
full-time in-state, $5,381
part-time in-state, $18,241
full-time out-of-state, $17,831
part-time out-of-state

Tuition per credit: $250
full-time in-state, $250
part-time in-state, $595
full-time out-of-state, $595
part-time out-of-state
Acceptance rate: 98.0%
Test scores required:
GMAT or GRE
Average GMAT: 456
Average GRE: 147 verbal,
147 quantitative
Average age of entrants: 32
Students with prior work
experience: 32.0%
Enrollment: 101, 55% men,
45% women, 65% minority,
5% international
Average class size: 22
Completion: Three year
graduation rate: 70%; credits
needed to graduate: 30; target
time to graduate: 1 year
College funded aid
available: Domestic: Yes;
International: Yes
Graduates with debt: 49%;
average amount of debt $28,599

Texas A&M University–Texarkana

Public

ONLINE MBA PROGRAM(S)

tamut.edu/admissions/
index.html
Admissions: (903) 223-3000
Email: admissions@tamut.edu
Financial aid: (903) 223-3000
Application deadline: N/A
Program can be completed
entirely online: Yes
Total program cost: $1,430
full-time in-state, $1,343
part-time in-state, $6,338
full-time out-of-state, $4,235
part-time out-of-state
Tuition per credit: $250
full-time in-state, $250
part-time in-state, $731
full-time out-of-state, $731
part-time out-of-state
Test scores required: GMAT
Enrollment: 176, 49% men,
51% women, 36% minority,
3% international
Completion: Credits
needed to graduate: 36
College funded aid
available: Domestic: Yes;
International: Yes

Texas Tech University (Rawls)

Public

ONLINE MBA PROGRAM(S)

www.depts.ttu.edu/gradschool/
admissions/howtoapply.php
Admissions: (806) 742-3184
Email: rawlsgrad@ttu.edu
Financial aid: (806) 742-3681
Application deadline: rolling
Program can be completed
entirely online: Yes
Total program cost: $15,065
full-time in-state, $15,065
part-time in-state, $15,065
full-time out-of-state, $15,065
part-time out-of-state
Tuition per credit: $326
full-time in-state, $326
part-time in-state, $326
part-time out-of-state

Test scores required:
GMAT or GRE
Completion: Credits needed
to graduate: 42; target time
to graduate: 2 years

ONLINE BUSINESS PROGRAM(S)

www.depts.ttu.edu/gradschool/
admissions/howtoapply.php
Admissions: (806) 742-3184
Email: rawlsgrad@ttu.edu
Financial aid: (806) 742-3681
Application deadline: rolling
Program can be completed
entirely online: Yes
Total program cost: $15,065
full-time in-state, $15,065
part-time in-state, $15,065
full-time out-of-state, $15,065
part-time out-of-state
Tuition per credit: $326
full-time in-state, $326
part-time in-state, $326
full-time out-of-state, $326
part-time out-of-state
Acceptance rate: 100.0%
Test scores required:
GMAT or GRE
Average GMAT: 380
Average age of entrants: 33
Enrollment: 5, 80% men,
20% women, N/A minority,
40% international
Completion: Credits needed
to graduate: 36; target
time to graduate: 1 year
College funded aid
available: Domestic: Yes;
International: Yes

Texas Wesleyan University

Private

ONLINE MBA PROGRAM(S)

txwes.edu/admissions/graduate/
Admissions: (817) 531-4930
Email: graduate@txwes.edu
Financial aid: (817) 531-4420
Application deadline: rolling
Program can be completed
entirely online: Yes
Total program cost: N/A
Tuition per credit: $886
full-time in-state, $886
part-time in-state, $886
full-time out-of-state, $886
part-time out-of-state
Acceptance rate: 74.0%
Average age of entrants: 34
Enrollment: 105, 38%
men, 62% women, 45%
minority, 4% international
Average class size: 20
Most popular MBA
concentrations: accounting,
health care administration,
supply chain management/
logistics
Completion: Credits needed
to graduate: 30; target
time to graduate: 1 year
College funded aid available:
Domestic: No; International: No

University of Dallas

Private

ONLINE BUSINESS PROGRAM(S)

www.udallas.edu/cob
Admissions: (972) 721-5004
Email: admiss@udallas.edu
Financial aid: (972) 721-5266
Application deadline: rolling
Program can be completed
entirely online: Yes

Total program cost: $37,500
full-time in-state, $37,500
part-time in-state, $37,500
full-time out-of-state, $37,500
part-time out-of-state
Tuition per credit: $1,250
full-time in-state, $1,250
part-time in-state, $1,250
full-time out-of-state, $1,250
part-time out-of-state
Acceptance rate: 41.0%
Test scores required: No
Average GMAT: 466
Average GRE: 147 verbal, 150
quantitative, 3.4 writing
Average age of entrants: 34
Students with prior work
experience: 90.0%
Enrollment: 174, 67% men,
33% women, N/A minority,
N/A international
Average class size: 24
Most popular business
concentrations: finance
Completion: Credits needed
to graduate: 30; target time
to graduate: 1.5 years
College funded aid
available: Domestic: Yes;
International: Yes

University of Houston–Clear Lake

Public

ONLINE MBA PROGRAM(S)

www.uhcl.edu/admissions
Admissions: (281) 283-2500
Email: admissions@uhcl.edu
Financial aid: (281) 283-2480
Application deadline: rolling
Program can be completed
entirely online: Yes
Total program cost: $19,640
full-time in-state, $38,180
part-time in-state, $19,640
full-time out-of-state, $38,180
part-time out-of-state
Tuition per credit: $467 full-time
in-state, $467 part-time in-state,
$982 full-time out-of-state,
$982 part-time out-of-state
Acceptance rate: 95.0%
Test scores required: No
Average GMAT: 448
Enrollment: 139, 41% men,
59% women, 47% minority,
0% international
Average class size: 38
Most popular MBA
concentrations: finance,
human resources
management, international
business, manufacturing and
technology management
Completion: Three year
graduation rate: 31%; credits
needed to graduate: 36; target
time to graduate: 2 years
College funded aid
available: Domestic: Yes;
International: Yes
Graduates with debt: 29%;
average amount of debt $33,144

ONLINE BUSINESS PROGRAM(S)

www.uhcl.edu/admissions
Admissions: (281) 283-2500
Email: admissions@uhcl.edu
Financial aid: (281) 283-2480
Application deadline: rolling
Program can be completed
entirely online: Yes
Total program cost: $19,640
full-time in-state, $38,180
part-time in-state, $19,640
full-time out-of-state, $38,180
part-time out-of-state

Tuition per credit: $467 full-time in-state, $467 part-time in-state, $982 full-time out-of-state, $982 part-time out-of-state
Acceptance rate: 94.0%
Test scores required: No
Enrollment: 72, 29% men, 71% women, 58% minority, 1% international
Average class size: 38
Most popular business concentrations: finance, human resources management
Completion: Three year graduation rate: 42%; credits needed to graduate: 36; target time to graduate: 2 years
College funded aid available: Domestic: Yes; International: Yes
Graduates with debt: 50%; average amount of debt $34,079

University of Houston–Victoria
Public

ONLINE MBA PROGRAM(S)
www.uhv.edu/admissions/
Admissions: (361) 570-4110
Email: admissions@uhv.edu
Financial aid: (361) 580-4125
Application deadline: rolling
Program can be completed entirely online: Depends
Total program cost: $13,334 full-time in-state, $13,334 part-time in-state, $29,519 full-time out-of-state, $29,519 part-time out-of-state
Tuition per credit: $342 full-time in-state, $342 part-time in-state, $757 full-time out-of-state, $757 part-time out-of-state
Acceptance rate: 65.0%
Test scores required: GMAT or GRE
Average GMAT: 430
Average GRE: 146 verbal, 148 quantitative
Average age of entrants: 35
Enrollment: 834, 46% men, 54% women, 46% minority, 2% international
Average class size: 25
Most popular MBA concentrations: accounting, entrepreneurship, finance, general management, international business
Completion: Credits needed to graduate: 39; target time to graduate: 2 years
College funded aid available: Domestic: Yes; International: Yes

ONLINE BUSINESS PROGRAM(S)
www.uhv.edu/admissions/
Admissions: (361) 570-4110
Email: admissions@uhv.edu
Financial aid: (361) 580-4125
Application deadline: rolling
Program can be completed entirely online: Yes
Total program cost: $13,886 full-time in-state, $13,886 part-time in-state, $26,336 full-time out-of-state, $26,336 part-time out-of-state
Tuition per credit: $342 full-time in-state, $342 part-time in-state, $757 full-time out-of-state, $757 part-time out-of-state
Acceptance rate: 44.0%

Test scores required: GMAT or GRE
Average GMAT: 360
Average GRE: 152 verbal, 150 quantitative
Average age of entrants: 32
Enrollment: 33, 70% men, 30% women, 55% minority, 9% international
Average class size: 12
Completion: Credits needed to graduate: 30; target time to graduate: 2 years
College funded aid available: Domestic: Yes; International: Yes

University of North Texas
Public

ONLINE MBA PROGRAM(S)
www.cob.unt.edu/programs/masters/onlinecourses.php
Admissions: (940) 369-8977
Email: MBACoB@unt.edu
Financial aid: (940) 565-2302
Application deadline: rolling
Program can be completed entirely online: Depends
Total program cost: $16,672 full-time in-state, $18,672 part-time in-state, $31,612 full-time out-of-state, $33,612 part-time out-of-state
Tuition per credit: $325 full-time in-state, $352 part-time in-state, $767 full-time out-of-state, $767 part-time out-of-state
Acceptance rate: 60.0%
Test scores required: GMAT or GRE
Average GMAT: 562
Average GRE: 157 verbal, 154 quantitative, 3.3 writing
Average age of entrants: 30
Students with prior work experience: 82.0%
Enrollment: 231, 58% men, 42% women, 31% minority, 0% international
Average class size: 20
Most popular MBA concentrations: finance, general management, human resources management, marketing
Completion: Three year graduation rate: 65%; credits needed to graduate: 36; target time to graduate: 2 years
College funded aid available: Domestic: Yes
Graduates with debt: 44%; average amount of debt $31,677

University of Texas of the Permian Basin
Public

ONLINE MBA PROGRAM(S)
www.utpb.edu/admissions/index.html
Admissions: (432) 552-2605
Email: admissions@utpb.edu
Financial aid: (432) 552-2620
Application deadline: rolling
Program can be completed entirely online: Yes
Total program cost: N/A
Tuition per credit: $327 full-time in-state, $327 part-time in-state, $661 full-time out-of-state, $661 part-time out-of-state
Test scores required: GMAT

Enrollment: 74, N/A minority, N/A international
Average class size: 95
Most popular MBA concentrations: accounting, finance, general management
Completion: Credits needed to graduate: 36; target time to graduate: 2 years
College funded aid available: Domestic: No; International: No
Graduates with debt: 82%

University of Texas–Arlington
Public

ONLINE MBA PROGRAM(S)
Admissions: (817) 272-3649
Email: rneilson@uta.edu
Financial aid: (817) 272-3568
Application deadline: rolling
Program can be completed entirely online: Yes
Total program cost: $42,250 full-time in-state, $42,250 part-time in-state, $42,250 full-time out-of-state, $42,250 part-time out-of-state
Tuition per credit: $1,174 full-time in-state, $1,174 part-time in-state, $1,174 full-time out-of-state, $1,174 part-time out-of-state
Test scores required: No
Completion: Credits needed to graduate: 36; target time to graduate: 2 years

University of Texas–Dallas
Public

ONLINE MBA PROGRAM(S)
jindal.utdallas.edu/
Admissions: (972) 883-6282
Email: mba@utdallas.edu
Financial aid: (972) 883-4037
Application deadline: rolling
Program can be completed entirely online: Yes
Total program cost: $46,816 full-time in-state, $49,178 part-time in-state, $83,084 full-time out-of-state, $83,428 part-time out-of-state
Tuition per credit: $717 full-time in-state, $764 part-time in-state, $1,402 full-time out-of-state, $1,410 part-time out-of-state
Acceptance rate: 43.0%
Test scores required: GMAT or GRE
Average GMAT: 621
Average GRE: 157 verbal, 157 quantitative, 3.9 writing
Average age of entrants: 29
Students with prior work experience: 99.0%
Enrollment: 295, 66% men, 34% women, 38% minority, 7% international
Average class size: 30
Most popular MBA concentrations: accounting, finance, marketing, management information systems, supply chain management/logistics
Completion: Three year graduation rate: 47%; credits needed to graduate: 53; target time to graduate: 4 years
College funded aid available: Domestic: Yes; International: Yes

Graduates with debt: 34%; average amount of debt $36,276

ONLINE BUSINESS PROGRAM(S)
jindal.utdallas.edu/
Admissions: (972) 883-6282
Email: mba@utdallas.edu
Financial aid: (972) 883-4037
Application deadline: rolling
Program can be completed entirely online: Yes
Total program cost: $31,592 full-time in-state, $33,264 part-time in-state, $56,264 full-time out-of-state, $56,538 part-time out-of-state
Tuition per credit: $717 full-time in-state, $764 part-time in-state, $1,402 full-time out-of-state, $1,410 part-time out-of-state
Acceptance rate: 62.0%
Test scores required: GMAT or GRE
Average GMAT: 599
Average GRE: 154 verbal, 153 quantitative, 3.9 writing
Average age of entrants: 30
Students with prior work experience: 92.0%
Enrollment: 637, 54% men, 46% women, 32% minority, 37% international
Average class size: 30
Most popular business concentrations: accounting, finance, marketing, management information systems, supply chain management/logistics
Completion: Three year graduation rate: 67%; credits needed to graduate: 36; target time to graduate: 3 years
College funded aid available: Domestic: Yes; International: Yes
Graduates with debt: 16%; average amount of debt $31,063

University of Texas–Tyler
Public

ONLINE MBA PROGRAM(S)
www.uttyler.edu/graduate
Admissions: (903) 566-7457
Email: ogs@uttyler.edu
Financial aid: (903) 566-7181
Application deadline: rolling
Program can be completed entirely online: Yes
Total program cost: $15,476 full-time in-state, $19,428 part-time in-state, $31,280 full-time out-of-state, $35,232 part-time out-of-state
Tuition per credit: $395 full-time in-state, $849 part-time in-state, $834 full-time out-of-state, $1,288 part-time out-of-state
Acceptance rate: 98.0%
Test scores required: GMAT or GRE
Average GMAT: 448
Average GRE: 148 verbal, 149 quantitative, 3.0 writing
Average age of entrants: 34
Students with prior work experience: 10.0%
Enrollment: 1,357, 41% men, 59% women, 45% minority, 2% international
Average class size: 65
Most popular MBA concentrations: general management, health care administration, marketing

University of the Incarnate Word
Private

ONLINE MBA PROGRAM(S)
sps.uiw.edu/admissions/graduate
Admissions: (210) 757-0202
Email: eapadmission@uiwtx.edu
Financial aid: (210) 829-3912
Application deadline: rolling
Program can be completed entirely online: Yes
Total program cost: $28,200 full-time in-state, $28,200 part-time in-state, $28,200 full-time out-of-state, $28,200 part-time out-of-state
Tuition per credit: $940 full-time in-state, $940 part-time in-state, $940 full-time out-of-state, $940 part-time out-of-state
Acceptance rate: 87.0%
Test scores required: No
Average GRE: 150 verbal, 142 quantitative, 3.5 writing
Average age of entrants: 34
Students with prior work experience: 100.0%
Enrollment: 319, 63% men, 37% women, 63% minority, 0% international
Average class size: 19
Most popular MBA concentrations: general management, human resources management, real estate, quantitative analysis/statistics and operations research
Completion: Three year graduation rate: 82%; credits needed to graduate: 30; target time to graduate: less than 1 year
College funded aid available: Domestic: Yes; International: No
Graduates with debt: 63%; average amount of debt $31,422

ONLINE BUSINESS PROGRAM(S)
sps.uiw.edu/admissions/graduate
Admissions: (210) 757-0202
Email: eapadmission@uiwtx.edu
Financial aid: (210) 829-3912
Application deadline: rolling
Program can be completed entirely online: Yes
Total program cost: $28,200 full-time in-state, $28,200 part-time in-state, $28,200 full-time out-of-state, $28,200 part-time out-of-state
Tuition per credit: $940 full-time in-state, $940 part-time in-state, $940 full-time out-of-state, $940 part-time out-of-state
Acceptance rate: 98.0%
Test scores required: No
Average GMAT: 390
Average GRE: 146 verbal, 146 quantitative, 3.5 writing
Average age of entrants: 35
Students with prior work experience: 100.0%

Enrollment: 716, 52% men, 48% women, 58% minority, 0% international
Average class size: 20
Most popular business concentrations: arts administration, health care administration, leadership, organizational behavior
Completion: Three year graduation rate: 72%; credits needed to graduate: 30; target time to graduate: less than 1 year
College funded aid available: Domestic: Yes; International: No
Graduates with debt: 65%; average amount of debt $34,644

West Texas A&M University

Public

ONLINE MBA PROGRAM(S)

www.wtamu.edu/graduateschool
Admissions: (806) 651-2731
Email: graduateschool@wtamu.edu
Financial aid: (806) 651-2059
Application deadline: rolling
Program can be completed entirely online: Yes
Total program cost: $13,935
full-time in-state, $15,300
part-time in-state, $14,400
full-time out-of-state, $16,035
part-time out-of-state
Tuition per credit: $335
full-time in-state, $380
part-time in-state, $365
full-time out-of-state, $410
part-time out-of-state
Acceptance rate: 76.0%
Test scores required: No
Average GMAT: 550
Average GRE: 154 verbal, 158 quantitative, 4.0 writing
Average age of entrants: 31
Students with prior work experience: 95.0%
Enrollment: 1,010, 60% men, 40% women, 47% minority, 1% international
Average class size: 40
Most popular MBA concentrations: general management, health care administration, marketing, management information systems, organizational behavior
Completion: Three year graduation rate: 83%; credits needed to graduate: 31; target time to graduate: 2 years
College funded aid available: Domestic: Yes; International: Yes
Graduates with debt: 34%; average amount of debt $12,600

ONLINE BUSINESS PROGRAM(S)

www.wtamu.edu/graduateschool
Admissions: (806) 651-2731
Email: graduateschool@wtamu.edu
Financial aid: (806) 651-2059
Application deadline: rolling
Program can be completed entirely online: Yes
Total program cost: $15,410
full-time in-state, $17,000
part-time in-state, $16,725
full-time out-of-state, $17,885
part-time out-of-state

Tuition per credit: $335
full-time in-state, $380
part-time in-state, $365
full-time out-of-state, $410
part-time out-of-state
Acceptance rate: 72.0%
Test scores required: No
Average GRE: 154 verbal, 156 quantitative, 4.5 writing
Average age of entrants: 31
Students with prior work experience: 93.0%
Enrollment: 244, 64% men, 36% women, 46% minority, 1% international
Average class size: 39
Most popular business concentrations: economics, finance, management information systems
Completion: Three year graduation rate: 83%; credits needed to graduate: 36; target time to graduate: 1.5 years
College funded aid available: Domestic: Yes; International: Yes
Graduates with debt: 36%; average amount of debt $11,800

UTAH

Southern Utah University

Public

ONLINE MBA PROGRAM(S)

www.suu.edu/business/mba/
Admissions: (435) 586-7740
Email: businessgrad@suu.edu
Financial aid: (435) 586-7734
Application deadline: rolling
Program can be completed entirely online: Yes
Total program cost: $13,442
full-time in-state, $14,570
part-time in-state, $13,442
full-time out-of-state, $14,570
part-time out-of-state
Tuition per credit: $448
full-time in-state, $548
part-time in-state, $448
full-time out-of-state, $548
part-time out-of-state
Acceptance rate: 85.0%
Test scores required: GMAT or GRE
Average GMAT: 553
Average GRE: 153 verbal, 146 quantitative
Average age of entrants: 31
Enrollment: 105, 72% men, 28% women, 11% minority, 0% international
Average class size: 23
Completion: Credits needed to graduate: 30; target time to graduate: 1 year
College funded aid available: Domestic: Yes; International: Yes
Graduates with debt: 41%; average amount of debt $27,787

ONLINE BUSINESS PROGRAM(S)

www.suu.edu/business/macc/
Admissions: (435) 586-7740
Email: businessgrad@suu.edu
Financial aid: (435) 586-7734
Application deadline: rolling
Program can be completed entirely online: Yes
Total program cost: $13,442
full-time in-state, $14,570
part-time in-state, $13,442
full-time out-of-state, $14,570
part-time out-of-state

Tuition per credit: $448
full-time in-state, $548
part-time in-state, $448
full-time out-of-state, $548
part-time out-of-state
Acceptance rate: 88.0%
Test scores required: GMAT or GRE
Average GMAT: 507
Average GRE: 147 verbal, 147 quantitative
Average age of entrants: 30
Enrollment: 141, 69% men, 31% women, 13% minority, 0% international
Average class size: 23
Most popular business concentrations: accounting, tax
Completion: Credits needed to graduate: 30; target time to graduate: 1 year
College funded aid available: Domestic: Yes; International: Yes
Graduates with debt: 49%; average amount of debt $16,687

University of Utah (Eccles)

Public

ONLINE MBA PROGRAM(S)

eccles.utah.edu/programs/mba/mba-online/admissions/
Admissions: (801) 587-8870
Email: mbaonline@utah.edu
Financial aid: (801) 581-6211
Application deadline: rolling
Program can be completed entirely online: Yes
Total program cost: $58,800
full-time in-state, $58,800
part-time in-state, $58,800
full-time out-of-state, $58,800
part-time out-of-state
Tuition per credit: $1,225
full-time in-state, $1,225
part-time in-state, $1,225
full-time out-of-state, $1,225
part-time out-of-state
Acceptance rate: 66.0%
Average GMAT: 557
Average GRE: 153 verbal, 154 quantitative
Average age of entrants: 35
Students with prior work experience: 100.0%
Enrollment: 121, 77% men, 23% women, 10% minority, 1% international
Average class size: 44
Most popular MBA concentrations: accounting, finance, leadership, management information systems, quantitative analysis/statistics and operations research
Completion: Three year graduation rate: 82%; credits needed to graduate: 48; target time to graduate: 2 years
College funded aid available: Domestic: Yes; International: Yes
Graduates with debt: 53%; average amount of debt $45,508

Westminster College

Private

ONLINE MBA PROGRAM(S)

www.westminstercollege.edu/graduate/programs/project-based-mba
Admissions: (801) 832-2200
Email: admissions@westminstercollege.edu
Financial aid: (801) 832-2500
Application deadline: rolling
Program can be completed entirely online: Depends
Total program cost: $54,600
full-time in-state, $54,600
part-time in-state, $54,600
full-time out-of-state, $54,600
part-time out-of-state
Tuition per credit: $1,400
full-time in-state, $1,400
part-time in-state, $1,400
full-time out-of-state, $1,400
part-time out-of-state
Acceptance rate: 87.0%
Test scores required: GMAT or GRE
Average age of entrants: 27
Enrollment: 84, 68% men, 32% women, 20% minority, 0% international
Average class size: 6
Most popular MBA concentrations: entrepreneurship, finance, international business, leadership, production/operations management
Completion: Credits needed to graduate: 39; target time to graduate: 1.5 years
College funded aid available: Domestic: Yes; International: Yes
Graduates with debt: 33%

VIRGINIA

College of William and Mary (Mason)

Public

ONLINE MBA PROGRAM(S)

Admissions: (757) 500-5532
Email: onlinemba@mason.wm.edu
Financial aid: (757) 221-2420
Application deadline: rolling
Program can be completed entirely online: No
Total program cost: $59,780
full-time in-state, $59,780
part-time in-state, $59,780
full-time out-of-state, $559,780
part-time out-of-state
Tuition per credit: $1,220
full-time in-state, $1,220
part-time in-state, $1,220
full-time out-of-state
Acceptance rate: 96.0%
Average GMAT: 600
Average GRE: 154 verbal, 161 quantitative, 4.5 writing
Average age of entrants: 35
Students with prior work experience: 100.0%
Enrollment: 401, 67% men, 33% women, 30% minority, 1% international
Average class size: 23
Completion: Credits needed to graduate: 49; target time to graduate: 2 years
College funded aid available: Domestic: No; International: No

Graduates with debt: 54%; average amount of debt $62,721

George Mason University

Public

ONLINE MBA PROGRAM(S)

business.gmu.edu/mba-programs/admissions/
Admissions: (703) 993-1856
Email: sbudgrad@gmu.edu
Financial aid: (703) 993-2353
Application deadline: rolling
Program can be completed entirely online: Yes
Total program cost: N/A
Tuition per credit: $950
full-time in-state, $950
part-time in-state, $950
full-time out-of-state, $950
part-time out-of-state
Most popular MBA concentrations: accounting, finance, marketing, management information systems, production/operations management
Completion: Credits needed to graduate: 48

ONLINE BUSINESS PROGRAM(S)

business.gmu.edu/msa/
Admissions: (703) 993-2136
Email: msa@gmu.edu
Financial aid: (703) 993-2353
Application deadline: Domestic: 04/01; International: 02/01
Program can be completed entirely online: No
Total program cost: N/A
Tuition per credit: $1,001
full-time in-state, $1,001
part-time in-state, $1,851
full-time out-of-state, $1,851
part-time out-of-state
Acceptance rate: 92.0%
Average age of entrants: 34
Students with prior work experience: 100.0%
Enrollment: 34, 29% men, 71% women, 47% minority, 3% international
Average class size: 14
Most popular business concentrations: accounting
Completion: Credits needed to graduate: 30; target time to graduate: 2 years
College funded aid available: Domestic: Yes
Graduates with debt: 60%; average amount of debt $40,267

James Madison University

Public

ONLINE MBA PROGRAM(S)

www.jmu.edu/cob/graduate/mba/infosec/admissions.shtml
Admissions: (540) 568-3058
Email: mccoynta@jmu.edu
Financial aid: (540) 568-7820
Application deadline: rolling
Program can be completed entirely online: No
Total program cost: $37,800
full-time in-state, $37,800
part-time in-state, $37,800
full-time out-of-state, $37,800
part-time out-of-state

Tuition per credit: $900
full-time in-state, $900
part-time in-state, $900
full-time out-of-state, $900
part-time out-of-state
Acceptance rate: 87.0%
Test scores required:
GMAT or GRE
Average GMAT: 550
Average age of entrants: 33
Students with prior work
experience: 100.0%
Enrollment: 33, 70% men,
30% women, 36% minority,
3% international
Average class size: 15
Most popular MBA
concentrations: accounting,
general management, marketing,
management information
systems, technology
Completion: Three year
graduation rate: 94%; credits
needed to graduate: 42; target
time to graduate: 2.5 years
College funded aid available:
Domestic: Yes; International: No
Graduates with debt: 23%;
average amount of debt $54,452

Liberty University

Private

ONLINE MBA PROGRAM(S)

www.luonline.com/
index.cfm?pid=21793
Admissions: (434) 582-9595
Email: luoadmissions@
liberty.edu
Financial aid: (434) 582-2270
Application deadline: rolling
Program can be completed
entirely online: Yes
Total program cost: N/A
Tuition per credit: $565 full-time
in-state, $615 part-time in-state,
$565 full-time out-of-state,
$615 part-time out-of-state
Acceptance rate: 32.0%
Test scores required: No
Average GRE: 154 verbal, 147
quantitative, 4.0 writing
Average age of entrants: 35
Enrollment: 3,942, 53%
men, 47% women, 27%
minority, 0% international
Average class size: 19
Most popular MBA
concentrations: accounting,
general management,
health care administration,
human resources
management, leadership
Completion: Three year
graduation rate: 41%; credits
needed to graduate: 45; target
time to graduate: 2.5 years
College funded aid
available: Domestic: Yes;
International: Yes
Graduates with debt: 79%;
average amount of debt $22,822

ONLINE BUSINESS PROGRAM(S)

www.luonline.com/
index.cfm?pid=21793
Admissions: (434) 582-9595
Email: luoadmissions@
liberty.edu
Financial aid: (434) 582-2270
Application deadline: rolling
Program can be completed
entirely online: Yes
Total program cost: N/A
Tuition per credit: $565 full-time
in-state, $615 part-time in-state,
$565 full-time out-of-state,
$615 part-time out-of-state

Acceptance rate: 61.0%
Test scores required: No
Average GMAT: 500
Average GRE: 151 verbal, 148
quantitative, 4.0 writing
Average age of entrants: 35
Enrollment: 4,935, 51%
men, 49% women, 31%
minority, 0% international
Average class size: 19
Most popular business
concentrations:
accounting, health care
administration, leadership,
marketing, management
information systems
Completion: Three year
graduation rate: 27%; credits
needed to graduate: 30; target
time to graduate: 2 years
College funded aid
available: Domestic: Yes;
International: Yes
Graduates with debt: 79%;
average amount of debt $22,822

Longwood University

Public

ONLINE MBA PROGRAM(S)

www.longwood.edu/
business/mba
Admissions: (434) 395-2043
Email: MBA@longwood.edu
Financial aid: (434) 395-2077
Application deadline: rolling
Program can be completed
entirely online: No
Total program cost: $21,816
full-time in-state, $21,816
part-time in-state, $44,676
full-time out-of-state, $44,676
part-time out-of-state
Tuition per credit: $360
full-time in-state, $360
part-time in-state, $995
full-time out-of-state, $995
part-time out-of-state
Acceptance rate: 70.0%
Test scores required:
GMAT or GRE
Average GMAT: 460
Average GRE: 144 verbal, 136
quantitative, 2.0 writing
Average age of entrants: 29
Enrollment: 34, 62% men,
38% women, 21% minority,
0% international
Average class size: 14
Most popular MBA
concentrations: general
management, real estate
Completion: Three year
graduation rate: 87%; credits
needed to graduate: 36; target
time to graduate: 2 years
College funded aid
available: Domestic: Yes;
International: Yes

Lynchburg College

Private

ONLINE MBA PROGRAM(S)

www.lynchburg.edu/graduate/
master-of-business-
administration/admission-
information/
Admissions: N/A
Financial aid: (434) 544-8228
Application deadline: rolling
Program can be completed
entirely online: Depends

Total program cost: $23,940
full-time in-state, $23,940
part-time in-state, $23,940
full-time out-of-state, $23,940
part-time out-of-state
Tuition per credit: $665
full-time in-state, $665
part-time in-state, $665
full-time out-of-state, $665
part-time out-of-state
Acceptance rate: 85.0%
Test scores required:
GMAT or GRE
Average GMAT: 470
Average age of entrants: 28
Students with prior work
experience: 100.0%
Enrollment: 15, 67% men,
33% women, N/A minority,
7% international
Average class size: 17
Most popular MBA
concentrations: accounting,
economics, human
resources management
Completion: Credits needed
to graduate: 36; target time
to graduate: 2 years
College funded aid
available: Domestic: Yes;
International: Yes
Graduates with debt: 43%;
average amount of debt $19,483

Marymount University

Private

ONLINE MBA PROGRAM(S)

www.marymount.edu/
admissions/graduate
Admissions: (703) 284-5901
Email: grad.admissions@
marymount.edu
Financial aid: (703) 284-1530
Application deadline: rolling
Program can be completed
entirely online: No
Total program cost: $39,780
full-time in-state, $39,780
part-time in-state, $39,780
full-time out-of-state, $39,780
part-time out-of-state
Tuition per credit: $1,020
full-time in-state, $1,020
part-time in-state, $1,020
full-time out-of-state, $1,020
part-time out-of-state
Acceptance rate: 94.0%
Test scores required:
GMAT or GRE
Average GMAT: 383
Average GRE: 146 verbal, 168
quantitative, 3.5 writing
Average age of entrants: 30
Enrollment: 128, 38% men,
63% women, 54% minority,
13% international
Average class size: 11
Completion: Credits needed
to graduate: 39; target time
to graduate: 1.5 years
College funded aid
available: Domestic: Yes;
International: Yes
Graduates with debt: 60%;
average amount of debt $53,362

ONLINE BUSINESS PROGRAM(S)

www.marymount.edu/
admissions/graduate
Admissions: (703) 284-5901
Email: grad.admissions@
marymount.edu
Financial aid: (703) 284-1530
Application deadline: rolling
Program can be completed
entirely online: Yes

Total program cost: N/A
Tuition per credit: $1,020
full-time in-state, $1,020
part-time in-state, $1,020
full-time out-of-state, $1,020
part-time out-of-state
Acceptance rate: 100.0%
Test scores required: No
Average age of entrants: 30
Students with prior work
experience: 94.0%
Enrollment: 115, 59% men,
41% women, 55% minority,
11% international
Average class size: 15
Most popular business
concentrations: general
management, leadership,
public policy, quantitative
analysis/statistics and
operations research
Completion: Three year
graduation rate: 54%; credits
needed to graduate: 36; target
time to graduate: 2 years
College funded aid
available: Domestic: Yes;
International: Yes
Graduates with debt: 42%;
average amount of debt $46,576

Old Dominion University

Public

ONLINE MBA PROGRAM(S)

odu.edu/business/departments/
mba/prospective-students/
admission
Admissions: (757) 683-3585
Email: mbainfo@odu.edu
Financial aid: (757) 683-3683
Application deadline: rolling
Program can be completed
entirely online: Yes
Total program cost: $20,920
full-time in-state, $20,920
part-time in-state, $22,720
full-time out-of-state, $22,720
part-time out-of-state
Tuition per credit: $523
full-time in-state, $523
part-time in-state, $568
full-time out-of-state, $568
part-time out-of-state
Acceptance rate: 74.0%
Test scores required:
GMAT or GRE
Average GMAT: 536
Average GRE: 158 verbal, 153
quantitative, 3.6 writing
Average age of entrants: 35
Students with prior work
experience: 100.0%
Enrollment: 86, 50% men,
50% women, 24% minority,
1% international
Average class size: 14
Most popular MBA
concentrations: health
care administration,
public administration,
supply chain management/
logistics, transportation
Completion: Three year
graduation rate: 55%; credits
needed to graduate: 40; target
time to graduate: 2 years
College funded aid
available: Domestic: Yes;
International: Yes
Graduates with debt: 38%;
average amount of debt $28,386

Regent University

Private

ONLINE MBA PROGRAM(S)

www.regent.edu/school-
of-business-and-leadership/
admissions-information/
Admissions: (757) 352-4400
Email: SBLAdmissions@
regent.edu
Financial aid: (757) 352-4125
Application deadline: rolling
Program can be completed
entirely online: Yes
Total program cost: $27,300
full-time in-state, $27,300
part-time in-state, $27,300
full-time out-of-state, $27,300
part-time out-of-state
Tuition per credit: $650
full-time in-state, $650
part-time in-state, $650
full-time out-of-state, $650
part-time out-of-state
Acceptance rate: 45.0%
Test scores required: No
Average age of entrants: 35
Enrollment: 529, 42%
men, 58% women, 54%
minority, 3% international
Average class size: 20
Most popular MBA
concentrations: finance,
general management,
health care administration,
human resources
management, marketing
Completion: Three year
graduation rate: 49%; credits
needed to graduate: 42; target
time to graduate: 1.5 years
College funded aid
available: Domestic: Yes;
International: Yes
Graduates with debt: 54%;
average amount of debt $19,229

ONLINE BUSINESS PROGRAM(S)

www.regent.edu/school-
of-business-and-leadership/
admissions-information/
Admissions: (757) 352-4400
Email: SBLAdmissions@
regent.edu
Financial aid: (757) 352-4125
Application deadline: rolling
Program can be completed
entirely online: Yes
Total program cost: $21,450
full-time in-state, $21,450
part-time in-state, $21,450
full-time out-of-state, $21,450
part-time out-of-state
Tuition per credit: $650
full-time in-state, $650
part-time in-state, $650
full-time out-of-state, $650
part-time out-of-state
Acceptance rate: 50.0%
Test scores required: No
Average GRE: 154 verbal,
149 quantitative
Average age of entrants: 38
Enrollment: 378, 38%
men, 62% women, 52%
minority, 2% international
Average class size: 18
Most popular business
concentrations: consulting,
human resources
management, leadership,
not-for-profit management
Completion: Three year
graduation rate: 54%; credits
needed to graduate: 33; target
time to graduate: 1.5 years
College funded aid
available: Domestic: Yes;
International: Yes

Graduates with debt: 64%; average amount of debt $37,283

Virginia Commonwealth University

Public

ONLINE MBA PROGRAM(S)

business.vcu.edu/admissions/masters-and-certificate-programs/
Admissions: (804) 828-4622
Email: gsib@vcu.edu
Financial aid: (804) 828-6669
Application deadline: rolling
Program can be completed entirely online: No
Total program cost: $39,500 part-time in-state, $39,500 part-time out-of-state
Tuition per credit: $878 full-time in-state, $878 part-time in-state, $878 full-time out-of-state, $878 part-time out-of-state
Acceptance rate: 100.0%
Average GMAT: 450
Average GRE: 147 verbal, 147 quantitative
Average age of entrants: 38
Students with prior work experience: 100.0%
Enrollment: 24, 38% men, 63% women, 17% minority, 0% international
Average class size: 21
Completion: Credits needed to graduate: 45; target time to graduate: 2 years
College funded aid available: Domestic: Yes; International: Yes

WASHINGTON

City University of Seattle

Private

ONLINE MBA PROGRAM(S)

www.cityu.edu/admissions-overview/admissions/
Admissions: (888) 422-4898
Email: info@cityu.edu
Financial aid: (206) 239-4535
Application deadline: rolling
Program can be completed entirely online: Yes
Total program cost: $33,504 full-time in-state, $33,504 part-time in-state, $33,504 full-time out-of-state, $33,504 part-time out-of-state
Tuition per credit: $698 full-time in-state, $698 part-time in-state, $698 full-time out-of-state, $698 part-time out-of-state
Acceptance rate: 73.0%
Test scores required: No
Enrollment: 790, 46% men, 54% women, N/A minority, N/A international
Average class size: 14
Most popular MBA concentrations: finance, general management, international business, marketing, technology
Completion: Three year graduation rate: 75%; credits needed to graduate: 48; target time to graduate: 2.5 years
College funded aid available: Domestic: Yes; International: No

Graduates with debt: 10%; average amount of debt $50,744

ONLINE BUSINESS PROGRAM(S)

www.cityu.edu/admissions-overview/admissions/
Admissions: (888) 422-4898
Email: info@cityu.edu
Financial aid: (206) 239-4535
Application deadline: rolling
Program can be completed entirely online: Yes
Total program cost: $33,504 full-time in-state, $33,504 part-time in-state, $33,504 full-time out-of-state, $33,504 part-time out-of-state
Tuition per credit: $698 full-time in-state, $698 part-time in-state, $698 full-time out-of-state, $698 part-time out-of-state
Acceptance rate: 71.0%
Test scores required: No
Enrollment: 92, 41% men, 59% women, N/A minority, N/A international
Average class size: 8
Most popular business concentrations: international business, management information systems, production/operations management, technology
Completion: Three year graduation rate: 41%; credits needed to graduate: 45; target time to graduate: 2.5 years
College funded aid available: Domestic: Yes; International: No
Graduates with debt: 38%; average amount of debt $43,042

Northwest University

Private

ONLINE MBA PROGRAM(S)

online.northwestu.edu
Admissions: (866) 327-0264
Email: online@northwestu.edu
Financial aid: (425) 889-5336
Application deadline: rolling
Program can be completed entirely online: Yes
Total program cost: $30,225 full-time in-state, $30,225 part-time in-state, $30,225 full-time out-of-state, $30,225 part-time out-of-state
Tuition per credit: $775 full-time in-state, $775 part-time in-state, $775 full-time out-of-state, $775 part-time out-of-state
Acceptance rate: 100.0%
Test scores required: No
Average age of entrants: 36
Students with prior work experience: 100.0%
Enrollment: 19, 53% men, 47% women, 47% minority, 5% international
Average class size: 7
Most popular MBA concentrations: general management, not-for-profit management
Completion: Three year graduation rate: 62%; credits needed to graduate: 39; target time to graduate: 2 years
College funded aid available: Domestic: No; International: No
Graduates with debt: 83%; average amount of debt $34,753

University of Washington (Foster)

Public

ONLINE MBA PROGRAM(S)

foster.uw.edu/academics/degree-programs/hybrid-mba/admissions/
Admissions: (206) 685-4622
Email: uwhybrid@uw.edu
Financial aid: (206) 543-6101
Application deadline: Domestic: 03/01
Program can be completed entirely online: Yes
Total program cost: $67,500 full-time in-state, $67,500 part-time in-state, $67,500 full-time out-of-state, $67,500 part-time out-of-state
Tuition per credit: $1,144 full-time in-state, $1,144 part-time in-state, $1,144 full-time out-of-state, $1,144 part-time out-of-state
Acceptance rate: 79.0%
Test scores required: GMAT or GRE
Average GMAT: 607
Average GRE: 160 verbal, 157 quantitative, 4.5 writing
Average age of entrants: 34
Students with prior work experience: 100.0%
Enrollment: 47, 38% men, 62% women, 34% minority, 4% international
Average class size: 47
Most popular MBA concentrations: finance, leadership, marketing, supply chain management/logistics, quantitative analysis/statistics and operations research
Completion: Credits needed to graduate: 59; target time to graduate: 2 years
College funded aid available: Domestic: No; International: No

Washington State University

Public

ONLINE MBA PROGRAM(S)

omba.wsu.edu
Admissions: (877) 960-2029
Email: admissions@wsumba.com
Financial aid: (509) 335-9711
Application deadline: rolling
Program can be completed entirely online: Yes
Total program cost: $35,000 full-time in-state, $35,000 part-time in-state, $35,000 full-time out-of-state, $35,000 part-time out-of-state
Tuition per credit: $813 full-time in-state, $813 part-time in-state, $813 full-time out-of-state, $813 part-time out-of-state
Acceptance rate: 60.0%
Test scores required: GMAT or GRE
Average GMAT: 551
Average GRE: 155 verbal, 149 quantitative, 4.1 writing
Average age of entrants: 36
Students with prior work experience: 99.0%
Enrollment: 840, 66% men, 34% women, 24% minority, 3% international
Average class size: 26

Most popular MBA concentrations: finance, hotel administration, international business, marketing
Completion: Three year graduation rate: 68%; credits needed to graduate: 32; target time to graduate: 2 years
College funded aid available: Domestic: Yes; International: Yes
Graduates with debt: 39%; average amount of debt $34,786

WEST VIRGINIA

Marshall University (Lewis)

Public

ONLINE MBA PROGRAM(S)

www.marshall.edu/admissions/
Admissions: (304) 746-1900
Email: Services@Marshall.edu
Financial aid: (304) 696-3162
Application deadline: rolling
Program can be completed entirely online: Yes
Total program cost: $15,500 full-time in-state, $15,500 part-time in-state, $15,500 full-time out-of-state, $15,500 part-time out-of-state
Tuition per credit: $406 full-time in-state, $406 part-time in-state, $406 full-time out-of-state, $406 part-time out-of-state
Acceptance rate: 85.0%
Test scores required: No
Average age of entrants: 31
Students with prior work experience: 71.0%
Enrollment: 24, 42% men, 58% women, N/A minority, N/A international
Completion: Credits needed to graduate: 36; target time to graduate: 2 years

West Virginia University

Public

ONLINE MBA PROGRAM(S)

be.wvu.edu/online-mba/index.htm
Admissions: (304) 293-5505
Email: eavitullo@mail.wvu.edu
Financial aid: (304) 293-5242
Application deadline: Domestic: 07/02; International: 07/02
Program can be completed entirely online: No
Total program cost: $49,104 full-time in-state, $49,104 part-time in-state, $49,104 full-time out-of-state, $49,104 part-time out-of-state
Tuition per credit: $1,023 full-time in-state, $1,023 part-time in-state, $1,023 full-time out-of-state, $1,023 part-time out-of-state
Acceptance rate: 94.0%
Test scores required: GMAT or GRE
Average GMAT: 640
Average GRE: 149 verbal, 151 quantitative, 3.6 writing
Average age of entrants: 32
Students with prior work experience: 87.0%

Enrollment: 169, 66% men, 34% women, 12% minority, 1% international
Average class size: 26
Completion: Three year graduation rate: 88%; credits needed to graduate: 48; target time to graduate: 2 years
College funded aid available: Domestic: Yes; International: No
Graduates with debt: 68%; average amount of debt $61,441

ONLINE BUSINESS PROGRAM(S)

www.be.wvu.edu/graduate/index.htm
Admissions: (304) 293-2333
Email: mba@wvu.edu
Financial aid: (304) 293-5242
Application deadline: Domestic: 07/02; International: 07/02
Program can be completed entirely online: No
Total program cost: $24,552 full-time in-state, $24,552 part-time in-state, $24,552 full-time out-of-state, $24,552 part-time out-of-state
Tuition per credit: $1,023 full-time in-state, $1,023 part-time in-state, $1,023 full-time out-of-state, $1,023 part-time out-of-state
Acceptance rate: 75.0%
Test scores required: GMAT or GRE
Average GMAT: 526
Average GRE: 155 verbal, 154 quantitative, 4.6 writing
Average age of entrants: 34
Students with prior work experience: 89.0%
Enrollment: 46, 59% men, 41% women, 24% minority, 2% international
Average class size: 20
Completion: Credits needed to graduate: 30; target time to graduate: 1 year
College funded aid available: Domestic: Yes; International: No
Graduates with debt: 59%; average amount of debt $46,638

WISCONSIN

Cardinal Stritch University

Private

ONLINE MBA PROGRAM(S)

www.stritch.edu/admissions/request-information
Admissions: (414) 410-4040
Email: admissions@stritch.edu
Financial aid: (414) 410-4048
Application deadline: rolling
Program can be completed entirely online: Yes
Total program cost: $24,840 full-time in-state, $24,840 part-time in-state, $24,840 full-time out-of-state, $24,840 part-time out-of-state
Tuition per credit: $690 full-time in-state, $690 part-time in-state, $690 full-time out-of-state, $690 part-time out-of-state
Test scores required: No
Completion: Credits needed to graduate: 36

Concordia University Wisconsin

Private

ONLINE MBA PROGRAM(S)

online.cuw.edu
Admissions: (877) 437-8175
Email: onlineadmissions@cuw.edu
Financial aid: (262) 243-4215
Application deadline: rolling
Program can be completed entirely online: Yes
Total program cost: $27,261 full-time in-state, $27,261 part-time in-state, $27,261 full-time out-of-state, $27,261 part-time out-of-state
Tuition per credit: $699 full-time in-state, $699 part-time in-state, $699 full-time out-of-state, $699 part-time out-of-state
Acceptance rate: 52.0%
Test scores required: No
Average age of entrants: 32
Enrollment: 203, 36% men, 64% women, 24% minority, 0% international
Average class size: 7
Most popular MBA concentrations: accounting, finance, general management, health care administration, human resources management
Completion: Three year graduation rate: 36%; credits needed to graduate: 39; target time to graduate: 2 years
College funded aid available: Domestic: Yes; International: No

ONLINE BUSINESS PROGRAM(S)

online.cuw.edu
Admissions: (877) 437-8175
Email: onlineadmissions@cuw.edu
Financial aid: (262) 243-4215
Application deadline: rolling
Program can be completed entirely online: Yes
Total program cost: $22,368 full-time in-state, $22,368 part-time in-state, $22,368 full-time out-of-state, $22,368 part-time out-of-state
Tuition per credit: $699 full-time in-state, $699 part-time in-state, $699 full-time out-of-state, $699 part-time out-of-state
Acceptance rate: 66.0%
Test scores required: No
Average age of entrants: 40
Enrollment: 162, 28% men, 72% women, 31% minority, 2% international
Average class size: 5
Most popular business concentrations: leadership
Completion: Credits needed to graduate: 32; target time to graduate: 1.5 years
College funded aid available: Domestic: Yes; International: No
Graduates with debt: 40%

Edgewood College

Private

ONLINE MBA PROGRAM(S)

www.edgewood.edu/admissions/graduate-students
Admissions: (608) 663-3297
Email: tkantor@edgewood.edu
Financial aid: (608) 663-4300
Application deadline: rolling
Program can be completed entirely online: Depends
Total program cost: N/A
Tuition per credit: $963 full-time in-state, $963 part-time in-state, $963 full-time out-of-state, $963 part-time out-of-state
Test scores required: GMAT or GRE
Average class size: 12
Most popular MBA concentrations: finance, general management, health care administration, human resources management, marketing
Completion: Credits needed to graduate: 37; target time to graduate: no time period

ONLINE BUSINESS PROGRAM(S)

www.edgewood.edu/academics/programs/details/business/graduate
Admissions: (608) 663-3297
Email: jalsteen@edgewood.edu
Financial aid: (608) 663-4300
Application deadline: rolling
Program can be completed entirely online: Yes
Total program cost: N/A
Tuition per credit: $963 full-time in-state, $963 part-time in-state, $963 full-time out-of-state, $963 part-time out-of-state
Test scores required: GMAT or GRE
Average class size: 14
Most popular business concentrations: accounting, organizational behavior
Completion: Credits needed to graduate: 30; target time to graduate: 2 years

Herzing University

Private

ONLINE MBA PROGRAM(S)

www.herzing.edu
Admissions: (866) 508-6748
Email: admissions@herzing.edu
Financial aid: (866) 508-0748
Application deadline: rolling
Program can be completed entirely online: Yes
Total program cost: $26,130 full-time in-state, $26,130 part-time in-state, $26,130 full-time out-of-state, $26,130 part-time out-of-state

Tuition per credit: $670 full-time in-state, $670 part-time in-state, $670 full-time out-of-state, $670 part-time out-of-state
Acceptance rate: 89.0%
Test scores required: No
Average age of entrants: 38
Enrollment: 243, 26% men, 74% women, 55% minority, 0% international
Average class size: 15
Most popular MBA concentrations: general management, health care administration, human resources management, technology
Completion: Three year graduation rate: 66%; credits needed to graduate: 39; target time to graduate: 1.5 years
College funded aid available: Domestic: Yes; International: Yes
Graduates with debt: 78%; average amount of debt $32,949

University of Wisconsin MBA Consortium

Public

ONLINE MBA PROGRAM(S)

www.wisconsinonlinemba.org/
Admissions: (715) 836-6019
Email: mba@uwec.edu
Financial aid: (715) 836-5606
Application deadline: rolling
Program can be completed entirely online: Yes
Total program cost: $23,250 full-time in-state, $23,250 part-time in-state, $23,250 full-time out-of-state, $23,250 part-time out-of-state
Tuition per credit: $775 full-time in-state, $775 part-time in-state, $775 full-time out-of-state, $775 part-time out-of-state
Acceptance rate: 85.0%
Test scores required: GMAT or GRE
Average GMAT: 596
Average GRE: 155 verbal, 155 quantitative, 4.2 writing
Average age of entrants: 32
Students with prior work experience: 100.0%
Enrollment: 342, 61% men, 39% women, 11% minority, 2% international
Average class size: 25
Most popular MBA concentrations: finance, general management, health care administration, marketing, management information systems
Completion: Three year graduation rate: 78%; credits needed to graduate: 30; target time to graduate: 3 years

College funded aid available: Domestic: No; International: No
Graduates with debt: 34%; average amount of debt $40,159

University of Wisconsin–Platteville

Public

ONLINE BUSINESS PROGRAM(S)

www.uwplatt.edu/distance-education
Admissions: (608) 342-1468
Email: disted@uwplatt.edu
Financial aid: (608) 342-1836
Application deadline: rolling
Program can be completed entirely online: Yes
Total program cost: $20,250 full-time in-state, $20,250 part-time in-state, $20,250 full-time out-of-state, $20,250 part-time out-of-state
Tuition per credit: $675 full-time in-state, $675 part-time in-state, $675 full-time out-of-state, $675 part-time out-of-state
Acceptance rate: 75.0%
Test scores required: No
Average age of entrants: 37
Enrollment: 606, 53% men, 47% women, 23% minority, 4% international
Average class size: 13
Most popular business concentrations: general management, leadership, manufacturing and technology management, organizational behavior, supply chain management/logistics
Completion: Three year graduation rate: 37%; credits needed to graduate: 30; target time to graduate: 3 years
College funded aid available: Domestic: No; International: No

University of Wisconsin–Whitewater

Public

ONLINE MBA PROGRAM(S)

www.uww.edu/cobe/onlinemba
Admissions: (262) 473-1945
Email: gradbus@uww.edu
Financial aid: (262) 472-1130
Application deadline: rolling
Program can be completed entirely online: Yes
Total program cost: $22,968 full-time in-state, $22,968 part-time in-state, $22,968 full-time out-of-state, $22,968 part-time out-of-state
Tuition per credit: $638 full-time in-state, $638 part-time in-state, $638 full-time out-of-state, $638 part-time out-of-state

Acceptance rate: 73.0%
Test scores required: GMAT or GRE
Average GMAT: 543
Average age of entrants: 29
Students with prior work experience: 96.0%
Enrollment: 379, 59% men, 41% women, 14% minority, 3% international
Average class size: 39
Most popular MBA concentrations: finance, general management, marketing
Completion: Three year graduation rate: 75%; credits needed to graduate: 36; target time to graduate: 1.5 years
College funded aid available: Domestic: Yes; International: Yes
Graduates with debt: 28%; average amount of debt $11,989

WYOMING

University of Wyoming

Public

ONLINE MBA PROGRAM(S)

www.uwyo.edu/admissions/
Admissions: (307) 766-5160
Email: admissions@uwyo.edu
Financial aid: (307) 766-2116
Application deadline: rolling
Program can be completed entirely online: Yes
Total program cost: $23,640 full-time in-state, $23,640 part-time in-state, $23,640 full-time out-of-state, $23,640 part-time out-of-state
Tuition per credit: $788 full-time in-state, $788 part-time in-state, $788 full-time out-of-state, $788 part-time out-of-state
Acceptance rate: 97.0%
Average GRE: 150 verbal, 151 quantitative, 4.0 writing
Average age of entrants: 35
Students with prior work experience: 100.0%
Enrollment: 83, 58% men, 42% women, N/A minority, N/A international
Average class size: 45
Completion: Three year graduation rate: 72%; credits needed to graduate: 30; target time to graduate: 2 years
College funded aid available: Domestic: Yes; International: Yes

On-Campus MBA Programs

Online Business Programs